Design, Performance, and Analysis of Innovative Information Retrieval

Zhongyu (Joan) Lu
University of Huddersfield, UK

A volume in the Advances in Data Mining
and Database Management (ADMDM)
Book Series

Managing Director:	Lindsay Johnston
Senior Editorial Director:	Heather A. Probst
Book Production Manager:	Sean Woznicki
Development Manager:	Joel Gamon
Development Editor:	Christine Smith
Assistant Acquisitions Editor:	Kayla Wolfe
Typesetter:	Adrienne Freeland
Cover Design:	Nick Newcomer

Published in the United States of America by
Information Science Reference (an imprint of IGI Global)
701 E. Chocolate Avenue
Hershey PA 17033
Tel: 717-533-8845
Fax: 717-533-8661
E-mail: cust@igi-global.com
Web site: http://www.igi-global.com

Library of Congress Cataloging-in-Publication Data

Design, performance, and analysis of innovative information retrieval / Joan Lu, editor.
    p. cm.
 Includes bibliographical references and index.
 Summary: This book examines a number of emerging technologies that significantly contribute to modern Information Retrieval (IR), as well as fundamental IR theories and concepts that have been adopted into new tools or system--Provided by publisher.
  ISBN 978-1-4666-1975-3 (hardcover) -- ISBN 978-1-4666-1976-0 (ebook) -- ISBN 978-1-4666-1977-7 (print & perpetual access) 1. Information retrieval--Technological innovations. I. Lu, Zhongyu, 1955-
 ZA3075.D47 2013
 025.5'24--dc23
                                    2012009915

This book is published in the IGI Global book series Advances in Data Mining and Database Management (ADMDM) (ISSN: 2327-1981; eISSN: 2327-199X)

British Cataloguing in Publication Data
A Cataloguing in Publication record for this book is available from the British Library.

All work contributed to this book is new, previously-unpublished material. The views expressed in this book are those of the authors, but not necessarily of the publisher.

Advances in Data Mining and Database Management (ADMDM) Book Series

David Taniar
Monash University, Australia

ISSN: 2327-1981
EISSN: 2327-199X

MISSION

With the large amounts of information available to businesses in today's digital world, there is a need for methods and research on managing and analyzing the information that is collected and stored. IT professionals, software engineers, and business administrators, along with many other researchers and academics, have made the fields of data mining and database management into ones of increasing importance as the digital world expands. The **Advances in Data Mining & Database Management (ADMDM) Book Series** aims to bring together research in both fields in order to become a resource for those involved in either field.

COVERAGE
- Cluster Analysis
- Customer Analytics
- Data Mining
- Data Quality
- Data Warehousing
- Database Security
- Database Testing
- Decision Support Systems
- Enterprise Systems
- Text Mining

IGI Global is currently accepting manuscripts for publication within this series. To submit a proposal for a volume in this series, please contact our Acquisition Editors at Acquisitions@igi-global.com or visit: http://www.igi-global.com/publish/.

Titles in this Series

For a list of additional titles in this series, please visit: www.igi-global.com

Data Mining in Dynamic Social Networks and Fuzzy Systems
Vishal Bhatnagar (Ambedkar Institute of Advanced Communication Technologies and Research, India)
Information Science Reference • copyright 2013 • 412pp • H/C (ISBN: 9781466642133) • US $195.00 (our price)

Ethical Data Mining Applications for Socio-Economic Development
Hakikur Rahman (University of Minho, Portugal) and Isabel Ramos (University of Minho, Portugal)
Information Science Reference • copyright 2013 • 359pp • H/C (ISBN: 9781466640788) • US $195.00 (our price)

Design, Performance, and Analysis of Innovative Information Retrieval
Zhongyu (Joan) Lu (University of Huddersfield, UK)
Information Science Reference • copyright 2013 • 508pp • H/C (ISBN: 9781466619753) • US $195.00 (our price)

XML Data Mining Models, Methods, and Applications
Andrea Tagarelli (University of Calabria, Italy)
Information Science Reference • copyright 2012 • 538pp • H/C (ISBN: 9781613503560) • US $195.00 (our price)

Graph Data Management Techniques and Applications
Sherif Sakr (University of New South Wales, Australia) and Eric Pardede (LaTrobe University, Australia)
Information Science Reference • copyright 2012 • 502pp • H/C (ISBN: 9781613500538) • US $195.00 (our price)

Advanced Database Query Systems Techniques, Applications and Technologies
Li Yan (Northeastern University, China) and Zongmin Ma (Northeastern University, China)
Information Science Reference • copyright 2011 • 410pp • H/C (ISBN: 9781609604752) • US $180.00 (our price)

Knowledge Discovery Practices and Emerging Applications of Data Mining Trends and New Domains
A.V. Senthil Kumar (CMS College of Science and Commerce, India)
Information Science Reference • copyright 2011 • 414pp • H/C (ISBN: 9781609600679) • US $180.00 (our price)

Data Mining in Public and Private Sectors Organizational and Government Applications
Antti Syvajarvi (University of Lapland, Finland) and Jari Stenvall (Tampere University, Finland)
Information Science Reference • copyright 2010 • 448pp • H/C (ISBN: 9781605669069) • US $180.00 (our price)

Text Mining Techniques for Healthcare Provider Quality Determination Methods for Rank Comparisons
Patricia Cerrito (University of Louisville, USA)
Medical Information Science Reference • copyright 2010 • 410pp • H/C (ISBN: 9781605667522) • US $245.00 (our price)

www.igi-global.com

701 E. Chocolate Ave., Hershey, PA 17033
Order online at www.igi-global.com or call 717-533-8845 x100
To place a standing order for titles released in this series, contact: cust@igi-global.com
Mon-Fri 8:00 am - 5:00 pm (est) or fax 24 hours a day 717-533-8661

List of Reviewers

Professor Sabah, Jassim, *University of Buckingham, UK*
Professor Chen Lijun, *Peking University, China*
Professor Hongji Yang, *De Montfort University, UK*
Dr Geyong Min, *University of Bradford, UK*
Dr Margaret West, *University of Huddersfield, UK*

Table of Contents

Section 1
Keyword Search in XML and XML Stream Processing Techniques

Section 3
Automatic Mapping of XML Documents into Relational Database

Section 4
An Investigation in Multi-Feature Query Language Based Classification in Image Retrieval

Section 5
Business Process in Information Retrieval

Detailed Table of Contents

Section 1
Keyword Search in XML and XML Stream Processing Techniques

Chapter 1

Weidong Yang, Fudan University, China
Hao Zhu, Fudan University, China

It has become desirable to provide a way of keyword search for users to query structured information in an XML database (data-centric retrieval) by combining database and information retrieval techniques. Therefore, the key challenges of keyword search in the XML database are how to define appropriate result models meeting user's search intents, how to search the results by using efficient algorithms, and how to ranking the results. In this chapter, on one hand, the authors present the foundational knowledge of XML keyword search such as XML data models, XML query languages, inverted index, and Dewey encoding. On the other hand, some existing typical researches of keyword search in XML are presented, including the results models such as Smallest Lowest Common Ancestor (SLCA), Exclusive Lowest Common Ancestor (ELCA), Meaningful Lowest Common Ancestor (MLCA), the related search algorithms, and the ranking approaches.

Chapter 2

Weidong Yang, Fudan University, China
Hao Zhu, Fudan University, China

In this chapter, firstly, the LCA-based approaches for XML keyword search are analyzed and compared with each other. Several fundamental flaws of LCA-based models are explored, of which, the most important one is that the search results are eternally determined nonadjustable. Then, the chapter presents a system of adaptive keyword search in XML, called AdaptiveXKS, which employs a novel and flexible result model for avoiding these defects. Within the new model, a scoring function is presented to judge the quality of each result, and the considered metrics of evaluating results are weighted and can be updated as needed. Through the interface, the system administrator or the users can adjust some parameters according to their search intentions. One of three searching algorithms could also be chosen freely in order to catch specific querying requirements. Section 1 describes the Introduction and motivation. Section 2 defines the result model. In section 3 the scoring function is discussed deeply. Section 4 presents the system implementation and gives the detailed keyword search algorithms. Section 5 presents the experiments. Section 6 is the related work. Section 7 is the conclusion of this chapter.

Chapter 3

Weidong Yang, Fudan University, China
Hao Zhu, Fudan University, China

Massive heterogeneous XML data sources emerge on the Internet nowadays. These data sources are generally autonomous and provide search interfaces of XML query language such as XPath or XQuery. Accordingly, users need to learn complex syntaxes and know the schemas. Keyword Search is a user-friendly information discovery technique, which can assist users in obtaining useful information conveniently without knowing the schemas, and is very helpful to search heterogeneous XML data. In this chapter, the authors present a system called SKeyword which provides a common keyword search interface for heterogeneous XML data sources, and employs OWL ontology to represent the global model of various data sources. Section 1 introduces the context of keyword search for heterogeneous XML data source. In Section 2, the preliminary knowledge is given, and the semantics of keyword search result in ontology is defined. In section 3, the system architecture is described. Section 4 presents the approaches of ontology integration and index building used by SKeyword. Section 5 presents the generation algorithm of searching results and discusses how to rewrite the keyword search of global conceptual model to into the XQuery sentences for local XML sources. Section 6 discussed how to organize and rank the results. Section 7 shows the experiments. Section 8 is the related work. Section 9 is the conclusion of this chapter.

Chapter 4

Weidong Yang, Fudan University, China
Hao Zhu, Fudan University, China

The problem of processing streaming XML data is gaining widespread attention from the research community, and various XML stream processing methods are put forward, including automaton-based methods, index-based methods, and so forth. In this chapter, the basic concepts and several existing typical approaches of XML stream processing are discussed. Section 1 introduces the background and current research status of this area. Section 2 focuses on the discussion of automaton-based methods, for example, X/YFilter, XPush, et cetera. In section 3, the index-based methods are given. In section 4, other methods such us Fist and XTrie are discussed briefly. Section 4 discusses some optimization technique of XML stream processing. Section 5 summarizes this chapter.

Chapter 5

Weidong Yang, Fudan University, China
Hao Zhu, Fudan University,China

Chapter 5 presents a novel approach for processing complex twig pattern with OR-predicates and AND-predicates over XML document streams which a twig pattern is represented as a query tree. Its OR-predicates and AND-predicates are represented as a separate abstract syntax tree associated with the branch node, and all the twig patterns are combined into a single prefix query tree that represents such queries by sharing their common prefixes. Consequently, all the twig patterns are evaluated in a single, document-order pass over the input document stream avoiding the translation of the set of twig patterns into a finite state automaton. Chapter 1 introduces the background of this issue. Chapter 2 discusses the representation of complex twig pattern as a query tree, how to combine a set of twig patterns into a single query three, how to match multi twig patterns over the incoming XML document, and possible optimization of computing logical AND/OR predicates. In section 3, the architecture of a XML stream process system named LeoXSQ is given. Section 4 shows the conducted experiments. In section 5, the related work is discussed. Section 6 summarizes this chapter.

Chapter 6

Weidong Yang, Fudan University, China
Hao Zhu, Fudan University, China

Most existing XML stream processing techniques adopt full structured query languages such as XPath or XQuery, which are difficult for ordinary users to learn and use. This chapter presents an XML stream filter system called XKFitler, which uses keyword to filter XML streams. In XKFitler, we use the concepts of XLCA (eXclusive Lowest Common Ancestor) and XLCA Connecting Tree (XLCACT) to define the search semantic and results of keywords, and present an approach to filter XML stream according to keywords. In section 1, the background of keyword search in XML streams is introduced. Section 2 explains the searching results. In section 3, a stack-based keyword searching algorithm for XML stream filtering without schemas is presented in-depth. Section 4 presents a keyword search over XML streams by using schema information. The system architecture of XKFilter is described in section 5. Section 6 is the experiments to show the performance. Section 7 discusses the related work. Section 8 is the summaries of this chapter.

Section 2
Retrieving Information from Compressed XML Documents According to Vague Queries

Chapter 7

Badya Al-Hamadani, University of Huddersfield, UK
Joan Lu, University of Huddersfield, UK

The eXtensible Markup Language (XML) is a World Wide Web Consortium (W3C) recommendation which has widely been used in both commerce and research. As the importance of XML documents increase, the need to deal with these documents increases as well. This chapter illustrates the methodology that has been used throughout the research, discussing all its parts and how these parts were adopted in the research.

Chapter 8

Badya Al-IIamadani, University of Huddersfield, UK
Joan Lu, University of Huddersfield, UK

XML documents are increasing in usage during the last years since the structure of these documents has lots of important specifications. This chapter explains the importance of XML documents and their structure. It spotlights the difference between the traditional text retrieval and retrieving information from XML documents as well as the query languages used to access parts of these documents.

Since this research consists of two main parts, the XML compressor and the vague query processor, this chapter discusses the main XML compression techniques in its first part. It will highlight the advantages and disadvantages of these techniques and discusses the differences between them. The second part of this chapter will focus on the vague query processors used to retrieve information from XML documents.

Chapter 10

As shown in the literature review from the previous chapter, there are a good number of studies in the field of compressing XML documents and querying the compressed version without the need to fully decompress. However, vague queries, which are one of the most important query types, have been processed to retrieve information from raw XML documents and not from compressed ones. Depending on the SDM, the design of the complete system should be made, followed by its implementation which can be seen in Appendix B in chapter 12. This chapter illustrates the design architecture of the XCVQ (an XML Compressing and Vague Querying) which has the ability to compress the XML documents and use the compressed files in order to retrieve information according to vague queries. It starts with the main architecture of the system followed by the design of each of its parts, namely XCVQ's compressor, decompressor, and the query processor.

Chapter 11

Since the testing and evaluation processes are part of SDM, this chapter illustrates the detailed testing of XCVQ and its ensuing evaluation. Because the XCVQ model consists of three main parts, XCVQ-C, XCVQ-D, and XCVQ-QP, the testing strategy will involve testing each stage on its own. This chapter describes the testing of the three parts of the XCVQ model.

Chapter 12

This chapter introduces a new model which has the ability to compress an XML document efficiently and retrieve information from the compressed file according to vague queries and even various other types of queries. This chapter will outline the main conclusions of the research as well as the main advantages and limitations of the designed model. Finally, the chapter will also list possible future trends in this research in terms of developing the proposed model.

Section 3
Automatic Mapping of XML Documents into Relational Database

Chapter 13

Ibrahim Dweib, Sultan Qaboos University, Oman
Joan Lu, University of Huddersfield, UK

Extensible Markup Language (XML) nowadays is one of the most important standard media used for exchanging and representing data through the Internet. Storing, updating, and retrieving the huge amount of web services data such as XML is an attractive area of research for researchers and database vendors. In this chapter, the authors propose and develop a new mapping model, called MAXDOR, for storing, rebuilding, updating, and querying XML documents using a relational database without making use of any XML schemas in the mapping process. The model addressed the problem of solving the structural hole between ordered hierarchical XML and unordered tabular relational database to enable us to use relational database systems for storing, updating, and querying XML data. A multiple link list is used to maintain XML document structure, manage the process of updating document contents, and retrieve document contents efficiently. Experiments are done to evaluate MAXDOR model.

Chapter 14

Ibrahim Dweib, Sultan Qaboos University, Oman
Joan Lu, University of Huddersfield, UK

In this chapter, the research background is discussed. This includes XML model, XML query languages, XML schema languages, XML Application Program Interface, XML documents types, XML data storage approaches, relational database model, and the similarities and differences between XML model and relational database model. Finally the chapter summary is given.

Chapter 15

Ibrahim Dweib, Sultan Qaboos University, Oman
Joan Lu, University of Huddersfield, UK

This chapter presents the state of the art approaches for storing and retrieving the XML documents from relational databases. Approaches are classified into schema-based mapping and schemaless-based mapping. It also discusses the solutions which are included in Database Management Systems such as SQL Server, Oracle, and DB2. The discussion addresses the issues of: rebuilding XML from RDBMS approaches, comparison of mapping approaches, and their advantages and disadvantages. The chapter concludes with the issues addressed.

Chapter 16

Ibrahim Dweib, Sultan Qaboos University, Oman
Joan Lu, University of Huddersfield, UK

This chapter gives a full description of the proposed model introduced by the authors. The new model is called MAXDOR for mapping XML document into relational database. The description includes mathematical concepts that are used in this model, the labelling method used to label XML document and identify its content, and the design framework used to maintain the document structure, parent-child, ancestor-descendant, and siblings relations among document contents. It also presents a set of algorithms for mapping, reconstructing, updating, and retrieving XML documents.

Chapter 17

Ibrahim Dweib, Sultan Qaboos University, Oman
Joan Lu, University of Huddersfield, UK

This chapter presents the system architecture, and implementation tools used for evaluating the MAX-DOR model. The chapter also presents the main classes created to demonstrate the methodology for mapping XML document into relational database, rebuilding XML document from relational database, updating the content of XML document stored in relational database, XPath-To-SQL query translation, and building the result in XML format. Application on a case study is also presented. XML data sets from selected XML bench marks and XML data repository will be identified to be used for testing and evaluating the model. Finally, the chapter concludes with a summary.

Chapter 18

Ibrahim Dweib, Sultan Qaboos University, Oman
Joan Lu, University of Huddersfield, UK

In this chapter, the authors give a description of the experiment setup consisting of experiment environment and performance measurement. They perform experiments on mapping XML document into relational database, building XML document from relational database, updating XML document stored in relational database, and retrieving document content from relational database using XPath expressions. These experiments will be done to check the scalability and effectiveness of the model. Then they compare their model with the Global Encoding model and the Accelerating XPath model. The comparison consist of four stages: mapping, building, updating, and retrieving, as most of other studies just took one or two stage and forgot the others. Some of them took retrieving, others took updating, and others took updating and retrieving, but most of them did not consider mapping and rebuilding.

Chapter 19

Ibrahim Dweib, Sultan Qaboos University, Oman
Joan Lu, University of Huddersfield, UK

In this chapter, the authors characterize a new model for mapping XML documents into relational database. The model examines the problem of solving the structural hole between ordered hierarchical XML and unordered tabular relational database to enable use of the relational database systems for storing, updating, and querying XML data. The authors introduce and implement a mapping system called MAXDOR to solve the problem.

With rapid development of digital technologies, building an efficient and reliable image retrieval system is always challenging in computing science and related application disciplines. This book part presents an investigation in how "Content-Based Image Retrieval (CBIR)" queries could be designed in order to achieve an extensible language understandable by both humans and machines. The query language used applies concepts from established text search and image retrieval engines. The question of whether such a query language can be sufficiently expressive to formally describe certain real-life concepts is investigated. Sets of images from different classes are used to build "descriptor" queries that are supposed to capture a single concept.

The research field of "Content-Based Image Retrieval (CBIR)" is closely related to several others. This chapter provides an overview of the most relevant research fields and their interrelationship regarding this investigation. For each one, a summary of recent, related research is presented. In addition, the related preliminary work of the author is shortly presented. Based on this background information, major challenges in CBIR are discussed. The scope and the aims of this investigation have been adjusted to accommodate those challenges with respect to the given resources.

This chapter points out certain technologies that are often applied in a CBIR system. A prototypical retrieval system has been developed in order to evaluate the research hypothesis. Following common principles of information hiding, the software is designed to have multiple layers of abstraction. The top layer needs to be user friendly and also has the task to translate human understandable concepts into machine readable commands. As every user has a different level of expertise, the interface complexity should be adapted accordingly.

Chapter 23

Raoul Pascal Pein, University of Huddersfield, UK

Joan Lu, University of Huddersfield, UK

Wolfgang Renz, Hamburg University of Applied Sciences, Germany

In this chapter, a CBIR design based on previous work of the author is presented. The available system already allows for a retrieval by a query string. In the context of this investigation, the system has been extended to support alternative user interfaces as well as a testing module used in the case studies below. Being a pure research prototype, the retrieval engine is optimized for generating accurate results in order to have a reliable data foundation. Further, the query language syntax and the constraints for a practical application of the learning algorithm are presented.

Chapter 24

Raoul Pascal Pein, University of Huddersfield, UK

Joan Lu, University of Huddersfield, UK

Wolfgang Renz, Hamburg University of Applied Sciences, Germany

This chapter discusses several case studies to evaluate the methods introduced in chapter 23, Methods. Each case study focuses on a specific issue and the advanced cases build up on previous findings. The first ones are dealing with the low-level fv directly and then the scope widens to the interrelationship of multiple fv until their combination within a single query is used as a mapping rule for higher-level semantics (i.e. categories).

Chapter 25

Raoul Pascal Pein, University of Huddersfield, UK

Joan Lu, University of Huddersfield, UK

Wolfgang Renz, Hamburg University of Applied Sciences, Germany

In this final chapter of the section, the conclusion of this book section is given. It is summarized how the initial hypothesis has been investigated and which answer has been found. A brief summary of the achievements as well as the intended future work in this area are presented.

Section 5
Business Process in Information Retrieval

Chapter 26

Wei Zhou, Yunnan University, China

Yixuan Zhou, Yunnan University, China

Jinwu Yang, Yunnan University, China

Shaowen Yao, Yunnan University, China

BPM (Business Process Management) includes support for business process analysis, design, implementation, management methods, techniques, and tools. This chapter introduces the origin of BPM technology and development, covering four fields: Business Process Management benefits, the history of BPM, classification of Business process, the lifecycle of BPM, and Business Process Modeling Techniques. In addition, the authors also determine that the present workflow technology is not enough to exist in the root causes of some deficiencies; concluding the chapter with the future of workflow technology trends.

Business process modeling is that make use of graphics, formulas, tables and text to describe the characteristics of business process, and answer why to do, what to do, how to do. Business process modeling is the foundation of business process management. Implementation of business process management can improve the process and enhance competitiveness. In this chapter, the authors attempt to find current business process modeling methods' advantages and disadvantages by analyzing their feature and comparison of based on series important evaluation criteria. The goal is that it provides a reference to business process modeling methods in practice.

Workflow patterns contain basic features of business process. Advanced branching and synchronization patterns present a series of patterns, which characterize more complex branching and merging concepts which arise in business processes. Pi-calculus can be applied in business process modeling. In this chapter, this kind of workflow patterns is investigated using Pi-calculus.

In this chapter, process exception handling at work item level, exception handling at case level, and recovery action are discussed and represented in bigraphs for CCS. Based on the discussion, models for process exception patterns are proposed. The work intends to provide abstract models for analyzing the behavior of exception handling, and the result shows that some advanced features of bigraphs are introduced in representations.

Chapter 30

Gang Xue, Yunnan University, China
Zhongwei Wu, Yunnan University, China
Kun Zhang, Chuxiong Normal University, China
Shaowen Yao, Yunnan University, China

Up to the present, the modeling of business process manly focuses on the flow-control perspective, regardless of the logic relationships between models. Although the value of business rules in business process modeling has been recognized by many organizations, it is not fully clear how business rules can be used to model business process models. Business rules are powerful representation forms that can potentially define the semantics of business process models and business vocabulary. This chapter is committed to model the business process based on SBVR, then use the method mentioned below to transform a plain text rule statement into BPMN files.

Chapter 31

Yanjun Qian, Yunnan University, China
Wei Zhou, Yunnan University, China
Zhongwei Wu, Yunnan University, China
Shaowen Yao, Yunnan University, China

WS-CDL (Web Service Choreography Description Language) is a language to describe multiple party how to work with together to accomplish a work in the context of SOA. BEPL (Business Process Execution Language) can get the same point, but they are from different view. WS-CDL is from a global view, which describes how multiple parties communicate with each other. BPEL is from a point of view of a single role who participates to manage the process of the work. Usually these two ways work together to describe and implement the business process. But WS-CDL has more advantages to achieve the most important goal of SOA-flexibility. So, W3C gives a suggestion to create an algorithm mapping from WS-CDL to BPEL; this chapter describes such a way to accomplish this.

Foreword

I am very glad to have this opportunity to provide a foreword for this book in one of today's most important areas in computing and information science. I cannot wait for introducing it to my friends and students around my circle. The reasons are stated as follows.

The World Wide Web overwhelms us with immense amount of widely distributed data and interconnected, rich and dynamic hypertext information. People are beginning to be puzzled by the problem of information acquisition from internet. That is why Information Retrieval Technology catches great attention from academics and industries in recent years.

The title of this book is "Design, Performance, and Analysis of Innovative Information Retrieval." Different with others in the subject area, the book is started with a fundamental problem, XML stream data processing, followed by special issues, such as Compressed XML document information retrieval, XML documents and relational database mapping, multi-feature image query language for image classification, and finally ended at business process in information retrieval. This book summarizes these developments, presents the state of the art of the technology in the fields both in the algorithms and system design. Some essential problems are extremely important for the multimedia search, e.g. efficient data processing, specially facing a large amount of data, is a key for internet data process and management systems; query language must be able to capture the user's intentions and translate them into a machine-understandable format. Another interesting area presented in the book is the last section of the book, titled "Business Processing in Information Retrieval." Business process as well as related information retrieval seldom mentioned in the conferences of IR, and should be counted as a topic of interdisciplinary research. The 5th section of the book supports for the analysis, design, implementation, management methods, techniques and tools for business process. It should be worth reading, since with the development of scientific management in both enterprises and economic, some disciplines would be beneficial from Business Process Management. Thus, the history of BPM, classification of Business process, and the lifecycle of BPM, will be keys to survive the business. It follows that as information retrieval techniques will be one of the most important needs, this book brings some lights for readers.

I believe the book will draw attention from the intended audiences, such as academic researchers who are interesting in some special issues, graduate students and industry professionals who are learning XML stream data processing, investigating and designing information retrieval systems.

Xiaoyan Zhu
Tsinghua University, P.R. China

Xiaoyan Zhu *is Professor and PhD supervisor of the Department of Computer Science and Technology at Tsinghua University, China. She is Deputy Head of the State Key Laboratory of Intelligent Technology and Systems at the same University, and Head of the Tsinghua-Waterloo Joint Research Center for Internet Information Acquisition. Professor Zhu serves on the Editorial Board of the Journal of BMC Bioinformatics. She earned her BSc at University of Science and Technology Beijing, her MSc at Kobe University, and her PhD at Nagoya Institute of Technology. Her research interests are in pattern recognition, neural networks, machine learning, natural language processing, text mining, intelligent information processing on biomedical literature, and many more.*

Preface

OVERVIEW

Research into information retrieval has strong impact on both the social and economic world (Debons, 1971). Information Retrieval – IR involves a wide range of applications including social science, science, and engineering (Lu, 2005; Wang & Lu, 2009). The improvement in both methodology and technology in IR is tremendously demanding. The areas like scientific experiments, engineering productions, business processes, et cetera, could generate huge amount of data daily, hourly, or per second, which could lead to a huge problem in efficient search and retrieval or secure storage, for the scientists, engineers, doctors, librarian, managers, et cetera in the real world. In recent years, a number of emerging technologies significantly contribute to the IR, together with fundamental IR theories and concepts, which are adopted into new tools or systems in target applications, such as XML technology, content based image retrieval, and business processes management.

XML technology can be counted as one of key contributors to the modern IR technology because it operates based on meaning not like other computing languages, which are based on notation or human-unreadable binary code. Using XML, people can instruct computer to search information semantically within language itself. However, XML is not perfect. Typical examples are XML files look like a large amount of text, which may cause problem to reduce retrieval efficiency, waste storage space with redundant data, and lower the extent of security, particularly data integrity. Thus, research into XML data compression is of important in both users and researchers. Also, XML is strong in data representation and exchanging in database management systems. The native XML database or industrial supported XML documents are popular in the contemporary computing in both applications and development environments (Lu & Arabnia, 2009). Relational database – RDB - is simple and easy to manipulate database management systems, and still very popular for a large number of database users among the database markets. Thus, automatic mapping XML into RDB system could be useful to enable XML DB system can be deployed by RDB users who has no XML background.

Image retrieval is another important area in IR as image uses a special way to deliver the information to human beings. Image information is normally stored in a huge repository and retrieved when needed. Applications are involved in a wide range of areas, such as medical diagnoses, personal collections, space agencies, and geographic information from general to specific systems. Content Based Image Retrieval – CBIR - is one of emerging technologies in image retrieval areas (Pein & Lu, 2010). A typical application of CBIR is multimedia publishing and design. Query languages and learning algorithms extract new features based on low level information could be beneficial from semantic search and satisfactory of both machine and human understanding.

Traditional IR was not often extended into business process models. In fact, information fusion in the business world cannot be ignored. Life cycle for Business Process Management – BPM, marketing analysis, process design, sales reports, et cetera, may easily produce billions of data sets, documents, or even images in today's digital world. Design, implementation, and optimization of BPM models are crucial for the success of organizational business. Therefore, BPM becomes an important component to join the areas of IR research.

THE TARGET AUDIENCE

Immediate audiences for this book are from the area of information retrieval around the world. The book targets at the readers who are interested in the latest theories, methods, technologies and tools for IR in interdisciplinary and multidisciplinary research and applications; researchers who are working in higher education, industrial companies, and professional bodies can be also benefited from the book; professors, lecturers, and teachers from a wide range of subject areas can be benefited from the book if they are interested in IR. The book can be an inspiration for research initiatives and reading materials for educationists and students, and for a library collection for this fast developing subject area with emerging cutting age technologies.

THE IMPORTANCE OF EACH OF THE SECTIONS

This book is organized in 5 sections. Section 1 has 5 chapters. Section 2 has 6 chapters. Section 3 has 7 chapters. Section 4 has 6 chapters. Section 5 has 6 chapters. The importance of each part will be introduced as follows.

Section 1 introduces research in searchability and manipulation for XML data stream files. One current approach is to use keyword to query requested information. The following areas in query semantics, computing algorithms, the ranking of the results, view-based keyword search, and the comparison between data-centric and text-centric approaches are discussed within context. Another interesting approach is to build up XML filtering systems, which aim to provide fast, on-the-fly matching of XML-encoded data to large numbers of query specifications containing constraints on both structure and content. Approaches use event-based parsing and Finite State Machines (FSMs) to provide the basis for highly scalable structure-oriented XML filtering systems. Finally, optimization technique is shown to improve the processing efficiency.

Section 2 researches into a very common issue in XML world, i.e. dealing with large amount of XML documents generated by legend systems. This part focuses mainly on introducing compression of large documents and querying information without decompression through a system called *XCVQ-QP* that uses the path-dictionary, which contains all the elements and attributes names, to specify the relevant documents from thousands of XML documents. It is claimed that the system is able to retrieve information from unspecified document(s). To be against existing XML query processors that require the users to pre-specify the required documents to retrieve information, *XCVQ-QP* has the ability to retrieve information from one or more than one XML document without the need to specify exactly which document could contain the required information.

Section 3 presents a research outcome which can automatically map XML documents into relational database. The research aims to make people's lives easier, especially in the reasons for which they are using database without XML background. The system developed is called MAXDOR, which has achieved the following advantages:

- **High Flexibility of Updating:** MAXDOR approach performed updating processes of inserting new tokens in any location in the document and at any level of relevance to the candidate element (i.e. parent, child, left-sibling and right-sibling), updating token name and value at constant cost of execution time since there is no need to relabeling following tokens IDs or overwrite tokens paths.
- **Stability:** The approach worked fine in both directions; mapping and rebuilding for large documents: *"Auction"* document with 600MB size and 9244050 tokens can be processed without trouble.

Section 4 introduces a set of research work based on the emerging technology – Content Based Image Retrieval (CBIR). Investigation is against traditional machine learning approaches. The study has been evaluated by a number of case studies based on a developed query language. The achievements show that developed query language is good enough to deal with general retrieval tasks, e.g. mapping image similarity, merging multiple sub-queries, querying features semantically, through a set of advanced algorisms.

Section 5 presents a set of collaborative approaches in business process in information retrieval. The studies focus on the building up business model, developing advanced algorisms, implementing the theories and concepts into advanced service oriented architecture systems. The key methods used in the investigation are Petri-net for analysis of Business Process Modeling Methods; Pi-calculus for advanced branching and synchronization patterns description; rule based approach for process modeling; finally WS-CDL (Web Service Choreography Description Language) for describing multiple party how to work with together to accomplish a work in the context of SOA.

CONCLUSION

In conclusion, this book presents a picture for the latest concepts and the state of the art technology in the information retrieval and its related technologies and approaches. In particular, it addresses the following.

1. The contributions of key technologies to IR, i.e. XML, database, image retrieval, and business modelling process.
2. The contributions of key application areas to IR, i.e. data technology, document engineering, and business sectors.
3. New challenges in the research into retrieval efficiency, accuracy, and correctness for a wide range of disciplines.

REFERENCES

Debons, A. (1971). Command and control: Technology and social impact. *Advances in Computers, 11*, 319–390. doi:10.1016/S0065-2458(08)60634-8

Lu, Z. (2005). A survey of XML applications on science and technology. *International Journal of Software Engineering and Knowledge Engineering, 15*(1), 1–33. doi:10.1142/S0218194005001902

Lu, Z., & Arabnia, H. R. (2009). An introduction to contemporary computing with XML in science & technology . In *Natural language engineering & machine learning: Self adaptive systems pervasive computing*. Athens, GA: Elliott & Fitzpatrick.

Pein, R. P., & Lu, J. (2010). Multi-feature query language for image classification. *Procedia Computer Science, 1*(1), 2539–2547. doi:10.1016/j.procs.2010.04.287

Wang, L., & Lu, Z. (2009). *Efficient spatial patterns mining*. USA: Elliot & Fitzpatrick, Inc.

Acknowledgment

Special thanks are sent to reviewers. With their critical feedback, the book is able to be introduced to this challenging area. Great thanks also send to Professor Weifen Fan from University of Edinburgh for his great encouragement and support to enable this book to be born. Huge thanks are sent to the IGI Global team for their strong support, help, guidance, and patience.

Section 1
Keyword Search in XML and XML Stream Processing Techniques

Weidong Yang
Fudan University, China

Hao Zhu
Fudan University China

XML Keyword Search is a user-friendly information discovery technique, which has attracted much interest in recent years. Different from keyword search over flat documents, the search object is a single XML document/database with structure information inside, and the results are supposed to be fragments of it containing keywords. Since it is difficult and sometimes impossible to identify users' intentions through keywords, it is really a challenging task to determine which fragments should be returned. As a matter of fact, this is still an open issue of keyword search on structured and semi-structured data. Stream-based continuous query processing fits a large class of new applications, such as sensor networks, location tracking, network management, and financial data analysis. Stream based applications usually involve handling the infinite size and unpredictability of the data streams and requiring timely response, traditional database processing techniques cannot be used directly; thus, there has been plentiful of researches about data stream management. As extensible markup language (XML) is a standard for information exchange, the problem of processing streaming XML data is gaining widespread attention from the research community.

This section presents research on XML keyword search and XML stream processing techniques. It has six chapters altogether. In chapter 1, the authors describe the foundation of XML keyword search including the concepts of keyword search in XML and the research status in this area. In chapter 2, the LCA-based approaches for XML keyword search are analyzed and compared with each other, a system of adaptive keyword search in XML, called AdaptiveXKS is presented, which employs a flexible result model, and a scoring function. In chapter 3, the techniques of keyword search for heterogeneous XML data sources are discussed. Chapter 4 describes the basic concepts and techniques of XML stream processing, and the state of art of XML stream is also given. Chapter 5 presents an approach for processing complex twig pattern with OR-predicates and AND-predicates over XML document streams. In chapter 6, the techniques of XML stream filtering techniques based on keyword are given.

Chapter 1
Foundation of Keyword Search in XML

Weidong Yang
Fudan University, China

Hao Zhu
Fudan University, China

ABSTRACT

It has become desirable to provide a way of keyword search for users to query structured information in an XML database (data-centric retrieval) by combining database and information retrieval techniques. Therefore, the key challenges of keyword search in the XML database are how to define appropriate result models meeting user's search intents, how to search the results by using efficient algorithms, and how to ranking the results. In this chapter, on one hand, the authors present the foundational knowledge of XML keyword search such as XML data models, XML query languages, inverted index, and Dewey encoding. On the other hand, some existing typical researches of keyword search in XML are presented, including the results models such as Smallest Lowest Common Ancestor (SLCA), Exclusive Lowest Common Ancestor (ELCA), Meaningful Lowest Common Ancestor (MLCA), the related search algorithms, and the ranking approaches.

1.1 INTRODUCTION

As a standard for the representation and exchange of semi-structured data on the Internet, XML has attracted much research in XML retrieval, which enables information discovery in XML data.

With regard to the retrieval mode, traditional *structured query languages*, such as *XPath* and *XQuery*, are used to search XML data, which can convey complex semantic meanings and therefore retrieve precisely the desired results. Nevertheless, the syntax of such a language is often rather complicated which makes it not appropriate for a naive user. One still needs sufficient knowledge of the structure, role of the requested objects in

DOI: 10.4018/978-1-4666-1975-3.ch001

order to formulate such a meaningful query. In contrast, *keyword search* is a proven user-friendly way of querying XML data, since the user does not need to know either a query language or the structure of the underlying data. The main disadvantage lies in the lack of expressivity and inherent ambiguity, which also poses challenges in interpreting the semantics when performing keyword search on XML data.

Considering the organization of underlying XML data, *data-centric retrieval* and *text-centric (or document-centric) retrieval* are to be examined. While both text and structure are important, text-centric retrieval give higher priority to text. The premise of this approach is that XML document retrieval is characterized by long text fields and inexact matching. In contrast, data-centric XML retrieval can execute exact match conditions upon mainly numerical and non-text attribute-value encoded data. Therefore, this put the emphasis on the structural aspects of XML data and queries. In a word, text-centric approaches are appropriate for data that are essentially text documents, marked up as XML to capture document structure, while data-centric approaches are commonly used for data collections with complex structures that mainly contain non-text data. (Further comparisons can be referred in later sections).

In the chapter, some basic XML concepts will be described in Section 1.2. Then we will mainly discuss data-centric keyword search from several aspects, namely semantic model, search algorithms and relevance ranking, which be further presented during section 1.3-1.5. Other related issues can be found in Section 1.6.

1.2 BASIC XML CONCEPTS

1.2.1 XML Documents

The Extensible Markup Language (XML) is a general-purpose specification for creating custom markup language. Originally designed to meet the challenges of large-scale electronic publishing, XML is also playing an increasingly important role in the exchange of a wide variety of data on the Web and elsewhere. XML is recommended by the *World Wide Web Consortium (W3C)*, a fee-free open standard, which also specifies XML lexical grammar and parsing requirements.

1.2.1.1 XML Element and Attribute

An *XML element* is everything from (including) the element's start tag to (including) the element's end tag. An element can contain other elements, simple text or a mixture of both. Elements can also have attributes. *XML attributes* provide additional information about elements.

In the XML document showed in Figure 1, <bookstore> and <book> have element contents, because they contain other elements. <title> has text context since it only contains text. And <book> has an attribute (category="NOVEL").

1.2.1.2 XML Schema

An *XML document* can optionally have a schema to describe the structure of the document. An *XML schema* defines elements and attributes that can appear in a document, the child elements of a particular element, the child elements' order and number, data types of elements and attributes and their default or fixed values, etc. Figure 2 displays an example schema, which is used to describe the structure of the XML document showed in Figure 1.

1.2.1.3 Data Model

As an XML document is formed by a sequence of elements that enclose text values and other elements, it is typically represented by a *tree* structure where the nodes correspond to elements, attributes or text values, and the edges represent immediate element-subelement or element-value relationships. Thus, an XML database is then

Figure 1. An XML document

```
<bookstore>
 <book category="NOVEL">
  <title>Harry Potter</title>
  <author>J K. Rowling</author>
  <year>2005</year>
  <price>29.99</price>
 </book>
 <book category="WEB">
  <title>Learning XML</title>
```

modeled as a forest of unranked, node-labeled trees, one tree per document. Figure 3 displays such a model for the XML document in Figure 1.

Note that in an XML data tree, some nodes with the same name might be nested on the same path, called *recursion*. Conventional labeled *graph* notation is also a commonly used model to represent XML data. The nodes of the graph correspond to XML elements and are labeled with the tags of the corresponding elements and optional string values. The graph model is based on the intra-document and inter-document references in addition to the hierarchical element structure considered in the tree structure. Intra-document references are represented using ID/ IDREFs, where ID uniquely identifies an element, and

Figure 2. The XML schema for the XML document in Figure 1

```
<xsd: element name="book" type="bookType"/>


<xsd: complexType name="bookType">
    <xsd: sequence>
        <xsd: element name="title"  type="xsd: string"/>
        <xsd: element name="author"  type="xsd: string"/>
        <xsd: element name="year"  type="xsd: gYear"/>
```

Figure 3. Tree representation

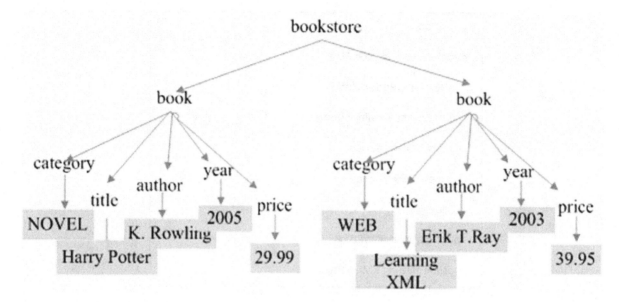

IDREF refer to other elements that are explicitly identified by their ID attributes. Inter-document references are represented using XLink. Thus, an edge of the graph denotes either containment (the general element-subelement or element-value relationship) or an ID/IDREF relationship or a cross-document XML Link.

1.2.2 XML Query Language

1.2.2.1 XPath

XPath is a standard for enumerating paths in an XML document collection. It is a basic XML query language that selects nodes from XML documents such that the path from the root to each selected node satisfies a specified pattern. XPath defines 13 axis types, namely *parent, child, ancestor, descendant, descendant-or-self, ancestor-or-self, following, preceding, following-sibling, preceding-sibling, self, attribute*, and *namespace*, among which *child* and *descendant* are the two most commonly used axes, where "A/B" denotes selecting B-tagged child nodes of A-tagged nodes

and "A//B" selecting B-tagged descendant nodes of A-tagged nodes.

A simple XPath query as a path pattern is formulated as a sequence of alternating axes and tags, while a general XPath query can specify a more complex twig pattern by using predicates in its expression. The following two examples are used to illustrate them separately.

Example 1: "/bookstore//title" would return all title elements under all top-level bookstore elements. The result of this query on the XML document in Figure 1 is two title nodes that have values "Harry Potter" and "Learning XML", respectively.

Example 2: "/bookstore/book[@ category="NOVEL"]/title", in such an XPath query, "/bookstore/book/title" is the main path of the query, and the content between "[" and "]" is a predicate. This query returns all book titles of those books belong to the category of "NOVEL". Only "Harry Potter" is returned.

1.2.2.2 XQuery

XQuery is a querying language designed specifically to work with XML data stores using a SQL-like syntax. It's more expressive than XPath.

In its simplest form, an XQuery query can simply be an XPath expression, however, the real power of XQuery shines through with FLWR expressions. FLWR stands for *For-Let-Where-Return*. The FLWR expression is akin to SQL's SELECT query; it allows for XML data to be queried with conditional statements, and then returns a set of XML elements as a result. Here is a relatively straightforward example, showing how to get all <book> elements whose category attribute equals "NOVEL":

Example 3: For $aBook in document ("bookstore. xml") /bookstore/book
Where $aBook/@category="NOVEL"
Return @aBook

1.2.3 The Indexing Techniques in XML Keyword Search

1.2.3.1 Inverted Index

An *inverted index* is an index data structure storing a mapping from content, such as words or numbers, to its locations in a database file, or in a document or a set of documents. Its purpose is to allow fast full text searches, at a cost of increased processing when a document is added to a database. It is the most popular data structure used in document retrieval systems, for example, in search engines.

The same holds for *XML keyword search*. Inverted list indices are always used to evaluate keyword search queries over XML documents. XML inverted list indices typically store each keyword in the document collection, and the list of XML elements that directly contain the keyword. As is shown in Figure 4, a typical inverted list index can be composed of two parts, with each keyword corresponds to a list of nodes which directly contain it. For example, there are k occurrences of keyword1 in the current document (or database), locating in loc11, loc12,..., loc1k.

In some cases, another index such as a *B+-tree* can be built on the top of each inverted list so that we can efficiently check whether a given element contains a keyword.

1.2.3.2 Path Index

While path indices are generally used to evaluate XML path and twig (i.e., branching path) queries, it can also used to improve the performance of *XML keyword search*. Also similar to the inverted list index, a particular path index can be of various structures. Some researchers Feng et al. (2007) have adopted the path indices based on the base

Figure 4. A sample inverted index

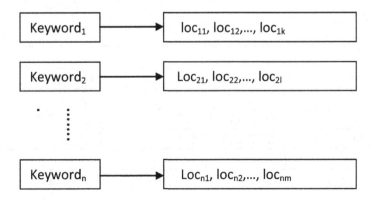

data to efficiently evaluate keyword search queries over virtual XML views. It implements path indices to store XML paths with values in a relational table and use indices such as B+-tree for efficient probes. Figure 5 shows a sample path index.

As shown in Figure 5, the Path-Value index table contains one row for each unique (Path, Value) pair, where path represents a path from the root to an element in the document, and value represents the atomic value of an element on the path. For each unique (Path, Value) pair, the table stores an IDList value, which is the list of ids of all elements on the path corresponding to Path with that atomic value (paths without corresponding values are associated with a null value). A B+-tree index is built on the (Path, Value) pair. Queries are evaluated as follows. First, a path query with value predicated such as /book/author/fn[.='Jane'] is evaluated by probing the index using the search key (Path, 'Jane'). Second, a path query without value predicates is evaluated by merging lists of IDs corresponding to the path, which are retrieved using Path, the prefix of the composite key. For path queries with descendant axes, such as /book//fn, the index is probed for each full data path (e.g., /book/name/fn), and the lists of result ids are merged. Finally, twig queries are evaluated by first evaluating each individual path query and then merging the results based on the dewey id.

1.3 SEMANTIC MODELS

As we have described in the introduction of this chapter, due to the lack of expressivity and inherent ambiguity, keyword search on XML databases can pose a great challenge in interpreting the semantics.

There are two possible semantics for keyword search queries. Under *conjunctive keyword query semantics*, elements that contain all of the query keywords are returned. Under *disjunctive keyword query semantics*, elements that contain at least one of the query keywords are returned. We focus on conjunctive keyword query semantics in the chapter.

In addition, since the user input is a set of keywords, each of which may match name or/and value nodes in the XML tree/graph, it is suitable for us to consider an *unordered* model. For instance, query (John, Design) and query (Design, John) have the same effect.

When we discuss the semantics of keywords search, we will focus on conjunctive keyword query semantics, which means the results of the keyword search should contain all of the query keywords. Since a reference to a whole XML documents is usually not a useful answer, the granularity of the search should be refined. Thus, instead of returning entire documents, an XML search engine should return fragments of XML documents. This is the basic requirement not only

Figure 5. Path-values table

B+-tree

Path	Value	IDList
...	...	...
/books/book/isbn	"111-111-1111"	1.1.1, 1.3.1
/books/book/isbn	"222-222-2222"	1.2.1
...	...	...
/books/book/author/fn	"Jane"	1.2.3, 1.7.3

for *XML keyword search*, but for a general XML search engine. Consequently, the query semantics defined must ensure that only the most specific results are returned. Finally, as *XML keyword search* results can be arbitrarily nested elements, the elements returned should be expected to be meaningfully-related. Intuitively, the "deepest" node containing all the keywords is regarded to give more context information than those "higher" nodes.

In this section, we will describe several existing semantic models, including the classical model *SLCA (Small Lowest Common Ancestor)* developed by Xu and Papakonstantinou (2005) and its variations. Some models issued based on XML graph will also be briefly discussed. In addition, it is necessary to give a brief introduction to Dewey Numbers, which is helpful for you to understand *XML keyword search*.

1.3.1 Dewey Encoding

*Dewey Number*s are always used to encode the element IDs of XML tree, since it can jointly capture ancestor and descendant information. Consider the tree representation of an XML document, where each element is assigned a number that represents its relative position among its siblings. The path vector of the numbers from the root to an element uniquely identifies the element, and can be used as the element ID. Figure 6 shows how Dewey element IDs can be generated for the XML document. This XML tree model is to be used in the latter few examples. An interesting feature of Dewey IDs is that the ID of an ancestor is a prefix of the ID of a descendant. Consequently, ancestor-descendant relationships are implicitly captured in the Dewey ID. The usual < relationship is assumed between any two Dewey numbers. For example, $0.1.0.0.0 < 0.1.1.1$.

1.3.2 Smallest Lowest Common Ancestor (SLCA)

SLCA (Smallest Lowest Common Ancestor) has been used widely as query semantic model for keyword search in XML (Xu & Papakonstantinou, 2005). A keyword search using the SLCA semantics returns nodes in the XML data that satisfy the following two conditions: (1) the subtrees rooted at the nodes contain all the keywords, and (2) the nodes do not have any proper descendant node that satisfies condition (1). The set of returned data nodes are referred to as the SLCAs of the keyword search query.

We first introduce the *Lowest Common Ancestor (LCA)* of k nodes (sets) before we formally define the SLCA query semantics. Assume that $lca(w_1,...,w_k)$ computes the Lowest Common Ancestor (LCA) of k nodes $w_1,...,w_k$. The LCA of sets $S_1,...,S_k$ is the set of LCA's for each combination of nodes in S_1 through S_k.

$$lca\left(S_1,...,S_k\right) = \{lca(w_k,...,w_k) \mid n_1 \in S_1,...,n_k \in S_k\}$$

A node w is called an LCA of sets $S_1,...,S_k$ if $w \in lca\left(S_1,...,S_k\right)$. (*Note:* We assume S_i denotes the keyword list of w_i, i.e., the list of nodes whose labels directly contains w_i sorted by id. The "id" refers to its Dewey ID.)

The Smallest Lowest Common Ancestor (SLCA) of k sets $S_1,...,S_k$ is defined to be

$$slca\left(S_1,...,S_k\right) = \{w \mid w \in lca\left(S_1,...,S_k\right) \wedge \forall w' \in lca\left(S_1,...,S_k\right) \quad w \not< w'\}$$

A node w is called a Smallest Lowest Common Ancestor (SLCA) of $S_1,...,S_k$ if $w \in slca\left(S_1,...,S_k\right)$. Note that a node in $slca\left(S_1,...,S_k\right)$ cannot be an ancestor node of any other node in $slca\left(S_1,...,S_k\right)$.

Figure 6. Dewey IDs

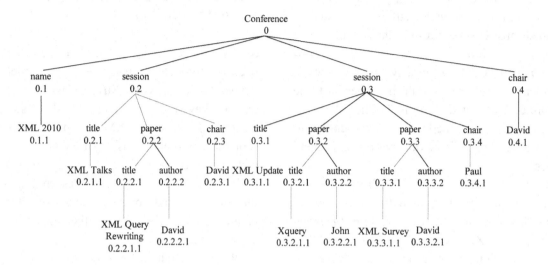

Thus, in this semantic model, two nodes matching to different keywords are considered to be meaningfully related if their LCA is an SLCA.

Example 4: In Figure 6, slca $(S_1,...,S_k)$= {0.2.2, 0.3.3}. Clearly, slca $(S_1,...,S_k) \subseteq$ lca $(S_1, ...,S_k)$. For example, consider S_1 and S_2 in Figure 6. The node 0.2 is not in slca $(S_1, ...,S_k)$ but in lca $(S_1,...,S_k)$.

Besides, SLCAs have some good mathematical properties, which provide some advantages for those algorithms computing them. We will focus on its four critical properties here, which we explain starting from the simplest case where k=2 and S_1 is a singleton {v}.

Property (1):

$$slca(\{v\}, S) = \\ \{descendant(lca(v, lm(v, S)), lca(v, rm(v, S)))\}$$

Property (2):

$$slca(\{v\}, S_2,...,S_k) = \\ slca(slca(\{v\}, S_2,...,S_{k-1}), S_k) \quad for \ k > 2$$

Property (3):

$$slca(S_1,...,S_k) = \\ removeAncestor(\cup_{v1 \in S1} slca(\{v_1\}, S_2,...,S_k))$$

Property (4):

$$slca(S_1,...,S_k) = \\ slca(slca(S_1,...,S_{k-1}), S_k) \quad for \ k > 2$$

The classical algorithms for keyword search using SLCA semantics are the Scan Eager (SE) and Indexed Lookup Eager (ILE) algorithms (Xu & Papakonstantinou, 2005), which were shown to be more efficient than stack-based algorithms (Guo et al., 2003; Yunyal et al., 2004).

1.3.2.1 The Indexed Lookup Eager Algorithm (ILE)

A brute-force solution to the SLCA problem computes the LCAs of all node combinations and then removes ancestor nodes. Besides being inefficient the brute-force approach is blocking. After it computes an LCA v = lca($v_1,...,v_k$) for some, $v_1 \in S_1,..., v_k \in S_k$, it cannot report v as an answer since there might be another set of k nodes $u_1,...,u_k$ such that $v \pi lca(u_1,...,u_k)$.

One of the most popular algorithms in *XML keyword search* areas for computing SLCA is the *Indexed Lookup Eager (ILE) algorithm*. Firstly, we investigate the relationships of these four properties. According to property (1), we compute the LCA of v and its left match in S, the LCA of v and its right match in S, and singleton formed from the deeper node from the two LCAs is slca({v},S). The property (2) is a recursive formula which generalizes property (1) to arbitrary k when the first set is a singleton. If the first singleton is generalized to arbitrary S_1, we get Property (3), which can straightforwardly leads to an algorithm to compute slca($S_1,...,S_k$). From analysis, we can find that the algorithm based on Property (3) is also a blocking one. The complexity of the Indexed Lookup Eager algorithm is $O(|S_1|kdlog|S|)$ where $|S_1|$ ($|S|$) is the minimum (maximum) size of keyword lists S1 through Sk.

1.3.2.2 Scan Eager Algorithm

When the occurrences of keywords do not differ significantly, the total cost of finding matches by lookups may exceed the total cost of finding matches by scanning the keyword lists. *Scan Eager Algorithm* is a variant of the Indexed Lookup Eager Algorithm, which takes advantage of the fact that the accesses to any keyword list are strictly in increasing order in the Indexed Lookup Eager algorithm. The Scan Eager algorithm is exactly the same as the Indexed Lookup Eager algorithm except that its lm and rm implementations scan keyword lists to find matches by maintaining a cursor for each keyword list. In order to find the left and right match of a given node with id p in a list S_j, the Scan Eager algorithm advances the cursor of S_j until it finds the node that is closest to p from the left or the right side. Notice that nodes from different lists may not be accessed in order, though nodes from the same list are accessed in order. The complexity of the

Scan Eager algorithm is $O(k|S_1|+d\sum_{2}^{k}|S_i|)$, or $O(kd|S|)$ because there are $O(\sum_{2}^{k}|S_i|)$ Dewey number comparisons, $O(k|S_1|)$ lca and descendant operations.

In a word, the Indexed Lookup Eager algorithm is important in practice since the frequencies of keywords typically vary significantly. In contrast, Scan Eager is tuned for the case where the occurrences of the query's keywords do not vary significantly.

1.3.2.3 Basic Multiway-SLCA Algorithm (BMS)

The Indexed Lookup Eager and Scan Eager algorithms are both based on the same principle of computing SLCAs for a query with k keywords in terms of a sequence of k-1 intermediate SLCA computations, where each SLCA computation takes a pair of data node lists as input and outputs another data node list. Chong at. Some researchers has classified these algorithms as binary-SLCA approach (BS) (Chong, Chee-Yong, & K.Goenka, 2007). As we have discussed in the previous part, the binary-SLCA algorithms compute the SLCAs for $w_1,...,w_k$ by computing the sequence $L_2, L_3, ..., L_k$, where each Li is computed by finding the SLCAs of L_{i-1} and S_i (with $L_1=S_1$), where Si denote the list of XML data nodes that are labeled with keyword k_i, $i \in [1,k]$; and Li denote the SLCAs for a query with the first i keywords, $i \in [1,k]$. An important observation exploited in the binary-SLCA algorithms is that the result size is bounded by min{$|S_1|, ..., |S_k|$}; therefore, by choosing the keyword with lowest frequency as k_1 (i.e., $|S_1| \leq |S_i|$ for $i \in [1,k]$), the algorithms can guarantee that each $|L_i| \leq |S_i|$ for $i \in [2,k]$. However, a drawback of the binary-SLCA approach is that by computing the SLCAs in terms of a series of intermediate SLCA computations, it can often incur many unnecessary SLCA intermediate computations even when the result size is small.

They have proposed a novel approach for processing SLCA-based keyword search queries called *Multiway-SLCA approach* (MS) (Chong et al, 2007). MS approach computes each potential SLCA by taking one data from each keyword list Si in a single step instead of breaking the SLCA computation into a series of intermediate binary SLCA computations. Conceptually, each potential SLCA computed by the BS approach can be thought of as being driven by some node from S1 (i.e., the keyword list with the lowest frequency); on the other hand, the MS approach proposed picks an "anchor" node, which is the central idea in the MS approach, from among the k keyword data lists to drive the multiway SLCA computation.

A set of nodes $S = \{v_1, ..., v_k\}$ is defined to be a *match* for $K = \{w_1, ..., w_k\}$ if $|S| = |K|$ and each $v_i \in S_i$ for $i \in [1,k]$. (S_i denotes the data node list associated with the keyword w_i as before.) A match $S = \{v_1, ..., v_k\}$ is said to be *anchored* by a node $v_a \in S$ if for each $vi \in S - \{v_a\}$, $vi = closest(v_a, S_i)$. Such a v_a is referred to as the *anchor node* of S. The function closest(v, S) computes the closest node in S to v. The anchor node is introduced to minimize redundant computations by maximizing the skipping of those redundant computations.

The MS algorithm computes the SLCAs iteratively. At each iteration, an anchor node v_m is judiciously selected to compute the match anchored by v_m and its LCA (denoted by α). If α is potentially an SLCA, it is maintained in an intermediate SLCA result list given by α1, α2, ..., $α_n$, $n \geq 1$, where all the LCAs $α_i$ in the list are definite SLCAs except for the most recently computed candidate αn. To minimize the computation of LCAs that not SLCAs, it is important to optimize the anchor node selected at each iteration. Besides, it has also developed several optimizations to future maximize the skipping of data nodes in the keyword list without compromising correctness of query results. For lack of space, we omit the further details of the algorithm.

MS approach has also proposed another algorithm called the Incremental Multiway-SLCA Algorithm (IMS) (Chong et al, 2007), which is an optimized variant of BMS that reduces the number of LCA computations. The readers interested in can refer to Chong et al. (2007) for any further details.

1.3.3 Exclusive Lowest Common Ancestor (ELCA)

The *Exclusive Lowest Common Ancestor (ELCA)* is proposed in Guo et al. (2003), which is also used as query semantics in Xu and Papakonstantinou (2008). Consider a keyword query Q consisting of k keywords w1,...,wk. According to ELCA query semantics, the result of the keyword query Q is the set of nodes that contain at least one occurrence of all the query keywords either in their labels or in the labels of their descendant nodes, after excluding the occurrences of the keywords in the subtrees that already contain at least one occurrence of all the query keywords.

According to Guo et al. (2003), the ELCA query semantic ensures that only the most specific results are returned for a keyword search query. It also ensures that an element that has multiple independent occurrences of the query keywords is returned, even if a sub-element of that element already contains all of the query keywords. This ensures that all independent occurrences of the query keywords are represented in the query result.

Example 5. In Figure 6, elca(S_1,S_2) = {0, 0.2, 0.2.2, 0,3,3}. Clearly, elca($S_1,...,S_k$) $\subseteq$ lca ($S_1,...,S_k$). For example, 0.3 is not in elca($S_1,...,S_k$) but in lca ($S_1,...,S_k$).

We can see that slca ($S_1,...,S_k$) $\subseteq$ elca ($S_1,...,S_k$) $\subseteq$ lca ($S_1,...,S_k$).

1.3.3.1 DIL (Dewey Inverted List) and RDIL (Ranked Dewey Inverted List)

Some researchers propose two core algorithms, *DIL (Dewey Inverted List)* and *RDIL (Ranked Dewey Inverted List)*, to return the top m answers from $elca(S_1,...,S_k)$ (Guo et al. 2003).

The DIL algorithm keeps an inverted list sorted by Dewey id for each keyword. DIL (conceptually) sort merges the k inverted lists of the k query keywords and reads each node v in the sorted merged list in order. Intuitively, it is easy to verify the correctness of the DIL algorithm since it reads all nodes in the k inverted lists in document order and has enough information to determine whether a lowest common ancestor of k nodes from the k inverted list is an ELCA node or not. Notice that the DIL algorithm has to scan to the end of all inverted lists. The complexity of the DIL algorithm is $O(kd|S|)$ where $|S|$ is the largest inverted list among $S_1,...,S_k$ and d is the depth of the tree.

The RDIL algorithm in Guo et al. (2003) maintains two separate data structures: inverted lists sorted by the individual nodes' ranking score in descending order and B+ trees built on inverted lists sorted by Dewey id in ascending order. The underlying assumption of RDIL is that higher ranked results (ELCA nodes) are likely to come from nodes in the front of inverted lists sorted by ranking score in descending order and query processing may terminate without scanning to the end of all of the inverted lists.

RDIL works as follows:

1. It reads a node v from the k inverted lists sorted by rank, in round-robin fashion.
2. Then it uses the B+ trees built on inverted lists sorted by Dewey id to find the lowest common ancestor l that contains v and all other keywords. The key observation is that given a node v, an inverted list S sorted by document order and the B+ tree BT built on S, it takes only a single range scan in BT to find the node v' in S whose id is the least that is greater than the id of v such that either v' or its immediate predecessor in S shares the longest common prefix with v which is the Dewey id of l.
3. However, the node l produced in the second step may not be an ELCA node. RDIL first determines whether each child of l contains all keywords or not. Then for each keyword w_i, RDIL checks that keyword witness nodes of l are not under any of its children that contain all keyword instances.

The complexity of RDIL is $O(k^2 d|S|p \log|S| + k^2 d|S|^2)$. Given a node v in an inverted list, as can be seen from the above explanation, the RDIL algorithm does not completely scan other inverted lists in order to find an LCA node that contains v and all other keywords. However, in order to guarantee correctness (not losing any answer nodes and not returning non-answer nodes), scan is repeatedly performed and that is why the complexity of the RDIL is high in the worst case. Furthermore, it is not guaranteed that individual nodes with higher ranking scores always lead to answer nodes higher overall ranking score because the combination ranking function takes into account the distance between witness nodes and answer nodes. Moreover, given a keyword query, there is no practical way to determine a priori whether the DIL or the RDIL algorithm will perform better.

1.3.3.2 Indexed Stack Algorithm (IS)

The *Indexed Stack Algorithm* is proposed in Xu and Papakonstantinou (2008) to answer a keyword query according to the ELCA query semantics. It takes advantage of the benefits of both stack based algorithms and indexed lookup based algorithms and is superior to DIL and RDIL we discussed in the former two sections both analytically and experimentally.

The Indexed Stack Algorithm, leveraging key tree properties, starts from the smallest list S_1, visits each node in S_1, but does not need to access every node in other lists. It achieves high efficiency, especially when the smallest list is significantly smaller than the largest list. The algorithm's efficiency is based on first discovering the nodes of a set elca_can(S_1; S_2, ..., S_k) (short for ELCA Candidates), which is a superset of elca(S_1, ..., S_k) but can be computed efficiently in $O(kd|S_1|\log|S|)$, where k is the number of keywords in the query, d is the depth of the tree and $|S_1|(|S|)$ is the occurrence of the lease (most) frequent keyword in the query.. A subroutine isELCA() is defined to determine whether a given node of elca_can(S_1; S_2, ..., S_k) is a member of elca(S_1, ..., S_k). The IS algorithm puts together the computation of elca_can and isELCA, avoiding redundant computations. More details about this algorithm can be found in Xu and Papakonstantinou (2008).

1.3.4 Meaningful Lowest Common Ancestor (MLCA)

Another work on keyword search based on the *meaningful LCA (MLCA)* (Yunyal et al., 2004) semantics also shares the similar principle as SLCA. A set of nodes consisting of one match to each keyword is meaningfully related if every pair is meaningfully related, and a MLCA is defined as the LCA of these nodes.

To formalize the idea, first of all, given two sets of nodes, where nodes within each set are of the same type, we define how to find pairs of nodes that are meaningfully related to each other from those two sets.

Definition 1 (MLCA of two nodes) Let the set of nodes in an XML document be N. Given A, B $\subseteq$ N, where A is comprised of nodes of type $\mathcal{A}$, and B is comprised of nodes of type $\mathcal{B}$, the Meaningful Lowest Common Ancestors Set C $\subseteq$ N of A and B satisfies the following conditions:

$\forall c_k \in C$, $\exists a_i \in A$, $b_j \in B$, such that $c_k = LCA$ (a_i, b_j). C_k is denoted as MLCA(a_i, b_j).

$\forall a_i \in A$, $b_j \in B$, if $d_{ij} = LCA$ (a_i, b_j) and $d_{ij} \notin$ C, then $\exists c_k \in C$, descendant(c_k, d_{ij}) = true.

The set C is denoted as MLCASET(A,B).

To extend the above definition 1 to define the MLCA of multiple nodes:

Definition 2 (MLCA of multiple nodes) Let the set of nodes in an XML document be N. Given A_1, A_2, ..., $A_m \subseteq$ N, where $\forall j$, $a_{ij} \in$ A_i is of type $\mathcal{A}_i$ ($i \in [1, ..., m]$), a Meaningful Lowest Common Ancestor c = MLCA(a_1, ..., a_m), where $a_i \in A_i$ ($i \in [1, ..., m]$), satisfies the following conditions:

- $\forall j,k \in [1, ..., m]$ ($j \neq k$), $\exists m$=MLCA(a_j, a_k), m $\neq$ null and descendant-or-self(m, c)=true.
- $\exists j,k \in [1, ..., m]$ ($j \neq k$), c=MLCA(a_j,a_k).

Schema-Free XQuery (Yunyal, et al., 2004) uses the idea of Meaningful LCA (MLCA), similar to SLCA, and proposes a stack based sorted merge algorithm which scans to the end of all inverted lists. The complexity of the algorithm in Yunyal, et al. (2004) is $O(kd|S|)$. Yunyal, et al. (2004) shows that keyword search functionality can be easily integrated into the structured query language XQuery as built-in functions, enabling users to query XML documents based on partial knowledge they may have over underlying data with different and potentially evolving structures. The recall and precision experiments shows that it is possible to express a wide variety of queries in a shema-free manner and have them return correct results over a broad diversity of schema.

1.3.5 Other Query Semantics

Besides, other LCA semantics are also proposed, using different techniques to determine which LCA nodes to include in the query result, such as Valuable Lowest Common Ancestor (VLCA) (Li, Feng, Wang, & Zhou,2007).

Yunyal, Cong and Jagadish (2008) introduce the notion of Meaningful Query Focus (MQF) for finding related nodes within an XML document. MQF enables users to take full advantage of the precise and efficiency of XQuery without requiring (perfect) knowledge of the document structure. Such a Schema-Free XQuery is potentially of value not just to casual users with partial knowledge of schema, but also to experts working in data integration or data evolution. In such a context, a schema–free query, once written, can be applied similar content under different schemas, and applied "forever" as these schemas evolve. Actually, the Meaningful Query Focus (MQF) is also a refinement of the Lowest Common Ancestor (LCA), except that the MQF is an XML fragment that meaningfully relates nodes corresponding to relevant variables in the XQuery expression.

There are also query semantics other than LCA for *XML keyword search*, which, for lack of space, will be shortly covered. XSEarch (Cohen, Mamou, Kanza, & Sagiv, 2003) introduces the concept of *interconnection*. Two matches are interconnected and therefore should be in the same group if there are no two distinct nodes with the same tag on the path between these two nodes (through their LCA), excluding themselves. XSeek (Ziyang & Yi, 2007) studies the problem of inferring the most relevant return nodes without elicitation of user preferences. It works for data with or without schema information. XSeek generaes two types of nodes: return nodes that can be inferred explicitly by analyzing keyword match patterns; and return nodes that can be inferred implicitly by considering both keyword match patterns and XML data structure. the experiments show that XSeek generates results with improved precision and recall over prior approaches with reasonable cost. We will not focus on the comparison of the quality of query semantics here.

1.4 RANKING

Since the keyword search may not always be precise and can potentially return a large number of query results. Consequently, an important requirement for keyword search is to rank the query results so that the most relevant results appear first. Different ranking mechanisms may consider different factors to score the query results. But a reasonable query semantic applied to the search results should guarantee that results with perceived higher relevance are returned to the user first.

There are some desired properties for ranking functions over hyperlinked XML documents (Guo et al. 2003):

1. **Result specificity:** The ranking function should rank more specific results higher than less specific results. For example in Figure 6, a <paper> result (which means that all query keywords are associated with the same paper) should be ranked higher than a <session> result (which means that the query keywords occur in the same session, but may associate with different papers). This is one dimension of result proximity.
2. **Keyword proximity:** The ranking function should take the proximity of the query keywords into account. This is the other dimension of result proximity. Note that a result can have high keyword proximity and low specificity, and vice-versa.
3. **Hyperlink awareness:** The ranking function should use the hyperlinked structure of XML documents.
4. In the following, we will describe XRank (Guo et al. 2003) in detail.

XRank (Guo et al. 2003) is a typical paper for ranking the results of XML keyword search, which applies the Exclusive Lowest Common Ancestor (ELCA), formalizes the notion of ranking for XML elements by taking all of the above factors into account. In the following, we will take XRank as an example to describe the ranking mechanisms of XML keyword search.

1.4.1 Ranking Function of XRank

Assume that *ElemRank(v)* is the objective importance of an XML element v computed using the underlying hyperlinked structure. Conceptually, ElemRank is similar to Google's PageRank (Brin & Page, 1998), except that ElemRank is defined at the granularity of an element and takes the nested structure of XML into account.

As before, consider a keyword search query $Q = \{k_1, k_2, ..., k_n\}$ and its result R = Result(Q). Now consider a result element $v_1 \in$ R. XRank first defines the ranking of v_1 with respect to one query keyword k_i, $r(v_1, k_i)$, before defining the overall rank, rank(v_1,Q).

From the definition of R, we know that for every keyword k_i, there exists a sub-element/value node v_2 of v_1 such that $v_2 \notin R_0$ and contains(v_2,k_i). Hence, there is a sequence of containment edges of the form $(v_1,v_2), (v_2, v_3), ..., (v_t,v_{t+1})$ such that v_{t+1} is a value node that directly contains the keyword k_i. Assume:

$$r(v_1, k_i) = ElemRank(v_t)*decay^{t-1}$$

Intuitively, the rank of v_1 with respect to a keyword k_i is ElemRank(v_t) scaled appropriately to account for the specificity of the result, where v_t is the parent element of the value node v_{t+1} that directly contains the keyword ki. When the result element v_1 is the parent element of the value node v_{t+1}(i.e.,$v_1=v_t$), the rank is just the ElemRank of the result element. When the result element indirectly contains the keyword (i.e., $v_1 \neq v_t$), the rank is scaled down by the factor decay for each level. Decay is a parameter that can be set to a value in the range 0 to 1.

The above discussion implicitly assumed that there is only one relevant occurrence of the query keyword k_i in v_1. In case there are multiple (say,

m) relevant occurrences of k_i, we first compute the rank for each occurrence using the above formula. Let the computed ranks be $r_1, r_2, ..., r_m$. The combination rank is:

$$r^{\wedge}(v_1,k_i)=f(r_1, r_2,..., r_m)$$

Here f is some aggregation function. We can set f = max by default, but other choices (such as f = sum) are also supported.

The overall ranking of a result element v_1 for query $Q = (k_1, k_2, ..., k_n)$ is computed as follows:

$$R(v_1,Q) = \left(\sum_{1\leq i\leq n} r^{\wedge}(v_1,k_i)\right) * p(v_1, k_1, k_2, ..., k_n)$$

The overall ranking is the sum of the ranks with respect to each query keyword, multiplied by a measure of keyword proximity $p(v_1, k_1, k_2, ..., k_n)$. The keyword proximity function $p(v_1, k_1, k_2, ..., k_n)$ can be any function that ranges from 0 to 1.by default, XRank sets the proximity function to be inversely proportional to the size of the smallest text window in v_1 that contains relevant occurrences of all the query keywords $k_1, k_2, ..., k_n$. For highly structured XML data sets, where the distance between query keywords may not always be an important factor, the keyword proximity function can be set to be always 1.

After a series of refinements to the PageRank algorithm (Brin & Page, 1998), XRank developed the final formula to compute ElemRank. Assume d1, d2 and d3 are the probabilities of navigating through hyperlinks, forward containment edges, and reverse containment edges, respectively. $N_{de}(v)$ is the number of elements in the XML documents containing the element v.

$$e(v) = \frac{1 - d_1 - d_2 - d_3}{N_d * N_{de}(v)} + d_1 \sum_{(u,v)\in HE} \frac{e(u)}{N_h(u)}$$
$$+ d_2 \sum_{(u,v)\in CE} \frac{e(u)}{N_c(u)} + d_3 \sum_{(u,v)\in CE^{-1}} e(u)$$

This formula has a more general interpretation in the context of random walks over XML graph. Consider a random surfer over a hyperlinked XML graph. At each instant, the surfer visits an element e, and performs one of the following actions: (1) with probability $1-d_1-d_2-d_3$, he jumps to a random document, and then to a random element within the document, (2) with probability d_1, he follows a hyperlink from e, (3) with probability d_2, he follows a containment edge to one of e's sub-elements, and (4) with probability d_3, he goes to e's parent element. Given this model, e(v) is exactly the probability of finding the random surfer in element v.

From the above detailed description of Elem-Rank – the core of XRank, we can see that this ranking scheme, which extends the PageRank hyperlink metric to XML, can be orthogonal to retrieval and be incorporated into other XML keyword query system.

Besides, ranking schemes have also been studied for keyword search on XML documents in other systems. Hristidis, Papakonstantinou, and Balmin (2003), Barg and Wong (2001) propose to rank query results according to the distance between different keyword matches in the original document. In the presence of XML schema, efficient algorithms to compute top k results are presented in (Hristidis, Papakonstantinou, & Balmin 2003). XSEarch (Cohen et al., 2003) employs a ranking scheme in the flavor of the information retrieval, considering factors like distance, term frequency, document frequency, etc. Cohen, Mamou, Kanza, and Sagiv (2003) shows how the theoretical results interconnection can be efficiently combined with Information Retrieval techniques to yield the system.

1.5 CONCLUSION

Keyword search is a user-friendly mechanism for retrieving XML data in web and scientific applications, comparing with traditional struc-

tured queries. Research on XML based keyword search has gained increasing attentions from many researchers.

In addition to the above mentioned issues, there are some other topics related to XML keyword search. For example, view –based keyword search is an interesting direction in the field of XML keyword search (Goldstein & Larson, 2001; Ziyang & Cheng, 2001; Feng et al., 2007). Ziyang and Cheng (2001) address an open problem of exploiting and maintaining materialized views for XML keyword search. They present the first XML keyword search engine that can answer queries using materialized views using SLCA semantics, and propose a polynomial time approximation algorithm for finding a good answer set of a given query form a set of materialized views. Feng et al. (2007) have proposed a approach to efficiently evaluate keyword search queries over virtual XML views. The key idea is to use regular indices, including inverted list and XML path indices that are present on the base data to efficiently identify the portion of the base data that is relevant to the current keyword search query so that only the top ranked results of the view are actually materialized and presented to the user.

Some novel approaches and techniques are still being proposed every year in each famous international conference on XML data management or databases. In this chapter, we have discussed keyword search issues from several aspects, namely, the query semantics, the computing algorithms, the ranking of the results and other related issues. The readers who are interested in any of them can refer to the corresponding references.

REFERENCES

Barg, M., & Wong, R. K. (2001). Structural proximity searching for large collections of semi-structured data. In *Proceedings of the 10th ACM conference on Conference on Information and Knowledge Management* (pp. 175-182).

Brin, S., & Page, L. (1998). The anatomy of a large-scale hypertextual web search engine. In *Proceedings of the 7th International World Wide Web Conference.*

Chong, S., Chee-Yong, C., & Goenka, A. K. (2007). Multiway SLCA-based keyword search in XML data. In *Proceedings of the 16th International Conference on World Wide Web.*

Cohen, S., Mamou, J., Kanza, Y., & Sagiv, Y. (2003). XSEarch: A semantic search engine for XML. In *Proceedings of the 29th International Conference on Very Large Data Bases.*

Feng, S., Lin, G., Chavdar, B., Anand, B., Muthiah, C., & Fan, Y. (2007). Efficient keyword search over virtual XML views. In *Proceedings of the 33th International Conference on Very Large Data Bases.*

Goldstein, J., & Larson, P. (2001). Optimizing queries using materialized views: A practical, scalable solution. In *Proceedings of the 2001 ACM SIGMOD International Conference on Management of Data.*

Guo, L., Shao, F., Botev, C., & Shanmugasundaram, J. (2003). XRank: Ranked keyword search over XML documents. In *Proceedings of the 2003 ACM SIGMOD International Conference on Management of Data.*

Hristidis, V., Papakonstantinou, Y., & Balmin, A. (2003). Keyword proximity search on XML graph. In *Proceedings of International Conference on Data Engineering.*

Li, G., Feng, J., Wang, J., & Zhou, L. (2007). Effective keyword search for valuable LCAs over XML documents. In *Proceedings of the 16th ACM Conference on Conference on Information and Knowledge Management.*

Xu, Y., & Papakonstantinou, Y. (2005). Efficient keyword search for smallest LCAs in XML database. In *Proceedings of the 2005 ACM SIGMOD International Conference on Management of Data.*

Xu, Y., & Papakonstantinou, Y. (2008). Efficient LCA based keyword search in XML Data. In *Proceedings of the 11th International Conference on Extending Database Technology.*

Yunyal, L., Cong, Y., & Jagadish, H. V. (2004). Schema-free XQuery. In *Proceedings of the 30th International Conference on Very Large Data Bases.*

Yunyal, L., Cong, Y., & Jagadish, H. V. (2008). Enabling schema-free XQuery with meaningful query focus. *The VLDB Journal, 17*(3), 355–377. doi:10.1007/s00778-006-0003-4

Ziyang, L., & Cheng, Y. (2001). Exploiting and maintaining views for XML keyword search. In *Proceedings of the 2001 ACM SIGMOD International Conference on Management of Data.*

Ziyang, L., & Yi, C. (2007). Identifying meaningful return information for XML keyword search. In *Proceedings of the 2007 ACM SIGMOD International Conference on Management of Data.*

Chapter 2
An Efficient and Flexible Approach of Keyword Search in XML

Weidong Yang
Fudan University, China

Hao Zhu
Fudan University, China

ABSTRACT

In this chapter, firstly, the LCA-based approaches for XML keyword search are analyzed and compared with each other. Several fundamental flaws of LCA-based models are explored, of which, the most important one is that the search results are eternally determined nonadjustable. Then, the chapter presents a system of adaptive keyword search in XML, called AdaptiveXKS, which employs a novel and flexible result model for avoiding these defects. Within the new model, a scoring function is presented to judge the quality of each result, and the considered metrics of evaluating results are weighted and can be updated as needed. Through the interface, the system administrator or the users can adjust some parameters according to their search intentions. One of three searching algorithms could also be chosen freely in order to catch specific querying requirements. Section 1 describes the Introduction and motivation. Section 2 defines the result model. In section 3 the scoring function is discussed deeply. Section 4 presents the system implementation and gives the detailed keyword search algorithms. Section 5 presents the experiments. Section 6 is the related work. Section 7 is the conclusion of this chapter.

2.1 INTRODUCTION AND MOTIVATION

XML Keyword Search is a user-friendly information discovery technique, which attracts many interests these years. Different with keyword search over flat documents, the search object is a single XML document/database with structure information inside and the results are supposed to be fragments of it containing keywords. Since it is difficult and sometimes impossible to identify users' intentions through keywords, it is really a hard task to determine which fragments should be returned. As a matter of fact, this is still an open issue of keyword search on structured and semi-structured data.

DOI: 10.4018/978-1-4666-1975-3.ch002

To define the results of XML keyword search many valuable models are proposed, and the most popular ones are the Smallest Lowest Common Ancestor (SLCA) model (Xu & Papakonstantinou, 2005) and its variants (Guo, Shao, Botev, & Shanmugasundaram, 2003; Hristidis, Koudas, Papakonstantinou, & Srivastava, 2006; Kong, Gilleron, & Lemay, 2009; Guoliang, Jianhua, Jianyong, & Lizhu, 2007; Yunyao, Cong, & Jagadish, 2004; Ziyang, Jeffrey, & Yi, 2007; Xu & Papakonstantinou, 2008), all of which are called as the *LCA-based models* in this paper. These researches regard the XML document as a rooted, labeled, unordered tree in which each inner node is an element or an attribute and each leaf is a value which may contain some keywords. In SLCA model a result is defined as a *subtree* that: (1) the labels of whose nodes contain all the keywords, (2) none of its subtree satisfies the first condition except itself. The root of such a subtree is called a SLCA node. It's recognized that SLCA model is definitely not a perfect one. After it s proposed, arguments have been aroused around the meaningfulness and completeness of its search results (Kong et al., 2009; Guoliang, Jianhua, Jianyong, Bei, & Yukai, 2008; Guoliang et al., 2007; Xu & Papakonstantinou, 2008). Judging from the examples illustrated, they claim that some results of the SLCA method are meaningless and some meaningful ones are missing. These are called the *false positive* and the *false negative* problems respectively. Interestingly, the remedy approaches they propose sometimes conflict with each other, and counterexamples can always be found to testify that the two problems still happen.

In order to explain these issues we employ the original examples from former researches (Kong et al., 2009; Guoliang et al., 2007; Xu & Papakonstantinou, 2008), which are illustrated in Figure 1 as three separate XML trees. In these trees keywords are marked in bold and only important nodes are identified by numbers. Besides, we use $node_i$ to denote the node with the number i in any of the trees. Consider keywords {"XML", "David"} issued on the XML document in Figure 1(a), apparently SLCA method can find two SLCA nodes: $node_7$ and $node_{17}$, and the subtrees rooted in them will be returned as the final results. In many cases the subtrees are not appropriate for users because their sizes are too large and plenty of meaningless information is involved. GDMCT (Hristidis et al., 2006) approach proposes a good way to handle this that it returns the Minimum Connecting Trees (MCTs) instead. As a SLCA node corresponds to a group of keyword nodes (the nodes whose labels contain keywords), a MCT is defined as a subtree which employs the SLCA node as root and the keyword nodes as leaves. Furthermore, a MCT can be expanded to fill more useful information through semantics reference or according to the feedback from users. We can see that in SLCA approach either a subtree or a MCT is determined by a group of keyword nodes, and in fact this rule suits the results of any LCA-based approach. Since the refining of the final results is not a topic in this paper, for convenience a search result is considered as a group of keyword nodes instead of a document fragment by us. In this example, SLCA method finds two results {$node_9$, $node_{11}$} and {$node_{19}$, $node_{21}$} which are two separate papers in semantics.

MLCA (Yunyao et al., 2004) method and GDMCT (Hristidis et al., 2006) method should agree with the answers because they both define a result model very similar to SLCA. But, ELCA (Guo et al., 2003; Xu & Papakonstantinou, 2008) method will claim that several reasonable results are missed. For instance {node3, node25} and {node16, node23}, which indicate a conference and one of its sessions respectively. Neither node1 nor node14 is a SLCA node due to at least one SLCA node is their descendant node, however seemingly they're both qualified results. As shown in Figure 1(a), these two new results along with the two SLCA results are all meaningful answers to the query {"XML", "David"}, besides they are perfectly exclusive to each other.

Figure 1. Original examples from LCA-based approaches

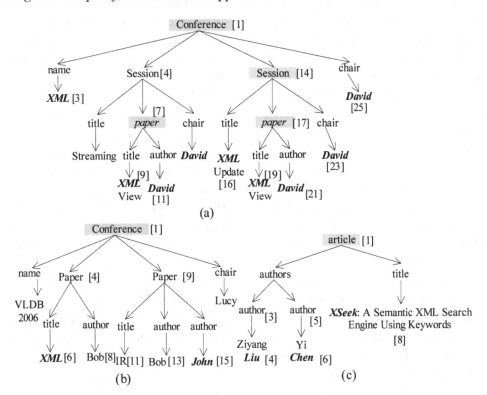

The semantics of Exclusive Lowest Common Ancestor (ELCA) is firstly proposed in (Guo et al., 2003), although it is not named as this. Afterwards, Xu and Papakonstantinou (2008) provide an efficient algorithm to retrieve all the ELCA nodes. Here is the formal definition of ELCA nodes. For an XML tree and any set of nodes $\{n_1, ..., n_k\}$ in it, we use $lca(n_1, ..., n_k)$ to denote their Lowest Common Ancestor (LCA) node. Moreover, for any two nodes n_i and n_j, $n_i \prec n_j$ implies that n_i is an ancestor node of n_j, and $n_i \leq n_j$ implies that n_i is an ancestor of n_j or n_i is n_j itself. Given a set of t keywords $\{w_1, ..., w_t\}$, K_i is the set of all the keyword nodes whose labels contain the keyword w_i. Let $lca(K_1, ..., K_t) = \{ lca(n_1, ..., n_t) \mid n_1 \in K_1, ..., n_t \in K_t \}$, then a node v is called an ELCA node of

$K_1, ..., K_t$ if and only if: (1) there exist nodes $n_1 \in K_1, ..., n_t \in K_t$ such that $v = lca(n_1, ..., n_t)$; (2) for every n_i ($1 \leq i \leq k$) there is not a node v' on the

path from v to n_i that satisfies $n' \leq l$, in which l is any node in $lca(K_1, ..., K_t)$. The definition looks complicated, nevertheless all the ELCA nodes can be retrieved through a straightforward two-step process: (1) find all the SLCA nodes, halt the process if if there isn't any; (2) remove all the SLCA nodes along with the subtrees rooted in them, then turn to the first step. It can be easily proved that the union of all the SLCA nodes obtained each time in the first step is indeed the set of ELCA nodes.

It seems ELCA model has fixed the false negative issue of SLCA model and thus can find results perfect enough. However, based on the example illustrated in Figure 1(b), Guoliang, Jianhua, Jianyong, and Lizhu (2007) claim that both SLCA and ELCA models are suffering from the false positive problem. Suppose {"XML", "John"} are the keywords, either SLCA or ELCA method returns $\{node_6, node_{15}\}$ as the only result which is thought as meaningless in (Guoliang et al., 2007). Actually, more examples can be found to support this point of view because in some cases the keyword nodes in a result could be really far from each other in the tree. Rather than implement semantics inference to improve the results as XSeek (Ziyang & Yi, 2007) does, Li et al. introduce a simple rule to filter all the ELCA nodes. For any two keyword nodes n_i and n_j in an ELCA result, if two nodes n_i' and n_j' which are from the paths "$lca(n_i, n_j) \rightarrow n_i$" and "$lca(n_i, n_j) \rightarrow n_j$" respectively satisfy that n_i' and n_j' have the same elementary type, then the result is unqualified. Accordingly, $\{node_6, node_{15}\}$ is not a qualified result because $node_4$ and $node_9$ have the same elementary type. After the filtering, the left ELCA nodes are called the Valuable Lowest Common Ancestor (VLCA) nodes.

The rule of VLCA method is actually first proposed by Cohen, Mamou, Kanza, and Sagiv (2003). They use this to determine if two keyword nodes are "meaningfully related". Indeed it is kind of overstrict, and more relaxed criteria could be used such as the LCA have to be low or the compactness should be high. Kong et al. present a counterexample in (Kong et al., 2009). To search the keywords {"Liu", "Chen", "XSeek"} in the tree from Figure 1(c), $\{node_4, node_6, node_8\}$ is a reasonable answer yet will be eliminated by VLCA method because $node_3$ and $node_5$ have the same elementary type "author". Kong, Gilleron, and Lemay (2009) also propose a concept called Related Tightest Fragments (RTF) as final search results, which is equal to representing the results of ELCA method in MCTs. Obviously, it keeps the vague problem of false positive results being existed.

Following the common sense that results should be returned to users as many as possible, we shouldn't care too much about the false positive issue actually. At least we can still return them to users with lower rank scores. On the other hand, another thing needs to be paid more attention to that is how to evaluate the results properly and so

that to judge if returned results are good enough or is there better ones can be found. No doubt out of the aforementioned models ELCA method can get the maximum number of results which is actually a superset of the results returned by any other LCA-based method. Next we use another synthetic example to discuss the ELCA results to explain the problem.

Example 2.1: Figure 2 illustrates another XML document in tree structure which stores the information of proceedings and journals in DBLP. There is a recursive situation in the document that a paper element could have a descendant which is also a paper. Given three keywords {"XML", "Bob", "David"}, there are four ELCA results could be found in the document which are illustrated in closed dashed curves. Apparently, $\{node_7, node_{10}, node_{12}\}$ is a very good answer which is a paper whose title is about "XML" and its authors are "Bob" and "David". From another point of view, the LCA node is appropriately low and the *compactness* (which is recognized as an important measure by many researches and can be calculated through dividing the number of keyword nodes by the number of all nodes in a result) is good. Another result $\{node_{15}, node_{18}, node_{25}, node_{27}, node_{29}\}$ consists of two connected papers and also can be regarded as a meaningful one. With respect to the other two results some people probably have different opinion. For $\{node_{32}, node_{35}, node_{37}\}$, although it satisfies the constraint VLCA model requires, it is hard to say that $node_{35}$ and $node_{37}$ are meaningful related. For $\{node_{40}, node_{43}, node_{46}, node_{50}\}$, many may argue that it will be better if it is split into two separate results $\{node_{40}, node_{50}\}$ and $\{node_{43}, node_{46}\}$. Suppose another keyword "SIGMOD" is added into the query, there will be a single large result for ELCA model which can be represented by the subtree rooted in $node_2$. It is too large to be an appropriate result for users, yet it cannot be divided since any of its subparts (such as the three in the closed dashed curves) is considered totally meaningless because it doesn't contain all the keywords. Besides, all the keyword nodes in the subtree rooted in $node_{38}$ are never included in any result because of the same reason. The false negative problem still happens in a way.

Here we enumerate the defects of ELCA model as follows which are actually the flaws of all LCA-based models. After that we propose a novel model which can void all of them.

1. **A lack of universal criteria to judge whether a result is qualified or not:** VLCA model tries to point out the false positive problem of ELCA model through the specific example in Figure 1(b) and afterwards provides a strict rule to filter results. The practicability of the rule is simply disconfirmed by the RTF model through another specific example. We don't think either of their arguments is convincing. In an extreme case, we can say that any fragment containing keywords is meaningful. However, to clarify which ones are qualified results and which ones are not, what we need is a quantifiable metric rather than some strict rules.

2. **Not enough features are considered:** In the ELCA model, a result is restricted to contain all the keyword nodes. Besides, only the LCA nodes of the results are considered. At least two important features are missed: the compactness and the size. Because the size doesn't mean anything in ELCA model (or any of other LCA-based models), large-size results keep showing. Although some work (Guo et al., 2003; Kong et al., 2009; Guoliang et al., 2008) consider several features in their ranking models, except for LCA nothing is taken into account when retrieving the results.

3. **Some useful information is omitted in the results:** For instance in Example 2.1 when the keywords {"XML", "Bob", "David", "SIGMOD"} are used to search the document any keyword node in the subtree rooted in $root_{38}$ is ignored despite they are more or less mea$ning_{ful}$l to users. Actually all the LCA-based models only serve the best results and refuse to organize and return the second-best ones. Although some work (Guoliang et al., 2008) supports the OR semantics and so that can find this information, this only can be utilized in a strict way that users have to

Figure 2. An example of XML tree

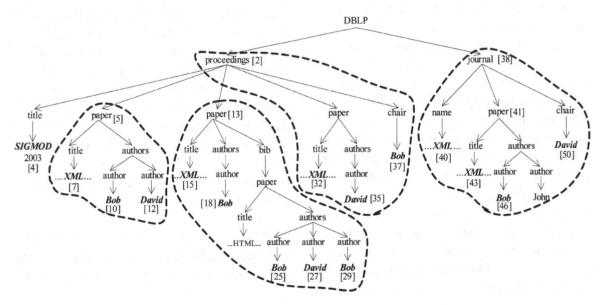

specify the AND/OR logic in their queries. In this example, users have to provide a query like "(XML *AND* Bob *AND* David) *OR* SIGMOD" even though they have *no* idea *of* what ex*ac*tly the real data is.

4. **Despite different users probably have distinct intentions with the same keywords, the search results are eternally determined and nonadjustable:** Check Example 2.1 again. When the keywords are {"XML", "Bob", "David", "SIGMOD"} we don't know which one is better: to return a proceeding with a lot of information or to generate smaller and compact papers. However with any LCA-based approach neither the administrator nor a user has a choose to improve their search results. Therefore, we need to provide a more flexible model in which we can adjust the results according to the context or the feedback of users.

In this chapter, we describe a novel result model for XML keyword search which can avoid all these defects perfectly, based on our previous work (Weidong, Hao, Nan, & Guansheng, 2011). Instead of applying restrictions upon the results such as each should contain all the keywords or the LCA must be the lowest, we give each result a score to evaluate the quality of it. Such a score considers sufficient features each of which is weighted and so that can be adjusted as necessary. As we investigate the optimal results could be distinct when the features are given different weights. Therefore we provide multiple algorithms to generate results and based on the values given to the parameters in the scoring function the most suitable algorithm will be chosen to get better results. Each of our algorithms is supposed to find not only the results with the highest scores as many as possible but also those second-best ones with lower scores. Furthermore, through the interface, the administrator or the users can arbitrarily modify the parameter values employed in the scoring function in order to catch specific

requirements. Finally, extensive experiments are done to compare the results of LCA-based approaches and the results of our approach. It shows that our approach dominates the LCA-based approaches in both result precise and recall.

2.2 RESULT MODEL

Before presenting the result model, we'd like to point out three rules any LCA-based model comply with.

Rule 1: A final result returned to users is considered to be a tree-structured XML fragment containing keywords.

Rule 2: Any result r contains a set of keywords R. Actually r is determined by R that it is a MCT of R or a transformed fragment built upon the MCT.

Rule 3: Overlapping and inclusion are not allowed between two individual results.

Rule 1 and Rule 2 are quite straightforward and reasonable that our result model follows them too. With respect to Rule 3, we have a different opinion that we think two results can share some common nodes as long as none of them is a keyword node, which means our model is more relaxed to the results. Next we provide the formal definition of search results. As explained before we use a set of keyword nodes to represent a final result for simplicity. Besides, rather than applying some restrictions upon the results, we give each result a score to evaluate its quality (how meaningful it is). Such a score of a keyword node set R is calculated through a function *score(R)*. R is a better result if it has a higher *score(R)*, and in our opinion any R satisfying *score(R)* > 0 can be regarded as a result.

Definition 1: (*XML Keyword Search Results*) T is an XML document/database which could be viewed as a tree. Given a set of t keywords

$\{w_1, ..., w_t\}$, K is the set of all the keyword nodes whose labels contain any keyword. Then, the result set of searching $\{w_1, ..., w_t\}$ in T is Υ which satisfies:

- $\forall R \in \mathbb{R}$ is a set of keyword nodes that $score(R) > 0$;
- $\forall R_i, R_j \in \mathbb{R}, R_i \cap R_j = \Phi$;
- $\bigcup_{R \in \mathbb{R}} R = K$.

From these three conditions in Definition 1 we can see that the XML tree is divided into separate fragments each of which is meaningful. In other words, XML keyword search can be regarded as a problem that dividing the set of all keyword nodes into groups that are meaningful. Clearly, excessive partitions of K can be qualified result sets in accordance with Definition 1 and we have to judge which ones are gratifying and which ones are not. However, comparing with the LCA-based models it has two advantages. First, each result is not given specific restrictions yet can be appraised. Second, all the keyword nodes are involved in the results which definitely brings a high recall. Next we define a concept of *the optimal result set* which is supposed to be a standard for our result-finding algorithms to pursue.

Definition 2: (*Optimal XML Keyword Search Result Set*) Suppose Υ is a partition set of K and $|\Upsilon| = n$. We arrange the items in Υ to be a sequence $S = \{R_1, ..., R_n\}$ which satisfies: for any $1 \leq i < j \leq n$, $score(R_i) \geq score(R_j)$. Then, Υ is called an optimal result set iff:

- $\forall R' \subset (R_k \cup ... \cup R_n)$, $1 \leq k \leq n$, $score(R_k) \geq score(R')$.

In other words, $score(R_1)$ is the biggest score can be found in the set of all the keyword nodes K, and $score(R_2)$ is the greatest score in the set $(K-R_1)$, and so on. The rationality of this definition is quite clear that users always prefer the best results and in our model the best results are those results with the largest scores.

2.3 SCORING FUNCTION

A proper *scoring function* represents a well-designed evaluation model, in which at least four metrics need to be involved: (1) the content information, which mainly refers to the keywords it contains; (2) the structure information, which specifically means the hierarchical position of the root (the LCA of the keyword node set); (3) the compactness, which usually can be calculated through dividing the number of keyword nodes by the number of all nodes in the fragment; (4) the size, which must not be too large. More importantly, the evaluation model should be adjustable to suit different contexts. As a matter of fact, in the evaluation model we can use as many features as possible when they are reasonable. Meanwhile, the LCA-based models only consider the first two features, the content and the structure information, and that's why they suffer from those defects aforementioned.

Next, we provide a universal scoring function for the result model. It is obvious that the four metrics have various priorities, and undoubtedly the content information possesses the highest one because users would most like to get the results containing as many keywords as possible. The structure information should be the second important one. Because the hierarchical position of the LCA node represents the semantics of the result, and a lower LCA indicates a more refined and compact result. This widely accepted by existing researches and is indeed the essential idea of LCA-based models. As for the compactness and the size, users are always reluctant to see the results with large size and few keyword nodes. Therefore, a result is considered better if the compactness is higher. Moreover, if some result have a really large size then it won't be appropriate to be returned to users.

Some extra notations have to be defined as follows before the scoring function is proposed:

- K is the set of all the keyword nodes;
- For any node v, *dpt(v)* returns the depth of v in the tree (the depth of the root is 1, and the height of the tree is h);
- For any set of keyword nodes N, *kn(N)* is the function to get the exact number of keywords N contains.
- For any set of keyword nodes N, *mct(N)* is the set of all the nodes contained by the MCT of N.

For any result R we provide separate formulas to evaluate the four kinds of features a result possesses: $\chi(R)$, $\phi(R)$, $\eta(R)$ and $\delta(R)$. Each of the functions returns a real number between [0, 1], and the greater the value is R is better in one respect.

- **Content Information:** $\chi(R) = kn(R) / t$;
- **Structure Information:** $\phi(R) = dpt(lca(R)) / h$;
- **Compactness:** $\eta(R) = |R| / |mct(R)|$;
- **Size:** $\delta(R) = \begin{cases} 1 & |mct(R)| \leq st \\ 0 & |mct(R)| > st \end{cases}$

In the formula of $\delta(R)$, st is an integer which is the size threshold of R's MCT. When the size exceeds the threshold, the result is considered inappropriate to be returned. Finally, the scoring function is defined as follows.

$$score(R) = \frac{(1 + \chi(R))^{\alpha} \times (1 + \phi(R))^{\beta} \times (1 + \eta(R))^{\lambda} \times \delta(R)}{2^{(\alpha+\beta+\gamma)}}$$

In formula (1) α, β, and γ are three adjustable parameters, each of which should be a positive real number greater than or equal to 1. Furthermore, according to former discussion under normal circumstances α should be set much greater than β, at the same time β is usually larger than γ. Hence we have $\alpha > \beta > \gamma \geq 1$. It is easy to find that any *score(R)* is either equal to zero or between $(1/2^{(\alpha+\beta+\gamma)}$ 1].

2.4 SYSTEM IMPLEMENTATION

Figure 3 shows our proposed system architecture. We implement AdaptiveXKS by using Java. In detail, we provide users several sample XML documents/datasets, including Synthetic DBLP, DBLP, TreeBank and XMark for retrieval. AdaptiveXKS returns such subtrees as search results that they root in the LCA of a certain keyword node set meeting user-specified requirements. AdaptiveXKS also allows user to select a particular searching algorithm from the Clustering Algorithm, the Content-Information-First Algorithm, and the Structure-Information-First Algorithm (all of them will be discussed later), according to their needs. As a most important merit, in order to refine search results, AdaptiveXKS allows users to update the values of parameters. In the remainder of this section, each critical component of our proposed system will be discussed in detail.

2.4.1 The Preprocess and Index Construction Component

In order to execute user queries efficiently, the parsing, storing and indexing of XML data is an important part of our proposed system. We now provide some necessary background on these techniques. In AdaptiveXKS, we use Apache Xerces XML SAX Parser to parse XML document. Rather than building a complete internal, tree-shaped representation of the XML document, like what DOM model does, SAX is an event-driven model for processing XML. A SAX parser fires off a series of events as it reads the document from beginning to end. Those events are passed to event handlers, which provide access to the contents of the document.

During the parsing of XML document, it is essential that each element is assigned with an ID, which is a way to uniquely identify an element. The AdaptiveXKS implementation uses Dewey numbers as the element IDs, since it is commonly used to label an XML document to facilitate XML query processing by recording information on

Figure 3. The AdaptiveXKS architecture

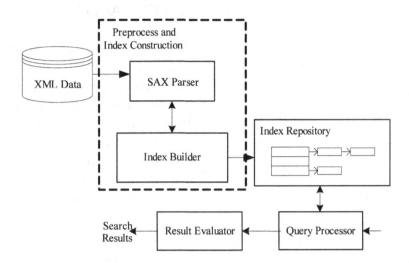

the path of an element. One interesting feature of Dewey numbers is that it is a hierarchical numbering scheme where the ID of an element contains the ID of its parent element as a prefix. At the same time, the Index Builder is employed to build the inverted index, which typically store for each term in the document/dataset, the list of XML elements that directly contain that term. In addition, an index with Dewey IDs as the keys, such as a B+-tree, is built on top of the inverted list so that we can efficiently check whether a given element contains a keyword. Lastly, the XML indices are stored in the Index Repository, which will be accessed once a keyword query is issued.

2.4.2 The Query Processor Component

The Query Processing component is the core of AdaptiveXKS system. Once a keyword query is issued, the system accesses the Index Repository and retrieves element list (These elements are so-called keyword nodes in this paper) matches to each keyword efficiently.

For an XML tree and given keywords, to find the optimal result set is certainly the ultimate goal of us. Nevertheless, there is a lack of an efficient

way to achieve this purpose due to a complicated situation that any feature in the scoring function is allowed to be weighted casually. In a naive approach, we have to enumerate all the possible subsets of K to find the result with the greatest score which alone has a time complexity of $O(2^n)$. Therefore, in this section we propose several heuristic algorithms with high efficiency to generate results hoped to be close to the optimal one. Especially, some of them are developed to adapt to specific circumstances. In the next section, many experimental results show the effectiveness of these algorithms.

2.4.2.1 Clustering Algorithm

From Definition 1, the XML keyword search problem is equivalent to dividing the set of all the keyword nodes into groups that are meaningful, which is actually the clustering techniques are supposed to handle. In this subsection, we provide a basic agglomerative hierarchical clustering algorithm to obtain the result set Υ. Before conduct the algorithm (or any algorithm we propose later) the nodes in the XML tree have been encoded by Dewey code and the inverted index of term-node

Algorithm 1. Clustering(K)

```
1: transform K to ℂ
2: build the score matrix M for ℂ
3: while there is a positive item in M
4: find the greatest m_{ij} in M ;
5: remove C_i and C_j from ℂ ;
6: add C_i ∪ C_j into ℂ ;
7: update M according to current ℂ ;
8: return ℂ ;
```

has been built. So that, each time the calculation of a score costs $O(1)$.

The input of the clustering algorithm is the set of all the keyword nodes K which is then transformed to a candidate set C that each entry $C \in \mathbb{C}$ is a node set and originally contains an individual keyword node. Afterwards, a *Score Matrix* of $\leq$ is built. Suppose $|K| = n$ and $\leq = \{C_1, ..., C_n\}$, then the score matrix of $\leq$ is an n-by-n matrix M that each item m_{ij} is set to be $score(C_i \cup C_j)$ if $score(C_i \cup C_j)$ is greater than both $score(C_i)$ and $score(C_j)$, otherwise m_{ij} is 0. At each step we find the highest m_{ij} in the matrix and merge C_i and C_j to be a new result in $\leq$. Then, the matrix is updated to be a $|\mathbb{C}| \times |\mathbb{C}|$ one for current $\leq$. The program stops when there is no positive value left in the matrix, then $\leq$ is the final result.

The *clustering algorithm* is shown in Algorithm 1. As we know the space complexity of this algorithm is $O(n^2)$, and in the worst case the time complexity is $O(n^3)$. If the scores are stored as sorted lists (or heaps), the time complexity is reduced to $O(n^2 logn)$. Still it is not as good as the performance of the algorithms from the LCA-based approaches. However, theoretically it generates much better results because it calculates possible scores as many as possible and always chooses the largest one.

2.4.2.2 Content-Information-First (CIF) Algorithm

Many believe that the Content information should be an overwhelming criterion to evaluate a result and thus in our scoring function they would prefer α to be much larger than β and γ. Under this circumstance, the results containing all the keywords should be returned as many as possible and a results with insufficient content information R will only be generated in two cases. First, there is no result R' can be found that satisfies: (1) $R \cup R'$ contains all the keywords; (2) $score(R \cup R') > score(R')$. Second, such a R' can be found however the size of $R \cup R'$ exceeds the limit. Among these results with insufficient content information one definitely dominates another when it contains more keywords. In this subsection, we present an algorithm called the Content-Information-First (CIF) algorithm to retrieve such results.

Given a set of t keywords $\{w_1, ..., w_t\}$ there are t sets of keyword nodes $K_1, ..., K_t$ possessed through the inverted index and each K_i stores all the keyword nodes containing the keyword w_i. Without loss of generality, let K_1 be the one with the smallest size out of them. In line with the principle that a keyword node only exists in a single result, we can only obtain $|K_1|$ results containing all the keywords at most. Thus, we employ a program that for each set from K_2 to K_t we distribute one or more keyword nodes in it to every node in K_1 which can form a result with highest score.

Let $K = \{K_1, ..., K_t\}$ and Υ to be the set of results which is empty originally, then the pseudocode of CIF algorithm is illustrated in Algorithm 2. Line 11 is what Example 4 wants to explain. In the best case (when the sizes of the keyword node sets are even) the time complexity of CIF is $O(|K_1| \times \sum_{2 \leq i \leq t}(|K_i|))$, and in the worst case the time complexity is $O(|K_1| \times \sum_{2 \leq i \leq t}(|K_i|^2))$.

Algorithm 2. CIF(K)

```
1: while $K \neq 0$
2: m=| $K$ |;
3: set $K_1$ as the set with the smallest size in $K$ ;
4: if (m==1)
5: $\mathbb{R} = \mathbb{R} \cup$ clustering( $K_1$ );
6: break;
7: else
8: remove $K_1$ from $K$ ;
9: transform $K_1$ to semi-results $S$ ;
10: for ( $2 \leq i \leq m$ )
11: transfer one or more nodes from $K_i$ into each set in $S$ ;
12: if $K_i = \Phi$ remove $K_i$ from $K$ ;
13: $\mathbb{R} = \mathbb{R} \cup S$ ;
14: return $\mathbb{R}$ ;
```

2.4.2.3 Structure-Information-First (SIF) Algorithm

In some specific cases, we concern what the structure of a result much more than how much keyword information inside. For example, it is quite reasonable to assume that no matter how many keywords a result contains only those papers are qualified when proceeding keyword search on DBLP data set. In this case, we can set α close to or even smaller than β and λ and then generate results based on some restrictions built on the structure. Here we provide an algorithm called the Structure-Information-First Algorithm (SIF) which actually comes from another work of us (Weidong et al., 2011) in which it is called the Core-driven Clustering Algorithm. To save space we don't explain the details here. Normally the time complexity of Algorithm SIF is $O(n)$, and $O(n_2)$ in the worst case.

2.5 EXPERIMENTS

Extensive experiments are performed to compare our approaches with SLCA and ELCA approaches. For SLCA and ELCA approaches the Indexed Lookup Eager Algorithm (Xu & Papakonstantinou, 2005) and the Indexed Stack Algorithm (Xu & Papakonstantinou, 2008) are implemented respectively.

We use two metrics to evaluate them: recall and precision. Since we presume any keyword node is meaningful to users, the recall value can be simply calculated by dividing the number of the keyword nodes in the result set with the number of all keyword nodes in the document. The standard definition of precision from Information Retrieval is difficult to be followed here. Because in any search, each result returned is believed to be a satisfying one, which means they all consider the precision of their result set to be 1. Therefore, we design a variation called the proximity precision. Out of the set of results we find the one with the greatest score which is then considered as the best result and used as a standard. For a certain small number k, the top k results with the largest scores are found and then an average score value is calculated which afterwards is divided by the greatest score to get the value of proximity precision.

The experiments show that the results generated by our approach have an overwhelming recall value comparing with SLCA and ELCA. We can see that SLCA always gets a poor value because lots of keyword nodes are abandoned. Our approach always has the largest recall since any keyword node is considered meaningful and included in a result. We also conduct the experiments to test how the proximity precision values change when we vary the number of keywords. The parameters are set to static values, and for any approach we only consider the scores of top-10 results. Obviously, Matrix and CIF overcome the other three. SIF doesn't act quite good since in the scoring function α is set much larger than β and γ. Similarly, when we give the parameters some static values and use three keywords to search each of the data sets, our experiments show how the proximity precision values change as the value of *k* varies. There is a dramatic decline while *k* is enlarged for SLCA and ELCA. This can be explained that they usually only find a few best results and omit those second-best ones. The most interesting thing is, for either CIF or SIF the proximity precision changes severely with different parameter values. That's why it is so important to select the appropriate algorithms according to them.

2.6 RELATED WORK

Extensive research has been conducted in XML keyword search, which can be done in either tree data model or the digraph data model. And the ranking of query results is another important issue in this area.

Keyword Search on XML Tree/Graph Databases. We have reviewed the most important LCAbased result models for XML keyword search, like SLCA (Xu & Papakonstantinou, 2005), ELCA (Xu & Papakonstantinou, 2008), VLCA (Guoliang et al., 2007), RTF (Kong et al., 2009), GDMCT (Hristidis et al., 2006), MLCA (Yunyao et al., 2004) in the Section 1. All of these works model the underlying XML data as a rooted, labeled, unordered tree. In addition, in other tree data model, XSeek (Ziyang et al., 2007) implements semantic inference to improve the results through the adoption of entities and keyword match pattern. It also works without schema information. XKeyword (Hristidis, Papakonstantinou, & Balmin, 2003), which is built on a relational database, is a typical one implementing XML keyword search on XML graph databases. It builds a set of keyword indices along with indexed path relations that describe particular patterns of paths in the graph. During query processing, plans that use a near optimal set of path relations are developed to efficiently locate the keyword

query results. Besides, XKeyword also use the graph's schema for optimization. BLINKS (Hao, Haixun, Jun, &Philip, 2007) adopts a completely different approach. It partitions a data graph into blocks and then builds a bi-level index, which stores summary information at the block level to initiate and guide search among blocks, and more detailed information for each block to accelerate search within each block. BANKS (Bhalotia, Hulgeri, Nakhe, Charkrabarti, & Sudarshan, 2002) uses bidirectional expansion heuristic algorithms to search as small portion of graph as possible. Different from the above approaches, EASE (Guoliang, Beng, Jianhua, Jianyong, & Lizhu, 2008) models not only semi-structured data, but also unstructured and structured data as graphs, thus can deal with indexing and querying large collections of heterogeneous data.

Ranking of Search Results. Ranking schemes have been studied for keyword search on XML documents. XRank (Guo et al., 2003) employs such a rank model that extends Googles's PageRank to XML element level to rank among all LCA results, which takes into account result specificity, keyword proximity and hyperlink awareness together. In addition, extended tf-idf techniques stemming from traditional information retrieval have mostly been adopted in many ranking schemes, though with different formulas. However, tf-idf-based ranking models can easily ignore the inherent hierarchical structural information of XML data, which may always indicate some important semantics. RACE (Guoliang et al., 2008) is a ranking mechanism to rank compact connected trees, by taking into consideration both the structural similarity and the textual similarity, thus leverage the efficiency and effectiveness of keyword proximity serach over XML documents. In XSEarch (Cohen et al., 2003), the XSEarch Ranker ranks the results by giving a score to each result N, considering both the structure of the result as well as its content. Moreover, in this paper, we present a proper scoring function for each potential result, involving four critical metrics, namely the content information, the structure information, the compactness and the size. Besides, our approach differs from previous ones in that our scoring function is more likely a well-designed evaluation model during the query processing phase, instead of an isolated ranking module after all the search results have been produced. Thus our work can generate results with improved precision.

2.7 CONCLUSION

In this chapter, several defects of LCA-based result models are explored. We present an flexible and effective XML keyword search system, named AdaptiveXKS, and develop a proper scoring function, which takes the content information, the structural information, the compactness and the size into consideration and it also functions as an evaluation model. We allow arbitrary modification of these considered metrics to catch any reasonable searching requirement of different users. Based on this novel result model, three heuristic algorithms are developed to retrieve answers. And also the most suitable algorithm can be selected to generate better results according to different values given to the parameters in the scoring function. The analytical results, as well as the experimental evaluation, show that our approach outperforms any LCA-based ones with higher precision and recall.

REFERENCES

Bhalotia, G., Hulgeri, A., Nakhe, C., Charkrabarti, S., & Sudarshan, S. (2002). Keyword searching and browsing in databases using BANKS. In *Proceedings of International Conference on Data Engineering.*

Cohen, S., Mamou, J., Kanza, Y., & Sagiv, Y. (2003). XSEarch: A semantic search engine for XML. In *Proceedings of the 29th International Conference on Very Large Data Bases* (pp. 1069–1072).

Guo, L., Shao, F., Botev, C., & Shanmugasundaram, J. (2003). XRANK: Ranked keyword search over XML documents. In *Proceedings of the 2003 ACM SIGMOD International Conference on Management of Data* (pp. 16–27).

Guoliang, L., Beng, C. O., Jianhua, F., Jianyong, W., & Lizhu, Z. (2008). EASE: Efficient and adaptive keyword search on unstructured, semi-structured and structured data. In *Proceedings of the 2008 ACM SIGMOD International Conference on Management of Data* (pp. 903–914).

Guoliang, L., Jianhua, F., Jianyong, W., Bei, Y., & Yukai, H. (2008). Race: Finding and ranking compact connected trees for keyword proximity search over XML documents. In *Proceedings of the 17th international conference on World Wide Web* (pp. 1045–1046).

Guoliang, L., Jianhua, F., Jianyong, W., & Lizhu, Z. (2007). Effective keyword search for valuable LCAs over XML documents. In *Proceedings of the 16th ACM Conference on Conference on Information and Knowledge Management* (pp. 31–40).

Hao, H., Haixun, W., Jun, Y., & Philip, S. Y. (2007). BLINKS: Ranked keyword searches on graphs. In *Proceedings of the 2007 ACM SIGMOD International Conference on Management of Data* (pp. 305–316).

Hristidis, V., Koudas, N., Papakonstantinou, Y., & Srivastava, D. (2006). Keyword proximity search in XML trees. *IEEE Transactions on Knowledge and Data Engineering, 18*(4), 525–539. doi:10.1109/TKDE.2006.1599390

Hristidis, V., Papakonstantinou, Y., & Balmin, A. (2003). Keyword proximity search on XML graphs. In *Proceedings of International Conference on Data Engineering* (pp. 367–378).

Kong, L., Gilleron, R., & Lemay, A. (2009). Retrieving meaningful relaxed tightest fragments for XML keyword search. In *Proceedings 2009 International Conference on Extended Data Base Technology* (pp.815–826).

Weidong, Y., Hao, Z., Nan, L., & Guansheng, Z. (2011). Adaptive and effective keyword search for XML. In *Proceedings of 15th Pacific-Asia Conference on Knowledge Discovery and Data Mining.*

Xu, Y., & Papakonstantinou, Y. (2005). Efficient keyword search for smallest LCAs in XML databases. In *Proceedings of the 2005 ACM SIGMOD International Conference on Management of Data* (pp. 537–538).

Xu, Y., & Papakonstantinou, Y. (2008). Efficient LCA based keyword search in XML data. In *Proc. 2008 International Conference on Extended Data Base Technology* (pp. 535–546).

Yunyao, L., Cong, Y., & Jagadish, H. V. (2004). Schema-free XQuery. In *Proceedings of the 30th International Conference on Very Large Data Bases* (pp. 72–83).

Ziyang, L., Jeffrey, W., & Yi, C. (2007). XSeek: A semantic XML search engine using keywords. In *Proceedings of the 33rd International Conference on Very Large Data Bases* (pp. 1330–1333).

Ziyang, L., & Yi, C. (2007). Identifying meaningful return information for XML keyword search. In *Proceedings of the 2007 ACM SIGMOD International Conference on Management of Data* (pp. 329–340).

Chapter 3
Ontology–Driven Keyword Search for Heterogeneous XML Data Sources

Weidong Yang
Fudan University, China

Hao Zhu
Fudan University, China

ABSTRACT

Massive heterogeneous XML data sources emerge on the Internet nowadays. These data sources are generally autonomous and provide search interfaces of XML query language such as XPath or XQuery. Accordingly, users need to learn complex syntaxes and know the schemas. Keyword Search is a user-friendly information discovery technique, which can assist users in obtaining useful information conveniently without knowing the schemas, and is very helpful to search heterogeneous XML data. In this chapter, the authors present a system called SKeyword which provides a common keyword search interface for heterogeneous XML data sources, and employs OWL ontology to represent the global model of various data sources. Section 1 introduces the context of keyword search for heterogeneous XML data source. In Section 2, the preliminary knowledge is given, and the semantics of keyword search result in ontology is defined. In section 3, the system architecture is described. Section 4 presents the approaches of ontology integration and index building used by SKeyword. Section 5 presents the generation algorithm of searching results and discusses how to rewrite the keyword search of global conceptual model to into the XQuery sentences for local XML sources. Section 6 discussed how to organize and rank the results. Section 7 shows the experiments. Section 8 is the related work. Section 9 is the conclusion of this chapter.

3.1 INTRODUCTION

More and more autonomous XML databases and systems emerge. Consider some data sources from a specific domain, which provide structural query interfaces and have heterogeneous schemas. The schemas mostly represent similar or even the same semantics. A reasonable requirement is requesting an identical query over them. However, distinct query interfaces and semantic conflicts bring difficulties. Moreover, the query results are heterogeneous and consequently cannot be sorted easily. In this chapter, we present a system called *SKeyword* which provide a common interface and

DOI: 10.4018/978-1-4666-1975-3.ch003

can meet the requirement. SKeyword employs keyword search as the query model and builds a global ontology upon the multiple data sources to solve semantic conflicts, and finally uniforms, sorts and returns the results to users.

Example 1: University A and university B both have a library management system with XML databases. Figure 1 illustrates the schemas of their XML databases. A has all data stored in one database, and B has two XML databases and hence has two corresponding schemas. In Figure 1 (b), the left schema is from the database which stores the information of books and employees, and the other one is from the database stores the information of students (assume only students borrow books). One thing should be noticed is: the dashed lines with an arc between them denote a "choice" relation. For example, in Figure 1 (b) each book could be written either by some authors or by an organization.

Suppose we have a common keyword search interface for two systems of A and B, and keywords "*Yang Maths Differential Geometry*" are submitted, then what kind of information should be returned?

Some reasonable search results could be deduced instantly, such as: "Is there a borrower whose name is *Yang* and now holds a *Maths* book about *Differential Geometry*?", or "Is there a *Maths* book about *Differential Geometry*, and one of its authors is *Yang*?" etc. For former XML keyword search systems cannot find integrated information on multiple XML databases, users can never know which book is now in which person's hand in university B (suppose Yang is a student of university B and he borrowed a Maths book about Differential Geometry). However even only one single database is considered (suppose the searching target is A), in former systems problems still exist: (1) they don't know "Maths"

means "Mathematics", so none match of this term would be found; (2) although "a borrower *Yang* has borrowed a *Maths* book about *Differential Geometry*" is a very reasonable query, considering most researches are based on structural distance of nodes on tree or graph, such semantics would be the last thing be considered because the information of book's name and borrower's name are so far from each other structurally in the schema (no matter their LCA or distance is considered); (3) they return XML document segments or variations as the results, which mostly cannot express meaningful semantics (in some cases, only a value node is returned).

SKeyword provides a solution to these problems. Suppose heterogeneous databases belong to multiple autonomous systems, and each system provides a search interface of XQuery. Firstly SKeyword employs semiautomatic ontology integration to integrate heterogeneous schemas into a global ontology. Implicit semantics in a single schema or between schemas can be revealed and described in the global ontology (e.g. the relation between borrower and book in Figure 1). Then, an inverted index of all terms along with a term-concept mapping table are built and stored in the SKeyword server (as illustrated in Figure 2)

When keywords are submitted, with the term-concept mapping table SKeyword classifies keywords into two kinds: concepts and values. A concept indicates a thing users are interested in, which is practically a *class* in the global ontology (e.g. library, book and borrower). After analysis of keywords, some concepts are figured out as targets. Then, some ontology segments called SCNs are generated according to the distance between concepts have keywords. Afterwards, these segments are translated to XQuery sentences which then are sent to autonomous systems. After receives all the query results, SKeyword organizes them into ontologies. At last they are sorted and sent to users as final results.

Figure 1. The XML schemata of library management systems

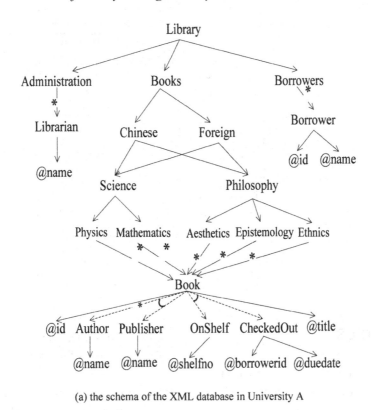

(a) the schema of the XML database in University A

(b) the schemata of XML databases in University B

Figure 2. Data exchange in SKeyword system

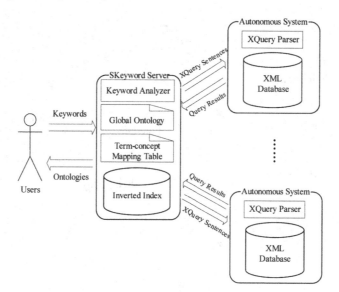

3.2 PRELIMINARIES

Firstly, we explain some basic knowledge and present the definitions of some concepts used in this chapter.

The purpose of our system is to provide a common keyword search interface for heterogeneous XML databases. We assume all these XML databases are from a specific domain and each XML database D consists of an XML document T and an XML Schema S to which T conforms. Moreover, all the XML databases provide a query interface supporting XQuery (XQuery 1.0, 2011) language (Figure 2).

An XML schema expresses shared vocabularies and allows machines to carry out rules made by human; also it provides a means for defining the structure, content and semantics of the XML documents which store the data. Rather than *ontology*, an XML schema can only expresses message formats. Actually, the specification is not designed to support reasoning outside the transaction context. For example, from an XML schema we will never know that an aesthetics book is a philosophy book. In contrast, *ontology* is a knowledge representation and can truly image the things and the relations in reality. Followed is the definition of *ontology* used in this chapter.

Definition 1 (Ontology): An *ontology* is an explicit specification of a shared conceptualization which is described in OWL (Web Ontology Language, 2007), and the ontology used here is a variation of it. An ontology consists of four elements: *Class*, *Instance*, *Property*, and *Constraint*.

- "Class" is a concept to denote general things. A class could be a *"concrete class"* or an *"abstract class"* which cannot have any instance. In SKeyword, the information of a class (class name and class attributes) is fully extracted from XML schemata. Moreover, there could be *inheritance relationships* between classes: (1) if class B inherits class A, we call that A is B's *superclass* and B is A's subclass; (2) a super class could have multiple subclasses, and a subclass also can have multiple *superclasses*; (3) a subclass has all the properties of all its superclasses.

- *"Instance"* denotes particular things. An instance always corresponds to a concrete class, and all its information is from XML documents.

- "Property" includes: *"Object Property"* which describe the relationships between things; "Datatype Property" which describe the attributes of things. The name of a property is from XML schemata and its value comes from XML documents. Otherwise, values only exist in instances.

- *"Constraint"* denotes the constraints and rules among things. In SKeyword, there are four of them: (1) *value constraints* which confine the relations between classes, for example panda eats only bamboo; (2) *cardinality constraints* which confine the existence frequency of a class, for example a book is written by one or more authors; (3) *connection disjoints* means some object properties of a certain class cannot coexist, only one of them can be subject to any instance of the class; (4) *connection conditions*, denotes the conditions under which two classes interconnect to each other, for example borrower only borrow book when borrower.id = book.borrowid. The first two kinds are defined in OWL, while the latter two are not.

An example is given to explain the definition of ontology used in SKeyword as follows.

Example 2: Figure 3 illustrates an ontology which is an integration of schemas in Figure 1.

In Figure 3, classes are represented as ellipses, of which grey ones illustrate abstract classes and dark ones denote concrete classes. From this example we can see that abstract classes usually denote more general things (person, book, etc.). Actually they are "generalized" from the concepts in real data, and they sometimes exist as "connection nodes" in XML schema. Inheritance relations are denoted as lines with triangle-arrows; the lines with open triangle-arrows denote object properties (ordinary relations except inheritance) and the number at their ends indicate the cardinalities. Each card of term list with a connection line to a class contains the datatype properties. For any subclass, only those properties which its superclasses don't have are displayed for the sake of simplicity. Moreover, an arc between two relations indicates a connection disjoint constraint (a book can be written either by some authors or by an organization). A dashed line between borrower and book indicates a connection condition constraint that a borrower only conditionally has a *"borrow"* relation with a book (only when its *id* equals to the book's *borrowerid*).

For two constraints (connection disjoints and connection conditions) are beyond the specification of OWL, we give them extra definitions. Using the ontolgoy in Figure 3 as an example, the syntaxes of them written in OWL are illustrated in Figure 4.

In SKeyword, ontologies are used in two ways: the global ontology which is generated from ontology integration, and the ontologies which are presented to users as searching results. A global ontology doesn't have any instance (just like the one in Figure 2); it is the schema of all possible ontologies and thus we also call it an "ontology schema." For the ontologies used as results, we name it with "SSR" (semantic search results) and define it as follows.

Definition 2 (Semantic Search Result): *A semantic search result (SSR)* of SKeyword is an ontology of definition 1 which satisfies: (1) it must contain some instances and each instance should contain some keywords; (2) all keywords must exist in a SSR; (3) each class should have at least one connection with another one; (4) if a class only has one connection with another class, it must have some instances.

Figure 3. An example of ontology

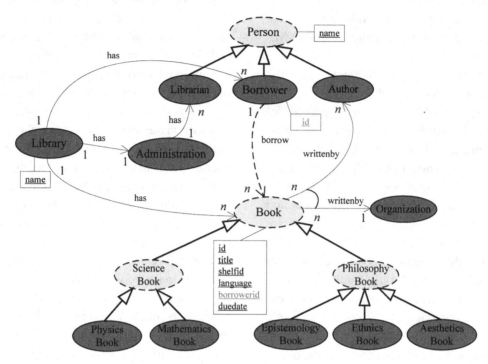

If we consider classes as nodes and relations as edges, a SSR is a directed connected graph. It is easy to find from definition 2 that we don't restrict the topology of the results. However, for users are searching the data for useful information, at least one class one a SSR should have some instance and all keywords must exist in one SSR. Besides, a class could have no instance but it should be used as a "bridge node", otherwise it is apparently useless. Accordingly, for the ontology in Figure 2, a SSR illustrated in Figure 4 could be a result of the query "*Yang Maths Differential Geometry*."

From Figure 5, it is easy to find that keyword "*Yang*" has been found as a borrower whose name is Weidong Yang, and keywords "*Maths Differential Geometry*" have been figured out as two maths books. Also, these three instances have relations close relations between each other.

Figure 4. Syntaxes beyond OWL specification

```
<owl:Connection Disjoint   rdf:about="#Book"   rdf:ID="CD1">
      <owl:class   rdf:resource = "#Author"   relation = "#writtenby"/>
      <owl:class   rdf:resource = "#Organization "   relation = "#writtenby"/>
</ owl:Connection Disjoint>

<owl:ConnectionCondition   rdf:ID="CC1">
      <rdfs:fromClass   rdf:resource = "#Borrower"   key = "id"/>
      <rdfs:toClass   rdf:resource = "#Book"   key = "borrowerid"/>
      <rdfs:condition>Borrower.id = Book.borrwerid</rdfs:condition>
</ owl:ConnectionCondition >
```

Figure 5. An example of SSR

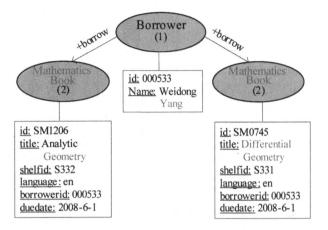

Obviously, this SSR is a reasonable answer and sufficient semantics can be easily obtained by users from it. Finally we propose the definition of XML keyword search in XKeyword. In section 3.5, we will formally define the search results as a semantic candidate network (SCN), which is a joining network (actually a tree) whose nodes are classes (excluding abstract classes) and edges are relations on ontology.

Definition 4 (XML Keyword Search): for k XML databases in a specific domain, $\{D_1, ..., D_k\}$ are XML documents and $\{S_1, ..., S_k\}$ are corresponding schemas. A global ontology O is generated from $\{S_1, ..., S_k\}$. Based on the databases and O, for certain keywords submitted by users, some ontologies which contain keywords and rich semantics are generated. Afterwards, these ontologies are ranked and exhibited to users.

3.3 SYSTEM ARCHITECTURE

The architecture of SKeyword is illustrated in Figure 6. It consists of two stages: the pre-processing stage and the query processing stage.

The pre-processing stage is an off-line processing and its purposes are to generate the global ontology and build the indices. We gather all the schemas from the databases, and integrate them into a global ontology through the ontology generator module. Actually the global ontology is the schema of all current XML databases, and each class of it corresponds to some XML data which can be integrated as the class's instances. The ontology generator also produces three mapping tables. The term-concept mapping table maps some terms to the classes of the global ontology (e.g., "Maths"→"Mathematics Book"), and the terms actually come from the thesaurus of all the classes' names in the global ontology. Moreover, if a term is mapped to a superclass then it is also mapped to all the superclass's subclasses. This setting indicates that if users are interested in "book", it means he is interested in all kinds of books. The second one is the schema-ontology map ping table, which is used to record detailed mapping information from schema elements and attributes to ontology classes and properties. The third one is the ontology–schema mapping table, which is used in query rewriting. Besides three mapping tables, a master index is built up by the index generator. It is an inverted index, and each item of it is a 3-tuple.

Figure 6. The architecture of SKeyword

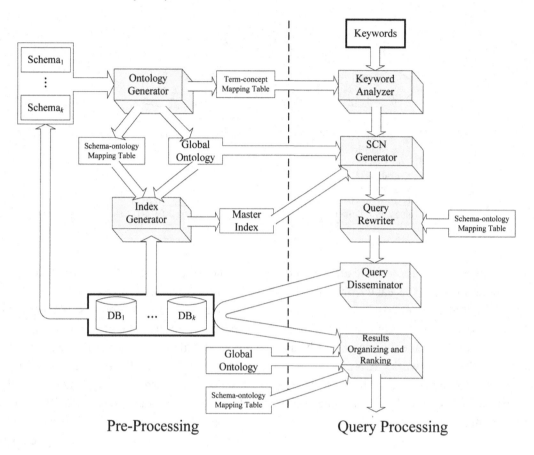

In the query processing stage, after receives the keywords, keyword analyzer extracts some concepts out of them through the term-concept mapping table. Afterwards, SCN generator considers all keywords as values and finds the classes contain them through the master index; accordingly the global ontology is divided into subparts (SCNs). Afterwards, the query rewriter rewrites the SCNs to some XQuery sentences and the query disseminator distributes them to the corresponding databases. Finally, results organizing and ranking module takes charge of collecting the XQuery results, converts them into ontolgies and sorts them in accordance with our ranking model.

3.4 ONTOLOGY INTEGRATION AND INDEX BUILDING

3.4.1 Ontology Integration

Ontology integration is currently a hot subject of research, and it is not a focus topic in this chapter. So, we only give a brief introduction of the technology we use.

We adopt a semi-automatic approach similar to PROMPT (Natalya & Mark, 2000). In our system SKeyword, the sources are XML files. We need to lift XML Schema into Ontology first, and OWL ontology language is employed. Each XML Schema *complexType* is mapped to an *owl:Class*. Elements of *simpleType* and all attributes are mapped to an *owl:DatatypeProperty*; elements of *complexType* are mapped to an *owl:ObjectProperty*. Cardinality restriction are mapped to *owl:minCardinality* and *owl:maxCardinality*. XML Schema also offers three compositors to combine elements: sequence, all and choice. They are mapped to appropriate OWL Boolean expressions. Sequence and All are both conjunctions and are both mapped to an *owl:intersectionOf* constructor. The mapping of the choice compositor is more verbose since there is no direct equivalent in OWL to an exclusive-OR. Hence, it needs to be constructed with a boolean expression (with *owl:intersectionOf*, *owl:unionOf* and *owl:complementOf*). At last, additional constraints defined in definition 1 also been expressed by extra OWL syntaxes.

Afterwards, all local ontologies are integrated into the global ontology. This process consists of four steps and requires users' interactions.

Now we explain how to integrate two ontologies. Firstly, it is certain to load two source ontologies O_1 and O_2. Secondly, we scan the class names in both ontologies to find linguistically similar names and create the initial list of suggested operations. Then we go to the merging process which is the third step. We can select an operation from the current list of suggestions or define a merge operation by ourselves as well. Furthermore, after performing the operation, new suggestions would appear. We also maintain a confliction list and gives possible solutions to resolve the conflicts. If step 4 is not terminal, we go back step 3 and execute in the cycle until the source ontologies O_1 and O_2 are fully merged. The basic merge operations we defined include *merge-class*, *deep-copy*, *shallow-copy* etc.

3.4.2 Building Indices

Totally, SKeyword contains four indices: master index, term-concept mapping table, schema-ontology mapping table, and ontology–schema mapping table.

Master index, what we call the *master index* is actually an inverted list of which every element is a 3-tuple *<term, schema node list, class list>*. *Schema node* list stores the schema nodes which have the *term* as values in corresponding XML data. Each schema node is actually expressed as a path from the schema root to the node along with the database name. Such information is recorded because we need to figure out the appearing places of the *term* in XML databases. *Class list* is a list of ontology classes, and each class corresponds a set of data which contains the term. The purpose of using *Class list* is to find relevant objects of keywords in the global ontology instantly. The following is an example of it.

<Yang, (DB2-Library-Books...-Writer, …), (Author, …)>

Term-concept mapping table maps a set of concepts to a specific term. In practical life, usually a simply concept have several ways to express. For instance, a man who writes a book or an article can be called an author or a writer. Generally each individual has his/her own habits of speaking and writing, therefore for a keyword search system the genuine concept of keywords need be figured out. This mapping table is built by firstly traverse each class in the global ontology and a reasonable thesaurus of it is gathered artificially. Afterwards, for each term in the thesaurus make up a term-concepts map. A piece of this mapping table is as follows.

<writer, Author>, <author, Author>,
<article, <Book, Science Book, …>>, …

Here is one thing must be paid attention to is: for the inheritance relationship between two classes, all the words in the superclass's thesaurus must exist in the subclass's thesaurus. This is a representation of the concept inclusion (a subclass is a *kind* of superclass).

Schema-ontology mapping table maps each schema path to an ontology class. It is generated in the ontology integration process and is used to build the master index.

Ontology–schema mapping table is the reverse form of the former mapping table. It is used in query rewriting process.

After some keywords are submitted by users, firstly term-concept mapping table is checked to find if users are interested in some objects (classes) in the ontology. Then the ontology classes whose instances have some keywords as values are marked by using master index. All these classes are considered as meaningful objects, and accordingly some SCNs (which described in the next section) are computed. Finally each SCN is translated into an XQuery sentence in virtue of ontology-schema mapping table.

3.5 GENERATING AND REWRITING SCNs

In this section, firstly we define the concept of SCN and provide a SCN generation algorithm; afterwards we discuss how to rewrite SCNs into XQuery sentences.

3.5.1 Semantic Candidate Network

In the research of keyword search in relational or XML databases, *candidate network* is a commonly used concept. Here we define a similar concept which is called "Semantic Candidate Network" on the ontology.

Definition 4 (Semantic Candidate Network): *A semantic candidate network (SCN) is a joining network (actually a tree) whose nodes are classes (excluding abstract classes) and edges are relations on ontology. It contains all the keywords and none of its sub-trees contain all the keywords.*

The concept of SCN is similar to CN defined by former researches on keyword search for relational database (Hristidis & Papakonstantinou, 2002). CN uses tables as nodes while SCN uses ontology classes. Each CN node corresponds to one data tuple, accordingly a SCN node only has one instance. It is obvious that SCNs are the

schemas of SSRs and they can be generated from the global ontology. We can easily find out classes have keywords in the global ontology through the master index and the term-concept mapping table, and hence can use a SCN generation algorithm to find all valid SCNs. However, not every SCN is useful for users (suppose a very large SCN which has only two substantial classes), so we define the number of classes in a SCN as the *size* of it, and before doing the SCN generation algorithm an up-bound of the size (denoted as $max(|SCN|)$) must be set.

3.5.2 Generating Semantic Candidate Network

SCN generation algorithm is based on a breadth-first traversal to find all possible SCNs from the ontology. It is similar to the algorithm described in DISCOVER (Hristidis & Papakonstantinou, 2002). But there are still some differences between them:

- SCN generation algorithm doesn't need to consider the pruning condition in CN's.
- SCN generation algorithm need to consider more than CN's since abstract class nodes should not be included in the SCN according to its definition. Therefore if an abstract class node is added into network, it should not affect the size of network and after this network is confirmed to be a SCN, all the abstract-class nodes need to be removed from it.

For a certain keyword query, we add the keywords into the global ontology graph using keywords and indices to form a SCN ontology graph. The SCN ontology graph is similar to the global ontology graph, and the only difference is the node in the SCN ontology graph may contain keywords which indicate that certain keywords may appear in corresponding instance.

The generation algorithm input a set of keywords, SCN ontology graph, the up-bound size of SCN and using a queue Q to make breadth-first traversal. The algorithm is described briefly in Figure 7.

S satisfies acceptance condition in algorithm indicates that a network satisfies the definition of SCN. S and N satisfies expansion condition indicates that node N contains no keywords or it contains keyword which is not in S. $|S|$ is the size of network S excluding abstract class nodes. Moreover, the disjoint constraint must be treated additionally. At the same time only one of the two edges with disjoint constraint can exist in a SCN. The unqualified SCNs must be deleted.

3.5.3 Query Rewriting

After executing the SCN generation algorithm with an up-bound size $max(|SCN|)$, we will get several SCNs with size smaller than $max(|SCN|)$. Now for each SCN, we should rewrite it into different XQuery sentences for each database. However, before that, if a SCN contains a constraint of "connection conditions" (as the edge named "borrow" illustrated in Figure 3), this kind of edge must be broken. Also, if the nodes of a SCN are from different databases, the SCN need to be separated into several sub-parts, and all nodes of each part are from a single database. After these processes,

a SCN would be divided to several parts which afterwards are translated into multiple XQuery sentences respectively.

Now we discuss about how to rewrite a SCN into an XQuery sentence for a database and its schema.

- In for clause, we get all the nodes that contain keywords in the SCN, and then we get schema node list from master index according to keyword and the node name. For example, if a SCN node 'Author' contains keyword 'Yang', for database DB2, we can get its schema path from master index is DB2-Library-Books-Writer. Then we can write for clause as *for $author in doc(DB2)/ Library/ Books/ Writer,…*

- In where clause, we just write a simple judgment like *where $author=Yang and …*

- In return clause, for all SCN nodes that contain keywords, we first find the LCA node of their corresponding schema path in schema. For example, for two SCN nodes 'Author' and 'Title', we can get their schema path from master index is DB2-Library-Books-Writer and DB2-Library-Books-Title. Then we can get their LCA node is DB2-Library-Books. Here we will return this node as a result.

Figure 7. The SCN generation algorithm

```
SCN Generation Algorithm
pick an arbitrary keyword k from keywords
put all the nodes in SCN ontology graph that contain  k into Q
while Q is not empty :
     get head network S from Q
        if S satisfies acceptance condition :
             remove all the abstract class node in  S
             output S
     else  for each node N adjacent to S:
          if S and N satisfies expansion condition
          and |S|<max(|SCN|):
               add N into S
                    put S into Q
```

After all XQuery sentences are obtained, we disseminate these XQuery sentences to each database. Then some XML segments are returned as query results, afterwards we organize them to form SSRs.

3.6 ORGANIZING AND RANKING RESULTS

After receives an XQuery sentence, each autonomous system would query local database by it, and then sends the results back to the SKeyword server. However this kind of query results cannot be regarded as final results, for actually a SCN is the result pattern what users are interested. Therefore, some transformations from XML segments to ontologies need to be done. It is easy to achieve it through schema-ontology mapping table.

Moreover, as explained in section 6.3, a SCN could be translated into multiple XQuery sentences because corresponding data are not from a single database, and they only can be related with some extra conditions. Accordingly, these query results returned from multiple databases need to be integrated. An example is as follows.

Example 3: Figure 8(a) illustrates a SCN which contains two classes and each one has some keywords. Moreover, these two classes are connected along with a "connection conditions" constraint. They are then translated into two XQuery sentences. Figure 8(b) illustrated two returned query results. Based on them the connection condition is used to integrate query results into an ontology as the final result which is illustrated in Figure 8(c). From Figure 8, it is easy to find that the final result is much more meaningful and expressive than XML document segments. Above all, implicit semantics is revealed.

A novel ranking model is proposed to sort results. We believe the ranking model can over-

match former ones because: (1) the topologies of SSRs are based on semantics rather than the structures of schemas; (2) the relations between concepts are contributive to the score. Obviously, each final result could be regarded as a connected graph whose nodes are ontology classes which respond some instances. Many excellent ranking models have been proposed to sort graph-like results in keyword search (Hristidis, Papakonstantinou, & Balmin, 2003; Hristidis, Gravano, & Papakonstantinou, 2003), and the most important criterion is the size of the graph. However, we consider our ranking model in SKeyword more effective, for an extra criterion is considered: the weight of edges. In the stage of integration from XML schemas to the global ontology, the administrator can give each edge a numerical value as a weight between ontology classes according to practical semantics. For example, the relationship between *Book* and *Author* is more closed than the relationship between *Book* and *Borrower*. Because the former one maybe only exist for a time but the latter would last forever. Accordingly, the edge "*writtenby*" can be given a greater value as a bigger weight.

In conclusion, we rank final results w.r.t two things: the size of the results, and the weights of edges.

3.7 EXPERIMENTS

Our experiments are designed for purpose of: (1) the comparison of results by using SKeyword and classic approach (SLCA); (2) to see if the results generated by SKeyword express richer semantics than the results obtained by search each database respectively.

1. To simulate the environment of heterogeneous XML databases, we adopt both real and artificial data, and each kind contains two databases. The first data set consists of *DBLP Computer Science Bibliography*

Figure 8. An example of result organization

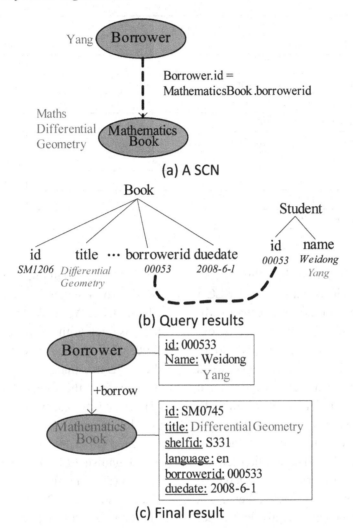

(a) A SCN

(b) Query results

(c) Final result

and *SIGMOD Record* from XML Data Repository, and the other one contains two databases illustrated in Figure 1. Besides, all data from the latter data group are generated from some vocabularies built by ourselves. We selected 10 queries as illustrated in Table 1 to search these two data groups. For each of the queries, we find out the top-10 best answers manually, and describe all of them in human language (e.g., a person named Yang borrowed a maths book, and the book's title is Differential Geometry.). Afterwards, we use these queries to search databases for

results through different approaches, and invite ten people to evaluate the results. The results of each group are compared with standard ones, and a score between 0 and 10 is given by each person in consideration of both precision and recall.

Figure 9 (a) and (b) illustrate the comparison of the effectiveness of SLCA method and SKeyword. From them we can see that the results of SKeyword are much more useful for users than that of SLCA. According to analysis, the reasons are: SKeyword is based on a graph algorithm

Table 1. Queries used in the experiments

Query ID	Keywords	Target DBs
Q_1	XML Database Efficient	DBLP&SIGMOD
Q_2	XML Jason Author	DBLP&SIGMOD
Q_3	Michael Writer Information Retrieval	DBLP&SIGMOD
Q_4	Chris Buckley Paper	DBLP&SIGMOD
Q_5	University of California 1993	DBLP&SIGMOD
Q_6	Yang Maths Differential Geometry	Libraries
Q_7	Zhu Yang Article	Libraries
Q_8	Zhu Author Ethnics	Libraries
Q_9	Yang XML HTML	Libraries
Q_{10}	Fang Borrower Book	Libraries

while SLCA is based on a tree algorithm; SKeyword can reveal implicit semantics which SLCA cannot find; SSRs are more expressive than XML segments. In one database group, we use SKeyword for each database and then simply add all the results; such method is called SKeyword (respective). We compare it with SKeyword and the results are showed in Figure 9 (c) and (d). From Figure 9 (c), we can find that the result scores are sheerly the same, because the two databases are both simple and no implicit semantics has been mined, furthermore they have no semantical connections with each other. As a result, these two methods have equivalent effectiveness. On the contrary, the schemas of the library databases hide much implicit semantics. That's why the result scores differ in Figure 9 (d).

In conclusion, from the experiments it is easy to find that SKeyword has a high effectiveness and can provide users meaningful results with sufficient semantics.

3.8 RELATED WORK

Keyword search on databases gains more and more attentions these years. For XML databases, most approaches are LCA-based. (Xu & Papakonstantinou, 2005; Yunyao, Cong, & Jagadish, 2004; Cohen, Mamou, Kanza, & Sagiv, 2003; Guo, Shao, Botev, and Shanmugasundaram, 2003; Chong, Chee-Yong, & Amit, 2007) are the most famous ones of them. Xu and Papakonstantinou (2005) defines the concept of SLCA as a node in the XML tree that: (1) contains all keywords in its label or in the labels of its descendant nodes, (2) none of its descendant nodes is a SLCA.

This means results only can be judged by the deep of LCAs in the tree. Yunyao, Cong, and Jagadish (2004) defines a concept called MLCA (Meaningful LCA), and Cohen, Mamou, Kanza, and Sagiv (2003) defines the concept of Interconnection Relationship. They are both the same as SLCA essentially. LCA-based approaches have many drawbacks, and the most serious one is the criterion of choosing results and consequent difficulty to explain the effectiveness of results. SKeyword is based on Ontology, and the global ontology is generated by semiautomatic process, which means semantics could be expressed precisely as long as enough energy is spent.

Proximity search on graphs also has been utilized extensively in keyword search on relational or XML databases (Hristidis et al., 2003; Bhalotia, Hulgeri, Nakhe, Chakrabarti, & Sudarshan, 2002; Hristidis & Papakonstantinou, 2002; Agrawal, Chaudhuri, & Das, 2002; Goldman, Shivakumar, Venkatasubramanian, & Garcia-Molina, 1998). In

Figure 9. Scores of search results

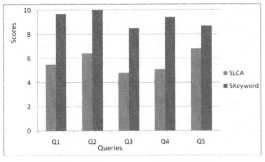

(a) Databases: DBLP & SIGMOD

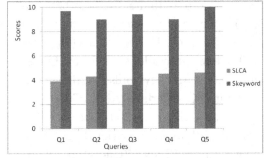

(b) Databases: the libraries

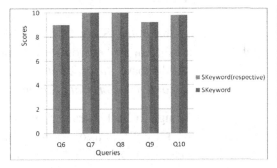

(c) Databases: DBLP & SIGMOD

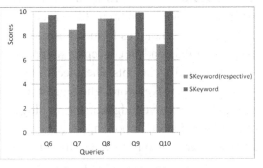

(d) Databases: the libraries

which, database is viewed as a graph with objects/tuples as nodes and relationships as edges. The distance between two nodes is regarded as the length of path. BANKS (Bhalotia et al., 2002) and (Goldman et al., 1998) can be applied to both relational and XML database, however, the algorithms are intrinsically expensive even some precomputation could be done. DISCOVER (Hristidis & Papakonstantinou, 2002) and DBXplorer (Agrawal et al., 2002) are developed as middleware working on top of DBMSs, and they only support keyword search in relational database. XKeyword (Hristidis et al., 2003) supports keyword search specifically for XML, and it defines a concept of target objects which are specific fragments of XML document as results. Moreover, the administrator needs to mark out Target Schema Segments (TSS) from the schema. SKeyword is similar to XKeyword in a way. However SKeyword employs OWL Ontology to express objects and relations,

and afterwards is more general and expressive than XKeyword.

There are mainly two forms of result organization for keyword search on databases currently: (Xu & Papakonstantinou, 2005), XSEarch (Cohen et al., 2003), and XRANK (Guo et al., 2003) return the subtrees rooted at LCAs of some keyword nodes; (Hristidis, Koudas, Papakonstantinou, & Srivastava, 2006) and BANKS (Bhalotia et al., 2002) return the trees similarly defined as MBT, which is actually a set of paths from LCA to keyword nodes. In XKeyword (Hristidis et al., 2003), the administrator decides the form of results through splitting the schema into TSSs. A recent work XSeek (Ziyang & Yi, 2007) discusses how to automatically infer the most relevant information from the results. SKeyword adopts a formation similar to ontology called Semantic Search Result (SSR) as returned results. Accordingly, more sufficient semantics can be delivered through results.

(Hristidis et al., 2003; Barg & Wong, 2001) rank the answers according to the distances between elements in one result; closer elements would receive a higher rank. In XKeyword (Hristidis et al., 2003), trees of smaller sizes denote higher association between the keywords. And the similar idea is used in SKeyword. XRANK (Guo et al., 2003), XSEarch (Cohen et al., 2003) and (Hristidis et al., 2003) use Information-Retrieval techniques in ranking results. XRANK (Guo et al., 2003) extends the PageRank metric (Brin & Page, 1998) from HTML to XML. XSEarch (Cohen et al., 2003) adopts two techniques from Information-Retrieval: tf-idf model and the concept of similarity between queries and documents. These techniques are all compatible to SKeyword. The biggest difference is SKeyword gives edges on the ontology weights, and use it as an importance criterion.

To solve heterogeneous problem of multiple databases, Guoliang, Beng, Jianhua, Jianyong, and Lizhu (2008), Sayyadian, LeKhac, Doan, and Gravano (2007) both propose excellent ideas. Sayyadian et al., (2007) supposes a circumstance of pure relational databases and connect multiple databases by deducing joins between databases. EASE (Guoliang et al., 2008) is the latest research in this field. It can be applied in any graph-based databases (unstructured, semi-structured, or structured data). The Authors defined a variation of Steiner tree problem to simplify the requirement, and accordingly results can be found efficiently. Other than EASE, SKeyword faces a number of autonomous systems which store XML databases and provide XQuery interfaces. Besides, EASE mainly cares about the search efficiency while SKeyword concerns the effectiveness of searching results.

3.9 CONCLUSION

This chapter proposes a system SKeyword for keyword search on heterogeneous XML data sources. SKeyword provides a common interface for multiple autonomous systems with XML databases, and can seek for semantics from the data furthest by employing OWL Ontology. SKeyword also can provide results with sufficient semantics, and the form of results is more expressive than any existing system. Furthermore, the architecture of this system is provided and the experiments prove that SKeyword has a high effectiveness.

REFERENCES

Agrawal, S., Chaudhuri, S., & Das, G. (2002). DBXplorer: A system for keyword-based search over relational database. In *Proceedings of 18th International Conference on Data Engineering.*

Barg, M., & Wong, R. (2001). Structural proximity searching for large collections of semi-structured data. In *Proceedings of the 10th International Conference on Information and Knowledge Management.*

Bhalotia, G., Hulgeri, A., Nakhe, C., Chakrabarti, S., & Sudarshan, S. (2002). Keyword searching and browsing in database using BANKS. In *Proceedings of 18th International Conference on Data Engineering.*

Brin, S., & Page, L. (1998). The anatomy of a large-scale hypertextual Web search engine. In *Proceedings of the 7th International World Wide Web Conference.*

Chong, S., Chee-Yong, C., & Amit, K. G. (2007). Multiway SLCA-based keyword search in XML data. In *Proceedings of the 16th International Conference on World Wide Web.*

Cohen, S., Mamou, J., Kanza, Y., & Sagiv, Y. (2003). XSEarch: A semantic search engine for XML. In *Proceedings of the29th International Conference on Very Large Data Bases* (pp. 1069–1072).

Goldman, R., Shivakumar, N., Venkatasubramanian, S., & Garcia-Molina, H. (1998). Proximity search in database. In *Proceedings of the 24th International Conference on Very Large Data Bases.*

Guo, L., Shao, F., Botev, C., & Shanmugasundaram, J. (2003). XRANK: Ranked keyword search over XML documents. In *Proceedings of the 2003 ACM SIGMOD International Conference on Management of Data* (pp.16–27).

Guoliang, L., Beng, C. O., Jianhua, F., Jianyong, W., & Lizhu, Z. (2008). EASE: An effective 3-in-1 keyword search method for unstructured, semistructured and structured data. In *Proceedings of the 2008 ACM SIGMOD International Conference on Management of Data.*

Hao, H., Haixun, W., Jun, Y., & Philip, S. Y. (2007). BLINKS: Ranked keyword searches on graphs. In *Proceedings of the 2007 ACM SIGMOD International Conference on Management of Data* (pp.305–316).

Hristidis, V., Gravano, L., & Papakonstantinou, Y. (2003). Efficient IR-style keyword search over relational databases. In *Proceedings of the 29th International Conference on Very Large Data Bases.*

Hristidis, V., Koudas, N., Papakonstantinou, Y., & Srivastava, D. (2006). Keyword proximity search in XML trees. In *IEEE Transactions on Knowledge and Data Engineering.*

Hristidis, V., & Papakonstantinou, Y. (2002). DISCOVER: Key-word search in relational databases. In *Proceedings of the 28th International Conference on Very Large Data Bases.*

Hristidis, V., Papakonstantinou, Y., & Balmin, A. (2003). Keyword proximity search on XML graphs. In *Proceedings of 19th International Conference on Data Engineering.*

Natalya, F. N., & Mark, A. M. (2000). Prompt: Algorithm and tool for automated ontology merging and alignment. In *Proceedings of 17th National Conference on Artiðcial Intelligence.*

Sayyadian, M., LeKhac, H., Doan, A., & Gravano, L. (2007). Efficient keyword search across heterogeneous relational database. In *Proceedings of 23th International Conference on Data Engineering.*

Web Ontology Language (OWL). (2007). Retrieved from http://www.w3.org/2004/OWL/.

XML Data Repository. Retrieved from http://www.cs.washington.edu/research/xmldatasets/www/repository.html

XQuery 1.0: An XML query language (2nd ed.). (2011). Retrieved from http://www.w3.org/TR/xquery/

Xu, Y., & Papakonstantinou, Y. (2005). Efficient keyword search for smallest LCAs in XML databases. In *Proceedings of the 2005 ACM SIGMOD International Conference on Management of Data.*

Yunyao, L., Cong, Y., & Jagadish, H. V. (2004). Schema-free XQuery. In *Proceedings of the 30th International Conference on Very Large Data Bases* (pp. 72–83).

Ziyang, L., & Yi, C. (2007). Identifying meaningful return information for XML Keyword search. In *Proceedings of the 2007 ACM SIGMOD International Conference on Management of Data* (pp. 329–340).

Chapter 4
Foundation of XML Stream Processing Techniques

Weidong Yang
Fudan University, China

Hao Zhu
Fudan University, China

ABSTRACT

The problem of processing streaming XML data is gaining widespread attention from the research community, and various XML stream processing methods are put forward, including automaton-based methods, index-based methods, and so forth. In this chapter, the basic concepts and several existing typical approaches of XML stream processing are discussed. Section 1 introduces the background and current research status of this area. Section 2 focuses on the discussion of automaton-based methods, for example, X/YFilter, XPush, et cetera. In section 3, the index-based methods are given. In section 4, other methods such us Fist and XTrie are discussed briefly. Section 4 discusses some optimization technique of XML stream processing. Section 5 summarizes this chapter.

4.1 INTRODUCTION

4.1.1 Background

Nowadays, XML is considered as a standard of data representation and exchange, it is widely used in various fields such as SOAP and WSDL web services, business to business transactions and personalized content delivery. On the other hand, due to the demands from sensor network applications, information dissemination, content based routing, and processing of scientific data, efficient processing of XML stream data has attracted lots of attentions in recent years.

A data stream is defined as a massive unbounded sequence of data elements continuously generated at a rapid rate. A *data stream management system (DSMS)* registers queries in advance because it should execute them continuously perpetually rather than once on demand. The registered query is called a continuous query. It produces its query result whenever an incoming tuple of a target data stream satisfies it. Accord-

DOI: 10.4018/978-1-4666-1975-3.ch004

ingly, it should be evaluated in real-time, which requires strict time and space constraints.

Particularly, a data stream which is formatted by XML is called *an XML Stream*, its corresponding management system is called XML stream management system. If we treat XML as a tree, XML stream is a string sequence after a preorder traversal in this tree. XML stream data can be transmitted by two different ways: one is by character stream, the commoner one is by token or chunk. A token is made by several elements, and transmit together.

XML data is consisting of many nesting elements, which each one begins with a certain open tag and ends with the corresponding close tag. XML data is ordered, hierarchical and maybe recursive, so its processing is more complicated than the ordinary data. A well-formed XML stream is one in which every pure XML stream which is delimited by control tokens is a well-formed XML fragment. Most researches only consider well-formed streams and fragments. Well-formed XML fragments correspond to labeled ordered trees, with labels of inner nodes indicating the element name of a node and leaf nodes representing character content.

Generally, there are two different method to process XML data, *DOM (Document Object Model)* and *SAX (Simple API for XML)*. DOM treats XML data as an entire element tree, and keeps the whole tree in the memory for processing. Unlike DOM, SAX is an event-driven API for processing XML. Obviously, SAX is more suitable for processing XML stream data than DOM. In the most researches, XML stream data is modeled as a stream of SAX events: startElement(*id, tag, text*) and endElement(*id, tag*), where *tag* is the tag of the node being processed, *text* is text value of the node in the corresponding XML tree, and *id* is unique identifier of the node. By implementing these interfaces, whenever the open tag or close tag is reached, the above two events will be activated to processing the data.

For XML stream management systems, currently, most queries are expressed by some structured query languages such as XPath (XQuery 1.0, 2011) or (Su, Jinhui, & A. Rundensteiner, 2003). The core technical challenge in such systems is processing a large set of XPath queries over a continuously incoming XML stream. This challenge is related to, but different from, the more traditional stored XML data retrieval problem. XML stream is generated at a rapid rate and arrives continuously, therefore it requires the processing system has a better processing capability and lower memory used. XML streaming data are available for reading only once and are provided in a fixed order determined by the data source.

4.1.2 The State of Art

Several relational data stream management systems have been proposed since 2002, such as Aurora (Abadi et al., 2003), Telegraph (Madden, Shah, & Hellerstein, 2002) and STREAM (Motwani, et al., 2003). Similar to these systems, XML stream filtering is also based on the concept of continuous queries processing for streaming data. But XML data is ordered, recursive and hierarchical, mostly queried by XPath/XQuery language. The differences between XML data and ordinary relational data determine that the special techniques are needed for processing XML stream data.

Several studies have been concentrated on how to evaluate multiple and large amount of XPath queries over XML stream data. University of California at Berkeley proposed *X*Filter (Altinel & Franklin, 2000) at 2000 in the VLDB (one of most famous conference in the field of database), which builds a finite state machine (FSM) for each XPath query and employs a query index on all the FSMs. As the successor of XFilter, *YFilter* (Diao, & J. Franklin, 2003) combines all of the XPath queries into a single NFA(non-deterministic finite automaton), supporting shared processing of the common prefixes among all navigation paths. YFilter eagerly constructs the NFA with all the queried registered in the filtering system. On the contrary, XML Toolkit (Green, Miklau, Onizuka, & Suciu, 2003) proposes a single DFA (deterministic finite automata) that is collectively constructed from target XPath queries called lazy DFA. Unlike YFilter, lazy DFA constructs the automata at runtime to prevent the states of automata increasing exponentially with the amount of queries. Also in this paper, a Stream IndeX (SIX) that arranges simple binary offset data for the elements of an input XML document is proposed for rapid access to the XML document as an optimization. Similarly, the XPush (Gupta & Suciu, 2003) machine extends the lazy DFA approach to handle complex queries with nested paths using deterministic pushdown automaton in a bottom up fashion. Except the methods with automata, Index-Filter (Bruno, Gravano, Koudas, & Srivastava, 2003) uses indexes built over the document tags to filter out large portions of the input XML document that are not guaranteed to be part of any match. XTrie (Chee-Yong, Pascal, Minos, & Rajeev, 2002) handles tree-shaped path expressions involving predicates in a *trie* structure based on common substrings.

There are several XPath/XQuery streaming engines such as XSQ (Peng & Chawathe, 2003), XSM (Ludascher, Mukhopadhay, & Papakonstantinou, 2002), SPEX (Daniela et al., 2003), BEA/XQRL (Salton & McGill, 1983). By using an enhancive and hierarchical automata, XSQ processes XPath queries with child and descendant axes, and predicates with the restriction that each query node can contain at most one predicate without axes. SPEX processes regular expressions, which are similar to the XPath queries of XSQ. XSM of University of California-San Diego is a XQuery streaming engine with an XML Stream Machine similar to FSM. XSM supports optimizations with DTD and returning of matching results. BEA/XQRL is a full implementation of XQuery. BEA/XQRL targets processing general XQuery queries on small XML messages.

In the remainder of this chapter, we classify the XML stream processing techniques into automaton-based methods, index-based methods and other methods. Also, we will describe the optimization of XML stream processing techniques.

4.2 AUTOMATON-BASED METHODS

4.2.1 X/YFilter

Many systems adapt the processing approach based on automaton. The typical works are X/YFilter (Altinel & Franklin, 2000; Diao & Franklin, 2003) which is proposed by University of California at Berkeley. In these systems, each data node causes a state transition in the underlying finite state automata representation of the filters. XFilter is implemented in the context of the Dissemination-Based Information Systems (DBIS) project which is developing a toolkit for constructing adaptable, application-specific middleware that incorporates multiple data delivery mechanisms in complex networked environments. XFilter developed indexing mechanisms and matching algorithms based on a modified Finite State Machine (FSM) approach that can quickly locate and evaluate relevant profiles. By converting XPath queries into a Finite State Machine representation, XFilter is able to handle arbitrary regular expressions in queries, efficiently check element ordering and evaluate filters in queries, and cope with the semi-structured nature of XML documents. XFilter (Altinel & Franklin, 2000) demonstrates how by using an index on profiles, one scan of a document can be used to drive the simultaneous execution of all candidate profiles. As stated previously, however, XFilter fails to exploit commonality that exists among the path expressions (recall that XFilter builds an FSM for each query). For large-scale filtering of XML data, exploiting such commonality can greatly reduce redundant processing.

Thus, YFilter (Diao & Franklin, 2003) proposes a new filtering approach that follows the event-driven philosophy of XFilter, but in addition, shares processing among path expressions to eliminate redundant work. YFilter extends XFilter to use a nondeterministic automaton (NFA) in which the state transitions for multiple queries are pre-computed instead of advancing an automaton for each query separately.

In the YFilter, rather than representing each query as an FSM individually, it combines all queries into a single Nondeterministic Finite Automaton (NFA). As such, the common prefixes of the paths are represented only once in the structure. In addition, the machine employs a stack-based mechanism to cope with non-determinism and support backtracking in the structure. It is important to note that because NFA construction in YFilter is an incremental process, new queries can easily be added to an existing system. This ease of maintenance is a key benefit of the NFA-based approaches

4.2.2 LazyDFA/ XPush

The difficulty in XML stream processing is that the number of XPath queries in the workload is very high. YFilter is capable with evaluating large workloads of XPath expressions, but there is a space guarantee that is proportional to the total size of all XPath expressions in the workload, but no guarantee on the throughput. As the number of queries increased, the size of NFA automaton will be larger and the processing time and space consumption will increase exponentially. LazyDFA (Green et al., 2003) described two techniques for processing linear XPath expressions on streams of XML packets: using a lazy Deterministic Finite Automaton, and a *Stream IndeX (SIX)*. The main problem with the DFA is that the worst case memory requirement is exponential in the size of the XPath workload. LazyDFA have presented a combination of theoretical results and experimental validations that together prove that the size

of the lazy DFA remains small, for all practical purposes. Some of the theoretical results offer insights into the structure of XPath expressions that is of independent interest. LazyDFA also validated lazy DFAs on streaming XML data and shown that they indeed have a very high throughput, which is independent on the number of XPath expressions in the workload. The SIX is a simple technique that adds some small amount of binary data to an XML document, which helps speed up a query processor by several factors.

The basic approach of LazyDFA is to convert a query tree into a *Deterministic Finite Automaton (DFA)*. Recall that the query tree may be a very large collection of XPath expressions: we convert all of them into a single DFA. This is done in two steps: convert the query tree into a *Nondeterministic Finite Automaton (NFA)*, and then convert the NFA to a DFA. The runtime processing of LazyDFA is quite similar with YFilter. It suffices to maintain a pointer to the current DFA state, and a stack of DFA states. SAX events are processed as follows. On a startElement(e) event it pushes the current state on the stack, and replace the state with the state reached by following the e transition; on an endElement(e) we pop a state from the stack and set it as the current state. Attributes and text values are handled similarly. At any moment, the states stored in the stack are exactly those at which the ancestors of the current node were processed, and at which one may need to come back later when exploring subsequent children nodes of those ancestors.

Then, we will analyze the size of the different DFA construction. For a general regular expression the size of the DFA including the NFA used by YFilter may be exponential. We call a DFA eager if it is obtained using the standard power-set construction. We call the DFA lazy if its states and transitions are constructed at runtime. The lazy DFA is constructed at run-time, on demand. Initially it has a single state (the initial state), and whenever we attempt to make a transition into a missing state we compute it, and update the transition. Thus, the size of the lazy DFA is determined by two factors: (1) the number of states, i.e. $| \text{states}(A_l) |$, and (2) the size of each state, i.e. $| A_n(w) |$, for $w \in L_{data}$. Recall that each state in the lazy DFA is represented by a set of states from the NFA, which we call an NFA table. In the eager DFA the NFA tables can be dropped after the DFA has been computed, but in the lazy DFA they need to be kept, since we never really complete the construction of the DFA. Therefore the NFA tables also contribute to the size of the lazy DFA. Finally, consider a simple graph schema with d, D, defined as above, and let Q be a set of XPath expressions of maximum depth n. Then, on any XML input satisfying the schema, the lazy DFA has at most $1 + D \times (1 + n)^d$ states.

Another technique proposed in the LazyDFA is the Stream Index(SIX). Parsing and tokenizing the XML document is generally accepted to be a major bottleneck in XML processing. An obvious solution is to represent an XML document in binary, as a string of binary tokens. In an XML message system, the messages are now binary representations of XML, rather than real XML, or they are converted into binary when they enter the system. Some commercial implementations adopt this approach in order to increase performance. The disadvantage is that all servers in the network must understand that binary format. This defeats the purpose of the XML standard, which is supposed to address precisely the lack of interoperability that is associated with a binary format. LazyDFA favors an alternative approach: keep the XML packets in their native text format, and add a small amount of binary data that allows fast access to the document. We will introduce the details of SIX in section 4.1.

Besides LazyDFA, another filtering system proposed by Washington University is a lazily construct single deterministic pushdown automaton, called the XPush (Gupta, & Suciu, 2003) Machine. Its goal is to process efficiently large numbers of XPath expressions with many predicates per query, on a stream of XML data. It

have described a new pushdown machine, called XPush that can express such workloads. If fully computed, the XPush machine runs extremely fast on the XML stream, since it processes each SAX event in O(1) time, independent of the query workload. However, in most practical applications the XPush machine cannot be pre-computed but needs to be computed lazily, at runtime. XPush have shown experimentally that by computing it lazily the memory requirements of the XPush machine are manageable.

The resulting machine is called the bottom-up XPush machine. It is obtained in two steps: (1) convert each of the XPath filters $P_1, ..., P_n$ into an Alternating Finite Automaton, AFA, $A_1, ..., A_n$, (2) translate the set of all AFAs, $A_1, ..., A_n$, to a single XPush machine. An Alternating Finite Automaton, AFA, is a nondeterministic finite automaton A where each state is labeled with AND, OR, or NOT.

X/YFilter is a predecessor of XML stream filtering using automaton. Then LazyDFA and XPush commonly construct their own automata lazily at runtime to prevent the rapid increase of states. Next we will introduce some single query processing systems that some of them support evaluating XQuery.

4.2.3 XSM

The *XML Stream Machine (XSM)* (Ludascher et al., 2002) system is a XQuery processing paradigm that is tuned to the efficient processing of sequentially accessed XML data (streams). The system compiles a given XQuery into an XSM, which is an XML stream transducer, i.e., an abstract device that takes as input one or more XML data streams and produces one or more output streams, potentially using internal buffers. XSM present a systematic way to translate XQueries into efficient XSMs: First the XQuery is translated into a network of XSMs that correspond to the basic operators of the XQuery language and exchange streams. The network is reduced to a single XSM by repeated application of an XSM composition operation that is optimized to reduce the number of tests and actions that the XSM performs as well as the number of intermediate buffers that it uses. Finally, the optimized XSM is compiled into a C program. XML stream machines resemble traditional transducers and translate one or more XML input streams into (usually) one output XML stream. Like transducers and finite state machines, they have finite sets of states Q and state transitions T. The latter are defined based on the content of the input, the current state, and some internal memory. In the case of XSMs, the memory is a finite set of buffers B = B1,…, Bn. Some buffers are distinguished input buffers and output buffers, which are associated with the input streams and output streams of the XSM, respectively.

4.2.4 XSQ

The *XSQ* (Peng, & Chawathe,2003) ystem is an XPath engine for streaming XML. XSQ supports XPath features such as multiple predicates, closures, and aggregation, which pose interesting challenges for streaming evaluation.

The XSQ system uses an automaton-based method to evaluate XPath queries over XML streams. The automaton, called an HPDT, is a finite state automaton augmented with a buffer. Its transitions are optionally associated with predicates and buffer operations. A transition is taken only if its predicate, if any, is satisfied. The buffer operation, if any, on a transition is executed when that transition is taken. For every input XPath query, XSQ constructs an HPDT hierarchically using a template-based method. Using the HPDT as a guide, a runtime engine responds to the incoming stream and emits the query result. The multiple matching problem is solved by associating with every buffer item its matching with the query and a flag indicates the current predicate results. Note that the HPDT is used simply as convenient conceptual machinery to describe the methods.

4.2.5 RAINDROP

RAINDROP (Su, Jinhui, & A. Rundensteiner, 2003) addresses the efficient evaluation of XQuery expressions over continuous XML data streams, which is essential for a broad range of applications including monitoring systems and information dissemination systems. This approach faces an intricate trade-off. On the one hand, we want to exploit automata theory to process streaming XML data on-the-fly. On the other hand, it needs to overcome the limitations imposed by the automata model and instead exploit query algebra for optimization. The key feature of this model is its power in flexibly integrating automata theory into an algebraic query framework. Unlike any of the previous work, this power facilitates various established query optimization techniques to be applied in the automata context. It also allows for novel optimization techniques such as rewrite rules that can flexibly change the functionality implemented by the automata-based operators.

4.3 INDEX-BASED METHODS

Automaton-based algorithms compute results by expressing the queries with automaton machine and analyzing an input document one tag at a time. In contrast, index-based algorithms take advantage of pre-computed numbering schemes over the input XML document.

4.3.1 Index-Filter

Index-Filter (Bruno et al., 2003) introduces a new index-based technique to answer multiple XML path queries. Index-Filter uses indexes built over the document tags to avoid processing large portions of the input document that are guaranteed not to be part of any match. After comparing Index-Filter against Y-Filter, the state-of-the-art automaton-based technique, we can see that both techniques have their advantages.

Index-Filter is a novel technique to answer multiple path queries by exploiting indexes that provide structural information about the tags in the XML document. By taking advantage of this additional information, Index-Filter is able to avoid processing certain tags in the document that are guaranteed not to be part of any match. Next we first discuss the index structure that used in Index-Filter, and then we present its main algorithm.

Index-Filter extend the classic inverted index data structure used in information retrieval (Joonho, Praveen, Bongki, & Sukho, 2005) to provide a positional representation of elements and values in the XML document. This representation allows it to efficiently check whether two tags in the XML documents are related by a parent/child or ancestor/descendant structural relationship. The position of an element occurrence in the XML document is represented as the pair (L: R, D) where L and R are generated by counting word numbers from the beginning of the document to the start and the end of the element being indexed, respectively, and D is the nesting depth of the element in the document.

We can easily determine structural relationships between tree nodes using this indexing scheme. Consider document nodes n1 and n2, encoded as (L1: R1; D1) and (L2: R2; D2), respectively. Then, n1 is an ancestor of n2 (and n2 is a descendant of n1) if and only if $L1 < L2$ and $R2 < R1$. To check whether n1 is the parent of n2 (n2 is a child of n1) we also need to verify whether $D1+1=D2$. An important property of this positional representation is that checking an ancestor-descendant relationship is computationally as simple as checking a parent-child relationship, i.e., we can check for an ancestor-descendant structural relationship without knowledge of intermediate nodes on the path.

In general, when the number of input queries is small (i.e., fewer than 500 queries), Index-Filter is much more efficient than Y-Filter if the required indexes are already materialized. The reasons for this behavior are as follows. First, in

these scenarios Index-Filter effectively traverses a small fragment of the input document, since it only processes the indexes whose tags are present in the input queries. Also, since each node in the prefix tree is relatively sparse (due to the moderate number of input queries), the efficiency of the priority queues is comparable to that of Y-Filter's hash tables. Finally, for larger document sizes, Index-Filter takes advantage of the structural (containment) properties of the index elements to avoid processing significant portions of the document that are guaranteed not to participate in any match.

In contrast, when we continue increasing the number of queries, the situation is reversed. The nodes in the prefix tree become more and more populated, and Y-Filter's hash tables start scaling better than Index-Filter's priority queues. Moreover, the prefix tree becomes larger, and Index-Filter spends more time analyzing its structure to decide which nodes to process next. For those reasons, in the scenario explained above, Y-Filter results in faster executions than Index-Filter, especially when using small documents. When we also consider the time spent for building indexes on the fly, the gap between both algorithms is reduced. If the number of queries is large, the results are similar to the precomputed-index case, because the index creation cost is small compared to the cost of answering the queries. In contrast, the largest differences between both scenarios occur for small numbers of queries. In fact, for a small number of input queries the creation of indexes is the actual bottleneck of Index-Filter. In any case, it is interesting to note that even when indexes over the input documents need to be created on the fly to answer queries, Index-Filter is still more efficient than Y-Filter in several situations. This behavior has an analogous counterpart in traditional relational query processing, where sometimes the most efficient plan for a join query is to create an index over one operand and then use an index-based join to get the results. Finally, it is interesting to note that for the TPC-H documents(this family of

XML documents was generated from the popular TPC-H benchmark for relational database), the relative performance of both Index-Filter and Y-Filter algorithms is insensitive to the document size. This is surprising given the large variations between both algorithms when considering other document families, and the fact that Index-Filter and Y-Filter are based on significantly different approaches.

4.4 OTHER METHODS

Unlike the above mentioned methods change queries into automaton, some processing methods represent the query as a string or a tree structure.

4.4.1 XTrie

XTrie (Chee-Yong et al., 2002) handles tree-shaped path expressions involving predicates in a trie structure based on common substrings. In Xtrie, each XPath expression is decomposed into a group of substrings, and each substring' prefix is '/'. A substring decomposition S is a minimal decomposition of p if each substring si of S is of maximal length; that is, there does not exist another longer substring in p's XPE-tree that contains si. Clearly, a minimal decomposition of p comprises the smallest possible number of substrings among all possible decompositions of p. XTrie index relies on substring decompositions for installing XPath expressions into the indexing structure. The choice of a specific class of substring decompositions impacts both the space and performance of the index. Minimal decompositions, in particular, have several important performance advantages. Their experiments show that the evaluation performance of XTrie is relatively better than XFilter. However, similar to XFilter, XTrie still only support a subset of the XPath which can process "/", "//" and simple predicate.

4.4.2 FiST

Another sequence-based XML stream filtering system *FiST* (Rao & Moon, 2004) (Filtering by Sequencing Twigs) performs holistic matching of twig patterns with each incoming XML document. The matching is holistic since FiST does not break a twig pattern into root-to-leaf paths. Rather the twig pattern is matched as a whole due to sequence transformation. FiST focuses on ordered twig pattern matching, which is essential for applications where the nodes in a twig pattern follow the document order in XML. For example, an XML data model was proposed by Bow et al. for representing interlinear text for linguistic applications, which is used to demonstrate various linguistic principles in different languages. Bow's XML model provides a four-level hierarchical representation for the interlinear text, namely, text level, phrase level, word level and morpheme level. For the purpose of linguistic analysis, it is essential to preserve linear order between the words in the text. Thus, there is a compelling need for ordered twig pattern matching. In addition to interlinear text, language treebanks have been widely used in computational linguistics. Treebanks capture syntactic structure of text data and provide a hierarchical representation of text by breaking them into syntactic units such as noun clauses, verbs, adjectives and so on.

FiST system matches twig patterns holistically using the idea of encoding XML documents and twig patterns into Prüfer sequences (Berglund et al., 2002). The Prüfer's method constructs a one-to-one correspondence between labeled trees and sequences. It was shown in the PRIX system (Berglund et al., 2002) that the above encoding supports ordered twig pattern matching efficiently. A collection of sequences for twig patterns are organized into a dynamic hash based index for efficient filtering. Our filtering algorithm involves two phases: Progressive Subsequence Matching and Refinement for Branch Node Verification.

While the first phase identifies a superset of twig patterns that potentially match an incoming document, the second phase discards false matches by performing post-processing for branch nodes in the twig patterns. The experiments in the Fist shows that the holistic matching approach enables FiST to outperform the state-of-the-art YFilter system by achieving better scalability under various situations.

4.4.3 TurboXPath

Another approach uses tree to reconstruct the queries in the memory is called *TurboXPath* (XQuery 1.0, 2001). TurboXPath system is a streamed processor for processing for-let-where constructs of XQuery. The features supported by TurboXPath were chosen by examining the emerging XMLquery standards and identifying a common core. A distinguishing feature of the TurboXPath system is its capability to process query trees constructed of several concatenated paths returning tuples as results. The tuple-based interface is suitable for integration in an XQuery database engine using existing virtual table interfaces. The TurboXPath system also presented an experimental evaluation of a prototype implementation of the TurboXPath processor, where it demonstrated orders of magnitude lower execution times and memory consumption compared to a DOM-based XPath processor and substantial performance improvement and richer set of features compared to other streamed XPath processors. Finally, the system presented a novel XPath processing technique that does not require the translation of queries to FSAs. This new technique may require exponentially less memory to process queries when compared to the previous streaming algorithms based on FSA. However, TurboXPath only support the single query evaluation within a subset of XQuery, and its space requirement is increased linearly with the size of query.

4.5 OPTIMIZATION AND OTHER TECHNIQUE

Optimizations in the XML stream processing include: (1) decrease the time of stream parsing; (2) enhance the time and space efficiency of query evaluation; (3) use efficient cache management; (4) Simprove the capability of result dissemination. Next we will introduce several techniques in order to make the query evaluation more efficient.

4.5.1 Stream Index

We have shown the LazyDFA (Green et al., 2003) in the previous section and its SIX. Given an XML document, a Stream IndeX (SIX) for that document is an ordered set of byte offsets pairs:(beginOffset, endOffset), where beginOffset is the byte offset of some begin tag, and endOffset of the corresponding end tag (relative to the begin tag). Both numbers are represented in binary, to keep the SIX small. The SIX is computed only once, by the producer of the XML stream, attached to the XML packet somehow, then sent along with the XML stream and used by every consumer of that stream (e.g. by every router, in XML routing). A server that does not understand the SIX can simply ignore it.

The SIX is sorted by beginOffset. The query processor starts parsing the XML document and matches SIX entries with XML tags. Depending on the queries that need to be evaluated, the query processor may decide to skip over elements in the XML document, using endOffset. Thus, a simple addition of two integers replaces parsing an entire subelement, generating all SAX events, and looking for the matching end tag. This is a significant savings. The SIX module offers a single interface: skip(k), where $k \geq 0$ denotes the number of open XML elements that need to be skipped. Thus skip(0) means "skip to the end of the most recently opened XML element".

The SIX for an XML document is constructed while the XML text output is generated, as follows. The application maintains a circular buffer containing a tail of the SIX, and a stack of pointers into the buffer. The application also maintains a counter representing the total number of bytes written so far into the XML output. Whenever the application writes a startElement to the XML output, it adds a (beginOffset, endOffset) entry to the SIX buffer, with beginOffset set to the current byte count, and endOffset set to NULL. Then it pushes a pointer to this entry on the stack. Whenever the application writes a endElement to the XML output, it pops the top pointer from the stack, and updates the endOffset value of the corresponding SIX entry to the current byte offset. In most cases the size of the entire SIX is sufficiently small for the application to keep it in the buffer. However, if the buffer overflows, then application fetches the bottom pointer on the stack and deletes the corresponding SIX entry from the buffer, then flushes from the buffer all subsequent SIX entries that have their endOffset value completed. This, in effect, deletes a SIX entry for a large XML element.

4.5.2 DTD-Based Optimization

In some condition, XML schema or DTD is available for stream processing system. We can make use of these XML structure information to optimize the query evaluation. For example in YFilter, it use eight queries(Q1=/a/b;Q2=/a/c;Q3=/a/b、 /c;Q4=/a//b/c;Q5=/a/*/c;Q6=/a//c;Q7=/a/*/*/c;Q8=/a/b/c) in the processing sample. If we now get the DTD of this XML document:

    <!ELEMENT a (b)>
    <!ELEMENT b (c)>

Then, we can directly remove the queries Q2 and Q7 since no results will match them. With this DTD in consideration, the nondeterministic "*" or "//" navigation steps can be replaced with deterministic ones. Therefore, we can simplify the queries into Q1=/a/b;Q4,Q4,Q5,Q6,Q8=/a/b/c, Q2

and Q7 just return no matching. It is meaningful to remove the "*" and "//" in the query expression. For example, "//" makes the size of NFA automaton in YFilter grow exponentially.

4.6 CONCLUSION

Nowadays, XML is considered as a representative textual information structure for exchanging data over the internet. The management of XML stream also attracts many attentions both in the research and industrial area. XML stream applications bring the challenge of efficiently processing queries on sequentially accessible token-based data streams. The automaton paradigm is naturally suited for pattern retrieval on tokenized XML streams, but other approaches have better performance under certain circumstances. In this chapter, we first introduce the background and foundation of XML stream and its query language. Next we introduce the automata-based filtering system X/YFilter. XML stream filtering systems are used for sifting through real-time messages to support publish/subscribe, real-time business data mining, accounting, and reporting for enterprises. XML filtering systems aim to provide fast, on-the-fly matching of XML-encoded data to large numbers of query specifications containing constraints on both structure and content. It is now well accepted that approaches using event-based parsing and Finite State Machines (FSMs) can provide the basis for highly scalable structure-oriented XML filtering systems. Then, many other filtering system such as LazyDFA, XPush, XSQ, XSM, RainDrop, Index-Filter, FiST etc. is introduced. Some of them are still based in the automaton approach, and others use some other effective method to evaluate the query. In the end, some optimization technique is shown to improve the processing efficiency.

REFERENCES

W3C Working Draft. (2001). *XQuery 1.0: An XML query language.* Retrieved from www.w3.org/TR/xquery/

Abadi, D. J., Carney, D., Cetintemel, U., Cherniack, M., Convey, C., & Lee, S. (2003). Aurora: A new model and architecture for data stream management. *The VLDB Journal, 12*(2), 120–139. doi:10.1007/s00778-003-0095-z

Altinel, M., & Franklin, M. J. (2000). Efficient filtering of XML documents for selective dissemination of information. In *Proceedings of the 26th International Conference on Very Large Data Bases* (pp. 53-64).

Berglund, A., Boag, S., Chamberlin, D., Fernandez, M. F., Kay, M., Robie, J., & Simon, J. (2002). *XML path language (XPath) 2.0 W3C working draft 16.* In World Wide Web Consortium.

Bruno, N., Gravano, L., Koudas, N., & Srivastava, D. (2003). Navigation- vs. index-based XML multiquery processing. In *proceedings of 19th International Conference on Data Engineering* (pp. 139-150).

Chee-Yong, C., Pascal, F., Minos, G., & Rajeev, R. (2002). Efficient filtering of XML documents with XPath expressions. [Special Issue on XML Data Management]. *The VLDB Journal, 11*(4), 354–379. doi:10.1007/s00778-002-0077-6

Diao, Y. L., & Franklin, M. J. (2003). Query processing for high-volume XML message brokering. In *Proceedings of the 29th International Conference on Very Large Data Bases.*

Florescu, D., Hiller, C., Kossman, D., Lucas, P., Riccardi, F., & Westmann, T. … Agrawal. G. (2003). The BEA/XQRL streaming XQuery processor. In *Proceedings of the 29th International Conference on Very Large Data Bases* (pp. 997–1008).

Green, T. J., Miklau, G., Onizuka, M., & Suciu, D. (2003). Processing XML streams with deterministic automata and stream indexes. [TODS]. *ACM Transactions on Database Systems, 29*(4), 752–788. doi:10.1145/1042046.1042051

Gupta, A., & Suciu, D. (2003). Stream processing of XPath queries with predicates. In *Proceedings of the 2003 ACM SIGMOD International Conference on Management of Data* (pp. 419-430).

Joonho, K., Praveen, R., Bongki, M., & Sukho, L. (2005). FiST: Scalable XML document filtering by sequencing twig patterns. In *Proceedings of the 31th International Conference on Very Large Data Bases* (pp. 217-228).

Ludascher, B., Mukhopadhay, P., & Papakonstantinou, Y. (2002). A transducer-based XML query processor. In *Proceedings of the 28th International Conference on Very Large Data Bases.*

Madden, S. R., Shah, M. A., & Hellerstein, J. M. (2002). Continuously adaptive continuous queries over streams. In *Proceedings of the 2002 ACM SIGMOD International Conference on Management of Data* (pp. 261–272).

Motwani, R., et al. (2003). Query processing, approximation, and resource management in a data stream management system. In *Proceedings of the Conference on Innovative Data Systems Research.*

Peng, F., & Chawathe, S. S. (2003). XSQ: A streaming XPath engine. *ACM Transactions on Database Systems, 30*(2), 577–623. doi:10.1145/1071610.1071617

Rao, P., & Moon, B. (2004). PRIX: Indexing and querying XML using Prsfer sequences. In *Proceedings of the 20th IEEE International Conference on Data Engineering* (pp. 288–299).

Salton, G., & McGill, M. J. (1983). *Introduction to modern information retrieval*. McGraw-Hill.

Su, H., Jinhui, J., & Rundensteiner, A. E. (2003). RAINDROP: A uniform and layered algebraic framework for XQueries on XML streams. In *Proceedings of the 12th International Conference on Information and Knowledge Management* (pp. 279 - 286).

Chapter 5
Matching of Twig Pattern with AND/OR Predicates over XML Streams

Weidong Yang
Fudan University, China

Hao Zhu
Fudan University, China

ABSTRACT

Chapter 5 presents a novel approach for processing complex twig pattern with OR-predicates and AND-predicates over XML document streams which a twig pattern is represented as a query tree. Its OR-predicates and AND-predicates are represented as a separate abstract syntax tree associated with the branch node, and all the twig patterns are combined into a single prefix query tree that represents such queries by sharing their common prefixes. Consequently, all the twig patterns are evaluated in a single, document-order pass over the input document stream avoiding the translation of the set of twig patterns into a finite state automaton. Chapter 1 introduces the background of this issue. Chapter 2 discusses the representation of complex twig pattern as a query tree, how to combine a set of twig patterns into a single query three, how to match multi twig patterns over the incoming XML document, and possible optimization of computing logical AND/OR predicates. In section 3, the architecture of a XML stream process system named LeoXSQ is given. Section 4 shows the conducted experiments. In section 5, the related work is discussed. Section 6 summarizes this chapter.

5.1 INTRODUCTION

Stream-based continuous query processing fits a large class of new applications, such as sensor networks, location tracking, network management and financial data analysis. Stream based applications usually involve handling the infinite size and unpredictability of the data streams and requiring timely response, traditional database processing techniques cannot be used directly, then there has been plentiful of researches about data stream management (for examples, Babcock, Babu, Datar, Motwani & Widom, 2002). As extensible markup language XML is a standard for information exchange, the problem of processing streaming XML data is gaining widespread attention from the

DOI: 10.4018/978-1-4666-1975-3.ch005

research community. Many researchers presented their work of processing XML stream based on automaton (Altinel & Franklin, 2000; Chan, Felber, Garofalakis & Rastogi, 2002; Green, Miklau, Onizuka & Suciu, 2003; Gupta & Suciu, 2003; Diao, Altinel, Franklin, Hao & Fischer, 2003). The XFilter system (Altinel & Franklin, 2000) used a separate FSM per path query to allow all of the FSMs to be executed simultaneously during the processing of a document. Building on the insights of the XFilter work, YFilter (Diao, et al., 2003) describes a new method, called "YFilter" that combines all of the path queries into a single Nondeterministic Finite Automaton (NFA).

XML stream systems aim to provide fast, on-the-fly matching of XML-encoded data to large numbers of query specifications containing constraints on both structure and content. An XML twig query is essentially a complex selection predicate on both structure and content of an XML document. Matching a set of twig patterns with the incoming XML stream is a core operation in XML stream system. Kwon, Rao, Moon & Lee (2005) recently presented a system called FiST, which performs holistic matching of twig patterns with incoming XML documents by transforming twig pattern into prufer sequences. But their work considers only twig patterns whose sibling edges are combined by AND logic.

Queries in real application, however, often contains logical-OR and logical AND in a single twig patter. For example, the following query

```
Q = /dblp/paper[title = 'XML
Stream' or (year = 2006 and conf =
'CAiSE')]//author
```

This twig pattern contains complex AND/OR logical operations. Although, theoretically, some existing systems, for example, YFilter (OR predicate is not implemented in YFilter) can deal with this case, but their approaches are not very efficient. YFilter treats twig-patterns as nested path expressions, which are processed by using query decomposition. In their approach, the nested paths are extracted from the main path expressions and processed individually. A post-processing phase is used to link matched paths back together to determine if an entire query expression has been matched. This approach has some disadvantage: a) many intermediate results may be produced; b) the intermediate results should be buffered, and then are linked together.

This chapter presents an approach to match complex twig pattern with OR-predicates and AND-predicates over XML document streams in a way of combining top-down and bottom-up process. In the approach, a twig pattern is represented as a query tree. Its OR-predicates and AND-predicates of a branch node are represented as a separate abstract syntax tree associated with the branch node and processed in a bottom-up way. For the improvement of the processing performance of twig patterns, all the twig patterns are combined into a single prefix query tree that represents such queries by sharing their common prefixes. Consequently, all the twig patterns are evaluated in a single, document-order pass over the input document stream efficiently avoiding the translation of the set twig patterns into a finite state automaton.

5.2 MULTIPLE TWIG PATTERNS PROCESSING OVER XML STREAM

In this section, we address the central topic: processing strategies for multiple twig patters over an XML stream. In 5.2.1, we describe a mechanism to represent the twig pattern with OR-predicates and AND-predicates as a query tree, and then they are combined into a single query tree with common prefix. In 5.2.2, we describe how to match the document stream with the twig patterns. In 5.2.3, we discuss the short-circuit evaluation for optimization.

5.2.1 Tree Representation for a Twig Pattern with AND/OR Predicates

An AND/OR *twig pattern* can be represented as a tree. We call it twig pattern query tree. Intuitively, the nodes of the tree fall into with three types of nodes: location step query node (QNode), logical-AND node (ANode) and logical-OR node (ONode) (Jiang, Lu & Wang, 2004):

```
Q = /dblp/paper[title = 'XML
Stream' or (year = 2006 and conf =
'CAiSE')]//author
```

For example, the above query Q can be represented as a twig pattern tree as follows.

For a complex twig pattern, this kind of tree representation may contain many ANodes/ORnodes. Furthermore, different from traditional XML database, a document stream will match a lot of queries and sharing common parts among these queries is very important for improving the performance of XML stream system. ANodes and ONodes in a query tree makes it difficult to share common parts among queries, for example, /a[b and c]; /a/[b or c].

In order to simplify the query tree representation and improve share among queries, we define a compact twig pattern query tree by removing ANodes and ONodes and associating them with their parent QNode.

Definition 1: A *compact twig query tree* is a rooted tree that consists of two types of nodes:

- ○ ***OQNode*** (Ordinary Query Node): A location step query node in the tree stands for one location step without associated predicates in the original twig query. An OQnode has the content /tagName or //tagName, where the tagName is the name of the corresponding label in the twig pattern, "/" denotes a child location step axis,

"//" denotes a descendant location step axis.

- ○ ***PQNode*** (Predicate Query Node): A location step query node in the tree stands for one location step with associated predicates in the original twig query. It has the additional contents of a logical expression for the representation of its associated predicates by an abstract syntax tree. It's a logical expression connects two or more child subtrees with AND and/or OR logic. A leaf node of the abstract syntax tree maintains a reference to its corresponding root of child subtrees.

Figure 2 shows the compact twig pattern query tree of Figure 1. The left part is an abstract syntax tree of a logical expression associated with PQNode 'paper'.

XML stream system should have the ability of processing a large number of queries simultaneously, therefore, it is likely that significant commonalities between queries exist. To eliminate redundant processing while answering multiple twig patterns, the query commonalities are identified and all twig patterns are combined into a single structure, which called *prefix compact twig pattern query tree*. Prefix twig pattern query tree can significantly reduce both the space needed to represent the input twig patterns and the bookkeeping required to answer them by sharing the prefix of all input compact twig pattern query trees, thus reducing the execution times of XML streams.

Consider the three queries in Figure 3. For simplicity, we associate a logical expression instead of abstract tree with a PQNode. We can obtain a single compact twig pattern query tree that represents such queries by sharing their common prefixes, as shown in Figure 4.

The detailed data structure of a node in will be described in the following section.

Figure 1. Twig pattern query tree

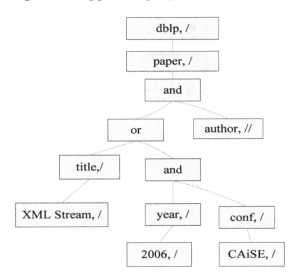

5.2.2 Matching Multiple Twig Patterns over XML Document Stream

The XML stream evaluator is the central component of **LeoXSQ**. It uses the prefix compact twig pattern query tree to process the stream of SAX events generated from the input document to identify the matched documents. We combine top-down and bottom-up query matching process in our approach: for an ordinary query without predicates, a top-down process is used; for predicate part (QNodes and any sub-nodes of

a QNodes) of a twig pattern, a bottom-up process is used. Consequently, all the twig patterns are evaluated in a single, document-order pass over the input document stream

Definition 2: *A predicate sub-tree* is a sub-tree of a compact twig pattern tree of a twig pattern, where the root of the predicate sub-tree is a PQNode, which has the shortest distance between it and the root of its compact twig pattern tree.

For example, the predicate sub-tree of Q2 in Figure 4 is a sub-tree rooted by QNode n2<b, />.

Definition 3: For a compact twig pattern query tree with AND/OR predicates, the root of its predicate sub-tree is its accepting node. If an XPath hasn't any predicates, its accepting node is the leaf node of its query tree.

An accepting node is represented as bold box in its query tree, as shown in Figure 4 and fig 5. For example, in Figure 4, Q1 is an ordinary query without any predicates, then n3 <c, /> is its accepting node; for query Q2, n2<b, /> is its accepting node. For a prefix compact twig pattern query tree, many queries may share an accepting

Figure 2. Compact twig pattern query tree

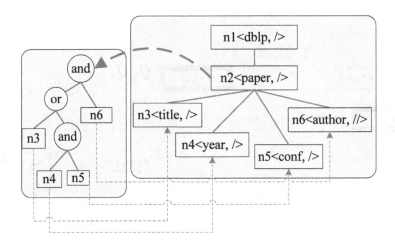

Figure 3. Original compact twig pattern query tree

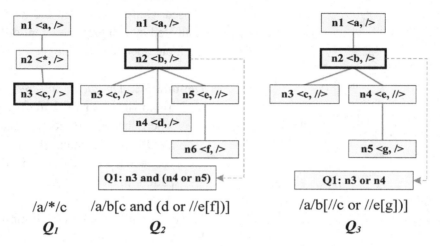

Q_1 /a/*/c

Q_2 /a/b[c and (d or //e[f])]

Q_3 /a/b[//c or //e[g])]

node. For example, in Figure5, node n2 <b, /> is the accepting node of queries Q2 and Q3.

Besides the prefix compact twig pattern tree, the XML stream evaluator needs a run time stack and the following data structure:

Each query node (include PQNode and QQNode) in the compact twig pattern query tree has a unique node ID and contains the following basic information:

- **Name:** it is the tag name.
- **Axis:** it is an integer: 0 means a child ("/") operator and 1 means a descendant ("//") operator.

- **DocumentLevel:** this is an integer that represents the level in the XML document at which this path node should be checked.

Each accepting node associates a set of query ID. If a node is a sub-node of a predicate sub-tree, a set of <QID, Status, LExpression> are also associated with the node (see node n3 in Figure 6), where

- QID is the query ID of associated query.
- Status indicates that if this node matched. Its value is FALSE initially

Figure 4. Prefix compact twig pattern query tree

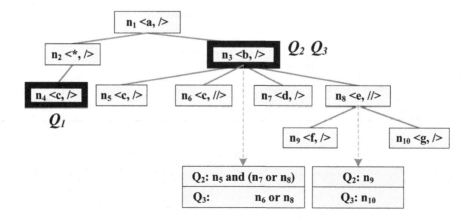

Figure 5. A running example

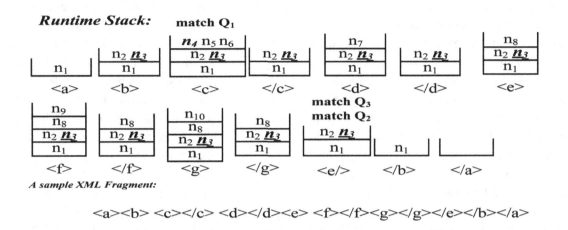

Runtime Stack:

A sample XML Fragment:

`<a><b> <c></c> <d></d><e> <f></f><g></g></e></b></a>`

- LExpression is its associated logical expression. Each term (that is, the leaf node in the abstract syntax tree of logical expression, see Figure 4) in the logical expression contains a reference to its corresponding child node.

For example, node n4 in Figure 5 associates a query ID "Q1" because that it is a accepting node of Q1; node n3 in Figure 5 associates query ID "Q2" and "Q3" because of same reason; n3 also associates logical expression "n3 and (n4 or n5)" for Q2 and "n3 or n4" for Q3. If a node is a sub-node of a PQNode (itself is not a QNode)

Figure 6. System architecture

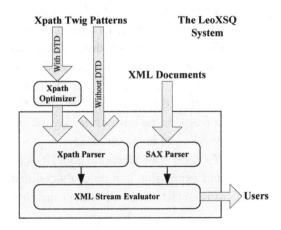

and is not a leaf node, it also contains a logical expression, but the logical expression here only contains a single term corresponding to its child (see node n8 in Figure 5). If a node is a sub-node of a PQNode (n5, n6, n7, n9, n10 in Figure6) and is a leaf node, it contains a status flag (its logical expression is null), used during processing to indicate if the corresponding document node has matched.

When a document arrives at LeoXSQ, it is run through an XML Parser that reports parsing events to the application through callbacks, and the events are used to translate to the form of (Name, Type, Document Level) to drive the query matching process, where the name is the node test name and type is the event type, which can be StartElement, EndElement, etc. The Document Level is maintained by the SAX event handler by simply counting StartElement and EndElement events. By convention, the document root appears at level 0. The processing of a document starts with a (ROOT, OPEN, 0).

Given a node of a query that is an OQNode and is not a sub-node of a PQNode of a twig pattern tree, a node match occurs when both the document levels and the names of the event and the node are same. A node match also occurs when only the names match if the node in the query tree contains a descendent operator. When the name of the matching node in query is "*", the name comparison always returns TRUE.

For each PQNode or each sub-node of a PQNode reached (that is, the basic information of <Name, IsChild, DocumentLevel> is matched), its logical expressions or status flags stored there are checked. If the logical expression or status flag is evaluated TRUE, a node match occurs. When a StartElement event is encountered, its value is FALSE initially, when an EndElement event is encountered, its final value is evaluated.

If the node match occurs, then the node passes. If this is the accepting node for a query (note that a node may be a accepting node for a query, and is not an accepting node for another query. Also note that a node may be a PQNode for a query and is not for another query), then the document is deemed to match the query.

For a query without AND/OR predicates (for example, Q1) its leaf node is the accepting node; the query is said to match a document if during parsing, an accepting node for that query is reached. The matching process of this kind of query is top-down.

For a twig pattern, the query is said to match the arriving documents until an accepting node is reached during the matching (top-down process), and only at that point, its associated logical expression is evaluated TRUE (the process of evaluating logical expression is bottom-up). Note that the prefix compact twig pattern query tree contains multiple accepting nodes, while each query in the query tree has only a single accepting node.

The algorithm for matching twig patterns over XML document stream consists two parts: StartElement and EndElement.

StartElement: An StartElement event calls this handler, passing in the name and level of the element encountered.

- For each node, it performs a node test and a level check. The purpose of the level check is to make sure that the element appears in the document at a level that matches the level expected by the query. If the node contains a child "/" operator, then the two levels must be identical in order for the check to succeed. Otherwise, the level for the node is unrestricted, so the check succeeds regardless of the element level.

- If a node match occurs, the node is pushed into the stack. If the node is a PQNode or a sub-node of a PQNode, its status is set to FALSE initially.

- When an accepting node is encountered, and if it is not a PQNode for a query, a query match occurs. Otherwise, we cannot determine if a query match is occurs until the result of the logical expression for associated query ID can be known.

CloseElement: A CloseElement event calls this handler, passing in the name of the element encountered

- For the leaf node the CloseElement event sets its status flag to TRUE. This change of the status indicates that the matching was satisfied. And then pops the node out of the stack, and set the corresponding term of logical expression to TRUE of its parent node.

- If a node is an intermediate node of a predicate sub-tree, its logical expression is evaluated (at this point, all its children have been processed) and the node is popped form the stack, and then the result value is set to the corresponding term of the logical expression of its parent node.

- If a node is an accepting node, its logical expression can be evaluated and if it is TRUE, the document matches to the query, if it is FALSE, the document does not match to the query.

○ Repeat the above steps until all PQNodes are evaluated.

A Running Example

We use the three queries in Figure 5 and a sample XML fragment to illustrate the processing. Each node in the runtime stack is represented by its corresponding node ID in the query tree. An italicized node ID indicates an accepting node. For a twig pattern, the node ID of its accepting node is also underlined.

When the b element is open due to the StartElement event of b, both n2 and n3 are pushed to the runtime stack, the associated information of n3 is: <Q2, FALSE, (n5 and (n7 or n8))> and <Q3, FALSE, (n6 or n8))>. The status flags are initially FALSE. When c element is open, n4, n5 and n6 are pushed to the stack. The status flag of n4 and n5 are set to FALSE initially. Because c is an accepting node of Q1 and the corresponding node of c is not a PQNode for Q1, therefore, Q1 matches the document.

When c element is closed, the status flag of n5 and n6 are set to TRUE, n4, n5 and n6 are popped form the stack and the associated information of n3 becomes: <Q2, FALSE, (TRUE and (n7 or n8))> and <Q3, FALSE, (TRUE or n8))>. Similarly, when f element is closed, the associated information of n8 is: <Q2, TRUE, TRUE> and <Q3, FALSE, n9))>. When b element is closed, it means that all the sub-nodes of b element have been processed, the associated information of b is: <Q2, TRUE, (TRUE and (TRUE or TRUE)) and <Q3, TRUE, (TRUE or TRUE))>, then Q2 and Q3 match the document.

5.2.3 Short-Circuit Evaluation of AND/OR Predicates

The evaluation of a logical expression can sometimes be performed even without the evaluation of all its sub-expressions. For example, TRUE or x, this logical expression are TRUE regardless of whether x is TRUE or FALSE; similarly, FALSE and x, is clearly FALSE regardless of the value of x.

Short-circuit evaluation of AND/OR predicate of a twig pattern has a number of benefits. One is that the evaluation of predicate part of a twig pattern can be improved. Another is that some elements can be skipped during parsing XML documents under some cases. For example (see Figure 6), when c element is closed, for query Q3, the associated logical expression becomes: TRUE or n8. At this point, we can know in advance that Q3 matches to the document, and the remainder evaluation can be ignored and some document parsing for Q3 can be skipped.

5.3 THE ARCHITECTURE OF LeoXSQ SYSTEM

XML stream systems are different from traditional database systems. In a traditional database system, a large set of data is stored persistently. Queries, coming one at a time, search the data for results. In a XML stream system, a large set of queries is persistently stored. Documents, coming one at a time, drive the matching of the queries. In this section, we provide an overview of LeoXSQ System architecture shown in Figure 6, and briefly explain its basic components.

There are two main sets of inputs to the system: a set of twig patters and XML document streams. In LeoXSQ, XML queries are a set of twig patterns represented by XPath expressions, which are parsed by XPath parser. The XPath parser takes a set of twig patterns, parses them and sends the parsed XPathes to the XML stream evaluator. When an XML document arrives at the system, it is run through the XML parser based on SAX interface for event-based XML parsing.

At the heart of the system, the XML stream evaluator takes the set of parsed twig patterns from the XPath parser and converts them to an internal tree representation. It also receives and reacts to events from the XML parser. These events call back the corresponding handlers implemented by the evaluator for XML stream processing, which perform the matching of documents against a set of twig patterns. All the twig patterns are combined into an internal prefix tree that represents such queries by sharing their common prefixes.

The internal representation of twig patterns is a query tree. When a lot of queries are processed simultaneously, it is likely that significant commonalities between queries exist. We identify query commonalities and combine multiple queries into a single query tree, which shares the common prefixes, and significantly reduce both the space needed to represent the input twig queries and the bookkeeping required to answer them, thus reducing the execution times.

When a document arrives at LeoXSQ, it is run through an XML Parser that reports parsing events to the application through callbacks, and the events are used to drive the query matching process. For a twig pattern, its predicate parts are processed in a bottom-up way, while the other parts are processed in a top-down way. Therefore, all twig patterns are evaluated in a single, document-order pass over the input document stream. We will delve into the related details in next section.

As XML stream systems are deployed on the Internet, the number of users for such systems can easily grow into the millions. A key challenge in such an environment is to efficiently and quickly search the huge set of user queries to find those for which the document is relevant. The dominant cost of a XML streams processing system includes the parsing of incoming XML documents and user's queries matching. The information of DTD can be used to optimize user's queries for reducing the cost of the he parsing of incoming XML documents and user's queries matching. The component of XPath Optimization in LeoXSQ system uses a set of twig patterns and DTD as its inputs, and its outputs are a set of simplified XPath queries. As a matter of fact, this is an extension to the

pre-processing technique since it is done before the processing of XML stream.

A DTD parser builds an internal representation (Tree Automaton) of the DTD, and then the related constraint information (child constraint, sibling constraint, etc) and possible path can be extracted form the DTD, which can be used to simplify the set of twig patterns.

- Eliminating any query that would not match the current document.
- Removing "*" completely and "//" partially in the XPath queries (when the recursion is encountered in DTD, the "//" can not be removed).
- Some constraint information (for example, cardinality constraints of DTD) is used to minimize the twig patterns.

The details of optimization of twig patterns under DTD are not discussed because of limited space of this paper.

5.4 EXPERIMENTS

This section presents experimental results on the performance of the approach we proposed in comparison with the existing state-of-art approach.

We have implemented LeoXQS using Eclipse 3.0.1 with Java virtual machine version 1.4.2. The YFilter package was implemented in Java and was obtained from the website of YFilter (Diao, et al., 2003). All of the experiments reported here were performed on a Pentium IV machine with 512 MB memory running Linux.

1. We use DTDs from the Xmark benchmark Busse, Carey, Florescu, Kersten, Manolescu, Schmidt & Waas, 2001) and the DBLP DTD (LEY, 2001) to generate the XML documents for our experiments. The data of XML documents were generated by an XML Generator from IBM D. XML Generator (Diaz &

Douglasl, 2004), which were categorized into three datasets base on the documents sizes from 10k to 30k. We also generated a large set of twig patterns using the XPath generator available in the YFilter Package.

We have evaluated the LeoXQS in three aspects comparing with YFilter: (1) by varying the total number of twig patterns, (2) by varying the number of PQNodes in the twig patterns, (3) by varying the size of input documents.

Figure 7 shows the comparison of performance between YFilter and LeoXSQ with respect to the varying number of twig patterns. Along the x-axis, we show the increase in the number of twig patterns, along the y-axis, we show the processing time of YFilter and LeoXSQ systems. The number of twig patters was varied from 50000 to 150000. The number of PQNodes in each twig pattern was varied from 3 to 7. The size of XML documents was 10k, 20k, 30k respectively.

For the same dataset, LeoXSQ was faster than YFilter. For examole, for 100000 twig patterns and 20k XML document, LeoXSQ was about 30% faster than YFilter. The processing time of LeoXSQ and YFilter grew as the number of twig patterns increased. But the observation that can be made from Figure 7 is that the processing time

of LeoXSQ increased more slowly than that of YFilter as the number of twig patterns were increased. This is consistent with the expected trend.

We now compare the performance of YFilter and LeoXSQ with respect to the varying number of PQNodes in the twig patterns. The results are shown in Figure 8. The processing cost of YFilter increased as the number of PQNodes in twig patterns increased from 3 to 15. On the contrary, the processing time for LeoXSQ just had a very small change as the number of PQNodes in twig patterns increased from 3 to 15. The reason for this was due to its post processing of nested paths of YFilter.

5.5 RELATED WORK

The XFilter system (Altinel & Franklin, 2000) was the first published FSM-based XML filtering approach. XFilter used a separate FSM per path query to allow all of the FSMs to be executed simultaneously during the processing of a document. Building on the insights of the XFilter work, YFilter (Diao, et al., 2003) described a new method, called "YFilter" that combines all of the path queries into a single Nondeterministic Finite Automaton (NFA). YFilter exploits commonality

Figure 7. Varying number of twig patterns

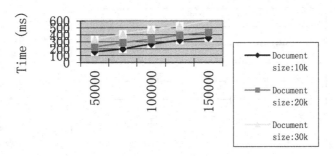

among queries by merging common prefixes of the query paths such that they are processed at most once. XFilter and YFilter system use query decomposition to handle nested path expressions. In their approach, when a query containing nested paths is parsed, it is decomposed into a list of absolute paths: the main path and any extended nested paths. Queries containing nested paths are processed in two phases, path matching and post-processing of the path matching results. The nested paths are processed separately by NP-Filter, and then,mach the filters.

XTrie (Chan, et al., 2002) indexes sub-strings of path expressions that only contain parent-child operators, and shares the processing of the common sub-strings among queries using the index. The "minimal decomposition" of queries in XTrie is identical to the decomposition of Hybrid method of YFilter. Because that NFAs could lead to performance problems due to (for example) the need to support multiple transitions from each state, Green, et al. 2003) converts the NFA into an equivalent DFA, and uses lazy DFA to process large set of queries.

Gupta et al. (2003) modified the definition of the pushdown automaton to an XPush Machine they called in order to adapt it to XPath queries and XML data and to save pace in the transition tables, and they presented a technique for con- structing a single XPush machine for all XPath queries and sharing large numbers common atomic predicates. Dan et al. Olteanu, Kiesling & Bry (2003) describes a technique for evaluating XPath expressions using state machine. In that approach one single XPath expression is translated into multiple pushdown automata that are connected by a network and need to be run in parallel and synchronized. Their technique dose not scale to large number of XPath queries.

XSQ (Josifovski, Fontoura and Barta, 2005) system handles multiple predicates, closures, and aggregations. XSQ uses a hierarchical net- work of push-down transducers augmented with buffers. Bruno et al. Bruno, Gravano, Koudas and Srivastava (2003) introduce an index-based technique, Index-Filter, to answer multiple XML path queries. Index-Filter uses indexes built over the document tags to avoid processing large portions of the input document. By comparing with YFilter, they show when the number of queries is small or the XML document is large, Index-Filter is more efficient than Y-Filter if the required indexes are already materialized, due to the focused processing achieved by the use of indexes; When the number of queries is large and the document is small, Y-Filter is more efficient due to the scalability properties of the Y-Filter's hash tables. The problem of nest paths in XPath

Figure 8. Varying number of PQNodes of twig patterns

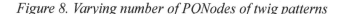
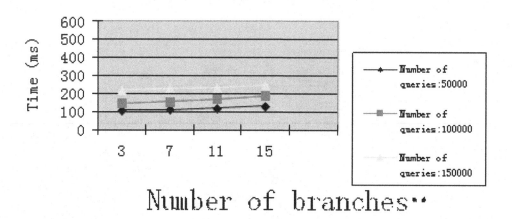

expression is not discussed further. TurboXPath (Josifovski, et al., 2005) uses a tree-shaped path expression with multiple outputs to drive the execution based on the bottom up processing of the tree. The result of a query execution is a sequence of tuples of XML fragments matching the output nodes. The problem of processing a large number of queries simultaneously was not considered further in their work.

Tian, Reinwald, Pirahesh, May rand Myllymaki (2004) proposed the use of a relational database system for XML-based publish/subscribe system. The XML filtering problem is turned into a join query that evaluates both the value predicate part and the tree structure part of the pattern which both stored in relational tables. Boom-filter system (Gong, Qian, Yan and Zhou, 2005) used a Bloom filter to store all queries of a user, and can filter input XML packets approximately with limited false positive. It is more efficient than automaton-based for low depth XML documents. But the capability of Boom-filter system is limited to the simple XPath expressions ($XP^{\{/,//,*\}}$).

A recent study by Kwon et al. (2005) presents a system called FiST which performs holistic matching of ordered twig patterns with incoming XML document by transforming twig pattern into prufer sequences. Their work outperformed YFilter system by yielding better scalability, but considers only twig patterns whose sibling edges are combined by AND logic

5.6 CONCLUSION

This chapter presents the LeoXSQ system, and addressed an approach for processing complex twig pattern with OR-predicates and AND-predicates over XML document streams. A distinguishing feature of the LeoXSQ system is its capability to process all the twig patterns with AND/OR predicates in a single, document-order pass over the input document stream avoiding the translation of them into a finite state automaton. In our

work, a twig pattern is represented as a compact twig pattern query tree. Our experimental studies showed that LeoXSQ outperformed the state-of-the-art systems.

As XML continues to gain acceptance in technologies such as Web Services, Event-based Processing, and Application Integration, this work will be of increasing commercial importance. There are many important problems to be addressed in future work. These include, the integration of filtering with dissemination, the extension of the LeoXSQ a wide-area distributed environment base on SOA (Service Oriented Architecture). Research on all of these issues is currently underway.

5.7 REFERENCES

Altinel, M., & Franklin, M. J. (2000). Efficient filtering of XML documents for selective dissemination of information. In *Proceedings of the 26th International Conference on Very Large Data Bases* (pp. 53-64).

Babcock, B., Babu, S., Datar, M., Motwani, R., & Widom, J. (2002). Models and issues in data stream systems. In *Proceedings of the 2002 ACM Symposium on Principles of Database Systems*.

Bruno, N., Gravano, L., Koudas, N., & Srivastava, D. (2003). Navigation- vs. index-based XML multiquery processing. In *Proceedings of 19th International Conference on Data Engineering*.

Busse, R., Carey, M., Florescu, D., Kersten, M., Manolescu, I., Schmidt, A., & Waas, F. (2001). *Xmark: An XML benchmark project*. Retrieved from http://monetdb.cwi.nl/xml/index.html

Chan, C., Felber, P., Garofalakis, M., & Rastogi, R. (2002). Efficient filtering of XML documents with XPath expressions. In *Proceedings of 18th International Conference on Data Engineering* (pp. 235-244).

Diao, Y. L., Altinel, M., Franklin, M. J., Zhang, H., & Fischer, P. (2003). Path sharing and predicate evaluation for high-performance XML filtering. *ACM Transactions on Database Systems, 28*(4), 467–516. doi:10.1145/958942.958947

Diaz, A. L., & Lovell, D. (2004). XML generator. Retrieved from http://www.alphaworks.ibm.com/tech/xmlgenerator.

Green, T. J., Miklau, G., Onizuka, M., & Suciu, D. (2003). Processing XML streams with deterministic automata. In *Proceedings of 6th International Conference on Data Theory* (pp. 173-189).

Gupta, A., & Suciu, D. (2003). Stream processing of XPath queries with predicates. In *Proceeding of 2003 ACM SIGMOD Conference on Management of Dat*a.

Jiang, H. F., Lu, H. J., & Wang, W. (2004). Efficient processing of XML twig queries with ORpredicates. In *Proceedings of the 2004 ACM SIGMOD International Conference on Management of Data*.

Josifovski, V., Fontoura, M., & Barta, A. (2005). Querying XML streams. *The VLDB Journal,* (14): 197–210. doi:10.1007/s00778-004-0123-7

Kwon, J., Rao, P., Moon, B., & Lee, S. (2005). FiST: Scalable XML document filtering by sequencing twig patterns. In *Proceedings of the 31th International Conference on Very Large Data Bases*.

Ley, M. (2001). *DBLP DTD*. Retrieved from http://www.acm.org/sigmod/dblp/db/about/dblp.dtd

Olteanu, D., Kiesling, T., & Bry, F. (2003). An evaluation of regular path expressions with qualifiers against XML streams. In *Proceedings of 19th International Conference on Data Engineering*.

Tian, F., Reinwald, B., Pirahesh, H., Mayr, T., & Myllymaki, J. (2004). Implementing a scalable XML publish/subscribe system using a relational database system. In *Proceedings of the 2004 ACM SIGMOD International Conference on Management of Data* (pp. 479-490).

Chapter 6
Keyword Search in XML Streams

Weidong Yang
Fudan University, China

Hao Zhu
Fudan University, China

ABSTRACT

Most existing XML stream processing techniques adopt full structured query languages such as XPath or XQuery, which are difficult for ordinary users to learn and use. This chapter presents an XML stream filter system called XKFitler, which uses keyword to filter XML streams. In XKFitler, we use the concepts of XLCA (eXclusive Lowest Common Ancestor) and XLCA Connecting Tree (XLCACT) to define the search semantic and results of keywords, and present an approach to filter XML stream according to keywords. In section 1, the background of keyword search in XML streams is introduced. Section 2 explains the searching results. In section 3, a stack-based keyword searching algorithm for XML stream filtering without schemas is presented in-depth. Section 4 presents a keyword search over XML streams by using schema information. The system architecture of XKFilter is described in section 5. Section 6 is the experiments to show the performance. Section 7 discusses the related work. Section 8 is the summaries of this chapter.

6.1 INTRODUCTION

Stream-based continuous query processing (Babcock, Babu, Datar, Motwani & Widom, 2002) fits a large class of new applications, such as sensor networks, publish-subscribe systems. As eXtensible markup language – XML is a standard for information exchange, the problem of processing streaming XML data is gaining widespread attention from the research community (Diao, Altinel, Franklin, Zhang & Fischer, 2003). An XML stream system (XSS) aims to provide fast and on-the-fly matching of XML-encoded data to user's query, which is different from traditional XML database management systems. The XSS usually involves handling the XML stream coming online at any moment and any order, and requiring timely response without incurring more memory cost.

DOI: 10.4018/978-1-4666-1975-3.ch006

Therefore, the numbering schemes like Dewey numbers and XML indexing techniques for accelerating query process in XML databases don't apply to XML data streams processing generally. For XSS, currently, most existing researches adopt full structured query languages such as XPath (Berglund, Boag, Chamberlin, Fernandez, Kay, Robie & Simon, 2002) or XQuery Chamberlin, D. (2003). These query languages can convey complex meaning in the query specifications containing constraints on both structure and content of an XML document, thus, can precisely retrieve the desired results. However, for an ordinary user, especially for a web user, it is difficult to learn the complex query languages, it is also impossible to write a correct query without knowing the exact structure of an XML document.

Keyword search is a user-friendly information retrieval technique that has been extensively studied for text documents. Unlike structured queries on database which adopts exact match approach, the keyword search adopts best match approach which has to "guess" the best search results and provide an appropriate rank model; different from traditional information retrieval systems, keyword search on database, instead of retrieving whole documents, aim at retrieving content components of the whole database, i.e. joined tuples (for relational database) or XML elements (for XML database) of varying granularity that fulfill the user's query. Recently, many researchers in database field extended this technique into relational database (Liu, Yu, Meng & Chowdhury, 2006) and XML database (Xu & Papakonstantinou, 2005) by combining information retrieval techniques and database techniques, and proposing various approaches to define and rank the keyword search results, and developing algorithms to accelerate the execution of keyword search. It is noted that keyword search is also well-suited to some applications under streams data processing environment. Alexander et al (Markowetz, Yang & Papadias, 2007) presented

a system called "S-KWS" for keyword search on relational data streams.

In this chapter, we focus on keyword search on XML Stream, including:

- A prototype system called *XKFilter* is introduced, which can process XML streams with or without schemas.

- When XML DTD is not available, XKFilter lets users register their queries by writing several keywords simply (called pure keyword search), and we define the search results as eXclusive Lowest Common Ancestor Connecting Tree (XLCACT) based on our previous work (Xu, Lu, Wang & Shi, 2006). Also, we design an algorithm "S-XSF" based on stack to process XML stream and buffering return results efficiently in a single pass.

- XKFilter provides a user-friendly search interface based on both keyword search and DTD, if the XML DTD is available. This search interface is a simple expansion of pure keyword search syntax which contains a list of search terms. Each search term is composed of a keyword and the label containing keyword directly. By using the search terms of users and XML DTD, the keyword search can be refined to a Keyword Query Graph (KQG). As a result, the XML fragment unrelated to the keywords search will be ignored. It has two benefits: (i) effectively reducing the search space of XML streams; (ii) effectively reducing the parsing amount of XML streams. In order to process XML stream in a single pass, base on the KQG, the Keyword Query State Machine (KQSM) is built. The KQSM supports state forward transition and backward transition, and use a run-time stack to process the XML stream and buffering return results effectively.

6.2 KEYWORD SEARCH RESULTS ON XML STREAM

It is often difficult, even sometimes impossible to convey precise meaning in the keyword proximity search. Therefore, one of the key techniques of keyword search on database is defining the search results of a set of keywords. Many current researches regard XML document as a tree, definite the XML keyword search results base on the Lowest Common Ancestor (LCA) of all keywords [7, 8, 9]. For example, XKSearch (Xu & Papakonstantinou, 2005) defines the keyword search as the search for Smallest Lowest Common Ancestor (SLCA) of an XML document tree. The SLCAs are the set of nodes that (i) contain the keywords either in their labels or in the labels of their descendent nodes and (ii) they have no descendant node that also contains all keywords.

However, if the concept of SLCA is applied to an XML document that has recursive structure or there is some element names shared by a node of same type, it may lose some meaningful information. For instance, as the XML fragment shown in Figure 1, if a user give a query including keywords: "a", "b", "title". Then, the information he expects possibly is 1) The paper with its title "t2" and with its author "a" and "b". 2) The paper "t3" cited by "t2" with the same author "a" and "b". 3) The conference "t1" with its editor "a" and "b". However, according to the concept of SLCA, the information of paper "t2" and conference "t1" will be lost even if they exist.

To solve the above-mentioned problem, our previous work (Xu, et al, 2006). defined the concept of XLCA (eXclusive Lowest Common Ancestor) based on SLCA as follows: first of all, find out all the SLCAs in XML document tree T; these SLCAs are just XLCAs; second, remove from T the fragments rooted at these SLCA nodes, and then find out again all the SLCAs of T; these SLCAs are also XLCAs; the second step repeats until there is no SLCA in T. It can be seen that all the XLCAs are exclusive, i.e. non-overlapped. Based on XLCA, we define the results of a set of keywords over XML stream as XLCA Connecting Tree (XLCACT), which are the minimum subtrees that rooted at the XLCAs of the nodes that contain the keywords.

6.3 S-XSF: STACK BASED ALGORITHM FOR XML STREAM FILTERING

Stack based algorithms are used in some research work for processing XML keyword search, for instance, Stack Algorithm (Xu & Papakonstantinou,

Figure 1. Sample XML document 1

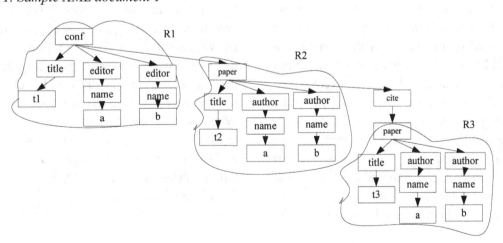

2005) for finding SLCAs in XML document. In these work, Dewey numbers are used for locating the LCA of two nodes. But under the XML stream processing environment, for processing XML streams in a single pass, it is not suitable to load the whole XML document into memory for coding and indexing. Therefore, by modifying the above-mentioned algorithms, we design an algorithm (called S-XSF) based on stack to process the pure keyword search over XML stream and return the XLCACTs to users.

S-XSF accepts the SAX events of an XML stream produced by parsing the input document in a pre-order traversal of the XML tree and transforms the SAX events into the form of (tagName, type), where tagName is the node being tested and type is the event type, which can be "Start Element", "End Element", etc. We use a runtime stack to buffer the processed node and potential results. The data structure of each entry in stack contains three components (N, B=<flag1,…,flagn>, RT), where N indicate the node name being processed. B is an array containing a series of flags (TURE or FALSE) corresponding to a list of keywords of a query, the number of elements in array B is equal to the number of inputting keywords, the flags are initialized as FALSE. RT is the candidate output of the query, which is implemented as a tree structure maintained by S-XSF algorithm dynamically.

S-XSF consists of two parts corresponding to the SAX event handlers of "Start Element" and "End Element", and the "Attribute" events are produced by iterating over the attributes in the "Start Element" SAX handler. When a "Start Element" event or an "Attribute" event is encountered, the stack entry corresponding to the node being processed is pushed onto the stack, the node pushed into the stack becomes an active node. An active node is an XML node whose start tag has been processed but end tag has not yet been processed by the SAX parser. If a keyword match occurs, which means the node name (the

element name, the content of an element, or the attribute value) and the keyword are same, we set the corresponding flag in B to TRUE, and add the node into RT. When an "End Element" event is encountered, if all flags of the top entry in the stack are TRUE, the stack item is popped and the node is added to the RT. At this point in time, the node is a XLCA, and the buffered result in RT of the popped entry is a XLCACT, which should be returned to users. Otherwise, if there are some TRUE flags in this entry, the entry is popped from the stack, and then the corresponding flags of the current top item in the stack are set to TRUE. If there are no any TRUE flags in this entry, just pop it from the stack.

To illustrate the processing of the algorithm S-XSF, we use a sample document shown in Figure 1 and a simple query Q("a", "b", "title"). The state of its runtime stack after each event is represented in the Figure 2. Firstly, when the startElement(conf) is encountered, since no keywords match occurs, the entry (conf, <F,F,F>,"conf") is just pushed into the stack. When the startElement(title) is encountered, the entry (title,<F,F,F>,"title") is pushed, and the first flag of array B is set to TRUE due to a keyword match is found, then the "title" and its content "t1" are added into the R. Next, when the endElement (title) is encountered, the entry is popped from the stack and the corresponding flag of current top entry of the stack is set to TRUE, and its result is linked to the R of current top entry of the stack (Figure 2(3)). When the endElement of last "paper" is encountered, the entry (paper,<T,T,T>,R3) is pop from stack, and its R is an answer of query (Figure 2(4)) due to all the flags of the entry are TRUE (For clarity, the results are represented as R1, R2, R3 respectively). When the close tag of "conf" is encountered, entry (conf,<T,T,T>,R1) is pop and its R is another and last answer of query(Figure 2(6)). Then we will get three answers of Q Q("a", "b", "title"): R1,R2,R3 (shown in Figure 1).

Figure 2. A running example of S-XSF

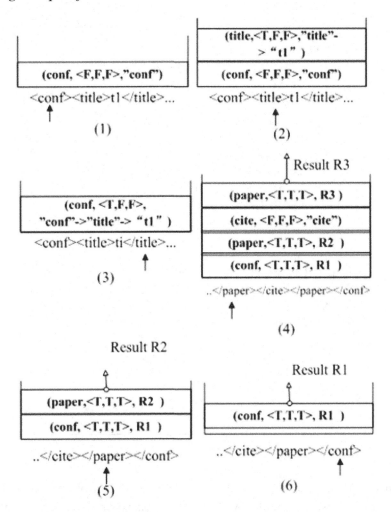

Theorem 3.1: For the given XML Document Tree D and a set of keywords Q(kw1, kw2, …, kwn), the outputs of algorithm S-XSF are a set of XLCACTs of KW, where KW={kwi|i∈1…k}.

To prove the correctness of S-XSF, we define N as the set of nodes of D, RS as the output set of S-XSF, and give the following propositions.

Proposition 3.1: In the processing of "End Element" events in the algorithm S-XSF, the first node n ∈ N, which all the flags in its stack entry are TRUE, is a SLCA of KW.

Proof Sketch: S-XSF algorithm processes the "Start Element" events of an XML stream in a pre-order traversal of the XML tree and processes the "End Element" events in a post-order traversal. When an "End Element" event is encountered, the "first" means until the processing of "End Element" event of n, there are no other nodes have all true flags. Since all the flags are true, it means (i) n contains all the keywords in its descendent nodes. (ii) There is no descendant node of n that also contains all keywords. As n is the first node with all true flags and descendant nodes of n has been processed but none of

List 1. Search algorithm 1 for S-XSF

```
Algorithm 1: S-XSF
Input: XML stream data;
An array KWS(kw1, kw2, ···, kwn) ;
Output: XLCACTs.
Method startElement(n)
  1.  push new entry en as (N=n, B=<F,···,F>,R=n) into S;
// S is the runtime stack
  2.  for each keyword kwi in the query
  3.  if v matches kwi; // v represents the content,
tagName, or attribute value of current element;
  4.  set en.Bi to TRUE;
  5.  link v to en.R as its child branch;

Method endElement (n)
  6.  pop the top entry enpop form S;
  7.  if all the flags of enpop.B are TRUE then   // n is a
XLCA
  8.  output enpop.R as an answer;
  9.  else                 // n is not a XLCA
 10. for each TRUE flags Bi in the enpop
 11. set the flag top(S).Bi to TRUE;    // keep
information in its parent node
 12. link enpop.R to the top(S).R as its child branch;
 13 drop en;
```

them has all true flags. According to the definition of SLCA, n is a SLCA of KW. A SLCA must be a XLCA, therefore, the first node n with all true flags in the processing of "End Element" events is a SLCA of KW.

Proposition 3.2: In the processing of "End Element" events in the algorithm S-XSF, any node $n \in N$, which all the flags in its stack entry are TRUE, is a XLCA of KW.

Proof Sketch: According to the S-XSF algorithm, when an "End Element" event of a node n is encountered and the flags of the n are all TRUE, its stack entry is popped and its result is returned to users, any information of the node n and its descendents (including its flag states) is not kept in the runtime stack. It just likes that the subtree rooted at the node n is removed from the XML document. On the basis of proposition 3.1, in the processing of "End Element" events, the first node with all TRUE flags is a XLCA, because of the post-order processing of "End Element" events, all the remainder nodes with all TRUE flags are also XLCAs in turn.

On the basis of proposition 3.1 and proposition 3.2, we can prove the correctness of Theorem 3.1 straightforward. Initially, the output set RS is empty. When the first XLCA is met, we can get the first XLCACT in RS; Repeat these steps until the whole document has been processed, we can get all the XLCACTs of KW.

6.4 SCHEMA-AWARE KEYWORD SEARCH FOR XML STREAMS

By using the algorithm S-XSF in section 3, users just need to input a list of keywords simply with pure keyword search approach and do not need to know any information for XML Schema. Nevertheless, this makes the pure keyword search approach of XML Stream has to parse the whole document, then its processing time will be directly proportional to the size of the XML document. An XML document can optionally have a schema. In many applications of XML stream processing, service providers know the Schema of XML document in advance if it is available, therefore, we expand the pure keyword search approach to a schema-aware approach in order to reduce the search space and optimize the performance of XML stream process.

6.4.1 Simplified DTD Entity-Attribute Graph

Besides XML Schema, Document Type Description (DTD) is a commonly used method to describe the structure of an XML document and acts like a schema. A DTD specifies the structure of an XML element by specifying the names of its sub-elements and attributes. Sub-element structure is specified using the operators * (set with zero or more elements), + (set with one or more elements), ? (optional), and | (or). There is a special attribute, id, which can occur once for each element.

To decide what information should be returned to users, XSeek (Liu, Walke &Chen, 2007) mimics the Entity-Relationship model in relational databases, which recognized XML documents as a set of real world entities, each of which has attributes. What users really want is the information related entities, therefore, similar to XSeek, we classify the nodes (a node means an element, a sub-element, or an attribute) in DTD into entities, entity attributes and connection nodes according to their node relationships by using the classifying rules: (i)If a node with name n1 has a one-to-many relationship ("*" operator, or "+" operator) with nodes with name n2, then n2 represents an entity; (ii) If a node with name n has only one child which is a value, then the node n denotes an entity attribute;(iii) if a node has attributes, then the node represents an entity; (iv) if a node with name n represents neither an entity nor an attribute, then the node n is a connection node.

To filter XML stream effectively based on keywords by using DTD, what we only need to consider is the possible paths containing the keywords. The operators "*", "+", "#", "?", "|", all the operators imply there is a possible path at least between two nodes, therefore, we ignore the difference among operators of DTD and treat them as a contain relations between the elements and its sub-elements uniformly. We use a concise graph structure to describe a DTD of an XML document.

Definition 1: A Simplified DTD Entity-Attribute Graph SDEAG is a pair (V, E), where nodes V is a finite set, and edges E is a binary relation on V: $E \subseteq V \times V$. The set V consists of elements and attributes in a DTD, each edge $e \in E$ represents the relation of an element contains a sub-element or an element has an attributes. In addition, the set V is divided into four categories:

- $r \in V$ is the designated root of SDEAG.
- $VE \subseteq V$ represents the set of the entity nodes of SDEAG.
- $VA \subseteq V$ represents the set of the entity attribute nodes of SDEAG.
- $VC \subseteq V$ represents the set of the connection nodes of SDEAG.

The DTD fragment of Figure 1 is shown in Figure 3. The SDEAG of Figure 3 is shown in Figure 4, where the entity node is shown as a rectangle (for example, "paper"), the entity attribute node is shown as a circle (for example,

Figure 3. A DTD fragment of Figure 1

```
<!ELEMENT conf    (title, editor*, paper*)>
<!ELEMENT title   (#PCDATA)>
<!ELEMENT editor  (name)>
<!ELEMENT name    (#PCDATA)>
<!ELEMENT paper   (title, author+, cite?)>
<!ATTLIST paper   id  ID #REQUIRED>
<!ELEMENT author (name, (email|phone)?)>
<!ELEMENT email  (#PCDATA)>
<!ELEMENT phone  (#PCDATA)>
<!ELEMENT cite (paper*)>
```

"title"), and the connection node is shown as a triangle (for example, "cite").

6.4.2 Entity Search Term

If the DTD of an XML document is available, XSEarch (Sara, Jonathan, Yaron, Yehoshua. 2003) uses a simple extension of the pure keyword search approach to search XML documents, which allows a user to specify labels and keyword-label combinations that must or may appear in a satisfying document in addition to specifying keywords. A keyword-label combination is called a *search term*, which has the form l: k formally, where l is a label and k is a keyword.

In order to filter XML stream based on key-words effectively by using DTD, we adopt the similar idea in our approach, but here comes another problem: there are too many labels in the DTD due to a large and complex document structure possibly, and many of them are not meaningful for users (for example, label "cite" in Figure 1) or represent more than one meaning due to different contexts (for example, label "title" in Figure 1 may can mean a paper's title or a conference's title). For giving a meaningful selection and provide a concise interface for the user, we combine the concepts of search term and entity.

Definition 2: An Entity Search Term (EST) has the form e: a: k, where "e" is a entity label defined in SDEAG, "a" is the attribute of the entity and "k" is a keyword which is the value of the attribute. The query Q(S) submitted by user is a set of entity search terms S={ e_1: a_1: k_1, e_2 :a_2: k_2, …, e_n: a_n: k_n}.

For example, in the user registration interface of XKFilter, user can select an entity in drop list box and an attribute of the entity, and then input a keyword in the text field. A user can add an EST by clicking the "add" button and register his keyword search by clicking the "submit" button. If a user selects an entity and an attribute of the entity, but the inputted keyword is empty, then it means that the user wants to get the value of the attribute.

6.4.3 Revise the Keyword Search Results

Each entity node in SDEAG may have multiple entity instances (i.e. XML elements) in its corresponding XML document. As aforementioned, what the users really want is the information related to entities. In order to reflect this idea, we revise

Figure 4. The SDEAG of Figure 3

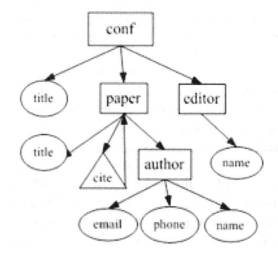

the keyword search results described in section 6.2 by using entities.

Definition 3: Most Related Entity Instance (MREI) of XLCA. Given an XML document tree D and a list of entity search terms S={ e_1: a_1: k_1, e_2 : a_2: k_2, ..., e_n: a_n: k_n}. X is the set of XLCAs of keywords in S. If $x_i \in X$ is an entity instance, then x_i is a most related entity instance; If $x_i \in X$ is not an entity instance, then the nearest ancestor entity instance of xi is the most related entity instance. e is the nearest ancestor entity instance of x_i means: e is an ancestor of x_i and e is an entity instance, and e has no descendant node that is both an ancestor and an entity instance of x_i.

According to the definition above, we revise the search results as a Most Related Entity Instance Connecting Tree (MREIMCT), which is a minimum connecting tree rooted at the MREI that contains the keywords.

6.4.4 Refining Keyword Search by Using DTD

In the pure keyword search over XML streams, the filter system has to parse and process the whole XML document due to lacking the structured information of the XML document. By using the DTD of an XML document and a set of EST submitted by users, the filter system can ignore the unrelated portions of an XML document with the keywords, therefore can constrain the keyword search to a restricted space of the XML document.

Given an input XML tree T, the SDEAG of T, and a query Q(S) containing a list of EST, where S={ e_1: a_1: k_1, e_2: a_2: k_2, ..., e_n: a_n: k_n}. A=a_1,...,a_2 is called matched attribute nodes in the SDEAG which contain keyword directly. We refine the keyword search Q(s) by taking the following steps roughly:

- Mark the matched attribute nodes a_1,...,a_2 in the SDEAG, and link the keywords to the corresponding matched attribute node.
- For each node that has been marked, mark its parent nodes and the edges between them if they are unmarked.
- Delete the unmarked nodes and edges in the graph.

For example, the SDEAG of Figure 1 is shown in Figure 4. Suppose a user submits a list of EST: S={author: name: a, author: name: b, paper: title}, its matched attribute nodes in the SDEAG are "title" and "name". After the refining process abovementioned, we get a graph structure shown in Figure 5.

Definition 4: A Keyword Query Graph KQG is a ten-tuple, KQG = (V, E, $\sum$, λ, ψ, ρ, τ, r, K, A), where
- V represents a finite set of nodes, E is a binary relation on V: E$\subseteq$V×V.
- $\sum$ represents a finite set of node labels
- λ: V→$\sum$ is a label function, λ(n) returns the name of label of node n.
- ψ(n) returns the type of the node n. The types include entity, attribute and connection.
- ρ: V→$\sum \cup \varepsilon$ is a parent function, ρ(n) returns the parent nodes of node n.
- τ: V→$\sum \cup \varepsilon$ is a child function, τ (n) returns the child nodes of node n.
- r$\in$V is the designated root of KQG.
- K=k_1,...,k_n is the list of keywords.
- A= a_1,...,a_m is the attribute nodes containing K directly.

6.4.5 XML Stream Filtering by Using DTD

By using KQG, we can reduce the search space due to ignoring the irrelevant parts of a coming XML document. In the process of filtering the XML document, we consider the KQG as a finite state

Figure 5. A sample KQG and its KQSM

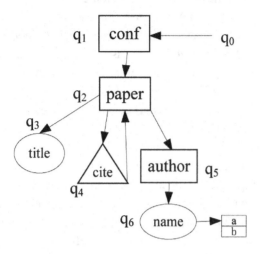

machine, called Keyword Query State Machine (KQSM). The nodes in KQG become the states of KQSM, meantime, the root node r of KQG is treated as the initial state of KQSM. The system accepts the SAX events of an XML stream and computes the solutions for keyword search driven by KQSM. The SAX events are transformed into the state transition function of KQSM. The child function $\tau(n)$ and parent function $\rho(n)$ in KQG can be used as the transition functions in KQS, separately corresponding to the "Start Element" and "End Element" event. For clarity, we define KQSM formally below:

Definition 5: *Keyword Query State Machine KQSM*(Q, q_0, F, I, δs, δe, Σ', λ', κ, QA) is constructed from KQG, where

- Q is the state identity corresponding to the nodes V in KQG.
- $q_0 \in Q$ is the initial state of KQSM.
- F is a sub set of Q, represents the accepting state of KQSM corresponding to the entity nodes in KQG.
- I is the SAX event (tagName, type), tagName represents name of current parsing tag, type represents event type, include "Start Element", "End Element" etc.

- δ_s and δ_e represents the state transition function separately corresponding to the parent function ρ and child function τ in KQG. δ_s is a forward transition function which means it only reacts to the "Start Element" event, and δ_e is a backward transition function which means it only reacts to the "End Element" event.
- Σ' represents finite input symbol, corresponds to the Σ in KQG.
- $\lambda':Q \rightarrow \Sigma'$ is a name function, returns the label name of the state corresponding to the λ function in KQG.
- ψ' corresponds to the type function ψ in KQG. q_0 is a special state $\psi'(q_0)=0$. Given $q \in Q$, If q's type is Entity, then $\psi'(q)=1$; If q's type is Connection node, then $\psi'(q)=2$; If q's type is Attribute, then $\psi'(q)=2$.
- QA $\subseteq$ Q, corresponds to the attribute nodes containing the list of keywords K=$k_1,...,k_n$ in KQG
- κ: QA$\rightarrow$K, is a keyword function, returns the contained keywords.

Similar to S-XSF, the process of filtering XML stream based on KQG (called Schema-XSF) also uses a run-time stack, but each entry in the stack contains four components (ID, Type, B=<flag$_1$,...,flag$_n$>, RT), where ID indicates the state identify of a state in KQSM; the Type indicates the type of a state node (1 represents Entity type, 2 represents Connection type, 3 represents Attribute type). The execution process of Schema-XSF is similar to the process of S-XSF, but there are some main differences:

- Schema-XSF is driven by KQSM, which means only matched incoming XML document nodes with KQSM states can be pushed into the runtime stack. When an element's open tag matches with a state in KQSM (denoted as a state match occurs), then invokes δ_s transition function; when a state match occurs in an element's close tag, the δ_e function will be invoked.

- When a state's flags are all TRUE and state's corresponding node is an entity, an accepting state of KQSM is reached, we call a query matching occurs. Noted that if an accepting state is reached, the KQSM doesn't stop, but keep running until the entire XML stream has been processed.

For making out the difference between Schema-XSF and S-XSF, we use the same sample XML document and query to illustrate the process of Schema-XSF. Suppose a query registered by a user is a list of ESTs: S={author: name: a, author: name: b, paper: title}. Its corresponding KQG and is shown in Figure 6. Its KQSM is also shown in Figure 6, where an arrow indicates a forward state transition, for clarity, all backward state transitions (corresponding to the "End Element" event) are omitted.

The processing is illustrated in Figure 7. Firstly, the initial state q_0 is pushed in the stack, when the startElement(conf) is encountered, a state match occurs, the state of KQSM is transformed from q_0 to q_1, i.e. δs (conf, q_0) $\rightarrow q_1$. Likewise, when the startElement(title) is encountered, δs (title, q_2) $\rightarrow q_3$, in the same time, the flag of title is set to true due to a keyword match occurs. When the endElement(title) is encountered, δe (title, q_3) $\rightarrow q_2$, the entry of q_3 is popped up and its true flag is set to corresponding flag of q_2. When the first endElement(paper) is encountered (shown in Figure 7(4)), δ_e(paper, q_2) $\rightarrow q_4$, the (q_2,1,<T,T,T>,R_3) is pop from stack as an answer of the query due to all the flags of the entry are TRUE and it is a Entity type. Note that by using the list of ESTs as the user's query, the results can reflect the user's intent more accurately. In this example, the results of Schema-XSF are R_2 and R_2.

Theorem 4.1: For the given XML Document Tree D and a set of keywords Q(kw$_1$, kw$_2$, …, kw$_n$), the outputs of algorithm S-XSF are a set of XLCACTs of KW, where KW={kw$_i$|i∈1…k}.

Due to the proof of this theorem is similar to the proof of theorem 3.1 it is the proof is not presented here.

6.5 THE SYSTEM ARCHITECTURE

The architecture of XKFilter is shown in Figure 7. The component of XML parser is event-based: when an XML document arrives at the system, it is run through the XML parser and treated as a linear sequence of events mark the beginning and the end of the parse of a document and its elements. The component of DTD Processor is implemented based on an automaton for parsing the DTD of an XML document, extracting entities and attributes, and constructing the SDEAG. The component of user register accepts the lists of entities and attributes of the DTD outputted from the component and present the lists to the users, then, the users can submit the keywords for getting useful information. The component of KQG Constructor accepts the SDEAG from the DTD processor and the ESTs from the user register, and then constructs the KQG.

The component of filtering engine is at the heart of the system. It takes the KQG as its input and converts it to the KQSM by using the KQSM Constructor component. It also receives and reacts to events from the XML parser. These events call back the corresponding handlers implemented by the filtering engine, which perform the matching of documents against keywords registered by users. When the input of the filtering engine is the pure keywords from the user register, the S-XSF algorithm is used; when the input is the KQG from the KQG constructor, the Schema-XSF is used. The implementation of KQSM in Schema-XSF

Figure 6. A running example of schema-XSF

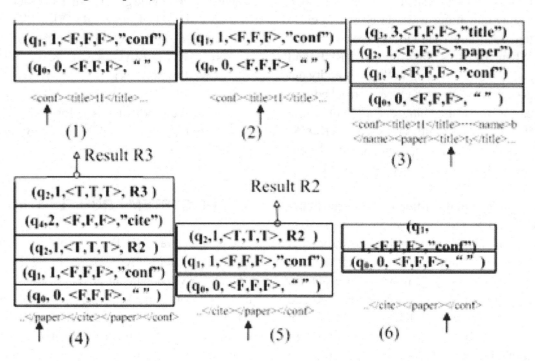

adopts the way based on state transition table. The Strategy Pattern (Gamma, Helm, Johnson & Vlisides, 2005) is used to organize the algorithms for adapting XKFilter to the future changes.

Once the matching results have been identified for a document, the results must be sent to the appropriate users by using the data dissemination component. Our current implementations simply send the matched results to each interested user. As for the effective delivery mechanism so they are not addressed further here.

6.6 EXPERIMENTS

XKFilter is implemented by using Java 1.5, with the IDE Eclipse Platform 3.3.0 and SAX XML parser (Xerces2-Java XML Parser 2.9.1). We run all the experiments on a machine with 2GHz *2 CPU and 2GB memory, Windows XP professional. To the best of our knowledge, XKFilter is the first system filtering XML streams based on keywords.

So, we evaluated XKFilter by comparing the performance between S-XSF and Schema-XSF.

We used the synthetic XMark (Busse, Carey, Florescu, Kersten, Manolescu, Schmidt & Waas, 2001) and DBLP (LEY, 2001) data for our experiments. The datasets were used generated by an XML generator (Angel and Douglas, 2004). We generated XML documents of different sizes by using the DTD of XMark and DBLP. S-XSF and Schema-XSF were evaluated in two different aspects: (a) by varying the size of input documents; (b) by varying the number of input keywords.

First, we used small document for the experiments. The size of document varies from 500K to 8000K, the number of keywords is 3, and the frequency of keywords in document is 1000, 1000, 1000 (it means each keyword occurs 1000 times in the document). The result is shown in Figure 8, which illustrates that, Schema-XSF is more efficient than S-XSF. The execution time of S-XSF is increasing with the increase of document size, while the execution time of Schema-XSF is

Figure 7. The architecture of XKFilter

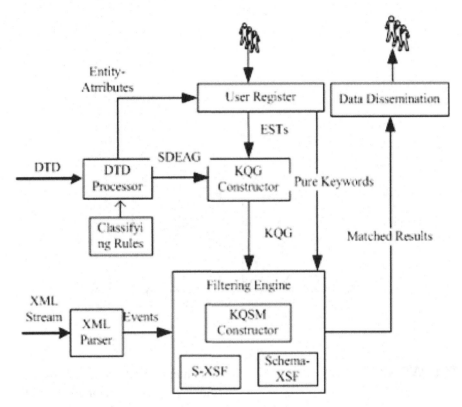

increasing more slowly. Second, we test the execution time of large document. The size of document varies from 11MB to 56MB and other parameters remain the same. The result is shown as Figure 9. Similar to the smaller document, S-XSF grows much faster than Schema-XSF. Finally, we vary the number of keywords from one to five and let the size of document be 22.8MB. The experiment result is shown in Figure 10. We can see that the processing time of S-XSF is going up with the increase of the number of keywords obviously, but Schema-XSF is not sensitive to the number of keywords, it's process time is almost constant while the number of keywords is increasing from 1 to 5. (this is a very good section with strong quantitative discussion. If these numbers can be summarized into a table, that would be much better and convincing).

S-XSF includes startElement and endElement method. For each node in an input XML docu-ment, the startElement method is invoked when the node's open tag is encountered, it's entry is pushed into the runtime's stack, and each keyword match is computed; when the node's close tag is encountered, the endElement method is invoked to do necessary process. Therefore, the processing time of S-XSF is increasing proportional to the size of input XML document and more sensitive to the number of keywords. Schema-XSF refines a list of keywords to the KQG by using DTD and constructs its KQSM from KQG, then the execution process of Schema-XSF is driven by the KQSM. Then, only the nodes of input document matching to the states of KQSM will be pushed into the runtime stack and the keywords match will be computed, the unrelated parts of input document to the KQSM are ignored. Therefore, the process time of Schema-XSF is not sensitive to the size of entire document, but only to the related parts to the KQSM.

Figure 8. Experiments for small document

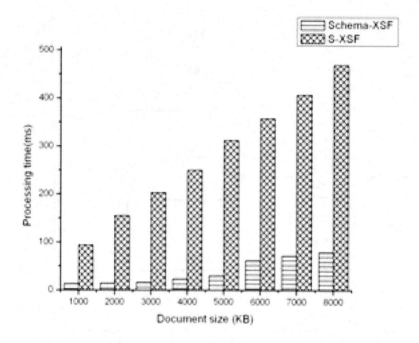

6.7 RELATED WORK

XKSearch (Xu & Papakonstantinou, 2005), XSearch (Cohen, et al. 2003), XRANK (Guo, Sha, Botev & Shanmugasundaramm, 2003) etc. Keyword search adopts the best match approach, which means that the most related results to the list of keywords should be selected. Most existing researches regard VLCA (Variation of LCA) as the meaningful XML fragment to the keywords. For example, XKSearch (Xu & Papakonstantinou, 2005) defines search results as the searching for SLCA of all keywords. XKFilter adopts XLCA approach based on our previous work (Xu, Lu, Wang & Shi,2006) [11] for pure keyword search. For identifying more meaningful results, XSeek(Liu, et. al., 2007) mimics the Entity-Relationship model in relational databases, which recognized XML documents as a set of real world entities. XKFilter combines the concept of entities into its schema-aware search approach

XML keyword search also focus on finding more efficient algorithms to search the XML

documents. XKSearch proposed two algorithms, Indexed Lookup Eager and Scan Eager, for keyword search in XML documents according to the SLCA semantic by using Dewey numbers as the index. XRANK (Guo, et al., 2003) presented stack based sort-merge algorithm (DIL). Because these works need to build the index (often use Dewey numbers) before searching the documents, they are not suitable for the environment of processing XML streams.

So far, all XML stream systems (Diao, et al., 2003) adopted structured query languages to represent user's profiles (such as XQuery, XPath) which can convey complex meaning by containing constraints on both structure and content, but is difficult to learn for an ordinary user, it is also impossible to write a correct query without knowing the exact structure of a document. XKFilter combines keyword search techniques and stream processing techniques to provide the abilities of filtering XML streams by using keywords, and proposes an algorithm named S-XSF based on runtime stack for pure keyword filtering on XML

Figure 9. Experiment for large document

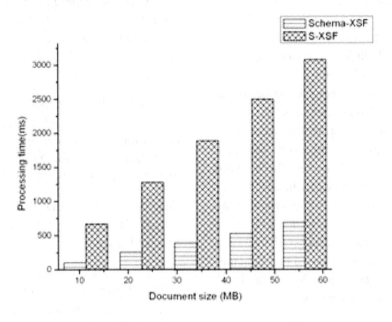

Figure 10. Varying the keyword number

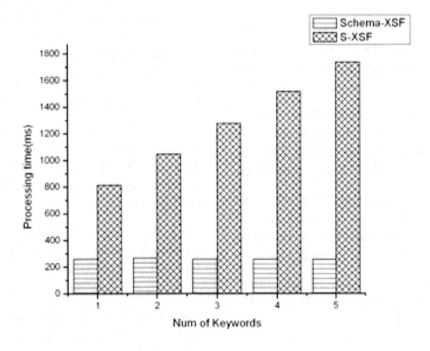

streams. Different from the stack based sort-merge algorithm presented in XRANK (Guo, et al., 2003), S-XSF uses event-based parsing to filter an input XML document in a single pass without building document index in advance, which can be fit for stream processing systems. XKFilter also proposes schema-aware approach called Schema-XSF for filtering XML streams if the DTD of the input documents is available.

6.8 CONCLUSION

This chapter presents a system named XKFilter which can support both pure keyword search and schema-aware keyword search. For the pure keyword search approach, we presented a stack based algorithm S-XSF to process the input document in a single pass and return the results to the users; for the schema-aware keyword search approach, we presented Schema-XSF to refine the keyword search to a constrained query structure KQG. For processing streams efficiently, the special finite state machine KQSM was constructed from the KQG to drive the execution process of document filtering. The experiments showed that Schema-XSF was more efficient than S-XSF if the DTD of the input document is available.

REFERENCES

Babcock, B., Babu, S., Datar, M., Motwani, R., & Widom, J. (2002). Models and issues in data stream systems. In *Proceedings of the 2002 ACM Symposium on Principles of Database Systems*.

Berglund, A., Boag, S., Chamberlin, D., & Fernandez, F. M., Kay, M., Robie, J., & Simon, J. (2002). *XML path language (XPath) 2.0 W3C working draft 16*. In World Wide Web Consortium.

Busse, R., Carey, M., Florescu, D., Kersten, M., Manolescu, I., Schmidt, A., & Waas, F. (2001). *XMark: An XML benchmark project*. Retrieved from http://monetdb.cwi.nl/xml/index.html

Chamberlin, D. (2003). XQuery: An XML query language. *IBM Systems Journal, 41*, 597–615. doi:10.1147/sj.414.0597

Cohen, S., Mamou, J., Kanza, Y., & Sagiv, Y. (2003). XSEarch: A semantic search engine for XML. *VLDB '03 Proceedings of the 29th International Conference on Very Large Data Bases, Vol. 29*.

Diao, Y. L., Altinel, M., & Franklin, J., M., Zhang, H., & Fischer, P. (2003). Path sharing and predicate evaluation for high-performance XML filtering. *ACM Transactions on Database Systems, 28*(4), 467–516. doi:10.1145/958942.958947

Diaz, A. L., & Lovell, D. (2004). *XML generator*. Retrieved from http://www.alphaworks.ibm.com/tech/xmlgenerator

Gamma, E., Helm, R., Johnson, R., & Vlisides. (1994). *Design patterns - Elements of reusable object-oriented software*. Addison-Wesley.

Guo, L., Shao, F., Botev, C., & Shanmugasundaram, J. (2003). XRANK: Ranked keyword search over XML documents. In *Proceedings of the 2003 ACM SIGMOD International Conference on Management of Data* (pp.16–27).

Ley, M. (2001). *DBLP DTD*. Retrieved from http://www.acm.org/sigmod/dblp/db/about/dblp.dtd

Liu, F., Yu, C., Meng, W. Y., & Chowdhury, A. (2006). Effective keyword search in relational databases. In *Proceedings of the 2006 ACM SIGMOD International Conference on Management of Data*.

Liu, Z. Y., Walker, J., & Chen, Y. (2007). Xseek: A semantic XML search engine using keywords. In *Proceedings of the 33th International Conference on Very Large Data Bases*.

Markowetz, A., Yang, Y., & Papadias, D. (2007). Keyword search on relational data streams. In *Proceedings of the 2007 ACM SIGMOD International Conference on Management of Data*.

Xu, J. J., Lu, J. H., Wang, W., & Shi, B. L. (2006). Effective keyword search in XML documents based on MIU . In Lee, M. L., Tan, K. L., & Wuwongse, V. (Eds.), *Database system for advanced applications* (pp. 702–716). doi:10.1007/11733836_49

Xu, Y., & Papakonstantinou, Y. (2005). Efficient keyword search for smallest LCAs in XML databases. In *Proceedings of the 2005 ACM SIGMOD International Conference on Management of Data.*

Section 2
Retrieving Information from Compressed XML Documents According to Vague Queries

Badya Al-Hamadani
University of Huddersfield, UK

Joan Lu
University of Huddersfield, UK

XML has become the standard way for representing and transforming data over the World Wide Web. The problem with XML documents is that they have a very high ratio of redundancy, which makes these documents demand large storage capacity and high network bandwidth for transmission. Because of their extensive use, XML documents can be retrieved according to vague queries by naive users with poor background in writing XPath query. The aim of this section is to present the design of a system named "XML Compressing and Vague Querying (XCVQ)," which has the ability of compressing the XML document and retrieving the required information from the compressed version with less decompression required according to vague queries.

XCVQ first compressed the XML document by separating its data into containers and then compressed these containers using the GZip compressor. The compressed file could be retrieved if a vague query is submitted without the need to decompress the whole file. For the purpose of processing the vague queries, XCVQ decomposes the query according to the relevant documents and then a second decomposition stage is made according to the relevant containers. Only the required information is decompressed and submitted to the user.

To the best of the authors' knowledge, XCVQ is the first XML compressor that has the ability to process vague queries. The average compression ratio of the designed compressor is around 78% which may be considered competitive compared to other queriable XML compressors. Based on several experiments, the query processor part had the ability to answer different kinds of vague queries ranging from simple exact match queries to complex ones that require retrieving information from several compressed XML documents.

Chapter 7
Introduction

Badya Al-Hamadani
University of Huddersfield, UK

Joan Lu
University of Huddersfield, UK

ABSTRACT

The eXtensible Markup Language (XML) is a World Wide Web Consortium (W3C) recommendation which has widely been used in both commerce and research. As the importance of XML documents increase, the need to deal with these documents increases as well. This chapter illustrates the methodology that has been used throughout the research, discussing all its parts and how these parts were adopted in the research.

1.1 INTRODUCTION

The eXtensible Markup Language (XML) is a World Wide Web Consortium (W3C) recommendation which has widely been used in both commerce and research. In recent years, we have witnessed a dramatic increase in the volume of XML digital information that is either created directly as an XML document or converted from another type of data representation. The importance of XML is mainly due to its ability to represent different data types within one document, solving the problem of long-term accessibility, and providing a solution to the problem of interoperability (Al-Hamadani et al., 2009).

Due to the replication of the XML schema in each record, the XML document is considered to be one of the self-describing data files, which means that these kinds of files have a lot of data redundancy in relation to both its tags and attributes (Ray, 2001). For the above reason the need to compress XML documents is becoming increasingly dramatic. Furthermore, what has evolved is the urgent need to retrieve information directly from the compressed documents and then decompress only the retrieved information (Ferragina et al., 2006).

DOI: 10.4018/978-1-4666-1975-3.ch007

Because of the wide range of XML documents in use and the different kinds of users, being able to deal with all kinds of queries has become a key issue. Some of these queries may have imprecise constraints which cannot be processed directly due to the grammar restriction in the existing query languages. However, these types of queries, which are known as *vague queries*, appear to be common when the users of the XML documents have little knowledge about the document structure, or may lack the skills to write a precise and meaningful query. Another type of vague queries occurs when the query is presented without the presence of a Schema or the data type definition (DTD) of the document.

According to the relevant literature, there are a number of techniques that compress the XML documents and query the compressed version with no or partial decompression. These techniques process almost all types of queries but not the vague queries; admittedly, there are a number of researchers now trying to process vague queries on the original XML document.

The research carried out in this thesis primarily concerns designing and implementing a new technique called XML Compressing and Vague Querying (*XCVQ*) which consists of two stages. In the first stage, it separates the data part of the XML document into several containers according to the path of that data within the document. Then each of the containers is compressed separately using a back-end compressor. The second stage processes the vague queries by decomposing them into multiple sub-queries, retrieves information from the compressed XML document according to each sub-query, combines the retrieved information according to the given query, and finally decompresses only the most relevant information.

To eliminate the amount of technologies associated with the XML documents and to make the process of compressing and retrieving information easier for the inexperienced users, *XCVQ* is designed to be schema independent in both phases of the compressor and the query processor.

1.2 RESEARCH HYPOTHESIS AND RESEARCH METHODOLOGY

This thesis is based on the following hypotheses:

1. The existing XML compression techniques can be improved to construct a new schema independent XML compressor with a higher compression ratio.
2. The redundancy in the XML documents significantly affects the size of those documents and can be reduced to more than half of the original file size.
3. The compressed XML document can be retrieved according to vague queries. Vague queries are those queries which do not follow the semantic rules of current query languages. They occur when the exact matching user's query does not retrieve the required information either because of the lack of experience in writing a query or the absence of the document's schema.
4. The necessity of retrieving information from more than one XML documents without the need to specify an exact relative document.

The above hypotheses are tested throughout this research by using the System Development Methodology (SDM) (Nunamaker et al., 1991; Morrison and George, 1995; Hevner et al., 2004). This methodology has been widely used by software developers and information system specialists (Meersman et al., 2008;.Yousof et al., 2011) As depicted in Figure 1, this methodology consists of four main stages:

1. **Identifying research problems:** This stage focuses on drawing up the research questions due in part to the lack of theories in the research field and/or build upon existing theories. In this thesis, the research questions are set from two XML fields, compressing the XML documents and querying them. As a result, a new XML compressor is introduced

Figure 1. System development methodology (Morrison and George, 1995)

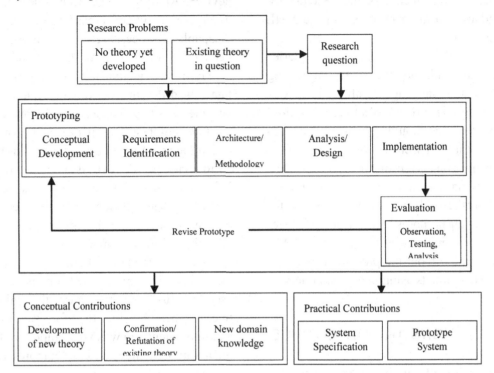

(CHAPTER-4) with the ability to retrieve information from the compressed document according to vague queries. The designed system may improve the querying process to retrieve information from XML documents.

2. **Prototyping and evaluation:** In the second stage, SDM spotlights the implementing or prototyping the proposed system. It starts by designing the conceptual model of the proposed system, identifying the necessary requirements, designing the complete architecture of the system, and then implementing the system to prepare it for the evaluation process by testing and analysing it. In this thesis, the complete architecture and the detailed design of the system are laid out in CHAPTER-4, the implementation part is in Appendix-F, and the evaluation process is given in CHAPTER-5.

3. **Conceptual and practical contributions:** As a final stage, SDM sets the main contribution to the knowledge. In this thesis all the contributions, conclusions, and future developments are presented in CHAPTER-6.

1.3 RESEARCH QUESTIONS

Following the SDM as shown in Figure 1, outlining the research questions should be made before proceeding further with defining the actual prototype. The research into this thesis focused on two main parts, each of which has its own set of questions to be addressed:

1. Is it possible to design a new compression technique that has the ability to compress XML documents and achieve a better compression ratio without the need for the document's schema or its DTD?

2. What is the influence of the structure redundancy on the overall size of the XML document?

3. What are the main types of vague queries and when could they occur? Has the existing XPath query language the ability to answer vague queries? If not, what is the required expansion that should be made on XPath to provide it with such ability?

4. How does one determine the relevant XML document(s) from thousands of documents without the need to scan them completely for time saving purposes? And is it possible to retrieve information from more than one XML document without the pre-specification of these documents using one XPath query?

1.4 MOTIVATIONS AND OBJECTIVES

This work is initially motivated by the need to expand the XML query languages. These languages are treating the user's query in Boolean nature (Campi et al., 2009) in which a specific XML node is selected if and only if it satisfies exactly the query or part of it. This case applies more restrictions to the inexperienced user or in the case of schema absence.

XML has become a focus for research in both the database as well as the document research communities (Harrusi et al., 2006; Moro et al., 2008). This research is motivated by the strength of XML such as its simplicity, the separation of data from the structure, interoperability, and human and machine readability. All these features and more make the XML document a reliable way for data transformation on the web. However, the redundancy in the structure of the XML documents enlarges their sizes, the very reason that inspired researchers to produce compression techniques dedicated to XML. Other researchers were interested in retrieving information from the compressed XML document to make it easier to use these fairly large documents with low resource devices. Although these techniques succeeded in answering several types of queries, they are incapable of processing vague queries, which is yet another motivation for this research.

The main objective of this research is to investigate the different types of vague queries and set new methods to solve these queries in the case of existing compressed XML document. The design and implementation of a system that has the ability to compress the XML document and retrieve information from the compressed file according to vague queries, let alone the need to decompress only the retrieved relevant information, is another objective of this research.

Since it was very difficult to have access to the source code of an XML compressor to be used as a first stage to achieve the main objective, another objective therefore was to design and implement a new XML compressor that has the ability to achieve a better compression ratio than the existing techniques.

1.5 RESEARCH CONTRIBUTIONS

This research will contribute to the fields of XML compression and XML retrieving in the following areas:

1. A new XML compression technique is introduced that compresses XML documents efficiently and independently from their Schema or the DTD. The designed compressor achieved a compression ratio of 1.83 which is higher than the best existing techniques.

2. Identify the exact ratio of the redundancy of the XML structure. This redundancy is abridged by up to half the size of the original file.

3. The main contribution of this research is the introduction of a new method to answer vague queries, a kind of queries that can be submitted by naive users or via the absence

of the document's schema. The new method is adjusted to process the vague queries under the compressed XML documents and retrieve the most related results.

4. Introduce the idea of retrieving information from XML documents without specifying the exact documents that have the required information.

REFERENCES

Al-Hamadani, B. T., Alwan, R. F., Lu, J., & Yip, J. (2009). *Vague Content and structure (VCAS) retrieval for XML electronic healthcare records (EHR).* Paper presented at the 2009 International Conference on Internet Computing, USA.

Campi, A., Damiani, E., Guinea, S., Marrara, S., Pasi, G., & Spoletini, P. (2009). A fuzzy extension of the XPath query language. *Journal of Intelligent Information Systems, 33*(3), 285–305. doi:10.1007/s10844-008-0066-3

Ferragina, P., Luccio, F., Manzini, G., & Muthukrishnan, S. (2006). *Compressing and searching XML data via two zips.* Paper presented at the 15th International Conference on World Wide Web.

Harrusi, S., Averbuch, A., & Yehudai, A. (2006). *XML syntax conscious compression.* Paper presented at the Data Compression Conference (DCC'06).

Hevner, A., March, S., Park, J., & Ram, S. (2004). Design science in information systems research. *Management Information Systems Quarterly, 28*(1), 75–105.

Meersman, R., Tari, Z., Herrero, P., Abdelaziz, T., Elammari, M., & Branki, C. (2008). MASD: Towards a comprehensive multi-agent system development methodology. In *On the Move to Meaningful Internet Systems: OTM 2008 Workshops* (Vol. 5333, pp. 108–117). Berlin, Germany: Springer. doi:10.1007/978-3-540-88875-8_30

Moro, M. M., Ale, P., Vagena, Z., & Tsotras, V. J. (2008). *XML structural summaries.* Paper presented at the PVLDB '08, Auckland, New Zealand.

Morrison, J., & George, J. (1995). Exploring the software engineering component in MIS research. *Communications of the ACM, 38*(7), 80–91. doi:10.1145/213859.214802

Nunamaker, J., & Chen, M. (1991). Systems development in information systems research. *Journal of Management Information Systems, 7*(3), 89–106.

Ray, E. T. (2001). *Learning XML guide to creating self-describing data.* O'Reilly Media Inc.

Yousof, M. M., Shukur, Z., & Abdullah, A. L. (2011). CuQuP: A hybrid approach for selecting suitable information systems development methodology. *Information Technology Journal, 10*(5).

Chapter 8
Research Background

Badya Al-Hamadani
University of Huddersfield, UK

Joan Lu
University of Huddersfield, UK

ABSTRACT

XML documents are increasing in usage during the last years since the structure of these documents has lots of important specifications. This chapter explains the importance of XML documents and their structure. It spotlights the difference between the traditional text retrieval and retrieving information from XML documents as well as the query languages used to access parts of these documents.

1.1 XML COMMENCEMENTS AND IMPORTANCE

Before the rise of the internet, 1980s witnessed the invention of Standard Generalized Markup Language (SGML) as a way to display information dynamically. Later, in 1995, W3C recommended SGML to be used for the internet. Problems occurred when using SGML included the lack of widely supported style sheets, complexity and instability in the software that were using it, and the difficulties in interchanging SGML data due to its varying levels among SGML software packages.

In 1996, the first XML working draft was intended to be a powerful substitute to SGML.

It was first recommended by the World Wide Web Consortium (W3C) in 1998 to be used as a mark-up language for storing and exchanging data through the web. The most recent recommendation was published in 2008, which is the fifth edition of the XML (W3C, 2008). In a very short period of time, XML has become the basis for data exchange through the Internet. This is due to its several features such as the following (NG et al., 2006; Gerlicher, 2007; Groppe, 2008):

- **Readability:** XML is readable by both human and machine. This means that the data represented by XML can be used by different users and by different parsing code.

DOI: 10.4018/978-1-4666-1975-3.ch008

- **Interoperability:** This is the ability of the hardware and software to use XML documents without the need to make any changes to the software or the data itself. This means that XML data is stripped of any dependency on software and machine.
- **Long term usability:** Since XML documents are represented using the Unicode; these documents are expected to stay in secure storage and usage for years (Augeri et al., 2007; De Meo et al., 2007).
- **Extensibility:** This means that there are no fixed set of tags that should be used to represent data.
- **Generality:** XML documents have the ability to represent different kinds of data representation such as images, sounds, videos, texts, etc.
- **Internationality:** Almost all written languages can be represented in XML documents since they support Unicode (Norbert and Kai, 2004).

In spite of all these advantages, XML has also some weaknesses:

- They have a huge amount of redundancy which makes these documents demand high storage memory to be archives, high band width to be transmitted, and high cost to be processed.
- The huge amount of technologies surrounding it complicates the use of these documents such as schema, DTD, XSLT, SAX, DOM, XPath, XQuery. These technologies render the use of these documents somewhat difficult especially with naive users or in cases where these technologies are absent, it would be just as difficult as they are considered necessary for dealing with XML documents.
- The problems that can occur when dealing with the document namespace should be carefully sorted out otherwise other problems and complications could occur during the processing of these XML documents.

1.2 XML DOCUMENT TYPES

The main building blocks of any well-formed XML document are nested open tags and their equivalent close tags. These tags can be formed as follows (Hunter, 2000; Anders, 2009; Goldberg, 2009):

1. **Elements:** each element starts with an open tag ($<p>$) and ends with an end tag ($</p>$). Everything between and including these tags are an element. The general structure of an element is as follows:
   $<e\ at_1="v_1"\ at_2="v_2"\ at_n="v_n">d_1d_2d_3...d_m</e>$
2. **Such that** $n \geq 0$, and $m \geq 0$ (1)

Each element has an *element-name* (e) which should follow the following rules:

- Case sensitive names.
- Consist of characters, numerals, underscores and tabs.
- Start with a character or an underscore.
- Should not start with *xml* or *XML*.

Elements can have optional *element-value* ($\{d_1d_2d_3...d_m\}$ in (1)) which represent the actual data values for the XML document.

3. **Attributes:** attributes (if any) appear within an element and they provide more information about that element. Each attribute has an *attribute-name* ($\{at_1, at_2, at_n\}$ in (1)) which should follow the same rules for an *element-name*, and an *attribute-value* ($\{v_1, v_2, ... v_n\}$ in (1)) which can be any printable character between a pair of quotations.
4. **Data text:** the data in a XML document could either be *attribute-values* or *element-*

values. This text can be a list of any keyboard printable character from the Unicode set ($\{d_1 d_2 d_3 \ldots d_m\}$ in (1)). Some escape character should be used to embed some of the characters in the data text such as (*<*), (*>*), (*&*), (*"*), and (*')* to represent (<), (>), (&), ("), and (') respectively.

5. **Comments:** comments can be added anywhere in the XML document to provide any further description but is not part of the main document. In XML, the comment start tag is (<!--) and the end tag is (-->).

6. **Declaration:** this single statement (if any) should be the very first line of the document. It supplies the XML processor with information such as the version, encoding and other information about the document. Its start tag is (<?xml) and its end tag is (?>).

Depending on the amount of data (*attribute-values* and *element-values*) in the XML document, Bourret (2005); and Manning et al. (2008) classified XML documents into two types, either data-centric or document-centric. Table 1 lists the main differences between these two types according to certain criteria. With data-centric XML documents the roles of the XML elements and attributes are to arrange these data in atomics. These documents are usually created and used by machines such as the XML documents that are generated by a Database Management System, or those used to transfer data between different databases.

In contrast, XML role in document-centric XML documents is very important since it is the only way to organize this document into large units of information. The order of the elements inside these documents is important since any change in the order can produce a completely different document.

1.3 JAVA API FOR XML (JAXP)

Java programming language, and some other languages, provides different types of XML Application Programming Interface (API) such as SAX, DOM, and XSLT (Violleau, 2001; McLaughlin and Edelson, 2006; Williams, 2009) in order to process the XML documents by means of writing a computer programme using several programming languages. SAX (*Simple API for XML*) scans the XML document sequentially and throws up events that the programmer can handle. These events are thrown by the parser when it detects the start-document, end-document, start-element including a list of all its attributes, end-element, and characters. The programmer should write suitable codes for each event to process an entire XML document. Since each event occurs only once for each element, all the required work needed to process the document should be done in one cycle.

By using DOM (*Document Object Model*) parser, the document is represented in the main memory of the computer as a tree-like structure. The programmer can write the code to traverse this tree as many times as s/he needs. Table 2 sets out the main features of SAX and DOM. It shows that using DOM parser is memory consuming

Table 1. Differences between data-centric and document-centric XML

Criteria	Data-centric	Document-centric
XML role	Superfluous	Significant
Order	Not very important	Significant
Consumption	Machine	Human
Data granularity	Fine	Large
Examples	Catalog and flight schedules	Books and advertisements

and since the aim of this research is to reduce the amount of memory used to process the XML documents, the designed system used SAX parser to process these documents.

While SAX and DOM parsers should be used through a programming language, XSLT (*XML Style-Sheet Language Transformation*) is a declarative language which is used to transform the XML document into another document type (Tidwell, 2008; Williams, 2009). Its two main purposes are: (1) produce HTML documents from XML documents for browsing purposes, and (2) retrieve information from the XML document using the XPath.

1.4 XML RETRIEVAL

XML retrieval is considered to be one of the semi-structured retrieval techniques (Manning et al., 2008). This adds more challenges to meeting the user's needs. The first difficulty in structured retrieval is that the user requires only parts of the documents and not the entire document like unstructured retrieval techniques do (Stamatina et al., 2006). This challenge leads to another, which is the identification of the most relevant parts from the document to the user's query. To solve this difficulty there are two approaches, either to retrieve the largest units of the document that contains the required information (top down) (Norbert and Kai, 2004; Jiaheng, 2006), or to retrieve the smallest unit by starting the search from the leaves of the XML tree (bottom up) (Fuhr et al., 2006).

Retrieving information from XML documents provides the users with the extra abilities to specify the exact piece of information needed or to combine different parts from of the document that meet the user's need. The user's queries can specify the required information as well as the place where this information is to be found inside the document. For instance the user may ask about *"a table of all XPath functions in XPath description chapter"*. In this case the *"XPath functions"* and

the *"XPath description"* are about the content of the document, while the *"table"* and the *"chapter"* are about its structure.

XML documents can be retrieved according to their type either text-centric or data-centric retrieval. In text-centric, an approximate matching process is used to match the text of the query with the text of the document while the structure role is as a framework within this process (Manning et al., 2008). Since the matching process is done with the data part of the XML document, the retrieved information is expected to be long and they should be ranked. On the other hand, data-centric retrieval retrieves only attribute values and numeric data using exact match. The retrieved information from this type is short and the ranking is not significant.

Another classification for XML retrieving techniques is done according to which part is more significant in the user's query: the content part or the data part (Hunter, 2000; Sanz, 2007). Content-Only (CO) queries are rich of text and focus on the data part of the XML document. The user can add some structural constraints to the query to specify the granularity of the required information. As seen in Figure 1 (a), the XPath query focuses on retrieving the title and the content of a paragraph which is considered the data content of the document. To process these queries, some of the techniques use the traditional IR techniques by completely ignoring the structural constraints and treat the XML document as a traditional text file, while other techniques decompose the query

Table 2. SAX and DOM features

SAX	DOM
Event based model	Tree-like structure
Sequential access	Random access
Required low memory	Memory intensive
One scan for the document	Multiple traverse for the document
1998, David Megginson's	1998, W3C's

into several small queries and process each one separately.

Content-And-Structure (CAS) retrieval takes into their considerations the structural part of the XML document and provides the user with extra advantages to accurately specify the exact part required from the relevant document. The XPath example in Figure 1 (b) concentrates on finding the first paragraph which is in a section for the specific article.

1.5 XML QUERY LANGUAGES

Different kinds of query languages have been proposed in order to retrieve specific information from an XML document. All these languages have a common feature in that the user should specify the exact XML document(s) wherefrom s/he would like to retrieve the information. This section spotlights the main features of some of the query languages which are either recommended by W3C (XPath, XQuery, XPoint, and XLink) or used by Initiative Evaluation of XML retrieval (INEX) working group (NEXI).

1.5.1 XPath

Standing for XML Path language, it is a descriptive language which takes an XML document and a user query as an input and produces specific nodes from this document as output (Kay, 2004).

It is considered to be the core to all other XML query languages, as illustrated in Figure 2 (W3Schools.com, 2006a). The main building blocks for an XPath expression are: (1) expressions deal with atomic values which include comparative and arithmetical operations, (2) expressions for selecting specific nodes from a tree, and (3) operation on every item in a specific sequences, such as using the *"for"* expression.

In 1990, W3C recommends XPath 1.0 as an XML query language (W3C, 1999). In 2010 W3C recommend the last version of XPath 2.0 to be a standalone query language or to be embedded with XSLT or XQuery (W3C, 2010a). It comes with some developments on the first version. These changes make XPath easy to use, improve its interoperability, simplify the manipulation of string contents and Schema-typed content, and to increase its efficiency. These developments include: (Holman, 2002; Kay, 2004; W3C, 2007b; Kay, 2008)

1. **Data types:** XPath 2.0 offers new data types such as integers, single precision, date, time, and any data type that can be defined by the user through XML Schema.
2. **Path expressions:** Not very big changes on path expression compared to XPath 1.0, only

Figure 1. XPath queries examples. (a): CO query; (b) CAS query

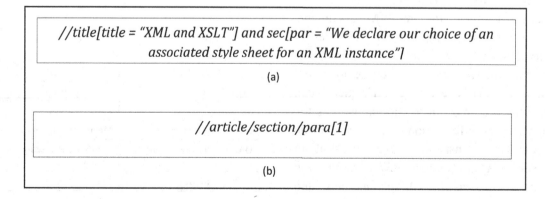

Figure 2. The role of XPath between other XML query languages (W3Schools.com, 2006a)

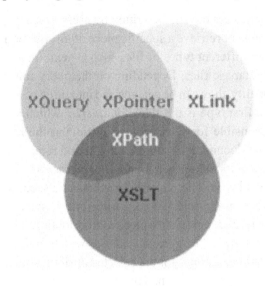

the ability to use the function call within the path expression is a slight change.

3. **Operators:** addition operators are used to support XPath 2.0 functions. Examples of these operators are: *"is"* to test if two expressions return the same set of nodes, *"<<" and ">>"* to test the order of the two operands, *"except" and "intersect"* to find the difference and the intersection between two node sets, and *"eq", "ne", "lt", "le", "gt", "ge"* to make a comparison between atomic values and return a node set.

4. **Functions:** Some new functions are added to the list of the available ones in XPath 1.0 such as: *"max()", "min()", "avg()"*, functions to manipulate the new data types like *date*, *time*, and *QNames*, generalization of string manipulation functions to deal with user-defined types.

Path expressions thus provide a very powerful mechanism for selecting nodes within an XML document, and this power lies at the heart of the XPath language (Sigurbjornsson and Trotman, 2003; Kay, 2004).

1.5.2 XQuery

In 2007, W3C first recommended XQuery as an XML query language and they made the last recommendation in 2010 (W3C, 2010b). This querying and descriptive language uses XPath to retrieve information from XML documents whereas the simplest XQuery expression is an XPath expression. The main engine in XQuery is the *"FLWOR"* expressions which stand for For-Let-Where-Order-Return. In these expressions, the *"for"* expression selects a specific node list from a specific document which can be repeated several times within the same expression. The *"let"* expression associates with each node in the node list(s) generated by the first expression or another node retrieved from another XML document. The *"where"* expression filters the resulting list according to a specific condition. The *"order"* expression sorts the list according to a specific atomic. Finally, the *"return"* expression specifies the required information from the node list(s).

The main advantage of XQuery over XPath is that XPath by its own cannot organize the output of the query in a specific format while XQuery does (McGovern et al., 2003). Although XML Style sheet Language Transformation (XSLT) can do organize the format of the retrieved information, but it could be difficult for the user to use it due to its recursive-structure and mixed name-spaces.

Another feature in XQuery is its capability to retrieve information from more than one specified XML documents. XPath is suffering from the lack of this feature.

Although it is considered to be very easy to use, XQuery is a read-only query language. This means that XQuery does not have the ability to exchange or create an XML document like SQL to the databases.

1.5.3 XLink and XPointer

XLink stands for Linking Language and recommended by W3C in 2001 (W3C, 2001). The main purpose of XLink is to make either *"simple"* links between two XML resources, or *"extended"* links between more than two XML resources (W3Schools.com, 2006a). With the *"simple"* links, any element inside the XML document can be linked with another resource such as an image, a text file or even another XML document just like the *"a"* element in HTML which performs Unidirectional link. When the link type is *"extended"* this means that the link will be bidirectional between the XML document and the other resource(s).

XPointer stands for XML Pointer Language and recommended by W3C in 2003 (W3C, 2002). It uses XLink to point to specific data part within the XML document. This means that XPointer query should starts with the URI of the document followed by *"#"* sign which indicates the starting of the XPointer query which is actually an XPath query with some extra functions.

1.5.4 NEXI

Stands for Narrowed Extended XPath I is an XML query language that follows the steps of XPath with some modifications. First, the NEXI retrieval engine designed to deduce the semantics from the query in reverse to XPath which has predefined semantics. Furthermore, NEXI extended the use of the contains() function, which is used by XPath to indicate an element that is contain a specific content, to be about() function to indicate the element to be about the content. This adjustment allows NEXI to deal with fuzzy queries. NEXI has been used for several purposes, such as question answering, multimedia searching, and searching heterogeneous document collections. (Trotman and Sigurbjornsson, 2005)

1.6 TYPES OF QUERIES

Queries are questions written by users to search, change or retrieve a specific piece of information from different types of files such as text, image, or database files. Depending on the query functionality, they can be categorized into three types. The first type is the *selection queries* which are responsible for selecting and retrieving the relevant document or sub-documents and returning the results to the user. The *action queries* are the second type. These queries implement a specific action on the selected file or document, such as delete, add, or update a piece of information. The third type is the *aggregate queries* which find the statistical amount for the selected attributes such as average, max, min...etc.

Depending on their complexity, selection queries can be categorized into five main types. Table 3 lists these types and describe their features supported by an example for each type and its equivalent XPath query (written in *Italic* in the table). The amount of the retrieved information varies according to the query's level of complexity such that the simplest query retrieves general information while the more complex query tries to retrieve more specific information.

Since vague queries are the central issue in this research, the following section provides a brief description of such queries and how they can appear in information retrieval domain.

1.7 VAGUE QUERIES

XML query languages force the users to follow their rigid rules to write a syntactically true query. This process is not easy to be maintained even for expert users (Huh et al., 2000). Moreover, in order to retrieve the required information these languages require previous full knowledge about the document's schema what is considered to be

Table 3. Query types

Query type	Description	XPath Example
Simple queries (SQ)	Retrieve part of the document according to general specification	List countries names *//countries/country/name*
Criteria queries (CQ)	Retrieve part of the document according to a specific criterion.	List countries with less than 10 million population *//countries/country[population < 10000000]*
Conjunctive queries (JQ)	Retrieve part of the document according to conjunction of two or more criteria.	List industrial countries with less than 10 million population *//countries/country[economy="industry"] and //countr[population < 10000000]*
Range queries (RQ)	Retrieve information according to a range between given minimum and maximum values.	List countries with population between 6 million and 15 million *//countries/country[population > 6000000] and //countries/country[population < 15000000]*
Vague queries (VQ)	Retrieve information when there is no Boolean matching between the user's query and the relevant XML document (Stasiu et al., 2005; Rajpal et al., 2007).	List countries with population between 6 million and 15 million */country/population between(6000000, 15000000)*

difficult to ordinary users. If the query does not follow the semantic rules of the querying language or it does not meet the document's schema, null information will be retrieved because these query languages use Boolean conditions wherein a condition is either true (exact match) or false (no match) (Campi et al., 2009). On the other hand, handling the fault-tolerant for the user's query makes it easier for the user to retrieve approximate information when vague conditions appear in the query (Zhao and Ma, 2009).

Vague queries are those that occur when exact matching queries fail to retrieve the required information (Fuhr, 1999; Bodenhofer and Küng, 2001; Zhang and Kankanhalli, 2003; Dutta et al., 2009). In this case the vague query needs to be generalized to retrieve the relevant information and rank this information in the bases of their relevancy. Vague queries can be cause by several factors:

1. **Schema:** Although XML Schema or its DTD are very important when creating and developing the document, their absence during the retrieving process leads to null information retrieved since all XML query languages demand complete knowledge over them. Even if the schema exists, it is difficult to figure out the exact structure of its XML document (Sakr, 2009; Al-Hamadani et al., 2011).

2. **Users:** There are two main kinds of XML retrieval users, the experts and the naïve. The experts have the ability to write syntactically true queries depending on their knowledge of the rules of the query language and have the ability to navigate the document's schema and write the appropriate query. However, different kinds of XML schema available such as XML Schema, DTD, and RNG, and even expert users are only aware of one or two of them. On the other hand, the naïve users have low experience in the rules of the language and in the schema navigation. The latter case could produce vague

queries which has spelling errors in either the structure or the content of the document, different case used in the query and in the original document, or out of order or weak path (Florescu et al., 2000; Campi et al., 2009).

3. **The query Language:** All XML query languages do not have the ability to retrieve approximate answers according to a user's query. Moreover, the functions in the query languages sometimes do not meet the user requirement. All these restrictions in the languages can lead to vague queries (Buneman et al., 2003; Norbert and Kai, 2004).

4. **Unknown document:** Whenever a query is submitted, it should specify the XML document(s) that has the required information. If the user does not know the exact document or the information is disseminated in more than one document, a vague query occurs (FAZZINGA et al., 2009).

1.8 SUMMARY

This chapter described the origins of the XML technique and its development. It showed the importance of the XML documents and their usage as well as their drawbacks. Since these documents have a special structure, this chapter provided a brief description of this structure and the different types of documents. To deal with XML documents, many APIs have appeared. This chapter listed the well known APIs and described their features and differences. Because this research lies in the field of XML retrieval, the chapter highlighted different kinds of XML retrieval techniques and query languages used to retrieve parts of the entire XML document. The main features of all types of queries are illustrated with the focus being on vague queries.

REFERENCES

W3C. (1999). *XML path language (XPath) - Version 1.0*. Retrieved from http://www.w3.org/TR/xpath/

W3C. (2002). *XML pointer language (XPointer)*. Retrieved from http://www.w3.org/TR/xptr/

W3C. (2008). *Extensible markup language (XML) 1.0* (5th ed.). Retrieved September 22, 2010, from http://www.w3.org/TR/REC-xml/

W3C. (2010a). *XML path language (XPath) 2.0*. Retrieved October 19, 2010, from http://www.w3.org/TR/xpath20/

W3C. (2010b). *XQuery 1.0 and XPath 2.0 functions and operators*. Retrieved September 26, 2010, from http://www.w3.org/TR/xpath-functions/

W3Schools.com. (2006). *XLink and XPointer*. Retrieved September 27, 2010, from http://www.w3schools.com/xlink/default.asp

Al-Hamadani, B., Lu, J., & Alwan, R. F. (2011). (in press). A new schema-independent XML compression technique. *International Journal of Information Retrieval Research*.

Anders, M. (2009). *An introduction to XML and Web technologies*. Pearson Education.

Augeri, C. J., Bulutoglu, D. A., Mullins, B. E., Baldwin, R. O., & Baird, I. (2007). *An analysis of XML compression efficiency*. Paper presented at the 2007 Workshop on Experimental Computer Science.

Bodenhofer, U., & Küng, J. (2001). *Enriching vague queries by fuzzy orderings*. Paper presented at the European Society for Fuzzy Logic and Technology - EUSFLAT.

Bourret, R. (2005). *XML and databases*. Retrieved September 23, 2010, from http://www.rpbourret.com/xml/XMLAndDatabases.htm

Buneman, P., Grohe, M., & Koch, C. (2003). Path queries on compressed XML. In F. Johann-Christoph, L. Peter, A. Serge, C. Michael, S. Patricia & H. Andreas (Eds.), *Proceedings 2003 VLDB Conference* (pp. 141-152). San Francisco, CA: Morgan Kaufmann.

Campi, A., Damiani, E., Guinea, S., Marrara, S., Pasi, G., & Spoletini, P. (2009). A fuzzy extension of the XPath query language. *Journal of Intelligent Information Systems*, *33*(3), 285–305. doi:10.1007/s10844-008-0066-3

De Meo, P., Palopoli, L., Quattrone, G., & Ursino, D. (2007). Combining description logics with synopses for inferring complex knowledge patterns from XML sources. *Information Systems*, *32*(8), 1184–1224. doi:10.1016/j.is.2007.03.003

Dutta, A. K., Idwan, S., & Biswas, R. (2009). A study of vague search to answer imprecise query. *International Journal of Computational Cognition*, *7*(4), 70–75.

Fazzinga, B., Flesca, S., & Pugliese, A. (2009). Retrieving XML data from heterogeneous sources through vague querying. *ACM Transactions on Internet Technology*, *9*(2), 7–35. doi:10.1145/1516539.1516542

Florescu, D., Kossmann, D., & Manolescu, I. (2000). Integrating keyword search into XML query processing. *Computer Networks, 33*(1-6), 119-135.

Fuhr, N. (1999). *A probabilistic framework for vague queries and imprecise information in databases.* Paper presented at the 16TH International Conference on Very Large Databases.

Fuhr, N., Lalmas, M., & Trotman, A. (2006). *Comparative evaluation of XML information retrieval systems* (5th ed.). Springer.

Gerlicher, A. R. S. (2007). *Developing collaborative XML editing systems.* London, UK: University of the Arts London.

Goldberg, K. H. (2009). *XML: Visual quickstart guide* (2nd ed.). Peachpit Press-Pearson Education.

Groppe, J. (2008). *Speeding up XML querying.* Berlin, Germany: Zugl Lübeck University.

Holman, G. K. (2002). *XSLT and XPath*. Prentice Hall PTR.

Huh, S. Y., Moon, K. H., & Lee, H. (2000). A data abstraction approach for query relaxation. *Information and Software Technology*, *42*(6), 407–418. doi:10.1016/S0950-5849(99)00100-7

Hunter, D. (2000). *Beginning XML*. Wrox Press Ltd.

Jiaheng, L. (2006). *Efficient processing of XML TWIG pattern matching*. National University of Singapore.

Kay, M. (2004). *XPath 2.0 programmers reference*. Canada: Wiley Publishing, Inc.

Manning, C. D., Raghavan, P., & Schütze, H. (2008). *Introduction to information retrieval*. Cambridge University Press.

McLaughlin, B., & Edelson, J. (2006). *Java and XML* (3rd ed.). O'Reilly.

Ng, W., Lam, W.-Y., & Cheng, J. (2006). Comparative analysis of XML compression technologies. *World Wide Web: Internet and Web Information Systems*, *9*, 5–33.

Norbert, F., & Kai, G. (2004). XIRQL: An XML query language based on information retrieval concepts. *ACM Transactions on Information Systems*, *22*(2), 313–356.

Sakr, S. (2009). XML compression techniques: A survey and comparison. *Journal of Computer and System Sciences*, *75*(5), 303–322. doi:10.1016/j.jcss.2009.01.004

Sanz, I. (2007). *Flexible technique for heterogeneous XML data retrieval*. Universitat Jaume.

Sigurbjornsson, B., & Trotman, A. (2003). *Queries: INEX 2003 working group report.* Paper presented at the 2nd Workshop of the Initiative for the Evaluation of XML Retrieval (INEX).

Stamatina, B., Mounia, L., Anastasios, T., & Theodora, T. (2006). *User expectations from XML element retrieval.* Paper presented at the 29th Annual International ACM SIGIR Conference on Research and Development in Information Retrieval.

Trotman, A., & Sigurbjornsson, B. (2005). *Narrowed extended XPath I (NEXI).* Paper presented at the Advances in XML Information Retrieval, Berlin.

Violleau, T. (2001). *Java technology and XML.* Retrieved October 1, 2010, from http://java.sun.com/developer/technicalArticles/xml/JavaTechandXML/

Williams, I. (2009). *Beginning XSLT and XPath: Transforming XML documents and data.* Wrox Press.

Zhang, Q., & Kankanhalli, M. S. (2003). *Semantic video annotation and vague query.* Paper presented at the 9th International Conference on Multimedia Modeling (MMM 2003)

Zhao, F., & Ma, Z. M. (2009). *Vague query based on vague relational model.* Paper presented at the AISC.

Chapter 9
State of the Art Technology in Compressing and Querying XML Documents

Badya Al-Hamadani
University of Huddersfield, UK

Joan Lu
University of Huddersfield, UK

ABSTRACT

Since this research consists of two main parts, the XML compressor and the vague query processor, this chapter discusses the main XML compression techniques in its first part. It will highlight the advantages and disadvantages of these techniques and discusses the differences between them. The second part of this chapter will focus on the vague query processors used to retrieve information from XML documents.

1.1 XML COMPRESSION TECHNIQUES

Recently, large numbers of XML compression techniques have been proposed. Each of which has different characteristics. This section discusses the differences between these compressors and their main features.

XML compressors can be classified into two classes either to be *XML-blind* or *XML-conscious* compressors. XML-blind or general purpose

compressors deal with the XML document as a traditional text document ignoring its structure and apply the general purpose text compression techniques to compress them. These techniques can be classified into two main classes (Salomon, 2007), either to be statistical or dictionary based compressors (Augeri et al., 2007; Augeri, 2008). The statistical or the arithmetic compressors represent each string of characters using a fixed number of bits per character. PPM, CACM3, and PAQ are examples of this kind of compressors (Cleary and Witten, 1984; Moffat., 1990; Alistair et al., 1998). On the other hand, dictionary compres-

DOI: 10.4018/978-1-4666-1975-3.ch009

sion techniques substitute each string in the input by its reference in a dictionary maintained by the encoder. WinZip, GZIP, and BZIP2 are examples of this compression class (WinZip, 1990; GZip, 1992; BZip2, 1996).

On the other hand, XML-conscious compressors try to utilize the structural behaviour of XML documents in order to achieve better compression ratio and less time in comparative with the XML-blind type. Table 1 sets the main differences between the two aforementioned compressors types.

The main theory of data compression, which described in (Shannon, 1948), is the formulation of the entropy rate *(H)* which indicates the limit to lossless data compression. The value of *(H)* depends on the probability of each symbol in the information source. The most popular entropy value is (Shannon, 1948):

$$H = \sum_{i=1}^{n} P_i log \frac{1}{P_i} \qquad (1)$$

where, P_i is the probability of the symbol a_i.

In this paper, Shannon proved that the compression ration cannot exceed the value of *(aH)*, where *(a)* is the number of symbols in the source.

Since XML are heterogeneous data, the theory of XML compressors is to separate the data from the structure, separate the data into containers according to the type of the data, and apply a general purpose compressor for each container. This pro-

cess can lead to produce an optimal compressor over heterogeneous data. (Liefke and Suciu, 2000) developed the entropy value for XML compression to be (Liefke and Suciu, 2000):

$$H = \frac{1}{2}\left(H_0 + p_1 H_1 + ... + p_k H_k\right) \qquad (2)$$

where, $H_0, H_1, ..., H_k$ are the entropies for the sources, and $p_1, p_2, ..., p_k$ are the probabilities of these sources.

XML-conscious compressors can be classified according to their ability to querying the compressed documents into two main subclasses; these are queriable and non-queriable compressors. While the queriable compressors have the ability to retrieve information from the compressed XML document without the need to completely decompress the document, the non-queriable XML compressors are used to compress the XML documents for archival purposes only and they achieved better compression ratio than the queriable compressors.

1.1.1 Queriable XML Compressors

The main goal of this type of compressors is to provide the ability to the compressed version of the XML document to be queried without complete decompression them. The compression ratio for

Table 1. The main differences between XML-conscious and XML-blind compressors

XML-conscious compressors	XML-blind compressors
Information about XML documents is usually available in schema which can be optimized by XML-conscious compressors to get better compression.	Cannot take advantage of the schema to get useful information about the file.
They utilize the structure of XML document and the type of the data inside.	They do not take in consideration the entire file structure or data types.
Some of them abridge the original XML tree in a summary or compact tree for better ratio.	They cannot exploit redundancies in the XML tree structure.
Most of them are powerful in compressing small or large files.	They do not efficiently compress small files that can be used in transactions for e-business. (Hung, 2009)

these compression techniques is lower than the blind-XML or the non-queriable techniques.

However, these techniques are important when dealing with resource-limited applications and mobiles. Some of these techniques are homomorphic compressors, which mean that the compressed file is a semi-structured one. In the next section, a brief description of some of these techniques will be given, and Table 2 explains their main limitations.

The first queriable compressor is *XGrind* by (Tolani and Haritsa, 2000). This technique replaces the elements and attribute names with the letters *"T"* and *"A"* respectively, followed by a unique identifier which represents the substituted element or attribute name. Moreover, it replaces the end tags with *"/"* sign. The data part of the document is encoded using Huffman encoding. For the purpose of querying the compressed document, XGrind's query processor finds the simple path to check whether it satisfies the path in the given query. The main drawback with XGrind is that while it has the ability to process exact-match and prefix-match queries on the compressed documents, a whole range of or

partial-match queries require partial decompression to be handled.

In order to solve *XGrind's* partial decompression problem, *Xpress* (Min et al., 2003) uses the *reverse arithmetic encoding* method to encode the label paths of the XML document as a distinct interval in [0.0, 1.0). Using the relationships between these intervals will allow for the ability to evaluate path expressions more efficiently on the compressed XML document. Furthermore, by using this method, *XPress* uses path-by-path matching instead of element-by-element matching that has been used in *XGrind*. To encode the data part of the XML document, *XPress* uses different compression techniques depending on the type of the data and without the need to the human interference. (Min et al., 2009)

Because *XGrind* and *Xpress* are homomorphic, the relationship between the size of the compressed document and the size of the original one is linear. To solve this problem (Cheng and NG, 2004) proposed a new technique (*XQzip*) that depends on extracting the *Structure Index Tree (SIT)* from the tree structure of the original document. The SIT depth is non-linear to the structure tree

Table 2. The main limitations of some queriable XML compressors

Compression technique	Limitations
XGrind	o Requires partial decompression to handle range and partial-match queries. o Lower compression ratio comparative with other compressors.
XPress	o Limited experimented data corpus to depth 5 and 6 only and large documents (>12MB). o Handles only exact-match, partial-match, and range queries.
XQzip	o Ignoring IPs and comments from being compressed. o Critical in choosing the appropriate block size to balance between the good compression ratio and efficient query processing. o The need for partial decompression to handle string matching queries.
XQueC	o Using too many structures with their pointers which yield to huge space overhead. o Long compression and decompression time.
XSAQCT	o Lossless compressor since it does not taking into consideration the order of the attributes in an element. o Queries only the exact match queries.
SXSI	o Designed to increase the querying speed. o The compression ratio has not been tested. o Supports only navigational queries and string matching predicates.

which makes this technique accomplishes higher compression ratio and faster query evaluation.

Instead of using (SIT), *XQueC* (Arion et al., 2007) uses the *structure summary tree* in order to efficiently stores the XML documents. The space needed to store the structure summary (*SS*) is (Arion et al., 2007):

$$CSaux = \sum_{n \in SS} \left(\left| tag(n) \right| + \log_2 \left(\left| SS \right| \right) \right) \qquad (3)$$

This represents the summation of the space needed to store a tag node plus the space needed to store all its successive nodes. Furthermore, instead of using hash table to store the tags and attribute names, *XQueC* used the *structural identifiers*, which has been used in some querying techniques (Al-Khalif A et al., 2002; Grust, 2002; Halverson et al., 2003; Paparizos et al., 2003) in order to uniquely identify a node in the XML tree. This technique considered to be the first one that uses XQuery as a query language.

In their work, (Müldner et al., 2009) created an annotation tree to succinctly store the structure of the XML document and use the containers to store the data part of the document. Their compressor, named *XSAQCT*, has two versions; the first was dependent on the XML Schema and the second was schema-free. They showed that the first version is better than the second from the standpoint of compression ratio even though it was slower.

Finally, (Arroyuelo et al., 2010) proved in their proposed *SXSI* compressor that the XPath queries can be performed better when using an indexing technique to compress the XML document. This technique is based on producing a labelled tree from the XML Tree structure and then indexing this tree into a bit array and compressing the data part of the document using a general back-end compressor. Although the compression ratio of SXSI is not calculated, the querying time and the retrieving quality are better than traditional retrieving techniques.

Table 3 shows the main differences between the various compression techniques mentioned above. It is clear that the compression ratio of all XML-conscious compressors is better than traditional blind-compressors and the compression ratios of the queriable compressors are still less than those of non-queriable techniques.

Figure 1 demonstrates the distribution of the compression techniques over the years, where NQC and QC refer to the non-queriable and queriable compressors respectively. It shows that the years 2006 and 2007 witnessed an increasing amount of compression for both queriable and non-queriable techniques. The overwhelming rise in the number of queriable-XML compressions in the years 2008 and 2009 reflects the importance of this type of compressors.

1.2 PROCESSING VAGUE QUERIES TECHNIQUES

In order to elevate the flexibility of querying XML documents, many researchers have produced varied approaches to meet that need.

In their work (Damiani and Tanca, 2000) proposed a technique to solve what they called "blind queries" which refers to the queries submitted with the absence of XML schema. This technique first transforms the XML document into a labelled graph and provides each node a number which represent the importance of this node in the XML document. The graph then is expanded to perform a fuzzy graph. To process the vague queries, it creates a graph for the query and performed a similarity match between the two graphs.

According to the importance of approximate retrieval, (Schlieder, 2001) proposed a query language named *approXQL* since the existing XML query languages have the ability to answer queries according to exact matching only. This language is designed to answer vague queries on data-centric XML documents by encoding them into a labelled tree. It uses three pointers to encode

Table 3. A comparison of different compression techniques

Compression technique	XML-Conscious	Schema dependant	queriable	Compression technique	Back-end compressor	Average compression ratio
WinZip (WinZip, 1990)	No	No	No	Reducing algorithm+ AES encryption	-	0.48
BZip2 (BZip2, 1996)	No	No	No	Burrows-Wheeler+ Huffman	-	0.24
GZip (GZip, 1992)	No	No	No	LZ77+ Huffman	-	0.36
XMill (Liefke and Suciu, 2000)	Yes	No	No	Dictionary-based	Gzip, Bzip2, PPM	0.55
Millau (Girardot and Sundaresan, 2000)	Yes	Yes	No	Dictionary-based	GZip, deflate	0.58
xmlppm (Cheney, 2001)	Yes	No	No	Statistical models	PPM	0.57
dtdppm (Cheney, 2005)	Yes	Yes	No	Statistical models	PPM	0.58
XWRT (Skibinski et al., 2007)	Yes	No	No	Dictionary-based	Gzip, LZMA, PPM	0.54
RNGzip (League and Eng, 2007)	Yes	Yes	No	Deterministic automaton Tree	Gzip	0.58
LXC (Bonifati et al., 2009)	Yes	No	No	words abbreviation	-	0.59
XGrind (Tolani and Haritsa, 2000)	Yes	No	Yes	Dictionary-based	Huffman	0.57
Xpress (Min et al., 2003)	Yes	No	Yes	Dictionary-based	Reverse encoding	0.57
XQZip (Cheng and NG, 2004)	Yes	No	Yes	Dictionary-based	Gzip	0.66
XQueC (Arion et al., 2007)	Yes	No	Yes	Binary encoding	Depending on the type of data	0.68
XSAQCT (Müldner et al., 2009)	Yes	Yes	Yes	Tree-size elimination	Bzip2, gzip, PAQ8	0.80
SXSI (Arroyuelo et al., 2010)	Yes	No	Yes	FM indexing	BWT	n/t

each node of the document's tree by associating it with its pre-order number, the number of its ancestors, and the pre-order number of its most right leaf. To answer vague queries, it makes useful node transformation on them which are insertion, deletion and renaming. Each transformation is associated with its cost and the results that require less transformation cost are the most relevant once.

Figure 1. The distribution of the compression techniques over the years

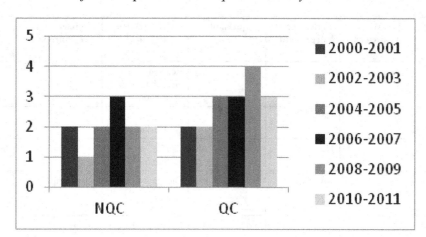

Instead of expanding a query language, (Amir-Yahya et al., 2002) proposed a new algorithm that depends on converting the XML document and the user's query into a tree-like structure and perform some relaxation process on the latest tree by deleting, inserting and renaming the nodes in that tree to be matched with the original XML document. Each of these processes attached with a score in order to compute the Top-k relevant answers. This technique solves the problem of generating large amount of sub-queries when using the query re-writing algorithm which has been used in *approXQL*. In this paper, the authors debate applying the traditional IR techniques to retrieve approximate answers and they prove that those techniques are not sufficient enough when dealing with XML documents, however, converting the document to a tree-like structure and applying approximate matching on it is more appropriate.

In 2004, *FleXPath* technique has been proposed by (Amer-Yahia et al., 2004). *FleXPath* depends on merging the XPath query language that has exact matching with full text search that has approximate matching. First, the query is converted to a tree and used it as a template to find the approximate matches within the XML document. The query relaxation process used by *FleXPath* depends on deleting a structural predicate if at least one of its nodes does not belong to the docu-

ment structure and the deletion process will not affect the tree structure of the query. Furthermore, this technique performs more relaxation such as *contains-relaxation* by replacing the parameter of the *contains()* function with its ancestor, *tag-relaxation* by replacing a tag with its super tag, *value-relaxation,* and *type-relaxation.*

Instead of relaxing the query, (Lalmas and Rolleke, 2004) transforms the query to a conjunction query by adding an "OR" between the query's path and its predicate and changes each "AND" in the query with an "OR" to increase the recall precision. In this technique the XML document passes into two probabilistic transformation processes. In the first pass, each element, attribute name, attribute value and element value is attached with a probability value to indicate the importance of this element in the whole document using probabilistic object-oriented logic. The output from the first pass is transformed into probabilistic relational algebra expressions. This technique changes the XML document into a new one which is much bigger than the original.

In the same year, (Mandreoli et al., 2004) proposed a new approach for answering approximate queries to retrieve all the relevant parts of the XML document not only the exact matching. This approach finds the syntactic similarity between the XML Schema and the user's query, written in XQuery query language, and rewrites the query to match this Schema. It works with the XML Schema instead of working with the XML document directly in order to retrieve relative information from a repository of documents. Although this technique has the ability to retrieve 90% of the relevant information, it shows conflicts when the root node of the different schemas are the same as the root node in the query.

In 2006 (Li et al., 2006) proposed *FLUX* to process only range queries in their fuzzy appearance. It uses B+-tree in order to identify the relevant leaf nodes to the given user's query. The path from the root to the relevant leaves is used as signatures to be matched with the path in the query to determine their relevancy. Using the Bloom filter, *FLUX* converts the path in the query and the path signatures into hash tables and compare between them to extract the most relevant paths. The implementation process for *FLUX* is limited only to two XML documents and the 100 tested queries include only the year and date range queries with random selections. Their test explains that *FLUX* perform good retrieval with higher speed that other relative techniques.

While *FLUX* tried to process fuzzy range queries, *TIJAH* (Mihajlovic et al., 2006) tried to process only two vague cases in NEXI query language. This technique finds the list of synonyms

for each element name in the user's query using WordNet "A Lexical Database for the English Language", and it uses these synonyms as new keywords to be searched in the XML document by rewriting the query using the new elements. Furthermore, this technique generalizes the path in the query in order to look for the elements in the whole XML tree.

Depending on the aforementioned *FleXPath* approach, (Campi et al., 2009) proposed a new technique called *FuzzyXPath* that expands XPath query language to include fuzzy cases. The main purpose of this work was to determine the degree of similarity between two trees by providing a weight to each node to determine its importance within the document. The weight is calculated depending on the level of the node within the XML document and the number of its children. *FuzzyXPath* adds new functions to the list of available functions in XPath such as *SIMILAR* to find the similarity between the given node and the nodes in the document, and *CLOSE* to find the similarity between the given value and the data in the document. It provides more flexibility in path structure by adding *NEAR* and *BELOW* functions.

In our previous work (Al-Hamadani et al., 2009) we proposed a new technique to process vague queries by decomposing it into CAS and CO queries and then apply the normal retrieval

Table 4. Query types with the compression techniques process each

Compression techniques/ query types	Simple queries (SQ)	Criteria queries (CQ)	Conjunctive queries (JQ)	Range queries (RQ)	Vague queries (VQ)
XGrind	☑	☑*	☑*	☑*	✖
Xpress	☑	☑	☑*	☑*	✖
XQZip	☑	☑	☑	☑*	✖
XQueC	☑	☑	☑	☑	✖
XSAQCT	☑	☑	✖	✖	✖
SXSI	☑	☑	☑	✖	✖

*Partial decompression required

process for each part. The results from the retrieval process are combined again to obtain the final results. The technique applied on health care record and it shows good retrieval precision.

(Fredrick and Dr.G.Radhamani, 2009) proposed a framework to extend XQuery language to include fuzzy queries. They tried to generalize the *FLWOR* to include natural language words, such as good, bad, etc. to get more precise results. It depends on the fuzzy-set theory by (Zadeh, 1965) to transfer each fuzzy word to a range of values and then retrieve the most relevant parts from the document.

1.3 PROBLEM IDENTIFICATION

The previous sections list several compression techniques that have the ability to process different kinds of queries. Table 4 lists all the discussed queriable compression techniques and shows the types of queries that can be processed by each technique. Some of the compressors require partial decompression to the compressed XML document in order to process some of these queries.

It is clear that the entire existing compressors do not have the ability to process vague queries since this type of queries is complex and needs intensive research to resolve it.

For this reason, the research in this thesis is focused on how to handle different types of vague queries in retrieving information from compressed XML documents.

1.4 SUMMARY

This chapter illustrated the main types of general purpose compressors and focused on XML compression techniques which rely on two types, either as queriable or non-queriable techniques. Since this research is dealing with a queriable compressor, this chapter concentrated on the

existing techniques, listed their main features and the differences between them and the types of queries in the process. Finally, the chapter also demonstrated different techniques that have the ability to process vague queries and the key differences between them.XML

REFERENCES

Al-Hamadani, B. T., Alwan, R. F., Lu, J., & Yip, J. (2009). *Vague content and structure (VCAS) retrieval for XML electronic healthcare records (EHR)*. Paper presented at the 2009 International Conference on Internet Computing, USA.

Al-Khalif, A. S., Jagadish, H., Patel, J., Wu, Y., Koudas, N., & Srivastava, D. (2002). *Structural joins: A primitive for efficient XML query pattern matching*. Paper presented at the 8th International Conference on Data Engineering.

Alistair, M., Radford, M. N., & Ian, H. W. (1998). Arithmetic coding revisited. *ACM Transactions on Information Systems*, *16*(3), 256–294. doi:10.1145/290159.290162

Amer-Yahia, S., Lakshmanan, L. V. S., & Pandit, S. (2004). *FleXPath: Flexible structure and fulltext querying for XML*. Paper presented at the ACM, SIGMOD, Paris, France.

Amir-Yahya, S., Cho, S., & Srivatava, D. (2002). *Tree pattern relaxation*. Paper presented at the EDBT 8th International Conference on Extending Database Technology. Retrieved from http://citeseerx.ist.psu.edu/viewdoc/summary?doi=10.1.1.8.4952

Arion, A., Bonifati, A., Manolescu, I., & Pugliese, Λ. (2007). XQuеC: A query-conscious compressed XML database. *ACM Transactions on Internet Technology*, *7*(2), 10. doi:10.1145/1239971.1239974

Arroyuelo, D., Claude, F., Maneth, S., M̈akinen, V., Navarro, G., Nguyen, K., et al. (2010). *Fast in-memory XPath search using compressed indexes.* Paper presented at the IEEE Twenty-Sixth International Conference on Data Engineering (ICDE 2010), California, USA.

Augeri, C. (2008). *On some results in unmanned aerial vehicle swarms. Unpublished Ph.D.* San Diego, CA, USA: Air Force Institute of Technology.

Augeri, C. J., Bulutoglu, D. A., Mullins, B. E., Baldwin, R. O., & Leemon, C. Baird, I. (2007). *An analysis of XML compression efficiency.* Paper presented at the 2007 Workshop on Experimental Computer Science.

Bonifati, A., Lorusso, M., & Sileo, D. (2009). XML lossy text compression: A preliminary study. *Proceedings of the 6ᵗʰ XML Database Symposium on Database and XML Technologies* (pp. 106-113).

BZip2. (1996). Retrieved October 10, 2009, from http://www.bzip.org/

Campi, A., Damiani, E., Guinea, S., Marrara, S., Pasi, G., & Spoletini, P. (2009). A fuzzy extension of the XPath query language. *Journal of Intelligent Information Systems, 33*(3), 285–305. doi:10.1007/s10844-008-0066-3

Cheney, J. (2001). *Compressing XML with multiplexed hierarchical models.* Paper presented at the IEEE Data Compression Conference (DCC 2001).

Cheney, J. (2005). *An empirical evaluation of simple DTD conscious compression techniques.* Paper presented at the Eighth International Workshop on the Web and Databases (WebDB 2005).

Cheng, J., & Ng, W. (2004). *XQZip: Querying compressed XML using structural indexing.* Paper presented at the International Conference on Extending Data Base Technology (EDBT).

Cleary, J., & Witten, I. (1984). Data compression using adaptive coding and partial string matching. *IEEE Transactions on Communications, 32*(4), 396–402. doi:10.1109/TCOM.1984.1096090

Damiani, E., & Tanca, L. (2000). *Blind queries to XML data.* Paper presented at the 11th International Conference on Database and Expert Systems Applications.

Fredrick, E. J. T., & Radhamani, G. (2009). Fuzzy logic based XQuery operations for native XML database systems. *International Journal of Database Theory and Application, 2*(3).

Girardot, M., & Sundaresan, N. (2000). Millau: An encoding format for efficient representation and exchange of XML over the Web. *Computer Networks, 33*(1-6), 747-765.

Grust, T. (2002). *Accelerating XPath location steps.* Paper presented at the ACM SIGMOD International Conference on Management of Data.

GZip. (1992). Retrieved October 12, 2009, from http://www.gzip.org/

Halverson, A., Burger, J., Galanis, L., Kini, A., Krishnamurthy, R., Rao, A., et al. (2003). *Mixed mode XML query processing.* Paper presented at the 29th International Conference on Very Large Data Bases.

Hung, P. C. K. (2009). *Services and business computing solution with XML.* Hershey, PA: IGI Global. doi:10.4018/978-1-60566-330-2

Lalmas, M., & Rolleke, T. (2004). Modelling vague content and structure querying in XML retrieval with a probabilistic object-relational framework. *Proceedings of the 6th International Conference on Flexible Query Answering Systems, LNCS 3055.* Springer.

Li, H.-G., Aghili, S. A., Agrawal, D., & Abbadi, A. E. (2006). *FLUX: Fuzzy content and structure matching of XML range queries.* Paper presented at WWW 2006, Edinburgh, Scotland.

Liefke, H., & Suciu, D. (2000). *XMill: An efficient compressor for XML data.* Paper presented at the ACM.

Mandreoli, F., Martoglia, R., & Tiberio, P. (2004). *Approximate query answering for a heterogeneous XML document base.* Paper presented at the 5th International Conference on Web Information Systems Engineering, Brisbane, Australia.

Mihajlovic, V., Hiemstra, D., & Blok, H. E. (2006). Vague element selection and query rewriting for XML retrieval. *Proceedings of the 6th Dutch-Belgian Information Retrieval Workshop* (DIR 2006).

Min, J.-K., Park, M.-J., & Chung, C.-W. (2003). *XPRESS: A queriable compression for XML data.* Paper presented at the 2003 ACM SIGMOD International Conference on Management of Data.

Moffat, A. (1990). Implementing the PPM data compression scheme. *IEEE Transactions on Communications, 38*(11), 1917–1921. doi:10.1109/26.61469

Müldner, T., Fry, C., Miziołek, J. K., & Durno, S. (2009). *XSAQCT: XML queryable compressor.* Paper presented at the Balisage: The Markup Conference 2009.

Paparizos, S., Al-Khalifa, S., Chapman, A., & Jagadish, H. V., Lakshmanan, L. V. S., Nierman, A., et al. (2003). *TIMBER: A native system for querying XML.* Paper presented at the ACM SIGMOD International Conference on Management of Data.

Salomon, D. (2007). *Data compression: The complete reference* (4th ed.). Springer.

Schlieder, T. (2001). *Similarity search in XML data using cost-based query transformations.* Paper presented at ACM SIGMOD WebDB.

Shannon, C. E. (1948). A mathematical theory of communication. *The Bell System Technical Journal, 27*, 379–423.

Tolani, P. M., & Haritsa, J. R. (2000). *XGRIND: A query-friendly XML compressor.* Paper presented at the IEEE 18th International Conference on Data Engineering.

WinZip. (1990). Retrieved November 15, 2009, http://www.winzip.com/

Zadeh, L. A. (1965). Fuzzy sets. *Information and Control, 8*, 338–353. doi:10.1016/S0019-9958(65)90241-X

Chapter 10
Compressing and Vague Querying (XCVQ) Design

Badya Al-Hamadani
University of Huddersfield, UK

Joan Lu
University of Huddersfield, UK

ABSTRACT

As shown in the literature review from the previous chapter, there are a good number of studies in the field of compressing XML documents and querying the compressed version without the need to fully decompress. However, vague queries, which are one of the most important query types, have been processed to retrieve information from raw XML documents and not from compressed ones. Depending on the SDM, the design of the complete system should be made, followed by its implementation which can be seen in Appendix B in chapter 12. This chapter illustrates the design architecture of the XCVQ (an XML Compressing and Vague Querying) which has the ability to compress the XML documents and use the compressed files in order to retrieve information according to vague queries. It starts with the main architecture of the system followed by the design of each of its parts, namely XCVQ's compressor, decompressor, and the query processor.

1.1 SYSTEM ARCHITECTURE

As illustrated in Figure 1, the *XCVQ* system consists of two main stages. The first is designing a new XML compression technique which converts the normal XML documents to a compressed version. The second is designing a retrieving technique that processes the XPath vague queries in order to retrieve the relevant information from the compressed document accordingly.

The design of the *XCVQ* does not rely on the XML Schema or the DTD of the document. This is due to several reasons:

DOI: 10.4018/978-1-4666-1975-3.ch010

Figure 1. Preliminary architecture of XCVQ

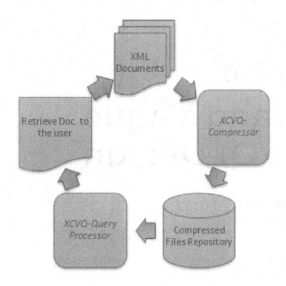

1. The main purpose of designing *XCVQ* is to process vague queries which are usually written, as illustrated in a previous section, by inexperienced users who may not want to have another technology linked with their documents.
2. Even if the schema for a document exists, it could not have been accessible to the user.
3. Since the main purpose of any compressor is to reduce the storage memory and the transition bandwidth, *XCVQ* saves the amount of memory required to store the schema.

As illustrated in the design of the *XCVQ*, all the compressed XML documents are stored in a repository which is going to be used in the retrieving process. To the best of our knowledge, *XCVQ* may well be considered to be the first retrieving technique that has the ability to retrieve information from more than one XML document without requiring the pre-specification of the documents needed to be retrieved and without dependence on the document's schema. This approach helps users retrieve more relative information no matter which documents contain this information.

The complete design of the XCVQ is illustrated in Figure 2.

The following sections demonstrate the design of each part of the system starting with *XCVQ-Compressor (XCVQ-C)*, passing by *XCVQ-Decompressor (XCVQ-D)*, and ending with *XCVQ-Query Processor (XCVQ-QP)*.

1.2 XCVQ-C DESIGN

XCVQ-C compressor takes an XML document as the input and creates the compressed version from this document by passing through several steps. An example in Figure 3 from (W3Schools.com, 2006b) will be used in the following sections in order to simplify the exact process of each step.

1.2.1 Creating the Structured-Tree and its Abridgment

As illustrated in Figure 2, the first step in compressing the XML document is to create the structured-tree using the SAX parser. This parser scans the XML documents only once and it cached several events such as start-document, start-element, end-element, and end-document. Section 0 contains more details about this parser and its advantages. During this parsing process the complete *path-dictionary* was created and separates the data part of the XML document from its structure to be abridged to the structured-tree. The structured-tree for the running example is shown in Figure 4. The data under each root-leaf path are stored in containers linked to that path.

Each data item is accompanied with a number ID_{order} that represents the order of this item within the document (the number between the brackets in Figure 4). ID_{order} counts each start element, data value, attribute name, attribute value and end element. According to this number, each node is uniquely identified for the purposes of decompression process and in the querying process. Previous XML compressors used two

Figure 2. The complete design of XCVQ

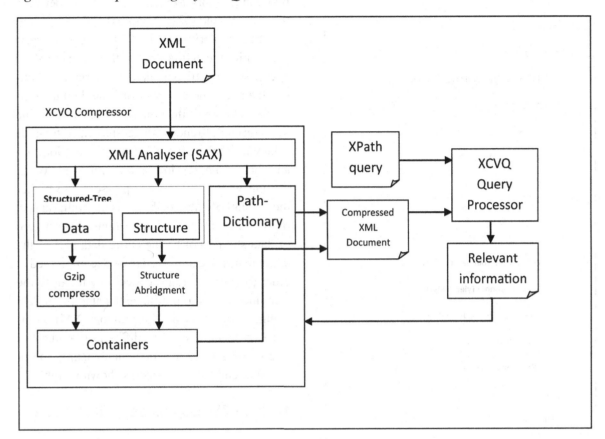

numbers for each node in the structured-tree to identify this node uniquely. These numbers represented by the pre-order and post-order traversal of that node $[ID_{pre}, ID_{post}]$ (Cheng and NG, 2004; Arion et al., 2007; Arroyuelo et al., 2010) which required:

$$S_{SIT} = 2(N * \log_2 N) \qquad (1)$$

where S_{SIT} represents the number of bits needed to store the structured-tree that contains N nodes. While the number of bits required to store the same structured-tree in *XCVQ-C* is shown in Equation (6).

$$S_{SIT} = (N * \log_2 N) \qquad (2)$$

Since *XCVQ-C* uses only one number to store a node, the number of bits required to store a single node is $\log_2 N$. In this stage *XCVQ-C* saves half the number of bits required to store the structured-tree.

1.2.2 Creating the Containers

XCVQ-C creates the containers from the structured tree, as seen in Figure 6. First each node is replaced with a number that represents the entry of that node's name in the *path-dictionary*. The structured-tree is traversed to create the containers. Each container has an index and data set. The path from the root to a leaf is used as index to the container and all the data under that path are the data set to this container.

Figure 3. An XML example

```
<CATALOG>

    <CD no="1">

        <TITLE>Empire Burlesque</TITLE>

        <ARTIST>Bob Dylan</ARTIST>

        <COUNTRY>USA</COUNTRY>

        <PRICE>10.90</PRICE>

        <YEAR>1985</YEAR>

    </CD>

    <CD no="2">

        <TITLE>Hide your heart</TITLE>

        <ARTIST>Bonnie Tyler</ARTIST>

        <COUNTRY>UK</COUNTRY>

        <PRICE>9.90</PRICE>

        <YEAR>1988</YEAR>

    </CD>

    <CD no="3">

        <TITLE>Romanza</TITLE>

        <ARTIST>Andrea Bocelli</ARTIST>

        <COUNTRY>EU</COUNTRY>

        <PRICE>10.80</PRICE>

        <YEAR>1996</YEAR>
```

For the running example, the *path-dictionary* and the containers are illustrated as in Figure 5, (a) and (b) respectively.

1.2.3 Compressing the Containers

After preparing all the containers and replacing the element's names in the containers with their entry in the *pathDictionary*, now the contents of the containers should be compressed using a back-end compressor. To do this, *XCVQ-C* uses

two compressors to make comparison between them, LZW and GZIP compressors.

The granularity used by *XCVQ-C* is container/ path, which means that after all the data parts of the document are settled in their appropriate containers, the back-end compressor is applied to compress each one of the containers separately. The decision made to choose this granularity is towards achieving a balance between the compression ratio and the decompression process required. When dealing with back-end compressors, the higher the amount of data, the better is the compression ratio achieved. At the same time, this amount of data should not be the entire data part of the document, since they need to be decompressed in order to answer queries concerning them, so the technique needs to minimize the amount of data being decompressed. The previous XML compression techniques used different granularities to compress the XML documents using one of the back-end compressors, as shown in Table 1.

1.2.3.1 LZW Compression Technique

This is one of the dictionary-based lossless compressors which developed in 1984 from LZ78 by Lempel, Ziv and Welch (Salomon, 2007). It has been used in UNIX as a program compressor in 1986 and it is still being used by GIF, TIFF and PDF files to compress images (Murray and Van-Ryper, 1996). The tokens in LZW are pointers to their entries in the dictionary which starts with the first 256 positions occupied by the first 256 ASCII characters before any other entry.

Although it performs good compression ratio it suffers from problems. All the pointers to the dictionary should be larger than 8-bit since the first 256 entries are occupied from the beginning. This makes these pointers to be at least 3-bytes to accommodate all the entries in a document. Moreover, this technique is considered to be slow since its progress is one character at a time.

Figure 4. The structured-tree for the example in Figure 3

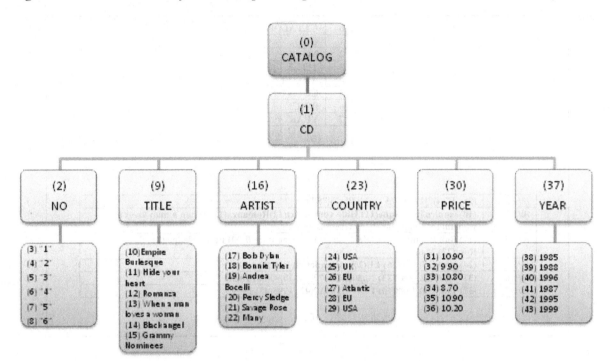

1.2.3.2 Gzip Compression Technique

This is another example of dictionary-based lossless compression software which is based on *Deflate* compression algorithm. This software used by many applications such as HTTP protocol, the PNG (Portable Network Graphics), PNG images, and PDF files. The *Deflate* algorithm was designed in 2003 by combining the LZ77 and

Huffman algorithms (PKWare, 2003; Salomon, 2007). *Deflate* uses different block sizes in order to compress the input data. The size of the blocks is determined according to the available memory and the size of the data. This algorithm provides three modes for each block, (1) No compression when the file is already compressed or it is random; (2) A fast mode that uses two fixed code tables in the encoder and they will not been written in the compressed file; and (3) A powerful mode that uses several code tables generated by the encoder and they should be written in the compressed file.

1.3 XCVQ-C ALGORITHMS AND THEIR CORRECTNESS

Since putting the complete compressing process in one algorithm could not be very clear, the designed algorithm is separated into three sub-algorithms. The separation process is made depending on the main parts of the XML document:

Table 1. Compression granularity comparison

XML compression technique	Compression granules
XGrind	Value/tag
XPress	Value/path
XQzip	Blocks
XQueC	Container item/tag
XSAQCT	Container/tree-structure
SXSI	-
XCVQ	Container/path

Figure 5. Creating containers process: (a) the path-Dictionary; (b) the container

0	CATALOG
1	CD
2	NO
3	TITLE
4	ARTIST
5	COUNTRY
6	PRICE
7	YEAR

(a)

/0/1/@2	(3) "1"(4) "2" (5) "3" (6) "4" (7) "5" (8) "6"
/0/1/3	(10)Empire Burlesque(11) Hide your heart(12)Romanza(13) When a man loves a woman(14) Black angel(15) Grammy Nominees
/0/1/4	(17) Bob Dylan(18) Bonnie Tyler(19) Andrea Bocelli(20) Percy Sledge (21) Savage Rose(22) Many
/0/1/5	(24) USA(25) UK(26) EU(27) Atlantic(28) EU(29) USA
/0/1/6	(31) 10.90(32) 9.90(33) 10.80(34) 8.70(35) 10.90(36) 10.20
/0/1/7	(38) 1985(39) 1988(40) 1996(41) 1987(42) 1995(43) 1999

(b)

Figure 6. (startElement) algorithm

```
1.      Algorithm startElement(String eName, String data)
2.      let pathDictionary=[i₀, i₁, ..., iₙ]
3.      let structured-Tree=[j₀, j₁, ..., jₘ]
4.      let pathStack=[kₚ, kₚ₋₁, ..., k₀]
5.      let IDOrder= the current order
6.      if (eName ∉ pathDictionary)
7.          pathDictionary=[i₀, i₁, ..., iₙ] ∪ eNameₙ₊₁
8.          Q"= n+1
9.      else
10.         Q"= q where iq =eName
11.     pathStack=[kₚ, kₚ₋₁, ..., k₀] ∪ [Q"ₚ₊₁]
12.     currentPath ← k₀ + k₁ + ...+ kₚ
13.     if (currentPath ⊄ structured-Tree)
14.         Add currentPath to structured-Tree
15.     IDOrder++
16.     if (data is not empty)
17.         Add (IDOrder,data) to the leaf node of [j₀, j₁,
            ..., jₘ]
18.     End.
```

start-element or attribute name, end-element, data, and end-document. This section illustrates the design of the algorithms in each of the previous XML parts and the formal correctness proof of each one of them. The process of correctness proof depends on specifying the set of preconditions $P:\{P_1, P_2, ..., P_n\}$ and the postconditions $Q:\{Q_1, Q_2, ..., Q_n\}$ and the algorithm A such that $P \xrightarrow{A} Q$ [ref]. The algorithm is considered to be true is it terminates and all the postconditions are true upon completion.

1.3.1 startElement Algorithm

This algorithm in Figure 6 is processed whenever a start element or an attribute name occurs in the XML document. In this algorithm, each element or attribute name (*eName*) encountered in the XML document must be added to the list of *path-dictionary* if it is not added before (lines 6-8). The index of (*eName*) in the *path-dictionary* is used from now on instead of the element's name itself to be added to the structured-tree (lines 11-14). When there is a value in *data* this means that the algorithm is dealing with an attribute. In this case, the attribute value alongside with its order is added to the leaf of the current path in the *Structured-Tree* (lines 16-17).

To proof the formal correctness of this algorithm, the preconditions and the postconditions should first be specified:

```
P:{ eName=a, data=b are two strings,
pathDictionary=[i₀, i₁, ..., iₙ]=c
represents the current pathDiction-
ary,
structured-Tree=[j₀, j₁, ..., jₘ]=d
represents the current structure-
tree,
pathStack=[kₚ, kₚ₋₁, ..., k₀]=e repre-
sents the current path elements
stored in a stack}
Q: {a ∈ c,
```

```
a ∈ e,
e ∈ d,
In case of attributes, b ∈ d}
Correctness:
{eName=a, data=b, pathDictionary=c,
structured-Tree=d, pathStack=e}
if (eName ∉ pathDictionary)
        {a ∉ c, data=b,
pathDictionary=c, structured-Tree=d,
pathStack=e}
        pathDictionary=[i₀, i₁, ...,
iₙ]∪ eNameₙ₊₁
        Q"= n+1
                {a ∈ c, data=b,
pathDictionary=c, structured-Tree=d,
pathStack=e}
else
        Q"= q where i_q =eName
                {a ∈ c, data=b,
pathDictionary=c, structured-Tree=d,
pathStack=e}
pathStack=[kₚ, kₚ₋₁, ..., k₀] ∪ [Q"ₚ₊₁]
{a ∈ c, data=b, structured-Tree=d, a
∈ e}
currentPath ← k₀ + k₁ + ...+ kₚ
if (currentPath ⊈ structured-Tree)
        Add currentPath to structured-
Tree
        {a ∈ c, data=b, e ∈ d, a ∈
e}
IDOrder++
if (data is not empty)
        Add (IDOrder,data) to the leaf
node of [j₀, j₁,
..., jₘ]
        {a ∈ c, b ∈ d, e ∈ d, a ∈ e}
= Q
```

1.3.2 endElement Algorithm

The algorithm in Figure 7 is processed when the end of an XML element encountered which means that there is a piece of data ready to be inserted in a leaf node of the structured-tree (if that element holds data). The suitable current path can be known from the contents of the *pathStack* and the *data* should be added in the leaf node of that path.

```
P:{ eName=a, data=b are two strings,
pathStack=[k_p, k_{p-1}, ..., k_0]=c repre-
sents the current path elements
stored in a stack,
structured-Tree=[j_0, j_1, ..., j_m]=d
represent the current structured-
tree}
Q: {b ∈ d}
Correctness:
{eName=a, data=b, pathStack=c, struc-
tured-Tree=d }
If data ≠ null
     {eName=a, data=b, pathStack=c,
structured-Tree=d }
     Add (IDOrder,data) to the leaf
node of [k_p, k_{p-1}, ..., k_0]
          { b ∈ d }= Q
```

1.3.3 endDocument Algorithm

When the whole XML document traversed, the algorithm in Figure 8 is processed. First the complete pathDictionary should be added to the output compressed file (line 7). The second step is to create the containers from the structured-tree and fill them with the compressed data (lines 6-10).

```
P:{ pathDictionary=[i_0, i_1, ..., i_n]=a
represent the complete pathDiction-
ary,
structured-Tree=[j_0, j_1, ..., j_m]=b
represent the current structure-tree,
F = ∅ }
Q: {a ∈ F, N Containers ∈ F }
Correctness:
{PathDictionary=a, structured-Tree=b
F=∅ }
Add pathDictionary to F
{a ∈ F, structured-Tree=b }
```

```
For all the N branches in structured-
Tree
     {a ∈ F, structured-Tree=b }
     index= Collect all the nodes
[j_0, j_1, ..., j_k]
     {a ∈ F, structured-Tree=b,
index=path nodes}
data= the contents of the leaf node
for the path [j_0, j_1, ..., j_k]
     data = GZipCompress(data)
          {a ∈ F, structured-
Tree=b, index=path nodes, data is
compressed}
Add a Container(index, data) to F
{a ∈ F, structured-Tree=b, a con-
tainer∈ F}
end
{a ∈ F, structured-Tree=b, N Con-
tainers ∈ F }=Q
```

1.4 XCVQ-D DESIGN

As shown in Figure 9, to decompress the compressed XML file, *XCVQ-D* first applies the back-end decompression technique, either LZW or Gzip, to decompress only the contents of all the containers in order to get the data shown in the running example.

The second step is to reconstruct the XML document from the indexes and the contents of the containers, and the *path-dictionary*. The main operation here is to determine the order of each element, attribute, and data value within the XML document. This order is the ID_{order} which is accompanied with the data in the containers but it should be checked against the number of data items written in the decompressed XML document $\left(D'\right)$ so far. To check the consistency of the order, *XCVQ-D* uses Equation (7) such that:

Definition-1: *If* XCVQ-D *has a piece of data [(σ)d], where σ denotes the ID_{order} accompanied with the data in a container, $\tilde{A}$ is the*

Figure 7. (endElement) algorithm

```
1.    Algorithm endElement(String eName, String data)
2.        let pathStack=[kₚ, kₚ₋₁, ..., k₀]
3.        let structured-Tree=[j₀, j₁, ..., jₘ]
4.        If data ≠ null
5.            Add (IDOrder,data) to the leaf node of [kₚ, kₚ₋₁, ...,
          k₀]
```

ID'_{order} *which denotes the order of the data written so far in* $\left(D'\right)$, *then the new order of D should be calculated by getting the difference between (σ) and the ($\tilde{A}$) taking into consideration the number of the elements and attribute names still not written in* $\left(D'\right)$, *such that:*

$$C_{order} = \sigma - \left(\sigma' + [\mu_P - \mu_C]\right) \qquad (3)$$

where:

μ_P : *The number of elements and attribute names written in* D'.

μ_C : *The number of elements and attribute names in the index of the container having this data.*

Then the value of C_{order} is checked and a performance made as shown in Equation 8.

$$if\, C_{order} \begin{cases} = 0 & newID_{order} = \sigma \\ \neq 0 & D' = D' \cup \left([\mu_P] - [\mu_C]\right) \end{cases} \qquad (4)$$

If C_{order} equals to (0) this means that the current ID_{order} is consistent with the number of elements and attribute names in D'. Otherwise, the difference between the current path in D' and the index

path for the current container should be added to D' before adding the required data.

Since the decompression method depends on the existence of data, the resulted decompressed XML document is lossless from the data side while the dummy nodes (the element that has no data but consists of an open tag and a close tag) could be lost. This case appears in documents that are converted from a database system with poorly structured documents.

1.5 XCVQ-D ALGORITHM AND ITS CORRECTNESS

The algorithm in Figure 10 illustrates the process of *XCVQ-D* which takes the *pathDictionary* and the compressed containers as its parameter list. The main idea of the decompression algorithm is to look for a data value which has the minimum ID_{Order} and put it in the decompressed file in its appropriate place. From the design of the *XCVQ-C* the first data value in each container always has the minimum order within this container, the process of looking for the minimum order will check only *(n)* item, where *(n)* represents the number of containers instead of searching all the data in the containers. This process reduces the time required to decompress the containers to *O(n)* instead of

Figure 8. (endDocument) algorithm

```
1.      Algorithm endDocument ()
2.          let pathDictionary=[i₀, i₁, ..., iₙ]
3.          let structured-Tree=[j₀, j₁, ..., jₘ]
4.          let F be the compressed file = ∅
5.          Add pathDictionary to F
6.          For all the N branches in structured-Tree
7.              index= Collect all the nodes [j₀, j₁, ..., jₖ]
8.              data= the contents of the leaf node for the path
         [j₀, j₁, ..., jₖ]
9.              data = GZipCompress(data)
10.             Add a Container(index, data) to F
11.     End.
```

$O(n \times m)$ where m represents the number of data items in each container.

If this piece of data is the first data value in the XML document (line 9) then, all the path's elements in the index of the container holding this data are pushed in a stack which represent the current working path and add these elements (or attribute names) to the new XML document (D') as an open tags (lines 10-12).

Before adding the data to the output file, a consistency check is made, by following the instructions in lines 16-19, where ({}) means set difference between the contents of the stack and the index path. If there is no consistency (line 17) then the difference between the stack content and the index path is added to the output file as losing tags and then the piece of data is added to the output file. In every addition to the output file, the value of (*dataOrder*) is updated (lines 12, 19, and 21) to check the consistency between them each time.

After adding the data to the output file, this data alongside with its order is deleted from the container. This process is done to keep the order of the first data items in all the containers in their minimum values and to release the memory storage used by these data values.

This process is continued until all the containers are empty, then all the content of the stack is added to the output file as closed tags to finish the new decompressed XML document.

The next paragraph discuss the correctness of the decompression algorithm by guarantee the one-to-one mapping from the compressed document to the decompressed document.

The core of the decompression technique is to make sure that each part of the compressed XML document should return to its place in the original XML document. This is done in *XCVQ* by using the ID_{Order} which counts the order of each single part of the original document, such that:

$$O_{data}(ID_{Order}) = D_{data}(ID_{Order})$$

Figure 9. Architecture of XCVQ-D

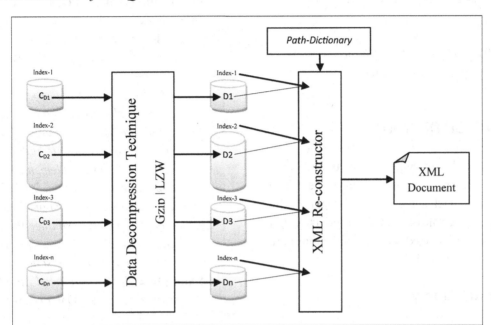

where, O_{data} and D_{data} represent a single piece of data in the original and the decompressed XML documents, respectively.

As seen in Figure 5, the only $O_{data}(ID_{Order})$ stored in the compressed document are for the data part of the document to save the storage required. For instance, in the first container indexed *(/0/1/@2)* in Figure 5, the first data item ("1") has its $O_{data}(ID_{Order})=3$. This means that there are three pieces should be transferred to the decompressed XML document before transferring this part of data. These pieces are the three nodes in the container's index *(/0, /1, and /@2)*.

To make this balance between $O_{data}(ID_{Order})$ and $D_{data}(ID_{Order})$ in the decompression algorithm, the *dataOrder* variable was used (to represent $D_{data}(ID_{Order})$) to count every single piece of data written in the XML document. Before adding a data value to the decompressed XML document, the decompression algorithm checks if it is in its right place (i.e. if $O_{data}(ID_{Order})=D_{data}(ID_{Order})$ after taking onto consideration the expected number of pieces from the). Otherwise a process is required

to solve this inconsistency between the two values and as follows:

Find the difference between the two $ID_{Order}s$

$$D=O_{data}(ID_{Order}) - D_{data}(ID_{Order})$$

This means that there are D pieces should be added to the decompressed file first.

2. Add the D pieces of data that are in the current working path but not in the container's index.

Update $D_{data}(ID_{Order})$

$$D_{data}(ID_{Order})= D_{data}(ID_{Order})+D$$

Since

$$D=O_{data}(ID_{Order}) - D_{data}(ID_{Order})$$

Then

$$D_{data}(ID_{Order}) = D_{data}(ID_{Order}) + O_{data}(ID_{Order}) - D_{data}(ID_{Order})$$

$D_{data}(ID_{Order}) = O_{data}(ID_{Order})$ Which is the target of the decompression technique.

1.6 XCVQ-QP DESIGN

The design of the query processor, as illustrated in Figure 11, consists of various stages. The output(s) from each stage is used as input for the other stages. The role of each stage and its design are discussed in the next sections using the same running example in Figure 3.

1.6.1 XPath Query

The current XPath query language does not have the ability to answer vague queries, since its work is based on a restricted Boolean matching; either the query matches part(s) of the existing document and retrieves those parts, or no retrieval at all is achieved if there is no match. *XCVQ-QP* uses XPath as a query language after expanding the original language to give it the ability to solve vague user's queries. This expansion includes adding more flexibility in both path matching and data value matching in addition to adding some functions to the list of available XPath functions.

1.6.1.1 Path Matching Expansion

To increase the flexibility of XPath axes matching, *XCVQ-QP* provides some generalization to the XPath query that gives the users of *XCVQ-QP* the ability to retrieve the most relevant information to their queries (Grust, 2002; Amer-Yahia et al., 2004; Campi et al., 2009). These generalizations are the following:

1. Eliminating the use of the recursive descent sign (//) and replacing it with the child operator (/) sign. This elimination increases

the flexibility of *XCVQ* as shown in the following examples:

Example 1: *to retrieve all the (TITLE) elements from the XML example in Figure 7, an XPath query should be (/CATALOG/CD/TITLE). In this case the user should have a complete idea about the XML schema for that file to indicate the complete path from the root to the (TITLE) element. To retrieve the same information, XCVQ query is either (/CD/TITLE) or (CATALOG/TITLE), which is simpler than XPath queries and does not need any previous knowledge about the schema.*

Example 2: *if the user need the (TITLE) element for the CD with (no) equals to "2". The XPath query is (CATALOG/CD[@no="2"]/TITLE) while the XCVQ query is (/CD[@no="2"]/TITLE) which is again much simpler than XPath query.*

2. If the query tries to retrieve sibling elements, then using XPath would need to write two separate queries or one query with two parts connected by logical (and) operator.

Example 3: *The elements (TITLE) and the elements (YEAR) are both siblings in the XML tree. The XPath query to retrieve all the data from the two elements is (CATALOG/CD/TITLE | CATALOG/CD/YEAR), while the XCVQ query to retrieve the same information is (/TITLE/YEAR).*

Example 4: *if the user interesting in retrieving all the (TITLE) elements only for the CD published after (1990). The XPath query is (/CATALOG/CD/TITLE and /CATALOG/CD[YEAR>1990]), while the relevant XCVQ query is (/TITLE[YEAR>1990]).*

3. If the order of the path is not arranged properly, XPath query does not have the ability

Figure 10. XCVQ-decompression algorithm

```
1.      Algorithm XCVQ-D (pathDictionary [P₀, P₁, ...,Pₘ], containers
        [C₀, C₁, ...,Cₙ])

2.      let currentPathStack=[Sₖ, Sₖ₋₁, ...,S₀]

3.      let dataOrder= number of elements, attribute names, and data

        values in the outputFile D

4.      While (the containers are still having data) Do

5.       for i=0 to n

6.           let minDataSet[(O₀,D₀), (O₁,D₁),... (Oₙ,Dₙ)] ← first
             element in each container

7.           minOrder=min(O₀, O₁,..., Oₙ)

8.           minData ← Dᵢ from (minOrder, Dᵢ)

9.        if currentPathStack=∅

10.           currentPathStack ← Cᵢ.index

11.           D ← open tags of Cᵢ.index

12.           dataOrder=dataOrder+ number of open tags added

13.        }

14.       Else

15.           currentPathStack ← [Cᵢ.index]-[currentPathStack]
```

$$16. \quad \text{dataCons} = \boldsymbol{minOrder - (dataOrder + \{[C_i.index] - [currentStackPath]\})}$$

```
17.       if dataCons ≠ 0
```

$$18. \quad \boldsymbol{D \ \leftarrow \ close\ tag\{[C_i.index] - [currentStackPath]\}}$$

```
19.          dataOrder=dataOrder+ number of close tags added
```

$$20. \quad \boldsymbol{D} \leftarrow \text{Di}$$

```
21.          dataOrder=dataOrder+1

22.       remove (minOrder, Dᵢ)

23.    }
```

$$24. \quad \boldsymbol{D} \leftarrow \text{close tag } [S_k, S_{k-1}, ...,S_0]$$

```
25.    End.
```

to retrieve information from the specified document, while *XCVQ* does.

Example 5: *using the same requirements of* Example (3), *XPath user should follow the same path from the root to the required element, while* XCVQ *query could be written as follows: (TITLE/CD/YEAR)*

4. Using XPath queries, the user should follow the case of the letters, since the XPath query is case sensitive language. This feature adds more complexity to the user and to the XML creator who has to follow those specific rules. *XCVQ* queries are case insensitive, which retrieve the information from the XML document even if the case is different.

Example 6: *all the* XCVQ *queries in* Examples (1-5) *can be written as following:*

```
cd/TITLE
/CD[@no="2"]/title
/TITLE/year
title[year gt 1990]
title/cd/YEAR
```

5. When the system does not find a specific element within the XML compressed database, it tries to look for elements that are similar to it. For that reason, *XCVQ-QP* uses a *string-similarity* algorithm (White, 2008) in order to match any misspelling in the elements or attribute names. If an element within the path is written in a wrong way, then the system will look for the nearest spelling element in the retrieved documents such that the similarity ratio should not be below 40%. After many experiments, we noticed that this percent is the best for retrieving the required element. If this number is less than 40, then non-related elements could be retrieved. The choice of *string-similarity* algorithm is made on the ground that it meets most of *XCVQ*-QP needs since this algorithm has the following features:

a. If two strings have minor differences, they are considered to be similar (ex: heap, heard).

b. If two strings have the same words but in different order, they are considered to be similar (ex: data base management system, managing data base).

As shown in Figure 12, the *string-similarity* match algorithm takes two strings, and for each string it produces sets each of which has two adjacent letters in that string. Then the similarity is computed as in line (5) to determine the similarity ratio between them.

6. *XCVQ-QP* has the ability to retrieve information from more than one file (FAZZINGA et al., 2009) even if the user does not specify these files in prior. As a simple example, if the user has the query (title/year) then s/he might get information about the titles and year of publication for CDs, movies, books or journals. Moreover, *XCVQ-QP* has the ability to compare the results from one file with the data from another file and retrieve the results accordingly.

Example 7: *Suppose the following user query: (catalog/book/author/bookstore[author="Erik Ray"]). This query is considered to be a merged from two queries, (catalog/book/author="Erik Ray") and (bookstore/book/author="Erik Ray"). Each one is to retrieve all the books for the author's name ("Erik Ray") from two separate XML documents that follow different schemas.*

Example 8: *suppose the following user query:*

```
(cars/car/price lt carType/Ford[model
eq 2008]/price)
```

In this query the user is interesting in looking for all the cars that their pricees are less than (*lt*)

Figure 11. The architecture of the query processor

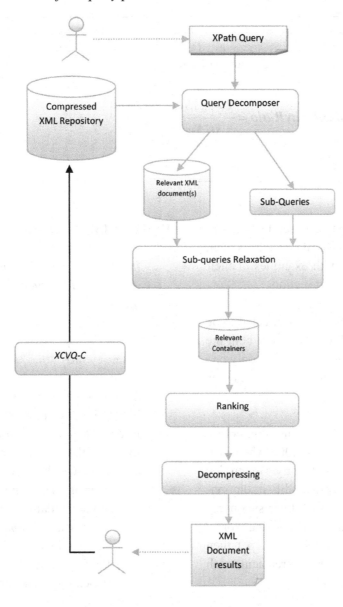

the 2009 Ford car price. *XCVQ-QP* first looks for the smallest price (*x*) in the path (carType/ Ford[model eq 2008]/price) and then retrieve all the information from the path (cars/car/price) which are less than (*x*). Notice that the two paths are from two separate XML documents.

1.6.1.2 Data Value Matching Expansion

In order to make more expansion on XPath queries to retrieve more relevant data from the XML document, *XCVQ-QP* adds a set of functions that deal with the data part of the document (Campi et

Figure 12. String-similarity match algorithm

```
1. Algorithm string-similarity (String st1, st2)
2. let st1= [s₁s₂s₃ ... sₙ]   and st2= [c₁c₂c₃ ... cₘ]
3. st1Set= [s₁s₂][s₂s₃][s₃s₄]...[sₙ₋₁sₙ]
4. st2Set= [c₁c₂][c₂c₃][c₃c₄]...[cₘ₋₁cₘ]
```

$$5. \quad \textbf{\textit{SimilarityRatio}} = \frac{2 \times \left| \textit{st1Set} \cap \textit{st2Set} \right|}{\left| \textit{st1Set} \right| + \left| \textit{st2Set} \right|}$$

```
6. End.
```

al., 2009). Although some of these functions are adopted to be used in structural retrieval as well. The extended functions with examples of their use are illustrated in the next section.

1. *Synonym(x):* This function is created to be used to retrieve information from both the structure and the data parts. It has only one parameter *x* and returns a list of synonyms for *x*.

To do so, *XCVQ-QP* uses the WinterTree thesauruses engine (WinterTree, 2006) which provides a wide multipurpose dictionary. This engine provides the user the ability to modify its dictionary by adding new words with their synonyms or adding more synonyms to the existing words.

If the list of synonyms is (S₁, S₂, ..., Sₙ), then *XCVQ-QP* processes (n) queries by replacing each Si instead of the function call.

Example 9: *Suppose the query /cd/title/ synonyms("time"). XCVQ-QP replaces this query with 3 queries:*

```
/cd/title/duration
/cd/title/interval
/cd/title/date
```

It is clear that the use of the function in this example is for structure retrieving purposes.

Example 10: *Suppose the query /cd/country eq synonyms("Britain"),which retrieves information from the data part of the XML document. This query is replaced with two queries:*

```
/cd/country eq "UK"
/cd/country eq "The United Kingdom"
```

2. *Similar(x):* This function uses the String-Similarity algorithm, shown in Figure 12 in order to retrieve information according to one of the following conditions:
   a. If the user has doubt on the spelling of a string as shown in *Example (11)*.
   b. If the similar strings to *x* are required as shown in *Example (12)*. This function works on both the structure and the data parts of the XML documents depending on the previous conditions.

Example 11: *In the query /cd/title/similar(artest), the word artest has spelling error. The role of XCVQ-QP here is to find the similar element name from the retrieved documents and retrieve the required information accordingly. This query is replaced with /cd/ title/artist for the running example.*

Example 12: *In the query /cd/year/title eq similar("keep your heart") for the running example, the data required is similar to "keep* *your heart" which is replaced by* XCVQ-QP *with cd/year/title eq "hide your heart"*.

1.6.1.3 Function Set Expansion

The list of available functions in XPath query language includes string, Boolean and number functions. *XCVQ-QP* adds four functions to the number functions set.

1. **Average(x):** the *avg()* function in XPath provides the user the ability to get the average of a list of numbers specified as a parameter list for the function. This function is expanded by *XCVQ-QP* to provide the user the ability to specify an element from the XML document and find the average of the numerical values under that element.

    Example 13: The query /cd/title/average(price) retrieves all the data values of the title element and the average of the numbers of the price element.

2. **Median(x):** This function is used to find the median for the list of numbers in the selected path.

    Example 14: If the query /catalog/cd median(year)is applied, the user will get the median number for all the data values of the year element.

3. **Between(x,y):** Instead of using and logical operator to retrieve information lying between two different intervals, *XCVQ-QP* introduce this function. It has two parameters which represent the data interval.

    Example 15: *The query /cd/title[price=between(9.0,10.0)] retrieves all the title elements if and only if the value of its price element is between the given interval.*

1.6.2 Query Decomposer

This part of the *XCVQ-QP* is responsible for decomposing the XPath query into several sub-queries. This stage consists of two decomposition stages, as shown in Figure 13. Each stage has specific roles and results in a set of sub-queries as in the following:

Decomposition Stage -1: *The main purpose of this stage is to specify the relevant documents from the compressed XML repository. This case occurs when the user's query does not specify the exact XML document to retrieve information from it.* XCVQ-QP *decomposes this query into (n) queries, where (n) represents the number of the relevant documents.*

Definition- 2 (relevant document): *If* $Q = [e_1, e_2, e_3, \ldots e_n]$ *is the set of elements in the user's query, and* $X = [x_1, x_2, x_3, \ldots x_m]$ *is the set of all the compressed XML documents in the repository.* $x' \in X$ *is considered to be relevant document if* $\exists e_i : e_i \in x'_j.PD$, *where* **PD** *is the path-dictionary for the specified document. If so, add* x'_j *to the relevant repository and add* e_i *to* q'_j.

          ■

According to the definition above, a XML document is considered to be relevant if it has one or more of the query elements in its path-dictionary. All the relevant documents $X' = x'_1, x'_2, \ldots x'_l$ are collected in a small repository for relevant XML documents each of which is accompanied with its relevant sub-query $Q' = q'_1, q'_2, \ldots q'_l$. All the elements and attribute names in Q' are replaced with its location in the path-dictionary of the relevant document. This process is done to prepare the sub-queries for the second decomposition stage. As an example, if a sub-query is: title/cd/year from the running example, it is replaced with /3/1/7 where 3, 1, and 7 represent the entries of title, cd, and year respectively as shown in Figure 9.

In the case when the user's query Q is submitted to retrieve information from a specific document, then the query does not pass by this stage and the list of sub-queries Q' has only the original query, i.e. $Q' = [Q]$ and the related document's repository contains only the specified document.

Decomposition Stage -2: *After specifying the relevant documents, the role of this stage is to specify the relevant containers within these documents. This process causes further decomposition to the sub-queries*

Definition-3 (Relevant Container): *Given* $C = \{c_1, c_2, \cdots c_n\}$ represents the set of n containers for a relative document and each of these containers has an index with k elements $P = \{p_1, p_2, \cdots p_k\}$, and $q_i' = \{e_1, e_2, \cdots e_m\}$ represents the set of m elements in the sub-query accompanies C, to select the relevant container follow the steps:

$\forall c_i \in C$

$k =$ *the last element in the set*

if $p_k \in q_i'$

Add c_i to C' to denote the list of relevant containers

$\forall e_k$ *if* $e_k \in P$, *copy e_k and add it to the list of the elements in $q_{i,j}'$ to denote a new sub-query.*

$k = k - 1$

Repeat the above steps until the entire element in q_i' are copied to a new sub-query.

∎

At the end of this stage only the relevant containers taken from the relevant documents are

uploaded into the memory for ranking process. Each of these containers is accompanied with is sub-query as shown in Figure 13.

1.6.3 Query Relaxation

In this stage, the list of sub-queries Q' is being relaxed to determine the relevancy of each of these queries to the document. To do so, *XCVQ-QP* relaxes all the members of Q' according to each of the containers in x' to compute the cost of this relaxation process for ranking purposes. To reach this goal, *XCVQ-QP* adopts different kinds of relaxation processes. These types and their costs are listed below:

1. **Node insertion:** This type of relaxation is done by inserting one node or more in the list of available query nodes. To do so, *XCVQ-QP* compares each container of the relevant XML documents with its sub-query.

Definition-4 (Node-Insertion): *Given a container* $c_j \in C'$ has an index with k elements $P = \{p_1, p_2, \cdots p_k\}$ and given $q_{i,j}' = \{e_1, e_2, \cdots e_m\}$ represents the set of m elements in the sub-query accompanies the ith relevant document and j[th] relevant container. The relaxed sub-query $q_{i,j}'' = q_{i,j}' \bigcup (P \setminus q_{i,j}')$

∎

The cost of the insertion node(s) in a single sub-query is specified as follows:

$$cost_{In} = \frac{\left| (P \setminus q_{i,j}') \right|}{|P|} \quad (5)$$

2. **Node renaming:** After completing the first stage of relaxation, each sub-query is going to pass through the following procedure:

Figure 13. The design of XCVQ-query decomposer

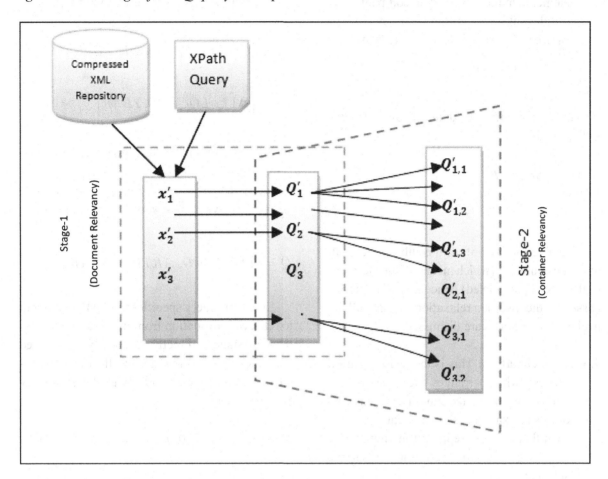

Let $q_{i,j}^{''} = \left\{e_1, e_2, \cdots e_m\right\}$ be the set of elements in the current sub-query, $P = \left\{p_1, p_2, \cdots p_k\right\}$ be the set of elements of the index for the current container associated with $q_{i,j}^{''}$.

For all $e_i \in q_{i,j}^{''}$,

if $e_i \notin P$ then find the value of *SimilarityRatio* by applying the *string-similarity(e_i, p_j)* algorithm in Figure 16 such that $1 \le j \le m$.

if *(SimilarityRatio>50%)* then

　　　replace e_i with p_j

changes++

The cost of the node renaming process is calculated as follows:

$$cost_{Ren} = \frac{changes}{\left|q_{i,j}^{''}\right|} \qquad (6)$$

3.　**Node deletion:** After inserting all the required nodes from the index of a container, the extra nodes from the query should be removed.

Definition-5 (Node-deletion): *Given a* container $c_j \in C'$ has an index with k elements $P = \left\{p_1, p_2, \cdots p_k\right\}$ a n d　　g i v e n $q_{i,j}^{'} = \left\{e_1, e_2, \cdots e_m\right\}$ represents the set of m elements in the sub-query accompanies the ith relevant document and j[th] relevant container. The relaxed sub-query $q''_{i,j} = q''_{i,j} - \left[q''_{i,j} \setminus P\right]$.

.

The cost required to delete node(s) from a sub-query is:

$$cost_{Del} = \frac{\left|q''_{i,j} \setminus P\right|}{\left|q''_{i,j}\right|} \qquad (7)$$

The deletion cost of all the sub-queries will never be equal to 1 (which means all the elements in the query are deleted), since all these queries passed by the insertion relaxation first and all the irrelevant containers are dismissed.

4. **Order relaxation:** This is the last relaxation process which arranges the order of the nodes in each resulted sub-queries. The cost of this relaxation is shown in equation (11) such that *changes* represent the number of changing in the order of the elements in the sub-query.

$$cost_{Order} = \frac{changes}{\left|Q''\right|} \qquad (8)$$

Example 16: *For the running example, the lists of containers indexes are as follows:*

$C_1 = \left\{CATALOG, CD, NO\right\}$

$C_2 = \left\{CATALOG, CD, TITLE\right\}$

$C_3 = \left\{CATALOG, CD, ARTIST\right\}$

$C_4 = \left\{CATALOG, CD, COUNTRY\right\}$

$C_5 = \left\{CATALOG, CD, PRICE\right\}$

$C_6 = \left\{CATALOG, CD, YEAR\right\}$

Suppose the following vague query:

```
Q1=document("cdcatalog.xml")/title/
cd/artest[year between(1990, 1996)]
```

$Q = \{TITLE, CD, ARTIST, YEAR\}$

Since this query specifies the XML document to retrieve information from it, it is going to pass through stage-2 directly to specify the related containers. The following list illustrates the related containers alongside with the sub-query accompanied it:

$C_2 = \left\{CATALOG, CD, TITLE\right\} \Leftrightarrow q'_{1,2} = \{TITLE, CD\}$

$C_3 = \left\{CATALOG, CD, ARTIST\right\} \Leftrightarrow q'_{1,3} = \{CD, ARTEST\}$

$C_6 = \left\{CATALOG, CD, YEAR\right\} \Leftrightarrow q'_{1,6} = \{CD, YEAR\}$

The insertion relaxation process updates the sub-queries to be as follows:

$q''_{1,2} = \{CATALOG, TITLE, CD\}$

$q''_{1,3} = \{CATALOG, CD, ARTEST\}$

$q''_{1,6} = \{CATALOG, CD, YEAR\}$

The cost of insertion the required nodes are as follows:

$$\text{cost}_{In_{q_{1,2}}^*} = \frac{\left|\{CATALOG,\ CD,\ TITLE\} \setminus \{TITLE,\ CD\}\right|}{\left|\{CATALOG,\ CD,\ TITLE\}\right|} = \frac{1}{3}$$

$$\text{cost}_{In_{q_{1,3}}^*} = \frac{\left|\{CATALOG,\ CD,\ ARTIST\} \setminus \{CD,\ ARTEST\}\right|}{\left|\{CATALOG,\ CD,\ ARTIST\}\right|} = \frac{1}{3}$$

$$\text{cost}_{In_{q_{1,6}}^*} = \frac{\left|\{CATALOG,\ CD,\ YEAR\} \setminus \{CD,\ YEAR\}\right|}{\left|\{CATALOG,\ CD,\ YEAR\}\right|} = \frac{1}{3}$$

The node renaming relaxation process updates the sub-queries to be as follows:

$$q_{1,2}^{''} = \{CATALOG,\ TITLE,\ CD\}$$

$$q_{1,3}^{''} = \{CATALOG,\ CD,\ ARTIST\}$$

$$q_{1,6}^{''} = \{CATALOG,\ CD,\ YEAR\}$$

The only sub-query affected by this stage is $q_{1,3}^{''}$ and the cost of this process is as follows:

$$\text{cost}_{Ren_{q_{1,3}}^{''}} = \frac{1}{\left|\{CATALOG,\ CD,\ ARTEST\}\right|} = \frac{1}{3}$$

The node reordering relaxation process updates the sub-queries to be as follows:

$$q_{1,2}^{''} = \{CATALOG, CD, TITLE\}$$

$$q_{1,3}^{'} = \{CATALOG, CD, ARTIST\}$$

$$q_{1,6}^{'} = \{CATALOG, CD, YEAR\}$$

The only sub-query affected by this stage is $q_{1,2}^{''}$ and the cost of this process is as follows:

$$\text{cost}_{Order_{q_{1,2}}^{''}} = \frac{1}{\left|\{CATALOG, TITLE, CD\}\right|} = \frac{1}{3}$$

1.6.4 Ranking

After relaxing all the sub-queries, the process of finding the similarity between the containers' index and the sub-queries is computed according to the following equation:

Definition-6 (Query Similarity): *To find the similarity between the given query (Q) and the relevant XML document, first the cost of all the relaxation process, that has been done on (i) sub-queries, should be found as follows depending on the previous equations in (9), (10), (11), and (12):*

$$cost_R = \frac{\left(\sum_{i=1}^{n} \frac{\left(cost_{In}\right) + \left(cost_{Ren}\right) + \left(cost_{Del}\right) + \left(cost_{Order}\right)}{4}\right)}{i} \tag{9}$$

Then the similarity is computed as follows:

$$sim\left(X, Q\right) = 1 - cost_R \tag{10}$$

All the sub-queries are sorted according to their value of $sim\left(X, Q\right)$, the higher similarity the sub query has, the higher order it takes.

Example (16): continue

To find the similarity of the query *Q1*, first find the value of $cost_R$ as follows:

$$cost_R =$$

$$\frac{\left(\left(\frac{\frac{1}{3}+0+0+\frac{1}{3}}{4}\right) + \left(\frac{\frac{1}{3}+\frac{1}{3}+0+0}{4}\right) + \left(\frac{\frac{1}{3}+0+0+0}{4}\right)\right)}{3}$$

$$= 0.134$$

And the similarity between the query *Q1* and the pre-specified XML document is:

$$sim\left(cdcatalog.xml, Q1\right) = 1 - 0.134 = 0.866$$

1.6.5 Decompression

During all the previous stages no decompression required except when the query has to retrieve information about the data part of the document. In this case only the relevant containers were decompressed to answer the sub-query having that part of data.

To retrieve the relevant parts of the XML document to the user, all the retrieved, ranked containers were decompressed using the same decompression technique discussed in section 1.4 in this chapter.

Although there may be more than one relevant containers retrieved from one or more XML documents, all these containers were combined and decompressed into one XML document to perform one tree instead of a forest of multiple XML trees.

If the user needs more queries to be processed on the resulted document, then this document should be compressed first to be within the XML repository and then it can be used in its compressed version. This feature is called *composition* and is borrowed from XQuery, in which the retrieved information is stored in a temporary XML file for further retrieving.

1.7 SUMMARY

This chapter sets forth the main features in the design of the *XCVQ* system which has the ability to compress and/or decompress an XML document without losing its data. The significant feature of *XCVQ* is its ability to retrieve information from the compressed version according to different kinds of queries and especially vague queries. This required an expansion of the existing XPath queries through adding certain features to provide it with the ability to answer imprecise queries.

REFERENCES

W3Schools.com. (2006). *XML examples*. Retrieved October 7, 2010, from http://www.w3schools.com/XML/cd_catalog.xml

Amer-Yahia, S., Lakshmanan, L. V. S., & Pandit, S. (2004). *FleXPath: Flexible structure and fulltext querying for XML*. Paper presented at the ACM, SIGMOD., Paris, France.

Arion, A. (2007). *XML access modules: Towards physical data independence in XML Databases*. Paris, France: University of South Paris.

Arroyuelo, D., Claude, F., Maneth, S., M¨akinen, V., Navarro, G., Nguyen, K., et al. (2010). *Fast in-memory XPath search using compressed indexes*. Paper presented at the IEEE Twenty-Sixth International Conference on Data Engineering (ICDE 2010), California, USA.

Campi, A., Damiani, E., Guinea, S., Marrara, S., Pasi, G., & Spoletini, P. (2009). A fuzzy extension of the XPath query language. *Journal of Intelligent Information Systems*, *33*(3), 285–305. doi:10.1007/s10844-008-0066-3

Cheng, J., & NG, W. (2004). *XQZip: Querying compressed XML using structural indexing.* Paper presented at the International Conference on Extending Data Base Technology (EDBT).

Grust, T. (2002). *Accelerating XPath location steps.* Paper presented at the ACM SIGMOD International Conference on Management of Data.

Murray, J. D., & VanRyper, W. (1996). *Encyclopedia of graphics file formats.* O'Reilly.

PKWare. (2003). *Website.* Retrieved March 1, 2011, from http://www.pkware.com/

Salomon, D. (2007). *Data compression: The complete reference* (4th ed.). Springer.

Chapter 11
XCVQ Testing, Evaluation and Discussion

Badya Al-Hamadani
University of Huddersfield, UK

Joan Lu
University of Huddersfield, UK

ABSTRACT

Since the testing and evaluation processes are part of SDM, this chapter illustrates the detailed testing of XCVQ and its ensuing evaluation. Because the XCVQ model consists of three main parts, XCVQ-C, XCVQ-D, and XCVQ-QP, the testing strategy will involve testing each stage on its own. This chapter describes the testing of the three parts of the XCVQ model.

1.1 TESTING STRATEGY

For the purposes of testing the complete model, the testing strategies are to be specified first. The next sections describe the behaviour testing strategy used (state graph) and then the functional testing strategies (white and black boxes).

1.1.1 Testing XCVQ's Behaviour

For the purposes of testing the complete model, first the state diagram was defined to describe the behaviour of *XCVQ* and to implement the State

Graph testing strategy (Beizer, 1990; Farrell-Vinay, 2008).

The following is the detailed description of each state of the state graph in Figure 1.

State-A: This state is the GUI of the designed model. It represents the starting state in order to deal with all the other states. This state has three outputs:

Out-1: to compress an XML document, go to state-B.

Out-2: to decompress an XML document, go to State-C. This output is true only if (Out-1) is performed at least one time.

DOI: 10.4018/978-1-4666-1975-3.ch011

Figure 1. XCVQ state graph

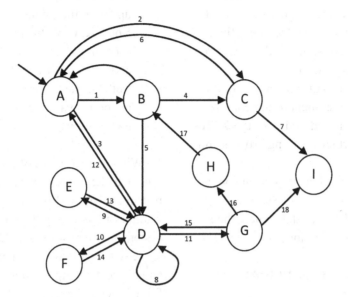

Out-3: to write a query, go to State-D. This output is true only if (Out-1) is performed at least one time.

State-B: This state represents the process of compressing an XML document. It has two outputs:

Out-4: to decompress an XML document, go to State-C.

Out-5: to submit a query, go to State-D.

State-C: This stage represents the process of decompressing an XML document and it has two outputs:

Out-6: return to the starting state.

Out-7: submit the decompressed document to the user, go to State-I.

State-D: this is the most important state in the system which represents the query submission and checking its syntax. It has the following five outputs:

Out-8: if the submitted query has syntactical error(s), return to the same stage to resubmit another query.

Out-9: if the syntactically true query specifies the exact XML document to retrieve information from, go to Stage-E.

Out-10: if the syntactically true query does not specify the exact XML document to retrieve information from, go to Stage-F.

Out-11: take the out-of-errors query and the relevant XML document(s) as inputs to State-G.

Out-12: from this stage the user can return back to the starting state.

State-E: This state is responsible on retrieving the required XML document which specified by the query. It has only one output:

Out-13: carry the unique XML document which is specified by the query to State-D.

State-F: In the state, the set of relevant XML document is specified depending on the submitted query. This state has one output:

Out-14: carry the set of the relevant XML document(s) retrieved from the repository to State-D.

State-G: In this state, the query is processed and the required information is retrieved from the relevant XML document(s). It has three outputs:

Out-15: to ignore the current query, return to State-D.

Out-16: if more retrieval process required for the retrieved document, go to State-B to decompress the retrieved document first.

Out-18: to submit the results of the querying process to the user, go to State-I

State-H: This state returns the retrieved information as an XML document to the compressor to compress it and add it to the XML repository for further querying process and it has only one

Out-17: if the user required more querying on the retrieved information, go to State-B.

State-I: This state is the final state where the resulted document(s) are submitted to the user.

1.1.2 Testing *XCVQ*'s Structure and Functionality

Both White-Box and Black-Box testing strategies are used in order to test the structure and the functional of *XCVQ* respectively. In the White-Box testing strategy all the subroutines in the system were tested to check every single statement. Depending on this testing strategy, different kinds of XML documents were derived to guarantee that all paths, logical decisions, loops, and data structures have been tested at least once. Firstly, the complete *XCVQ* system was divided into three main sub-systems: *XCVQ-C, XCVQ-D, and XCVQ-QP* in order to make it easier to follow the white-box testing strategy. Secondly, each sub-system was divided into small units to follow the *unit white-box testing type*. For each unit three white-box tests were made:

1. **Conditional test:** In this test all the condition statements were tested checking the values of the Boolean variables and the correctness of the conditions.

2. **Data lifecycle & data structure test:** the second white-box tests the lifecycle of the variables, their initializations, their value changing, and their expiring. It also checks the created data structures by testing their boundaries, applicability, initializations, and updating their data.

3. **Loop testing:** In this box all the loops in each unit were tested. The test includes the control variable initialization value, the truth of the control condition, the change in control variable, and the guarantee of its termination.

While the structure of the designed system is crucial to the White-Box testing strategy, it has no role in the Black-Box strategy since this strategy is aimed at observing the outputs of the designed system for certain inputs. The main aim of this strategy is to test all the functional requirements, and hence it attempts to derive the necessary data for achieving that aim. In this chapter, the intensive test for the chosen XML data corpus and the independent test were both achieved.

During both previous strategies, a huge amount of XML data was used to cover different data ratios, depths, resources, and sizes. The overall tested data amounted to more than 1500 MB with 45 XML documents (see Appendix-C)

1.2 TESTING FACTORS

To test the performance of the *XCVQ*, all the factors listed in Table 1 were used. The following is the complete description of these factors and their importance in the testing process.

Compression Ratio (CR): this factor is used to test the difference between the original XML file size and the compressed file size as illustrated in Equation (15) (Salomon, 2007). It is used in two stages. In the first stage, only the structure part of the document was compressed and in the second stage the data and the structure parts were compressed. Depending on this factor, the relation between CR and the Data Ratio (DR) and the relation between CR and the size of the file were found. For this purpose a corpus of XML documents was used. Its complete description is discussed in the next paragraph.

Table 1. XCVQ Testing factors

Sub-system	Testing factor
XCVQ-C	- Structure Compression Ratio - Structure Compression Time - Compression Ratio - Compression Time
XCVQ-D	- Structure Decompression Time - Decompression Time
XCVQ-QP	- Functionality test - Performance Test

$$CR = 1 - \left(\frac{Size\ of\ compressed\ file}{Size\ of\ original\ file} \right) \qquad (1)$$

- **Compression Time (CT):** This factor is used to determine the time required to compress each XML document in seconds (s) and to specify its relation with the file size.
- **Decompression Time (DT):** This is the measure of the time required to decompress the XML document in order to obtain the original one. The effect of the file size on DT was obtained.
- **Query Functional Test (QFT):** The purpose of this test is to determine the main types of queries that can be processed by *XCVQ-QP*. For this purpose, a query benchmark was tested.
- **Query Performance Test (QPT):** This factor is used to determine the time required to process each of the XPath query in the benchmark and retrieve the relevant results.

All the time comparison factors shown in the following figures are scaled by ($\log_{10}$) to make the figures clearer. All the negative values in these figures mean that the actual time values were less than (1).

1.3 DATA PREPARATION

To test the *XCVQ* model, a set comprising of different types of XML documents has been chosen. These documents should have different sizes, number of elements, number of nodes, the depth of the longest path, and the data ratio (DR) which is calculated as follows (Sakr, 2009):

$$DR_d = (D_d\ /\ Si_d)\ /\ 100 \qquad (2)$$

where DR_d is the data ratio for the XML document (*d*), (*D*) is the data, and (*Si*) represents the size of the XML document.

According to their main characteristics, XML documents can be categorized into three types (Maneth et al., 2008; Sakr, 2009):

1. **Textual documents (TD):** The DR_d of this type of documents exceeds 70%. The structure of these documents is very simple. Books and articles are examples of this type.
2. **Structural documents (SD):** In this type of XML documents, the DR_d is less than 30%. Baseball box score and line-item shipping are two examples of this type.
3. **Regular documents (RD):** These documents have DR_d between 40% and 60%. Relational databases are examples of this type.

The complete descriptions of the XML corpus with all the required information and the detailed description of all the groups in the corpus are listed in Appendix-C in chapter 12.

1.4 TESTING ENVIRONMENT

All the testing were carried out on a personal computer with Intel(R) Core(TM)2 Due CPU processor that has the speed of 5.50 GHz. The RAM memory of the tested environment is 4.00GB and 300GB of hard disk drive. It has 32-bit Windows Vista operating system.

1.5 XCVQ-C AND XCVQ-D TESTING

The testing technique for the *XCVQ-C* is made in two stages. The first stage is done by compressing only the structure of the XML document and creating the *path-dictionary* without compressing the data part of the document. The second stage is done by compressing the structure and the data parts to obtain the final XML compressed document which will be used in the querying process.

1.5.1 XCVQ-C and XCVQ-D Testing: Stage-1

The main purpose of this stage is to examine the effect of redundancy on the structure of the XML document and its overall size. In this stage, the data part of the document has not been compressed and thus keeps its original size, while the structure part is abridged and replaced with the elements index and the attribute name entries in the *path-dictionary*. The compressed XML document, at this stage, contains the *path-dictionary* and the created containers except that the data inside these containers are not compressed.

This test includes finding the Structure Compression Ratio (SCR), specifying the Structure Compression Time (SCT) and its relationship to the size of the XML document, as well as determining the Structure Decompression Time (SDT) and its relationship to the size of the XML document.

Figure 2 explains the Structure Compression Ratio (SCR) for the XML corpus. By keeping the data in its original size and compressing only the structure part of each document, the resulted SCR is between *0.003* and *85.43* and the average SCR is *49.47*. The value of SCR depends on the structure ratio of each document, which is listed in appendix-D, and the repetition of the schema in this document. This test explains the role of the redundancy in the structure of the XML document.

Figure 3 (a) shows the relation between the size of the XML document (X) and the structure compression time (Y), while Figure 3 (b) illustrates the time (Y) required for decompressing the XML document and restoring the original one. It is clear from the above figures that the relationships between the two variables in both cases are expanding almost linearly. The correlation coefficient between X and Y was $r = 0.886607$ in the compression case and $r = 0.996626$ in the decompression case. These values indicate the strong positive relationship between the size of the XML document in the one hand and the compression and decompression time on the other. The actual SCR, SCT, and SDT for the complete XML corpus are listed in Appendix-D.

1.5.2 XCVQ-C and XCVQ-D Testing: Stage-2

In this testing stage, the fully designed *XCVQ-C* and *XCVQ-D* were tested. The main aims of this test is to determine the average compression ratio for the XML corpus and the compression ratio for each of the documents, to specify the compression and decompression time and their relationship to the size of the XML document, and to generate the XML repository which is going to be used in the testing of *XCVQ-QP*.

The compression ratio of the complete XML corpus is shown in Figure 4. The resulted compressed file contains the *path-dictionary* and the containers after compressing their data using Gzip back-end compressor. The minimum resulted compression ratio is *68.51* for Richard II and the maximum is *93.52* for Sweden-meta. The average compression ratio for the complete XML corpus is *78.45*.

Figure 5 (a) shows the compression time for the complete XML corpus according to the size of the XML document while Figure 5 (b) shows the time required to decompress the XML docu-

Figure 2. SCR for the XML corpus

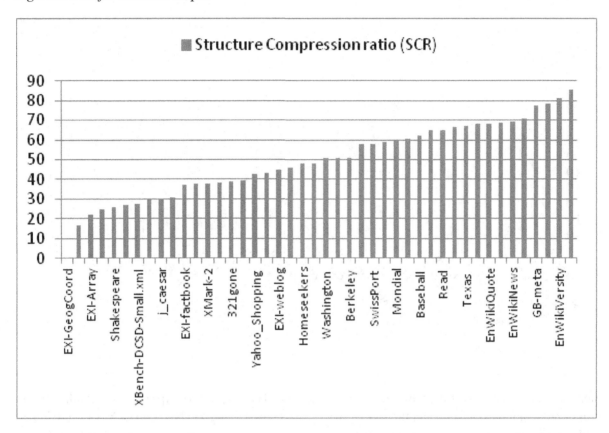

Figure 3. (a) Structure compression time for the XML corpus and (b) Structure decompression time for the XMLCcorpus

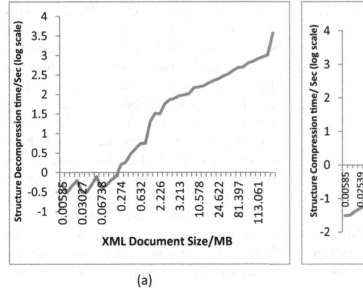

(a)

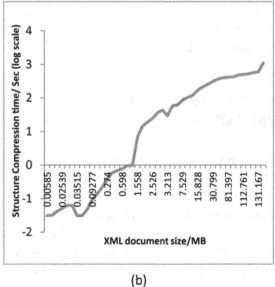

(b)

Figure 4. CR for the XML corpus

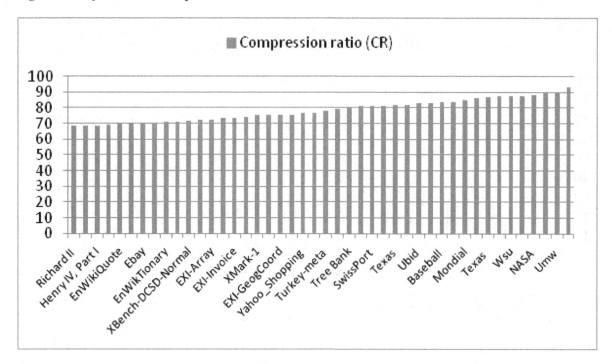

ments. Again, the relationship between the compression/decompression time and the size of the XML document is almost linear and the correlation coefficient between the compression time and the XML document size is: r=0.971702, while it is r=0.888598 in the case of decompression. This illustrates the strong positive relation between the two tested variables. The complete tested files alongside with their CR, CT, and DT are listed in Appendix-D in chapter 12.

1.6 XCVQ-C AND XCVQ-D EVALUATION

For the purpose of evaluating *XCVQ-C* and *XCVQ-D*, comparisons were made between *XCVQ* and other competitive techniques. Depending on the availability of the techniques and the XML corpus used in the testing of these techniques, four queriable XML compressors were chosen for the purpose of comparison: XGrind (Tolani

and Haritsa, 2000), Xpress (Min et al., 2003), XQzip (Cheng and NG, 2004), XQueC (Arion et al., 2007), and (Müldner et al., 2009). The XML corpus used in the testing and the compression ratio for each document is shown in Figure 6. The evaluation of the XCVQ includes comparing the following factors: CR, CT, and DT.

It is clear that *XCVQ-C* achieved a better compression ratio than other compressors except when dealing with high structural documents, since *XSAQCT* achieved better ratio. But when dealing with querying the compressed XML document, *XSAQCT* has the ability to answer only exact match queries since it transfers the structure of the document into an annotated-tree which can be compressed better than structured-tree. The average CR of the *XCVQ-C* is considered to be the best between all the other techniques for the selected documents, as listed in Table 2.

As seen in Figure 7, the time required by the *XCVQ-C* to compress the XML document was higher than the other compressors in most cases.

Figure 5. (a) Compression time and (b) the Decompression time for the XML corpus

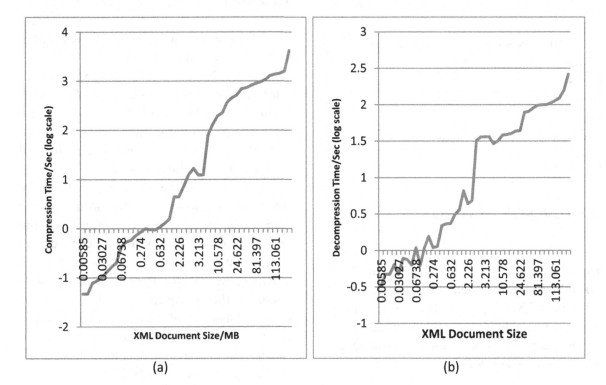

(a)   (b)

This is due to the SAX parser being used by *XCVQ-C*, which traverses the XML document only once, during which time the complete containers and the structured tree were constructed.

While the time required to decompress and regenerate the XML document, shown in Figure 8, was better than some of the XML compressors.

Figure 6. Evaluating XCVQ-C CR

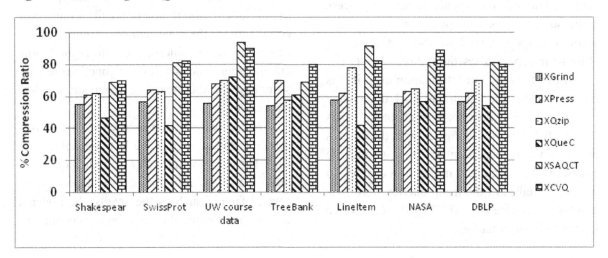

Table 2. Average CR for all the tested XML compressors

XML compressor	Average CR
XGrind	57.39
XPress	57.55
XQzip	66.95
XQueC	68.4
XSAQCT	80.02
XCVQ	81.85

1.7 XCVQ-QP TESTING

For the purpose of testing the performance of the *XCVQ-QP*, a XPath benchmark is used from XPathMark (Franceschet, 2005) since it covers all types of XML queries. The queries in this benchmark are divided into two main categories either Query Functional Test (*QFT*) or Query Performance Test (*QPT*).

1.7.1 QFT

XPath-FT queries are used to check the completeness and correctness of the query processor and are grouped into five aspects. Table 3 illustrates these five aspects. Since the main concern of *XCVQ-QP* is to process vague queries, only the vague cases in each of the aspects are tested. Since the third aspect could not be as vague, the testing process at this stage ignores this aspect. Furthermore, one additional aspect was added to the existing aspects (Multi-File aspect) to test the ability of *XCVQ-QP* to retrieve the required information even if it is disseminated in more than one XML document.

Table C-2 in Appendix-C in chapter 12 lists all the QFT concepts alongside with the queries associated with each concept by applying the example XML document in Fig. 3 in chapter 10 as a case study. All the listed queries were successfully processed by *XCVQ-QP* and retrieve the required information.

1.7.2 QPT

The QPT queries test the exact time required to answer a specific query (Franceschet, 2005). For this purpose, the same concepts in Table were used to test the performance of the *XCVQ-QP* by testing the time required to process the set of queries for each concept and retrieve the information from a specific XML document chosen from the used XML corpus with different sizes.

The testing results in Figure 9 includes all the concepts of the selected benchmark after averaging the time required to process the set of queries within each concept. These sets were applied to retrieve information from various XML documents with different sizes. It is clear from the aforementioned figure that the axes queries need less time to be processed than the other concepts. This is due to the structure of the compressed XML document which requires searching only the indexes of the containers to process these queries.

Since the queries belonging to the Filter concepts required partial decompression only for the retrieved containers, this set of queries needs more time than the queries in the first set. Because the set of queries in the Operation concept needs partial decompression for the relevant containers plus filtering the values in the retrieved information according to the given operation, they need even more time to be processed. Finally, the set of queries containing function calls require processing either the synonym or similarity of the given parameter which needs the highest time among other concepts as these functions require searching the dictionary or other similar data respectively.

Another test was made to check the performance of the queries in the last concept (multi-file). The test concludes that the time required to process a query from that set was dependent on several factors such as the size of the relevant documents, the number of relevant documents,

Figure 7. Evaluating XCVQ-C CT

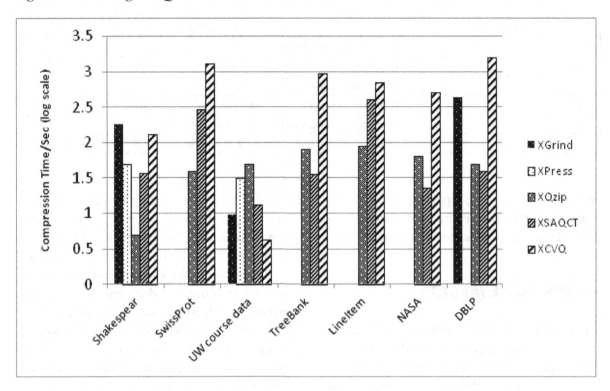

Figure 8. Evaluating XCVQ-D DT

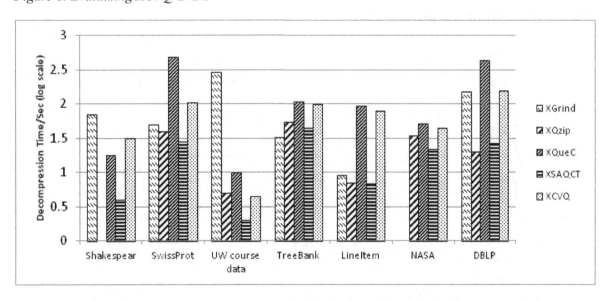

Table 3. XPathMark-FT query benchmark

QFT concepts	Description
Axes	**parent, descendant, preceding**
Filters	**predicates**
Node Test	**Comment(), text(), node()**
Operators	**Relational operators (<, =,...) and Boolean operators (and, or)**
Functions	**String manipulating functions and mathematical functions**
Multi-File	**Retrieving information from more than one XML document**

and the size of the XML repository. It could thus be concluded that these entire factors have a positive relationship with the query processing time.

1.8 XCVQ-QP EVALUATION

To evaluate *XCVQ-QP*, a test was first made to check the functionality of the model and its capability to process different kinds of queries. All the existing XML queriable compressors were tested to determine the types of queries each compressor can process. All the existing queriable compressors have the ability to process SQ, while some of them were designed to process specific types of queries. As discussed before, *XCVQ-QP* has the ability to process the vague queries plus all the other kinds of queries which renders it the only queriable XML compressor with such a feature.

Another evaluation test was made to compare the time required to process a query and retrieve the relevant information accordingly. Since each of the previous XML compressors used a different set of queries and documents to test their querying

Figure 9. Testing XCVQ-QP querying time

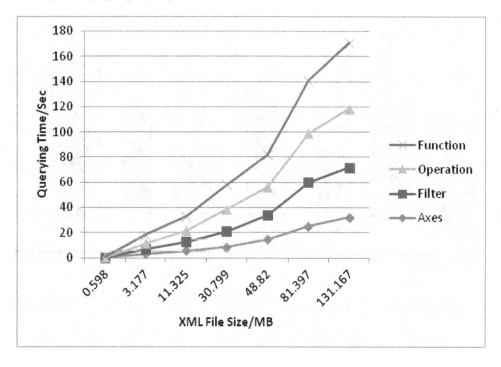

Figure 10. XCVQ query processing time against (a) XGrind and Xpress, (b) XQZip, and (c) XSAQCT

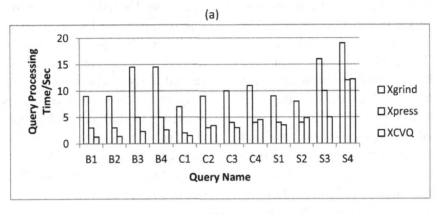

(a)

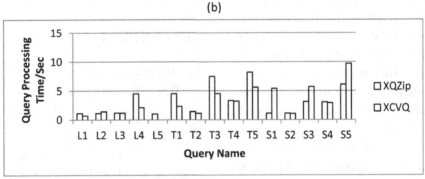

(b)

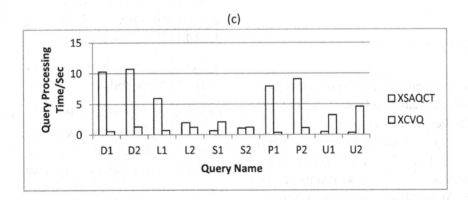

(c)

time, several tests were made to compare *XCVQ-QP* with these compressors using their queries and XML document sets.

The evaluation tests were made to compare the querying time with XGrind and Xpress, XQZip, and XSAQCT using the set of queries and the XML documents listed in Appendix-E (Set-1)

(Min et al., 2003), (Set-2) (Yang et al., 2006), and (Set-3) (Müldner et al., 2009) respectively.

As declared in Figure 10, the time required to process the queries using *XCVQ-QP* was less than the time required to process the same queries using almost all the previous XML queriable compressors, except for the queries that require data retrieval such as the queries in the filter concept. This is due to the fact that *XCVQ-QP* needs to decompress the relevant containers in order to retrieve the required information. The time of *XCVQ-QP* was even more than the other compressors when retrieving information from the textual XML documents since the size of the containers in these documents were higher than other types of documents.

The designed query processor is considered to be the first processor which has the ability to retrieve information according to all types of queries from the compressed XML documents. Comparing it with the techniques that retrieve information from the original XML documents, *XCVQ-QP* covers different sides of vague queries (path expansion, data value expansion, and function set expansion). On the other hand, the previous techniques are dedicated to solving only one side (path expansion as in (Grust, 2002; Amer-Yahia et al., 2004) and or two sides (path expansion and function expansion as in (Campi et al., 2009) or path expansion and data value expansion as in (Brisaboa et al., 2010).

1.9 SUMMARY

In this chapter, extensive tests were carried out to check the performance and functional abilities of *XCVQ*. In the compressor part of the model, the model was tested using a corpus of XML documents that have different features. After comparing the compression ratio with other XML compressors, *XCVQ* showed better ratios in most of the tested documents and its average ratio was higher than all other tested techniques. On the other hand, the compression time was high and needs further development in the future. An independent test was also made to test the compression ratio of *XCVQ-C* and the results of the tested data are listed in Appendix-F in chapter 12.

From the decompression side, *XCVQ-D* was fast enough compared to the existing techniques and the decompressed documents were lossy

when there were dummy elements in the XML document. The ratio of the dummy elements and that of the structure loss are listed in Appendix-G.

Finally, *XCVQ-QP* was tested to check for its ability to retrieve information according to several kinds of vague queries and other kinds of queries. A benchmark of queries was chosen and tested for the functional and the performance abilities of the designed model. The results were very encouraging, since the model proved its ability to process different kinds of queries in a competitive processing time.

REFERENCES

Amer-Yahia, S., Lakshmanan, L. V. S., & Pandit, S. (2004). *FleXPath: Flexible structure and fulltext querying for XML.* Paper presented at the ACM, SIGMOD, Paris, France.

Arion, A., Bonifati, A., Manolescu, I., & Pugliese, A. (2007). XQueC: A query-conscious compressed XML database. *ACM Transactions on Internet Technology, 7*(2), 10. doi:10.1145/1239971.1239974

Beizer, B. (1990). *Software testing techniques* (2nd ed.). New York.

Brisaboa, N. R., Cerdeira-Pena, A., Navarro, G., & Pasi, G. (2010). *An efficient implementation of a flexible XPath extension.* Paper presented at the Recherche d'Information Assistee par Ordinateur - RIAO.

Campi, A., Damiani, E., Guinea, S., Marrara, S., Pasi, G., & Spoletini, P. (2009). A fuzzy extension of the XPath query language. *Journal of Intelligent Information Systems, 33*(3), 285–305. doi:10.1007/s10844-008-0066-3

Cheng, J., & Ng, W. (2004). *XQZip: Querying compressed XML using structural indexing.* Paper presented at the International Conference on Extending Data Base Technology (EDBT).

Farrell-Vinay, P. (2008). *Manage software testing.* Auerbach. doi:10.1201/9781420013849

Franceschet, M. (2005). Lecture Notes in Computer Science: *Vol. 3671. XPathMark: Functional and performance tests for XPath* (pp. 129–143). Berlin, Germany: Springer.

Grust, T. (2002). *Accelerating XPath location steps.* Paper presented at the ACM SIGMOD International Conference on Management of Data.

Maneth, S., Mihaylov, N., & Saker, S. (2008). *XML tree structure compression.* Paper presented at the XANTEC'08, IEEE Computer Society.

Min, J.-K., Park, M.-J., & Chung, C.-W. (2003). *XPRESS: A queriable compression for XML data.* Paper presented at the 2003 ACM SIGMOD International Conference on Management of data.

Müldner, T., Fry, C., Miziołek, J. K., & Durno, S. (2009). *XSAQCT: XML queryable compressor.* Paper presented at the Balisage: The Markup Conference 2009.

Sakr, S. (2009). XML compression techniques: A survey and comparison. *Journal of Computer and System Sciences, 75*(5), 303–322. doi:10.1016/j.jcss.2009.01.004

Salomon, D. (2007). *Data compression: The complete reference* (4th ed.). Springer.

Tolani, P. M., & Haritsa, J. R. (2000). *XGRIND: A query-friendly XML compressor.* Paper presented at the IEEE 18th International Conference on Data Engineering.

Yang, Y., Ng, W., Lau, H. L., & Cheng, J. (2006). *An efficient approach to support querying secure outsourced XML information.* Paper presented at the 18th Conference on Advanced Information Systems Engineering (CAiSE).

Chapter 12
Conclusions and Future Work

Badya Al-Hamadani
University of Huddersfield, UK

Joan Lu
University of Huddersfield, UK

ABSTRACT

This thesis introduces a new model which has the ability to compress an XML document efficiently and retrieve information from the compressed file according to vague queries and even various other types of queries. This chapter will outline the main conclusions of the research as well as the main advantages and limitations of the designed model. Finally, the chapter will also list possible future trends in this research in terms of developing the proposed model.

1.1 CONCLUSION

As the importance of XML usage for storing and transferring data via the World Wide Web becomes increasingly clear, there is a corresponding need to compress the size of XML documents, dealing with them in their compressed mode so as to make them accessible to devices with limited resources. When these compressed documents are used by simple users, in a situation where there is absence of schema, or if such a user has no exact idea of what s/he is looking for, there should be a special technique available to adequately deal with these

types of queries. The questions had been raised by this research and their answers are as follows:

1. Is it possible to design a new compression technique that has the ability to compress the XML documents and achieve better compression ratio without the need to the document's Schema or its DTD?

    The answer to this question is *XCVQ* compressor. The design of the model showed the best average compression ratio (78.45) among the other XML queriable compressors without the need to the XML schema to be available. This was due to several reasons, such as: (1) limiting the storage of each element and attribute name in the document

DOI: 10.4018/978-1-4666-1975-3.ch012

to only one number, which represents the order of that element or attribute in the XML document, instead of being two numbers, and (2) increase the granularity of the data to be compressed in order to perform better compression ratio. Although this design issue increased the compression ratio, but it affects the time required to compress the document by increasing this time to be higher than the time require to compress these documents using other techniques. However, the compression process usually made only once, while the querying process can be done hundreds of times to retrieve information from the compressed files.

2. What is the influence of the structure redundancy on the overall size of the XML document?

To answer this question, *XCVQ Structure Compressor* was designed. In the compression process of the XML documents, the research found the strong affect of the redundancy in the structure of the document on its overall size. By succinctly storing the structure part of the XML document and keeping the data part as it is, the experiments showed good compression ratios which were up to 85.43 and averaged 49.47 for the tested XML corpus. This shows the big redundancy in the structure part of the document, apart which is considered to be very important for several purposes and retrieving information is one of them.

3. What are the main types of vague queries and when they can be occur? Have the existing XPath query language the ability to answer vague queries? If no, what is the required expansion that should be made on XPath to give it this ability?

Vague queries are one of the important types of queries. They occur in different situations and require special ways to be processed since the existing query languages do not have the abil-

ity to answer these queries. The *XCVQ-QP* can deal with simple and complex queries by forcing each query to pass by two decomposition stages in order to make it easier to retrieve information from the relevant document(s) and then combine the sub-results to be decompressed and submitted to the user. This process required the expansion of XPath query language in different sides: the path expansion, the data value expansion, and the set of functions expansion. The time required to process the queries are very competitive especially when dealing with structure-based queries, since the compressed structure of the document helps in accelerating the retrieving process.

4. How to determine the relevant XML document(s) from thousands of documents without the need to scan them completely for time saving purposes? And is it possible to retrieve information from more than one XML document without the pre-specification of these documents using one XPath query?

Instead of scanning the complete document to search for a specific bit of data, *XCVQ-QP* uses the path-dictionary, which contains all the elements and attributes names, to specify the relevant documents from thousand of XML documents. In this way, it is now possible to retrieve information from unspecified document(s). While all the existing XML query processors required the user to pre-specify the required documents to retrieve information from them, *XCVQ-QP* has the ability to retrieve information from one or more than one XML document without the need to specify exactly which document could contain the required information.

1.2 RECOMMENDATIONS

*   The main purpose of designing *XCVQ* is to process vague queries on compressed XML documents. For that reason, the first

recommendation for the model is to be used in cases where vague queries could be submitted, such as when dealing with naive users, where there is absence of schema, and when the required information is scattered among many files.

- The model is recommended to be used in retrieving information from XML documents when these documents have to be stored in devices with limited resources. The required documents can be compressed once and then queried several times with very limited resources requirements.

1.3 FUTURE WORK

Several research issues can be explored to improve the model:

- The model in this research can be developed to convert *XCVQ* into a complete XML management system with the ability to manage XML document in its compressed stage. The management process includes adding, deleting, or editing elements or attributes names. This process does not require any decompression, since the change is only made to the structure part of the document. The management process can include editing in this part of the document. In this case, only the container(s) with the required data should be decompressed using the Gzip back-end decompressor. They could also be used for editing the data and re-compressing the container(s).

- Another development is providing the ability to retrieve information from XML documents written in languages other than English. This could be done by adding a translator to translate any data part into other languages and retrieve the information accordingly.

- The model can be enriched by adding a Natural Language Processor that can convert a user's query into a vague XPath query and then retrieve the required information from the compressed XML document.

- Remains to be fully implemented is the complete set of XPath statements such as "for" and "if".

APPENDIX-A: XPATH'S EBNF

The complete EBNF of the XPath query language is listed in this appendix (Table 1). This form had been used in *XCVQ* to check the correctness of the syntax of the submitted query.

APPENDIX-B: IMPLEMENTING XCVQ

The implementation of *XCVQ* is done using *Eclipse* environment for java programming language. The GUI for the system uses the (visualswing4eclipse) plug-in to makes the design more powerful, friendly, and easy to use. The main window of the system is shown in Figure 1. Using this GUI the user can compress, decompress and querying XML documents.

This section illustrates the implementation part of *XCVQ* compressor, decompressor, and the vague query processor.

1. Implementation of XCVQ-C

According to all the advantages of using SAX parser mentioned in section 1 to parse the given XML document, SAX parser (from *Eclipse* environment for java programming language) is used to scan the XML document. This type of parsing scans the document only once by detecting several events from that document. During each event *XCVQ-C* collects information from the document in order to use it in the compression process. The events and the work through each one are listed below and illustrated in the class diagram in Figure 2.

1. *(StartDocument):* this event is cached only once by SAX when it detects the first tag of the document. In this stage *XCVQ-C* only initializes the used variables and prepares the used data structures and the output file to receive the data. Furthermore it specifies the name space used in that document and save it for further processes.
2. *(startElement):* this event is coached by SAX each time it detects an open tag. It holds the name of the element (*qName*) and the list of attribute names and values associated with this element (if any). In this stage, *XCVQ-C* performs the algorithm in Figure 3.
3. *(characters):* this event occurs when a data value appeared in the XML document. SAX could process this event more than once to deal with the same data. The data value is accumulated and added to the list of data in a leaf node in its appropriate path as illustrated in Figure 3.
4. *(endElement):* SAX processes this event when it catches the end of an element, a case means that there is a piece of data ready to be inserted in a leaf node of the structured-tree (if that element holds data). The suitable path can be known from the contents of the *pathStack* as described in Figure 4.
5. **(endDocument):** this event is processed only once by SAX when it catches the very end of the XML document. In this stage the containers first are created from the structured-tree as illustrated in Figure 4. Each container has an index which represents the path from the root to the leaf for the data contained in this container. Secondly, the contents of each container are compressed using one of the back-end general purposes compression techniques either Gzip or LZW. The complete algorithm for LZW compressor is shown in Figure 4.

Table 1.

[1]	XPath	::=	Expr
[2]	Expr	::=	ExprSingle (“,” ExprSingle)*
[3]	ExprSingle	::=	ForExpr | QuantifiedExpr | IfExpr | OrExpr
[4]	ForExpr	::=	SimpleForClause “return” ExprSingle
[5]	SimpleForClause	::=	“for” “$” VarName “in” ExprSingle (“,” “$” VarName “in” ExprSingle)*
[6]	QuantifiedExpr	::=	(“some” | “every”) “$” VarName “in” ExprSingle (“,” “$” VarName “in” ExprSingle)* “satisfies” ExprSingle
[7]	IfExpr	::=	“if” “(” Expr “)” “then” ExprSingle “else” ExprSingle
[8]	OrExpr	::=	AndExpr (“or” AndExpr)*
[9]	AndExpr	::=	ComparisonExpr (“and” ComparisonExpr)*
[10]	ComparisonExpr	::=	RangeExpr ((ValueComp | GeneralComp | NodeComp) RangeExpr)?
[11]	RangeExpr	::=	AdditiveExpr (“to” AdditiveExpr)?
[12]	AdditiveExpr	::=	MultiplicativeExpr ((“+” | “-”) MultiplicativeExpr)*
[13]	MultiplicativeExpr	::=	UnionExpr ((“*” | “div” | “idiv” | “mod”) UnionExpr)*
[14]	UnionExpr	::=	IntersectExceptExpr ((“union” | “|”) IntersectExceptExpr)*
[15]	IntersectExceptExpr	::=	InstanceofExpr ((“intersect” | “except”) InstanceofExpr)*
[16]	InstanceofExpr	::=	TreatExpr (“instance” “of” SequenceType)?
[17]	TreatExpr	::=	CastableExpr (“treat” “as” SequenceType)?
[18]	CastableExpr	::=	CastExpr (“castable” “as” SingleType)?
[19]	CastExpr	::=	UnaryExpr (“cast” “as” SingleType)?
[20]	UnaryExpr	::=	(“-” | “+”)* ValueExpr
[21]	ValueExpr	::=	PathExpr
[22]	GeneralComp	::=	“=” | “!=” | “<” | “<=” | “>” | “>=”
[23]	ValueComp	::=	“eq” | “ne” | “lt” | “le” | “gt” | “ge”
[24]	NodeComp	::=	“is” | “<<” | “>>”
[25]	PathExpr	::=	(“/” RelativePathExpr?) | (“//” RelativePathExpr) | RelativePathExpr
[26]	RelativePathExpr	::=	StepExpr ((“/” | “//”) StepExpr)*
[27]	StepExpr	::=	FilterExpr | AxisStep
[28]	AxisStep	::=	(ReverseStep | ForwardStep) PredicateList
[29]	ForwardStep	::=	(ForwardAxis NodeTest) | AbbrevForwardStep
[30]	ForwardAxis	::=	(“child” “::”) | (“descendant” “::”) | (“attribute” “::”) | (“self” “::”) | (“descendant-or-self” “::”) | (“following-sibling” “::”) | (“following” “::”) | (“namespace” “::”)

continued on following page

Table 1. Continued

[31]	AbbrevForwardStep	::=	"@"? NodeTest
[32]	ReverseStep	::=	(ReverseAxis NodeTest) | AbbrevReverseStep
[33]	ReverseAxis	::=	("parent" "::") | ("ancestor" "::") | ("preceding-sibling" "::") | ("preceding" "::") | ("ancestor-or-self" "::")
[34]	AbbrevReverseStep	::=	".."
[35]	NodeTest	::=	KindTest | NameTest
[36]	NameTest	::=	QName | Wildcard
[37]	Wildcard	::=	"*" | (NCName ":" "*") | ("*" ":" NCName)
[38]	FilterExpr	::=	PrimaryExpr PredicateList
[39]	PredicateList	::=	Predicate*
[40]	Predicate	::=	"[" Expr "]"
[41]	PrimaryExpr	::=	Literal | VarRef | ParenthesizedExpr | ContextItemExpr | FunctionCall | FunctionCallList FunctionCallList::= "synonyms" " (" StrinLiteral ")" | "similar(" StrinLiteral ")" | "avg(" pathExpr ")" | "median" " (" pathExpr ")" | "between" " (" IntegerLiteral | DecimalLiteral | DoubleLiteral "," IntegerLiteral | DecimalLiteral | DoubleLiteral ")"
[42]	Literal	::=	NumericLiteral | StringLiteral
[43]	NumericLiteral	::=	IntegerLiteral | DecimalLiteral | DoubleLiteral
[44]	VarRef	::=	"$" VarName
[45]	VarName	::=	QName
[46]	ParenthesizedExpr	::=	"(" Expr? ")"
[47]	ContextItemExpr	::=	"."
[48]	FunctionCall	::=	QName "(" (ExprSingle ("," ExprSingle)*)? ")"
[49]	SingleType	::=	AtomicType "?"?
[50]	SequenceType	::=	("empty-sequence" "(" ")") | (ItemType OccurrenceIndicator?)
[51]	OccurrenceIndicator	::=	"?" | "*" | "+"
[52]	ItemType	::=	KindTest | ("item" "(" ")") | AtomicType
[53]	AtomicType	::=	QName

continued on following page

Table 1. Continued

[54]	KindTest	::=	DocumentTest | ElementTest | AttributeTest | SchemaElementTest | SchemaAttributeTest | PITest | CommentTest | TextTest | AnyKindTest
[55]	AnyKindTest	::=	"node" "(" ")"
[56]	DocumentTest	::=	"document-node" "(" (ElementTest | SchemaElementTest)? ")"
[57]	TextTest	::=	"text" "(" ")"
[58]	CommentTest	::=	"comment" "(" ")"
[59]	PITest	::=	"processing-instruction" "(" (NCName | StringLiteral)? ")"
[60]	AttributeTest	::=	"attribute" "(" (AttribNameOrWildcard ("," TypeName)?)? ")"
[61]	AttribNameOrWildcard	::=	AttributeName | "*"
[62]	SchemaAttributeTest	::=	"schema-attribute" "(" AttributeDeclaration ")"
[63]	AttributeDeclaration	::=	AttributeName
[64]	ElementTest	::=	"element" "(" (ElementNameOrWildcard ("," TypeName "?"?)?)? ")"
[65]	ElementNameOrWildcard	::=	ElementName | "*"
[66]	SchemaElementTest	::=	"schema-element" "(" ElementDeclaration ")"
[67]	ElementDeclaration	::=	ElementName
[68]	AttributeName	::=	QName
[69]	ElementName	::=	QName
[70]	TypeName	::=	QName
[71]	IntegerLiteral	::=	Digits
[72]	DecimalLiteral	::=	("." Digits) | (Digits "." [0-9]*)
[73]	DoubleLiteral	::=	(("." Digits) | (Digits ("." [0-9]*)?)) [eE] [+-]? Digits
[74]	StringLiteral	::=	('"' (EscapeQuot | [^"])* '"') | ("'" (EscapeApos | [^'])* "'")
[75]	EscapeQuot	::=	'""'
[76]	EscapeApos	::=	"''"
[77]	Comment	::=	"(:" (CommentContents | Comment)* ":)"
[78]	QName	::=	[http://www.w3.org/TR/REC-xml-names/#NT-QName][Names]
[79]	NCName	::=	[http://www.w3.org/TR/REC-xml-names/#NT-NCName][Names]
[80]	Char	::=	[http://www.w3.org/TR/REC-xml#NT-Char][XML]
[81]	Digits	::=	[0-9]+
[82]	CommentContents	::=	(Char+ - (Char* ('(:' | ':)') Char*))

The LZW algorithm starts with filling the first 256 positions in the *dictionary* with the 256 printable characters (line 3). The scanning process for the input string starts character by character in an attempt to look for the maximum sequence of characters belongs to the dictionary and add the index of this

Figure 1. The main screen of XCVQ

Figure 2. XCVQ-C Class Diagram

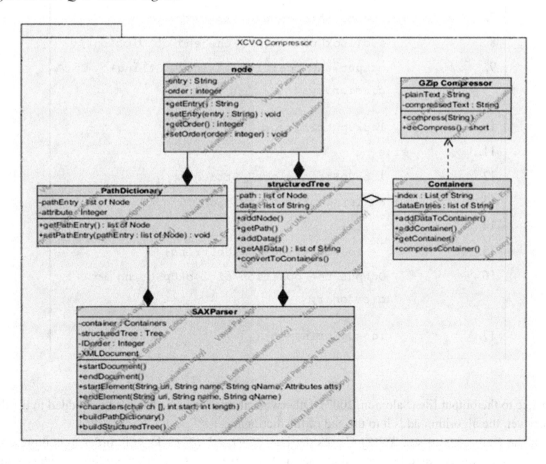

Figure 3. (character) algorithm

```
1.      Algorithm characters(chaArray ch[])
2.          data+=ch[];
3.          ignoreWhiteSpaces(data)
4.      End.
```

Figure 4. (LZW) algorithm

```
1.      Algorithm LZW(String input)
2.          input={c₁, c₂, …cₙ}
3.          let dictionary={all the 256 printable characters}
4.          lookUpString=c₁
5.          for all cᵢ ∈ input: i=2, 3, …n
6.              lookUpString=lookUpString+ cᵢ
7.              if (lookUpString) ∉ dictionary
8.                  add(lookUpString)to the end of dictionary
9.                  output the position of lookUpString+cᵢ in
                    dictionary
10.                 lookUpString= cᵢ₊₁
11.             else
12.                 lookUpString=lookUpString+ cᵢ₊₁
13.                 While (lookUpString + cᵢ₊₁ ∈ dictionary)
14.                     i++
15.                     lookUpString=lookUpString+ cᵢ
16.                 Output the position of lookUpString in
                    dictionary
17.                 lookUpString= cᵢ₊₁
```

sequence to the output file (Salomon, 2007). Otherwise, if this sequence has not been added to the dictionary yet, the algorithm adds it to the end of the dictionary.

For the Gzip compressor, *XCVQ-C* uses the java *(java.util.zip)* package in order to compress the required data. This package has several classes and one of them is *(GZIPOutputStream)* class which consists of more than one constructor, each of which is used to convert the input stream into a zip file.

Figure 5. GUI for compression results

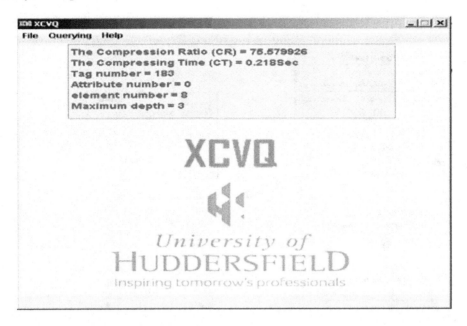

Figure 6. (XCVQ-D) class diagram

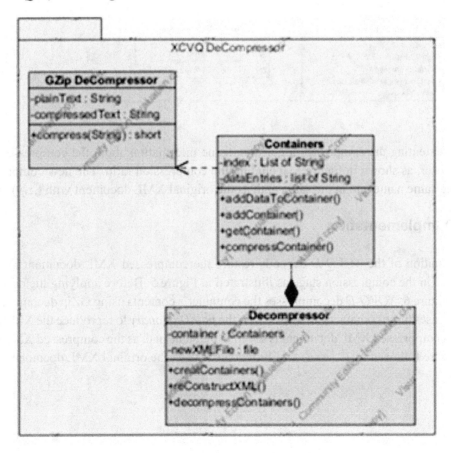

Figure 7. (XCVQ-D) class diagram

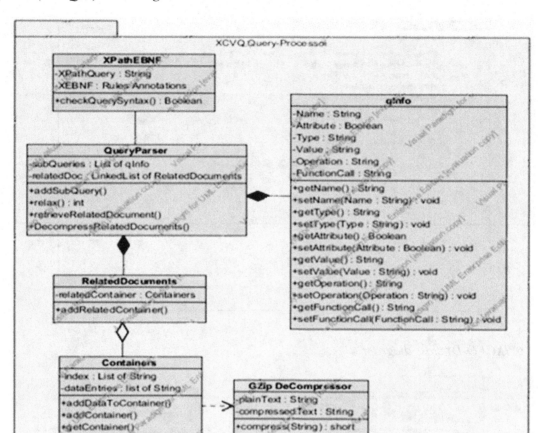

After implementing the compressor algorithm, some information about the compressed file is appeared to the user, as shown in Figure 5, including the compression ratio. The new compressed file is saved with the same name and in the same path as the original XML document with (*.zip*) extension.

2. XCVQ-D Implementation

The implementation of the *XCVQ-D* depends restore the compressed XML document into the same containers used in the compression stage as illustrated in Figure 5. Before applying the decompression algorithm in Figure 6, *XCVQ-D* decompresses the container's contents using GZip decompression technique and then uses these containers alongside with the *pathDictionary* to reproduce the XML document.

The new decompressed XML document is saved in the same path as the compressed XML document, carrying its name followed by (*_1.xml*) to differentiate it from the original XML document.

Figure 8. GUI for XCVQ-QP

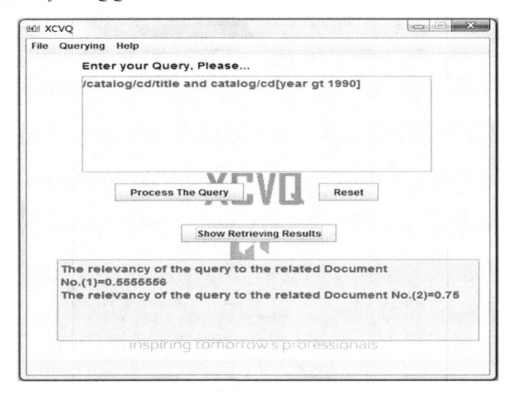

3. XCVQ-QP Implementation

The implementation of *XCVQ-QP* passes through several stages. Each stage has specific roles and certain classes which are illustrated in Figure 7.

The main steps of each stage and the detailed roles are listed in the following sections.

a.   XPath's EBNF expansion

When the user writes a vague query using the GUI in Figure 8, this syntax of this query is checked against the XPath Extended Backus-Naur Form (EBNF) (W3C, 2007a) which specifies the grammar of XPath language. The complete EBNF for XPath query language can be seen in Appendix-A.

Since *ZXCQ-QP* performs expansion on XPath grammars to provide it the capability of accept vague conditions, an expansion process is performed on the XPath EBNF. This expansion includes:

```
PrimaryExpr = Literal | VarRef | ParenthesizedExpr | ContextItemExpr | Func-
tionCall | FunctionCallList
FunctionCallList::= "synonyms" "("  StrinLiteral ")"
               | "similar("  StrinLiteral ")"
  | "avg("  pathExpr ")"
  | "median" "(" pathExpr ")"
```

Figure 9. An XPath query (a) and its semantic tree (b)

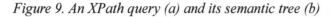

```
/CATALOG/CD/TITLE and /CATALOG/CD[YEAR > 1990]
```
(a)

```
XPath2

    XPath

      Expr

        AndExpr  and

          PathExpr

            Slash  /

            StepExpr

              AbbrevForwardStep

                NodeTest

                  NameTest

                    QName  CATALOG

            StepExpr

              AbbrevForwardStep

              NodeTest

                NameTest

                  QName  CD

          StepExpr

            AbbrevForwardStep

            NodeTest

              NameTest
```
(b)

```
| "between" "(" IntegerLiteral
                    | DecimalLiteral
     | DoubleLiteral "," IntegerLiteral
            | DecimalLiteral
                    | DoubleLiteral ")"
```

Using Java Compiler-Compiler (JavaCC), the expanded EBNF for XPath is converted into executable java source code to makes it possible to follow the instructions of the EBNF and checks the syntax

Table 2. The set of types provided by XCVQ-QP to qName

predicateLiteral	predicateString	comparisonLiteral	comparisonString
comparisonPath	functionName	andExpr	orExpr
ifVariable	forVariable	ifExpr	forExpr
pathExpr			

Table 3. The qInfo structure for the query in Figure 9

Name	Attribute	Type	Value	Operation	FunctionCall
CATALOG	False	andExpr			
CD	False	pathExpr			
TITLE	False	pathExpr			
CATALOG	False	andExpr			
CD	False	predicateLiteral			
YEAR	False	comparisonLiteral	1990	>	

Figure 10. Processing an XPath query algorithm

```
1.      Algorithm processXPathQuery(structure qInfo)
2.      let qInfo= [a₁, a₂, …, aₙ] such that:
3.      let fileDB=[f₁, f₂, …, fₘ]
4.      let relevant=[r₁, r₂, …, rₖ]
5.      for all aᵢ.Name ∈ qInfo
6.        for all fⱼ ∈ fileDB
7.           if aᵢ.Name ∈ fⱼ.pathDictionary
8.                relevant.pathDictionary ← fⱼ
9.                relevant.query ← aᵢ
10.     for all rᵢ ∈ relevant
11.          subQuery= Decpmpose(rᵢ.query)
12.          cost=relax(rᵢ.subQuery)
13.          if cost>threshold
14.              remove (rᵢ) from relevant
15.          tree=retrieveData
16.     allTrees=Combine all the retrieved trees
```

Figure 11. Query decomposition function

```
1.  Function decompose (query Q)
2.  let Containers=[c₁, c₂, …, cₙ]
3.  For all cᵢ
4.      If Q.nameⱼ ∈ cᵢ.index
5.          newSub-queries ← Q.nameⱼ
6.          newSub-query ← cᵢ
7.      }
8.  End.
```

and lexical errors in the user's query. If the query does not meet the XPath grammar, an error message appears to the user determining the exact place of the error within the query.

The syntactically correct query is converted into a tree structure depending on the semantic of the XPath query. As an example, Figure 9- (a) shows a query and (b) shows its semantic tree. The semantic tree for each query determines the type of each part of that query. In this example the query is divided into two main branches since it has the (AndExpr and), each branch is a (PathExpr). The first branch holds the (CATALOG, CD, and TITLE) QNames, while the second branch holds (CATALOG, CD, and Year) QNames with the (IntegerLiteral) accompanied the (YEAR) element.

The tree structure of the given query is used by *XCVQ-QP* to determine the type of each QName and to build the required data structure in order to process the query as discussed in the next section.

b.   Storing the Query

XCVQ-QP uses a pre-designed data structure named (*qInfo*) in order to store all the required information from the query. This structure has the fields as presented in Table 2.

1. *Name*: this field stores all the *QNames* appear in the query.
2. *Attribute*: it is a Boolean field which is true if the *QName* is an attribute and is false otherwise.
3. *Type*: in this field the type of each *QName* is stored. *XCVQ-QP* provides each *QName* a specific type according to its position and role in the query. The set of provided types is shown in Table 3. These types cover all the kinds of XPath query that can be processed by *XCVQ-QP*.
4. *Value*: if there is a literal or a string value in the query, then it is associated with the proper *qName*.
5. *Operation*: this field stores the arithmetical and logical operations in the query.
6. *FunctionCall:* stores the list of parameters for the function if there is one in the query.

Table 3 illustrates the *qInfo* structure for the query example in Figure 10.

Table 4. XML Corpus

Group#	XML file name	File Size/MB	%SR	Tag no	Element no	Attributes no	Max depth
1	321gone	2.441E-2	38.06	311	32	0	6
	Ebay	3.515E-2	11.14	156	32	0	6
	Ubid	2.050E-2	42.63	342	32	0	6
	Yahoo_Shopping	2.539E-2	34.1	342	32	0	6
	Homeseekers	2.603	58.12	59322	35	0	5
	Nky	3.213	70.43	112051	50	0	5
	Texas	3.177	58.7	84577	54	0	5
	Yahoo_Homes	0.419	56.77	11038	33	0	3
	XMark-1	11.325	30.16	520546	74	0	12
	XMark-2 (Schmidt et al., 2002; Washington, 2002)	113.061	30.03	5167121	74	0	12
2	Baseball (Washington, 2002)	0.632	92.95	28306	46	0	6
3	Berkeley	9.277E-2	32.96	1143	15	0	6
	Cornell	3.027E-2	45.64	833	15	0	6
	Michigan	6.738E-2	46.68	1899	15	0	6
	Texas	3.222E-2	44.88	859	15	0	6
	Washington	5.175E-2	33.28	1025	15	0	6
	Read	0.283	63.22	10546	16	0	5
	Uwm	2.226	58.41	66729	16	6	6
	Wsu (Washington, 2002)	1.558	73.99	74557	16	0	5
4	CD-Catalog	0.598	63.68	183	8	0	3
5	DBLP (Washington, 2002)	131.167	45.1	4718588	32	3	5
6	EnWikiNews	69.421	10.13	2103778	20	4	6
	EnWikiQuote	124.532	3.69	2672870	20	4	6
	EnWikiVersity	81.397	10.64	3333622	20	4	6
	EnWikTionary (Wikipedia, 2001)	556.612	26.26	28656178	20	4	6
7	EXI-Array	22.062	43.7	226523	47	0	14
	EXI-factbook	4.042	47.47	55453	199	0	8
	EXI-GeogCoord	15.828	0.003	17	30	0	11
	EXI-Invoice	0.934	65.41	15075	52	28	9
	EXI-weblog (EXI, 2009)	2.526	72.49	93435	12	0	3
8	GB-meta	48.82	71.32	886419	97	18	13
	Sweden-meta	3.35	71.14	60614	101	17	12
	Turkey-meta (European, 2003)	5.85E-3	73.66	100	48	2	8
9	Henry IV, Part I	0.274	34.21	4334	14	0	7
	Richard II	0.251	32.48	4116	16	0	8
	j_caesar	0.181	37.95	4455	16	0	8
	Shakespeare (plays, 2000)	7.529	36.56	179690	22	0	9
10	LineItem	30.799	83.47	1022976	18	0	3
	XBench-DCSD-Normal	105.368	57.24	2242699	50	0	10
	XBench-DCSD-Small (Washington, 2002; Waterloo, 2003)	10.578	57.3	2259292	50	0	10
11	Mondial (Washington, 2002)	1.778	48.74	22423	23	45	8

continued on following page

Table 4. Continued

Group#	XML file name	File Size/MB	%SR	Tag no	Element no	Attributes no	Max depth
12	NASA (Washington, 2002)	24.622	37.13	476646	61	0	11
13	SwissPort (Washington, 2002)	112.761	56.5	13917441	85	0	5
14	Tree Bank (Washington, 2002)	85.416	31.65	10795711	250	0	36

c. Query Decomposition: Stage-1

After collecting the important information from the query and store them in (*qInfo*) structure, the algorithm in Figure 11 is processed. This algorithm starts by collecting the relevant documents from the compressed XML repository. During this process each compressed document is scanned for one of the *Name* field in the *qInfo* structure, if it contains one of them in its *path-dictionary*, then this file is candidate to be one of the relevant documents. If *(n)* relevant document encountered, only the *path-dictionary* for these documents are loaded into the memory and the original *qInfo* structure is decomposed into *(n)* structures each of which is associated with its relevant document (lines 5-9). This process decomposes the XPath query into several sub-queries according to their relevancy to a specific document.

d. Query Decomposition: Stage-2

After completing the first stage decomposition, the second stage of the decomposition is started by applying the decomposition function in Figure B-14 on each sub-query to produce a new set of sub-queries (line 11 in Figure 11). This function determines the relevant containers from the compressed file. This is done through checking if any *Name* field of the given sub-query is contained within the index of that container. In this case the relevant container is uploaded into the memory alongside with its relevant part from the sub-query.

For all the new sub-queries, each one is relaxed against the index of its relevant container, (line 12). This relaxation is done by performing a matching process between the sub-query and the index of its relevant container. This process performs changes on the original sub-query in order to fit it with the index by adding, removing, renaming, or reordering position in the nodes of the query. After each change, the cost of that change is computed and the total cost of relaxation is checked against a predefined threshold to determine if this query should be removed from the list of relevant queries if it has high cost (lines 13-14).

e. Retrieving and Combining Results

At this stage, (line 17), each container accompanied with its sub-query is on the memory ready to be retrieved. The retrieving process taking into consideration the type of each *qName* and its operation and retrieve only the required information. If the query required retrieving information from the data set attached in the container, decompression process is performed only on this single container in order to retrieve the required data. The example query in Figure B-12 has a predicate requiring the values of the (*YEAR*) data to be greater than (*1990*) which requires the performance of the decompression only on one container that has the data and filter these data to retrieve only the data that meet the condition.

Until this stage no decompression required when the query is structured based one. After combining all the retrieved sub-documents, each one is decompressed, using the same decompression algorithm in Figure 11, and combined under one XML document to form single tree instead of a forest.

The resulted document can be compressed again if the user needs to make further querying on it.

APPENDIX-C: XML CORPUS AND XPATH BENCHMARK

This appendix contains the XML corpus that were used in the testing process (Table 4), the description of its groups, and the complete XPath benchmark that were used in the testing process (Table 5).

The selected XML documents in the corpus were organized into many groups according to their origins and the purpose of their use, as follows:

Group-1: It consists of many XML documents that are used in online shopping processes through different e-shopping and auction web sites. These documents are converted from database systems and they contain many empty elements with neither data nor sub-elements inside them.

Group-2: the XML document in this group provides a complete description to all the teams including all the details about their players who participated in 1998 national league.

Group-3: This group contains XML documents from different academic department. Some of the documents describe simple CVs for the academic staff in these departments and the courses they teach. The other documents describe the detailed information for the courses submitted by some academic departments in different universities.

Group-4: The Document in this group gives details about many songs CDs such as their name, publication year, and their country.

Group-5: This group has only one document that illustrates different papers published in proceeding of conferences and journals in the field of computer science.

Group-6: different backup documents from Wikipedia web site are collected in this group.

Group-7: This group contains sample documents from a collection of documents collected by the Efficient XML Interchange (EXI) working group which is part of the W3C. These documents contain the needed information in data exchanging.

Group-8: The XML documents that describe the detailed climate changes in different countries around the world are listed in this group.

Group-9: This group has some of Shakespeare's plays which considered being (TD) document type.

Group-10: This document contains a huge amount of shipping information for online shopping for different items taken from Google web site.

Group-11: The XML document in this group contains lots of statistical information about many countries around the world such as their population, area, available natural resources, etc.

Group-12: This document is transferred from NASA database which includes summarization of some of the NASA projects converted from text file.

Table 5. XPath query benchmark

QFT Concept	Query Name	Query	Description
Axes	Q1	/catalog/cd	normal path (exact matching)
	Q2	/catalog/title/cd	Path out of order
	Q3	/cd/year/catalog	Does not start from the root
	Q4	/catalog/title	a gap exists, the actual path is (/catalog/cd/title)
	Q5	/catalog/yeer	miss spelling in the element name
	Q6	/cd/cateloge/yeer	miss spelling in more than one element name
	Q7	/catalog/cd/year/title	Sibling elements(year, title)
Filters	Q8	/catalog/cd/year[5]	Normal partial match (position filter)
	Q9	/catalog/cd/year["1990"]	Normal partial match (value filter)
	Q10	/cd/catalog/country["uk"]	Out of order path + predicate
	Q11	/cd/title/year/country[8]	Siblings + predicate
	Q12	cataloge/yeer/cuntry["USA"]	Spelling errors + predicate
Operators	Q13	/catalog/cd[year lt 2000]	Normal predicate with comparative operator
	Q14	/cd/title/artist[year ge 1990]	Sibling + comparative operator
	Q15	/cd/title[year lt 1990][country eq "uk"]	More than one comparative operator
	Q16	/cd/title/country["uk"][yeer le 1990]	Predicate + comparative operator
	Q17	/cd/title/year eq 1990	comparative operator without predicate
	Q18	/cd/year=2000	Relational operator (the result is either True or False)
	Q19	cd/title/yeer !=1998	Siblings + miss spelling + operation
	Q20	/cd[year gt 1990] and /cd[country eq "uk"]	(and) operator
Functions	Q21	/cd/title/synonyms("date")	Find the synonyms of an element name
	Q22	cd/country eq synonyms("Britain")	Find the synonym of a data value
	Q23	/cd/title/similar(artest)	Find the similar element name
	Q24	/cd/similar(artest)/title	Find the similar element name
	Q25	/cd/year/title eq similar("keep your heart")	Find the similar data value
	Q26	/cd/artist/count(title)	Find the number of occurrences of an element
Multi-File	Q27	/cd/book/year/title	Exact match
	Q28	/cd/book/title/artist/author/year	Siblings
	Q29	book/title/cd/yeer/aother	Miss spelling
	Q30	/cd/book/title/year["1990"]	Data value predicate
	Q31	book/title/year[4] and /cd/title/year	Order predicate
	Q32	/cd/book[year lt 1990][country eq "uk"]	Multiple predicates

Table 6.

XML file name	SCR	SCT/Sec	SDC/Sec	CR	CT/ Sec	DT/Sec
Turkey-meta	48.02	0.031	0.47	78.17	0.047	0.32
Ubid	60.34	0.032	0.31	83.35	0.047	0.47
321gone	38.99	0.042	0.46	73.31	0.078	0.47
Yahoo_Shopping	42.47	0.051	0.62	76.54	0.087	0.64
Cornell	68.66	0.062	0.31	87.5	0.102	0.47
Texas	45.71	0.063	0.32	81.75	0.13	0.78
Ebay	16.51	0.031	0.48	70.29	0.163	0.75
Washington	50.55	0.031	0.78	81.1	0.2	0.63
Michigan	70.83	0.047	0.41	89.3	0.42	1.09
Berkeley	50.81	0.094	0.47	81.94	0.538	0.62
j_caesar	30.32	0.14	0.64	70.91	0.58	1.1
Richard II	24.9	0.22	0.8	68.51	0.72	1.56
Henry IV, Part I	26.85	0.37	1.59	68.8	0.85	1.1
Read	64.82	0.583	1.85	87.33	0.988	1.14
Yahoo_Homes	43.32	0.68	3.04	83.35	0.96	2.19
CD-Catalog	57.67	0.77	4.13	75.53	0.94	2.32
Baseball	62.19	0.95	5.53	83.56	1.078	2.34
EXI-Invoice	58.98	0.98	5.62	73.63	1.28	3.12
Wsu	64.81	21.85	20.62	87.35	1.56	3.59
Mondial	59.37	14.64	32.81	85.35	4.42	6.56
Umw	66.37	39.17	31.56	90.35	4.43	4.37
EXI-weblog	44.6	54.8	57.81	72.38	7.3	4.84
Homeseekers	47.9	36.98	72.75	86.21	12.6	32.41
Texas	67.24	42.93	79.7	86.8	16.75	36.04
Nky	50.75	29.54	92.1	83.69	12.3	36.4
Sweden-meta	78.23	57.53	97.6	93.52	12.4	36.41
EXI-factbook	37.5	61.71	103.94	74.2	80.8	29.07
Shakespeare	26.01	85.5	148.6	69.32	130.8	32.09
XBench-DCSD-Small	27.76	103.7	155.7	69.92	194.6	38.28
XMark-1	38.45	120.8	165.3	75.38	225.6	39.01
EXI-GeogCoord	0.0031	169.1	198.8	75.61	374.7	40.1
EXI-Array	22.062	210.9	226.4	72.56	458.5	43.4
NASA	39.18	256.3	254.2	88.51	517.3	43.9
LineItem	30.799	312.8	297.7	81.51	692.4	78.6
GB-meta	77.22	370.6	337.2	75.67	734.2	81
EnWikiNews	69.421	398.9	412.3	68.52	810.6	89.89
EnWikiVersity	81.397	417.7	489.8	70.55	894.7	97.39
Tree Bank	37.68	426.3	504.4	79.8	956.2	99.87
XBench-DCSD-Normal	30.19	486.9	645.6	71.38	1069.8	100.19

continued on following page

Table 6. Continued

XML file name	SCR	SCT/Sec	SDC/Sec	CR	CT/ Sec	DT/Sec
SwissPort	58.12	502.6	702.4	81.2	1296.4	105.75
XMark-2	37.89	524.5	826.9	77.02	1368.8	113.65
EnWikiQuote	68.25	565.8	924.3	69.69	1438.1	123.9
DBLP	68.16	605.1	1022.3	79.54	1578.7	157.45
EnWikTionary	85.43	1104.7	3750.7	70.85	4152.7	260.9

Table 7. Set-1: The queries listed in this set were used to test the performance of XGrind and Xpress compressors, and were used to evaluate XCVQ-QP and compare the results with these two techniques

XML document	Query Name	Query
BaseBall	B1	SEASON/LEAGUE/DIVISION/TEAM/PLAYER/GIVEN NAME
	B2	//TEAM/PLAYER/SURNAME
	B3	/SEASON/LEAGUE//TEAM/TEAM CITY
	B4	/SEASON/LEAGUE//TEAM[TEAM CITY >= Chicago and TEAM CITY <= Toronto]
Umw	C1	/root/course/selection/session/place/building
	C2	//session/time
	C3	/root/course//session/time/start time
	C4	/root/course//session/time[start time >= 800 and start time <= 1200]
Shakespeare	S1	/PLAY/ACT/SCENE/SPEECH/STAGEDIR
	S2	//PGROUP/PERSONA
	S3	/PLAY/ACT//SPEECH/SPEAKER
	S4	/PLAY/ACT//SPEECH[SPEAKER>= CLEOPATRA and SPEAKER <= PHILO]

Table 8. Set-2: this set of queries, listed in the following table, was used to evaluate XCVQ-QP against XQzip compressor

XML document	Query Name	Query
LineItem	L1	//table/T/L_TAX
	L2	/table/T[L_TAX = "0.02"]
	L3	/table/T[L_TAX[[. >= "0.02"]]]
	L4	//T[L_ORDERKEY = "100"]
	L5	//L_ DISCOUNT
TreeBank	T1	//_QUOTE_//_NONE_
	T2	//_QUOTE_//_BACKQUOTES_
	T3	//_QUOTE_//NP[_NONE_ = "FTTVhQZv7pnPMt+EeoeOSx"]
	T4	//_QUOTE_//SBAR//VP/VBG
	T5	//_QUOTE_//NP/PRP_DOLLAR_
Shakespeare	S1	//SPEAKER
	S2	//PLAY//SCENE//STAGEDIR
	S3	//SPEECH[SPEAKER = "PHILO"]/LINE
	S4	//SCENE/SPEECH/LINE
	S5	//SCENE[TITLE="SCENE II. Rome. The house of EPIDUS"]/LINE

Table 9. Set-3: the queries listed in the following table were used to evaluate XCVQ-QP against XSAQCT compressor

XML document	Query Name	Query
dblp	*D1*	*/dblp/article/cdrom*
	D2	*/dblp/mastersthesis/@key*
LineItem	*L1*	*/table/T/L_COMMENT*
	L2	*/table/T/L_ORDERKEY*
Shakespeare	*S1*	*/PLAYS/PLAY/TITLE*
	S2	*PLAYS/PLAY/ACT/SCENE/STAGEDIR*
SwissPort	*P1*	*/root/Entry/@id*
	P2	*/root/Entry/Ref/Comment*
uwm	*U1*	*/root/course_listing/course*
	U2	*/root/course_listing/restrictions/A/@HREF*

Group-13: The complete description of the DNA sequence is described in the XML document in this group.

Group-14: This document contains many parsed and encrypted English sentences taken from the Wall Street Journal.

APPENDIX-D: TESTING RESULTS

The complete set of data that had been used to test and evaluate *XCVQ-C* and *XCVQ-D* is listed in the following table. Table 6 contains all the actual results for these testing.

APPENDIX-E: XPATH QUERY EVALUATION BENCHMARK

This appendix contains the complete set of queries that had been used to evaluate *XCVQ-QP* and comparing the results with other queriable XML compressors. It consists of three sets of queries:

APPENDIX-F: INDEPENDENT TESTING

The following table contains the XML documents that have been used in an independent testing to find the compression ratio using *XCVQ*. To find the compression ratio, the following equation was used:

$$\text{Compression ratio} = \frac{\text{Original}_{\text{XML}} \text{file size} - \text{Compressed}_{\text{ZIP}} \text{file size}}{\text{Original}_{\text{XML}} \text{file size}}$$

Table 10.

XML File Name	Compression Ratio
Setup of points	50%
books1	50%
cd_catalog	60%
TURKY_meta	66.7%
data_20101111102811	57.9%
ubid	81%
321gone	0.72%
yahoo	73.1%
cornell	87.1%
texas	84.8%
ebay	69.4%
washington	81.1%
berkeley	81.4%
j_caesar	71%
rich_ii	68%
Hen_vi_1	68.7%
reed	87.2%
yahoo_homes	83.3%
BaseBall	83.4%
EXI-Invoice	79.8%
Mondial	85.3%
uwm	90.35%
EXI-weblog	88.3%
homeseekers	86.2%
texas_house	81.7%
nky.xml	83.7%
SWEDEN_meta	93.6%
EXI-factbook	81.5%

The independent testing was made on environment Quad-Core Intel Xeon processor that has the speed of 2.8 GHz. The operating system was Mac OS X 10.6.4 with 8GB of hard drive.

APPENDIX-G: XML DUMMY ELEMENTS RATIO

Table 11 lists the ratio of the dummy elements in the tested XML documents which is the same ratio that represents the loss in the structure of these documents.

Table 11.

XML file name	%Dummy elements ratio
321gone	7.4
Ebay	1.3
Ubid	16.8
Yahoo_Shopping	9.2
Homeseekers	6.2
Nky	3.8
Texas	6.3
Yahoo_Homes	2.2
XMark-1	1.5
XMark-2	0.4
Baseball	1.2
Berkeley	12.2
Cornell	19.3
Michigan	19.5
Texas	4.1
Washington	4.7
Read	4.3
Umw	14.6
Wsu	12.4
CD-Catalog	0.0
DBLP	0.0
EnWikiNews	0.9
EnWikiQuote	0.3
EnWikiVersity	1.2
EnWikTionary	1.1
EXI-Array	0.0
EXI-factbook	0.0
EXI-GeogCoord	0.0
EXI-Invoice	0.0
EXI-weblog	0.0
GB-meta	0.0
Sweden-meta	5.9

continued on following page

Table 11. Continued

XML file name	%Dummy elements ratio
Turkey-meta	0.0
Henry IV, Part I	1.6
Richard II	1.4
j_caesar	1.2
Shakespeare	2.4
LineItem	0.0
XBench-DCSD-Normal	0.0
XBench-DCSD-Small.xml	0.0
Mondial	9.2
NASA	0.0
SwissPort	0.0
Tree Bank	0.0

Section 3
Automatic Mapping of XML Documents into Relational Database

Ibrahim Dweib
Sultan Qaboos University, Muscat, Oman & University of Huddersfield, UK

Joan Lu
University of Huddersfield, UK

Extensible Markup Language (XML) nowadays is one of the most important standard media used for exchanging and representing data through the Internet. Storing, updating, and retrieving the huge amount of web services data such as XML is an attractive area of research for researchers and database vendors. In this section, the authors propose and develop a new mapping model, called MAXDOR, for storing, rebuilding, updating, and querying XML documents using a relational database without making use of any XML schemas in the mapping process. The model addresses the problem of solving the structural hole between ordered hierarchical XML and unordered tabular relational database to enable use of relational database systems for storing, updating, and querying XML data. A multiple link list is used to maintain XML document structure, manage the process of updating document contents, and retrieve document contents efficiently.

Experiments are done to evaluate MAXDOR model. MAXDOR is compared with other well-known models available in the literature using total expected value of rebuilding XML document execution time and insertion of token execution time.

Chapter 13
Automatic Mapping of XML Documents into Relational Database:
Introduction

Ibrahim Dweib
Sultan Qaboos University, Oman

Joan Lu
University of Huddersfield, UK

ABSTRACT

Extensible Markup Language (XML) nowadays is one of the most important standard media used for exchanging and representing data through the Internet. Storing, updating, and retrieving the huge amount of web services data such as XML is an attractive area of research for researchers and database vendors. In this chapter, the authors propose and develop a new mapping model, called MAXDOR, for storing, rebuilding, updating, and querying XML documents using a relational database without making use of any XML schemas in the mapping process. The model addressed the problem of solving the structural hole between ordered hierarchical XML and unordered tabular relational database to enable us to use relational database systems for storing, updating, and querying XML data. A multiple link list is used to maintain XML document structure, manage the process of updating document contents, and retrieve document contents efficiently. Experiments are done to evaluate MAXDOR model. MAXDOR will be compared with other well-known models available in the literature (Tatarinov et al., 2002) and (Torsten et al., 2004) using total expected value of rebuilding XML document execution time and insertion of token execution time.

DOI: 10.4018/978-1-4666-1975-3.ch013

INTRODUCTION

The World Wide Web (WWW) nowadays is an important medium used by many people for many activities in their daily life (i.e.; e-management, e-learning, e-mail, e-library and e-business). Many enterprises are working together using XML technologies for exchanging their web services data. Exchanging, sorting, updating and retrieving these huge data has become a source of concern for researchers and database vendors.

At present, storing and retrieving of XML documents can be done using mainly three approaches, i.e., native XML database (Jagadish et al., 2003; M. Grinev et al., 2004), Object Oriented Database (Chung and Jesurajaiah, 2005) and Relational Database (Zhang and Tompa, 2004a; Shanmugasundaram et al., 1999); (Fujimoto et al., 2005; O'Neil et al., 2004) (Tan et al., 2005) (Leonardi and Bhowmick, 2005; Atay, 2006; Atay et al., 2007a; Min et al., 2008, Yun and Chung, 2008; Ahlgren and Colliander, 2009).

The most important factor in choosing the target database is the type of XML documents to be stored, data-centric (e.g., bank transaction, airlines transactions) or document-centric (e.g., emails, books, manual).

Using a hybrid approach of relational database to store and retrieve data and XML to exchange and represent it. This will solve most of the data issues of integrity, multi-user access, retrieving, exchanging, concurrency control, crash recovery, indexing, security, storing semi-structure data, and reliability. The previous studies of this approach can also be studied. These are: Loss of information, difficulties in updating its contents and difficulties in rebuilding of original document. The mapping techniques of this approach can generally be classified into two tracks: Schemaless-centric technique and schema–centric (Dweib et al., 2008). Schemaless-centric technique is used to make use of XML document structure to manage mapping process (Zhang & Tompa, 2004; Yoshikawa et al.,

2001; Jiang et al., 2002; Tatarinov et al., 2002; Soltan and Rahgozar, 2006). In schema–centric, XML schema information is used to develop a relational storage for XML documents (Shanmugasundaram et al., 1999; Atay et al., 2005; Yahia et al, 2004; Lee et al, 2006; Knudsen et al., 2005; Fujimoto et al., 2005, Xing et al., 2007). Unfortunately, relational storages constructed from schema-centric approach need database reconstruction as any change in the XML schema is very expensive. Each approach introduced some solutions for the mapping process but failed to solve others.

In this thesis we will concentrate on a new approach for mapping XML documents into relational database which is called MAXDOR (i.e. Mapping XML Document into Relational database). The model does not make use of any XML schemas to manage mapping process. In this model, the document structure and document contents are stored in relational database tables. It uses multi-links to reserve document structure and elements relations within the document as parent-child, ancestor-descendant, left- sibling and right-sibling. The use of multi-links will make the insertion process cost for new elements and attributes anywhere in the document close to constant value, since there is no need to relabel the elements and the attributes following the inserted element or attribute. Other models (Tatarinov et al., 2002) (Torsten et al., 2004) which consider the element or attribute label as an identifier to reserve document structure, the cost of insertion in this case will vary depending on the position of insertion, since relabeling is needed after each insertion to maintain the document order.

The proposed model uses a process of four steps: (1) Mapping XML document into relational database. To achieve this objective, a fixed relational schema is presented and used to maintain document contents relations and manage the contents. (2) Building XML document from relational database without a need to the original document.

To achieve this objective, the document contents are retrieved from the relational database and a new XML document file is created for it, and its name is represented by the document identification. (3) Updating XML document contents within the relational database without going back to the original document. To achieve this objective, an editor is created to browse the document as tree structure with a tool bar identifying the position of insertion for the new token in reference to the candidate token. (4) Querying and retrieving document contents through the use of XPath language. To achieve this objective, an editor is created to write the XPath expression, execute and display the results as tree view and grid view.

PROBLEM DEFINITION

The transformation method of XML documents to RDB should fulfil many requirements while each requirement is to fulfil certain application needs. In some applications it is extremely important to maintain nodes' order such as properties of an XML tag. However, in others order is not so significant. Some of these requirements are the following:

1. Maintain document structure without losing information during shredding.
2. Ease of process, transforming a fresh document should be an easy task, and updating an already transformed document should also be straight forward.
3. To reconstruct the XML document or part of it from relational database.
4. To perform semantic search.
5. To preserve the ordering nature of XML data and its structure.

From previous sections, it can be seen that some studies work on optimizing query time (Torsten, 2002; Soltan and Rahgozar, 2006), but they fail to update XML document stored in

relational database. That is because each insertion requires a lot of nodes to be relabelled after insertion of new node or subtree. Others (Chung and Jesurajaiah, 2005; Li and Moon, 2001; O'Neil et al., 2004) solve partially the updating problem by creating a gap within the label, but there is still a need for relabeling after consuming the reserved space. Other studies (Fujimoto et al., 2005; Shanmugasundaram et al., 1999; Tan et al., 2005; Chen et al., 2003; Amer-Yahia et al., 2004; Xing et al., 2007a; Atay et al., 2007b) work on storage optimization and create a relational schema depending on XML schema. Redundant data are removed by creating new relation for each recursive child (or inlining some child in parent relation to reduce the number of created relation). Sometimes a large number of relations are needed to be created for some complex document. Consequently, large numbers of joins are needed to retrieve document information from a relational database. Also sometimes XML schema is not available for some documents which require reconstructing XML schema first from document structure, and creating relational schema based on it. XML reconstruction is considered as a time overhead in this case. In some studies like (Zhang and Tompa, 2004b), they do a map for some parts of the XML document. They used the query to optimize the mapping time from XML document to relational database. They did not store the entire content of a document in a relational database. This method requires a mapping for each query, and cannot make use of other data stored in relational database.

It can be concluded that there is still a problem while updating an XML document content stored in relational database. A lot of data in a relational database is needed to be overwritten after inserting each new element or attribute in XML document. That is done to maintain XML document structure and reserve elements and elements' attributes order within the document.

RESEARCH AIM

The aim of this research is to minimize the updating execution time cost of XML document without affecting its structure. It seeks to achieve this aim throughout fulfilling the following two goals:

- Building XML document contents relations in an efficient way to maintain document structure and minimize updating execution cost.
- Forwarding queries to a subset of nodes that is most likely to have relevant information.

The above goals are achieved in the current research by the following objectives:

1. Relational engine will not be modified that may result in consistency problem.
2. The model will be efficient and will perform well for large XML documents.
3. The model is schema-independent. The model design does not depend on the schema information for the mapping process, since relational storages based on schema-centric approach need database reconstruction as any change in the XML schema.
4. Identify fixed relational schema to reserve XML document contents and structure depending on the previous objective.
5. Build XML document from relational database after updating its contents without significant difference in the execution time of building the original one.
6. Make the scheme of objective 2 applicable to queries, in such away that a query is forwarded to a set of nodes that cache information about desired XPath expression.

CONTRIBUTIONS

The following are the main contributions presented throughout this thesis:

- **XML document mapping into relational database:** a novel method is introduced to partition XML document into tokens (elements and attributes). It relies on assigning a tuple in relational table for each token information and relations with its neighbours. The method works efficiently and performs well for large XML documents.
- **Building XML document from relational database:** a novel method is introduced to rebuild original XML document or update one from relational database. It relies on retrieving document contents depending on token links and token level which formulate XML document as a group of subtrees.
- **Updating XML document contents:** a novel method is used to update (i.e. insert new token or modify its name or value) XML document contents stored in relational database. It is based on creating links for each token with its neighbours to maintain document structure without a need to relabel or re-index document contents.
- **Querying and retrieving XML document:** a novel method is introduced to access most of XPath axes preceding-sibling, following-sibling and descendant without storing all possible XPath information for document contents. It relies on creating a dummy table "XPathQuery table" for the desired XPath expression storing all interested tokens.

THESIS OUTLINE

We present a brief outline of the thesis:

In Chapter 14, the research background is discussed. This includes XML model, XML query languages, XML schema languages, XML Application Program Interface, XML documents types, XML data storage approaches, relational database model, and the similarities and differences between XML model and relational database model.

In Chapter 15, the approaches for storing XML documents in relational databases and for querying and retrieving XML Data from relational databases will be discussed according to their classification into schema-based mapping and schema-less mapping. Commercial Database Management System such as, DB2, Oracle, and SQL Server solutions to support XML will be discussed and reviewed. Rebuilding XML from RDBMS, their issues and approaches will be reviewed. Comparison of mapping approaches, their advantages and disadvantages will be discussed in the last sections.

In Chapter 16, a full description of a novel model is given and introduced in the thesis for Mapping XML Document into Relational database. This is called MAXDOR. This includes the main mathematical concepts that are used in this model. A description of the labelling method used to label the XML document and identifying its contents, the design framework for maintaining document structure, (i.e. parent-child, ancestor-descendant and siblings relations) between document contents is given. Mapping XML to relational database algorithm, building XML document from relational database algorithms using SAX parser, and updating of XML document contents which is stored in relational database algorithm are presented. Translating XPath query to SQL statements algorithm is included along with the query results in XML format.

In Chapter 17, a presentation of the system architecture, and the tools used for implementing the system of MAXDOR model is given. Theory implementation on a case study is also presented. The main classes for mapping XML document into relational database, building XML document from relational database, updating XML document contents stored in relational database and XpathToSql query translation and building the result in XML format methods, are also presented. XML data sets from selected XML bench marks

and XML data repository will be identified to be used for testing and evaluating the model.

In Chapter 18, a description of the experiment setup is given through experiment environment and performance measurement. In fact, a set of experiments are performed on mapping XML document into relational database, building XML document from relational database, updating XML document stored in relational database and retrieving document contents from relational database using XPath expressions. These experiments are performed to check the scalability and effectiveness of our model. Then, the model will be compared with the Global Encoding model (Tatarinov *et al.*, 2002) and the Accelerating XPath model (Torsten *et al.*, 2004). The comparison is performed in four stages of mapping, building, updating and retrieving, since the other studies just took one or two stages and did not address the others. Some took retrieving, while others took updating or updating and retrieving, but most of them did not consider mapping and rebuilding.

Finally, in Chapter 19, a summary of the thesis and discussion of further research directions are presented.

CONCLUSION

In this Chapter, introductions to the approaches that can be used to store and retrieve XML documents are given including: native XML database, Object Oriented Database and Relational Database. The problem definition which is the research works on is presented with identification for the requirements that are needed in the method used for mapping XML document into Relational Database. An overview of the thesis approach which uses the Relational Database approach to store, rebuild, update and querying XML is presented including the processes used for presenting this approach. The research aim, goals and thesis contributions are given. Finally the thesis outline is presented.

REFERENCES

Ahlgren, P., & Colliander, C. (2009). Document-document similarity approaches and science mapping: Experimental comparison of five approaches. *Journal of Informatrics, 3*, 49–63. doi:10.1016/j.joi.2008.11.003

Amer-Yahia, S., Du, F., & Freire, J. (2004). *A comprehensive solution to the XML-to-relational mapping problem.* In WIDM'04, Washington, DC, USA.

Atay, M. (2006). *XML2REL: An efficient system for storing and querying XML documents using relational databases* (p. 127). Detroit, Michigan: Graduate School, Wayne State University.

Atay, M., Chebotko, A., Liu, D., Lu, S., & Fotouhi, F. (2007a). *Efficient schema-based XML-to-relational data mapping* (pp. 458–476). Elsevier Science Ltd.

Atay, M., Chebotko, A., Liu, D., Lu, S., & Fotouhi, F. (2007b). Efficient schema-based XML-to-relational data mapping. *Information Systems, 32*, 458–476. doi:10.1016/j.is.2005.12.008

Chen, Y., Davidson, S., Hara, C., & Zheng, Y. (2003). RRXS: Redundancy reducing XML storage in relations. In *Proceedings of the 29th International Conference on Very Large Data Bases* - Vol. 29. Berlin, Germany: VLDB Endowment.

Chung, S. M., & Jesurajaiah, S. B. (2005). Schemaless XML document management in object-oriented databases. *International Conference on Information Technology: Coding and Computing, ITCC 2005*, Vol. 261, (pp. 261-266).

Dweib, I., Awadi, A., Alrahman, S. E. F., & Lu, J. (2008). Schemaless approach of mapping XML document into relational database. *8th IEEE International Conference on Computer and Information Technology, CIT 2008*, (pp. 167-172).

Fujimoto, K., Yoshikawa, T., Kha, D. D., Yashikawa, M., & Amagasa, T. (2005). *A mapping scheme of XML documents into relational databases using schema-based path identifiers.* International Workshop on Challenges in Web Information and Integration (WIRI'05).

Grinev, M., Fomichev, A., & Kuznetsov, S. (2004). *Sedna: A native XML DBMS.* MODIS ISPRAS.

Jagadish, H., Al-Khalifa, S., Chapman, A., Lakshmanan, L., Nierman, A., & Paparizos, S. … Yu, C. (2003). *TIMBER: A native XML database.* In SIGMOD, San Diego, CA.

Jiang, H., Lu, H., Wang, W., & Yu, J. X. (2002). XParent: An efficient RDBMS-based XML database system. *International Conference on Data Engineering*, 2002, (pp. 335-336).

Knudsen, S. U., Pedersen, T. B., Thomsen, C., & Torp, K. (2005). RelaXML: Bidirectional transfer between relational and XML Data. *9th International Database Engineering* (IDEAS'05) (pp. 151-162).

Lee, Q., Bressan, S., & Rahayu, W. (2006). *XShreX: Maintaining integrity constraints in the mapping of XML schema to relational.* 17th International Conference on Database and Expert Systems Applications (DEXA'06).

Leonardi, E., & Bhowmick, S. S. (2005, Nov). XANDY: A scalable change detection technique for ordered XML documents using relational databases. *Data & Knowledge Engineering, 59*, 32.

Li, Q., & Moon, B. (2001). Indexing and querying XML data for regular path expressions. *Proceedings of the 27th International Conference on Very Large Data Bases* (pp. 361 - 370).

Min, J.-K., Lee, C.-H., & Chung, C.-W. (2008). XTRON: An XML data management system using relational database. *Information and Software Technology, 50*, 18. doi:10.1016/j.infsof.2007.05.003

O'Neil, P., O'Neil, E., Pal, S., Cseri, I., Schaller, G., & Westbury, N. (2004) ORDPATHs: Insert-friendly XML node labels. In *Proceedings of the 2004 ACM SIGMOD International Conference on Management of Data*. Paris, France: ACM.

Shanmugasundaram, J., Tufte, K., Zhang, C., He, G., DeWitt, D. J., & Naughton, J. F. (1999). Relational databases for querying XML documents: Limitations and opportunities. *VLDB Conference* (pp. 302–314).

Soltan, S., & Rahgozar, M. (2006). A clustering-based scheme for labeling XML trees. *International Journal of Computer Science and Network Security, 6*, 84–89.

Tan, Z., Xu, J., Wang, W., & Shi, B. (2005). Storing normalized XML documents in normalized relations. *The Fifth International Conference on Computer and Information Technology* (CIT'05) (pp. 123-129).

Tatarinov, I., Viglas, S. D., Beyer, K., Shanmugasundaram, J., Shekita, E., & Zhang, C. (2002). *Storing and querying ordered XML using a relational database system* (pp. 204–215). SIGMOD.

Torsten, G. (2002) Accelerating XPath location steps. In *Proceedings of the 2002 ACM SIGMOD International Conference on Management of Data*. Madison, WI: ACM.

Torsten, G., Keulen, M. V., & Jens, T. (2004). Accelerating XPath evaluation in any RDBMS. *ACM Transactions on Database Technology, 29*, 40.

Xing, G., Xia, Z., & Ayers, D. (2007a). X2R: A system for managing XML documents and key constraints using RDBMS. In *Proceedings of the 45th Annual Southeast Regional Conference*. Winston-Salem, NC: ACM.

Xing, G., Xia, Z., & Ayers, D. (2007b). *X2R: A system for managing XML documents and key constraints using RDBMS*. Winston-Salem, NC: ACMSE.

Yoshikawa, M., Amagasa, T., Shimura, T., & Uemura, S. (2001). XRel: A path-based approach to storage and retrieval of XML documents using relational databases. *ACM Transactions on Internet Technology, 1*, 32. doi:10.1145/383034.383038

Yun, J.-H., & Chung, C.-W. (2008). Dynamic interval-based labelling scheme for efficient XML query and update processing. *Journal of Systems and Software, 81*, 56–70. doi:10.1016/j.jss.2007.05.034

Zhang, H., & Tompa, F. W. (2004a). Querying XML documents by dynamic shredding. In *Proceedings of the 2004 ACM Symposium on Document Engineering*. Milwaukee, WI: ACM.

Zhang, H., & Tompa, F. W. (2004b). *Querying XML documents by dynamic shredding*. In DocEng'04, Milwaukee, Wisconsin, USA.

Chapter 14
Research Background

Ibrahim Dweib
Sultan Qaboos University, Oman

Joan Lu
University of Huddersfield, UK

ABSTRACT

In this chapter, the research background is discussed. This includes XML model, XML query languages, XML schema languages, XML Application Program Interface, XML documents types, XML data storage approaches, relational database model, and the similarities and differences between XML model and relational database model. Finally the chapter summary is given.

XML MODEL

"EXtensible Markup Language (XML), is a W3C Recommendation in 1998 for marking up data" (Bray et al., 2007). It is designed for publishing and exchanging a large scale of digital data over the Internet. It is a Markup language that is used to define the structure of information and its elements' contents, where HTML is used to define the way in which the elements are displayed on a web page. It can also be considered as an ideal format for server-to-server transfer of structured data (Bansal and Alam, 2001).

The importance of XML documents transformation is largely increased. Moreover different

XML models have common requirements and limitations as tools for data management. For rich data to be shared among different groups, all concepts need to be placed into a common frame of reference. XML schemas must be globally standardized among groups, or mapping must be created between all pairs of related data. Parsing and text conversion slows down the access of the data.

A well-formed XML document is one that corresponds to the XML 1.0 (Bray *et al.*, 2007) grammar specified by W3C. It has exactly one root element, which is called document element. Each starting element tag should have a corresponding closing tag. The elements should be nested within one another. The tags and nesting rules allow XML to represent information in a

DOI: 10.4018/978-1-4666-1975-3.ch014

hierarchical manner. Figure 1 shows an example for valid XML document.

In recent years, significant development in the XML domain has been achieved. Many languages based upon XML Markup have been designed; XML Schema and XML XQuery have been developed. These standardized technologies augment the data processing abilities of XML. The following sections give a brief description of a variety of XML based languages and technologies.

XML QUERY LANGUAGES

XML query languages are used to enable the user to retrieve data from a single XML document using XPath language, or from multi-documents using XQuery language.

XPath Language

XPath stands for the XML Path Language(Berglund et al., 2007). It is used for retrieving parts of a single XML document by using a path notation, like those used in URLs. Every XPath expression evaluates to one of four basic types:

- Node-set (An unordered list of nodes)
- Boolean
- Number (floating-point number)
- String (a sequence of UCS characters)

An XPath location can be either a relative or an absolute location in an XML document. It can deal with seven node types:

- Root node
- Element nodes
- Attribute nodes
- Namespace nodes
- Processing instruction nodes
- Text nodes
- Comment nodes

The amount of nodes matched by an XPath location can be restricted further by specifying

Figure 1. An example of XML document

```xml
<?xml version="1.0" encoding="UTF-8" standalone="yes"?>
<Books>
        <Book Price="39.99" id="101">
                <Name>Visual Basic programming</Name>
                <Authors>
                        <Author id="A100">Tom, Criss</Author>
                        <Author id="A150">Jim, Divad</Author>
                </Authors>
                <ISBN>1254315121</ISBN>
        </Book>
        <Book Price="59.99" id="102">
                <Name>Visual C# with SQL</Name>
                <Authors>
                        <Author id="A150" >Mike, Roudy</Author>
                </Authors>
                <ISBN>487524545</ISBN>
        </Book>
</Books>
```

additional requirements for a match like comparison operators, functions or predefined variables. XPath supports equality operators and helper functions operating on the four basic types (i.e. node-set, Boolean, number and string), for instance substring extraction, summation of the values in a node-set or the number of nodes in a node-set to name a few. Table 1 shows an example of some XPath expressions to retrieve data from the XML document in Figure 1.

XML XQuery 1.0 Language

XQuery (Boag et al., 2007) is an XML Query Language according to W3C Candidate Recommendation on 23rd January 2007. The mission of the XML Query project is to provide flexible query facilities to extract data from real and virtual documents on the World Wide Web. Users can retrieve data from multiple XML documents using complex nested query expressions by XQuery. Therefore, it is providing eventually the needed interaction between the Web World and the database world.

XQuery is an extension of XPath version 2.0; it does not operate on the syntax of an XML document, but on its abstract, logical structure known as the XQuery 1.0 and XPath 2.0 data model. The XQuery language does not utilize XML Markup but has a syntactic grammar of its own.

The special feature of XQuery is that it has FLWOR expressions. FLWOR is a shortcut for FOR-LET-WHERE-ORDER BY-RETURN and it works similarly to SELECT-FROM-WHERE-ORDER BY statements in SQL. FLWOR expressions are used to combine and restructure XML data; it binds variables to values in "for" and "let", clauses. Such binding of a variable to some value is called a tuple. The "for" clauses produce a stream of tuples. This tuple stream can be stored by a let clause into a variable. This variable can be used later by "where", "order by" and "return" statements.

Table 2 shows some XQuery expressions that can be used to retrieve data from the XML document in Figure 1. The first three expressions look like XPath expressions and the last one looks like an SQL statement. The last two expressions give the same results, but they are different in form. So, users can use any one of the two forms to retrieve their data.

Table 1. Example of some XPath expressions

./author	All <author> elements within the current context. Note that this is equivalent to the expression in the next row.
author	All <author> elements within the current context.
/books	The document element (<books>) of this document.
//author	All <author> elements in the document.
book/ISBN	All <ISBN> elements that are children of a <book> element.
books//name	All <name> elements one or more levels deep in the <books> element (arbitrary descendants). Note that this is different from the expression in the next row.
books/*/name	All <name> elements that are grandchildren of <books> elements.
author[1]	The first <author> element in the current context node.
book/*	All elements that are the children of <book> elements.
book[@price < "60.0"]	All <book> elements where price attribute is less than "60.0".
ancestor::name[parent::book][1]	The nearest <name> ancestor in the current context and this <name> element is a child of a <book> element.

SCHEMA LANGUAGES FOR XML

XML Schema languages (i.e. DTDs, XML Schema (Fallside and Walmsley, 2004;Thompson et al., 2004), RELAX NG (Murata et al., 2001), DSD (Møller, 2005), Schematron (Jelliffe, 2006)) are used to validate XML documents. Validating a document is the process of verifying whether XML documents conform to a set of structural and content rules expressed in one of many schema languages; it works as firewall against invalid documents and allows skipping document validation in data processing applications because the parser will have already validated the document. Validation occurs on at least four levels: (Ray, 2003)

1. **Structure:** the use and placement of Markup elements and attributes.
2. **Data typing:** patterns of character data (e.g. numbers, dates, text).
3. **Integrity:** the status of links between nodes and resources.
4. **Business rules:** miscellaneous tests such as spelling checks, checksum results, and so on.

Document Type Definition (DTD) has been used for validating SGML structures (OASIS, 2002), and then it has become in use to provide validation for XML documents. It provides a regular expression language for imposing constraints on the content model (i.e. elements and subelements), but it is very limited in the control of attributes and data elements as it is not designed originally for XML data. Figure 2 shows a DTD example, which can be used to validate the XML document in Figure 1.

XML Schema is a W3C recommendation aimed for replacing DTDs as the official schema language for XML documents (Fallside and Walmsley, 2004;Thompson et al., 2004). It provides a large number of improvements over DTDs. The first and most evident improvement is the switch to an XML-based syntax, which improves it in terms of flexibility and automatic process ability. Moreover XML Schema is completely namespace-aware. Another major contribution of XML Schema is the Post Schema Validation Infoset (PSVI), i.e., the additional information that the validation adds to the nodes of the XML document so that downstream applications can make use of it for their own purposes. The most important advantage of PSVI is certainly the type, or the set of legal values that a node can have. Types in XML Schema are either simple (strings with various constraints) or complex (Markup substructures of the XML document including elements, attributes and text nodes). A large number of built-in simple types are provided, ranging from integers to dates, times, and URIs. Figure 3 shows an example for XML Schema, which can be used to validate the XML document in Figure 1.

RELAX NG is a schema language for XML developed by an international working group, ISO/

Table 2. Example for some XQuery expressions

doc("books.xml")/books/book/name	Select all the name elements in the "books.xml" file
doc("books.xml")/books/book[@price<30]	Select all the book elements under the books element that have a price attribute with a value that is less than 30
doc("books.xml")/books/book[@price>30]/name	Select all the name elements under the book elements that are under the books element that have a price attribute with a value that is higher than 30.
for $x in doc("books.xml")/books/book where $x/@price>30 order by $x/name return $x/name	Select exactly the same as the path expression above. Except names are sorted using order by clause.

Figure 2. DTD example

```
<!ELEMENT books (book*)
<!ELEMENT book (name, authors, ISBN)
<!ATTLIST book price CDATA #REQUIRED>
<!ATTLIST book id ID #REQUIRED>
<!ELEMENT name (#PCDATA) >
<!ELEMENT authors(author*)>
<!ELEMENT author(#PCDATA)>
<!ATTLIST author id ID #REQUIRED>
<!ATTLIST author address CDATA>
<!ELEMENT ISBN (#PCDATA)>
```

IEC JTC1/SC34/WG1 (Murata *et al.*, 2001). It is based on two preceding languages: Tree Regular Expressions for XML (TREX) (Clark, 2001), designed by James Clark, and Regular Language description for XML (RELAX) (Makoto, 2002), designed by Murata Makoto. Patterns are the central concept of RELAX NG. They widen the scope of the concept of content model, while in DTDs a content model is an expression over elements that are limited to text. In RELAX NG a pattern is an expression of elements, text nodes and attributes. External definitions of data types can be used for constraining the set of values of text nodes and attributes. Figure 4 shows an example for RELAX NG Schema, which can be used to validate the XML document in Figure 1.

Document Structure Description (DSD) is a schema language developed jointly by AT&T Labs and BRICS (Møller, 2005;Klarlund et al., 2000). Constraints are the central concept in DSD. A constraint is used to specify the content of an element, its attributes and its context (i.e. the sequence of nodes from the root to the element). An element definition is specified as a pair consisting of an element name and a constraint. The element content is constrained by a content expression, that is, a regular expression over element definitions. Context patterns are used to enforce constraints on the context of an element.

Schematron is a rule-based schema language created by Rick Jelliffe at the Academia Sinica Computing Centre (ASCC) (Jelliffe, 2006). It is mainly used to check co-constraints in XML instance documents. A Schematron document defines a sequence of <rule>s, logically grouped in <pattern> elements. Each rule has a context attribute where XPath pattern determines the elements in the instance document to which the rule applies. Within a rule, a sequence of <report> and <assert> elements is specified having a test attribute which is an XPath expression evaluated to a Boolean value for each node in the context. The content of both <report> and <assert> is an assertion which is a declarative sentence in natural language. When the test of a <report> succeeds, its content becomes output.

XML API

The XML Application Program Interfaces (XML APIs) has been designed to allow a programmer in most programming languages, such as Java, C++, and Perl, to access their XML documents information without writing a parser in their Programming Language.

Figure 3. Shows an example for XML schema

```
<?xml version="1.0" encoding="ISO-8859-1" ?>
<xs:schema xmlns:xs="http://www.w3.org/2001/XMLSchema">
<!-- definition of simple elements -->
<xs:element name="name" type="xs:string"/>
<xs:element name="author" type="xs:string"/>
<xs:element name="ISBN" type="xs:string"/>
<!-- definition of attributes -->
<xs: attribute name="price" type="xs:decimal"/>
<xs: attribute name="id" type="xs: positiveInteger "/>
<xs:attribute name="address" type="xs:string"/>
<!-- definition of complex elements -->
<xs:element name="books">
 <xs:complexType>
  <xs:sequence>
   <xs:element ref="book"/>
</xs:sequence>
 </xs:complexType>
</xs:element>
<xs:element name="book">
 <xs:complexType>
  <xs:sequence>
   <xs:element ref="name"/>
   <xs:element ref="authors"/>
   <xs:element ref="ISBN/>
  </xs:sequence>
<xs:attribute ref="price" use="required"/>
<xs:attribute ref="id" use="required"/>
 </xs:complexType>
</xs:element>
<xs:element name="authors">
 <xs:complexType>
  <xs:sequence>
   <xs:element ref="author" minOccurs="1"/>
  </xs:sequence>
<xs:attribute ref="id" use="required"/>
<xs:attribute ref="address" minOccurs="0"/>
 </xs:complexType>
</xs:element>
</xs:schema>
```

DOM Parser

DOM (Document Object Model) parser is used as a hierarchical object model to access the XML document information. It reads the entire document information and forms its corresponding DOM object tree of nodes in the main memory.

This approach makes XML parser suitable for small XML document that can fit in the memory. DOM parser can be used for the documents in which the sequence of elements is very important (i.e. document centric documents) since it preserves the sequence of elements that it reads from the XML documents. It contains functions

Figure 4. Shows an example for RELAX NG schema

```
<?xml version="1.0" encoding="UTF-8"?>
<element name="books"
xmlns="http://relaxng.org/ns/structure/1.0">
   <element name="book"
   <attribute name="price"/>
   <attribute name="id"/>
   <element name="name"><text/></element>
   <element name="authors"
      <element name="author"><text/>
      <attribute name="id"/>
      <optional>
        <attribute name="address"/>
      </optional>
      </element>
   </element>
   <element name="ISBN"><text/></element>
   </element>
</element>
```

for traversing XML trees, inserting, deleting, and accessing nodes. Table 3 shows some properties and methods used by DOM parser. (Hégaret et al., 2005;W3C, 2005)

SAX Parser

SAX (Simple Application Interface for XML) parser gives access to XML document information as a sequence of events, which makes it faster than DOM parser. It fires an event for every open tag, every closing tag, #PCDATA and CDATA section. The document handler will have to interpret these events and the sequence in which these events are fired. SAX can be used for large XML documents, since the documents do not need to be parsed in the main memory first. It can also be suitable for structured XML documents since elements order is not necessary. Another point of difference between SAX and DOM is worth mentioning here. SAX has a limitation in that no insertion of new contents can be done on the document, i.e., read only. DOM has the ability to do that through some methods and function for

accessing, inserting and deleting nodes, i.e., read and write over XML document. Table 4 shows main methods used by most XML SAX parsers. (www.Altova.com/XMLSpy, 2008)

XML DOCUMENTS TYPES

Using of XML technology in most web services such as e-business, e-commerce, e-banking, e-mail, e-library, e-government generates different types of XML data. These data can be classified according to their structure into: 1) Document centric documents, 2) Data centric documents, and 3) Mixed documents. (Bourret, 2005)

A comparison between XML document types are shown in Table 5. Characterizing XML documents as data-centric or document centric will help in deciding the kind of database to use. As a general rule, data can be stored in a traditional database, such as a relational, object-oriented, or hierarchical database. This can be done by third-party middleware or by capacity built into the database itself. In the latter case, the database

Table 3. Some properties and methods used by DOM parser

Some XML DOM properties:	
• x.nodeName	- the name of x
• x.nodeValue	- the value of x
• x.parentNode	- the parent node of x
• x.childNodes	- the child nodes of x
• x.nextSibling	- the right sibling of node x
• x.attributes	- the attributes nodes of x
• x.previousSibling	- the left sibling of node x
Some XML DOM Methods:	
• x.getElementsByTagName(*name*)	- get all elements with a specified tag name
• x.appendChild(*node*)	- insert a child node to x
• x.removeChild(*node*)	- remove a child node from x
Where x is referring to a node object.	

is said to be XML-enabled. Documents can be stored in a native XML database, (i.e. a database designed especially for storing XML), or a content management system (i.e. an application designed to manage documents and built on top of a native XML database).

These rules are not absolute. Data, especially semi-structured data, can be stored in native XML databases and documents can be stored in traditional databases where few XML-specific features are needed. Furthermore, the boundaries between traditional databases and native XML databases are beginning to fade away, as traditional databases add native XML capabilities and in turn native XML databases support the storage of document fragments in external databases, which are usually relational databases.

XML Data Storage Approaches

Since XML inception in 1998, a lot of research studies have looked for efficient storage and query medium for storing XML documents. Athena Vakali discussed existing options of XML storage which depends on the underlying framework's particular level showing their storage format, main advantages and main disadvantages (Vakali et al., 2005). Table 6 summarises these options. The discussion shows that Relational Database Management System (RDBMS), Object Oriented Database Management System (OODBMS) and native XML database are the most accepted approaches.

RDBMS

Relational Database Management System (RD-BMS) which has been proposed by Codd in 1970s is reliable, widespread and a well established medium for storing and retrieving data in the business area. Some approaches have been proposed to store XML documents into relational database and retrieve its content again from relational database (Fujimoto et al., 2005; Shanmugasundaram et al., 1999; Tan et al., 2005; Zhang and Tompa, 2004b; Xing et al., 2007b). Relational database has power capabilities in indexes, triggers, data integrity, security, multi-user access, query optimization by SQL query language, and crash recovery. The youth XML technology is looking for achieving some of these capabilities.

Table 4. Some methods used by SAX parser

startDocument ()	Invoked when the Parser encounter document start
endDocument ()	Invoked when the Parser encounter document end
startElement (String name, AttributeList attrs)	Invoked when the Parser encounter element starting tag> The attributeList parameter has the list of all attributes declared for the current element in the XML File
endElement (String name)	Invoked when the Parser encounter element closing tag.
characters (char buf [], int offset, int len)	Invoked when the Parser encounter extra characters like space or enter character are encountered.
processingInstruction (String target, String data)	Invoked when the parser encounters a processing Instruction which is declared like

OODBMS

Object Oriented Database Management System (OODBMS) can deal with complex applications such as multimedia data and geographic information systems. However, there are some limitations: 1) OODBMS is language dependent often, (i.e. a specific API of specific language is used only to access the data), 2) it is schema dependent, (i.e. any modification to the schema or any class should be done to the classes interacting with instances of this class) This will involve the system in a wide recompile and will extend the time for updating the entire instance object within the database according to its size. But there are some works for storing XML documents in OODBS since both of XML and OODBS are hierarchical in their nature structure (Chung and Jesurajaiah, 2005).

XML Database

A new set of languages are dedicated for XML documents which are the native XML database (Jagadish et al., 2003;Grinev et al., 2004). These languages which include XLink, XPath, XQuery and XSLT are designed for the particular purpose of storing and querying XML documents (Bray *et al.*, 2007). Also XML languages do not reach the power capabilities of existing relational database system; they do not allow users to query data in XML documents and other data in RDBMS simultaneous.

Table 5. Overview of XML documents types

	Document type	Used for	Document characteristics	Order of sibling element	Document originality	Examples
1.	Data-Centric	data transportation, machine consumption	fairly regular structure, fine-grained data	generally not significant, except when validating the document	database	Sales orders, flight schedules, scientific data
2.	Document-centric	data publishing, human consumption	less regular or irregular structure, larger grained data	significant	RTF, PDF, or SGML, Documents then converted to XML	Books, emails, advertisements, user's manual, and almost any hand-written XHTML documents.
3.	Mixed Document	A + B types, or B + A types	A + B types, or B + A types	insignificant part + significant part	database & other document types (A + B)	- Invoice, might contain large-grained, irregularly structured data, such as a part description. - Books, might contain fine-grained, regularly structured data, such as an author's name and a publication date

The above discussion has shown that RDBMS is the most suitable storage for XML data until now; in addition, it has a widespread implementation as a storage and retrieval medium in the business area. But there is a difference in the structure between the hierarchical ordered XML and tabular unordered RDB. This difference expresses the need for mapping techniques from XML documents to RDB in order to utilize their advantages and make the XML technology more acceptable by the RDB users.

RDBMS Model

A database can be defined as a collection of related files. The relation between these files depends on the model used to describe these data, relational, hierarchical network or object-oriented model. Currently, RDBMS is the one used most often (Codd, 1970; Codd, 1971; Delobel, 1978; Codd, 1983). The relational model can be determined by some rules and facts such as:

1. Database is a collection of related tables (relations).
2. Each table consists of a set of records (tuples).
3. Each record consists of a fixed number of fields (attributes) which give descriptions for an object or a person.
4. Each field gives a specific characterization of data for the object, (i.e. single data type: name, age, or date). Relational model supports many data types including number, string, varchar, memo, date and Boolean.
5. One of those fields should uniquely identify the object; for example, student number in student table. This field is called the primary key.
6. The primary key in a table can be used as an additional field in other tables to create relations among them. This field is called a secondary key. So, the relations inside the database can be preserved using those primary and secondary keys.
7. The relation type between tables can be one-to-one relation or one-to-many relation which depends on the number of occurrence of the secondary key in one of them.
8. The relational model provides a set of relational operators' including selection, production, join, and cartesian product to process data in the database.
9. Database normalization helps to reduce data duplication and to increase data integrity.

Table 6. Overview of popular XML storage approaches (Vakali et al., 2005)

Framework	XML Storage Format	Main Advantages	Main Disadvantages
File-system-oriented	- ASCII files stored in the file system or database - management system (DBMS) as binary large objects (Blobs) or character large objects (Clobs)	- Easy implementation - Suitable for small XML sets	- Accessing and updating are difficult
Relational DBMS	- Tables	- Scalability and reliability - Easy implementation	- Requires many joins due to XML document factorization
Object-relational DBMS	- Tables and objects	- Easy implementation - Abstract data type support	- XML document factorization
Native XML	- Ad hoc data models or typical database models	- Flexibility - Improved access performance	- Less mature than conventional DBMSs (such as RDBMSs)
Directory servers	- Tree structure	- Optimized for queries - Effective data retrieval	- Low update performance

10. Structured Query Language (SQL) offers a set of commands for accessing database through inserting, deleting and updating data.

THE SIMILARITIES AND DIFFERENCES BETWEEN XML MODEL AND RDB MODEL

XML was originally proposed to represent, publish and exchange data between business applications on the Internet (Bray *et al.*, 2007) in 1998. RDB was proposed by Codd in the 1970s for storing and retrieving data (Codd, 1971;Codd, 1970). XML and its related technologies provide something found in database as XML documents for storing, DTDs and XML Schema for validating, XPath and XQuery for querying, and DOM and SAX for parsing XML documents. But, XML languages lack many things that are found in traditional databases such as indexes, triggers, data integrity, security, crash recovery, and multi-user access (Zhou et al., 2006).

XML can organize data in a hierarchical, object-oriented, and multidimensional way in the form of a tree with an arbitrary depth and width (Chen et al., 2006;Wang and Meng, 2005) as shown in Figure 5. Meanwhile, a traditional relational database table can be thought of as a tree of depth two with unbounded fan-out at the first level, and fixed fan-out at the second level, with the first level representing tuples (rows) and the second level representing fields (columns). Figure 6 and Figure 7 show a sample of relational database representation (i.e., as tree and table respectively). An XML tree is clearly a more expressive way of representing data as no constraints are placed on either depth or width.

A comparison between XML technology and RDB technology was given in (Bansal and Alam, 2001) as shown in Table 7. The comparison in Table 7 shows that there is a structural hole between hierarchical ordered XML and tabular unordered RDB. As a result, mapping between the XML and RDB is the best solution to exploit their advantages, and makes the XML technology more acceptable by the RDB users. For this reason, mapping XML documents to RDB has been

Figure 5. A sample of XML tree representation (Chen et al., 2006)

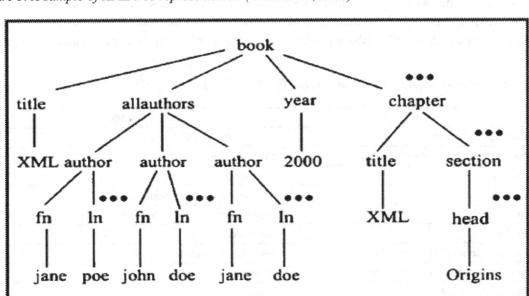

Figure 6. A sample of relational database tree representation

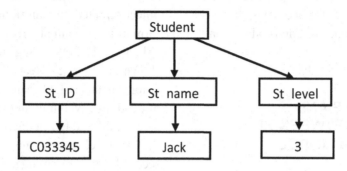

Figure 7. A sample of relational database table representation

Students table

St_ID	St_name	St_level
C03334	Jack	3

studied by many researchers, and relational database vendors (e.g., Oracle, DB2, and SQL Server).

CONCLUSION

In this chapter, a review of the XML language and other supporting languages, XPath, XQuery, XSLT, and XML schema were given. This review shows that XML technology has received a lot of attention from researchers and database vendors to improve and to make this technology available to the market and user in a highly standard form. Also, it shows that this technology needs a lot of work to solve data processing problems such as multi-user access, security, crash recovery, concurrency control, data querying and retrieving, and data integrity, which have been already solved by database management and object oriented databases. These issues show the need to think of other storage options for storing and retrieving XML data. Reviews of these options were presented in this chapter and a comparison

Table 7. A comparison between XML and RDBMS (Bansal and Alam, 2001)

XML	RDBMS
Data in single hierarchical structure	Data in multiple tables
Nodes have element and/or attribute values	Cells have a single value
Elements can be nested	Atomic cell values
Elements are ordered	Row/column order not defined
Elements can be recursive	Little support for recursive elements
Schema optional	Schema required
Direct storage/retrieval of XML documents	Joins often necessary to retrieve data
Query with XML standards (XQuery, XPath)	Query with SQL
Human and machine readable	Machine readable

between them was made. Relational database is the mostly expected candidate for this choice since it solves most problems of data access issues. Some rules and facts about the relational database model were raised, and a comparison with XML model was introduced. The comparison shows the need for mapping techniques to map XML data to relational database to take advantages of their attributes since there is a gap between the two models. In chapter three, different mapping techniques for storing, rebuilding, and retrieving XML data from relational databases are discussed.

REFERENCES

W3C. (2005). *Document object model* (DOM).

Bansal, V., & Alam, A. (2001). *Study and comparison of techniques to efficiently store and retrieve XML data.*

Berglund, A., Boag, S., Chamberlin, D., Fernández, M., Kay, M., Robie, J., & Siméon, J. (2007). *XML path language (XPath) 2.0.* W3 Consortium.

Boag, X., Chamberlin, D., Fernández, M., Florescu, D., Robie, J., & Siméon, J. (2007). *XQuery 1.0: An XML query language.* W3 Consortium.

Bourret, R. (2005). *XML and databases.*

Bray, T., Paoli, J., Sperberg-McQueen, C. M., Maler, E., & Yergeau, F. (2007). *Extensible markup language (XML) 1.0* (4th ed.). W3 Consortium.

Chen, Q., Lim, A., Ong, K. W., & Tang, J. Q. (2006). Indexing graph-structured XML data for efficient structural join operation. *Data & Knowledge Engineering, 58*, 21. doi:10.1016/j.datak.2005.05.008

Chung, S. M., & Jesurajaiah, S. B. (2005). Schemaless XML document management in object-oriented databases. *International Conference on Information Technology: Coding and Computing, ITCC 2005,* Vol. 261, (pp. 261-266).

Clark, J. (2001). *Tree regular expressions for XML.* TREX.

Codd, E. (1970). A relational model of data for large shared data banks. *Communications of the ACM, 13*, 11. doi:10.1145/362384.362685

Codd, E. (1971). A database sub-language founded on the relational calculus. *ACM SIGFIDET Workshop Data Description, Access and Control* (pp. 35-61).

Codd, E. (1983). *A relational model of data for large shared data banks* (pp. 64–69). ACM.

Delobel, C. (1978). *Normalization and hierarchical dependencies in the relational data model* (pp. 201–222). ACM.

Fallside, D., & Walmsley, P. (2004). *XML schema part 0: Primer* (2nd ed.). W3 Consortium.

Fujimoto, K., Yoshikawa, T., Kha, D. D., Yashikawa, M., & Amagasa, T. (2005). *A mapping scheme of XML documents into relational databases using schema-based path identifiers.* International Workshop on Challenges in Web Information and Integration (WIRI'05).

Grinev, M., Fomichev, A., & Kuznetsov, S. (2004). *Sedna: A native XML DBMS.*

Hégaret, P. L., Whitmer, R., & Wood, L. (2005). *Document object model* (DOM). W3 Consortium.

Jagadish, H., Al-khalifa, S., Chapman, A., Lakshmanan, L., Nierman, A., & Paparizos, S. … Yu, C. (2003). *TIMBER: A native XML database.* In: SIGMOD, San Diego, CA.

Jelliffe, R. (2006). *Resource directory (RDDL) for Schematron 1.5.*

Klarlund, N., Møller, A., & Schwartzbach, M. (2000). A schema language for XML. In *FMSP '00, ACM.* Portland, Oregon: DSD.

Makoto, M. (2002). *RELAX (Regular Language description for XML).*

Møller, A. (2005). *Document structure description*.

Murata, M., Walsh, N., & McRae, M. (2001). *TREX and RELAX unified as RELAX NG, a lightweight XML language validation specification*.

OASIS. (2002). *SGML: General introductions and overviews*.

Ray, E. T. (2003). *Learning XML: Creating self-describing data*. O'Reilly.

Shanmugasundaram, J., Tufte, K., Zhang, C., He, G., DeWitt, D. J., & Naughton, J. F. (1999). Relational databases for querying XML documents: Limitations and opportunities. *VLDB Conference* (pp. 302–314).

Spy, X. M. L. (2008). *SAX & DOM*. Retrieved from www.Altova.com/XMLSpy

Tan, Z., Xu, J., Wang, W., & Shi, B. (2005). Storing normalized XML documents in normalized relations. *The Fifth International Conference on Computer and Information Technology* (CIT'05) (pp. 123-129).

Thompson, H. S., Beech, D., Maloney, M., & Mendelsohn, N. (2004). *XML schema part 1: Structures*, 2nd ed. W3 Consortium.

Vakali, A., Catania, B., & Maddalena, A. (2005). XML data stores: Emerging practices. *IEEE Internet Computing, 9*(2). doi:10.1109/MIC.2005.48

Wang, H., & Meng, X. (2005). *On the sequencing of tree structures for XML indexing*. 21st International Conference on Data Engineering (ICDE 2005).

Xing, G., Xia, Z., & Ayers, D. (2007a). X2R: A system for managing XML documents and key constraints using RDBMS. In *Proceedings of the 45th Annual Southeast Regional Conference*. ACM, Winston-Salem, North Carolina.

Xing, G., Xia, Z., & Ayers, D. (2007b). *X2R: A system for managing XML documents and key constraints using RDBMS*. Winston-Salem, NC: ACMSE.

Zhang, H., & Tompa, F. W. (2004a). Querying XML documents by dynamic shredding. In *Proceedings of the 2004 ACM Symposium on Document Engineering*. Milwaukee, WI: ACM.

Zhang, H., & Tompa, F. W. (2004b). *Querying XML documents by dynamic shredding*. In DocEng'04, Milwaukee, Wisconsin, USA.

Zhou, J., Zhang, S., Wang, M., & Sun, H. (2006). XML-RDB driven semi-structure data management. *Journal of Information and Computing Science, 1*, 9.

Chapter 15
State of the Art Technology

Ibrahim Dweib
Sultan Qaboos University, Oman

Joan Lu
University of Huddersfield, UK

ABSTRACT

This chapter presents the state of the art approaches for storing and retrieving the XML documents from relational databases. Approaches are classified into schema-based mapping and schemaless-based mapping. It also discusses the solutions which are included in Database Management Systems such as SQL Server, Oracle, and DB2. The discussion addresses the issues of: rebuilding XML from RDBMS approaches, comparison of mapping approaches, and their advantages and disadvantages. The chapter concludes with the issues addressed.

APPROACHES FOR STORING AND QUERYING XML

A number of different techniques for storing XML documents in a RDB have been established. These techniques can be divided into two groups: the schemaless-centric technique and the schema–centric technique (Dweib *et al.*, 2008). The first one makes use of XML document structure to manage the mapping process (Tatarinov et al., 2002;Dweib et al., 2008;Soltan and Rahgozar, 2006; Zhang and Tompa, 2004b;Jiang et al., 2002;Yoshikawa et al., 2001). The second one depends on schema

information to develop a relational schema for XML documents (Fujimoto et al., 2005; Shanmugasundaram et al., 1999; Amer-Yahia et al., 2004; Atay et al., 2007b; Xing et al., 2007b; Knudsen et al., 2005; Lee et al., 2006).

The aim of mapping XML documents into relational database is to make use of the capabilities of the relational database which are: indexes, triggers, data integrity, security, multi-user access, and query optimization by SQL query language. In the meanwhile XML technology is trying to gain the above-mentioned capabilities, developed for RDBs, and efficiently store, retrieve, and rebuild XML data from RDBs.

DOI: 10.4018/978-1-4666-1975-3.ch015

The studies that address the problem of mapping XML document into RDB take care of the above issues, and attempt to translate users' XML queries, either XPath expression (Berglund *et al.*, 2007) or W3C's recommendation XQuery expression (Boag *et al.*, 2007), into SQL queries (Oracle, n. a.). XQuery gives power to the translation method since XQuery comprises XPath, and it is recommended by W3C, while XPath is not. The translation method should also consider its ability to rebuild, the stored XML document without losing information, and retrieve it in an acceptable time. Many studies have tried to address translation and restore constructing labelling methods. Labelling methods aim to reserve nodes order, parent-child and ancestor-descendant relationships, and document structure(Tatarinov et al., 2002;Chung and Jesurajaiah, 2005;Soltan and Rahgozar, 2006;Li and Moon, 2001;O'Neil et al., 2004;Wu et al., 2004;Kobayashi et al., 2005).

Schema-Based Mapping

One of the early studies in this area was conducted by (Shanmugasundaram *et al.*, 1999) from the University of Wisconsin-Madison. They proposed three mapping techniques: Basic, Shared, and Hybrid Inlining. These are proposed to map DTDs into relational schemas. Basic Inlining proposed building a separated table for each element in the DTD while in the Shared Inlining each element is represented in one table. The Hybrid Inlining technique inlines shares an element which is not repeated or recursively related. These techniques are different from one another in the degree of redundancy; they vary from being highly redundant in Basic Inlining, to containing no redundancy in Hybrid Inlining.

The above approach offers limited structures to represent the features of XML data, such as nested relationships, ordering of XML documents, and the DBMS schema representations. Querying these structures is usually complex since the end users are not familiar with them.

Mapping algorithms for XML DTDs to relational schemas were proposed by Atay *et al.* (2007b) from Wayne State University. They attempted to enhance the shared-inlining algorithm (Shanmugasundaram *et al.*, 1999), in away to overcome its incompleteness and eliminate redundancies caused by the shared elements. They claimed that the algorithm can deal with any DTDs including arbitrary cyclic DTDs, but shared-inlining algorithm deals merely with two mutually recursive elements. Dealing with cycles which involve more than two elements in a DTDs is not clear. Figure 1 shows the three cases they considered in their inlining procedure. In case 1, a node *a* is connected to a node *b* by a normal edge, and *b* has no other incoming edges. In this case, node *b* is inlined into its parent node *a*, and the parent-child relationships are maintained between *b* and its children. In case 2, node *a* is connected to node *b* by a normal edge where *b* has other incoming edges (i.e. *b* is a shared node). In this case node *b* is not inlined into its parent node *a* since *b* has multiple parents. In case 3, node *a* is connected to a node *b* by a star edge, such that every node of *a* can contain multiple occurrences of *b*. In this case, the node *b* is not combined into its parent node *a* in order to avoid redundancy. Figure 2 gives an example of the idea of the inlining procedure clear. Figures 2.A and 2.C show the DTD graphs, where the inlining results are shown in Figures 2.B and 2.D after applying the inlining algorithm. It could be noted from figures that nodes which are connected by, -edge or *-edge and,-edge must point to a shared node.

Redundancy reduction XML storage in relations (RRXS) within XML Functional Dependency (XFD) was proposed by (Chen *et al.*, 2003). They defined constraints to capture the structural constraints as well as semantic information. It makes use of XML schema semantic constraints. Using the semantics of a document could reduce the redundancy since node identifiers can be removed where value based keys are still available for particular elements. Unfortunately the sug-

Figure 1. The three case of inlining (Atay et al., 2007b)

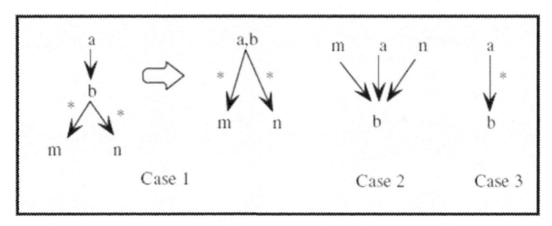

gested rewrite rules are not complete. So, this algorithm cannot guarantee redundancy reduction.

SPIDER (Schema-based Path IDentifiER) is an approach for a node labelling scheme identified by Fujimoto *et al.* (2005), from Nagoya University and the Nara Institute of Science and Technology. They aimed to preserve XML tree structure. The approach used document's DTD information to give unique numbers for all paths from the root node. It assigns unique integers to each sequence of elements and attributes from the root node to any node in the XML tree. Since SPIDER could not distinguish between multiple nodes appearing in the same path, *Fujimoto et al.* introduced Sibling Dewey Order to identify such nodes. Consequently, several nodes are to be relabelled in order to insert a new node into an XML document, and to maintain nodes order. Only Sibling Dewey Order is relabelled but SPIDER is not affected. Figure 3 and Figure 4 show the difference between SPIDER labels and SPIDER and Sibling Dewey Order labels for XML tree. And Figure 5 shows the relational schema used by SPIDER. Four relational tables are used each of which handles a different type of information; one for elements, one for attributes, one for texts and the last for paths of the document.

SPIDER uses string matching to handle the path that contains ancestor relation "//." This matching requires joining "element" and "path" relations, causes degradation of the approach performance. Moreover, this method cannot exactly preserve node order in some cases such as in the case of multiple components in the DTD declaration which have the same name but appear in different places. On the other hand, node indexing involves large extra space relative to the size of the original data. And indexing a document with a large number of nodes is very difficult. As a consequence, this method needs extra time overhead that is consumed to rebuild the original XML document.

Space reduction is needed to store XML documents which is a requirement to improve the performance of querying data. To reduce the space that is used to store the labels, and to make rebuilding of original XML documents easier, methods for indexing a group of XML nodes have been proposed by (Xing *et al.*, 2007a). These methods include: using path information to refine the storage, indexing a group of XML nodes instead of an individual node, and query evaluation based on the "nodes of interest."

Introducing nodes of interest can reduce the number of path joins required to process the query. Figure 6 shows the way of grouping nodes in the XML tree. Each group of nodes is stored in one

Figure 2. Inlining DTD graphs (Atay et al., 2007b)

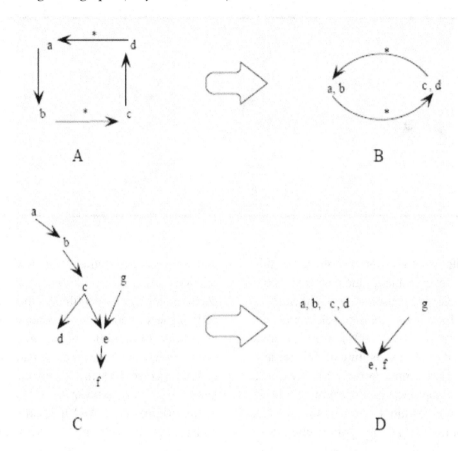

or at most two tables which can be linked together under the *"label"* field.

Amer-Yahia *et al.* (2004) at the AT & T Labs, proposed ShreX a mapping framework which stores the XML document in a RDBMS. XML schema was used to simplify the mapping process in ShreX by using a generic shredding process, which also translated XQuery into SQL. An extension of Shrex Mapping, called XShreX was proposed by Lee *et al.* (2006), from the National University of Singapore. Thus, XShreX mapped more constraints. They also developed semantic keys to replace the auto-generated keys of the ShreX in order to reduce redundancy and to decrease the size of the generated database.

Schema-Less Mapping

One of the issues of mapping XML to RDB is the loss of information due to the XML documents' shredding and inlining into RDB tables (Shanmugasundaram *et al.*, 1999). A dynamic shredding was proposed by Zhang and Tompa (2004b) in order to preserve the original XML document information and to solve the problem of the document size limitation. Documents are shredded to meaningful fragments according to users' judgement. These fragmentations are stored depending on relational schema. XML queries in XQuery are also needed to be translated by the users into SQL statements to retrieve shredded documents. The main idea of this approach is to keep the original document untouched; so, there

Figure 3. Node labelling using SPIDER (Fujimoto et al., 2005)

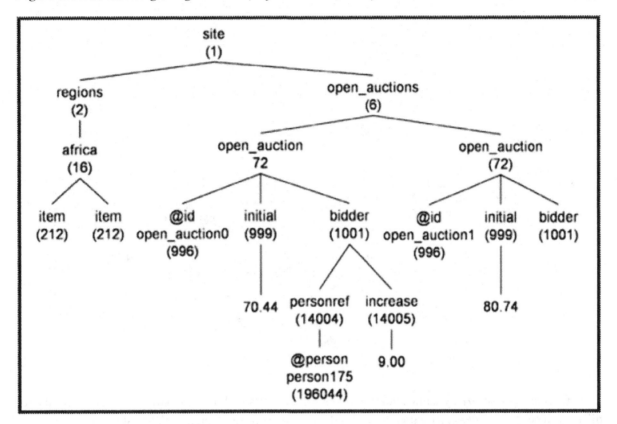

will be no need to rebuild it. But that will make it impossible to connect with the data which already exists in the relational database since the XML document will not be saved in the relational database. In addition, there will be a need to translate each XQuery with a support of appropriate structured text operators.

XRel (Yoshikawa *et al.*, 2001) and XParent approaches (Jiang *et al.*, 2002) are used to store XML documents in RDB. Both approaches are path-based approaches and use predefined fixed relational schema for storing the XML tree information. The relational schemas that are used in both approaches are shown in Figure 7 and Figure 8 respectively. In XRel, elements, attributes and text are stored in different tables (i.e. element, text and attributes tables). The region (i.e. starts and end positions) of each node of element, attribute and text along with its ordinal and pathID are

stored in the tables. The fourth table is used as a path table for document paths where the path is the sequence of elements from the root to the candidate element.

In XParent, element table stores each element in the document, and data table stores attributes and text values. LabelPath table stores all paths in the document and the length of each path. DataPath table stores all parent-child relations.

XRel and XParent make a path expression to be easily evaluated by comparing path IDs. But allocating one code for each element in both approaches result in larger storage for large XML documents, and larger number of path joins to process a query.

Tatarinov et al. (2002) proposed Global, Local and Dewey for labelling XML tree. In Global label each node is assigned a number that represents the node's absolute position in the document as in

Figure 4. Node labelling using SPIDER and Sibling Dewey Order (Fujimoto et al., 2005)

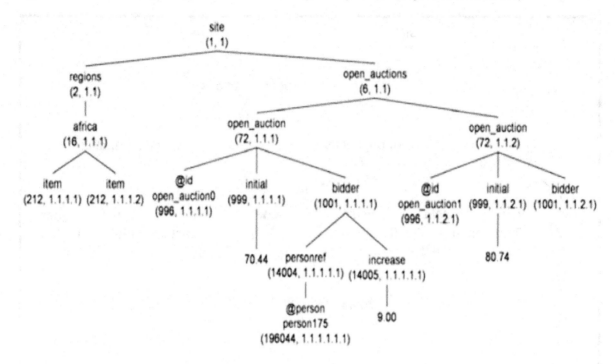

In this label (Figure 9), dynamic update is very difficult since all the nodes placed after the inserted node, need to be relabelled. And extracting the parent-child and ancestor-descendant relationship is also impossible.

In the Local Labelling, each node is assigned a number that represents its relative position among its siblings, as in Figure 10. In this label, a combination of node's position and that of its ancestors forms a path vector that identifies the absolute position of the node within the document. Updating the Local label has led to better performance than in the Global label because only the following siblings of the new node need to be renumbered.

But it is still hard to extract the parent-child and ancestor-descendant relationships.

In the Dewey label, a node label is generated by combing its parent label and private integer number.

Figure 11 shows an example of labelling using Dewey labels. Extracting node label from its ancestors is very easy. But a large sized RDB could be generated in this case because a private label is given for each node, and an update of the following nodes labels is needed when new node is inserted.

ORDPATH, a hierarchical labelling schema implemented in Microsoft SQL Server 2005, was introduced by O'Neil *et al.* (2004). Nodes label-

Figure 5. SPIDER relational schema

Element (docID, nodeID, spider, sibling, parentID)
Attribute (docID, nodeID, spider, sibling, parentID, value)
Text (docID, nodeID, spider, sibling, parentID, value)
Path (spider, path, pathexp)

Figure 6. Grouped nodes

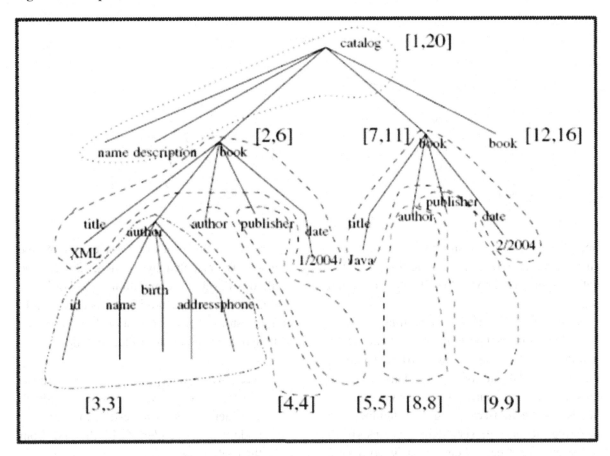

Figure 7. XRel relational schema

Path (PathID, PathExp)
Element (DocId, PathID, start, End, Index, Reindex)
Text (DocID, PathID, Start, End, Value)
Attribute (DocID, PathID, start, End, Value)

Figure 8. XParent relational schema

LabelPath (ID, Len, Path)
DataPath(PID, CID)
Element (PathID, DID, Ordinal)
Data (PathID, DID, Ordinal, Value)

Figure 9. Global labels for XML tree

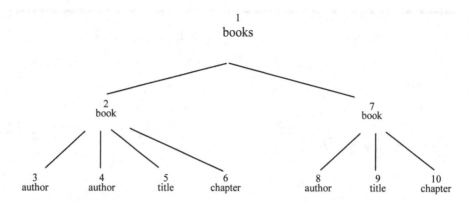

ling of XML tree in this approach does not need an XML schema. It used two tables to store XML data. Figure 12 shows ORDPATH relational schema.

Contrast to the Dewey Labelling method, ORDPATH makes it possible to insert new nodes in uninformed locations in the XML tree without the need to update old nodes labels. This is because only positive odd integers are assigned to the nodes for the first scan, and even-number and negative integers are reserved for future insertions in the existing tree. Labels are assigned during initial loading. Figure 13 shows ORDPATH labelling for an XML document. ORDPATH labelling update is efficient and it can maintain XML document structure. But it fails to perform semantic search or path search.

Pre-order and post-order traversing of tree structure is presented by Torsten, (2002). The method is designed to maintain nodes' ordering within the document, and identifies parent-child and ancestor-descendant relationships. The idea of this method can be described as follows:

1. **Area A:** where (post-order > Node(post-order)) and (pre-order < Node(pre-order)), consider nodes as ancestors to candidate node, which are identify by the path from the root to this node.

2. **Area B:** where (post-order > Node(post-order)) and (pre-order >Node(pre-order)), consider nodes as following the candidate node.

Figure 10. Local labels for XML tree

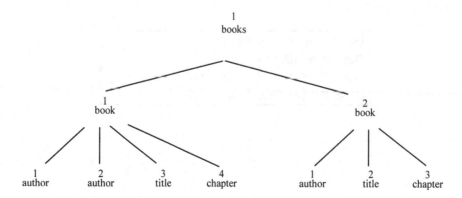

Figure 11. Dewey labels for XML tree

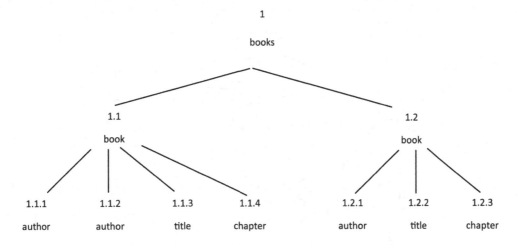

Figure 12. ORDPATH relational schema (O'Neil et al., 2004)

Node (OrdPathCode, Tag, NodeType, Value, PathID)
Path (PathID, PathExp)

3. **Area C:** where (post-order < Node(post-order)) and (pre-order >Node(pre-order)), consider nodes as descendant of the candidate node, i.e. they are forming a subtree rooted by the candidate node. Subtrees are used to form the nested subtree that fragments the XML document.

4. **Area D:** where (post-order < Node (post-order)) and (pre-order <Node (pre-order)), consider nodes as preceding the candidate node.

Figure 13. ORDPATH labels for XML tree

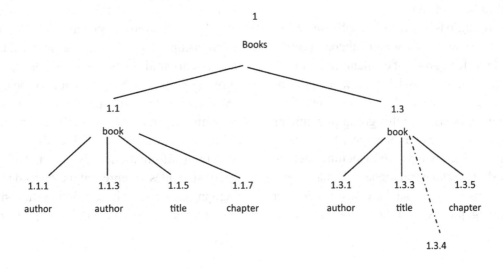

Figure 14. Tree representation for XML document with pre-order post-order labelling

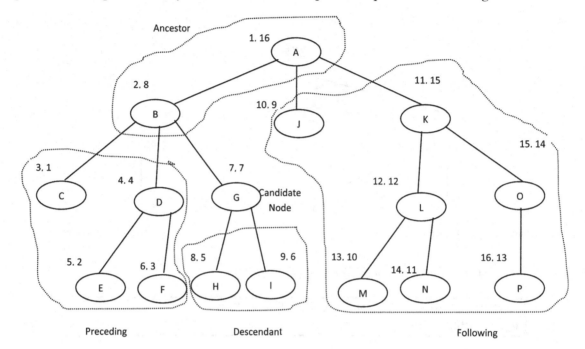

Pre-order and post-order method optimizes the XML query by minimizing the area of search.

Figure 14 and Figure 15 highlight how the pre-order and post-order method could minimize the area of search in the XML document. But this method encounters high cost of inserting a new node or new subtree since all nodes of pre-order label following the inserted node are to be relabelled and all nodes of post-order label for the following nodes and ancestors nodes for inserted node are to be relabelled.

A clustering-based scheme for labelling XML trees was proposed by Soltan and Rahgozar (2006). It uses a label for a group of elements not for each single element, and classifies elements into different groups in which each group is assigned for all sibling elements. And this group of elements are stored in a single relational record. Figure 16 and Figure 17 show clustered labelling method for an XML tree and its relational schema respectively. In this way, the database size needed for the mapping process is reduced because rela-

tional records numbers are less than those of using single record for each node. It also reduces the number of path joins needed to process the query, and makes the rebuilding of XML document from RDMB faster. But it experiences a problem of dynamic update; i.e. many nodes should be relabelled when a new node is inserted. But it fails in performing path and semantic search.

XTRON Min *et al.* (2008) is a schemaless system to manage XML data as relational database. It merges the edge and the region approaches to manage parent-child and ancestor-descendant relationships. The edge approach is used to manage parent-child relationship, and the region approach is used to manage ancestor-descendant relationship. An extra space is used to maintain renumbering at each new node insertion. If the XML schema is not available, then document structural information is extracted. The system needs six tables to represent the merged numbering approach. The path information is transformed into intervals to speed up the query performance.

Figure 15. Pre-order post-order label optimization areas

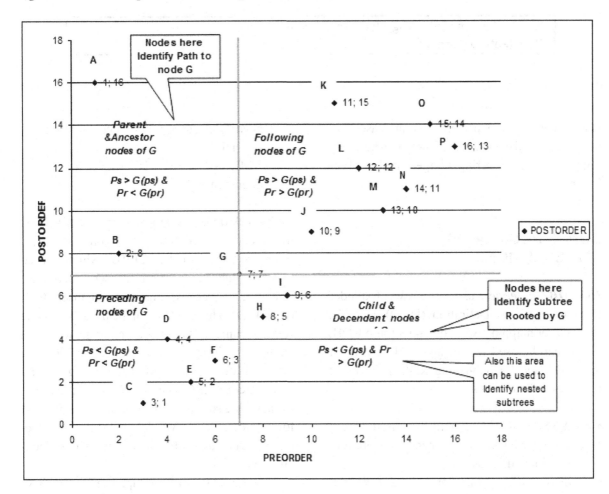

Figure 16. Clustered labels for XML Tree (Soltan and Rahgozar, 2006)

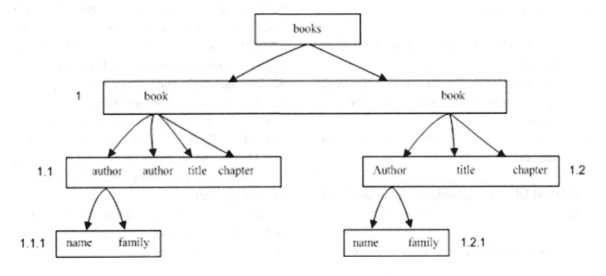

Figure 17. Clustered relational schema (Soltan and Rahgozar, 2006)

Node (ClusteredCode, Tag, NodeType, Value, PathID)
Path (PathID, PathExp)

But enhancing query performance increases size of the relational database. And there will be a very high cost of renumbering a larger number of relational fields.

COMMERCIAL DBMS
XML SOLUTIONS

IBM DB2 Extender: using the XML Extender Document Access Definition (DAD) as XML Schema for mapping XML document into RDB. DADs can be used for storing XML document into RDB and for publishing RDB as XML. It provides two functions:

- dxxShredXML() function is used to decompose an XML document and store it in relational database, and
- dxxGenXML() function is used to build a shredded XML from relational database.

IBM DB2 provided some procedures for handling XML columns:

- XMLVarCharFromFile() is used for type conversion.
- Varchar(XMLVarChar) is used for retrieval.
- Update(xmlobj, path,value) is used for update.
- ExtractVarChar() is used as selection function.

In IBM DB2, XML columns can be assigned a type of:

- XMLCLOB is used for large documents;

- XMLFile is used for documents stored outside DB2.
- XMLVARCHAR is used for small documents

XML Extender also provides an XML DTD repository. Each XML database contains a DTD reference table called DTD REF which is used to store Meta information on users' mappings. The user can access this table to insert their own DTDs. These DTDs can be used to validate XML documents. Given the mapping, the system reads an arbitrary XML document and loads it into a DB2 database. IBM DB2 is using CLOBs (Character Large OBjects) and some extra tables for indexing structured data contained in the text for mixed content XML documents. These extra tables are updated automatically when new documents are added.

Oracle: XML was first supported in Orcale8i. This support was limited for publishing relational data in XML format. In Oracle9i Database Release 1 XDK, a number of tools are added for storing XML into relational database and generating XML from relational database. These tools include: XML Parsers, XSLT Processor, XML Schema Processor and XML SQL Utility to generate XML documents, DTDs and schemas from SQL queries. New data types for supporting XML storage were added to the kernel, which are XMLType and URI-Ref types. Several operators are linked to XMLType to facilitate processing XML data such as extract(), getNumberVal(), getStringVal() and existsNode().

Oracle XML DB was introduced in Oracle9i Database Release 2 (Oracle 9iR2). XML DB offers two options for mapping XML Schema

either created automatically or by the user. Then, XML DB loads the schema file, stores mapping information internally and creates SQL types and tables' indexes.

Oracle 10g gave two solutions through Oracle XMLDB (DB, n.a). In the first solution, XML document is stored as CLOB in a single special type field (XMLType), or shredding the content of an XML document in a set of rows. The second gives an option for XML document shredding, either automated or controlled by the user, depending on the XML schema. SQL standards have been developed such as to be compatible with XML features. Database connectivity for SQL, XPath, XQuery and ODBC are provided. But XML schema is required before transmission to relational schema for shredding options. Oracle solutions are adapted only to Oracle systems which is expensive and not available for other DBMS.

Microsoft SQL Server

To publish relational data as XML documents, Microsoft SQL Server uses the FOR XML clause as extension to the SQL. It uses three publishing modes: RAW, AUTO and EXPLICIT:

- RAW creates flat XML documents by converting each SQL result row into an XML element and each non-NULL column value to an attribute.
- AUTO mode uses query results to build nested documents where each table in the FROM clause is represented as an XML element. The columns listed in the SELECT clause are mapped onto attributes or sub-elements.
- EXPLICIT mode defines an SQL view to gather related rows. Special column names such as Tag and Parent are used. Nesting is explicitly specified as part of the query.

Microsoft implements three solutions for storing XML documents:

- The generic Edge technique.
- Users' annotation of an XML schema in order to determine the XML-to-relations mapping.
- OpenXML that compiles an XML documents into an internal DOM representation using *sp_xml_preparedocument* procedure.

These solutions are created using the XML Schema Definition (XSD), and are used to create the mapping schema that could be used for validating the XML document that is loaded in the relational database.

SQL Server 2005 adds a new XML data type to the relational table by using Transact SQL (T-SQL) or SQL Server Management Studio (Pal et al., December 2005). Adding a new XML data type incorporates a definition of the following options:

1. **The type of the XML field:** Either typed (specify a Schema collection) or un-typed (well-formed XML).
2. **Document storage:** Either stores the complete documents or fragment of it.
3. **Schema:** To store XML document depending on either a single or multiple schemas.

Microsoft provides storing XML documents as CLOBs. But, unlike IBM DB2 Extender, no extra tables are provided for indexing mixed content data.

In SQL Server, the relational database schema is constructed from XSD, which makes it difficult to query the XML data from other resources. SQL Server XML side cannot be applied to other DBMSs such as DB2 or Oracle.

Consequently, each database vendor has to carry out special research for the development of XML support. Solutions are dedicated to the vendor's products and cannot be used in other products. Therefore, many research efforts are needed to leverage and utilize relational database and XML technologies and their advantages.

REBUILDING XML FROM RDB

Storing XML documents into relational databases makes use of relational database management systems facilities, (i.e. multi-user access, data integrity, security, crash recovery) and makes use of its high potential query language SQL. Using original XML document after the mapping process will be out of use if any updating is done on the document. This makes rebuilding of XML documents from relational databases is equally important as a big deal. The rebuilding process raises a lot of issues to be considered, such as: 1) Reserving the structure of the original document, including nodes order and relationships when efficient labelling methods are used for rebuilding (i.e., parent-child, ancestor-descendant and preceding-following relationships), 2) Making sure that all document contents are stored (elements, attributes, comments … etc), 3) The rebuilding process should be efficient for the entire document or some parts of it.

These rebuilding solutions depend on the method used for mapping, and the way of labelling the contents of XML document in relational database.

COMPARISON OF MAPPING APPROACHES

Table 1 and Table 2 show a comparison between some procedures of mapping of XML documents into relational database. The bases that are used for comparison are: schema-less or schema-based, number of tables used in relational schema, recursive consideration, and the query language (XPath or XQuery) used for retrieving the data. Mapping could be classified also according to the method used for labelling XML documents because the efficiency of the labelling method affects the performance of querying and updating documents' contents. Table 2 reviews some methods presented in the literature for labelling XML document contents including elements and elements attributes.

Advantages and Disadvantages of Previous Approaches

Schema-less centric techniques reviewed above do not require an XML DTD or XML Schema. Present proposals depend on XML document's structure to manage the mapping process. In such approaches, XML document is entirely stored as a large solid object data type (CLOBs, BLOBs for example), which are provided by most relational database vendors (e.g., Oracle interMedia Text, DB2 Text Extender). Another way is to map the tree or graph of the XML document generically onto predefined relations. These approaches depend on using a long-character-string data type, such as CLOB in SQL, to store XML documents or fragments as texts in columns of tables. The advantages of these approaches are: (1) They could provide textual fidelity since they preserve the original XML at the character string level, and (2) there is no need for an XML schema in the storing process. The drawbacks of these methods are: (1) They cannot make use of the XML Markup structural information, (2) they don't take into account the query workload while constructing the relational schema, (3) the XML document structure is not preserved, and (4) it is difficult to deal with huge XML documents.

Schema centric techniques need XML schema to develop the relational schema. Such techniques need to create a relational schema to store the XML schema. The created schema is used during and after shredding the XML documents. The data that is captured from the XML document is stored in the created relational tables. The advantages of these techniques are: (1) They restrict XML structure to the defined schema (i.e. assign and use of Markup elements and attributes according to the defined schema), (2) they enforce referential constraints,

Table 1. A summary of XML to RDB related work

Technique	Schema/ Schemaless	No. of Tables	Cost-based	Preserve Order	preserve Constraints	Recursive consideration	XML query XPath/ XQuery
(Shanmugasundaram *et al.*, 1999)	Schema	> 2	yes	no	yes	no	XPath
XRel (Yoshikawa *et al.*, 2001)	Schemaless	4	no	Yes	No	no	XPath
Dewey (Tatarinov *et al.*, 2002)	Schemaless	4	no	Yes	No	no	XPath
XParent (Jiang *et al.*, 2002)	Schemaless	4	no	Yes	Yes	no	N/A
(Zhang and Tompa, 2004b)	Schemaless	> 2	no	yes	yes	no	XQuery
ORDPATH (O'Neil *et al.*, 2004)	Schemaless	2	no	Yes	Yes	No	XPath
ShreX (Amer-Yahia *et al.*, 2004)	Schema	> 2	No	Yes	No	no	Partial XPath
RELAXML (Knudsen *et al.*, 2005)	Schema	> 2	yes	yes	no	no	N/A
SPIDER (Fujimoto *et al.*, 2005)	Schema	4	yes	Yes	yes	no	XPath
(Atay *et al.*, 2007b)	Schema	> 2	yes	yes	yes	yes	N/A
LegoDB & FleXMap (Ramanath, 2006)	Schema	> 2	yes	No	No	yes	XPath
XShreX (Lee *et al.*, 2006)	Schema	> 2	yes	Yes	Yes	yes	XPath
(Soltan and Rahgozar, 2006)	Schemaless	2	no	Yes	Yes	No	N/A
Oracle interMedia Text, 2006	Schemaless /Schema	1	no	Yes	yes	-	XPath, XQuery
DB2 Text Extender, 2006	Schemaless /Schema	1	no	Yes	No	-	N/A
XTRON (Min *et al.*, 2008)	Schemaless	6	no	Yes	Yes	No	Partial XQuery

primary and foreign key relationships, and (3) they simplify the mapping process because users are not involved in addressing a new mapping language. But, the techniques reviewed above are (1) all heuristic; (2) do not consider multiple possible relational mappings so as to choose the optimal one; (3) moreover, fixed shredding of XML documents will lead to a loss of information from the original one, (Atay *et al.*, 2007b is an exception), (4) XML schemas are sometimes not available, so there is a need to construct the schema first and then do the mapping. 5) A reconstruction of database schema is needed as any change in the XML schema happens, which makes it very expensive in this case. 6) Sometimes, a large number of relations need to be created depending on the XML schema; consequently, a lot of joins are needed to retrieve XML document information.

CONCLUSION

In this chapter, a review and discussion of related methods and techniques for mapping XML documents into relational database have been presented. Maintaining document structure and reserving nodes' order within XML documents are too important as in document-centric documents (i.e. books, emails). Nodes labelling is another issue in mapping XML document into relational database, since relational database structure is an unordered tabular form, and XML document has a hierarchically ordered structure by nature. Some labelling methods for XML documents contents have also been discussed in this chapter.

The discussion shows that most of the labelling methods are concerned with the increase of query performance, but they ignore or fail to achieve

Table 2. A summary of XML labelling methods

Technique	Name	Advantages	disadvantages
(Li and Moon, 2001)	Interval encoding based on the number of words	Partially solves dynamic update problem	Relabeling of many nodes is needed in case of inserted data size exceeding reserved space
(Tatarinov *et al.*, 2002)	Global order label	It can help in answering XPath queries such as following and following-sibling.	All nodes of higher label than inserted node must be relabelled. It is difficult to answer ancestor-descendant relationship
(Tatarinov *et al.*, 2002)	Local order label	Only the following siblings of the inserted node need to be relabelled.	Just Sibling nodes following inserted node must be relabelled. Maintain parent-child relation is not easy.
(Tatarinov *et al.*, 2002)	Dewey order label	It is easy to maintain parent-child and ancestor-descendant relation	Sibling nodes right to the inserted node and their descendant must be relabelled
(Torsten, 2002)	Pre-order post-order	It minimizes the searching area within the document to accelerate XPath location step	All following nodes are needed to be relabelled after an insertion of new node. So, an insertion cost depends on the location where the new node is inserted.
(O'Neil *et al.*, 2004)	ORDPATH	It provides an ability for nodes insertion without a cost to relabel any existing node. Also it reserved parent-child relation	Many nodes need to be relabelled after the reserved space is used up. It fails in performing path and semantic search
(Wu *et al.*, 2004)	Prime number labelling	It is easy to identify ancestor-descendant relationship as it depends on whether their labels are divisible or not. Also insertion of new node and giving it prime number is easy.	- Large space size since candidate node label is self-label product from the root to node. - To reflect document order, they use simultaneous congruence value based on Chinese Reminder Theorem. And these value need to be re-calculated is considered time consuming. - Insertion between parent and child nodes is not supported.
(Kobayashi *et al.*, 2005)	Variable Length Endless Insertable (VLEI Code)	Parent-child and ancestor-descendant relationship are reserved. It reduces insertion cost since relabelling it not needed. Using octal number with "9" delimiter reduces the space needed for labelling.	Using octal and "9" delimiter instead of "." As character reduces the space but increases the time for relabeling since it as Dewey without space
(Soltan and Rahgozar, 2006)	Cluster based order	It is easy to maintain parent-child and ancestor-descendant relation. Also it decreases the # of records in the table	All sibling cluster right to the inserted cluster and their descendant must be relabelled
(Chung and Jesurajaiah, 2005)	Dynamic interval-based labelling	Parent-child and ancestor-descendant relationship are reserved. It solves partial insertion and updating issues.	Still some nodes need to be relabelled if no space available at the position of insertion. Also, extra space is needed for identifying each element. The querying process becomes high when the label is too long

efficient updating of XML document. The reason for that fail is a lot of elements and attributes are needed to be overwritten in case new elements or attributes are inserted into the document.

In general, transformation methods from XML document to relational database should satisfy many requirements. The significance of each requirement is application-dependant. In some applications it is extremely important to maintain order of nodes such as emails, books, journals and documents. In other applications, such as bank transactions, sales order and flight schedules documents, order is insignificant. Some of the requirements that should be met are the following:

1. Maintain document structure without loss of information while shredding.
2. Make the process of transforming a fresh document an easy task, and the updating of an already transformed document done with a constant time cost.
3. Ability to reconstruct the XML document or part of it from relational database.
4. Ability to perform semantic search.
5. Preserve the ordering nature of XML data and its structure.

In next chapters, the mapping model (MAX-DOR) and the labelling technique introduced in this thesis will be represented. This model attempts to meet some of these requirements which are not available in the literature including the update problem.

REFERENCES

Amer-Yahia, S., Du, F., & Freire, J. (2004). *A comprehensive solution to the XML-to-relational mapping problem*. In WIDM'04, Washington, DC, USA.

Atay, M., Chebotko, A., Liu, D., Lu, S., & Fotouhi, F. (2007b). Efficient schema-based XML-to-relational data mapping. *Information Systems, 32*, 458–476. doi:10.1016/j.is.2005.12.008

Berglund, A., Boag, S., Chamberlin, D., Fernández, M., Kay, M., Robie, J., & Siméon, J. (2007). *XML Path Language (XPath) 2.0*. W3 Consortium.

Boag, X., Chamberlin, D., Fernández, M., Florescu, D., Robie, J., & Siméon, J. (2007). *XQuery 1.0: An XML query language*. W3 Consortium.

Chen, Y., Davidson, S., Hara, C., & Zheng, Y. (2003). RRXS: Redundancy reducing XML storage in relations. In *Proceedings of the 29th International Conference on Very Large Data Bases*, Vol. 29. Berlin, Germany: VLDB Endowment.

Chung, S. M., & Jesurajaiah, S. B. (2005). Schemaless XML document management in object-oriented databases. *International Conference on Information Technology: Coding and Computing, ITCC 2005,* Vol. 261, (pp. 261-266).

Dweib, I., Awadi, A., Alrahman, S. E. F., & Lu, J. (2008). Schemaless approach of mapping XML document into Relational Database. *8th IEEE International Conference on Computer and Information Technology, CIT 2008*, (pp. 167-172).

Fujimoto, K., Yoshikawa, T., Kha, D. D., Yashikawa, M., & Amagasa, T. (2005). *A mapping scheme of XML documents into relational databases using schema-based path identifiers*. International Workshop on Challenges in Web Information and Integration (WIRI'05).

Jiang, H., Lu, H., Wang, W., & Yu, J. X. (2002). XParent: An efficient RDBMS-based XML database system. *International Conference on Data Engineering 2002,* (pp. 335-336).

Knudsen, S. U., Pedersen, T. B., Thomsen, C., & Torp, K. (2005). RelaXML: Bidirectional transfer between relational and XML data. *9th International Database Engineering* (IDEAS'05) (pp. 151-162).

Kobayashi, K., Wenxin, L., Kobayashi, D., Watanabe, A., & Yokota, H. (2005). VLEI code: An efficient labeling method for handling XML documents in an RDB. *Proceedings 21st International Conference on Data Engineering, ICDE 2005,* (pp. 386-387).

Lee, Q., Bressan, S., & Rahayu, W. (2006). *XShreX: Maintaining integrity constraints in the mapping of XML schema to relational*. 17th International Conference on Database and Expert Systems Applications (DEXA'06).

Li, Q., & Moon, B. (2001). Indexing and querying XML data for regular path expressions. *Proceedings of the 27th International Conference on Very Large Data Bases* (pp. 361 - 370).

Min, J.-K., Lee, C.-H., & Chung, C.-W. (2008). XTRON: An XML data management system using relational database. *Information and Software Technology, 50*, 18. doi:10.1016/j. infsof.2007.05.003

O'Neil, P., O'Neil, E., Pal, S., Cseri, I., Schaller, G., & Westbury, N. (2004). ORDPATHs: Insert-friendly XML node labels. In *Proceedings of the 2004 ACM SIGMOD International Conference on Management of Data*. Paris, France: ACM.

Oracle (n.d.). *Oracle XML DB developer's guide 10g*.

Oracle Technology Network. (n.d.). *Oracle XML DB*.

Pal, S., Fussell, M., & Dolobowsky, I. (December 2005). *XML support in Microsoft SQL server 2005*.

Ramanath, M. (2006) Schema-based statistics and storage for XML, (p. 175). In Faculty of Engineering. Indian Institute of Science, Bangalore, India.

Shanmugasundaram, J., Tufte, K., Zhang, C., He, G., DeWitt, D. J., & Naughton, J. F. (1999). Relational databases for querying XML documents: Limitations and opportunities. *Conference on Very Large Data Bases,* (pp. 302–314).

Soltan, S., & Rahgozar, M. (2006). A clustering-based scheme for labeling XML trees. *International Journal of Computer Science and Network Security, 6*, 84–89.

Tatarinov, I., Viglas, S. D., Beyer, K., Shanmugasundaram, J., Shekita, E., & Zhang, C. (2002). *Storing and querying ordered XML using a relational database system* (pp. 204–215). SIGMOD.

Torsten, G. (2002). Accelerating XPath location steps. In *Proceedings of the 2002 ACM SIGMOD International Conference on Management of Data*. Madison, WI: ACM.

Wu, X., Lee, M. L., & Hsu, W. (2004). A prime number labelling scheme for dynamic ordered XML trees. *Proceedings 20th International Conference on Data Engineering*, 2004, (pp. 66-78).

Xing, G., Xia, Z., & Ayers, D. (2007a). X2R: A system for managing XML documents and key constraints using RDBMS. In *Proceedings of the 45th Annual Southeast Regional Conference*. Winston-Salem, NC: ACM.

Xing, G., Xia, Z., & Ayers, D. (2007b). *X2R: A system for managing XML documents and key constraints using RDBMS. Winston. Salem*, NC: ACMSE.

Yoshikawa, M., Amagasa, T., Shimura, T., & Uemura, S. (2001). XRel: A path-based approach to storage and retrieval of XML documents using relational databases. *ACM Transactions on Internet Technology, 1*, 32. doi:10.1145/383034.383038

Zhang, H., & Tompa, F. W. (2004b). *Querying XML documents by dynamic shredding*. In DocEng'04, Milwaukee, Wisconsin, USA.

Zhou, J., Zhang, S., Wang, M., & Sun, H. (2006). XML-RDB driven semi-structure data management. *Journal of Information and Computing Science, 1*, 9.

Chapter 16
MAXDOR Model

Ibrahim Dweib
Sultan Qaboos University, Oman

Joan Lu
University of Huddersfield, UK

ABSTRACT

This chapter gives a full description of the proposed model introduced by the authors. The new model is called MAXDOR for mapping XML document into relational database. The description includes mathematical concepts that are used in this model, the labelling method used to label XML document and identify its content, and the design framework used to maintain the document structure, parent-child, ancestor-descendant, and siblings relations among document contents. It also presents a set of algorithms for mapping, reconstructing, updating, and retrieving XML documents

MAXDOR THEORY

Storing XML document into relational database means storing ordered, hierarchical and structured information into an unordered tables. XML manipulation is still facing some problems such as retrieving information, updating data contents, concurrency control and multi-user access. These problems can be overcome by using relational database to store, update and retrieve XML documents contents. Labelling techniques are used in order to preserve XML document structure, and the relations among its contents. MAXDOR adopts the Global Labelling method with some modifications (Tatarinov *et al.*, 2002). Global Labelling is modified to make the cost of the execution time of XML document updating constant, and to preserve parent-child and ancestor-descendant relationships. The modified method uses document structure information to guide the mapping process, Consequently DTD or XML Schema information availability is not required.

DOI: 10.4018/978-1-4666-1975-3.ch016

Figure 1. Composite parent-child relations (P:: Parent, C:: Child, A:: Ancestor, D:: Descendant)

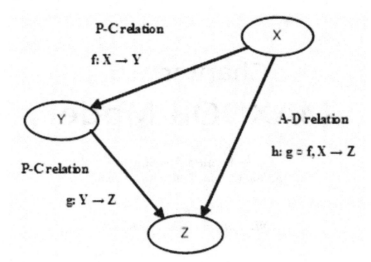

Theory Background

The hierarchy of XML document could be represented as a tree structure. XML tree can clearly represent the relationships between nodes of document content. Definitions 1 and 2 identify composite and associative relations between XML document elements, both as parent-child and ancestor-descendant relations. These relations help retrieve XML document contents as regular XPath expressions, and optimize query process. More details are given in section 4.2.4.

Definition 1: Composite relation: Given that f is a parent-child relation between X and Y, in a way that f: X → Y, and g is a parent-child relation between Y and Z, g: Y → Z, then the composition h: g ○ f is ancestor-descendant relation between X and Z as h: X → Z, (Oosten, July 2002). Figure 1 illustrates this composite relation.

Definition 2: Associative relation: Suppose f is a parent-child relation between X and Y as f: X → Y, g is a parent-child relation between Y and Z as g: Y → Z, and h: is a parent-child relation between Z and W as h: Z → W, then the composition i: g ○ f is

ancestor-descendant relation between X and Z, j: h ○ g is ancestor-descendant relation between Y and W, and K: (h ○ g) ○ f = h ○ (g ○ f) is also ancestor- descendant relation between X and W, (Oosten, July 2002). Figure 2 illustrates this associative relation.

Definition 3: An XML tree is a collection of many nested subtrees of depth two. It can be denoted as follows:

$$T = \sum_{i=1}^{n} \sum_{j=1}^{m} S_{ij} \tag{1}$$

where:

- $J = 1, 2, 3 \ldots$ m represent the order of subtree number within i^{th} level;
- $I = 1, 2 \ldots$ n represents tree level number and 1 also represents the tree root; and

S_{ij} represents a subtree structure and is denoted as

$$S_{ij} = E_{ij}(\sum_{r=1}^{l_1} X_{jr}, \sum_{k=1}^{l_2} A_{jk}, \sum_{w=1}^{l_3} E_{jw}, \sum_{z=1}^{l_2+l_3} G_{iz}) \tag{2}$$

where:

Figure 2. Associative ancestor-descendant relations

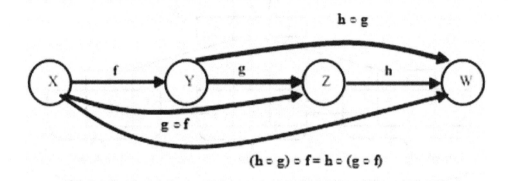

- E_{ij} *represents the root of the subtree* S_{ij}
- l_1 *represents number of text (X) in subree* S_{ij}
- l_2 *represents number of attributes (A) in subree* S_{ij}
- l_3 *represents number of elements (E) in subree* S_{ij}
- $G_{i,z}$ *is a finite set of edges between* E_{ij} *and its childs representing parent-child relationship* (l_2+l_3).

An XML document is a tree of nested elements, each element can have zero or more attributes. There can only be one root element, which is called document element. Each element has a starting and ending tag, closed by angle brackets, with content in between:

```
<element>...content...</element>
```

The content can contain other elements, or can consist entirely of other elements, or might be empty. Attributes are named values which are given in the start tag, with the values surrounded by single or double quotations:

```
<element attribute1="value1"
attribute2="value2">
```

One of the important characteristics of XML document is 'well-formed'. A well-formed XML document conforms to some rules, such as:

- Having only one root element.
- All start tags have matching end tags.
- Elements must be nested properly.
- Attribute values must always be quoted.
- Tags are case sensitive.

These restrictions on XML document structure makes shredding process and storing of XML document in relational database easier.

Definition 3 moves the organization of XML document, from being a tree of multi-dimensional way with arbitrary depth and width, to a tree structure of depth two. The resultant tree is unbounded fan-out at first level and fixed fan-out at the second level. The first level can be represented in relational database as tuples (i.e. rows) and the second level can be represented by fields (i.e. columns).

The processing and handling XML content is very important in optimizing data updating and retrieval. The search space is reduced into a subtree instead of working with the entire document tree. Consequently, definitions 4 and 5 given below make it possible to deal with an XML document as a dynamic-sized partition.

Figure 3. Multiple linked list over view

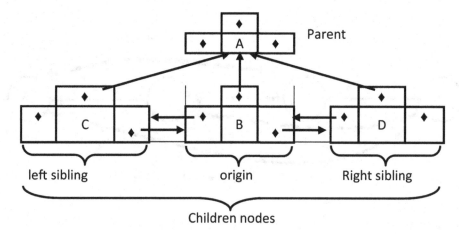

Definition 4: A dynamic fragment (shred) df(i) is defined to be the attributes and text (i.e. child leaves) of the subtree i of the XML tree plus its root r_{i-1}, as follows:

$$df(i) = (A_i, X_i, r_{i-1}) \qquad (3)$$

where:

- A_i *is a finite set of attributes in the level i*
- X_i *is a finite set of text in the level i.*
- r_{i-1} is the root of the leaves in level *i*.

Definition 5: The root of the fragment (shred) is the node that has an out-degree more than one.

Definition 6: A multiple linked list is a data structure in which each node has its data and contains links to the preceding node, the following node, and to the parent node.

Multiple linked lists give the ability to access its content in different directions, and to insert a new node in constant number of operations. This makes it possible to update document in contact time cost, and efficiently retrieve preceding sibling element, following sibling, and parent-child. But more space is needed to create this type of linked list than single and double linked list. This issue is considered as a drawback for multiple linked list over single and double linked list.

Figure 3 gives an overview on the multiple linked list and the relations between its nodes.

MAPPING FRAMEWORK

The mapping framework includes an algorithm to map XML documents into relational database and an algorithm to reconstruct XML documents from relational database. It also includes a method for updating stored XML document in relational database and querying and retrieving stored data from relational database. User's queries in XQuery or XPath languages are transformed into SQL statements, and SQL results are constructed into XML data format. Our approach considers well-formed XML documents, which are shredded and decomposed into elements and attributes, and then these elements and attributes are inserted into the relational database tables. It does not consider the XML schema for the following reasons:

- Many applications need highly flexible XML documents whose structure is not easy to define by DTD or fixed schema. Therefore, schema-less approach is better to deal with such XML documents.

- It is not practical to design many candidate relational schemas for all potential XML data which may have different XML schema.

Labelling Method

Four Dimensional Links (FDLs) are used to maintain the XML document contents. FDLs' uses a global labelling approach that gives labels for XML elements and attributes. A unique label is given for each element and attribute. The sequence of label is not essential as (Tatarinov et al., 2002; Soltan and Rahgozar, 2006). Point out, an initial pre-order traversing for the XML document is performed to assign a label for each element or attribute. No re-labelling is needed for XML document elements and attributes (tokens) in case of adding new element or attribute. In contrast (Tatarinov *et al.*, 2002), (Torsten, 2002), (Soltan and Rahgozar, 2006), and (Torsten *et al.*, 2004); proved the reverse, all tokens that follow the new inserted token should be relabelled. In pre-order, post-order two labels are to be updated. In order to achieve this objective, FDLs uses the following format to identify a token:

- Token *(tokenID, leftID, parentID, rightID, prevID)*
- *tokenID* is a unique label given to identify each token.
- *leftID* (Left-sibling) is the *tokenID* of the preceding sibling token.
- *parentID* (Parent) is the *tokenID* of the current token parent.
- *rightID* (Right-sibling) is the *tokenID* of the following sibling token.
- *prevID* is the *tokenID* of the previous token of the current token in the document structure.

Figure 4 shows an example of FDLs labelling method for XML tree structure and identifies the relationships between its contents.

The *tokenID* and *parentID* are used to maintain the parent-child and ancestor-descendant relationships, while *leftID* and *rightID* together with *tokenID* are used to maintain elements and attributes order as siblings and brothers relationships within the documents structure.

A fixed relational schema consisting of three tables is used to store XML documents' contents and their structure. The first table is called "documents table"; it preserves XML documents information. The second table is called "tokens table"; it preserves XML documents contents and structure. The third table is called "XpathQuery table"; it is a temporary table used to preserve token paths for a desired XPath expression from a document's root down to the desired token.

Relational Schema

This section gives a description of the relational schema used in FDLs, which consists of the following tables:

1. **Document master table:** It is called "documents table". This table keeps information about documents themselves; its minimal structure is:

Documents (<u>documentID</u>*, documentName, Header, docElement, schemaInfo, maxTokenId, XpathCount)*

   a. *DocumentID* is a unique ID generated for each document.
   b. *DocumentName* is the external name for XML document.
   c. *Header* is used to keep document header which specifies document encoding.
   d. *SchemaInfo* keeps the document's schema if it exists for documentation purpose.
   e. *DocElement* represents the document's root.

Figure 4. A tree representation for XML document

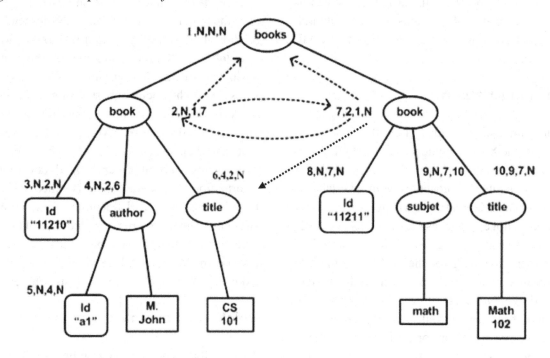

Where the sequence of numbers appears next to each node identify:
tokenID, leftID, parentID, and rightID

f. *MaxTokenId* represents the number of tokens in the document (i.e. total number of elements and attributes). It is used for future insertion, since a new inserted token is given a new ID following the last token number given in the document.

g. *XpathCount keeps the number of paths created for a specified query.*

2. **"Tokens table":** A table to store the actual content and structure for all documents. Documents will be shredded into pieces of data called tokens. Each document element, or element attribute will be considered as a token. The "tokens table" will have the following structure:

Tokens(documentID, tokenID, leftID, parentID, rightID, treeLevel, prevID, tokenName, tokenValue, tokenType)

a. *TokenID* field is the primary generated ID for each token.

b. *DocumentID* field is a foreign key linking the "tokens table" with the "documents table" to achieve referential integrity constraint.

c. *LeftID* (left-sibling) field keeps the ID of the left sibling token of current node. It is used to preserve tokens' order and document's structure.

d. *ParentID* field keeps the ID of parent's node. It is used to preserve parent-child and ancestor-descendant relations.

e. *RightID* (Right-sibling) field keeps the ID of the right sibling token of current node. It is to preserve the document's structure and tokens' order.

f. *PrevID* field keeps the ID of the previous token in the document structure.

g. *TreeLevel* field reserved the token level in the document or tree. It is starting from 1 for document element and increases by 1 for the nested element.

h. *TokenName* field is the tag name or the property name as found in the original XML document.

i. *TokenValue* field is the text value of the XML tag property.

j. *TokenType* field is used to differentiate between elements and attributes. (1 = element, 2 = attribute).

3. **"XpathQuery table":** A dummy table that is used to store all tokens involved in desired XPath expression. This table will have the following structure:

*XpathQuery(*documentID*, XpathID, tokenID, TreeLevel, ParentID, tokenName, TokenValue, TokenType)*

a. *DocumentID* field is a foreign key linking the "XpathQuery table" with the "documents table" to achieve referential integrity constraint.

b. *TokenID* field is the primary generated ID for each token.

c. *ParentID* field keeps the ID of parent's node. It is used to preserve parent-child and ancestor-descendant relations.

d. *TreeLevel* field reserved the token level in the document or tree. It is starting from 1 for document element and increases by 1 for the nested element.

e. *TokenName* field is the tag name or the attribute name as found in the original XML document.

f. *TokenValue* field is the text value of the XML tag property.

g. *TokenType* field is used to differentiate between elements and attributes. (1 = element, 2 = attribute).

Figure 5 represents the Entity-Relationship (ER) diagram for MAXDOR model showing the entities and the relation types connecting them. While Figure 6 represents the relational schema used in MAXDOR model and shows the three tables (i.e., "Documents table", "Tokens table", and "XpathQuery table"), their attributes and primary keys.

SAX-Based Approach

SAX parser (Megginson, 27-April 2004) is used for parsing XML document in order to store it in relational database. It is used instead of DOM (Document Object Model) to deal with large XML documents. SAX parses XML document as a sequence of events (i.e., startDocument, endDocument, startElement, endElement … etc), in the contrary of DOM that constructs the whole document tree (in memory) first and then parses it. DOM has an advantage over SAX that it offers XML update, but SAX provides XML for read only. In our approach updating XML contents is provided over the data stored in relational database and not on the XML document itself.

Mapping XML Document to Relational Database Algorithm

In this algorithm, the XML document is scanned once and is shredded into tokens. Each token represents one element or an element attribute in the document. The hierarchical structure of XML document imposes the use of a stack data structure. The stack is used to preserve element information that establishes links between sibling elements. These links (ParentID, leftID and rightID, prevID) are used to preserve document structure and the order of elements within the document.

The system automatically assigns each document a unique identification (DocumentID). During document scanning, maximum token identification is automatically generated for each new token. And any new inserted element or attribute will be assigned a new token ID following the maxTokenID value.

Figure 5. The entity-relationship diagram ER of MAXDOR model

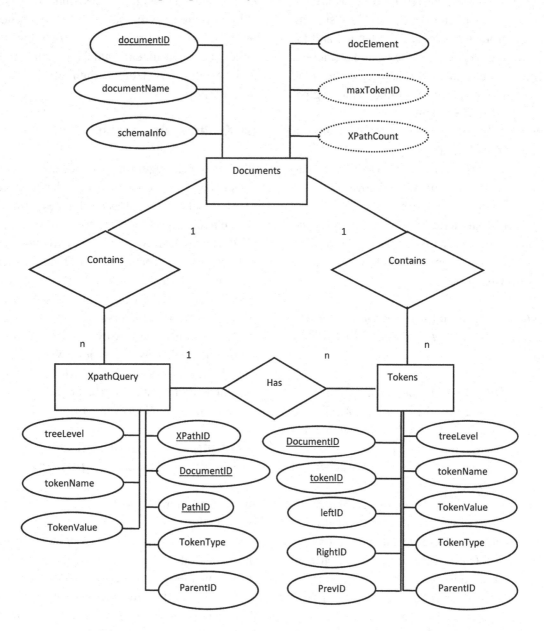

Figure 6. Relational schema

- **Documents**(<u>documentID</u>, documentName, docElement, maxTokenId, maxPathId, schemaInfo)
- **Tokens**(<u>documentID, tokenID</u>, leftID, parentID, rightID, treeLevel, prevID, tokenName, tokenValue, tokenType)
- **XpathQuery**(<u>documentID, XpathID, tokenId, TreeLevel, ParentId, tokenName, TokenValue, TokenType</u>)

A document is scanned sequentially as tree structure in pre-order traversal. And the generated elements and elements' attributes are assigned token IDs in that order. As the document scanned sequentially, all descendant elements are pushed into the stack buffer formulating a full path from the document root (i.e. document element) going down through descendant element until reaching leaf nodes.

Attributes of elements are written directly to the "Token table", since they are leaf nodes listed in order at the starting tag of an element, and their relations (Parent-child, preceding-sibling, and following-sibling) are easily formulated at this stage. The left-sibling of the first attribute is assigned zero identifier. While the right-sibling and left-sibling links between element attributes are assigned incremental identifiers as a new attribute is caught. The right-sibling of the last attribute is assigned zero identifier.

The stack reserves information of elements in order to create the links between sibling elements. A right-sibling of the current element cannot be assigned until the next sibling is caught, which cannot be done until all the descendant elements of the current element are scanned. Once the right sibling of an element is caught, or an element whose tree level is less than the element's level which is found at the top of the stack, all elements in the stack will have tree levels. This is greater or equal to that element level which popped from the stack and the appropriate links are established for these elements. Finally, the new element is pushed to the stack.

Stack size depends on two factors:

1. The depth of the document; stack size is directly proportional in this case to the document depth.
2. The length of elements' names and values. Also in this case, stack size is directly proportional to the length of elements' names and values.

Stack size can be managed as follows: In most document-centric XML, document depth is less than that of data-centric document, while elements' names and elements' values are larger than that of data-centric document. Experiments in Chapter 6 applied to selected data sets will give more clarification on this statement.

An implementation of this algorithm is described in Chapter 5 as XML2Base class, and experiments on different data sets are done in Chapter 6 to test the algorithm usability and performance.

Rebuilding XML Document from RDB

The rebuilding process of XML document from relational database is needed for the following reasons:

1. To make sure that the mapping method, used in the research, efficiently maintain the entire XML document without losing information.
2. To update document content after being mapped into relational database; updating takes place in the relational database. So, the original XML file become obsolete; i.e. not reflecting the current state of the content of database table.

For the preceding factors, a rebuilding algorithm is used to:

1. Rebuild the entire XML document that can be exchanged or exported by the user somewhere, or
2. Rebuild part or some parts of the document as a result of user queries using XPath or XQuery that are translated into SQL statements retrieved by relational database system.

Reconstruction or rebuild algorithm depends on the labelling method and the relational schema described in previous sections used for MAXDOR model. It manages the rebuilding process in two ways:

1. **Fresh document or un-updated (un-changed) document:** In this case, the document is built as it was read from relational database, and in the sequence it was stripped in. A stack data structure is used to reserve ending tags of ancestor elements. As a starting tag of the element and its attributes (if it exists) are written directly to the output XML document file. The algorithm uses treeLevel in order to manage nested elements. As new element is identified to be next element, its treeLevel is compared to the top element of the stack; if it is less than the top of the stack, then pop the stack, write the popped element to the output file, write elements' closing tag, until the top of the stack becomes less than or equal to the new element. Finally, the new element closing tag is pushed into the stack. The process is repeated until building the entire document is completed.

2. **Updated document:** to manage document fragmentation that resulted from updates (insertion and deletion) on a document, three stack data structure are being used because no relabeling is allowed for document contents after insertion to reserve element order. These stacks are:

   a. A stack for pending elements: It is used to hold elements that cannot be written directly to the output file since new inserted elements are assigned labels not in the same order of their predecessor elements in the document structure. Those elements should be written to the output file before their new successors after pended elements on the stack.

   b. A stack for element attributes: It is used to manage element attributes in their logical order to be written in the same order as their order is in the element starting tag.

   c. A stack for nested elements closing tags: It is used to reserve ancestors' closing tags because processing goes from parent to child. If a new element is caught and its treeLevel is less than that of the element treeLevel in the stack, then all elements of treeLevel greater than that or equal to treeLevel of the new element pop and their closing tags are written to the output file as XML document.

Whenever a new element is caught, and before writing it to the output file, its attributes are popped from the attributes' stack and appended to it.

An implementation of this algorithm is described in Chapter 17 as xbsXML2Base class. In addition, some experiments on reconstructing XML documents from relational database are conducted in Chapter 18.

UPDATING XML DOCUMENT CONTENTS

Insertion of New Token

This section gives more evidence that the method used in this research makes insertion time cost of new token, anywhere in the document, constant; this, one of the main objectives of the research is achieved. The insertion process can be clarified by the following rules:

a. Insertion of a new token to the left of a subtree, left to S1:

   1. The new token T gets a label tokenID following the maxTokenID in the document. $TokenID(T) = maxTokenID + 1$.
   2. $RightID(T) = RightID(S1)$
   3. $LeftID(T) = 0$
   4. $LeftID(S1) = tokenID(T)$

5. ParentID(T) = ParentID(S1)
6. prevID(T) = prevID(S1)
7. PrevID(S1) = tokenID(T)

b. Insertion of a new token to the right of a subtree, right to S1:
   1. The new token T gets a label tokenID following the maxTokenID in the document. *TokenID(T) = maxTokenID + 1.*
   2. LeftID(T) = TokenID(S1)
   3. RightID(T) = 0
   4. RightID(S1) = tokenID(T)
   5. ParentID(T) = ParentID(S1)
   6. prevID(T) = prevID(followS1)
   7. PrevID(followS1) = tokenID(T)

c. Insertion of a new token T as a leaf and child of S1:
   1. The new token T gets a label tokenID following the maxTokenID in the document. *TokenID(T) = maxTokenID + 1.*
   2. LeftID(T) =0
   3. RightID(T) = 0
   4. ParentID(T) = TokenID(S1)
   5. prevID(T) = tokenID(S1)
   6. PrevID(followS1) = tokenID(T)

d. Insertion of a new token T as a parent of S1:
   1. The new token T gets a label tokenID following the maxTokenID in the document. *TokenID(T) = maxTokenID + 1.*
   2. LeftID(T) =LeffID(S1)
   3. RightID(T) = RightId(S1)
   4. ParentID(T) = ParentID(S1)
   5. TreeLevel(T) = TreeLevel(S1)
   6. prevID(T) = prevID(S1)
   7. PrevID(S1) = tokenID(T)
   8. LeftID(S1) = 0
   9. RightID(S1) = 0
   10. Look for all descendant and update treeLevel by 1

Figure 7 gives an overview of inserting new token (i.e. element or attribute) in the XML document. In the figure, the new element "subject" is inserted between "author" (labelled [4, N, 2, 6]) and "title" of label [6, 4, 2, N]. The new element is

given tokenID equals to maxTokenID + 1, which is 11. And the token links are updated as follows:

1. rightID(subject) = rightID(author)
2. leftID(subject) =leftID(title)
3. rightID(author) = tokenID(subject)
4. leftID(title) = tokenID(subject)
5. prevID(subject) = prevID(title)
6. prevID(title)= tokenID(subject)
7. ParentID(subject) = ParentID(title)

As seen from the previous example, there is no need for relabeling the tokens that follow the inserted token "subject". All tokens' labels in the document remain as they were before the insertion process. While in (Tatarinov *et al.*, 2002) (Torsten, 2002) (Soltan and Rahgozar, 2006), all the following nodes of new inserted element "subject" must be relabelled, and the cost of relabeling depends on the location of the new inserted element. The highest cost is gained when the insertion happens at the beginning of the document, and the lowest cost is gained when the insertion takes place at the end of the document.

An implementation of this algorithm is described in Chapter 17 as dbxTokens class. And an evidence of the previous claim that insertion of new tokens anywhere in the document is done on constant time cost is shown as the experiments in Chapter 18 demonstrate.

Deletion of a Token

Deletion of existing tokens from any location or level in the XML document can be done also with constant cost. This deletion process follows the following rules:

Note: The maxTokenID field will not be changed (i.e. not decremented), since no relabeling of the tokens within the document will be done.

1. Deletion of a token T between two siblings, S1 and S2:
   a. RightID(S1) = RightID(T)

Figure 7. Inserting new token in XML tree

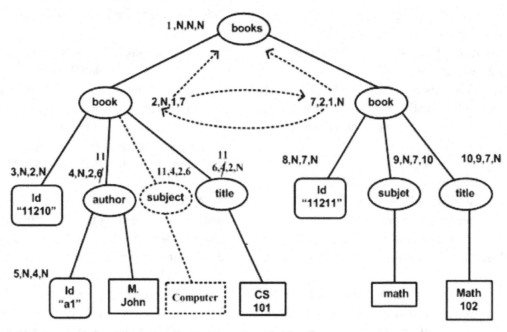

Where the sequence of numbers appears next to each node identify:
tokenID, leftID, parentID, and rightID

b.   LeftID(S2) = LeftID(T)
c.   prevID(s2) = prevID(T)
2.   Deletion of a token from the left side of a subtree, to the left of S1:
a.   LeftID(S1) = 0
b.   prevID(followT) = prevID(T)
3.   Deletion of a token from the right of a subtree, to the right to S1:
a.   RightID(S1) = 0
b.   prevID(followT) = prevID(T)
4.   Deletion of a complex element:

Deletion of a subtree can be handled as a single token by one of the previous three cases, but all its descendants should also be deleted.

RETRIEVING AND QUERYING XML DATA STORED IN RELATIONAL DATABASE

Mapping XML documents into relational database is not just for storage and back-up. This data is stored so as to be efficiently updated and retrieved. In our proposed method, the XML Path Language (XPath) is used as a source tool for retrieving and querying the XML data stored in the relational database. The XPath expressions will be translated into its equivalent SQL statements in order to get the results from the relational database.

"XpathQuery table" is used as a temporary table to isolate XPath query results at run time from the database main tables. Its content is the result of walking through the tree side by side according to the XPath command, filtered as required, and getting the records (nodes) while doing so. This method has minimal cost, since in path methods we have to select the records too. It is different from Path table methods since those approaches building a table of all expected queries in the DBMS during the mapping time will result in increasing the database size (O'Neil et al., 2004; Jiang et al., 2002; Yoshikawa et al., 2001),.

In the following sub-section, a discussion for XPath axes (i.e. parent, child, ancestor, descendant, following, following-sibling, preceding, and preceding-sibling), translating of XPath expression to SQL statements, and building their results in XML format are also presented.

XPath Axes

XPath has mainly 8 axes used for retrieving XML document content. Figure 8 gives a clearer view of these axes. Consider G as a candidate node, and the nodes:

- Node B is a parent of G.
- Nodes H and I are children of G.
- Nodes A and B are ancestor of G.
- Nodes H, I and J are descendant of G.
- Nodes C, D, E and F are preceding of G.
- Nodes C and E are preceding-sibling for G.
- Nodes K, M, L and N are following for G.
- Nodes K and M are following-sibling for G.

Here is an explanation of how MAXDOR labelling method supports these axes. Given x and y as nodes in the XML document n:

1. **Parent and child axes:** node x is a parent of node y if and only if its tokenID is assigned as parentID of node y and its level is greater than its parent level by 1.
2. **Ancestor axis:** All ancestor nodes of node x can be retrieved as nested parent axes starting from node x in reverse order. All ancestor nodes of x are formulated and located on the same path.
3. **Descendant axis:** All descendant nodes of a node x can be retrieved as nested parent-child axes. They are retrieved recursively from left

to right, as each of its children is a subtree. The left most child of x has leftID equal to zero. Move right until the right most child having rightID = 0.

4. **Following axis:** All nodes following a node x can be retrieved as follows:
   a. If RighID of x is not equal to zero, then the right node of x is considered as a starting node to be retrieved, and retrieve all of its following nodes. The process applies in the same way building the whole document, but the resultant XML document may not be well-formed.

Document ID	TokenID	ParentID	LeftID	RightID	TokenName	TokenValue	TokenType
n	1	0	0	1	x	B	1
n	6	1	4	10	y	G	1

   b. If RightID of x is equal to zero, then find the node whose prevID equals the ID of node x. If it exists, consider it as the starting node to be retrieved and retrieve all of its following nodes. As in case 1, the process applies to building the whole document, but resultant XML document may not be well-formed

5. **Preceding axis:** All preceding nodes of a node x can be retrieved as follows:
   a. The process goes through the candidate node path starting from it up to the root node (i.e., node x and its ancestor nodes in reverse order), check the left-sibling of each parent. If its leftID is not equal to zero then push it to the stack.
   b. The parent nodes starting from the top are popped from the stack, and their preceding-sibling nodes are retrieved along with their descendant nodes according to cases VII and III.

Figure 8. Nodes relationship in XML tree structure

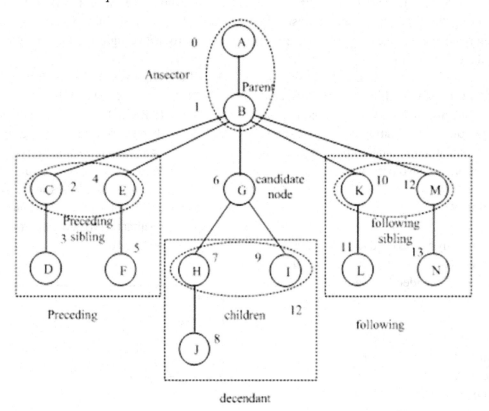

6. **Following-sibling axis:** All following-sibling nodes of a node x that has the same parent as x can be retrieved from rightID link, starting from rightID node of node x, as a sequence, until the right most sibling node(with rightID equals to zero) is reached.

7. **Preceding-sibling axis:** All preceding-sibling nodes of node x, which has the same parent as x, can be retrieved from leftID link, starting from leftID node of node x, as a sequence, until the left most sibling node (with leftID equals to zero) is reached. In this case a stack data structure can be used to retrieve preceding sibling from left to right instead of right to left.

8. **Attribute Axis:** All attributes of a node x can be retrieved as an attribute whose parentID equals X's tokenID. To retrieve them from

left to right, start by the attribute of leftID= 0, and move right by following rightID links until the right most attribute is reached.

Other Axes, as ancestor-or-self axis and descendant-or-self axis can be processed as ancestor or descendant axes including the context node.

XPath Syntax

XPath uses path expression to select a node or a set of node from the XML document by following a path or a step. According to W3C (Berglund *et al.*, 2007), this selection can be performed as follows:

1. **Nodes selection:** This selection can be done through some expressions which appear in Table 1.

Table 1. XPath expressions (Berglund et al., 2007)

Expression	Description	Comments
nodename	Selects children nodes of the named node	
/	Selects nodes from the root node	This expression is considered as absolute expression
//	Selects document nodes from the current node no matter where they are	This expression is considered as relative expression
.	Selects the current node	
..	Selects the parent of current node	
@	Selects attributes of the current node	

In this case retrieving XPath results can be dealt with as follows:

a. Expression of one step like /books or // name, the process can directly use the tokens table as:

```
SELECT t1.* FROM tokens as t1
WHERE t1.tokenName = x
And t1.documentId=n;
```

Where x is the specified token name and n represents the current document ID. But if the expression has multi step as /books/book or //book/authors/author, then nested inner joins on "Tokens" table and relation between "XPathQuery" table is needed to retrieve the desired tokens which have this path.

b. For "." expression to select current node, the SQL statement for this expression is:

```
SELECT t1.tokenName, t1.tokenValue
FROM tokens as t1
WHERE t1.tokenID = x   And
t1.documentId= n;
```

Where x represents the current token ID

c. For "@" expressions, the SQL can be:

```
SELECT t1.tokenName, t1.tokenValue
FROM tokens as t1, token AS t2 WHERE
```

```
t1.parentId = t2.tokenID
And t2.tokenID = x
And t1.documentID = n
And t1.tokenType= 2;
```

2. **Path expression including predicates:** Predicates in XPath are used to find a specific node, or a node that has a specific value. Usually, predicates are surrounded by square brackets.

Table 2 shows some path expressions that use predicates. In this case retrieving XPath results can be dealt with as follows:

a. For path expressions number 1 and 2, a nested inner joins between "XPathQuery" table and "Tokens" table are used to retrieve the desired elements that have this path. Left link or right link of selected tokens is also retrieved. In expression 1, leftID should be zero for the selected token, while in expression 2 rightID should be zero for the selected token. The following two SQL statements represent expression 1 and expression 2 respectively.

b. For path expressions number 3 and number 4, the process goes for expression 1 and 2, and after identifying the desired tokens. Then a selection of tokens whose parent is in the selected set will be performed.

Table 2. Path expressions with predicate

No.	Path expression	Description
1.	/books/book[1]	Select the first book element that is a child of books element.
2.	/books/book[last()]	Select the last book element that is a child of books element.
3.	/books/book[last()]/isbn	Select the isbn element of last book element that is a child of books element.
4.	/books/book[isbn='425168']/title	Select the title element of book element which its isbn = '425168' and is a child of books element

Where x represents the left part of "[", and y represents the right part of "]".

For both expressions 3 and 4 farther step is needed to identify the desired child.

An implementation of mapping XPath expressions into SQL statements algorithm is described in Chapter 5 as *frmQuery* class. And some experiments on different forms of XPath expressions are conducted in Chapter 18.

XML Sub-Tree Reconstruction (Query's Result Translation to XML)

A user query result could be a group of separated single elements, or attributes or nested elements that can be consider in this case as a subtree. In case of group of separated elements or attributes, a "starting tag" and "closing tag" can be used to group the results as a single level tree which rooted by query result. This procedure helps in forming the result as a well-formed document. In case the result is a nested element, it can be built the same way as building an entire document, starting by the lowest level element as a root node instead of the document element. In both cases, the algorithm that is used for reconstructing XML document from relational database can be used also for building queries' results from relational format into XML format.

CONCLUSION

In this Chapter, a detailed description is given for the MAXDOR model. The description includes: the theory used for this model and tree facilities for representing and accessing XML document as the two structures are both hierarchical and nested. The labelling method used in designing the MAXDOR model is represented as Four Dimensional Links (FDLs), since a multiple linked list is used in our case. The links are used for parent node, left node, right node and previous node in the structure. Those links make the insertion time cost of new element or attributes anywhere in the document realized with a constant number of operations. Also the retrieving process of document contents can be done smoothly as the relations between its nodes are identified through those links. For example, left-sibling can be identified by leftID, right-sibling by rightID, parent by parentID, complex element by previous ID. The relational model used in the model is introduced as Entity-Relational diagram and relational schema. As three relational tables are used, two used to store document metadata, which are "documents table" and "XpathQuery table" while the third one "tokens table" is used to store document contents. A description of mapping XML document into relational database algorithm has been given with the data structure that is used to optimize the process. The rebuilding of XML document from relational database algorithm has been presented with two options. The first option is to reconstruct updated documents and the other to reconstruct documents that are updated within insertion or deletion processes. The update of XML document contents in relational database include inserting, deleting and allocating processes algorithm have been presented, and operations on different locations in the document have been done to show that the updating time cost is constant. At the end, a querying and retrieving document contents algorithm has been presented with some XPath axes and XPath expressions translated into SQL statements.

An implementation of MAXDOR model will be offered in the next chapter, (i.e. Chapter 5). This includes system architecture, the tools used, software needed for implementation, classes implemented for the model, data structure used for enhancing the model performance and the XML data set used for testing.

REFERENCES

Berglund, A., Boag, S., Chamberlin, D., Fernández, M., Kay, M., Robie, J., & Siméon, J. (2007). *XML path language (XPath) 2.0*. W3 Consortium.

Jiang, H., Lu, H., Wang, W., & Yu, J. X. (2002). XParent: An efficient RDBMS-based XML database system. *International Conference of Data Engineering*, (pp. 335-336).

O'Neil, P., O'Neil, E., Pal, S., Cseri, I., Schaller, G., & Westbury, N. (2004). ORDPATHs: Insert-friendly XML node labels. In *Proceedings of the 2004 ACM SIGMOD International Conference on Management of Data*. Paris, France: ACM.

Oosten, J. v. (July 2002). *Basic category theory.* Department of Mathematics, Utrecht University, The Netherlands. Megginson, D. (27 April, 2004). *Simple API for XML*. SAX.

Soltan, S., & Rahgozar, M. (2006). A clustering-based scheme for labeling XML trees. *International Journal of Computer Science and Network Security*, *6*, 84–89.

Tatarinov, I., Viglas, S. D., Beyer, K., Shanmugasundaram, J., Shekita, E., & Zhang, C. (2002). *Storing and querying ordered XML using a relational database system* (pp. 204–215). SIGMOD.

Torsten, G. (2002) Accelerating XPath location steps. In *Proceedings of the 2002 ACM SIGMOD International Conference on Management of Data*. Madison, WI: ACM.

Torsten, G., Keulen, M. V., & Jens, T. (2004). Accelerating XPath evaluation in any RDBMS. *ACM Transactions on Database Technology*, *29*, 40.

Yoshikawa, M., Amagasa, T., Shimura, T., & Uemura, S. (2001). XRel: A path-based approach to storage and retrieval of XML documents using relational databases. *ACM Transactions on Internet Technology*, *1*, 32. doi:10.1145/383034.383038

Chapter 17
System Architecture and Implementation

Ibrahim Dweib
Sultan Qaboos University, Oman

Joan Lu
University of Huddersfield, UK

ABSTRACT

This chapter presents the system architecture, and implementation tools used for evaluating the MAXDOR model. The chapter also presents the main classes created to demonstrate the methodology for mapping XML document into relational database, rebuilding XML document from relational database, updating the content of XML document stored in relational database, XPath-To-SQL query translation, and building the result in XML format. Application on a case study is also presented. XML data sets from selected XML bench marks and XML data repository will be identified to be used for testing and evaluating the model. Finally, the chapter concludes with a summary.

SYSTEM ARCHITECTURE AND THE USED TOOLS

System Architecture

System architecture consists of four main components each of which represents one of the project requirements. Those components are:

1. **Mapping XML document into relational database:** the system loads the XML document and parses it using XML SAX parser as a sequence of events, shreds the document content into tokens, and inserts these tokens into predefined relational database schema. Detail of the relational schema has been given in chapter 4.

2. **Reconstructing XML document from relational database:** this component goes through the relational tables and reconstructs the requested XML document to check the method for lossless of XML document information in Part one or to exchange or export the document to other location.

DOI: 10.4018/978-1-4666-1975-3.ch017

3. **Updating XML document stored in relational database:** by this component, the user is given the facility to update the XML document stored in relational database. Update includes: inserting new tokens as element or element attributes, delete tokens or tokens' re-allocation within the document, and modify tokens' name and values.

4. **Retrieving and querying XML document stored in relational database:** throughout this component, XPath queries are translated into SQL statements. The resultant SQL statements are fired against the database engine so as to retrieve XML data results. The retrieved results are reconstructed as XML hierarchical format and returned to the user. Figure 1 gives an overview of the system architecture.

The above listed components will be tested and evaluated in Chapter 6 for the MAXDOR model described in chapter 4. The following points are taken into consideration during system design; i.e. components of the system should be:

- **Testable against requirements:** every requirement should be easy to test.
- **Structured:** the system structure should be clear, read and its code should be easy and understandable.
- **Reusable:** the system design should be reusable and repeatable.

Tools Used

The tools used in the project can be classified into:

1. XML interface: both input and output documents are XML format and relational database technology is a target tool for storing XML documents' contents and structure; so, the relational database capabilities are used for internal processing of data.

2. XPath or XQuery as source languages provided for users to represent their requests. SQL query language is a target language used against relational database to answer users' queries. XPath is used for the following two reasons:
   a. XPath is simpler than XQuery, and hence would be better to achieve the objective of testing our model in current situation.
   b. Its structure is included in XQuery, so it is easier to be upgraded into XQuery.

3. Visual Basic 6.0 programming language is used as a tool to create the GUI and to implement the system components. It is used for the following reasons:
   a. VB structure is simple, mainly as to the executable code.
   b. VB is easy for building graphical user interfaces.
   c. VB application is easily connected with Microsoft Access database.

4. Microsoft Office Access is used as a relational database management system (RDBMS). It is used for the following reasons:
   a. It can be easily used with visual basic programming language.
   b. Access database can be easily sited on a website for access by remote users. Simple screens can be built in Access, Data Access Pages. Or it can be employed using Active Server Page (ASP) scripting.

SYSTEM IMPLEMENTATION

Requirements for System Implementation

1. Microsoft Office 2003 or 2007 is required since we are using Microsoft Access as the development DBMS for the system.

Figure 1. MAXDOR architecture

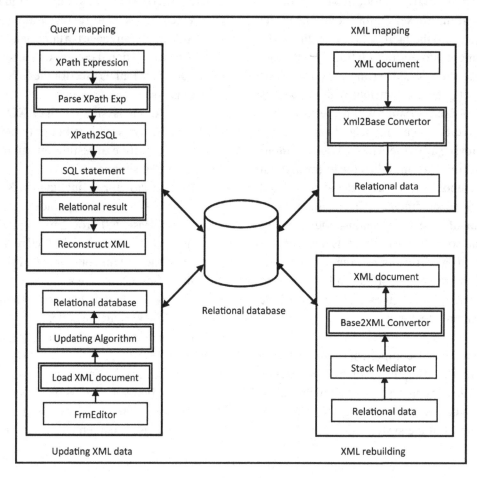

2. Microsoft Windows 2000 with service pack 3 (sp3), Windows XP, or later, because Microsoft Office Access 2003 is used, and this is its minimum requirement of the operating system.
3. Minimum hardware requirements are given in Table 1.

Classes of the MAXDOR Model

In the following sections a description of the main classes used for system implementation is given. These classes are *xbsXml2Base*, *xbsBase2XML*, *dbxTokens* classes and *frmQuery*.

XbsXml2Base Class

The data model used for the mapping algorithm uses the W3C's Simple Application Program Interface for XML (SAX parsing) (Megginson, 2004). A stack is also used to traverse the XML document. Each child of the element is pushed to preserve and identify nodes' order, element siblings and parent-child relationship. SAX parser fires actions on many events including document start, document end, element start, element end, characters, element attributes, and processing instruction. These events help in shredding XML document and store its contents into relational database tables. Four more links are added to token description, its parent ID, left sibling ID,

Table 1. Hardware requirements for Microsoft Office 2003 (Corporation, 2009)

Computer and processor	Personal computer with an Intel Pentium 233-MHz or faster processor (Pentium III recommended)
Memory	128 MB of RAM or greater
Hard disk	150 MB of available hard-disk space; optional installation files cache (recommended) requires an additional 200 MB of available hard-disk space
Drive	CD-ROM or DVD drive
Display	Super VGA (800 × 600) or higher-resolution monitor

right sibling ID, and previous token ID in the document structure. Left and right sibling IDs are used to make the time needed for future insertion in the document constant since these IDs could be updated as new node or subtree is added or relocated in the document. Previous token ID helps in rebuilding XML document with minimum cost because the document is built in sequential order, on top-down bases, (i.e. moving down through parent-child relationship and forward through sibling relationship).

A description of xbsXML2Base class is given below. The class takes XML document as input and generates its relational database tables as output. It mainly depends on the XMLSAX *Contenthandler* class (i.e. a custom class implementing the IVBSAXContentHandler interface). Figure 2 shows the state transition diagram for this class. Few private methods are added to the class and their description is given below. The coding of the class is presented in Appendix B in chapter 19.

The startDocument method is called just one time for each document. As it is called by SAX parser, the relational database tables are prepared to receive document information in "document table" and "tokens table".

The three methods, *startElelment, characters* and *endElement* are called back by SAX parser depending on the document contents and contents sequences.

1. The *startElement* method is called by SAX parser whenever it encounters an XML start tag as <book id="bk210">. The parser gives

tag name and the list of attributes if any. In this method, a stack data structure is used to manage document structure and build relations between document contents in our model.

2. The *characters* method is called whenever text content is seen as input in the document.

3. The *endElement* method is called whenever the corresponding end tag </book> is seen. In this method, a return to previous level is performed.

Figure 2. State transition diagram for xbsXml-2RDB class

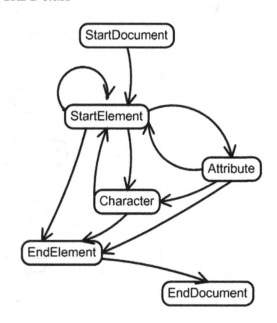

If SAX parser encounters Document end, it calls *endDocument* method. In this method, all pending elements in the stack are inserted into "Tokens table".

The stack data structure in this class is used to preserve parent-child and sibling relationships. The stack is used to hold the tokens' information of all elements for one path of the document, (i.e., ancestors' nodes of the current node). And that path identifies the size of the stack since the path size depends on the tree level or depth. In this case, the relation between the path size and the stack size can be considered proportional, and may decrease the performance of the method for documents with very deep levels.

XbsBase2Xml Class

The class is used to rebuild XML documents back from relational database to create new XML document from scratch since original document contents could be updated. The class depends mainly on two methods: *DirectBuild* and *BuildProps*. Figure 3 shows the main processes of this class.

A brief description for these processes is given below and the coding of the class is presented in Appendix B in chapter 19:

- The *select document elements* process is used to select the entire candidate document elements from "*tokens table*".
- *Open output file* process is used to open an output XML file for writing the candidate document contents in XML format.
- *Buildprops method:* This method is used to read all attributes and put them on a stack for later use in a form of "*attribute vectors*"; each vector corresponds to a unique element (i.e. the attributes parent) and is composed of an ordered list of attributes in their original order.
- The *building elements process:* This is used to rebuild document elements depending on the prevID and treeLevel for elements in order to identify elements sequence and parent-child relation. The element starting tag, its attributes (if any is found on the "attribute vectors"), and value are written to

Figure 3. Rebuilding XML document from relational database state diagram

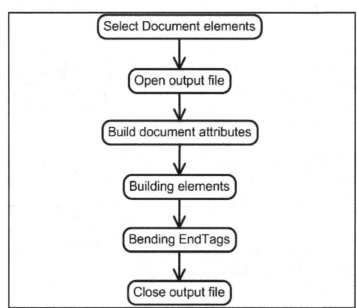

240

output file. If the current element has children, its closing tag will not be written out but put onto a stack till all sub-children are processed. The process uses a stack called Clpending to temporarily hold the elements that cannot be written directly to XML file since newly inserted elements would break the sequence order of the labels.

- The *bending EndTags* process: This is used to write all bending closing tags off the stack to the output files.
- The *closing output file* process: This is used to close the output file and terminates the building process.

DbxTokens Class

This class consists of three groups of subroutines for editing XML documents: *inserting*, *updating* and *deleting* the tokens. Figure 4 shows the state transition diagram for this class and the coding of the class is presented in Appendix B in chapter 19.

The editing process starts by loading the XML document contents from relational database using the *"frmeditor"*. When the document is loaded

into the editor and a candidate element is selected, any one of the following processes can be performed:

1. **Adding (i.e. inserting) new elements:** Four different methods are used to perform this process depending on the position of insertion which are *InsTagBefore*, *InsTagAfter*, *InsTagBelow* and *InsTagAbove*. These four methods are used to insert new elements as left-sibling, right-sibling, child and parent respectively for the candidate element. The methods are different since different links have to be updated depending on the position of insertion. Insertion of new elements as a parent needs to update all descendent tokens level of candidate element.

2. **Update element:** Candidate element's name and value can be updated in this process.

3. **Deleting selected token:** This process is used to delete a candidate element and its entire descendant tokens (if any).

4. **Adding an attribute:** This process is used to add an attribute to the candidate element.

Figure 4. State transition diagram for updating the XML document

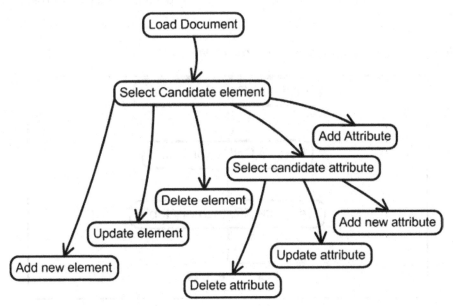

5. Select candidate attributes for selected elements. In this process any one of the following can be performed:
   a. Add (i.e. insert) new attribute before or after the candidate attribute.
   b. Delete the candidate attribute.
   c. Update the candidate attributes name or value.

FrmQuery Form

Executing XPath queries pass through four stages: validating XPath expression, parsing XPath expression, generating "XPathQuery table", and building the results in XML tree format. Figure 5 shows the state transition diagram for these main processes and the coding of the form is presented in Appendix B in chapter 19.

A brief description of these processes is given below:

1. *"Validate XPath expression"* process is to ensure that the given XPath expression conforms to XPath expression structure rules before parsing it.
2. *"Parsing XPath expression"* process is used to parse and simplify the XPath expression into multiple steps and identify relevant

conditions in order to create equivalent SQL statements. These SQL statements will be used to generate the output into a temporary dummy table for the next stage (i.e. cursors alternative).

3. *"Generate XPathQuery table process"* is used to dynamically create result subtree(s) on the fly using the records from the temporary table generated on the previous step.
4. *"Show results process"* is used to show the query results in two forms, grid view and tree view. In grid view, the results of the query, (i.e. *XPathQuery table* contents) are displayed in tabular format which shows tokenIDs, parentID, token name and token value. While in tree view, the results are shown in a tree-like format representing the XML structure.

CASE STUDY

In this section, a case study is presented to illustrate the implementation of MAXDOR model. Consider the sample XML document (i.e. *books. xml*) in Figure 6. The hierarchical structure of XML document makes it possible to represent

Figure 5. Main processes of XPath expression execution

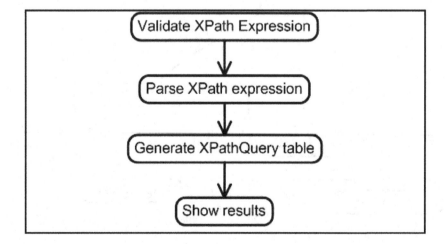

it as a rooted, labelled tree. Figure 7 presents an XML tree for the XML document in Figure 6. Our approach gives each node a global label in pre-order traversal in the first scan while any new inserted token is given an identification label following the last label used for the document. This label can be taken from *maxTokenID* from *"documents table"*. So the label of a token does not reflect its location in the document structure. Consequently, a label, in our approach, is used to identify a token where each token represents an element or attribute of the XML document. Other researchers use a label to represent the structure of the contents of a document and nodes order (cf. Tatarinov *et al.*, 2002; Torsten et al., 2004; Soltan and Rahgozar, 2006).

After mapping, a single record is assigned for this document in *"documents table"*, for example with *documentID* = 1, as in Figure 8, and document elements and elements' attributes are represented as records in the *"tokens table"*, as shown in Figure 9. Each record gives a full description of an element or element's attribute and its structure.

After storing XML document content and structure in a relational database, MAXDOR gives the ability to update document contents. Update includes inserting new elements or elements' attributes, deleting elements or attributes, modifying elements' names or values and modifying attributes names or values in a way to keep the document in well-formed condition. The update is performed on the relational database version of the document. Thus, there will be no need to keep the original XML document as it does not reflect the contents of the relational database.

Inserting New Element

Inserting a new element can be executed in four locations in reference to the selected element; these locations can be as a child, parent, left-sibling or right-sibling. The following discussion shows how to insert new "book" element between the

Figure 6. XML document

```
<books>
   <book id="bk210" >
      <author id="a1" >M. John</author>
      <title>C++ </title>
   </book>
   <book id="bk211">
      <subject>Math</subject >
      <title> Calculus </title>
      <price> 45.50 </title>
   </book>
</books>
```

two existing ones, (i.e. before token # 7). Figure 10 shows the XML element "book", Figure 11 reflects the XML modification after inserting the new element. It is a complex element (i.e. subtree) of one attribute and 2 simple elements. Subtree tokens (i.e. elements and attributes) are assigned new IDs that succeed the last assigned label in the previous shredding process for initial mapping or element insertion. For example, the "Book" elements' tokenID becomes 12, and the "book id" elements' tokenID will be 13, the "author" tokenID will be equal to 14, while the "title" elements' tokenID will be equal to 15. Figure 12 shows the equivalent relational tuples for the "book" element and the required updated links for this operation. The right sibling of token number 2 points to the new element which is 12 and the left sibling of node 7 points to the new element which is 12. The left sibling of the new element (i.e. subtree root) points to the element whose TokenID equals to 2 and the right sibling of the new element points to the element whose TokenID equals to 7. PrevID of token 7 is changed to point to the last token in the new subtree which is 15. And prevID of token number 12 points to token number 6. Other tokens' links of the new complex element are shown in Figure 12.

The process is trivial for updating selected element's name or value as this process does not involve updating of document structure. To delete

Figure 7. A tree representations for XML document

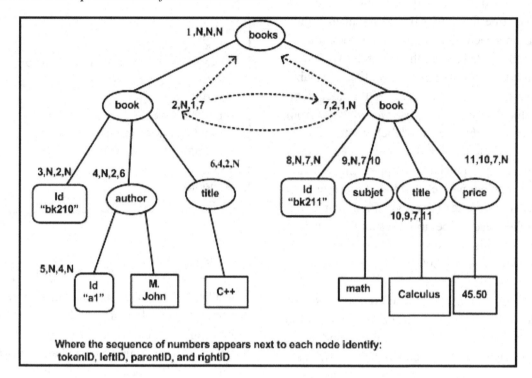

XML DATA SETS USED FOR TESTING THE MODEL

In order to assess the usability and efficiency of our MAXDOR model, three XML benchmarks are used: XML benchmark from Washington University (Washington University, 2002), XMark benchmark (Busse et al., 2002) and Michigan XML benchmark (Runapongsa et al., 2006). XML document generator *XMLgen* from XMark is used to create documents of different sizes using factors of the original one.

"Tree-bank" document is taken from Washington benchmark, "Auction documents" from XMark, and "Xbench-TCSD-small" and "Xbench-TCSD-normal" from Michigan benchmark. These documents characteristics are shown in Table 2.

Michigan XML benchmark data sets are used for evaluating the performance of the model against the complicated characteristics of XML documents such as depth, fan-out in "tree-bank" document. The tree depth has significant effect on performance in cases, of creating and evaluating containment relationships between nodes, namely identifying nodes with ancestor-descendant relations. Nodes fan-out can affect the way in which the DBMS stores data, and affect queries based on retrieving children in precise order, such as the first or last child of a node (Runapongsa *et al.*, 2006). Scaling a benchmark data set in the relational model is done by increasing the number of records. Scaling in XML, however, can be done by increasing depth, number of nodes, or fan-outs. The data sets in Table 2 and Table 3 are used to evaluate the model performance and usability in

Figure 8. Documents table

documentID	documentName	docElement	maxTokenID
1	Catalog	Books	11

Figure 9. Tokens table

documentID	tokenId	leftID	parentID	RightID	prevID	treeLevel	tokenName	tokenValue	tokenType
1	1	0	N	0	0	1	books	Null	1
1	2	0	1	7	1	2	book	Null	1
1	3	0	2	0	2	3	id	bk210	2
1	4	0	2	6	3	3	author	M. John	1
1	5	0	4	0	4	4	id	a1	2
1	6	4	2	0	5	3	title	C++	1
1	7	2	1	0	6	2	book	Null	1
1	8	0	7	0	7	3	id	bk211	2
1	9	0	7	10	8	3	subject	Math	1
1	10	9	7	11	9	3	title	Calculus	1
1	11	10	7	0	10	3	Price	45.50	1

Figure 10. XML document element (subtree)

```
<book id="bk106">
  <author>Mike</author>
  <title>Applied Geometry </title>
</book>
```

both directions, for mapping the documents into relational database and for rebuilding the mapped documents from relational database.

For evaluating the update performance of our model, we used the set of documents in Table 4.

The documents are created from auction document using *XMLgen*. We choose small factor between 0.001 and 0.006 to get small size document that can be managed by our editor. Many experiments can be performed to insert new tokens in different

Figure 11. A tree representation for updated XML document

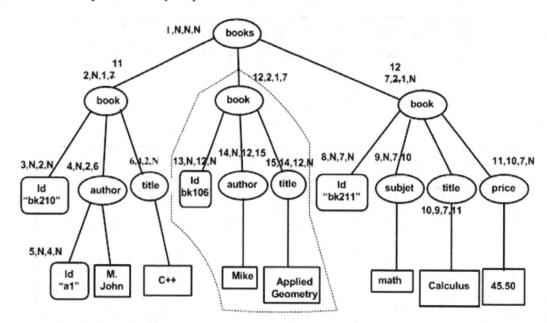

Where the sequence of numbers appears next to each node identify:
tokenID, leftID, parentID, and rightID

Figure 12. Updated "tokens table"

documentId	tokenId	leftId	parentId	RightId	prevId	treeLevel	tokenName	tokenValue	tokenType
...	...	...	...	...	...	...	...	...	...
...	...	...	...	...	...	...	...	...	...
1	2	0	1	12	1	2	book	Null	1
...	...	...	...	...	...	...	...	...	...
1	7	12	1	0	15	2	book	Null	1
...	...	...	...	...	...	...	...	...	...
1	12	2	1	7	6	2	book	Null	1
1	13	0	12	0	12	3	Id	bk106	2
1	14	0	12	15	13	3	Author	Mike	1
1	15	14	12	0	14	3	title	Applied Geometry	1

Table 2. XML data sets of equally sizes

Document	Size(MB)	# of Token	# of Paths	Max depth
Auction11	11	200358	502	12
Xbench-TCSD-small	11	283312	26	8
Auction82	82	1485699	502	12
Tree-bank	82	2437667	168123	36
Auction107	107	1946203	502	12
Xbench-TCSD-Normal	107	2757084	26	8

Table 3. XML datasets of equal depths and different sizes

Document Name	Factor used	Document Size (MB)	Max depth	# of nodes
Auction_1	0.1	11.3	12	206130
Auction_2	0.2	22.8	12	413111
Auction_3	0.3	34.0	12	616229
Auction_4	0.4	45.3	12	820438
Auction_5	0.5	56.2	12	1024073
Auction10	1.0	113.0	12	2048193

Table 4. Auction documents of small factor

Document Name	Factor used	Document Size (KB)	# of nodes
Auction_0.001	0.001	115	2086
Auction_0.002	0.002	210	3684
Auction_0.003	0.003	318	6284
Auction_0.004	0.004	457	7957
Auction_0.005	0.005	567	10492
Auction_0.006	0.006	682	11911

Table 5. XPath expression sets

XPath expression	name	Used for
/root/listing	Q1	Short simple path
/root/listing/auction_info/higher_bidder/bidder_rating	Q2	Long simple path
//higher_bidder/bidder_name	Q3	Regular expression, single '//'
//auction_info//bidder_rating	Q4	Regular expression, double '//'
/root/listing/seller_info[seller_rating='2']	Q5	Text matching
/root/listing[last]	Q6	index
/root/listing/seller_info[seller_rating='2']/seller_name	Q7	Text matching

places: In the beginning, in the middle and at the end. They can also have different relationship with the candidate element such as parent, child, left-sibling and right-sibling.

For evaluating the query performance of our model, a set of XPath queries are selected from different resources, Table 5 shows those XPath queries and the features which they evaluate.

CONCLUSION

In this chapter, a description of the system architecture, and the tools used in building the project are given in section 1. These tools include XML tools for generating XML documents, XPath tools for querying and retrieving an XML document or parts of it. RDBMS tools (i.e. Microsoft Access) for storing XML document and SQL for retrieving XPath expression from relational database. To this end, Visual Basic programming language is used as a programming tool.

System implementation description is given in section 2. Software and hardware requirements for system implementation have been presented. A description of the classes implemented in Visual Basic for the four main components of the project is offered. *XbsXml2Base* Class is used for mapping XML document into relational database. *XbsBase2XML* Class is used for rebuilding XML document from relational database. *DbxTokens* Class is used for editing XML document contents within a relational database. That includes update, insert or delete of document element's name, element's value, attribute's name or value. "*fmrquery*" form is used for parsing XPath expression, formulating of equivalent SQL statement, getting the results and building it in XML tree format.

Section 3 presents theory implementation on a sample case study which shows the process of mapping an XML document into relational database and the process of how to update the XML document within the relational database.

Section 4 shows different XML data sets from various XML benchmarks and XPath expression sets for testing and evaluating the usability and performance of MAXDOR model.

The experiments and their resultant assessments will be given in the next chapter, Chapter 18.

REFERENCES

Busse, R., Carey, M., Florescu, D., & Kersten, M. (2002). *XMark- An XML benchmark project.*

Megginson, D. (27 April 2004). *Simple API for XML*. SAX.

Microsoft Corporation. (2009). *Microsoft Office Word 2003 system requirements*. Microsoft Corporation.

Runapongsa, K., Patel, J. M., Jagadish, H., Chen, Y., & Al-Khalifa, S. (2006). The Michigan benchmark: Towards XML query performance diagnostics. *Information Systems, 31*, 73–97. doi:10.1016/j.is.2004.09.004

Soltan, S., & Rahgozar, M. (2006). A clustering-based scheme for labeling XML trees. *International Journal of Computer Science and Network Security, 6*, 84–89.

Tatarinov, I., Viglas, S. D., Beyer, K., Shanmugasundaram, J., Shekita, E., & Zhang, C. (2002). *Storing and querying ordered XML using a relational database system* (pp. 204–215). SIGMOD.

Torsten, G., Keulen, M. V., & Jens, T. (2004). Accelerating XPath evaluation in any RDBMS. *ACM Transactions on Database Technology, 29*, 40.

Washington University. (2002). *XML data repository.*

Chapter 18
Experiments and their Assessment

Ibrahim Dweib
Sultan Qaboos University, Oman

Joan Lu
University of Huddersfield, UK

ABSTRACT

In this chapter, the authors give a description of the experiment setup consisting of experiment environment and performance measurement. They perform experiments on mapping XML document into relational database, building XML document from relational database, updating XML document stored in relational database, and retrieving document content from relational database using XPath expressions. These experiments will be done to check the scalability and effectiveness of the model. Then they compare their model with the (Tatarinov et al., 2002) and the Accelerating XPath model (Torsten et al., 2004). The comparison consist of four stages: mapping, building, updating, and retrieving, as most of other studies just took one or two stage and forgot the others. Some of them took retrieving, others took updating, and others took updating and retrieving, but most of them did not consider mapping and rebuilding.

EXPERIMENT SETUP

Experiment Environment

All experiments tests are conducted on a PC of an Intel Core2 Quad Q9550 2.83 GHz CPU, 4.00 GB RAM, running Windows 7 Professional. Visual Basic 6 programming language is used to implement MAXDOR model, and Microsoft Access 2007 is used as a target relational database for storing XML document contents on local hard drive. In addition, a disk file is named with document number in the document table and with an XML extension created for reconstructed XML document from relational database.

DOI: 10.4018/978-1-4666-1975-3.ch018

Performance Measurement

- Mapping XML document into RDB execution time.
- Rebuilding of XML document from RDB execution time.
- Dealing with any document size.
- Inserting nodes processing time (number of nodes to be relabelled).
- Query processing execution time.

The execution time is used as an evaluation scale in this research rather than storage space since the former is crucial nowadays for the users, while storage space is available in a very huge size with reasonable prices.

TESTING STRATEGIES

Mapping XML Document into Relational Database Performance

The experiment is performed as follows:

Face 1, scalability test: An XML document generator from XMark (Busse *et al.*, 2002) is used to create documents of different sizes with factors of 0.1, 0.2, 0.3, 0.4 and 0.5. The documents characteristics are shown in Table 1. In this experiment, our model shows performance in a linear and scalable manner as document size is increasing. The mapping result over different sizes of the same document is shown in Figure 1.

Face 2, effectiveness test: Three groups of documents of different sizes 11MB, 82MB and 107MB but with different structure and different numbers of token are included in this experiment. Table 2 shows documents properties and their mapping and rebuilding time. Figure 2 shows the time required for mapping XML documents into relational database which consistently increases as the number of tokens increases in the document.

Considering the results shown in Figure 1 for homogenous documents and those shown in Table 2 and Figure 2 for heterogeneous documents coupled with calculating the correlation coefficient between document size and mapping time in the two cases $r_1 = 0.99988$ and $r_2 = 0.8751$ on the one hand, and the number of tokens and mapping time in the two cases $r_3 = 0.99991$ and $r_4 = 0.9991$ on the other hand, we can conclude that the time required for mapping the document largely depends on the number of tokens (i.e., elements and attributes) in the document, the document size and document depth ($r = 0.1752$) respectively.

Now let us compare MAXDOR model with Global Encoding for (Tatarinov *et al.*, 2002) and Accelerating XPath for (Torsten *et al.*, 2004), since the three models are using the same general number encoding to identify the XML document of elements and attributes (tokens). A detail description for Global Encoding and Accelerating XPath is given in Chapter 15.

The three models use one scan to shred the document contents, assign an identifier for each token, reserve node information, (i.e. token name and token value) to store them in one tuple in relational database. Global Encoding adds another table for tokens path from the document element

Table 1. Different sizes of auction document

Document Name	Factor used	Document Size (MB)	# of nodes
Auction_1	0.1	11.3	206130
Auction_2	0.2	22.8	413111
Auction_3	0.3	34.0	616229
Auction_4	0.4	45.3	820438
Auction_5	0.5	56.2	1024073

Figure 1. Mapping time for dataset in Table 1

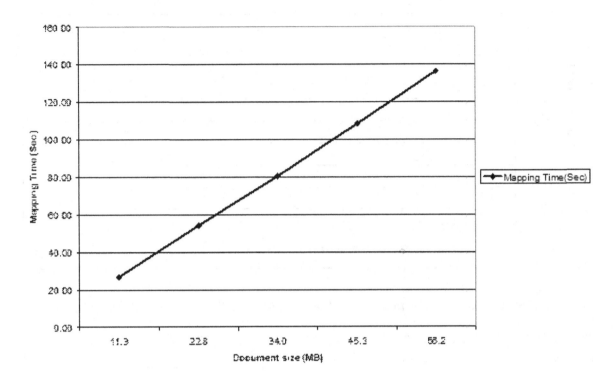

passing through until the candidate token. MAX-DOR and Accelerating XPath are similar in using just one table to store documents contents. Both also use a stack collection to manage post-order label in Acceleration XPath and RightID link in MAXDOR.

Based on previous experiment, one finds that mapping time mainly depends on the number of tokens in the document. Based on that, we may consider the following assumptions:

$$T \begin{cases} t & \text{for both MAXDOR and Accelerating XPath,} \\ t + tp & \text{for Global encoding,} \end{cases} \tag{1}$$

where T is the mapping time and tp is the time required to process the tokens path.

$$tp = (t \mathbin{/} n) * m \tag{2}$$

Table 2. XML dataset of different structures

Document	Doc Size (MB)	# of Token	# of XPath	Mapping (Sec)	Building (Sec)
Auction11	11	200358	502	25.50	13.41
Xbench-TCSD-small	11	283312	26	36.75881	17.39469
Auction82	82	1485699	502	186.7157	141
Tree-bank	82	2437667	168123	325.2331	150
Auction107	107	1946203	502	260.3572	200
Xbench-TCSD-Normal	107	2757084	26	376.7195	181

Figure 2. Mapping time for documents in Table 2

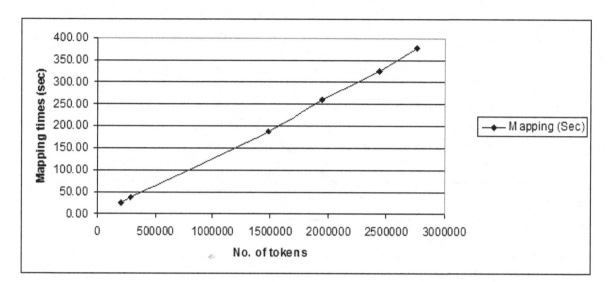

Figure 3. Mapping comparison between MAXDOR, accelerating XPath and global encoding

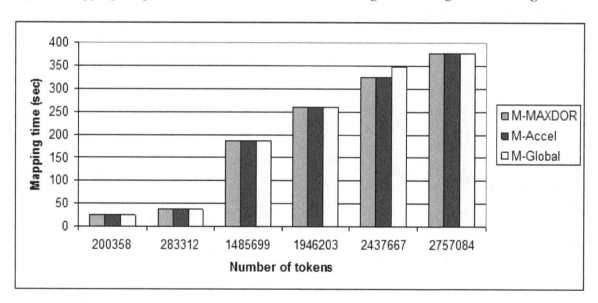

Table 3. Mapping time for MAXDOR, accelerating XPath and global encoding in seconds

Doc. Size (MB)	# of Token	Different path	M-MAXDOR	M-Accel	M-Global
11	200358	502	25.4965	25.4965	25.56038
11	283312	26	36.7588	36.7588	36.76218
82	1485699	502	186.7157	186.7157	186.77879
107	1946203	502	260.3572	260.3572	260.42436
82	2437667	168123	325.2331	325.2331	347.66404
107	2757084	26	376.7195	376.7195	376.72305

Figure 4. Building time for documents in Table 1

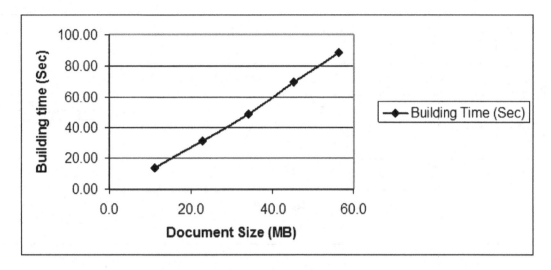

Figure 5. Mapping and building time for XML documents of different sizes

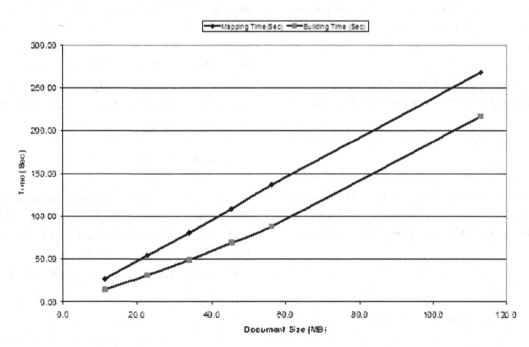

where n is the number of tokens in the document and m is the number of distinct paths in the document.

Now we can use the results of experiments 1 and 2 for mapping XML documents into relational database and compare our model with the other two models.

From Table 3 and Figure 3 we can see that MAXDOR and Accelerating XPath are identical while Global Encoding is closed to the other two models in homogeneous documents where the

Figure 6. Building time for documents in Table 2

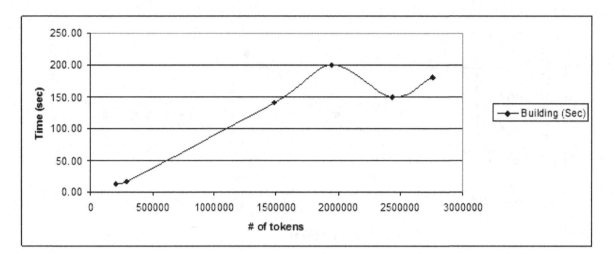

number of paths is small and the gap becomes larger for heterogeneous documents where the number of paths becomes very large as in tree_bank document.

Rebuilding XML Document from Relational Database Performance

The experiment is done at different stages as follows:

Face 1, scalability test: the auction documents in Table 1 mapped before will be built in this experiment to see the scalability of MAXDOR in rebuilding XML documents from relational database.

From the results shown in Figure 4, we find that our model performs well for rebuilding the XML document. The time for rebuilding a document of 11.3MB size is 14.14 seconds and for 56.2MB size is 88.00 seconds. This shows that the relation between rebuilding time and document size is approximately linear as it passes through the origin and is given as follows:

$$t = 1.644989s \qquad (3)$$

where t is the time in seconds for rebuilding the document and s is the size of the document in MB.

Figure 5 is a combination of Figure 1 and Figure 4 for mapping and rebuilding of the same XML documents, in addition to an extra document

Table 4. Building time after update

Document Size (KB)	# of Tokens	Before insertion	Insertion Location		
			Begin	**Middle**	**End**
115	2086	0.1256	0.1598	0.1384	0.12623
210	3684	0.2264	0.2759	0.2474	0.22581
318	6284	0.3854	0.4799	0.4341	0.37913
457	7957	0.4963	0.6134	0.5671	0.49238
567	10492	0.6419	0.8116	0.7307	0.64538
682	11911	0.7295	0.8924	0.8245	0.73666

Table 5. Differences in building time

Document Size (KB)	Differences			Percent		
	Begin L1	Middle L2	End L3	Begin	Middle	End
115	0.03425	0.01281	0.00067	27%	10%	1%
210	0.04950	0.02100	-0.00056	22%	9%	0%
318	0.09450	0.04869	-0.00631	25%	13%	-2%
457	0.11719	0.07088	-0.00388	24%	14%	-1%
567	0.16969	0.08875	0.00344	26%	14%	1%
682	0.16291	0.09497	0.00716	22%	13%	1%

which is the original auction document of 113.0MB. From the Figure we can conclude that our model still behaves linearly for both mapping and rebuilding of large sizes of documents.

Face 2, effectiveness test: The same sets of documents from Table 2 are also used to check the ability of MAXDOR in dealing with different XML document types. The documents are grouped by size and every two have the same size.

From the experiments done and results shown in Figure 6, it can be concluded that the time of rebuilding the document is influenced by the number of tokens formulating the document because two documents of the same size need different amounts of time for rebuilding.

Figure 7. Comparison of building after insertion in different location

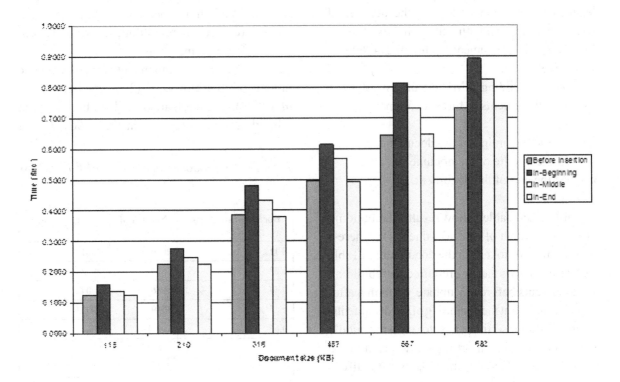

Table 6. Time cost of insertion of a token in different location

Location in Document	Insert Location (time in Sec)				# of token in Document
	Parent	**Child**	**Before**	**After**	
In-Beginning	0.046875	0.015625	0.015625	0.015625	2086
At-Middle	0.015625	0.015625	0.015625	0.015625	
At-End	0.015625	0.015625	0.015625	0.078125	
In-Beginning	0.0625	0.015625	0.015625	0.03125	3684
At-Middle	0.015625	0.015625	0.015625	0.015625	
At-End	0.015625	0.015625	0.015625	0.015625	
In-Beginning	0.046875	0.015625	0.015625	0.03125	6284
At-Middle	0.0625	0.015625	0.015625	0.015625	
At-End	0.015625	0.015625	0.015625	0.015625	

From the results shown in Figure 4 for homogenous documents and results shown in Table 2 and Figure 6 for heterogeneous document, and after calculating the correlation coefficient between document size and rebuilding time ($r_1 = 0.998795203$, $r_2 = 0.926455747$), and number of tokens and rebuilding time ($r_3 = 0.999311324$, $r_4 = 0.308485455$), we can conclude that the time required for rebuilding the document mainly depends on the document size, the number of tokens (elements and attributes) that exist in the document and the document depth ($r = 0.214860654$) respectively.

Face 4, Building XML document after the insertion of elements in three locations:

1. At the beginning of the document.
2. In the middle of the document
3. At the end of the document.

Table 4 and Table 5 show results of rebuilding auction document of several values of n, where n is the number of tokens in the document. In Table 4, column 3 shows the time required for rebuilding the documents before any update, column 4 after inserting a token at the beginning of the documents, column 5 after inserting a new token at the middle and column 6 after inserting a new token at the end of the documents. Table 5 shows the difference between the required time for rebuilding the document after inserting the defined location and the rebuilding time of the original document and the percentages of that difference.

The averages of percentages are different. The cost of rebuilding the document depends mainly on the location of inserting the new tokens. The cost decreases from $1.24*t$ at location L_1 to t at location L_3, where L_1 denotes token number 2 and L_3 denotes token number $n + 1$, and t represents the time required for rebuilding the original document before any insertion.

Next, we will compare our model with the models of Tatarinov *et al.* (2002) and Torsten *et al.* (2004). The comparison will be based on the rebuilding document cost in time (*BCDT*) and

Table 7. XML documents sizes and # of tokens in them

Document size (MB)	Number of Nodes	Factor value
0.11	2086	0.001
0.22	3684	0.002
0.44	7956	0.004
0.55	10492	0.005
0.66	11911	0.06
1.1	21051	0.01
11.0	200358	0.1

Table 8. XPath expressions under evaluation

XPath expression	name
/site/regions	Q1
/site/regions/Africa/item/location	Q2
/site/regions/Africa/item[@id="item1"]/location	Q3

Table 9. XPath traversals for query Q1

Document size (MB)	# Result Nodes	# of interest result	t(ms)
0.11	2	1	7.8125
0.22	2	1	4.882813
0.44	2	1	6.835938
0.55	2	1	7.8125
0.66	2	1	5.859375
1.1	2	1	7.8125
11.0	2	1	7.8125

the time of inserting a new token (element or attribute) (*ICDT*). The comparison will make use of the discussion above. In the following results, we will give the expected value of the *BCDT* and *ICDT* for the models under study.

THEOREM-6.1

Under the following assumptions:

We will assume that the locations of insertion have the same probability,

$$P\left[X = x\right] = 1 / n, x = 2, 3, \ldots n + 1 \quad (4)$$

where X denote the location of insertion.

We will assume that the time decreases from $1.24*t$ at location 2 to t at location $n+1$ uniformly, i.e.

$$P[Y = 1.24 - [0.24 * (y - 2) / (n - 1)] * t] = 1 / n, y = 2, 3, \ldots n + 1 \quad (5)$$

where Y denotes the time required to build the document after inserting a new token at position y, we have:

$$E_{11} = E_{MAXDOR}[BCDT] = 1.24 * t - 0.12 * t(n - 1) / n \quad (6)$$

$$E_{12} = E_{Global}[BCDT] = t \quad (7)$$

$$E_{13} = E_{Acc}[BCDT] = t \quad (8)$$

where E_{model} denotes the expected value of *BCDT* under the model. The Proof of Theorem 6.1 (a) will be given in Appendix A in chapter 19.

For E_{12} and E_{13}, in both cases the tokens there are sorted in sequential order and the time needed for building the document is equal to t

Remark

The motivation of the assumptions 1 and 2 in the theorem are based on the experiment results in Table 4 and Table 5.

Updating Performance

To evaluate our model updating performance, the experiment is performed as follows:

1. Inserting a child node in different location in the document and at different levels.
2. Inserting a preceding-sibling (i.e. before) node in different locations in the document and at different levels.
3. Inserting a following-sibling (i.e. after) node in different locations in the document and at different levels.
4. Inserting a parent node in different location in the document and for different levels.

Table 6 shows the time in seconds needed to process the inserting nodes in documents that

Table 10. XPath traversals for query Q2

Document size (MB)	# Result Nodes	# of interest result	t(ms)
0.11	5	1	7.8125
0.22	5	1	11.23047
0.44	7	2	11.23047
0.55	7	2	7.8125
0.66	9	3	11.23047
1.1	13	5	11.23047
11.0	113	55	15.625

Table 11. XPath traversals for query Q3

Document size (MB)	# Result Nodes	# of interest result	t(ms)
0.11	5	1	23.4375
0.22	5	1	31.73828
0.44	5	1	38.08594
0.55	5	1	46.875
0.66	5	1	45.89844
1.1	5	1	70.3125
11.0	5	1	60.15625

have 2086, 3684, 6284 tokens. The figures in the table show that the number of tokens (i.e. size of the document) has an influence on the processing time wherever the insert on process occurs, in the beginning of the document, in the middle or at the end. For cases of inserting a token as a child or before (i.e. left-sibling), the time cost is constant, but for the other two cases, parent and after (i.e. right-sibling), the cost is variable. For the parent node since we have an identifier for token level in the document, all descendant nodes tree level should be updated (i.e. incremented by 1). While for after nodes (right-sibling) we should look at

descendant nodes for the proper PrevID link for the new node. That means, there is an increase in the cost of insertion time depending on the size of the candidate node (i.e. number of descendant nodes) for the two cases. The differences in cost for *parent* and *after* tokens are shown in Table 6.

Theorem-6.2

Under the following assumptions:

We will assume that the locations of insertion have the same probability,

Figure 8. Total expectation time for the three models, MAXDOR, global encoding, and accelerating XPath

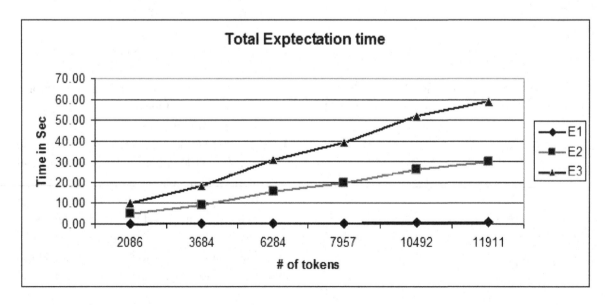

Table 12. Total expectation time for building and inserting tokens for the three models (in Sec)

n	t_0	t	t_1	E_1	E_2	E_3
2086	0.015625	0.1256	0.00488	0.15882	5.21734	10.30907
3684	0.015625	0.2264	0.00488	0.27373	9.21870	18.21099
6284	0.015625	0.3854	0.00488	0.45499	15.72405	31.06270
7957	0.015625	0.4963	0.00488	0.58142	19.91858	39.34086
10492	0.015625	0.6419	0.00488	0.74740	26.25188	51.86185
11911	0.015625	0.7295	0.00488	0.84726	29.80312	58.87674

$$P\left[X = x\right] = 1 \,/\, n, x = 2, 3, \ldots n + 1 \qquad (9)$$

where X denotes the location of insertion.

We will assume that the time decreases from $n * t_0$ at location 2 to t_0 at location $n+1$ uniformly, i.e.

$$P\left[Z = t_0[n - z + 2]\right] = 1 \,/\, n, y = 2, 3, \ldots n + 1 \qquad (10)$$

where Z denotes the time required to insert the new node at position z, we have:

$$E_{22} = E_{Global}[ICDT] = t_1 n \,/\, 2 + t_0 \,/\, (n + 1) \qquad (11)$$

$$E_{21} = E_{MAXDOR}[ICDT] = t_0 \qquad (12)$$

$$E_{23} = E_{Acc}[ICDT] = t_1 n + t_0 \,/\, (n + 1) \qquad (13)$$

where E_{model} denotes the expected value of *ICDT* under the model:

Proof of Theorem 6.2 will be given in Appendix A. For E_{21}, since there is no relabeling needed after insertion of a new token. Then, the

Figure 9. Snapshot for mapping and building of XML document

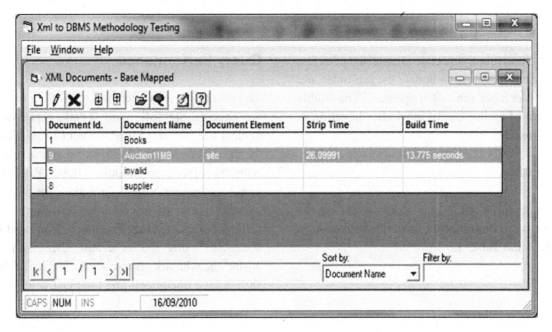

Figure 10. Snapshot for inserting new element before candidate one

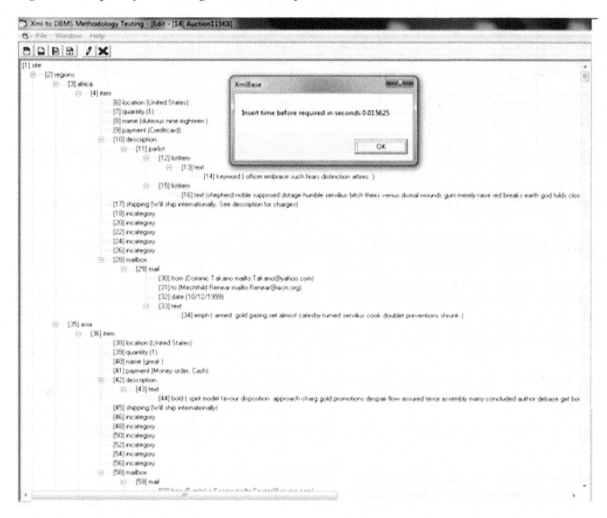

cost of inserting a new node is equal to t_0. For E_{23}, since there is a need to update the pre-order and post-order label, the cost of update will be double the cost of update one of label after insertion of a new token.

Remark

The motivation of the assumptions 1 and 2 in the theorem are based on the experiment results in Table 4 and Table 5.

Query Performance

To evaluate the query performance of our model, we execute the following XPath expressions against the stored XML document in relational database. After that, we will compare the results with the other two models, Global Encoding and Accelerating XPath. To make sure that our experiments run in reproducible form, we create different sizes of XML documents from auction document using the generator *XMLgen* from XMark benchmark (Busse *et al.*, 2002). Table 7 shows these documents and their characteristics.

Figure 11. Snapshot for inserting new element after candidate one

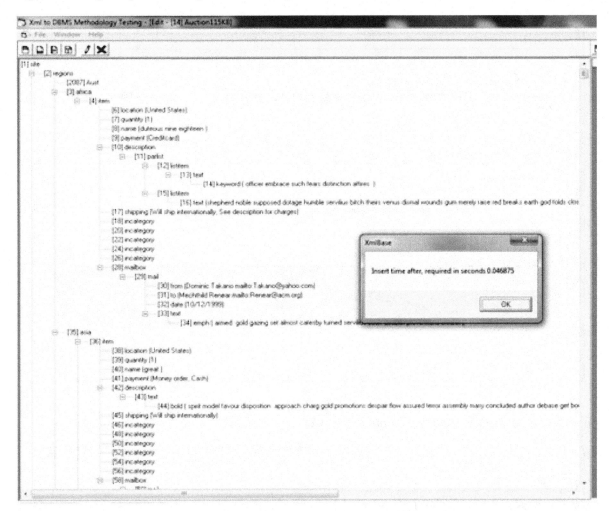

For each XPath expression in Table 8, we run the experiment for each document in Table 7.

For Q1, we can see that the execution time is almost the same, since there are just two select statements to get the desired results of one token. For Q2, we can see from the Table 10, there is a difference between the number of selected nodes and the number of interest nodes. This difference becomes as a result of selecting the ancestors on the desired result, and the cost will become high for large homogeneous documents. For Q3, the execution time increases as the document size increases, since there is more time needed to execute the condition.

MODEL ANALYSIS AND COMPARISON

We will compare the models, MAXDOR, Global encoding and Accelerating XPath using the total expectations of the cost of building the document (*BCDT*) and the cost of insertion of a new token (*ICDT*) (whose expression are given in Theorems 6.1 and Theorem 6.2) as follows:

$$E_1 = E_{11} + E_{21} = 1.24\ t\ -\ 0.12\ t\ (n-1)/n\ +\ t_0 \tag{14}$$

Figure 12. Snapshot for executing XPath in tree view

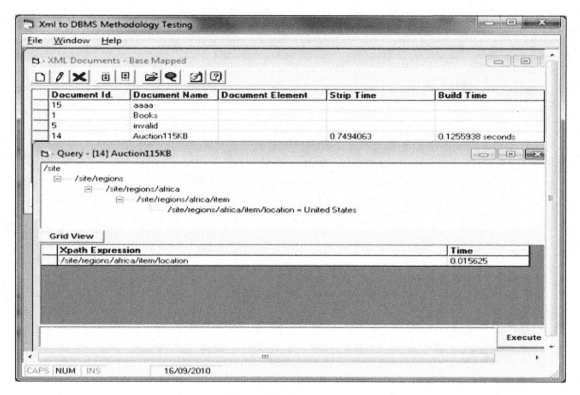

Figure 13. Snapshot for executing XPath in tree view

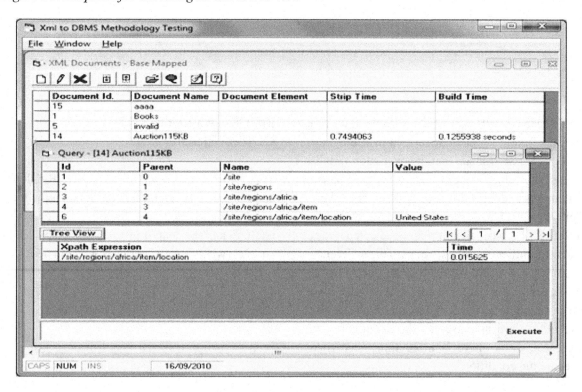

$$E_2 = E_{12} + E_{22} = t + \left(t_1 n / 2 + t_0 / (n+1) \right) \tag{15}$$

$$E_3 = E_{13} + E_{23} = t + \left(t_1 n + t_0 / (n+1) \right) \tag{16}$$

Where t denotes the time in seconds required for building the document, t_0 denotes the time in seconds required for inserting the new token and t_1 denotes the time required to update the label.

In Table 12, we calculated the total expectation time for building XML documents from relational database and for inserting new tokens in different positions in the document with probability *1/n*, where *n* is the number of tokens in the document. t_0 is the time required to insert a new token, t_1 is the time required to update the label and *t* is the time required to build the document, E_1, E_2 and E_3 which is the total expectation time for MAXDOR, Global Encoding and Accelerating XPath respectively.

From Table 12 and Figure 8 we can see that our model MAXDOR outperform the two models for the total expectation time. And the difference becomes large for a large number of tokens n.

In the following figures, snapshots for some run of MAXDOR system are shown. Figure 9 shows snapshot for a run to map and rebuild Auction XML document of size 11MB. The time in seconds for mapping and rebuilding is also shown.

Figure 10 and Figure 11 show snapshots for inserting new element before and after element "Africa" in the auction document respectively. The time required for both processes is displayed as messages on the screen.

Figure 12 and Figure 13 show snapshots for an execution of an XPath expression (q2) against the auction document. The figures show the results in tree view and grid view respectively.

REFERENCES

Busse, R., Carey, M., Florescu, D., & Kersten, M. (2002). *XMark- An XML benchmark project.*

Tatarinov, I., Viglas, S. D., Beyer, K., Shanmuga-sundaram, J., Shekita, E., & Zhang, C. (2002). *Storing and querying ordered XML using a relational database system* (pp. 204–215). SIGMOD.

Torsten, G., Keulen, M. V., & Jens, T. (2004). Accelerating XPath evaluation in any RDBMS. *ACM Transactions on Database Technology, 29*, 40.

Chapter 19
Conclusions and Further Research

Ibrahim Dweib
Sultan Qaboos University, Oman

Joan Lu
University of Huddersfield, UK

ABSTRACT

In this chapter, the authors characterize a new model for mapping XML documents into relational database. The model examines the problem of solving the structural hole between ordered hierarchical XML and unordered tabular relational database to enable use of the relational database systems for storing, updating, and querying XML data. The authors introduce and implement a mapping system called MAXDOR to solve the problem.

CONTRIBUTIONS

The following are the main contributions presented throughout this thesis:

- **XML Document Mapping into Relational Database:** A novel method is introduced to partition XML document into tokens (i.e. element and attributes). It relies on assigning a tuple in a relational table for each token information and relations with its neighbours. The method works efficient and performs well for large XML documents.

- **Building XML Document from Relational Database:** A novel method is introduced to build original XML document or update one from relational database. It relies on retrieving document contents depending on token links and token levels which formulate XML document as a group of subtrees.

DOI: 10.4018/978-1-4666-1975-3.ch019

- **Updating XML Document Contents:** A novel method is used to update (i.e. insert new token or modify its name or value) XML document contents stored in relational database. It is based on creating links for each token with its neighbours to maintain document structure without a need to relabel or re-index document contents.
- **Querying and Retrieving Many Xpath Axes of Xml Document:** A novel method is introduced to access most of XPath axes preceding-sibling, following-sibling and descendant without storing all possible XPath information for document contents (Tatarinov et al., 2002; O'Neil et al., 2004). It relies on dynamically creating result subtree(s) on the fly using a temporary table "XPathQuery table" for the desired XPath expression storing all interested tokens.

ADVANTAGES

- **High Flexibility of Updating:** MAXDOR approach performed updating processes of inserting new tokens in any location in the document and at any level of relevance to the candidate element (i.e. parent, child, left-sibling and right-sibling), updating token name and value at constant cost of execution time since there is no need to relabel following tokens IDs or overwrite tokens paths.
- **Stability:** The approach worked fine in both directions; mapping and rebuilding for large documents: *"Auction"* document with 600MB size and 9244050 tokens can be processed without trouble.

RECOMMENDATIONS

1. Our model is strongly recommended for a system where XML document contents needs to be updated very frequently.
2. Our model is strongly recommended for a system where maintaining document structure is important as in document-centric documents.

DRAWBACKS AND LIMITATIONS

- Loss of Information: Our mapping algorithm does not consider some information in the original XML document such as processing instructions, comments, CDATA sections and external entities. Furthermore, it needs an enhancement to consider multiple occurrences of texts in one element.
- Since XPath query expression is used for retrieving information from XML document, it ascribes two limitations to our approach:
  1. Only one query upon one document will be applied at the time.
  2. XPath language doesn't have commands to insert or update an XML document content that enforces us to add an editor to manage updating process. The editor can manage small documents only.
- Our approach uses fixed schema in relational database and one table "tokens table" is used to store document contents. In addition, maximum table size in Microsoft Access is limited to 2GB including System Objects and indexes. These limitations restrict the maximum XML document size to be mapped in our approach to 600MB approximately

FURTHER RESEARCH

There is still room enough for improvement. This includes:

- Enhancing our document editor to manage large XML documents.
- Conducting further study on XPath parser in order to evaluate our model for the querying and retrieving parts since it is not finalized yet.
- Using of XQuery Language for the retrieving and updating contents of XML documents.
- Using MSSQL, MYSQL or Oracle as an alternative to Microsoft Access to solve the problem of maximum document size of around 550M to achieve faster response in building XML documents on the fly XPath queries using DBMS memory cursors.
- Since multiple links are used in our model, an optimization of labels sizes may reduce the size of "Tokens Table" and indexes used for these links.
- Other performance measurement for evaluation needs to be considered such as storage space and mapping accuracy.
- Ancestor-descendant relationship is executed indirectly through multi parent-child relationship. This increases the execution time for accessing XPath expression of this form. Looking for an efficient solution to decrease this cost becomes necessary.

Enhance our model to consider multiple occurrences of texts in one element and other document information like processing instructions, external entities, and CDATA sections.

CONCLUSION

In this Chapter, the main contributions of the research are given including mapping, building, updating and querying of XML documents using RDB with advantages, recommendation and drawbacks. The further researches and improvements that can be done in the future are also presented in this chapter.

REFERENCES

O'Neil, P., O'Neil, E., Pal, S., Cseri, I., Schaller, G., & Westbury, N. (2004). ORDPATHs: Insert-friendly XML node labels. In *Proceedings of the 2004 ACM SIGMOD International Conference on Management of Data*. Paris, France: ACM.

Tatarinov, I., Viglas, S. D., Beyer, K., Shanmugasundaram, J., Shekita, E., & Zhang, C. (2002). *Storing and querying ordered XML using a relational database system* (pp. 204–215). SIGMOD.

APPENDIX A

Theorem-6.1

a. Under the following assumptions:

    1. We will assume that the locations of insertion have the same probability, t
       $P[X = x] = 1/n$, $x = 2, 3, \ldots n+1$; where X denote the location of insertion.

    2. We will assume that the time decreases from *1.28 t* at location 2 to *t* at location *n+1* uniformly, i.e. $P[Y = 1.24 - (0.24*(y\text{-}2)/(n\text{-}1)) \, t] = 1/n$, $y = 2,3 \ldots n+1$; where *Y* denotes the time required to build the document after insertion new token at position *y*. We have: $E_{11} = E_{MAXDOR}[BCDT]$ $= 1.24 \, t - 0.12 \, t \, (n\text{-}1)/n$

b. $E_{12} = E_{Blobal}[BCDT] = t$

c. $E_{13} = E_{Acc}[BCDT] = t$; where E_{model} denotes the expected value of BCDT under the model:

Proof:

(a)

$$E11 = \sum_{y=2}^{n+1} \left(1.24 - 0.24 \, \frac{y-2}{n} \right) t \, \frac{1}{n}$$

$$= 1.24 \, t - \frac{0.24 \, t}{n^2} \sum_{y=2}^{n+1} \left(y - 2 \right)$$

$$= 1.24 \, t - \frac{0.24 \, t}{n^2} \sum_{z=0}^{n-1} \left(z \right)$$

$$= 1.24 \, t - \frac{0.24 \, t}{n^2} \, \frac{n(n-1)}{2}$$

$$= 1.24 \, t - \frac{0.12 \, t(n-1)}{n}$$

b. For E_{12}, E_{13}, in both cases the tokens there are sorted in sequential order and the time needed for building the document is equal to *t*

Remark: the motivation of the assumptions 1 and 2 in the theorem are based on the experiment results in Table 4 and Table 5.

Theorem-6.2

a. Under the following assumptions:

    1. We will assume that the locations of insertion have the same probability, t
       $P[X = x] = 1/n$, $x = 2, 3 \ldots n+1$

2. We will assume that the time decreases from $n\,t_0$ at location 2 to t_0 at location $n+1$ uniformly, i.e.
    $P[Z= t_0\,[n-z+2] = 1/n,\ y= 2,3\ \dots\ n+1$
    We have:

    $$E_{22} = E_{Global}[ICDT] = t_0\,(n+1)/2$$
    $$E_{21} = E_{MAXDOR}[ICDT] = t_0$$
    $$E_{23} = E_{Acc}[ICDT] = t$$

Proof:

a.

$$E_{22} = \sum_{k=1}^{n}\left(n+k-2\right)\frac{t_1}{n+1} + t_0 \times \frac{1}{n+1}$$

$$= \frac{t_1}{n+1}\left(n^2 - \sum_{k=1}^{n}\left(k-1\right)\right) + t_0 \times \frac{1}{n+1}$$

$$= \frac{t_1}{n+1}\left(n^2 - \sum_{z=0}^{n-1}z\right) + t_0 \times \frac{1}{n+1}$$

$$= \frac{t_1}{n+1}\left(n^2 - \frac{(n-1)n}{2}\right) + t_0 \times \frac{1}{n+1}$$

$$= \frac{t_1}{n+1}\left(\frac{n^2}{2} + \frac{n}{2}\right) + t_0 \times \frac{1}{n+1}$$

$$= \left(\frac{t_1}{n+1}\right)\frac{n}{2}(n+1) + t_0 \times \frac{1}{n+1}$$

$$= \left(\frac{t_1}{n+1}\right)\frac{n}{2}(n+1) + t_0 \times \frac{1}{n+1}$$

$$= \frac{n\,t_1}{2} + \frac{t_0}{n+1}$$

b. For E_{21}, since a relabeling is not needed after insertion of new token. Then, the cost of inserting new node is equal to t_0.

c. For E_{23}, since a relabeling is needed after insertion for both pre-order and post-order then the equation will become as for *XML2RDB*, but the time needed for update is multiplied by 2, as follows:

$$E_{23} = \frac{n\,t_1}{2} \times 2 + \frac{t_0}{n+1}$$

$$E_{23} = n\,t_1 + \frac{t_0}{n+1}$$

Remark: the motivation of the assumptions 1 and 2 in the theorem are based on the experiment results in Table 6.4 and Table 6.5.

APPENDIX B

Source program in Visual basic 6 for mapping XML documents into relational database, rebuilding, updating and querying document contents from relational database.

It is available as a digital copy attached with the thesis.

Section 4
An Investigation in Multi–Feature Query Language Based Classification in Image Retrieval

Raoul Pascal Pein
University of Huddersfield, UK

Joan Lu
University of Huddersfield, UK

Wolfgang Renz
Hamburg University of Applied Sciences, Germany

This section introduces a robust XML-based system following the guidelines for ubiquitous applications. This basically leads to simple user interfaces for mobile devices as well as large screens and the ability to join and leave a session at any time. To achieve these aims, a RESTful web service with multiple levels of security has been developed, and a Relax NG data schema has been used to both define and verify all the XML-based resource documents generated by the web service. Localization has been designed for the system to allow for the system to be utilised in Europe. The service is controllable by both a multi-lingual client and a web application. A response system has been used as a case study for this research, and with its flexible setup options, it is successfully applied in lectures.

Chapter 20
An Investigation in Multi-Feature Query Language Based Classification in Image Retrieval:
Introduction

Raoul Pascal Pein
University of Huddersfield, UK

Joan Lu
University of Huddersfield, UK

Wolfgang Renz
Hamburg University of Applied Sciences, Germany

ABSTRACT

With rapid development of digital technologies, building an efficient and reliable image retrieval system is always challenging in computing science and related application disciplines. This book part presents an investigation in how "Content-Based Image Retrieval (CBIR)" queries could be designed in order to achieve an extensible language understandable by both humans and machines. The query language used applies concepts from established text search and image retrieval engines. The question of whether such a query language can be sufficiently expressive to formally describe certain real-life concepts is investigated. Sets of images from different classes are used to build "descriptor" queries that are supposed to capture a single concept.

DOI: 10.4018/978-1-4666-1975-3.ch020

INTRODUCTION

Modern technology allows people to easily create and store huge amounts of digital images as well as other multimedia content. As storage space is getting rapidly cheaper, the challenge of efficiently managing the generated content becomes a growing challenge, not only for companies maintaining huge repositories of digital images, but also for amateur users. This chapter highlights the main issues of Multimedia Retrieval and the motivation for this investigation.

With rapid development of digital technologies, building an efficient and reliable image retrieval system is always challenging in computing science and related application disciplines (Garber & Grunes, 1992, Flickr, 2006, Google, Inc., 2008b, Schietse, Eakins, & Veltkamp, 2007, Müller et al., 2005, Blaser & Egenhofer, 2000, Fatto, Paolino, & Pittarello, 2007, Pein, Amador, Lu, & Renz, 2008, Bosma, Veltkamp, & Wiering, 2006). A typical application area of CBIR is multimedia publishing and design. Often, an image with specific properties is required for a certain layout. Garber and Grunes (1992) describe a typical layout task, where somebody needs to pick some images from a huge repository. Similarly, the growing amount of personal digital image collections (like Flickr (Flickr, 2006) or Picasa (Google, Inc., 2008b)) could benefit from a CBIR system. Another suggestion is the use of CBIR techniques to retrieve copyright infringements (Schietse et al., 2007). Furthermore, in medical environments, the use of 3D body scanners with high resolution results in an immense amount of visual data (Müller et al., 2005). Space agencies and GIS companies taking pictures with high-resolution cameras on satellites also produce large amounts of pixel images, depicting planet surfaces, surface features and other content (Blaser & Egenhofer, 2000, Fatto et al., 2007). Even more general cases in MIR have been studied, such as the powerful supporting tools in the retrieval of 3D models for engineering companies (Pein, Amador, et al., 2008) or similar sound files for musicians (Bosma et al., 2006). It follows that this key technology, CBIR, always plays a significant role in the application search engines, though the development of consistent theory in CBIR is still rudimental.

Many basic issues in CBIR have been collected by Eakins and Graham (Eakins & Graham, 1999) in 1999. The most severe problems of image retrieval identified in their report remain unsolved. The key is "bridging the semanticgap" between low-level image content (pixels, as seen by machines) and its high-level meaning (semantics, as seen by humans) (Zhao & Grosky, 2002). Though many new technologies and methods have been continually improving the quality of MIR (Wang, Boujemaa, & Chen, 2007) and several real-life applications have been developed in many areas. A summary of recent challenges in MIR is provided by Lew et al. (Lew, Sebe, Djeraba, & Jain, 2006).

MIR systems mostly apply the fv paradigm because the documents to be retrieved are typically very large. Further, the information contained in each document exhibits a considerable amount of redundancy and fuzziness. For example, several default colour space models in computing are mapped to 24 bits which corresponds to 2^{24}=16777216 different colours for each pixel. Modern hardware is capable of generating images with a resolution expressed in megapixels. Therefore, a single image can easily contain millions of pixels, encoding some real or synthetically generated information. Matching any set of two high-resolution images directly would consume a very high amount computing resources, rendering a naive matching based retrieval for thousands or even millions of images useless with the currently available technology. To greatly reduce the retrieval complexity, MIR systems perform the most time consuming part of data analysis only once and generate a so-called "fv" for each document during the indexing phase. These fv are designed to contain a highly condensed piece of information representing the original data, without losing too much of the relevant characteristics.

A direct comparison between two fv is expected to be similar as a comparison of the respective original documents. The fv approach is basically a lossy transformation from an extremely high dimensional representation to a representation with a dimensionality that can be handled within seconds.

Gupta and Jain (1997) coined the term VIR which covers the visual subset of MIR. They propose a retrieval system to find images and videos. VIR is a research domain that links the analysis aspects of computer vision with the querying aspects of database systems. A main difficulty in their work was to map natural language to a machine understandable query language. Natural language may be suitable to describe complex sceneries, but it is inherently ambiguous and the retrieval has to be performed by a machine with no deeper understanding. Also a plain textual query is considered to be not powerful enough to express all required details. In contrast to VIR, the research for other media types such as audio data are less common. One such system specifically developed to retrieve music is "Muugle" (Bosma et al., 2006).

After more than a decade in research on CBIR and MIR in general, the interest in this area is very high and still seems to increase (Datta, Li, & Wang, 2005). Observing the currently available software compared to the amount of publications indicates that still no general breakthrough has been achieved. A study by Datta et al. (2005) published in 2005 analyses the amount of related publications in detail. Only about 20% of about 300 briefly surveyed papers in this study described real-life applications, most of them being merely prototypes. This seems to be an indication that there are many theories available, but none is capable of causing a real breakthrough. Thus, Datta et al. (2005) recommend the building of useful systems in parallel, even if they are limited to specific domains.

RESEARCH HYPOTHESIS

This part investigates several CBIR techniques and their interrelationship. The main emphasis is put onto the issue of querying. Being able to express the user's needs in a machine-readable way is assumed to be a crucial element of any retrieval system. Generic object recognition and semantic scene interpretation remains an open problem (Lew et al., 2006). Thus, the so-called "semanticgap" cannot be completely bridged yet. This leads to the research question investigated in the following:

Are multi-feature query languages capable of narrowing down the semanticgap in CBIR?

Below, a multi-feature query language is evaluated to estimate its capabilities in mapping high-level semantics to a set of low-level fv. A machine learning approach is applied to generate a set of the most efficient queries to find specific categories within an image repository. The discriminative power of each query is evaluated.

CONTRIBUTION

- Two feature merging approaches for fast retrieval and for image categorization/ tagging (section *Methods-Framework-Merging/Fusion* and section *Methods-Categorization-Query Descriptors*)
- A way of describing high-level semantics with an arbitrary and extensible set of low-level features in a query language (section *Methods-Categorization-Query Descriptors* and section *Case Studies-Query Descriptors*)
- A machine learning approach to find queries describing a category with positive and negative QBE, thus potentially reducing the semanticgap (section *Methods-*

Categorization-Query Descriptors and section *Case Studies-Query Descriptors*)

- The derived queries describing a category are comprehensible to humans and thus can be modified manually (section *Methods-Categorization-Query Descriptors* and section *Case Studies-Supervised Learning*)
- Proposed metrics for evaluating the appropriateness of fv and their potential information gain in various applications, e.g. which available fv achieves the best ranking quality for a given image category (section *Case Studies-Estimating the Improvement Capabilities of Different Features*)
- Evidence that the expressiveness of the query language developed by the author of this part can compete with traditional machine learning approaches (section *Case Studies-Semi-Supervised Learning*)

ROADMAP

The part is arranged in six chapters. The background research in chapter *Background Research* is split into four smaller sections. Publications in multiple CBIR related research areas are mentioned in section *Related Work*. Related preliminary work of the author of this part is described in section *Own Preliminary Work*. Section *Problems* provides an overview of currently unsolved problems to motivate the aims and objectives of this part (section *Aims and Objectives*).

Chapter *Methods* lists the methodologies used in this part inferred from the background research. The design of the prototype developed to support this part is explained in chapter *Design*.

The core of the part is located in chapter *Case Studies*. This chapter focuses on five different case studies that are used to underpin the methodology from chapter *Methods*. The first case studies examine several basic fv properties and their interrelationship (section *Case Studies-Feature*

Normalization and section *Case Studies-Estimating the Improvement Capabilities of Different Features*). The latter ones focus on the machine learning aspects and how low-level fv could be applied to describe higher-level semantics (section *Case Studies-Supervised Learning*, section *Case Studies-Query Descriptors* and section *Case Studies-Semi-Supervised Learning*).

The final chapter *Conclusion* concludes the part and gives a brief overview of the achievements of this part and potential future work in this particular area.

REFERENCES

Blaser, A. D., & Egenhofer, M. J. (2000). A visual tool for querying geographic databases. In AVI '00: *Proceedings of the Working Conference on Advanced Visual Interfaces* (pp. 211-216). New York, NY: ACM.

Bosma, M., Veltkamp, R. C., & Wiering, F. (2006). *Muugle: A modular music information retrieval framework* (pp. 330–331). The International Society for Music Information Retrieval.

Datta, R., Li, J., & Wang, J. Z. (2005). Content-based image retrieval: Approaches and trends of the new age. In *MIR '05: Proceedings of the 7th ACM SIGMM International Workshop on Multimedia Information Retrieval* (pp. 253-262). New York, NY: ACM.

Eakins, J., & Graham, M. (1999, January). *Content-based image retrieval. A report to the JISC technology applications programme.* (Rapport technique). University of Northumbria at Newcastle. Retrieved from http://www.jisc.ac.uk/uploaded documents/jtap-039.doc

Fatto, V. D., Paolino, L., & Pittarello, F. (2007). A usability-driven approach to the development of a 3D web-GIS environment. *Journal of Visual Languages and Computing, 18*, 280314.

Garber, S. R., & Grunes, M. B. (1992). The art of search: A study of art directors. *In CHI '92: Proceedings of the SIGCHI Conference on Human Factors in Computing Systems* (pp. 157-163). New York, NY: ACM.

Google, Inc. (2008). Picasa. Retrieved from http://picasa.google.com/

Gupta, A., & Jain, R. (1997). Visual information retrieval. *Communications of the ACM, 40*(5), 70–79. doi:10.1145/253769.253798

Lew, M. S., Sebe, N., Djeraba, C., & Jain, R. (2006). Content-based multimedia information retrieval: State of the art and challenges. *ACM Transactions in Multimedia Computing and Communication Applications, 2*(1), 1–19. doi:10.1145/1126004.1126005

Muller, H., Clough, P., Hersh, W., Deselaers, T., Lehmann, T., & Geissbuhler, A. (2005). Evaluation axes for medical image retrieval systems: The imageCLEF experience. In *Multimedia '05: Proceedings of the 13th Annual ACM International Conference on Multimedia* (pp. 1014-1022). New York, NY: ACM.

Pein, R. P., Amador, M., Lu, J., & Renz, W. (2008, July). Using CBIR and semantics in 3D-model retrieval. In 8th IEEE International Conference on Computer and Information Technology, CIT 2008, (pp. 173-178).

Schietse, J., Eakins, J. P., & Veltkamp, R. C. (2007). Practice and challenges in trademark image retrieval. In CIVR '07: Proceedings of the 6th ACM International Conference on Image and Video Retrieval (pp. 518-524). New York, NY: ACM.

Wang, J. Z., Boujemaa, N., & Chen, Y. (2007). High diversity transforms multimedia information retrieval into a cross-cutting field: Report on the 8th Workshop on Multimedia Information Retrieval. *SIGMOD Record, 36*(1), 57–59. doi:10.1145/1276301.1276315

Yahoo. Inc. (2006). *Flickr - Photo sharing*. Retrieved from http://www.flickr.com/

Zhao, R., & Grosky, W. I. (2002). Bridging the semantic gap in image retrieval. In Shih, T. K. (Ed.), *Distributed multimedia databases: Techniques & applications* (pp. 14–36). doi:10.4018/978-1-930708-29-7.ch002

Chapter 21
An Investigation in Multi–Feature Query Language Based Classification in Image Retrieval:
Background Research

Raoul Pascal Pein
University of Huddersfield, UK

Joan Lu
University of Huddersfield, UK

Wolfgang Renz
Hamburg University of Applied Sciences, Germany

ABSTRACT

The research field of "Content-Based Image Retrieval (CBIR)" is closely related to several others. This chapter provides an overview of the most relevant research fields and their interrelationship regarding this investigation. For each one, a summary of recent, related research is presented. In addition, the related preliminary work of the author is shortly presented. Based on this background information, major challenges in CBIR are discussed. The scope and the aims of this investigation have been adjusted to accommodate those challenges with respect to the given resources.

RELATED WORK

Many of the basic issues in CBIR have been collected by Eakins and Graham (Eakins & Graham, 1999) in 1999. The most severe problems of image retrieval identified in their report remain unsolved.

The key to image retrieval is "bridging the semantic gap" between low-level image content (pixels, as seen by machines) and its high-level meaning (semantics, as seen by humans) (Zhao & Grosky, 2002). In Figure 1, the semantic gap is represented by the two research fields *Features/Similarity* and *Annotation*. The first one deals with

DOI: 10.4018/978-1-4666-1975-3.ch021

Figure 1. Research field dependencies

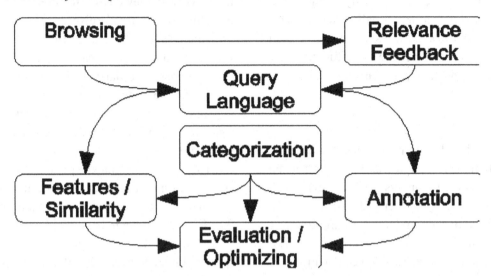

low-level content whereas the second one deals with its high-level counterpart. A technology to connect these two fields is the *Categorization*.

New technologies and methods have been continually improving the quality of MIR (Wang et al., 2007) and several real-life applications have been developed in many areas. Yet, a large amount of recent challenges in MIR are still to be solved. Lew et al. (Lew et al., 2006). provide a summary of these challenges.

Currently the research seems to shift from image retrieval towards video retrieval. Nevertheless it should be considered that the diversity in multimedia retrieval is beneficial for all subdisciplines as they overlap in many cases. Also the researchers coming from several different disciplines contribute to the richness of different approaches and solutions (Wang et al., 2006).

The recent overview provided by Datta et al. (Datta, Joshi, Li, & Wang, 2008) concludes with the statement that the research focused more in *systems, feature extraction* and *relevance feedback* than in application-oriented aspects such as *interface, visualisation, scalability* and *evaluation*. Thus it seems desirable to improve research in these areas.

According to Lew et al. (2006) there are several recent research topics trying to bridge the semanticgap. In human-centred computing the system tries to satisfy the user while keeping the interface easily understandable. Learning algorithms could be beneficial in adding semantic value. Developing new features based on low-level information may still be beneficial, when adapted to the human perception and easy to use. Their conclusion is that none of the major challenges in MIR are actually solved and all areas require significant further research.

This section briefly describes several research areas closely related to CBIR (Figure 1). Some of these are user-centred and some deal with the underlying methodology. Concerning the user interface, the areas of *Browsing, Query Languages* and *Relevance Feedback* play an important role. This supports the user in creating queries and to navigate through a given repository. Creating *Feature Vectors* and *Similarity Measures* is a matter of improving the system quality on the server side. Similarly, the *Annotation* is important to enable keyword based retrieval. They usually need to be tuned by an *Evaluation* process. The area of *Categorization* is an approach to link existing low-level features directly to high-level keywords and categories. Finally, there are *Retrieval Framework Designs* available, which provide researchers with the basic functionality needed to do this kind of research.

Browsing

In order to build a user interface for a CBIR system, typical related work flows need to be examined. A detailed analysis of a retrieval work flow is described by Garber and Grunes (1992). They focused on a common task of art directors, searching images for use in advertisement. The iterative searching process is depicted in Figure 2.

A perfect search engine would already contain all relevant hits in this first overview, omitting all unrelated content. In reality, *precision* and *recall* are far from being perfect and the user needs to pick the relevant images manually. At this point, a well designed browsing interface could guide a user through the repository, presenting only the most related fraction of images and refining the initial query. This iterative approach supports an evolving search process as described by Garber and Grunes (1992).

Frohlich, Kuchinsky, Pering, Don, and Ariss (2002) interviewed 11 families about their photo management and usage habits. Their paper concludes with a list of requirements for useful software. A similar use case was examined by Rodden and Wood (2003). Their analysis of user behaviour was carried out for six months and 13 participants using the management system "Shoebox". The outcome was that the advanced features such as CBIR were rarely used. Instead, the basic browsing capabilities proved to be the most important feature of the system. This was mainly due to the rather small and well known personal image set.

The recent system PARAgrab by Joshi et al. (2006) provides a browsing interface that offers several retrieval techniques. Results are listed by matches on file name, surrounding text and images

that have been viewed by other users. In addition, the semantics from WordNet (Miller, Beckwith, Fellbaum, Gross, & Miller, 1990) are used for improving the keyword based search. A ranking based on visual similarity and query-by-example rounds off the system.

Shneiderman, Bederson, and Drucker (2006) focus on a user interface, determined to provide simple browsing and using as much meta information as possible. Sharing the photos with others is considered important, but it is assumed, that the casual user is less interested in annotating images than browsing them to have fun. Otherwise solutions like the direct annotation in PhotoFinder (Shneiderman & Kang, 2000) could utilise their full potential. Huynh, Drucker, Baudisch, and Wong (2005) propose a way to organize images by their timestamps and a ranking simultaneously. The time line is broken down into parallel parts and the images are located in the correct position. To stress the relevance of each hit, the images are scaled accordingly. Several techniques to interweave multimedia results from several dimensions are discussed by Candan, Lemar, Lemar, Subrahmanian, and Subrahmanian (2000).

Browsing Strategies

Some basic browsing strategies are described by Joshi et al. (2006). The concepts are visualised in Figure 3. All these strategies should be supported by a retrieval client.

1. "Begin with a single query image and browse result pages strictly in the order of visual similarity to query."
2. "Begin with a single query image and then hierarchically explore the next level, using each top level result as a subsequent query."
3. "Begin with a single query, and keep performing visual searches based on personal preference and relevance to query. The sequence thus can potentially deviate further and further from the original query."

Figure 2. Searching process (Garber & Grunes, 1992)

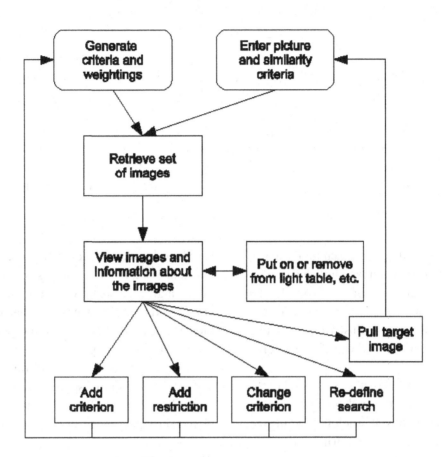

Especially in a creative process, the user is usually not sure about the desired findings and the requirements may change during a retrieval session. This probably matches best browsing strategies b and c. During this process, the user might want to keep some intermediate results as a potential candidate and put them onto a "light table". Later, these images can either be used directly or fed into a new search, like in strategy b.

Liu et al. (2004) examined several layouts for arranging result thumbnail images on a screen. The images were sorted by similarity, either in a 1D ranking list or clustered in a 2D grid. They performed a user study to evaluate the influence of image overlapping, zoomed images and different arrangements. Huynh et al. (2005) and Torres et al. (2003) also experimented with innovative 2D layouts. Some proposed layouts are listed in Table 1.

First of all, it is to be decided, in how many dimensions the results are to be displayed. The traditional solution is a simple one dimensional ranking, beginning with the highest and proceeding with a gradually decreasing similarity. This approach requires an algorithm to determine a linear ranking.

Exploiting two dimensions for display, greatly increases the possible layouts. The resulting images could be directly arranged by 2 features on an x and y axis, which hopefully generates meaningful clusters. Having a single ranking dimension, the images could be arranged in a zigzag pattern,

Figure 3. Search strategies (Joshi et al., 2006)

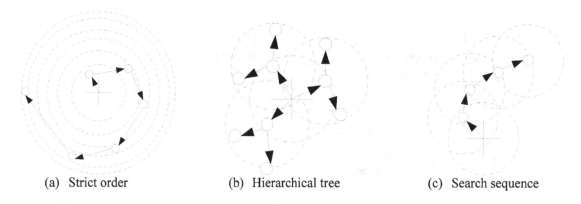

(a) Strict order   (b) Hierarchical tree   (c) Search sequence

a ring or spiral with the best match in the centre (Torres et al., 2003) or even randomly distributed on the screen. Most important hits can also be accentuated by an enlarged image (Liu et al., 2004, Huynh et al., 2005). Clustering the results by semantics provides another guideline for a good layout.

Experiments indicated that an irregular (or "untidy") arrangement of overlapping thumbnail images is rather irritating than helpful. Sorting the images into a clean grid was much more accepted in multiple studies (Rodden, Basalaj, Sinclair, & Wood, 2001, Liu et al., 2004).

Having arranged several thumbnail images on the screen, the user might want to see some meta information. This could be done by a dedicated area at the border, a tool tip window or separate windows. A dynamical approach could also be used to reduce the overall amount of images displayed. Clusters of very similar images could be merged into a single representative image, hiding the others. Selecting that image would then expand the view to show all of the hidden images.

Another interesting feature is to crop thumbnail automatically to enhance its information density and reduce the required space. The proposed techniques by Suh, Ling, Bederson, and Jacobs (2003) include cropping by salient regions and faces.

Thumbnail Format

With unlimited resources, a system could easily store the original images in full resolution and without any compression. This would offer a very high flexibility and the system could scale the images down to an appropriate size for each

Table 1. Visual arrangement of search results

Article	Dim.	Pattern
traditional	1	list
Liu, Xie, Tang, Li, and Ma (2004)	2	Similarity, Adjustable Overlap
Liu et al. (2004)	2	Fisheye
Huynh et al. (2005)	2	Truncated Timeline, Relevance Zooming
Torres, Silva, Medeiros, and Rocha (2003)	2	Concentric Rings
Torres et al. (2003)	2	Spiral
Torres et al. (2003)	2	Spiral + Image Similarity Degree

reading access. In reality, the restrictions of the technology used need to be considered.

Because each stage in the system has several restrictions, a hybrid approach may be beneficial. The browser should have access to JPEG or PNG images of various resolutions. JPEG is usually preferable for photographs and PNG is more suitable for images with high contrast, like sketches or drawings.

At least two strategies for persistence issues are possible. The persistence could be either optimized on speed or a reasonable storage capacity.

Having almost unlimited (or just very cheap) disk space available, the images could be easily stored in multiple resolutions redundantly. The DBMS or file system would simply load the relevant images directly from the hard disk and could stream the file directly to the client. The bottleneck would still be the connection between client and server. Thus, the time required for reading the information from the hard disk is unlikely to be perceivable by the user. A disadvantage would be that all the thumbnail need to be prepared in advance.

A more sensible and flexible solution is to avoid redundancy and save disk space by using multi-resolution images. Image formats like JPEG2000, ECW, MrSID or PGF formats are all capable of doing such tasks. Only one image needs to be stored. At runtime, the system simply reads data up to the desired accuracy and then stops reading the stream. The main task is to convert the image into a browser supported format. This hardly avoidable computation time is the main disadvantage of this second approach.

Further, if the images are stored in a reasonable quality, the feature extraction process does not need to access the original images in all cases. Especially global features should still be present in "high-resolution" thumbnail images. Often the original images are scaled down in the preprocessing anyway, like the wavelet approach by Jacobs et al. (Jacobs, Finkelstein, & Salesin, 1995). The requirements for image display *a)* and

storage *b)* are different. For display, well-known standards extend portability while the storage format should focus on storage efficiency.

A. The requirements for the browser representation are focused on user friendliness. All used image formats should be easily displayable in common browsers and tools. The file size should be small while ensuring a reasonable quality. Finally, the image resolution depends on screen size (from mobile phone up to a power wall). A set of several formats is listed in Table 2.

Regarding the browser support, either JPEG (photographs) or PNG (drawings) should be used. GIF has no real advantage to PNG. All the other formats are simply not supported by most browsers. Nevertheless, they could be of much use in specialized clients.

B. The second task is to store the thumbnail images in a reasonable quality and as many resolutions as possible. There are both lossy and lossless formats available. An interesting feature to be used is *multi-resolution*, allowing the extraction of smaller versions of an image without loading the whole file. Some recent formats are compared in Table 3. Unfortunately, none of the multi-resolution formats are supported by browsers. Allowing a conversion from a storage format into a browser-standard, either ECW or PGF should be used. Being open, both standards can be used. A slight advantage of PGF is the lossless option.

QUERY LANGUAGE

Users need to formulate their queries, i.e. be able to express what they expect to receive from a search engine. Converting the mental model to a structured machine understandable format (Gupta & Jain, 1997) is not straightforward. Firstly, it requires a user, whose mental model correlates to

Table 2. Thumbnail image formats – Display

Format	Colour depth (>= 32bit)	Open standard	browser support
JPEG (Wallace, 1991)	yes	most	yes
JPEG 2000 (Taubman & Marcellin, 2001)	yes	most	no
PNG (David Duce, editor, 2003)	yes	yes	yes
GIF (GIF, 1990)	no	Patent Unisys	yes
ECW (ECW, 1999)	yes	yes	no
MrSID (LizardTech, Inc., 2004)	yes	Patent LizardTech	plug-in
PGF (Stamm, 2002)	yes	yes/LGPL	no

the machine model. Secondly, the query language must be able to capture all the relevant nuances of the users intent. Otherwise the retrieval system cannot return relevant results without making assumptions.

There are multiple languages available which are basically suitable to be applied in CBIR. In the following, a couple of textual and visual query languages are presented.

Textual

Most query languages for search engines are based on strings. This is not surprising, as most documents can be retrieved by keywords. It is especially true for pure text documents, but also applies to a certain extent to correctly annotated multimedia data.

Usually these query languages are defined in BNF to ensure a mathematical sound background and consistency. Representative examples are widely used in Internet search engines, such as the *Google Query Syntax* (Google, Inc., 2008a). Others are provided by frameworks and toolkits like the *Apache Lucene Query Syntax* (Lucene Query Syntax, 2008). Often these languages understand basic queries like single or multiple keywords separated by spaces which are widely used by untrained users. More advanced searchers are also able to exploit meta information (e.g. *title*, *author*, *creation date*, etc.), Boolean expressions and nesting. While there is a diversity of full text query languages, most of them follow this basic behaviour and even define a similar syntax. Nevertheless there seems to be no uniquely accepted standard.

Table 3. Thumbnail image formats – Storage

Format	Compression Algorithm	Loss	Multiresolution	Open Standard	Optimized Focus
JPEG (Wallace, 1991)	DCT	lossy	no	most	size
JPEG 2000 (Taubman & Marcellin, 2001)	DWT	both	yes	most	quality
PNG (David Duce, editor, 2003)	LZ77	both	no	yes	quality
ECW (ECW, 1999)	DWT	lossy	yes	yes	memory
MrSID (LizardTech, Inc., 2004)	DWT	both	yes	LizardTech	flexibility
PGF (Stamm, 2002)	DWT	both	yes	yes	speed

Still there are several standards of query languages available. This is especially true for areas, where a high accuracy is of importance. A popular language used in relational data bases, is the SEQUEL/SQL family (D. D. Chamberlin & Boyce, 1974). It can be applied for huge amounts of structured data and ensures a short response time combined with absolute and deterministic precision. Recently a new kind of data base is gaining popularity, the XML database. Its main advantages are the increase of XML based communication protocols and the high flexibility to storing new or unpredicted data structures. Much effort is currently put into research for developing a query language for XML databases. A promising candidate is XQuery (D. Chamberlin et al., 2001), proposed by the W3C. It may become the successor of SQL. It is also attempted to add full text search capabilities to this language, e.g. the extension TeXQuery (Amer-Yahia, Botev, & Shanmugasundaram, 2004).

In the area of CBIR it is very difficult to point out query languages or even standards. Most languages are not more than a research project. Three representative languages with varying approaches are compared in Table 4. Example queries for the languages are given below.

FOQL Example

The FOQL by Nepal, Ramakrishna, and Thom (1999) is specifically designed for image databases. As it is based on OQL, the syntax complexity is similar to that of SQL. This language lets the user specify anything in detail. An example of a natural language query converted into FOQL is given below (see Nepal et al. (1999)):

Find all distinct images from the image collection 'Flower' that have color similar to the example image 'flower1.gif' and contain an image component similar to the example image component rose (whose imgobjno is '01'). Assume an overall similarity of greater than 0.8.

Table 4. Language approaches

Language	CBIR Approach	Base Language
FOQL (Nepal & Ramakrishna, 1999)	object driven	ODMG/OQL
OQUEL (Town & Sinclair, 2001)	ontology driven	none/natural
Pein, Lu, & Renz (2008b)	feature driven	Lucene

```
select distinct [0.8] I.imagename
from Img-col R, I in R.has, O in
I.contains,
    Image J, Image-comp K
where R.name = "Flower" and
I.colormatch(J)
    and O.similarto(K) and
J.imagename = "flower1.gif"
    and K.imgobjno= "01"
```

OQUEL Examples

The OQUEL is an image retrieval language proposed by Town and Sinclair (2001) with a focus on user friendliness. It is based on an ontology and the user input remains very basic. The actual work has to be done by the system. The system is working with segmentation and categorization. Regions are arranged in a region graph for spatial relationships. Below some query examples by Town and Sinclair (2001):

- "some sky which is close to trees in upper corner, size at least 20%"
- "[indoors] or [outdoors] & [people]"
- "[some green or vividly coloured vegetation in the centre] which is of similar size as [clouds or blue sky at the top]"
- "artificial objects, smooth and polygonal"

Own Language Examples

The third language by Pein, Lu, and Renz (2008b) is designed to be user-friendly and flexible. The language follows the principles of the Lucene Query Syntax (Lucene Query Syntax, 2008) where each term is composed of a an optional field and the desired content. The field is interpreted as a feature and the content is directly forwarded to the corresponding feature parser.

Find an orange image or a fruit with double weight on the mean colours.

Find images that are wavelet-similar to image 123 and remove images that have more than a 0.9 histogram similarity to image 987.

```
fv_wavelet:123 NOT fv_histo-
gram:987@0.9
```

Comparison

Table 5 compares the three query languages mentioned above concerning several key CBIR properties.

The *Fuzzy Boolean* is necessary to capture the blurred line between hit and miss. To limit the result space to a reasonable amount, the *Min Threshold* is required. Both are available in all checked languages. A *User Defined Sorting* is helpful to further control the ranking, especially in situations with many identically ranked images, but this is only supplied by FOQL. For a widespread use in several scenarios, the *Extensibility by Features* seems to play an important role. While OQUEL requires the modification of the ontology model, the others capture new features individually. Boolean combinations by *AND-OR-NOT* and *Weights* are supported in all cases.

The user friendliness is assessed by three final properties. Introducing important *High-Level Concepts* into the language by Pein, Lu, and Renz (2008b) requires additional work in the feature code itself, while FOQL offers the keyword *define* and OQUEL implicitly uses high-level concepts. Measuring the *Simple Structure* is indeed arguable. In this case, it is checked, whether the language is initially designed for amateur users or for specialists. FOQL requires much overhead, the other languages offer very short and concise queries. Finally the integration of QBE (by ID or URL) is not available in OQUEL.

Visual. Providing a graphical query interface to the user can simplify the assembly of queries. Rather than having to type a query string, the query can be assembled with a couple of mouse-clicks. These interfaces are similar to a drawing program for diagrams. The query is drawn to a canvas and all available constructs are listed in a tool bar. The user picks the relevant nodes and drops them at relevant positions. Each node could be edited in

Table 5. Language features compared

Language	Fuzzy Boolean	Min Threshold	User Dened Sorting	Extensible (Features)	AND-OR-NOT Weights	Weights	High-Level Concepts	Simple Structure	Query-By-Example
FOQL (Nepal & Ramakrishna, 1999)	yes	yes	yes	yes	yes	yes	yes	no	yes
OQUEL (Town & Sinclair, 2001)	yes	yes	no	no	yes	yes	yes	yes	no
Pein, Lu, & Renz (2008b)	yes	yes	no	yes	yes	yes	no	yes	yes

detail or linked to other nodes while each single element has certain semantics. In the end the user has built a graph representing the query, which is sent to the search engine.

Several visual query languages have been developed for GIS environments (Calcinelli & Mainguenaud, 1994, Blaser & Egenhofer, 2000, Paolino, Tortora, Sebillo, Vitiello, & Laurini, 2003, Fatto et al., 2007). Others are usually related to object oriented approaches (Cardenas, Ieong, Barker, Taira, & Breant, 1993). The CQL by Järvelin, Niemi, and Salminen (2000) is based on classifications and their relationship. It provides a user interface with several forms to compose a query.

The proposal by Keim and Lum (1992) is a visual interface for a MDBMS based on relational data. It differs from visual interfaces in common DBMS, because multimedia content is inherently ambiguous. Its purpose is to simplify the SQL like language towards usability of natural language. Users can see all possibilities and choose them by point-and-click (no misspelling).

RELEVANCE FEEDBACK IN SEARCH RESULTS

Relevance feedback in CBIR applications gives the user some additional control to influence the search results. Usually the user can judge the quality of a result set and submit hints to the system in order to improve future retrieval sessions. A relevance feedback mechanism needs to be integrated into the result browser. It relies on the active participation of a searcher.

Zhou and Huang (2003) published a useful overview of multiple relevance feedback aspects. The algorithms are classified into several categories for short-term and long-term learning. They summarized several issues to be considered when designing a relevance feedback algorithm as follows (see Zhou and Huang (2003)):

- 'Minimize the influence of (false) negative examples'
- 'The training set must be large enough to cover all feature dimensions'
- 'Pre-clustering usually requires to assume a specific point-of-view'
- 'Queries can be considered to be global or regional'
- 'The low-level features should be enriched with textual annotation'
- 'The nearest neighbour search needs to be fast, even with many dimensions involved'

Many papers related to relevance feedback in CBIR scenarios can be found. Some interesting contributions are recommended for further reading. An early article by Benitez, Beigi, and Chang (1998) gives a good idea of the basic problems involved. Müller, Müller, Marchand-Maillet, Pun, and Squire (2000) discuss the differences between positive and negative relevance feedback.

A couple of research systems using relevance feedback have been developed. One of the first systems was ImageRover by Taycher, Cascia, and Sclaroff (1997), which is an early image retrieval system with integrated relevance feedback for Internet use. Sciascio, Mingolla, and Mongiello (1999) additionally allowed query-by-sketch in their approach. A more recent approach is Cortina by Quack, Mönich, Thiele, and Manjunath (2004), a large-scale CBIR system which also included relevance feedback aspects. One of the latest researches in this area has been published by Chiang, Chan, Hung, and Lee (2007). They combined relevance feedback with an object movie retrieval.

A special variation of relevance feedback is the annotation by searchers. Instead of letting the originator of the image do all the hard work, it is delegated to all users. Russell, Torralba, Murphy, and Freeman (2008) developed the LabelMe system, which is suitable for region aware web based image annotation.

FEATURES AND SIMILARITY MEASURES

The selection of supported features and similarity measures is highly application specific (Datta et al., 2005). For this reason it should be possible to add them as needed to the retrieval engine used (Pein, 2008).

Many image features have been proposed so far. While earlier ones focused on single low-level features, later approaches tried to include more and more complex ones. Also the effort shifted from global to local features. In the following some exemplary features are described.

Jacobs et al. (1995) proposed a feature based on Haar wavelets. Their approach is performing a multi resolution decomposition of the images. Short signatures containing a set of wavelet coefficients with the highest amplitudes for each picture are extracted. Several other attempts are also based on wavelets (e.g. (Do & Vetterli, 2002)). Their strength is usually their sensitivity for the image texture.

Histogram approaches are a way to focus on colour-based similarity as well as providing rotation invariance. An examples is the fv proposed by (Al-Omari & Al-Jarrah, 2005), compressing the histogram into 12 stochastic moments (mean, variance, skewness, colour correlation) for three colour channels. Another one has been proposed by Berens, Finlayson, and Qiu (2000). Their fv compresses an opponent colour histogram with several transformations (Karhunen–Loêve, discrete cosine, Hadamard and hybrid) with a stated compression rate of up to 250:1.

A third field tries to get the grips on shape detection often based on an autocorrelograms. Typical instances are both the features by Latecki and Lakämper (2000) and Mahmoudi, Shanbehzadeh, Eftekha-ri-Mogha-dam, and Soltanian-Zadeh (2003). Other research even attempts to do some object recognition based on extracted shapes (Belongie, Malik, & Puzicha, 2002) by matching the contours of objects identified in an earlier

processing stage. A comprehensive overview of early descriptors for the MPEG-7 standard are presented by Manjunath, Ohm, Vasudevan, and Yamada (2001).

One representative for a more recent feature is the aesthetics measure by Datta, Joshi, Li, and Wang (2006). They do not try to find images based on similarities, but on higher visual aspects. This feature could be used as a filter to automatically reject poor quality images in advance.

1. The value s_{QI} is the similarity between query Q and image I respectively its features.
2. This is the second stage in the calculation to combine the more complex results "shape context", "appearance cost" and "bending energy".

Carefully choosing appropriate features for a use case is only the first step in designing a CBIR application. Afterwards it is to be considered, how the similarity between each of two image features can be calculated. Several basic metrics and their properties are collected and described by Santini and Jain (1999) as well as Jolion (2001). It is argued that the similarity (or dissimilarity) should not always be measured as a simple geometric distance. Santini points out that the four axioms for metrics (*self-similarity*, *minimality*, *symmetry* and *triangular inequality*) cannot be applied to both *perceived* and *judged similarity*. They state that several recognition experiments revealed the weaknesses of the distance approach. Still measures like varieties of the Minkowski/ L_m distances are widely interpreted as similarity. This is probably mostly done in order to minimize the effort to develop a whole new indexing structure for faster retrieval.

A major problem of many features is their retrieval performance. Having a simple structure and similarity metric, indexes can be based on generic solutions. Using the euclidean distance, allows for implementing one out of several multi dimensional index trees. The more specific a single feature gets, the more specific is the related index structure.

Early research in this field has been done by Seidl and Kriegel (1997). Recent results by Gelasca et al. (2007) already claim to handle image databases with more than 10 million entries.

Jain, Nandakumar, and Ross (2005) mention the problem of score merging when using multiple sources in biometrics. Each source would generate a different score depending on the technology and matching algorithm involved. Merging the results of multiple image unrelated fv in a CBIR system basically faces the same challenges.

Table 6 shows a concise comparison of diverse similarity measures. The value s_{QI} defines the similarity between the query representation Q and any image/document representation I. Below the notation of the related maths models are explained.

The similarity equation by Al-Omari and Al-Jarrah (2005) uses the two 12 dimensional vectors called V_{kf}. The " $\bullet$ " denotes the inner or dot product.

The fv proposed by Belongie et al. (2002) is matching sets of polygon points based on three values: "shape context", "appearance cost" and "bending energy". Each one is calculated by a different function, but the resulting 3 dimensional vectors Q and I are then merged into a single value.

In the vector dot product of Berens et al. (2000), the value q represents the vector of weights generated by the histogram compression algorithm. The similarity between those weights is proven to be equivalent to the similarity of the original histograms.

The KLD based similarity measure of Do and Vetterli (2002) sums all distances D from all analyzed sub bands j into a single value. The values $\alpha^{(j)}$ ("scale paramater") and $\beta^{(j)}$ ("shape parameter") are defined as the extracted texture

features from the wavelet sub band j. Both are assigned to a fv $p()$.

In the fv by Jacobs et al. (1995), w denotes the relative weight of a single value. The notation X[i,j] describes a single two-dimensional coefficient for image X. Quantized coefficients are written as $\tilde{X}$.

The equation by Latecki and Lakämper (2000) uses the tangent function $T(X)$ of the turning function X. Further, $l(X)$ is the relative arclength of an arc and Θ_0 is a constant minimizing the integral.

Mahmoudi et al. (2003) also use the L_1 distance for the extracted matrices. The similarity is measured by the summed distance of all value pairs.

ANNOTATION

The annotation carried out by humans is an important way to tell computers something about the *ground truth* of images. In the end, every learning algorithm requires some input for validation. In the simpler case, a search engine can directly use existing annotation information for text based retrieval (Zhao & Grosky, 2002). A current meta data standard is the IPTC description, which will most likely be succeeded by the more flexible XMP (IPTC [International Press Telecommunications Council], 2008).

The annotation itself can be done for whole image files or bounded objects within. Simple annotation for each image is relatively straightforward and can be easily supported. Several commercial or experimental systems adopt this scheme, especially for private photo books (Flickr, 2006, Rodden & Wood, 2003). Advanced user interfaces may even provide drag&drop solutions (Shneiderman & Kang, 2000, Shneiderman et al., 2006).

The support of bounded objects requires much more effort, as the regions need to be defined

Table 6. Similarity measures

Citation	Similarity Measure	Feature	Data Format	Maths Model ($s_{QI} = \dots$)[1]	Symmetric
Al-Omari and Al-Jarrah (2005)	vector dot product	histogram moments	vector (12 dim)	$$\frac{2\left(V_{kf}^{Q} \cdot V_{kf}^{QI}\right)}{V_{kf}^{Q} \cdot V_{kf}^{Q} + V_{kf}^{I} \cdot V_{kf}^{I}}$$	yes
Belongie et al. (2002)	L_1 Distance[2]	polygons	vector (3 dim)	$$\sum_{i=1}^{n} \left| Q_i - I_i \right|$$	yes
Berens et al. (2000)	vector dot product	compressed histogram	vector (n)	$$\left\| \underline{q_Q} - \underline{q_I} \right\|^2$$	yes
Do and Vetterli (2002)	Kullback-Leibler divergence (KLD)	wavelet coefficients	18 values	$$\sum_{j=1}^{B} D\left(p\left(.; \alpha_Q^{(j)}; \beta_Q^{(j)}\right) \| p\left(.; \alpha_I^{(j)}; \beta_I^{(j)}\right) \right)$$	no
Jacobs et al. (1995)	average colour	wavelet coefficients	coefficient bins	$$w_0 \left| Q[0,0] - I[0,0] \right| - \sum_{i,j: Q[i,j] \neq 0} w_{bin(i,j)} (Q[i,j] = I[i,j])$$	no
Latecki and Lakämper (2000)	integral	polygons	tangent function	$$\left(\int_0^1 (T(Q)(s) - T(I)(s) + \tilde{\ }_0)^2 ds \right) \max(l(Q), l(I)) \max\left(\frac{l(Q)}{l(I)}, \frac{l(I)}{l(Q)} \right)$$	yes
Mahmoudi et al. (2003)	L_1 Distance	edges	matrix (n,m)	$$\sum_{i=1}^{n} m \left| Q_i - I_i \right|$$	yes

somehow. These regions are usually represented as rectangles, polygons or pixel-based overlays. Algorithms are able to find several regions in an image. Based on those regions, humans only have to select and maybe edit them to define the proper boundaries. The next logical step is to annotate each image region separately (Russell et al., 2008).

EVALUATION OF RETRIEVAL SYSTEMS

As soon as a CBIR prototype has been developed, the question arises how to evaluate its quality. There are several synthetic benchmarks available.

Benchmarks

A very popular, yet non standardized benchmark is using the *Corel Stock Photo* collection. It contains several images, already assigned to several categories. This data is especially useful to measure classification algorithms.

Other than the Corel dataset, the Caltech 101 collection (Fei-Fei, Fergus, & Perona, 2004) has been specifically developed for benchmarks. It consists of 101 categories (plus a background category) with about 40 to 800 images per category. In addition, the outlines of each object and further annotation are available. Recently an updated version of the collection has been released, named Caltech 256 (Griffin, Holub, & Perona, 2007). The amount of categories has been increased to

256 and each category now holds at least 80 images. Another Caltech database contains several thousand images of planes, motorbikes cars and general background (Fergus, Perona, & Zisserman, 2003).

Further image databases are the UIUC Image Database for Car Detection (Agarwal & Roth, 2002, Agarwal, Awan, & Roth, 2004), the TU Darmstadt Database (formerly the ETHZ Database) (Leibe, Leonardis, & Schiele, 2004), the TU Graz-02 Database (Opelt, Pinz, Fussenegger, & Auer, 2006, Opelt & Pinz, 2005) and the MIT-CSAIL Database of Objects and Scenes(Torralba, Murphy, & Freeman, 2004). The PASCAL Object Recognition Database Collection uses some of the collections above to compile different test sets used in the Visual Object Classes Challenges ("Machine Learning Challenges. Evaluating Predictive Uncertainty, Visual Object Classification, and Recognising Textual Entailment", 2006, Everingham, Van Gool, Williams, Winn, & Zisserman, 2007). Some collections also contain images from Google, Flickr and the Microsoft Research Cambridge database.

The Benchathlon framework (Müller, Müller, Marchand-Maillet, Pun, & Squire, 2003) is another attempt to generate and collect benchmarks for a fair and general comparison of various retrieval systems, such as BIRDS-I (Gunther & Beretta, 2001).

Several conferences (e.g. ImageCLEF (Clough, Grubinger, Deselaers, Hanbury, & Müller, 2007), TRECVID (Hauptmann & Christel, 2004, Smeaton, Over, & Kraaij, 2006)) are especially dedicated to competitive multimedia retrieval solutions. These conferences develop challenging tasks closely related to real-world applications. Each participant needs to submit a prototype system solving certain tasks and the results are then compared to each other.

ImageCLEF (Clough et al., 2007) is focused on CLIR and CBIR. In the last workshop, the topics were: "photographic retrieval", "medical retrieval", "photographic concept detection", "medical automatic image annotation" and "image retrieval task from a collection of Wikipedia images". The TRECVID (Hauptmann & Christel, 2004, Smeaton et al., 2006) is essentially dedicated to video retrieval.

Metrics and Analysis. The performance of CBIR systems is usually measured by calculating values as PR, ROC, F-Measure/F-Score and Fall-Out. They use the amount of true/false positives and true/false negatives in the result set. Some metrics are dependent on other values like the result size or cannot be reduced to a single number. Each metric must be applied carefully regarding its specific strengths and weaknesses. A comprehensive discussion about these measures, especially ROC has been done by Fawcett (2006).

Retrieval Frameworks

All technologies described so far are different building blocks for a CBIR system. Except for the optional relevance feedback, each part is required. Research in the CBIR area often requires a prototype implementation and thorough testing of the outcome. Instead of building a search engine from scratch each time, the application of an existing framework should be considered.

An early solution was the Virage search engine (Bach et al., 1996, Gupta & Jain, 1997). It already allowed to extend the basic system by simple or complex primitives. MetaSEEk (Beigi, Benitez, & Chang, 1997) is a meta search engine, supporting the systems VisualSEEk (Smith & Chang, 1997), WebSEEk (Chang, Smith, Beigi, & Benitez, 1997), QBIC (Niblack et al., 1998) and Virage.

The Viper retrieval system (Müller et al., 2000) from the University of Geneva is based on the open GIFT framework. It uses altered techniques from traditional information retrieval. The idea is to merge several sources of information for the retrieval itself, such as textual as well as visual features. Currently the system is being replaced by a new development, called "ComMon SensE: Cross-Modal Search Engine".

Joshi et al. (2006) describe the recent, scalable web architecture PARAgrab for image retrieval, able to handle CBIR and keywords as well as interactive image tagging. It is part of a research group supervised by James Z. Wang at the Carnegie Mellon University, who also developed SIMPLIcity (Wang, Li, & Wiederhold, 2001) and other CBIR related research.

Merging/Fusion

When merging multiple sub queries into a single one, there are several possibilities to do so. "Multimodal fusion" is a recent research area emerging from the needs of modern retrieval systems.

Kim and Chung (Kim & Chung, 2003) distinguish three kinds of merging multiple query points in a single feature space for relevance feedback (Figure 4). In Figure 4(d), the model used by the author of this part is visualized. It can be argued that all given query points are within the desired cluster. The search engine must now decide how the final similarity should be calculated. In the simplest case, all query points are averaged in the feature space to get a new query point. The generation of convex or concave similarity shapes is more complex, but provides advantages if the cluster has no circular borders. Especially the first two methods require the use of a simple distance measure. Otherwise the calculations may become overly complex.

The Rocchio's formula (Rocchio, 1971) is based on the vector space model and represents the query type in Figure 4(a):

$$Q_1 = Q_0 + \beta \sum_{i=1}^{n_1} \frac{R_i}{n_1} - \gamma \sum_{i-1}^{n_2} \frac{S_i}{n_2}$$

where Q_0 is the original query, R_i is the fv for the relevant document i and n_1 the number of relevant documents. This formula also considers non-relevant documents S_i by subtracting them

from the query. The importance of the two sums can be justified by the weights β and γ (Ishikawa, Subramanya, & Faloutsos, 1998). A second formula for query point movement by Porkaew, Chakrabarti, and Mehrotra (1999) would be:

$$C[j] = \frac{\sum_{i=1}^{n} w_i E_i[j]}{\sum_{i=1}^{n} w_i}$$

where E_1 to E_n are the n query objects/fv and w_1 to w_n are the corresponding weights. C denotes the resulting centroid to be used as the next query. Parameter j stands for a single dimension of the fv. The second approach depicted in Figure 4(b) assumes, that all relevant documents lie close to each other in the feature space. The query points are clustered to a maximum of N clusters. For each cluster, the point closest to the centroid is used and weighted according to the cluster size. These form the next multi point query $M = \langle n, P, W, D \rangle$, where P is the set of points, W the corresponding weights and D is the distance function between two points. In this case — also proposed by Porkaew et al. (1999) — the distance between M and any point x x is:

$$D(M, x) = \sum_{i=1}^{n} w_i D(P_i, x)$$

The third approach (Figure 4(c)) is a multi point query, where each query point is taken as a separate query and the final result is merged from the sub results. This could be done by applying weighted sums, fuzzy sets or else. An example is the approach by Fagin (Fagin, 1996), who interprets results as *graded sets*. They are basically lists sorted by similarity and set characteristics. He proposes to apply the basic Fuzzy rules defined by Zadeh (Zadeh, 1996):

Figure 4. Query shape

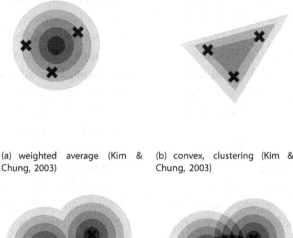

(a) weighted average (Kim & Chung, 2003)

(b) convex, clustering (Kim & Chung, 2003)

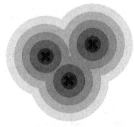
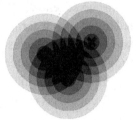

(c) concave, disjunctive (Kim & Chung, 2003)

(d) concave, conjunctive

Conjunction:

$$\mu_{A \wedge B}(x) = min\{\mu_A(x), \mu_B(x)\} \, (\text{AND})$$

Disjunction:

$$\mu_{A \vee B}(x) = max\{\mu_A(x), \mu_B(x)\} \, (\text{OR})$$

Negation:

$$\mu_{\neg A}(x) = 1 - \mu_A(x) \, (\text{NOT})$$

Using the disjunction would directly produce the concave shape depicted in Figure 4(c).

In general, the merging approach which is most suitable for a given use case cannot be decided. This highly depends on the nature of the implemented features. Systems designed for experts should offer a choice, but for occasional use a decision has to be made by the administrator or the system itself.

This problem applies to a single feature with multiple query points and also to multiple disjunct features for a single query image. Further a more complex combination of these cases can be imagined. The proposed query language (Pein, Lu, & Renz, 2008b) offers the ability to create and use those queries. Though, it does not define the way of merging. A fourth merging alternative is the weighted sum of sub results (Figure 4(d)), where the similarities for all query points are added up and normalized (Pein & Lu, 2007). Another, non-linear fusion approach called "super-kernel fusion" has been presented by Y. Wu, Chang, Chang, and Smith (2004).

Communication Protocols. It is remarkable that even after several years the existing prototypes are not yet established in daily life. Probably one reason is the diversity of approaches and the lack of interoperability. Recently emerged communication protocols could be the key to link many smaller systems together.

A communication protocol for this purpose, called MRML, is proposed by Müller et al. (2000). It is based on XML, has a formal specification and is already in use. The most recent proposal is version 2.0.

Currently, a de-facto standard for textual retrieval is emerging and gaining popularity. The Open Search Interface (OpenSearch, 2006) is developed by *A9.com*. It wraps up several XML formats in order to allow federated search across the web. The whole standard is based on the assumption, that specialized engines are best suited to certain domains. Hence, a unified communication between clients and search engines is meant to be the best approach.

CATEGORIZATION

Automatic image categorization — letting a machine determine, which semantic category an image belongs to — always involves some kind of more or less sophisticated machine learning. Common techniques are ANN (Doulamis, Doulamis, & Kollias, 1999), SVM (Weston et al., 2000, Zhou & Huang, 2001, Hoi & Lyu, 2004) and SOFM (Chandramouli & Izquierdo, 2006) or DT (Schapire & Singer, 1999). Besides other techniques, there are two main approaches for machine learning, supervised and unsupervised.

Unsupervised techniques have no real need of training sets and manual annotation. They take a given set of input and try to find a describing model. A common way of doing this is clustering the data where no additional information is needed. The supervised techniques have in common that they are optimizing certain parameters to satisfy a training set with respect to certain classes as

good as possible. A given input should lead to a defined output. An intermediate discipline is the semi-supervised learning, where a labelled training set is provided to learn a set of samples. This approach is a trade-off between the effort of annotating large amounts of data and the lack of semantic information.

In this investigation it is attempted to automatically build up descriptors based on a multi-feature query language. It is essential to provide at least a minimal ground truth, if certain concepts are to be learned in conjunction with a keyword. It can either be manually prepared for this purpose or has to be derived from the information context. This feeds essential information into the learning algorithm to optimize the descriptors. Thus, a supervised or semi-supervised approach is required if high-level semantics are to be learned. Semi-supervised learning has been successfully applied in image retrieval software, such as the "Multimedia Analysis and Retrieval System" (Smith, 2004) by IBM. The aspect of semi-supervised learning is further expanded in section *Case Studies-Semi-Supervised Learning*.

PRELIMINARY WORK

This section gives a quick overview of previous related work of the author (Pein, 2008).

Query Language

A CBIR query language has been developed by the author of this part (Pein, Lu, & Renz, 2008a). It is based on the Lucene Query Parser (Lucene, 2006) which defines a common language for full text search. The language allows queries similar to those used in traditional search engines and the parser is generated by JavaCC. This approach tries to merge key design principles of different languages. Like in OQUEL (Town & Sinclair,

2001), queries are kept as simple and natural as possible. Yet, to provide a high machine readability, a strict grammar like in SQL is defined. The main extensions to provide CBIR functionality are:

Fuzzy related operators and a nested two-layer grammar. The boost parameter for terms in the Lucene parser (Lucene, 2006) has been extended in the master thesis of the author to multiple TermParams allowing additional control of fuzzy result sets (Pein, 2008).

To provide a high extensibility the grammar is split into two different layers. The basic layer (see section Grammar) is parsed and interpreted by the search engine directly. This part of the grammar is predefined and fixed. Users may specify which meta information should be searched for by simply using fields. Typically these are fields like *title*, *content*, *author*, *creationdate*. Images hold other fields than normal text documents, typically EXIF and IPTC information. In the near future, this information may be replaced by the XML based XMP (Riecks, 2005). Additionally, a CBIR environment provides one or multiple fv holding low-level information about the pixels. These fv can be added by plug-ins, each one having a unique identifier which is the field name for content based queries. The difficulty now lies in specifying how the query fv is entered. There are at least three different ways possible:

- ID of an image stored in the repository
- URI of a query image
- specification of the fv itself

The simplest way is to use an existing image for a query (*query-by-example*). Images already in the repository have the prepared fv available. Specifying the URI of an image requires the engine to load the image and to extract the fv. The most advanced and complicated way is to let the user specify a fv in detail.

As a custom fv may contain any kind of proprietary data, offering an all-embracing language is not possible. Thus a second layer is added to the query language. A *Term* may contain the string *<FEATURE_START> [<FEATURE_CONTENT>] <FEATURE_END>*. The parenthesized part *<FEATURE_CONTENT>* is extracted by the search engine and passed to the responsible plug-in. The plug-in is fully responsible for parsing and interpreting this string to return the object representation of the fv.

Grammar

Below, the grammar of the query language in EBNF.

```
Conjunction::=  [ <AND> | <OR> ]
Modifiers::= [ <PLUS> | <MINUS> |
<NOT> ]
Query::= (Conjunction Modifiers
Clause)*
Clause::=
  [ LOOKAHEAD(2)
  (<TERM> <COLON> | <STAR> <COLON>)
  ]
  (Term | <LPAREN> Query <RPAREN>
[TermParams]
  )
Term::=
  (
    (<TERM>  | <STAR> | <PREFIXTERM>
|
      <WILDTERM> | <NUMBER>  |
<URI>)
    [ <FUZZY_SLOP> ]
    [ TermParams [ <FUZZY_SLOP> ] ]
  | (<RANGEIN_START>
      (<RANGEIN_GOOP>|<RANGEIN_
QUOTED>)
      [ <RANGEIN_TO> ]
      (<RANGEIN_GOOP>|<RANGEIN_
QUOTED>)
      <RANGEIN_END>)
    [ TermParams ]
  | (<RANGEEX_START>
      (<RANGEEX_GOOP>|<RANGEEX_
```

```
QUOTED>)
       [ <RANGEEX_TO> ]
         (<RANGEEX_GOOP>|<RANGEEX_
QUOTED>)
         <RANGEEX_END>)
       [ TermParams ]
    |
      (<FEATURE_START>
       [ <FEATURE_CONTENT> ]
       <FEATURE_END>)
       [ TermParams ]
    | <QUOTED>
      [<FUZZY_SLOP> ]
      [ TermParams ]
  )
TermParams::=
    (
     <CARAT> boost (
       ([ <HASH> maxCount ]  [ <AT>
threshold ])
       | ([ <AT> threshold ]  [ <HASH>
maxCount ])
      )
    |   <HASH> maxCount (
       ([ <CARAT> boost ]  [ <AT>
threshold ])
       | ([ <AT> threshold ]  [ <CARAT>
boost ])
      )
    |   <AT> threshold (
       ([ <CARAT> boost ]  [ <HASH>
maxCount ])
       | ([ <HASH> maxCount ]  [ <CARAT>
boost ])
      )
  )
```

Plug-Ins

The plug-in concept of the retrieval framework described in (Pein, 2008) allows the definition of any new feature. To make such a plug-in available in this language, only a few requirements need to be met. The plug-in needs an identifier which is automatically used as a term field. With this information it is already possible to formulate queries containing an example image (either by internal id or URI). The tricky part is to develop a syntax for user defined fv information embedded in a query. As features can be arbitrarily complex, each plug-in should use a simple default language to describe the contents of a fv. Otherwise the embedded data string of a query is forwarded directly to the feature plug-in where it needs to be converted into a valid feature object.

Identification of Problems

This section highlights major problems in the research fields analyzed above. This collection of issues is used to identify the aims presented in section *Aims and Objectives*.

The whole MIR area has to deal with fuzziness and uncertainty. Both approaches — either using primitives or semantics — are not yet suitable to create satisfying results on large data bases. A retrieval system based on low-level information is too imprecise, as a deeper understanding of the content is missing. A semantic based approach requires a lot of human annotation effort to be correct. Semantics created automatically also rely basically on low-level analysis and some human annotation.

A great deal of the problems in MIR seem to be caused by an imperfect human-machine interaction, missing machine intelligence and a lack of standards.

Most papers in section *Related Work* indicate that human beings are still better in generic object recognition than machines. Thus, the information which is already available should be used in the best way possible.

Browsing

For browsing, the search engine must present an initial overview of the contents. In pure CBIR, this is usually done by generating an initial image subset of the database. This can either happen at random or by a specific query from the user. Based on the user input, a more specific overview of probably related items must be generated.

In CBIR, often a number of thumbnail images is presented to the user (Niblack et al., 1998, Gupta & Jain, 1997). It is even possible to present a quite large number of images. Unlike text, image content can often be perceived at a glance. The user may now scan the results for potential matches. It is still an open question, as to how the results should be arranged. Several different ways (Combs & Bederson, 1999, Leuski & Allan, 2000, Liu et al., 2004) have been already proposed, each one with certain advantages and drawbacks. Sorting these hits by categories or visual similarity seems to be beneficial in many cases. To find eye-catching images, a random distribution seems to be even more useful, while the user does not necessarily need to know the arranging method (Rodden et al., 2001, Rodden, 2002). The challenge is to find a convenient solution.

Query Language

Independent from the user interface, each search engine needs to support queries. Usually they define a string representation covering the whole set of parameters. Internally the string is parsed and probably optimized before it is executed. The application area has a strong influence on each individual grammar. Image retrieval systems often provide a visual interface to compose queries.

Currently, the CBIR systems available mostly seem to use a proprietary query language, specifically adapted to each particular implementation. Several attempts have been made (e.g. FOQL (Nepal & Ramakrishna, 1999), OQUEL (Town & Sinclair, 2001)), but none of the proposed languages was highly successful in CBIR yet. The main reason for that seems to be the immense variability of requirements to such a language, as each system focuses on a certain field. In the current research the most important aspects about querying are:

- How to formulate a meaningful query?
- How to support as many useful queries as possible?
- How to support the user in searching/ browsing the results?

Another issue is the possible variety of user expertise. People working at workplaces with an immense amount of data, such as travel agencies or libraries are used to deal with complex query strings. But these queries are only special to a single application area and require a good deal of training.

Relevance Feedback in Search Results

Relevance feedback requires user interaction to work properly. The system behaviour is adapted to the user. For this reason the newly provided information must be more correct than the current situation. Otherwise the future results cannot be improved in quality. Further, the user is probably forced to do additional work which actually slows down a current retrieval session. In such a case, the search engine taxes the user's patience.

Features and Similarity Measures

There are two important characteristics of a feature in retrieval scenarios. The fv requires to be highly descriptive for a given document and there needs to be a similarity measure for each two fv of the same kind. A fv usually captures one certain document feature in a highly condensed format. This format does not allow a reconstruction of the original data, but it is describing a certain part of it.

The multi dimensional nature of many fv turns out to be very difficult to define a generally valid similarity measure. Each feature has its own structure and every dimension in the structure may reflect specific semantics, which cannot be easily captured. In the case of simple mathematical vectors, a default distance measure could be applied. Often a low dimensional Minkowski/L_m distance is used. Very popular measures are the Euclidean distance (L_2) and the Manhattan distance(L_1)(Pein, 2008). Standard index structures like multi dimensional trees such as the R-Tree (Guttman, 1984) could be applied.

In some cases, the vector representation is too coarse to capture all aspects of a feature. A more complex distance calculation between two features could be based on another feature model. The similarity function does not even have to be inverse.

An example is a set of keywords attached to each image interpreted as image feature. It has been implemented by Pein (2005) in an earlier CBIR prototype. The image to be retrieved is represented by the set $I = \{a, b, c, d\}$ and the search query is $Q = \{a, c\}$

The similarity between these sets could be defined as $s_{IQ} = \dfrac{|I \cap Q|}{|Q|}$, which is the relative occurrence of the query terms in the image feature. In this example, the resulting similarity would be $s_{IQ} = \dfrac{\{a, c\}}{\{a, c\}} = \dfrac{2}{2} = 1$. Swapping image and query set, the result is different: $s_{QI} = \dfrac{|Q \cap I|}{|I|} = \dfrac{\{a, c\}}{\{a, b, c, d\}} = \dfrac{2}{4} = 0.5$.

From a users point of view, this behaviour appears consistent. By specifying several keywords, one would expect, that the highest ranked results would contain all of them. Consequently, the relative amount of matches should be taken into account.

In these cases none of the basic fv theories can be applied without care. This disqualifies these features for many standard optimizations. But sometimes other ways of feature specific, but more efficient indexing can be found. E.g. for keywords, the reverse index is a highly efficient structure.

Annotation

The annotation problem is the foundation of all object recognition effort. Single images and small repositories can be easily annotated by humans whereas a growing amount of information cannot be handled any more by a single person. Due to the fact that object recognition is still an open problem, it is necessary to find a practicable workaround for the time being.

Evaluation of Retrieval Systems

It is claimed that benchmarking in CBIR is a very controversial topic (Wang et al., 2006). Due to the immense fan out of use cases and application areas, the aims of all the systems vary. It is a common opinion that synthetic benchmarks could kill innovation and causing new systems to be focused on solving the pre-defined tasks. For this reason, generic benchmarks should only apply to already established and small application areas. Judging the whole of research by a set of standardized benchmarking criteria would probably slow down innovation.

Retrieval Frameworks

It is obvious that until now no CBIR framework has made a final breakthrough. This might also be caused by the diversity of objectives. An important problem is the lack of a generic indexing structure for features. Possible approaches are not implemented within the boundaries of the part but are going to be considered in the future. Examples are used in the prototypes by Joshi et al. (2006) and Quack et al. (2004).

Which merging approach for sub-queries is most suitable for a given use case, cannot be decided generally. This highly depends on the nature of the implemented features. Systems designed for experts should offer a choice, but for occasional use a decision has to be made by the administrator or the system itself. The proposed query language (Pein, Lu, & Renz, 2008b) offers the ability to create and use complex Boolean queries. However, it does not define the way of merging.

Categorization

In the field of image recognition, several case specific problems arise. A major problem is to find suitable samples representing a certain object. For optimal learning, the object has to be totally isolated from the image background. Otherwise, the algorithm may also learn to recognize irrelevant noise instead of the relevant object only.

Further, most images do contain more than a single object. In that case, it is important to distinguish them and inform the learning algorithm which region represents which object. Overlaps, irregular shapes and high-contrast patterns increase the difficulty of automatically clustering images.

It is also important to keep in mind, that multiple samples of a single concept could differ significantly from each other. Using low-level descriptors and simply calculating a single average value or centroid is not sufficient in many cases. Then a "divide-and-conquer" approach for detailed modelling is required, as investigated by B. Wu and Nevatia (2007). They propose an iterative algorithm to subsequently add specific classifiers to a classification tree. If the category to be learned cannot be matched by a simple classifier, the training samples are spilt into smaller and more specific clusters. As a result, the classifier complexity grows with each single split and methods for joining them afterwards are required.

Aims and Objectives

The recent overview provided by Datta et al. (Datta et al., 2008) concludes with the statement, that the research focused more in *systems*, *feature extraction* and *relevance feedback* than in application-oriented aspects such as *interface*, *visualisation*, *scalability* and *evaluation*. Thus it seems desirable to improve research in these areas. According to Lew et al. (2006) there are several recent research topics trying to "bridge the semanticgap". In human-centred computing the system tries to satisfy the user while keeping the interface easily understandable. One possible approach is to apply machine learning to connect low-level features to high-level semantic concepts

The currently available technology can be applied to a CBIR system. This part examines a possible way of reducing the semanticgap. It focuses on how to link low-level features to high-level semantics. Key technologies to achieve this aim are:

- A user interface allowing guided browsing of an image repository
- A query language that can handle arbitrary features
- A core retrieval system supporting multiple fv types simultaneously
- A decision tree based learning algorithm to build category-related queries

User Interface

The user interface to be developed needs to address the problems stated in the former sections. The section *Identification of Problems-Browsing* indicates that the process of retrieving images depends on the user's needs and the particular use-case. Thus, the user interface should offer guidance for inexperienced users and detailed control for experts.

Query Language

In section *Identification of Problems-Query Language* the query language is identified to be the main connection between user interface and retrieval system. It is attempted to determine the crucial parts of a versatile language and to define a grammar covering them. Further, this language should be easily convertible between human-readable, XML and machine representations. The recently developed query language (Pein, Lu, & Renz, 2008b) is used as a foundation and is examind in detail.

Core System

The core system relies on mathematical models rather than human interaction. The back end of the project deals with the problems arising on pixel-level and fuzzy definitions. Having no universal feature covering all requirements in a single feature, it seems to be necessary to keep on researching new feature models and similarity measures. Also, these different features need to be mergeable.

A CBIR framework should wrap up all of the aims above into a fully functional system. The optimal system would be flexible enough to be set up in many different use-cases.

Categorization

To reduce the need of building up a suitable and annotated image repository, some prepared image collections with category annotation are used in this investigation. These images usually represent a single concept and the object of interest is either located in the centre or fills almost the complete image. This approach largely avoids the trouble of image segmentation.

A couple of previously implemented low-level features are then used as a basis for classification. Having various features available for optimization allows for determining the best ones for each single object class. The use of a query language with Boolean operators allows the learning algorithm to specify multiple independent clusters at the same time. Each single cluster may vary in its boundaries and the feature used.

The resulting query descriptors should be describing a given concept as well as possible. As with most learning algorithms, the problems of over-fitting and unpredictable run times have to be addressed. Thus, suitable heuristics for this learning scenario need to be developed.

Image collections containing several images for a single concept are used. Two candidates are the Caltech-101 (Fei-Fei et al., 2004) and the ETH-80 (Leibe et al., 2004) repository. Both contain between 31 and 800 samples for each contained category and the main object is centred in the images. As all fv used within this part are global features and no segmentation is applied, it is important for the image sets to fulfil the following preconditions:

1. Each image represents a single object/ concept
2. The object/concept to be learned fills most of the image area, is centred and completely visible
3. The ETH-80 collection provides additional mask files which define the relevant segment

Finally, the developed system is evaluated. This is done by comparing the query descriptors learnt in the categorization stage to an existing approach.

REFERENCES

Apache Software Foundation. (2006). *Apache Lucene*. Retrieved from http://lucene.apache.org/

Combs, T. T. A., & Bederson, B. B. (1999). Does zooming improve image browsing? In DL '99: *Proceedings of the Fourth ACM Conference on Digital Libraries* (pp. 130-137). New York, NY: ACM.

Datta, R., Joshi, D., Li, J., & Wang, J. Z. (2008, April). Image retrieval: Ideas, influences, and trends of the new age. *ACM Transactions on Computing Surveys, 40*(2), 1–60. doi:10.1145/1348246.1348248

Fei-Fei, L., Fergus, R., & Perona, P. (2004). *Learning generative visual models from few training examples: An incremental Bayesian approach tested on 101 object categories.* In International Conference on Computer Vision and Pattern Recognition (CVPR'04). (Workshop on Generative-Model Based Vision).

Gupta, A., & Jain, R. (1997). Visual information retrieval. *Communications of the ACM, 40*(5), 70{79.

Guttman, A. (1984). R-trees: A dynamic index structure for spatial searching. In ACM SIGMOD Conference on the Management of Data (pp. 47-57).

Joshi, D., Datta, R., Zhuang, Z., Weiss, W. P., Friedenberg, M., Li, J., et al. (2006). PARAgrab: A comprehensive architecture for web image management and multimodal querying. In VLDB '06: *Proceedings of the 32nd International Conference on Very Large Data Bases* (pp. 1163-1166). VLDB Endowment.

Leibe, B., Leonardis, A., & Schiele, B. (2004, May). Combined object categorization and segmentation with an implicit shape model. In *Proceedings of the Workshop on Statistical Learning in Computer Vision*, Prague, Czech Republic.

Leuski, A., & Allan, J. (2000). Improving interactive retrieval by combining ranked lists and clustering. In *Proceedings of RIAO'2000* (pp. 665{681). Retrieved from citeseer.ist.psu.edu/leuski00improving.html

Lew, M. S., Sebe, N., Djeraba, C., & Jain, R. (2006). Content-based multimedia information retrieval: State of the art and challenges. *ACM Transactions in Multimedia Computing and Communication Applications, 2*(1), 1–19. doi:10.1145/1126004.1126005

Liu, H., Xie, X., Tang, X., Li, Z.-W., & Ma, W.-Y. (2004). Effective browsing of web image search results. In *MIR '04: Proceedings of the 6th ACM SIGMM International Workshop on Multimedia Information Retrieval* (pp. 84-90). New York, NY: ACM.

Nepal, S., & Ramakrishna, M. (1999). Query processing issues in image (multimedia) databases. *International Conference on Data Engineering*, (pp. 22-29).

Niblack, W., Zhu, X., Hafner, J., Breuel, T., Ponceleon, D., & Petkovic, D. (1998). Updates to the QBIC system. *Retrieval for Image and Video Databases VI, 3312*, 150–161.

Pein, R. P. (2005). *Multi-modal image retrieval - A feasibility study*. Diplomarbeit.

Pein, R. P. (2008). *Hot-pluggable multi-feature search engine. Memoire de Master non publie*. Hamburg University of Applied Sciences.

Pein, R. P., Lu, J., & Renz, W. (2008a, July). An extensible query language for content based image retrieval. *The Open Information Science Journal, 3*(17), 81–97.

Pein, R. P., Lu, J., & Renz, W. (2008b, July). An extensible query language for content based image retrieval based on Lucene. In 8th IEEE International Conference on Computer and Information Technology, CIT 2008, (pp. 179-184).

Quack, T., Monich, U., Thiele, L., & Manjunath, B. S. (2004). Cortina: a system for large-scale, content-based web image retrieval. In *Multimedia '04: Proceedings of the 12th Annual ACM International Conference on Multimedia* (pp. 508-511). New York, NY: ACM.

Riecks, D. (2005). *IPTC Core schema for XMP - Version 1.0 (Rapport technique)*. International Press Telecommunications Council.

Rodden, K. (2002). *Evaluating similarity-based visualisations as interfaces for image browsing*. These de doctorat non publiee, University of Cambridge.

Rodden, K., Basalaj, W., Sinclair, D., & Wood, K. (2001). Does organisation by similarity assist image browsing? In *CHI '01: Proceedings of the SIGCHI Conference on Human Factors in Computing Systems* (pp. 190-197). New York, NY: ACM.

Town, C., & Sinclair, D. (2001, 14 December). Ontological query language for content based image retrieval. In IEEE Workshop on Content-Based Access of Image and Video Libraries, CBAIVL 2001, (pp. 75-80).

Wang, J. Z., Boujemaa, N., Bimbo, A. D., Geman, D., Hauptmann, A. G., & Tesic, J. (2006). Diversity in multimedia information retrieval research. In *MIR '06: Proceedings of the 8th ACM International Workshop on Multimedia Information Retrieval* (pp. 5-12). New York, NY: ACM.

Wu, B., & Nevatia, R. (2007, Oct.). Cluster boosted tree classifier for multi-view, multi-pose object detection. In *IEEE 11th International Conference on Computer Vision, ICCV 2007* (pp. 1-8).

Chapter 22
Methods Employed

Raoul Pascal Pein
University of Huddersfield, UK

Joan Lu
University of Huddersfield, UK

Wolfgang Renz
Hamburg University of Applied Sciences, Germany

ABSTRACT

This chapter points out certain technologies that are often applied in a CBIR system. A prototypical retrieval system has been developed in order to evaluate the research hypothesis. Following common principles of information hiding, the software is designed to have multiple layers of abstraction. The top layer needs to be user friendly and also has the task to translate human understandable concepts into machine readable commands. As every user has a different level of expertise, the interface complexity should be adapted accordingly.

INTRODUCTION

Typically, a CBIR system consists of *user interface, query-processing-module* and the *image database* (Figure 1). The user interface is probably the most important part of a search engine. An engine producing perfect results is of no value, if it cannot be handled. It is necessary to reduce the *perceived* complexity for the user. The approach is to provide graphical guidance while hiding the complex background theories as much as possible. This is especially useful for inexperienced users. Experts have usually far less difficulties in understanding and using complex interfaces. A real life example is the comparison between graphical user interfaces and console applications. Programs started from a console offer several parameters for detailed configuration. This requires knowledge of the program name and the parameter syntax. Their graphical representations are in many cases much easier to handle, but they offer less parameters and actions. For this reason, expert users should always be able to have a lower level access than the beginner.

DOI: 10.4018/978-1-4666-1975-3.ch022

Figure 1. Ranking in a typical CBIR-system (Torres et al., 2003)

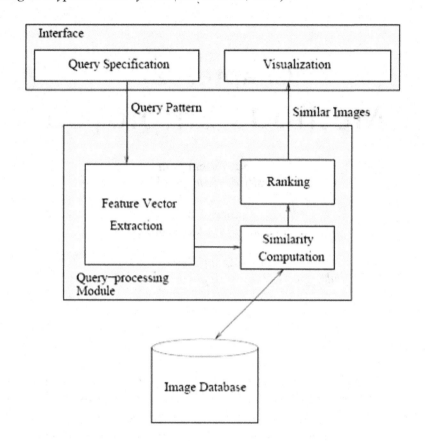

BROWSING

A basic browsing loop during retrieval is shown in Figure 2. The user starts with an initial query, waits for the results and then checks the results. In the best case, the desired content is already displayed on a prominent position on the screen. If not, the user may navigate through more results that are not yet visible on the screen. To improve the results, the initial query may be refined or even rewritten completely to initiate a new search.

This work flow contains all the important stages that need to be presented to the searcher. Each stage requires some methodology and techniques applied in the retrieval system.

For efficient browsing, the user needs to see some content of the available repository. This could be a structure of available categories, the results of a preceding search or other information.

The developed system does only provide a one dimensional list of results, as the aspect of browsing cannot be investigated in depth within this part. This list is always generated by a query which either generates a set of random results or represents a normal retrieval.

QUERY LANGUAGE

In section *Identification of Problems-Query Language*, a set of important aspects for the design of a query language is mentioned. The requirements for the query language applied in this part are derived from these aspects. Converting the users mental model into something machine readable

Figure 2. Retrieval-workflow (Pein, Amador, et al., 2008)

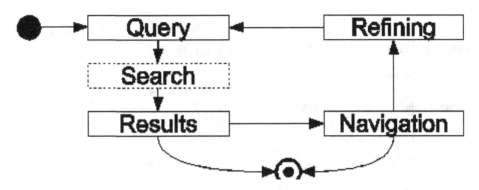

inevitably causes a loss of information. The task of a query language is to minimize this loss. Based on this assumption, the requirements are composed and presented below.

QUERY LANGUAGE REQUIREMENTS

Which Aspects does a Query Language for a CBIR System need to Cover?

- Boolean Queries
- Nested Queries
- Feature Vector Queries
- Keyword, Tag Queries
- Querying Concepts ("discrete"/fuzzy):
- Weights and Preferences
- Filters
- Temporal Aspects (Hibino & Rundensteiner, 1995)
- Technology:
- Query-By-Example (existing image/upload tool)
- Query-By-Sketch (drawing tool)
- Query-By-Feature (input tool)

As the level of user expertise may differ, the interface needs to provide multiple levels of complexity. Thus, is seems to be necessary to provide several user interface levels (Figure 3). The users can be split into three main categories:

- **Specialist Users:** Basic query language with all possible parameters and constructs, string based "console."
- **Intermediate Users:** Complex visual language constructs to compose queries close to the abilities of the underlying language, some tool support.
- **Amateur User:** Simplified visual language, containing only the essentials and much guidance/tools.

Beginning with the lowest level, more and more complexity of the underlying query language will be hidden. This usually leads to better usability as well as less freedom of manipulation. In fact, the whole retrieval system has to rely on a sound and powerful query language.

On higher abstraction levels, the user may be guided through a use case dependent work flow. The system could decide in the background, which low-level features suit the users needs and how they should be weighted. This functionality needs either to be set up by an experienced administrator, or by a learning algorithm. These could be realized with techniques like use neural or Bayesian networks. The training is usually performed by relevance feedback or dedicated training sets (Buijs & Lew, 1999, Rui & Huang,

Figure 3. User experience levels

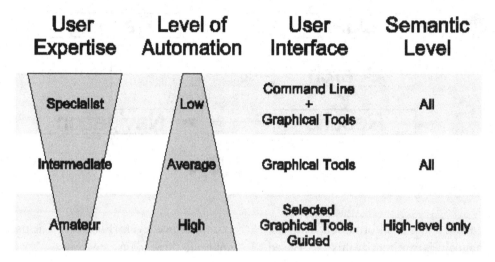

2000, Doulamis et al., 1999, Peng & DeClaris, 1997, Sheikholeslami, Chatterjee, & Zhang, 1998). In section *Methods-Categorization*, a learning approach is presented.

QUERY COMPOSING

Especially amateurs expect to see a well designed interface. The learning curve ought to incline very gently. Otherwise the user might be discouraged before even entering the first query. Being all about images, the CBIR scenario virtually suggests itself a visual query interface. Several query types related to CBIR are listed in Table 1. Though the most flexible approach, plain query strings are only of use, if they are easy-to-use or for experts. QBE is still feasible with URL and QBF could also be represented by a serialized representation. The QBS finally requires a graphical interface. To complete the collection of query types, the random and meta data queries are also important. Without any random capabilities, QBE could not work properly. No one can expect that the user has suitable example images at hand to be uploaded.

Composing queries by drawing them with objects from a toolbox directly, shows the user the most important possibilities. Without reading any documentation, the user can see useful constructs and try them out directly. Further, a visual query is not based on natural language. This keeps specifications clear and allows high complexity without any parsing errors.

The main task is to reflect all essentials of the underlying query grammar. Special nuances should always be possible by falling back to a basic query string. With a sound query grammar, the mapping from query objects to visual components and back is not a difficult task. Even the generation of basic input forms automatically created by the use of formal field definitions can be applied.

In addition, the visual query language should at least provide support for Boolean queries, image features and some parameters. Especially the features require attention, because entering them manually can be a very tedious work. There should be a visual tool to create and alter features. Otherwise, it can only be used for QBE. Considering the fuzzy nature of CBIR, these features need to understand range queries and wild cards.

Having graph like queries, it is of importance, how the objects are spatially arranged. The amount of overlaps and crossing joints should be low.

Table 1. Query composing

Type	Advantages	Disadvantages
Query String	highly flexible	must be learned complex feature tedious
Query-By-Example	simple	seed image by upload or other query
Query-By-Sketch	no image required	relies on user's painting skills requires canvas
Query-By-Feature	no image required	user needs basic feature understanding
Random	trivial rough overview	trivial
Browsing by	good overview	requires structured/
meta data	directed search	annotated content

Of course, incremental query building should be also supported, allowing to integrate newly found information into the query. This way, the query might grow very complex. In this case, sub-queries should be visually collapsed to hide details of an internal sub-query.

Query Language Principles

According to the problems mentioned in section *Identification of Problems-Query Language*, the query language should follow these basic principles:

- Keep it simple
- Keep flexible
- Keep it parseable
- Avoid ambiguities
- Stick to a reasonably sound mathematical grammar

This ensures both a reasonably understandable language as well as a sound theoretical background. The basis chosen for this is the language proposed earlier (Pein, Lu, & Renz, 2008b). Designed to be a flexible CBIR language, it provides all the functionality needed for the next steps. It is also easily convertible into an object-oriented format. These objects will be the nodes of the query graph. These nodes can hold and display all the information of the query. That is a visual representation of query images or a given feature as well as additional parameters.

Relevance Feedback

Relevance feedback gives the user some control to influence the search results. Usually the user can judge the quality of a result set and give the system hints to improve future retrieval sessions. The feedback mechanism is always closely related to the user interface, either to allow direct input or to analyse the users behaviour in the background.

Short-term relevance feedback can be implemented by simply altering the query in the background. If the user dislikes certain images, they are added as a negative example with a certain threshold to remove a couple of images from the result set.

Long-term approaches require much more attention, as the index itself is altered. The impact of wrong information needs to remain low and the weight of positive must be higher than negative ones Müller et al. (2000).

The integration of relevance feedback in the developed system is not considered due to resource constraints. Nevertheless, a short-term relevance feedback mechanism is technically available on a low level. The boolean structure of the query language itself offers a couple of parameters to alter results.

Features and Similarity Measures

As the application areas for CBIR are multifaceted, it seems to be necessary to use multiple fv to describe similarity.

Feature Normalization

It is obvious that every fv developed has different characteristics. section *Related Work-Features and Similarity Measures* and section *Identification of Problems-Features and Similarity Measures* discuss some examples, where data format and the maths model are of various kinds. Also, calculating the similarity of two fv highly differs. Earlier tests with implemented fv indicated that the similarity values of two different fv models cannot be compared directly. While one fv model may usually rank the first 100 hits with a similarity of 0.99, another fv model may hardly ever return such a high value except from identical images (Pein, 2008). Thus, it seems to be beneficial to provide a normalization mechanism for fv plug-ins.

The challenge is to determine a useful normalization function that can be applied to every similarity calculation to make the results comparable with other, completely unrelated features. To do so, the behaviour of the similarity distribution of each fv is required.

Similarity Profiles

An empirical approach is used in order to determine the individual characteristics of a given fv model. This information is needed to normalize the similarity distribution of the model.

Every feature is tested against the same image dataset. Every image is used as a query to gener-

ate a full result set of the complete repository. These results are sorted by decreasing similarity. For each ranking position, the similarities of all search runs are accumulated, i.e. the average, the highest and lowest similarity.

The resulting profile consists of three monotonic decreasing discrete functions with $rank \in [1, |I|]$ and $average(rank) \in [0.0, 1.]$; $min(rank) \in [0.0, 1.0]$; $max(rank) \in [0.0, 1.0]$. These functions can be easily compared against each other and are the starting point for a normalization function. Naturally, these profiles depend on the image dataset used and may look significantly different with another repository. In section *Case Studies-Feature Normalization*, two image collections, mainly consisting of photographs are used.

Determining a Normalization Function

Aim of the normalization is to achieve a steadily decreasing profile. The first ranked image should have a similarity of 1.0 whereas the last ranked image should be at 0.0. In between, the profile should decrease steadily. In terms of a function, the optimal normalized profile would be:

$$s(x) = 1 - x; x = \frac{rank}{|I|}$$

Where rank is the ranking position of an image, |I| is the size of the repository and s is the similarity of the image to the query. The optimal profile from the equation above is visualized in Figure 4.

A normalization function requires to have the following characteristics:

- Every value $x \in [0.0, 1.0]$ must be mappable to an $f(x) \in [0.0, 1.0]$
- $f(0.0) = 0.0, f(1.0) = 1.0$
- $f(X)$ must be monotonic ascending
- Determinable by an algorithm
- Fast calculation

Figure 4. Optimal similarity profile

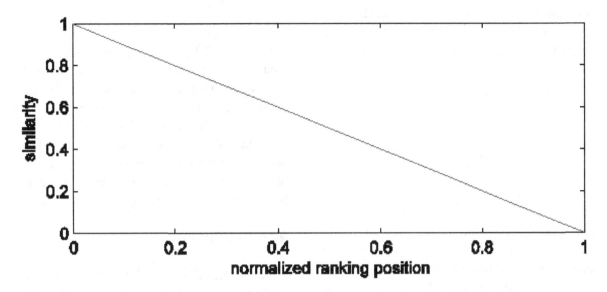

The retrieval system requires every fv plug-in to return only similarity values in the range [0.0, 1.0] (section *Methods-Framework-Merging/Fusion*). Thus, every normalized value must also lie in between these boundaries. The end points of this range are fixed and must not be changed. Further, the original ranking order must also be maintained. This demands for a monotonic ascending function, preferably strict. To allow the system to adapt to changing environments, the normalization function should be automatically generated by an algorithm. Finally, the normalization should be fast to compute as it needs to be performed for every result in every search request.

In order to generate a normalization function, a set of data points $\sum_{i=1}^{n} P_i(x_i, y_i)$ for interpolation can be extracted from the profile. These data points should be chosen carefully to ensure a high quality. If too few points are chosen, the interpolated function may become inaccurate. Too many points may unnecessarily slow down the calculations.

For interpolation between each two points $P_0(x_0, y_0)$ and $P_1(x_1, y_1)$ in the normalization function, the common linear model $y = y_0 + (x - x_0)\dfrac{y_1 - y_0}{x_1 - x_0}$ is chosen. It is fast and ensures keeping the monotonic characteristics of the profile. Polynomial or spline interpolation may cause overshooting of the curve, thus changing the ranking order. Also, a perfectly smooth normalization function is not mandatory, as a very high accuracy is not demanded and the functions does not need to be differentiated.

Evaluation of Retrieval Systems

The current effort put in the development of benchmarks is immense. Whole conferences are determined to apply benchmarks to restricted application areas. It is almost impossible to find a globally useful benchmark.

Nevertheless, default metrics such as precision/recall should always be used when testing the performance of a system. Also it is in the responsibility of each researcher to pick an appropriate data base for testing. Each available benchmark has its right to exist, but one must carefully choose the right ones.

In this part two existing databases (i.e. eth80 and caltech101) are used for evaluation. The basic metrics used are precision π and recall ρ that are defined as follows according to Rijsbergen (1979):

$$\pi = \frac{tp}{tp + fp} = \frac{R \cap retrieved}{|retrieved|}$$

$$\rho = \frac{tp}{tp + fn} = \frac{R \cap retrieved}{|R|}$$

where tp stands for the *true positives*, fp for the *false positives* and fn for the *false negatives*. The *true negatives* tn are not used in these equations. In order to capture both precision π and recall ρ in a single value, the fmeasure or the effectivity measure by van Rijsbergen (Rijsbergen, 1979) is applied:

$$F_{\beta} = 1 + \beta^2 * \frac{\pi * \rho}{\beta^2 * \pi + \rho} \quad E = 1 - \frac{1}{\alpha\left(\frac{1}{\pi}\right) + (1 - \alpha)\frac{1}{\rho}}$$

where β and α are weights to modify the balance between precision and recall. In section *Case Studies-Semi-Supervised Learning*, the results of the system are also compared to a reference learning approach.

Framework

The retrieval engine is supposed to be powerful enough to handle both textual and content-based queries. Primarily the engine needs to fulfil the requirements given by the user interface. Mainly the previous prototype (Pcin, 2008) and the Lucene tool kit (Lucene, 2006) were used.

Similarity Search

The main problem is the lack of a generic indexing structure. While small repositories can handle a linear scan, large ones require better solutions. Approaches like pre calculating clusters of similar images and the use of multidimensional trees are to be implemented. Examples are the prototypes by Joshi et al. (2006) and Quack et al. (2004). In order to minimize potential side effects of index based retrieval, no indexing technique is applied. Instead, a full scan is performed during ranking.

Merging/Fusion

The main difficulty of combining sub results from a CBIR system is the fuzzy nature of the results. Some simple features with filtering character (e.g. keywords) deliver a rather clean set of hits. But it is essential to have a a fuzzy model for merging these with highly similarity based features. Those results are usually a sorted list (Fagin, 1996, Ramakrishna, Nepal, & Srivastava, 2002). The approach by Fagin (Fagin, 1996) interprets results as *graded sets*, which are lists sorted by similarity and set characteristics. He uses the basic rules defined by Zadeh (Zadeh, 1996).

The text retrieval concept of *boosting* single terms by any float value is adapted to the extended engine. Before merging sub results, the similarities are boosted as specified to shift the importance into the desired direction.

An additional acknowledgement to the fuzzy nature is the use of additional set operators to keep the results at a reasonable size. The *minimum similarity* is a value between 0.0 and 1.0 and forces the engine to drop all results below this similarity threshold. As the efficiency of the threshold highly depends on the available images and features, a *maximum size* parameter limits the result to the specified size.

In the current prototype, a query q (eqn. 8) is defined in the following way:

$$q = C \cup C^+ \cup C^-$$

$$c = subquery\,or\,term$$

$$C = \left\{ c \mid c \in q \right\}$$

$$t = field\,or\,feature\,name\,and\,data\,f(i)$$

$$f\left(i\right) = feature\,of\,image\,i$$

where c is a subquery or term and t is a single term that can be processed as a single retrieval request. The subsets C, C^+ and C^- contain the clauses for $SHOULD\_HAVE$, $MUST\_HAVE$ and $MUST\_NOT\_HAVE$. The similarity is defined as:

$$s(f\left(i_q, f\left(i_x\right)\right) = similarity\,of\,i_q\,to\,i_x\,by\,f = s_x$$

where $s(f\left(i_q, f\left(i_x\right)\right)$ is the similarity between two images i_q and i_x. It is defined for each feature f independently. The result sets are defined as:

$$r\left(q\right) = [r(C^+) \cap r(C)] \setminus r(C^-)$$

$$r\left(t\right) = \{(i_x, s_x) \mid i_x \in I \wedge s_x \in [0.0, 1.0]\}$$

$$r\left(c\right) = \begin{cases} r\left(q\right) & if\,c\,is\,subquery \\ r\left(t\right) & if\,c\,is\,term \end{cases}$$

where the results $r(c_x)$ of each boolean clause c_x are a set of tuples (i_x, s_x). Each one contains a retrieved image i from the repository I and the similarity s to the query feature. These sub results are merged according to the unary operators of each clause:

$$r\left(C^+\right) = I \bigcap_{x=1}^{n} r(c_x^+)$$

$$r\left(C\right) = I \bigcup_{x=1}^{n} r(c_x)$$

$$r\left(C^-\right) = I \bigcup_{x=1}^{n} r(c_x^-)$$

First, the $MUST\_HAVE$ results $r(C^+)$ (eqn. 17) are intersected, which hopefully reduces the total search space for the $SHOULD\_HAVE$ clause that generate $r(C)$ (eqn. 18). This possibility of optimization is the main reason why no established fuzzy concept as proposed by Fagin (1996) or Zadeh (1996) is currently used. Based on this subspace, the second part of sub results is collected. These are joined and obtain a new weighted relevance. Finally, the $MUST\_NOT\_HAVE$ results $r(C^-)$ (eqn. 19) are removed from the final results r(q) (Pein, 2008).

CATEGORIZATION

According to Schapire (Schapire, 1990), classification tasks can be successful when using multiple "weak learning" algorithms. An important requirement for each weak learning algorithm is the ability of having at least a small classification advantage over random guessing. This section describes a learning approach published by the author of the part in more detail (Pein & Lu, 2010).

Unsupervised Learning

A totally unsupervised learning is not feasible for directly linking keywords to learned categories. Yet, it could be applied in order to build unlabelled clusters of similar images for each feature space. These clusters may be useful as an index for fast retrieval or to provide a quick overview of the repository (Saux & Boujemaa, 2002). They could also be manually annotated afterwards, if they are mainly describing a single concept.

Within the boundaries of this part this type of learning is not applied.

Supervised Learning

The proposed theoretical model is based on the following assumptions which are essential to justify the decisions described below. Most of which are necessary simplifications to tackle the still unsolved problem of the "semanticgap" (Smeulders, Worring, Santini, Gupta, & Jain, 2000, Jin, Khan, Wang, & Awad, 2005).

1. High-level semantics can be described by a set of low-level features
2. Certain low-level features are efficient in separating a set of relevant images from irrelevant ones
3. A reasonably large number of mutually independent features must be available to choose from to capture specific types of similarity
4. A single semantic concept can be represented by highly dissimilar images or image features (i.e. there is not necessarily a single "best describing feature")

Following these assumptions, a feature based query language (e.g. (Pein, Lu, & Renz, 2008a)) can be used in machine learning. Each concept to be learned can be mapped to a query containing low-level features only. The learned query itself would be a set of (boolean) combined low-level characteristics extracted from a training set. The algorithm suggested in this part analyses the results of CBIR queries to build a classifier. It is similar to the Cluster Boosted Tree approach by Wu and Nevatia (B. Wu & Nevatia, 2007), which is based on the AdaBoost algorithm by Freund and Schapire (Freund & Schapire, 1997). In their

algorithm, the training set is clustered according to the features before extracting the most suitable features for each sub cluster. A drawback of their approach is, that complex features may not be directly suitable for clustering, as the similarity measure is not necessarily identical to a multi-dimensional distance.

Capturing disjunctive sample sets of a single concept can be described with a disjunction (*OR*) operator. Samples of a semantic set are likely to have different low-level features. But according to the theory of fv based retrieval, series of samples are expected to be organized in clusters. These clusters are bounded by the features used. Often, a specific feature can be further optimized by removing irrelevant information (Praks, Izquierdo, & Kucera, 2008), making it more expressive. Yet, it should not be the task of a single low-level feature to capture all possible samples and merge them into a single "all-knowing" descriptor. Instead, a higher level descriptor should merge them into a single semantic concept. According to Zhang and Izquierdo (Zhang & Izquierdo, 2006), this usually cannot be done by simply merging low-level descriptors directly, because many low-level features show a non-linear behaviour.

Some low-level features are very efficient in filtering a certain concept from a given repository. But inevitably, using only a single feature, the filtered results may still be cluttered by several false positives. Further filtering may be required and two cases should be considered separately. If the false positives are very similar to each other, a negated term (*NOT*) could remove the unwanted parts from the result. Another approach to improve a filter is to specify further, unique features to the desired concept. This can be modeled by a conjunction (*AND*) to define boundaries in multiple feature dimensions. Rather than trying to create a single "multi-feature centroid", the proposed approach tries to find multiple relevant centroids, regardless of the features used.

The learning algorithm requires a training and an evaluation set. In the case of supervised learning, both sets are identical. For each image of a concept, the suitability as a representative query term or "centroid" is checked. This is determined by the ability of containing many other related images in the query result set. In other words, precision and recall should be as high as possible.

The best describing retrieval terms can then be further optimized by calculating a suitable similarity threshold. These optimized terms are then combined in a single query by the boolean "OR". If the low-level features applied are suitable to capture the relevant characteristics for the learned concept, the resulting query should be able to return a set of concept related images with only a few errors.

In some cases, a set of unrelated images may find its way into the results. This effect could be reduced by adding representative "AND" or "NOT" terms to a query. This term should not be closely related to an existing feature in the positive query part to stress the desired or to "cut out" the unwanted parts with a high accuracy.

The final classification query then needs to be tested against the remaining evaluation set. The main target is to find the optimal balance between maximum query length and retrieval accuracy. The more terms are used, the slower the final retrieval will be and the risk of over fitting increases. The query can then be used to calculate the similarity of any unknown input image to the query-related class, which can also be interpreted as the probability of belonging to that particular class.

Semi-Supervised Learning

The transition from supervised learning to semi-supervised learning would essentially be to shrink the labelled training set to a small size. According to Smith (2004), a reasonable size trade-off would be approximately 10%. An alternative way of testing is the leave-one-object-out cross validation. Such a test, leaving one of the objects of a category out has been published by Leibe and Schiele (2003) using the ETH-80 dataset. A

similar test is performed in section IV for direct comparison.

The semi-supervised learning generally follows the same principles as the supervised approach section *Methods-Supervised Learning*. The main difference is the change in the training set T and the evaluation set E. Semi-supervised learning uses disjunct sets generated from the known relevant images.

DEFINITIONS

The proposed learning algorithm uses several sets of images. A repository contains a set of images $i \in I$. In order to start a training session, the repository is split twice. The concept to be learned is represented by the set of relevant images R. The remaining images N are considered to be non-relevant. For later evaluation, R is again split into two sets: the training set T and the evaluation set E. The describing features are contained in the feature set F.

$$T \cup E = R$$

$$T = E \left(supervised \right)$$

$$T \cap E = \left\{ \; \right\} (semi - supervised)$$

$$R \cup N = I$$

$$R \cap N = \{\}$$

Example

A schematic visualization of the concept is depicted in Figure 5. It shows a 2 dimensional space, where each dimension represents the similarity for a single feature. The simplified example features *A* and *B* are extracted from each image and are represented by a single natural number. The similarity between two fv is a direct mapping from the distance: $s_{xy} = \left| f(i_x) - f(i_y) \right|$. The features *A* and *B* are assumed to be largely independent, i.e. the y are not (closely) related to each other.

Description of the relevant documents (black squares) by the use of features A and B. Irrelevant documents (white circles) should be excluded. Each box depicts a describable cluster.

An example for sufficiently independent features are a "colour histogram" and the "contour" of an object which have no direct relationship among each other.

Relevant images are represented by black squares, irrelevant images by white circles. The aim of the learning algorithm is to find a query, which contains as few parameters as possible covering as many relevant images as possible. At the same time, the amount of irrelevant images should be reduced to a minimum.

In the given example, the relevant images are forming clusters along certain values of each feature. This is an expected and necessary characteristic, which is required to learn a concept in the proposed way. It allows to describe a high-level concept with a set of low-level features. The resulting optimized query could look like this:

$$(f_A : [12.5]@1.5 \; NOT \; f_B : [16]@15) \; OR$$
$$f_B : [7]@1 \; OR$$
$$f_B : [28.5]@1.5 \; OR$$
$$(f_A : [8.5]@1.5 \; AND \; f_B : [21]@15)$$

Every term of this query is used to define a bounded area, where relevant images are located. The second and third term are the easiest ones. In both cases, they cover a reasonable amount of hits (5 respectively 3) and only a single false positive each. The fourth term exploits a useful coincidence, as the images satisfy both features at the same time very well. In that case, the target area can be reduced effectively by intersecting both features into a single result set. Term one illustrates a common problem when using low-level features. The term $f_A : [12.5]@1.5$ describes a large number of relevant images. Unfortunately, about one third of the results are in fact irrelevant. A considerable part of the unwanted result can be described by feature *B*. Subtracting the hits which satisfy the term $f_B : [16]@1.5$ removes two thirds of the false positives, boosting the precision of the remaining cluster.

The final result set based on the assembled query contains 22 relevant images and a single miss. In addition, this query generated only 4 false positives. This can only be achieved by a clever combination of both features instead of using a single one. Finding a suitable query is a typical optimization problem.

Interpretation as Decision Tree

Building a categorization query can be interpreted as the process of constructing a decision tree. A single binary tree represents the likelihood that an image belongs to the learned concept.

Node

Each node v in the tree contains a set of retrieved images $\iota \subseteq I$, which are either a representative of the concept or not. During training, the precision $\pi(v)$ and recall $\rho(v)$ of each node can be calculated, as the relevant training images T_v are known.

$$\prod(\nu) = \frac{\left| T \cap \iota \right|}{\left| \iota \right|}$$

Figure 5. Feature space separation

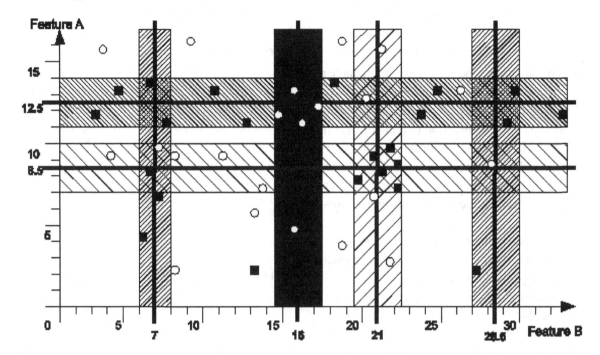

$$P\left(\nu\right) = \frac{\left|T \cap \iota\right|}{\left|T\right|}$$

$$\pi\left(\nu\right) = \frac{\left|T_\nu \cap \iota\right|}{\left|\iota\right|}$$

$$\rho\left(\nu\right) = \frac{\left|T_\nu \cap \iota\right|}{\left|T_\nu\right|}$$

$$\lambda = F_\beta$$

$\pi(\nu)$ (equation 27) is a measure for the categorization strength of a single node. If $\pi(\nu)=1$ the node only contains relevant images and if $\pi(\nu)=0$, the node does only contain irrelevant ones. In both cases, the nodes can be labelled as positive ν^+ or negative ν^- example. In reality, the precision is likely to be somewhere between these two ex-

tremes, which indicates an uncertainty $\nu^?$ about the categorization. The precision is interpreted as the equivalent to the local information gain in the ID3 algorithm by Quinlan (1986). The recall $\rho()$ (equation 28) is less important for each single node, as it is likely, that other nodes are containing some of the relevant images. A derived quality λ (equation 29), e.g. the F-Measure by Rijsbergen (1979) can be calculated for each single node. If it is based on the based on the precision and recall for the original training set T, λ is a measure for the global classification strength of a single node.

Node Splitting

Each node which cannot definitely be categorized as positive or negative example needs to be examined in more detail. A split criterion has to be found to divide the node into two more distinctive sub nodes. This criterion can be defined by a CBIR-query q over the still uncategorized ι_{parent} images. The query generates a result set $r(q)$ and the remaining data $r(q)^{-1} = \iota_{parent} \backslash r(q)$. These two sets are representing the content of the two child nodes. Assuming a strong query q, the set r(q) should have a higher precision and is stored in the "left" sub node. The set $r(q)^{-1}$ should have a lower precision than the original set and is stored in the "right" sub node. The aim is to push the precision as close as possible to either 1 or 0 in order to label the nodes accordingly. The "left" nodes should move towards 1 and the "right" ones towards 0. The splitting can be recursively performed until one of the following situations occurs:

1. The node contains no more images.
2. The precision π of the node either reached the upper or lower boundary.
3. Generating new splitting queries is not possible.

These situations are "hard boundaries", where further splitting is not possible or required anymore. For practical use, working against these boundaries may be unrealistic and cause an extremely long or even infinite processing time. For that reason, a set of arbitrary thresholds should be defined, e.g.:

1. Maximum query size.
2. Maximum tree depth.
3. Minimum information gain on a split.
4. Upper threshold of π to flag a node as positive: v^+
5. Lower threshold of π to flag a node as negative: v^-
6. Lower threshold of similarity s to create split query q.

After termination, the resulting binary tree should have all uncertainties resolved in the leaf nodes. The "left" leaves are considered to contain positive examples and the "right" leaves negative examples for the learned concept. A possible deci-

sion tree for the example (subsection *Example*) is shown in Figure 5.

Root Node

The root node v_{root} contains all images used in the learning process, both relevant T and irrelevant N ones. For this node, the precision can be calculated as follows.

$$\pi\left(v_{root}\right) = \frac{|T \cap I|}{|I|}$$

$$\rho\left(v_{root}\right) = \frac{|T \cap I|}{|T|} = 1$$

Null Query

The learning algorithm starts with an empty query q_{null}. By definition, this query is undefined and always returns an empty result set $r(q_{null})=\{\}$. Splitting by q_{null} generates an empty child node $v_{q_{null}}$ and another node $v_{\neg q_{null}}$ containing the same images as its parent. It follows $v = v_{\neg q_{null}}$. The root node can be interpreted as the "right" child of a parent node. The null query is also an example for an infinite recursion that can occur during learning.

LEARNING ALGORITHM

```
Algorithm 1.
findClassificationQuery(T,N)
1:  allA ← T
2:  result ←{}
3:  repeat
4:  queryq,λ,TruePositivesTP,FalsePos
itivesFP ← findBestQuery(T,N)
5:  if q = {} or |TP| < minTruePosi-
```

Figure 6. Decision tree

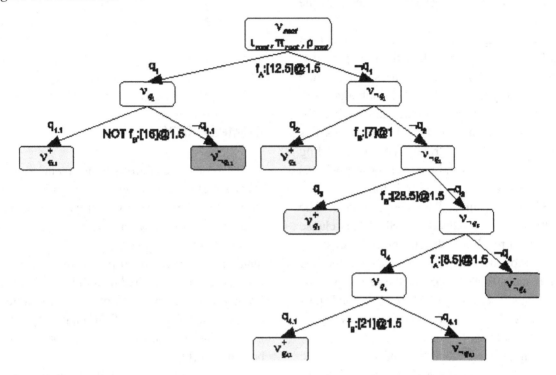

```
tives then
6:    return  result
7:    end if
8:    q,λ,TP,FP ←
addMustClauses(q,λ,TP)
9:    q,λ,TP,FP ←
addMustNotClauses(q,λ,A,FP)
10:   result ← result ∪ q
11:   T ← T \ TP
12:   until (|T| < minTermSize)
OR(|result| > maxQuerySize)
13:   return  result
```

Quinlan (1986) published an algorithm for building decision trees from a given training set. These trees are based on a probabilistic model and usually have problems with inaccurate or unclear definitions. A fuzzy approach by Yuan and Shaw (1995) tries to reduce this issue. Instead of using hard boundaries for separating nodes, a less strict separation is used.

In comparison, the learning algorithm 1 suggested in this part determines boundaries to split nodes into relevant and irrelevant data. These boundaries are represented by a single threshold which is set at a point, where the system assumes a reasonable trade-off to get a highly relevant image set after the split. As this threshold is used to cut off less relevant results in each single retrieval process, this boundary is not necessarily fixed. It can easily be moved towards creating either a smaller or larger result set, if required.

The algorithm tries to find a good, but not necessarily optimal query for a given concept. It is constructed to generate results in an acceptable amount of time that allows for realistic testing (i.e. ideally run times not longer than a day). The main aim of this algorithm is to examine the potential of the implemented fv and the query language for categorization tasks.

A concept is fed to the algorithm by providing a representative training set T and the negative set N. The resulting query should return a result set with a very high precision and recall for the target concept.

The training set T is copied to the local set of all relevant images A. Based on the provided data, the algorithm repeatedly tries to determine the best query for T and N. If the sub algorithm 2 is returning a query q and the true positives TP size is above the threshold minTruePositives, it is attempted to refine it further. The corresponding quality *quality* and the true and false positives TP and FP are used to search for MUST and MUST_NOT clauses that may extend q. The resulting q is then added as a SHOULD clause to the final result and the successfully retrieved TP is removed from T. This loop ends if the size of T reaches *minTermSize* or the result exceeds a previously set *maxQuerySize*. The conditions introduced in this algorithm are necessary to avoid over fitting.

The algorithm 2 attempts to find the best atomic query q for the given T and N. This is done by generating all possible stub queries q for each training image $t \in T$ and each feature vector $f \in F$. The sorted retrieval results S are then analyzed to find the best similarity threshold. Starting with a size of 2 and ending with $\min(|T|,|S|)$ (precision is expected to drop at bigger sizes), the result set size with the highest quality (e.g. F-Measure) is determined. The corresponding similarity value s for the lowest rank is then set as the threshold of the optimized query q. Finally, the best query is returned.

Algorithm 2. findBestQuery(T,N)

```
1:   q_result ←{},λ_result ← 0.0,TP_result
←{},FP_result ←{}
2:   for all t ∈ T, f ∈ F do
3:   q ← f(t)
4:   S ← getResults(q,T ∪ N)
5:   s,λ,TP,FP ←
calculateThreshold(S,T,N)
6:   q.threshold = s
7:   if λ > λ_result then
```

```
8:   q_result,λ_result,TP_result,FP_result ←
q,λ,TP,FP
9:   end if
10:   end for
11:   return  q_result,λ_result,TP_result,FP_result
```

COMPLEXITY

The proposed algorithm contains 2 main loops and at least one time consuming retrieval process. The execution of the repeat-until loop can be controlled by many factors. In essence, every iteration adds a clause to the query and further refines the result quality. For practical purposes, the amount of clauses should be limited to counter over fitting. From a complexity point of view, this loop is independent of the size of the image repository I. Thus, the runtime of this loop is considered to be constant ($O(1)$).

The crucial runtime is within the for loop. It iterates through all permutations of training images and features, raising the complexity with both the amount of training images $|T|$ and features $|F|$ involved. In the worst case, the complexity of this loop is $O(|T|*|F|)$. Realistically, the amount of features used is limited and the training set should be small. The most crucial factor in the training algorithm is the getResults() function, which performs the CBIR queries. If this function does not use an index, the execution time is linear, as every single image in the repository needs to be compared to the query. The index-less complexity would be $O(|I|)$, but in some cases, the index could guarantee a complexity of $O(1)$.

The optimization functions addMustClauses() and addMustNotClauses() both contain a restricted version of the learning algorithm. They are only called for already found base clauses. Thus, in the worst case, their complexity is the same, but usually a small subset of images needs to be checked. By adding sophisticated caching mechanisms and reuse of previous result sets, the execution time could be reduced significantly.

Query Descriptors

The proposed learning algorithm is one possible way to generate a feature-based query for each category to be learned. This query can be considered to be a low-level "descriptor" for a category. Using it in combination with an unknown image, a fuzzy probability of belonging to a certain category could be calculated. This value could be determined by finding the single best describing clause in the query descriptor or by applying the whole query descriptor to the fv of the unknown image. Query descriptors are defined as:

$$\omega = \left(q, category \right)$$

$$\Omega = \{\omega_1, \dots\}$$

where ω is a tuple of the query q and the category being represented. Ω is the set of all query descriptor tuples.

Classifying unknown images with a set of query descriptors encounters similar problems as in biometric systems with multiple sensors. Jain et al. (2005) describe several types of information fusion, split into "pre-classification" and "post-classification".

Pre-Classification Fusion

The first stage of fusion occurs when an unknown image is fed to a single query descriptor. This is done by a "feature level fusion" (**Jain et al., 2005**). Instead of creating a simple "weighted summation" or "concatenation" of the features, the calculations in a query descriptor are more complex. Each descriptor contains similarity thresholds, weights and Boolean rules to combine the results from the basic features. The resulting probability φ is a value in the range [0.0, 1.0]. A drawback of this approach would be the use of multiple feature vectors from different domains

that are insufficiently fine-tuned towards each other with respect to the similarity measures. While certain feature vectors may rank many images with values above 0.99, another one may only assign a value of 0.75 to highly similar images. This problem is addressed in section Case Studies-Feature Normalization.

Further, the thresholds of the Boolean clause in the query need to be considered. Their initial purpose is to suppress all results below that threshold from appearing in the result set of a search. The threshold of each positive clause is chosen in a way to be a reasonable trade-off between a high precision and recall in the remaining results. Thus, many relevant images may still lie below this threshold which is especially true for unknown objects from the same category. A classificator should still be able to recognize these relevant images. The retrieval algorithm simply pulls the similarity value of images below the threshold to 0.0, effectively removing them from the result set. The classification is less radical and min-max normalizes the calculated similarity according to the threshold θ.

$$\phi(\omega, i) = normalize_{(sq(i), \Theta)}$$

$$normalize\left(x, \Theta\right) = \begin{cases} \dfrac{1}{1-\Theta}\left(x - \Theta\right) if\, x \geq \Theta \\ \dfrac{0.5}{\Theta}\left(x - \Theta\right) if\, x < \Theta \end{cases}$$

where $s_q(i)$ is the calculated similarity between query and image i, φ(ω,i) is the probability of i to be a member of the category of the descriptor q and θ is the top level similarity threshold within q. The normalized probability is set to be 0.5 at θ by using linear interpolation. This normalization is performed recursively for each Boolean clause in the original query. As a result, the probability value is a direct indication as to how well an unknown item matches the descriptor. If $\phi \geq 0.5$, the image would appear in the result set of the query and if $\phi < 0.5$ it would be removed. The set of all probabilities Φ is defined as:

$$\Phi\big(i\big) = \{\phi(\omega,i) \mid \omega \in \Omega\}$$

where $\phi(\omega,i)$ is the probability of image i to be described by the query in ω,.

Post-Classification Fusion

At the second stage, multiple probabilities ϕ_q need to be considered and the system uses the information to make a decision. In the pure classification use-case, the output is a single category to describe the previously unknown object. A sophisticated fusion of probabilities is not required and a "dynamic classifier selection" also known as "winner-takes-all" (Woods, Bowyer, & Jr, 1996) is applied. The major disadvantage of this approach is the loss of accuracy by ignoring other categories which also may have high probability values:

$$category\big(i\big) = \{category \mid \big(q, category\big) = \\ \omega \wedge \phi\big(\omega,i\big)\arg\max{}_\phi(\Phi(\omega,i))\}$$

where category(i) is the set of categories that are assigned to the image i. In this case, it contains the category with the highest probability.

In retrieval related use-cases, it is desirable to tag unknown images automatically with a set of possible labels. Various systems automatically assign label sets to unknown images, assuming that most of them are correct, allowing the user to find those images by label while accepting a couple of false positives in the result (Smith, 2004, Jin et al., 2005).

REFERENCES

Apache Software Foundation. (2006). *Apache Lucene.* Retrieved from http://lucene.apache.org/

Buijs, J. M., & Lew, M. S. (1999). Visual learning of simple semantics in ImageScape. In Visual '99: *Proceedings of the Third International Conference on Visual Information and Information* Systems (pp. 131-138). London, UK: Springer-Verlag.

Doulamis, N., Doulamis, A., & Kollias, S. (1999). A neural network approach to interactive content based retrieval of video databases. Proceedings 1999 International Conference on Image Processing, ICIP 99, Vol. 2, (pp. 116-120).

Fagin, R. (1996). Combining fuzzy information from multiple systems (extended abstract). In PODS '96: *Proceedings of the Fifteenth ACM SIGACT-SIGMOD-SIGART Symposium on Principles of Database Systems* (pp. 216-226). New York, NY: ACM.

Freund, Y., & Schapire, R. E. (1997). A decision-theoretic generalization of on-line learning and an application to boosting. *Journal of Computer and System Sciences, 55,* 119–139. doi:10.1006/jcss.1997.1504

Hibino, S., & Rundensteiner, E. (1995). *A visual query language for identifying temporal trends in video data.* International Workshop on Multimedia and Database Management Systems.

Jain, A., Nandakumar, K., & Ross, A. (2005). Score normalization in multimodal biometric systems. *Pattern Recognition, 38*(12), 2270–2285. Retrieved from http://www.sciencedirect.com/science/article/B6V14-4G0DDW4-1/2/d922960ee7ed8928744113dd9494d37a doi:10.1016/j.patcog.2005.01.012

Jin, Y., Khan, L., Wang, L., & Awad, M. (2005). Image annotations by combining multiple evidence & wordNet. In Multimedia '05: Proceedings of the 13th Annual ACM International Conference on Multimedia (pp. 706-715). New York, NY: ACM.

Joshi, D., Datta, R., Zhuang, Z., Weiss, W. P., Friedenberg, M., Li, J., et al. (2006). PARAgrab: A comprehensive architecture for web image management and multimodal querying. In *VLDB '06: Proceedings of the 32nd International Conference on Very Large Data Bases* (pp. 1163-1166). VLDB Endowment.

Leibe, B., & Schiele, B. (2003, June). *Analyzing appearance and contour based methods for object categorization.* In International Conference on Computer Vision and Pattern Recognition (CVPR'03).

Muller, H., Muller, W., Marchand-Maillet, S., Pun, T., & Squire, D. (2000). Strategies for positive and negative relevance feedback in image retrieval. *Proceedings 15th International Conference on Pattern Recognition,* 2000, Vol. 1, (pp. 1043-1046). Retrieved from citeseer.ist.psu.edu/327327.html

Pein, R. P. (2008). *Hot-pluggable multi-feature search engine. Memoire de Master non publie.* Hamburg University of Applied Sciences.

Pein, R. P., Amador, M., Lu, J., & Renz, W. (2008, Juillet). Using CBIR and semantics in 3D-model retrieval. In *8th IEEE International Conference on Computer and Information Technology, CIT 2008,* (pp. 173-178).

Pein, R. P., & Lu, J. (2010). *Multi-feature query language for image classification.* In International Conference on Computational Science, ICCS 2010. Elsevier. (Accepted for publication)

Pein, R. P., Lu, J., & Renz, W. (2008a, July). An extensible query language for content based image retrieval. *The Open Information Science Journal, 3*(17), 81–97.

Pein, R. P., Lu, J., & Renz, W. (2008b, July). An extensible query language for content based image retrieval based on Lucene. In *8th IEEE International Conference on Computer and Information Technology, CIT 2008,* (pp. 179-184).

Peng, W., & DeClaris, N. (1997, October). Heuristic similarity measure characterization for content based image retrieval. *1997 IEEE International Conference on Computational Cybernetics and Simulation, Systems, Man, and Cybernetics, 1,* (pp. 7-12).

Praks, P., Izquierdo, E., & Kucera, R. (2008, October). The sparse image representation for automated image retrieval. In *IEEE International Conference on Image Processing* (pp. 25-28).

Quack, T., Monich, U., Thiele, L., & Manjunath, B. S. (2004). Cortina: a system for large-scale, content-based web image retrieval. In *Multimedia '04: Proceedings of the 12th Annual acm international Conference on Multimedia* (pp. 508-511). New York, NY: ACM.

Quinlan, J. R. (1986, March). Induction of decision trees. *Machine Learning, 1*(1), 81–106. doi:10.1007/BF00116251

Ramakrishna, M. V., Nepal, S., & Srivastava, P. K. (2002). A heuristic for combining fuzzy results in multimedia databases. In *ADC '02: Proceedings of the 13th Australasian Database Conference* (pp. 141-144). Darlinghurst, Australia: Australian Computer Society, Inc.

Rui, Y., & Huang, T. (2000). *Optimizing learning in image retrieval (Vol. 1,* p. 1236). IEEE Computer Society on Computer Vision and Pattern Recognition.

Saux, B. L., & Boujemaa, N. (2002). Unsupervised robust clustering for image database categorization. *International Conference on Pattern Recognition,* Vol. 1, (p. 10259).

Schapire, R. E. (1990). The strength of weak learnability. *Machine Learning, 5*, 197–227. doi:10.1007/BF00116037

Sheikholeslami, G., Chatterjee, S., & Zhang, A. (1998, August). NeuroMerge: An approach for merging heterogeneous features in content-based image retrieval systems. *Proceedings International Workshop on Multi-Media Database Management Systems*, 1998, (pp. 106-113).

Smeulders, A. W., Worring, M., Santini, S., Gupta, A., & Jain, R. (2000). Content-based image retrieval at the end of the early years. *IEEE Transactions on Pattern Analysis and Machine Intelligence, 22*(12), 1349–1380. doi:10.1109/34.895972

Smith, J. R. (2004). *MARVEL: Multimedia analysis and retrieval system (Whitepaper)*. Hawthorne, NY: IBM T. J. Watson Research Center Intelligent Information Management Dept.

Torres, R. S., Silva, C. G., Medeiros, C. B., & Rocha, H. V. (2003). Visual structures for image browsing. In *CIKM '03: Proceedings of the Twelfth International Conference on Information and Knowledge Management* (pp. 49-55). New York, NY: ACM.

van Rijsbergen, C. (1979). *Information retrieval*. London, UK: Butterworths.

Woods, K., Bowyer, K., & Jr, W. P. K. (1996). Combination of multiple classifiers using local accuracy estimates. In *CVPR '96: Proceedings of the 1996 Conference on Computer Vision and Pattern Recognition* (p. 391). Washington, DC: IEEE Computer Society.

Wu, B., & Nevatia, R. (2007, Oct.). Cluster boosted tree classifier for multi-view, multi-pose object detection. In *IEEE 11th international Conference on Computer vision, ICCV 2007* (pp. 1-8).

Yuan, Y., & Shaw, M. J. (1995). Induction of fuzzy decision trees. *Fuzzy Sets and Systems, 69*(2), 125–139. Retrieved from http://www.sciencedirect.com/science/article/B6V05-4007D5X-C/2/62fa7de5b67d27ad22a38a1f4e6ba0e6 doi:10.1016/0165-0114(94)00229-Z

Zadeh, L. A. (1996). *Fuzzy sets*. River Edge, NJ: World Scientific Publishing Co., Inc.

Zhang, Q., & Izquierdo, E. (2006, April). *A new approach to image retrieval in a multi-feature space*. In International Workshop on Image Analysis for Multimedia Interactive Services.

Chapter 23
Design

Raoul Pascal Pein
University of Huddersfield, UK

Joan Lu
University of Huddersfield, UK

Wolfgang Renz
Hamburg University of Applied Sciences, Germany

ABSTRACT

In this chapter, a CBIR design based on previous work of the author (Pein, 2008) is presented. The available system already allows for a retrieval by a query string (Pein, Lu, & Renz, 2008a). In the context of this investigation, the system has been extended to support alternative user interfaces as well as a testing module used in the case studies below. Being a pure research prototype, the retrieval engine is optimized for generating accurate results in order to have a reliable data foundation. Further, the query language syntax and the constraints for a practical application of the learning algorithm are presented.

RETRIEVAL FRAMEWORK DESIGN

Most retrieval systems follow a basic work flow cycle (see section *Methods-Browsing*). A successful retrieval is performed as follows: users submit a query to the engine to trigger a search and receive a set of results. Those results may be satisfying and the user finds the required information. If not, the user may navigate through the results and eventually refines the previous query to trigger a new search.

Figure 1 illustrates the internal search steps performed by the retrieval engine. Three differ-

ent abstraction levels are employed (Pein, Lu, & Renz, 2008a).

At a very high abstraction level, a simple retrieval system receives a query from the user, parses it somehow to understand the meaning, gathers the most relevant documents and finally returns them. This work flow is very common and can be offered by a generic framework, which simply offers all the basic functionality required. These framework components do not have to be specialized. They only need to understand standardized input and generate standardized output. All the details and optimizing are meant to be implemented in exchangeable plug-ins on the use-case dependent implementation level.

DOI: 10.4018/978-1-4666-1975-3.ch023

Figure 1. Layers in the retrieval process (Pein, Lu, & Renz, 2008a)

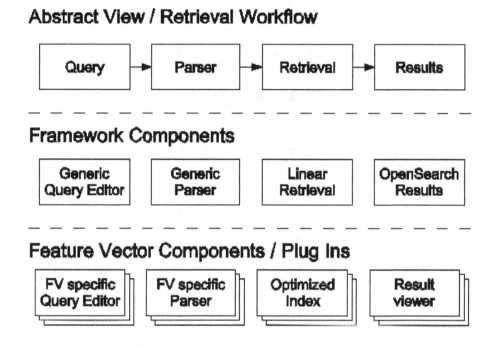

MAIN COMPONENTS

The main components of the system and their dependencies are presented in Figure 2. This diagram is a simplification of the true dependencies to ensure readability. Every single component makes use of "util." Several system components developed for the preceding master thesis have been extended within this part: "core," "admin," "client," "util," "plugins," "web" and "server." These have mainly been extended by an optional indexing structure for the plugins, XML support and additional interfaces. Completely new are the components "parser," "tester" and "composer."

The "core" component contains all CBIR data structures. It also defines the generic interfaces for the "Framework Components" in Figure 1. The "util" is a loose collection of several useful methods that are required in several other components. The "plugins" are a collection of optional fv implementations. They are essential to

make the CBIR work, but the choice of these plug-ins is up to the user.

The other components provide the actual realizations for work flow and user interfaces. "server" and "parser" are purely to provide the work flow. The "server" encapsulates the linear retrieval work flow of Figure 1. It accepts queries, forwards it to the "parser," performs the retrieval and returns the results.

The "admin" component encapsulates the functionality to manage the image repository. The main tasks are adding new images and extracting the fv. This information is written into the repository for later use by the retrieval software.

The retrieval components usually require read-only access to the repository (without relevance feedback). Two retrieval clients have been developed by the author of this part. A fat client solution is contained in the "client" package, containing a full graphical user interface to access the "server." A thin client is provided by the "web" package, allowing to use the "server" without the need of

Figure 2. Main components

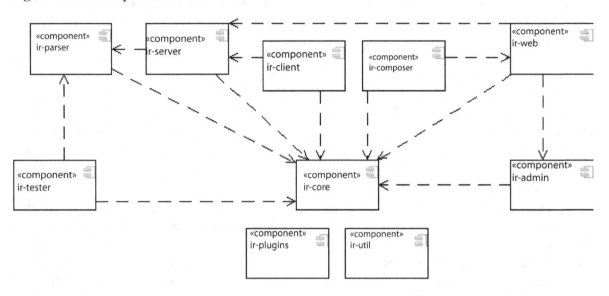

installing special software on the client machine. The UI of this package is supposed to be minimalistic, containing a user interface for directly submitting query strings and displaying results. On top of this service, a graphical query building software — the "composer" — is provided.

A special component is the "tester." It contains a collection of time-consuming algorithms for analyzing the repository and also for learning the query descriptors.

Speed and Quality

The earlier system developed by the author had been optimized for a high accuracy rather than a high processing speed (Pein, 2008). Each retrieval request is processed linearly by comparing the query fv to each stored fv. To provide a better scalability, the system is extended to support arbitrary indexes. Depending on the type of fv, an extremely feature specific index is required. However, a high accuracy is more important to optimize the feature normalization and learning methodology than a short response time. No user is required to be operating the system after starting a test, thus the algorithms are able to run automatically during the night.

Speed and Quality

The query language in the proposed system (Pein, Lu, & Renz, 2008a) is based on the Lucene Query Syntax (Lucene, 2006). It is intentionally chosen to provide beginners with a simple and familiar syntax.

Wildcards and Ranges

Wildcards and ranges can be used to express uncertainty or to allow the search engine to be less strict during retrieval. The meaning of those concepts depends on the described feature. Some features may well benefit, but for others they may not be required.

In text retrieval, wildcards stand for letters in a word that don't have to match an explicit query. In the example case of a RGB mean value, a wildcard can express, that a certain colour channel does not need to be considered. For spatial features it can be useful to define regions of interest as well as regions of non-interest.

Ranges are an intermediate concept between concrete queries and wildcards. They are used to specify a certain space where parameters can be matched. Searching for images with a creation time stamp is only feasible, if a range can be specified. It is very unlikely, that the searcher knows the exact time, especially when it is extremely accurate (i.e. milliseconds). In such a case, usually a time span is provided (e.g. "between 03/06/08 and 10/06/08" or "within the last week"). Analogous, image features such as the trivial RGB mean could specify a tolerance range for each colour channel.

Unfortunately, these definitely useful concepts cannot be fully generalized. At this point, the plug-in developer needs to decide how to address them. Taking the RGB means of an image, the user could specify an array like *"[36, 255, *]."* In this case the results should contain some red and dominant green. The rate of blue does not matter at all. Putting some more effort into the feature abstraction, a more convenient query like *"some red and very much green"* is also possible. This lies in the responsibility of the plug-in developer.

Parse Trees

Based on the grammar, the parser generates a hierarchy of sub queries wrapped up in a single root query object. By traversing the tree, the sub results can be merged accordingly. This section shows the decomposition on a relatively complicated query. The images used in this example are part of the Caltech-101 collection (Fergus et al., 2003).

```
(
  (
   histogram:"file://query.jpg" OR
   rgb_mean:([200, 50, *])^2.0
  )@0.8
  -wavelet:(89 244 345)@0.9
  +keywords:airplane
)#100
```

Verbally, this query can be read as follows:

"Find images, that have a similar histogram as the sample image query.jpg OR have a mean colour close to 200 red and 50 green. The blue channel can be anything. Rank the mean colour twice as high as normal. Both sub results should have at least a similarity value of 0.8. Please remove any result, that has a minimum wavelet similarity of 0.9 to the images 89, 244 and 345. Every result must be annotated with the keyword airplane. Find not more than 100 results in total."

After parsing, the query string is converted into a parse tree that contains all of the relevant concepts (Figure 3). The root node is represented by a *Query*, which is the single data object that is processed by the retrieval core. Each leaf is a *Term*, representing a partial search, which generates a sub result. The tree structure in between represents the rules how to merge the sub results into a final one.

The search engine then traverses the tree and generates the answer to this particular request. At this point, it is advisable to integrate a query optimizer to reduce the response time. In the current prototype, some straightforward query optimizing already takes place.

First, the *MUST* clause are processed, then the *SHOULD* and finally the *MUST_NOT* clause. This allows for an early reduction of the search space, which is especially of importance, if no index or only a slow index is available for certain features. Depending on the availability of indexes, the terms with the shortest processing time should be preferred. The optimization strategy should always be aimed at an early reduction of search space as well as preferring the use of fast indexes. The strategy applied in this case uses a strict definition of *MUST* and *MUST_NOT*. If an image is not part of all the *MUST* clause or part of a *MUST NOT* clause, it is removed from the final result. This approach is considered to be a useful trade-off between a perfect fuzzy algebra and speed optimizations.

Figure 3. Parse tree of a complex query

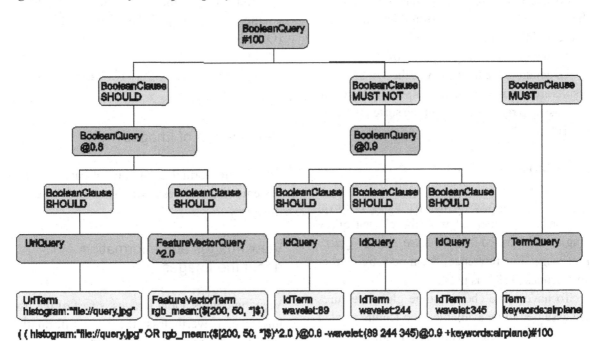

{ (histogram:"file://query.jpg" OR rgb_mean:($[200, 50, *]$)^2.0)@0.8 -wavelet(89 244 345)@0.9 +keywords:airplane}#100

In this case, the first term to be processed is "keywords:airplane." This triggers a keyword search, which is backed by a fast and efficient index, resulting in a list of matching images. As the parent *BooleanClause* is flagged as *MUST*, the final results of the query can only be amongst those sub results. Assuming, that only about 1% of the repository is related to the keyword "airplane," every subsequent linear search time can also be reduced to only 1% of the otherwise total scan time.

The second branch to be processed is the *SHOULD* clause on the left, that is split into a nested boolean query.

One leaf contains a *UrlTerm*, pointing at an external query image and requesting a comparison based on its histogram. To process this part, the engine reads the image from the URL and extracts the histogram automatically. This search only needs to compare the query histogram with the stored histograms from the previous sub result.

The other leaf contains a *FeatureVectorTerm*. The string embedded between the "(" ")" brackets is parsed by the *rgb_mean* plug-in. In this case, the string stands for the three mean colour values *red* (200), *green* (50) and *blue* ("don't care" wildcard) of an image. Again, the search space is drastically reduced by the first sub result.

After both terms have been processed, the sub results are merged into a single one. Their combined similarity must be at least *0.8*, otherwise the image is removed from the result set. There is no "best" rule to merge the sub results. Within this part the algorithm of merging described in section *Methods-Framework-Merging/Fusion* is used.

In this case, the *rgb_mean* branch has a weight of *2.0* and thus gains a higher importance in the merged result.

The last main branch is flagged as *MUST_NOT* and requires a minimum combined similarity of *0.9*. All of the three clause contain a plain *IdQuery* with an *IdTerm*. They require a retrieval on the wavelet feature and use sample images from the repository by stating the image id directly. Again, the search space is already limited, not only by the *MUST* branch, but also by the *SHOULD* branch. It is only necessary to check the images contained in the previously retrieved sub result. The sub results of the middle branch are merged accordingly and cropped at a minimum similarity of 0.9.

To generate the final answer, the *MUST_NOT* results are removed from the temporary sub result. The last step required is to cut the sorted list after the 100 best hits.

Browsing

This section analyses, which parts of a retrieval session can be realised with the chosen query language described in section *sec:Design-Query Language*. For reference, the model by Garber and Grunes (1992) is used.

To have some choice, some global features are assumed to be available. The feature related strings are bracketed within ($ and $).

Generate Criteria and Weightings

This can be done in several ways, depending on the feature extensions available.

Find red images:

```
fv_mean:($[255,0,0]$)
```

Find either an orange image or a fruit with double weight on the colours:

```
fv_mean:($orange$)^2
keywords:"fruit"
```

Enter Picture and Similarity Criteria

Find similar images to 123 based on wavelets (QBE):

```
fv_wavelet:123
```

Find similar images to the image "http://example.net/query.jpg" based on its histogram (QBE):

```
fv_histogram:"http://example.net/
query.jpg"
```

Retrieve Set of Images

This is the normal behaviour of each retrieval system. A set of results is generated based on the query.

View Images and Information about the Images

Viewing details about images is part of the user interface. Nevertheless, the meta information stored in the index should be readable.

Put on or Remove from Light Table, et cetera

Again, this is part of the user interface, not of the query processing.

Add Criterion

This can be done by adding a boolean term to the existing query.

Find images that are orange AND are tagged with the keyword "fruit."

```
fv_mean:($orange$) AND
keywords:"fruit"
```

Add Restriction

Restrictions can be added by specifying a NOT term.

Find images that are wavelet-similar to image 123 and remove images that have more than a 0.9 histogram similarity to image 987.

```
fv_wavelet:123 NOT fv_histo-
gram:987@0.9
```

Change Criterion

Changing a criterion is equivalent with changing the contents of a term. This could be the field/feature name or the data to be found.

Re-Define Search

Resetting the query and starting from scratch is no problem, as long as each search request is a single transaction.

Pull Target Image

This final step is again in the responsibility of the client software. If the results are returned with the URL of the images, this is easy to implement.

Most of the browsing aspects by Garber and Grunes (1992) can be represented by the chosen query language. Some functionality also requires support by the browser application itself, such as marking and remembering possible hits.

Learning Algorithm

The learning algorithm described in section *Methods-Categorization-Learning Algorithm* attempts to find the optimal result within the given parameters, e.g. minTermSize, maxQuerySize. To keep the complexity within reasonable boundaries and to prevent over fitting, these values are set manually.

The weighting factor β between precision and recall to measure the quality of each tested query (equation 7 and equation 29) is set to $\beta=0\_2$. This effectively shifts the threshold for each clause to a high value, resulting in small result sets with a high precision.

Concerning top-level SHOULD clauses, three parameters are set. In order to be able to ignore outliers, the amount of true positives found by a SHOULD clause must be $|r(c)| \geq 5$ to be included in the query. Equally, the training set must have at least a size of $|T| \geq 5$. A break condition in the main loop is the maximum amount of iterations generating positive SHOULD clauses. It is restricted to $|C| \leq 20$ to keep the query descriptors at a reasonable size and also ensuring reducing the maximum processing time of algorithm 1.

Similar considerations are valid for the additional MUST_NOT clauses. The amount of clauses added to each top level clause must be $|C^-| \leq 5$ to prevent a high amount of negative clauses. The training set must have a size of $|r(c)| \geq 2$. This value has been chosen, as tests indicated that often only a small group of related false positives appeared within the results. Similarly, each clause must remove at least $|r(c^-)| \geq 2$ false hits, i.e. every negative clause must remove at least two false positives from the intermediate result.

The last set of rules has been set for the MUST_HAVE clause. Constructing an intersected pair of results should always happen by using an unrelated fv. Using two independent fv would restrict the search space in both feature spaces and make the resulting intersection very robust (section *Methods-Supervised Learning*). As a very hard condition, not a single true positive must be lost by using a second clause. This prevents the algorithm to accidentally cutting out relevant images. Further, the amount of MUST_HAVE clause in the final query indicate, how well two independent fv are able to capture the same concept.

Multi Threaded Processing

Most tests can be parallelized. Every test with a high processing load is split into smaller work units. Dependent on the available processor cores and memory available, a semaphore (typically set to 2*cores) controls the amount of parallel threads. This is especially necessary when having a large number of threads or resource intensive ones. The default pattern works as follows:

1. Initialize system (e.g. CBIR service)
2. Assemble list of tasks to be done
3. Iterate through tasks
   a. Create runnable object ("work unit")
   b. Initialize work unit
   c. Wait for available semaphore
   d. Start work unit as thread
4. Wait for all threads to finish
5. Clean up system (e.g. database connections)

REFERENCES

Apache Software Foundation. (2006). *Apache Lucene*. Retrieved from http://lucene.apache.org/

Fergus, R., Perona, P., & Zisserman, A. (2003, June). Object class recognition by unsupervised scale-invariant learning. In *Proceedings of the IEEE Conference on Computer Vision and Pattern Recognition* (Vol. 2, pp. 264-271). Madison, Wisconsin.

Garber, S. R., & Grunes, M. B. (1992). The art of search: A study of art directors. In *CHI '92: Proceedings of the SIGCHI Conference on Human Factors in Computing Systems* (pp. 157-163). New York, NY: ACM.

Pein, R. P. (2008). *Hot-pluggable multi-feature search engine. Memoire de Master non publie*. Hamburg University of Applied Sciences.

Pein, R. P., Lu, J., & Renz, W. (2008, July). An extensible query language for content based image retrieval. *The Open Information Science Journal*, *3*(17), 81–97.

Chapter 24
Case Studies

Raoul Pascal Pein
University of Huddersfield, UK

Joan Lu
University of Huddersfield, UK

Wolfgang Renz
Hamburg University of Applied Sciences, Germany

ABSTRACT

This chapter discusses several case studies to evaluate the methods introduced in chapter 23, Methods. Each case study focuses on a specific issue and the advanced cases build up on previous findings. The first ones are dealing with the low-level fv directly and then the scope widens to the interrelationship of multiple fv until their combination within a single query is used as a mapping rule for higher-level semantics (i.e. categories).

INTRODUCTION

Section *Case Studies-Feature Normalization* investigates the feasibility of an empirical feature normalization as proposed in section *Methods-Feature Normalization*. The normalization is expected to reduce the differences in similarity calculations among the implemented fv, resulting in comparable similarity profiles. This is especially required for the interpretation of similarities as probabilities and thus a more accurate fusion when using the query descriptors for categorization tasks (see section *Methods-Categorization-Query Descriptors*).

DOI: 10.4018/978-1-4666-1975-3.ch024

Section *Case Studies-Estimating the Improvement Capabilities of Different Features* describes a way to estimate the discriminative power of each single fv for all of the given categories within a repository. The derived improvement factor is supposed to indicate which fv is expected to be most powerful for use in a query descriptor to be learnt. It basically represents the first iteration of the learning algorithm in section *Methods-Categorization-Learning Algorithm*, generating a query only containing a single term.

In section *Case Studies-Supervised Learning*, a machine learning algorithm based on DT (section *Methods-Supervised Learning*) is applied to construct a set of category related queries. This case study is used to fine-tune the behaviour of the algorithm and to find reasonable parameters to find a reasonable balance between precision and recall and to avoid over fitting.

The descriptors constructed during the learning are used for a simple categorization in section *Case Studies-Query Descriptors*. Other than performing a full retrieval on the database, the query is only used to categorize a single image into a fixed category. Instead of using a fast fusion approach (section *Methods-Framework-Merging/Fusion*), a more accurate approach is applied (section *Methods-Categorization-Query Descriptors*) to determine the most likely category. The results are not expected to be highly influenced by the similarity characteristics of distinct features, as they have been already normalized (section *Methods-Feature Normalization*).

The final case study in section *Case Studies-Semi-Supervised Learning* wraps up the findings of all previous ones into the semi supervised learning approach described in section *Methods-Semi-Supervised Learning*. It directly compares the proposed learning approach to an existing one on the same data. A leave-one-object-out cross validation is performed to evaluate, how well an unknown object can be categorized.

FEATURE NORMALIZATION

As mentioned in section *Methods-Feature Normalization*, each fv creates a different similarity curve between 100% match and the least relevant document. Similarities of features are not comparable to other features. For that reason, it is attempted to capture the fv specific similarity profiles and use them to normalize the similarity values within each retrieval.

Requirements

- Default image database with use-case related content (e.g. photographs)

Testing

First, the original similarity profile of each feature vector plug-in is determined for both image repositories (ETH-80 and Caltech-101). For each ranking position, the average, minimum and maximum value are collected. These profiles are used as reference to create the normalization functions and to measure the changes according to the normalized profiles. Each average curve is split into 20 segments of equal size. The selected boundaries are 1.0 for $rank_0$ and 0.0 for $rank_{|I|+1}$. In between, the average similarity of each of the 19 equidistant ranking positions are used as reference points for the later normalization. The feature vector modules used: RGB Mean, Histogram, Spatial Histogram, Wavelet

The normalized similarity profiles are expected to be close to the desired function in section *Methods-Features and Similarity Measures-Feature Normalization-Determining a Normalization Function*. Especially for the dataset specific normalizations, the average values should produce only a small error. Normalization parameters extracted from a different image set are expected to result at least in a better profile than without normalization.

Results

This section presents the similarity profiles of the two image collections. In subsection *Original Profiles*, the original profiles are listed. Subsection *Normalized by ETH-80* and subsection *Normalized by Caltech 101* contain the normalized profiles according to the original profiles of each collection.

Original Profiles

Figure 1 and Figure 2 show the similarity profiles for the four feature vector plug-ins in the ETH-80 image set containing 3280 images and the Caltech-101 image set containing 9144 images. Comparing the profiles for both datasets shows

Figure 1. Similarities cumulated by rank (ETH-80)

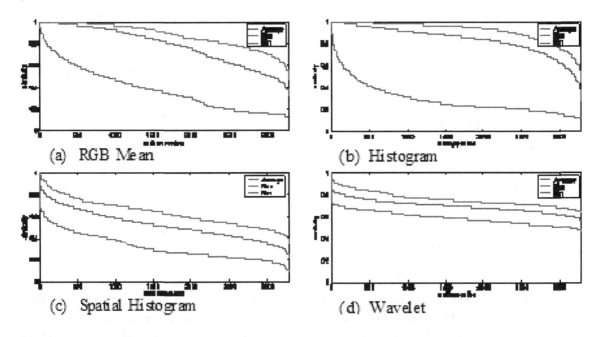

similar characteristics for each feature. Every single curve starts with a similarity of 1.0 (identity), as each query contains one of the images from the repository. Generally, all profiles are relatively smooth without obvious steps inside.

The RGB Mean produces a convex average profile with a relatively shallow decline until about 90% of the repository size. In the final part, the curve drops quickly to similarities near 0.2. The maximum value shows a similar trend, but on a slightly higher level. The minimum value

Figure 2. Similarities cumulated by rank (Caltech-101)

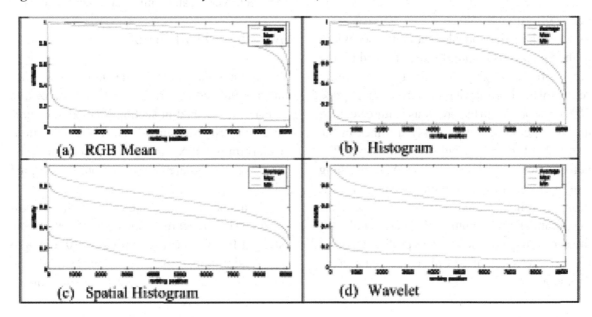

Figure 3. Similarities cumulated by rank (ETH-80, normalized by ETH-80)

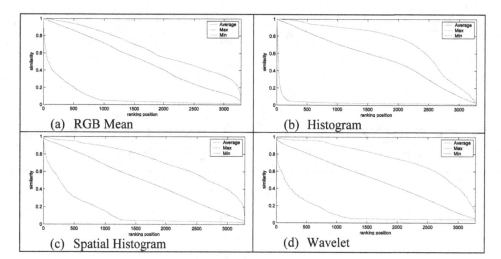

(a) RGB Mean

(b) Histogram

(c) Spatial Histogram

(d) Wavelet

drops quickly in the beginning and then the decline of the slope decreases. In general, the sections near the boundaries show a steep slope, which is even more evident in the Caltech-101 profile (Figure 1(a), Figure 2(a)).

The Histogram profiles are similar (Figure 1(b) and Figure 2(b)). In the ETH-80 profile, the decline of the three values is less steep in the central part compared to the ones of RGB Mean. In the Caltech-101 profile, the slope of average and max values is steeper than for the RGB Mean. Further, the minimum value drops very quickly below 0.1 (at rank 150).

The third pair of profiles shows the behaviour of the Spatial Histogram (Figure 1(c) and Figure 2(c)), forming roughly an "S"-shape. The central section of these profiles is relatively linear (approx. 80%). In contrast to the previous feature vectors, the average value very quickly declines in the first 10% of the profile below a similarity of 0.8 before entering the linear section. After reaching a similarity about 0.4, the average similarity starts dropping quickly again. For both data sets, the maximum and minimum profiles are roughly of the same shape as the average profile, whereas the extreme values of the Caltech-101 dataset are further apart.

The last feature vector to be tested is the Wavelet. Again, the profiles resemble an "S" (Figure 1(d), Figure 2(d)). Compared to the Spatial Histogram, the slope of the central section is shallower. For the ETH-80, most values lie in the corridor with a similarity between 0.6 and 0.8 and for the Caltech-101, the corridor is between 0.7 and 0.5. The maximum values are mostly 0.1 above the average values. For the minimum values, the ETH-80 profile is not much below the average profile, but on the Caltech-101 dataset, the gap between average and minimum values is about 0.5

Normalized by ETH-80

In Figure 3 and Figure 4, the similarity profiles are normalized according to the normalization function described in section Methods-Features and Similarity Measures-Feature Normalization-Determining a Normalization Function. The parameters used are extracted from the original similarity profile of the ETH-80 dataset.

As intended, the average values of the normalized ETH-80 (Figure 3) profile form a relatively straight line from (rank$_1$/similarity 1.0) down to (rank$_{|I|}$/similarity 0.0). Except from a slightly too quick drop near the first ranks and some minor

Figure 4. Similarities cumulated by rank (Caltech-101, normalized by ETH-80)

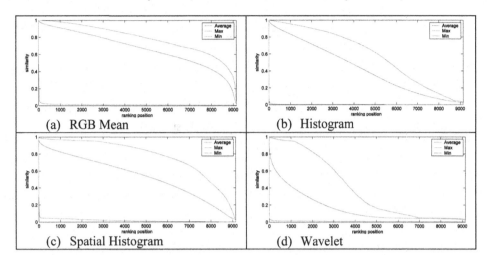

(a)　RGB Mean (b)　Histogram

(c)　Spatial Histogram (d)　Wavelet

bulges in the central section for RGB Mean (Figure 3(a)) and Histogram (Figure 3(b)), the normalized average values are close to the desired shape. In the central section, the extreme values are further apart from the averages than in the original profile.

The same normalization applied to the Caltech-101 image dataset is much less fitting the desired function Figure 4. Nevertheless, at least the actively used similarity range is clearly more evenly distributed between 1.0 and 0.0 than before (Figure 2). The average values of three profiles are closer to the intended function, but in the case of the Wavelet feature (Figure 4(d)), the profile is too steep in the beginning and too shallow in the second half. In all four profiles, the minimum drops to similarities below 0.1 very quickly.

Normalized by Caltech 101

In Figure 5 and Figure 6, the similarity profiles are also normalized according to the normalization function described in section *Methods-Features and Similarity Measures-Feature Normalization-Determining a Normalization Function*. The parameters used are extracted from the original similarity profile of the Caltech-101 dataset.

Applying the Caltech-101 normalization on the ETH-80 images generates profile not quite fitting the desired function (Figure 5). The average similarities take advantage of the full range from 0.0 to 1.0, but the curves are much less straight than in the ETH-80 normalized case (Figure 3.). Especially the Wavelet feature profile is not close to the intended function, but lies far above it (Figure 5(d)). The average similarity for $rank_{|I|}$ is 0.33.

As intended, the average values of the normalized Caltech-101 (Figure 6) profile form a relatively straight line from ($rank_I$/similarity 1.0) down to ($rank_{|I|}$/similarity 0.0). The most prominent deviations are the initial quick drop to similarities around 0.95 for the highest ranks. The maximum values do not show any special behaviour. Again, the minimum values drop extremely quick below a similarity of 0.1.

Analysis

Below, the results of the testing procedure are being analyzed. Especially the deviation from the reference function is calculated to determine the individual error for each test case. The figures below plot the four similarity profiles of the feature vectors and their absolute error compared to the

Figure 5. Similarities cumulated by rank (ETH-80, normalized by Caltech-101)

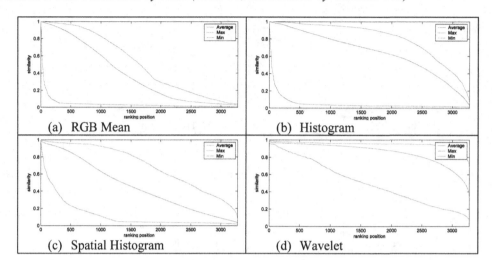

reference function (dotted line). In the summary (subsection Summary), the errors of all features are compared to each other.

The error $\in$ for each rank and the cumulated error E are defined as

$$\in_{rank} = \left| \left(1 - \frac{rank}{|I|} \right) - s\left(rank \right) \right|$$

$$E = \sum \in_{rank}$$

where s(rank) is the average similarity of all results at position rank.

Original Profiles

Figure 7 contains all similarity profiles for the average values for the ETH-80 image repository. In the range up to approximately rank 400 ($\approx 12\%$ of |I|), the Spatial Histogram and Wavelet features reach an error of about 0.2 because of their initial steep drop. With a growing rank, the error drops to 0 and then rises up to 0.57 (W) and 0.277 (SH).

Figure 6. Similarities cumulated by rank (Caltech-101, normalized by Caltech-101)

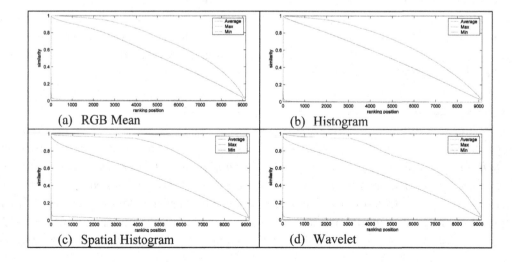

Figure 7. Error of original similarity profiles for ETH-80 images

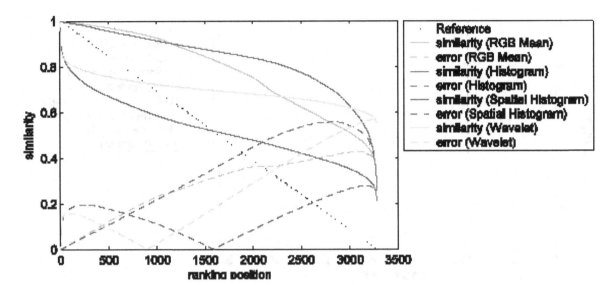

The error of the other features RGB Mean and Histogram ascend much slower and peak in the less relevant ranks around 3000 ($\approx$ 90% of |I|).

In Figure 8, all similarity profiles for the average of the Caltech-101 repository are contained. The error graphs have comparable characteristics to the previous profiles. Below the 2000 ($\approx$ 22% of |I|) Spatial Histogram and Wavelet both show

their first error peak above 0.2 and their second one around rank 8500 ($\approx$ 93% of |I|). Again, the error of the other features RGB Mean and Histogram ascend much slower and peak in the less relevant ranks around 8500.

Figure 8. Error of original similarity profiles for Caltech-101 images

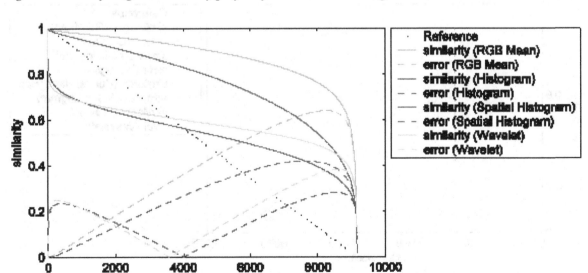

Figure 9. Error of normalized (ETH-80) similarity profiles for ETH-80 images

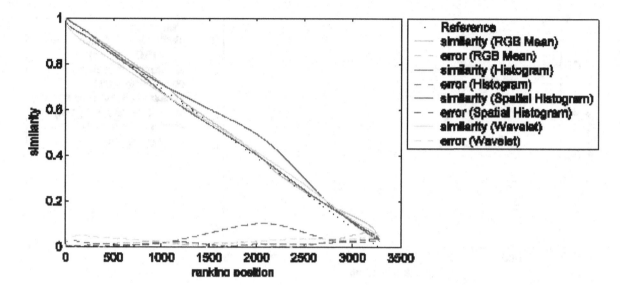

Normalized by ETH-80

In Figure 9, the error for the optimized ETH-80 dataset is depicted. It shows a very low error for all four features, whereas the Histogram feature vector shows a small error bulge around rank 2000 ($\approx$ 60% of $|I|$) with a peak deviation of 0.1.

Figure 10 is based on the Caltech-101 images, optimized by the ETH-80 parameters. Most features have an error below 0.1 for the first 2000 ($\approx$ 22% of $|I|$) ranked results. On later ranking posi-

Figure 10. Error of normalized (ETH-80) similarity profiles for Caltech-101 images

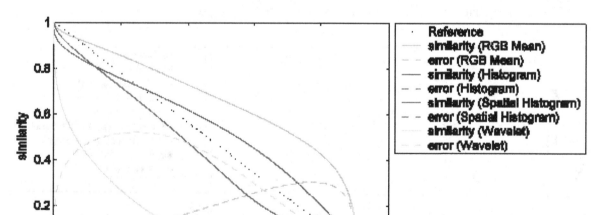

Figure 11. Error of normalized (Caltech-101) similarity profiles for ETH-80 images

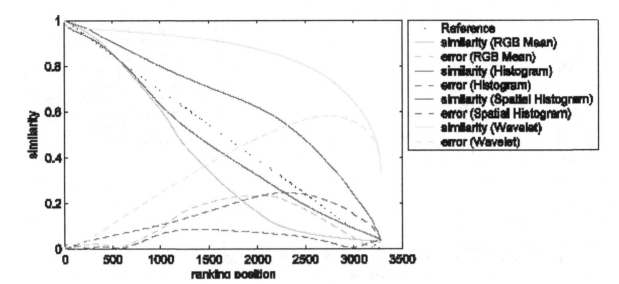

tions, the error of the RGB Mean feature keeps increasing, while Histogram and Spatial Histogram remain below 0.1. The worst performing feature is the Wavelet. At rank 2000, the error peaks at about 0.5 and then decreases again.

Normalized by Caltech 101

In the opposite way — the ETH-80 images profiled with the Caltech-101 function (Figure 11) — the results are less convincing than in Figure 10. While the Spatial Histogram always remains below 0.1, the RGB Mean and Histogram exceed the 0.2 in the second half of the results. Again, the worst normalized feature vector is the Wavelet. Opposed to the ETH-80 normalized Caltech-101 profile, the average similarity slope of the Wavelet feature is too shallow in the first half.

In Figure 12, the error for the optimized Caltech-101 dataset are plotted. As intended, the error for all four features is very low and always remains below 0.1. The strongest deviations can be seen for the Spatial Histogram and Wavelet features in the first 2000 results ($\approx$ 22% of |I|) where the average similarity is below the reference.

Summary

A concise overview of the results described above is given in Table 1 and Figure 13. In most test cases, the normalized similarities push the total error E below 50% of the original results. The only exception to this rule are the two Wavelet based errors while using the normalization parameters from the opposing image repository. If the matching normalisation parameters are chosen, E always remains below 0.056 (highest value for Caltech-101, RGB Mean). Using the "wrong" parameters, the best performing features generate an error twice above the optimized ones. The best improvement has been achieved for the RGB Mean feature in the ETH-80 dataset where the error is reduced to 6% of the original error.

Discussion

Generally, the expectations were satisfied by the test. Using database specific normalization parameters, the total error could be reduced in every case. This leads to much easier comparable feature vectors. The normalized similarity value between query and repository image is

Figure 12. Error of normalized (Caltech-101) similarity profiles for Caltech-101 images

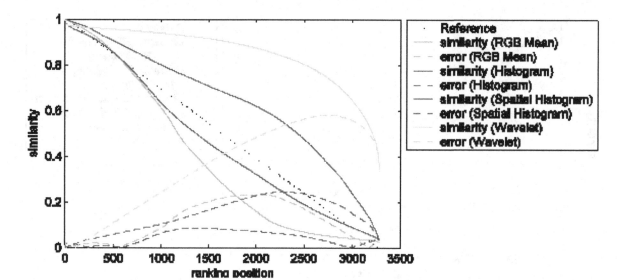

now roughly indicating the relative position of the image in the ranking independently from the feature vector used.

Using the normalization parameters of a different image set worked surprisingly well. At least, the similarity range [0.0,1.0] is used more evenly than before. The only real exception is the Wavelet feature. The main reason for this behaviour lies in the similarity calculation that returns values above 0.5 in almost any case (see Figure 1(d) and Figure 2(d)). This causes the normalization function to be inaccurate for values between 0.0

and 0.5 where in this case of the original range are mapped to only of the normalized range. Also, the lower boundary for $rank_{|I|+1}$ is arbitrarily mapped to 0.0 even if the similarity between two feature vectors may never be close to this value.

Another problem becomes evident in the highest ranks. Especially the features with higher dimensionality (i.e. Spatial Histogram and Wavelet) tend to drop too quickly at high similarities. A finer granularity of the normalization function in this range might reduce this effect. This issue also raises the question, if it is necessary to normalize

Table 1. Cumulated average error

dataset	feature vector	original	normalized ETh-80	normalized Caltech-101
ETH-80	RGB Mean	0 .28085	0 .0173	0 .11572
	Histogram	0.33513	0.040525	0.14398
	Spatial Histogram	0.14362	0.014856	0.044396
	Wavelet	0.24816	0.028131	0.35692
Caltech-101	RGB Mean	0.37754	0.055727	0.17042
	Histogram	0.26203	0.031286	0.075503
	Spatial Histogram	0.15737	0.03166	0.064893
	Wavelet	0.19342	0.031768	0.33909

Figure 13. Cumulated average error

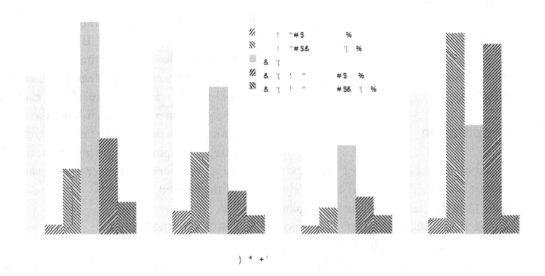

the similarities at less relevant ranks. A retrieval system is supposed to return a relatively small set of highly relevant results rather than a fully sorted list of all known documents. Even for the highly unclear boundaries of CBIR, it usually makes no sense to return everything. Instead of separating the whole range into equi-distant segments to determine the normalization function, another approach may be more useful. One possible approach would be a logarithmic segmentation by recursive binary splitting of the respective "upper" half of the ranking. This would easily scale to large databases without losing accuracy or storing too many normalization points. Also the error function should treat deviation in the highly relevant sections more than in the less relevant ones.

The minimum values have a tendency to be extremely low, especially in the caltech101 dataset (Figure 2). This can be explained by a collection containing at least one image having no similarity to any other image. As the minimum profile is generated by using each image of the repository, such an outlier far away from any cluster of similar images easily pulls the boundary down. Thus, the minimum values do not have a very high expressiveness for this case study except

from showing the extremes. More useful for future testing could be a set of given confidence intervals to determine statistical boundaries of how many similarity values are below or above a given threshold.

Summary

The above testing procedure can be applied during the development of new fv. In multi-feature applications, the similarity function for each pair of vectors may not easily be constructed to generate homogeneous distribution of similarities. Generating a set of normalization parameters would simplify this task and it would also allow for a use case specific optimization.

ESTIMATING THE IMPROVEMENT CAPABILITIES OF DIFFERENT FEATURES

This section evaluates the estimated improvement capabilities of each implemented fv. It is calculated, by which factor a fv can improve the retrieval performance for various categories. This information is a valuable help to select a certain fv to be used for searching a category.

Requirements

*   Default image database with annotated categories

Data Preparation

The fv used have various levels of complexity. The simplest one is a trivial RGB mean value, previously used for tests in a query language (Pein, Lu, & Renz, 2008a) (*mean*). Much more sophisticated is the use of 12 stochastic moments from the image histograms by Al-Omari and Al-Jarrah (Al-Omari & Al-Jarrah, 2005) (*stochastic2*). The same feature is also used in fv with added spatial awareness, by splitting the original image into a quad tree of histograms (Pein & Lu, 2006) (*stoch_quad*). Finally, a wavelet based feature is used (Jacobs et al., 1995) (*wavelet*). It is expected that the measured quality of the four fv is related to the complexity level.

These fv are applied on the Caltech 101 image repository (Fei-Fei et al., 2004). This collection consists of 101 categories with $|I| = 9144$ images, each one depicting a specific object. The images are reasonably well normalised by scaling, centring and rotating the objects into comparable positions. A set of more or less random background images is also included.

The testing has been carried out on a PC with "Intel Core2 Duo" CPU (2 * 2.33 GHz). A data collection run took approximately 4 hours. During this time, no speed-optimizing indexing has been used by the CBIR search engine and each query has been compared to every available image in the repository. Thus, the retrieval results represent the "optimal" quality without any loss caused by indexing techniques. Further, this case study does not use the normalized similarities.

Data Collection

For the benchmark preparation, the whole repository is imported into the CBIR system, extracting the image features and the category keywords. Then every single image feature is used as a query and the first 50 ranked results of each retrieval are stored in a database. Among the first 50 hits should be as many related images from the same category as possible. The higher the recall for the target category, the higher the measured quality of the fv used.

Data Normalization

A known issue of the Caltech 101 dataset is the strong variation of category sizes $|R_{category}|$. Some of which are under-represented with only as much as 31 images and others contain 800 samples. Therefore, the collected data needs to be normalized.

First of all, the under-represented images have to be adjusted to the other categories. This is done by calculating a normalized recall value $0 \leq \rho \leq 1$ for the first 50 results:

$$\rho_{normalized} = \frac{tp}{\min\{|R_{category}|; 50\}}$$

The second necessary step is the normalization of these recall values according to the size of each category set. The random precision π_{random} of picking an image of the required category depends both on the repository size n and the amount of samples for a category $|R_{category}|$:

$$\pi_{random} = \frac{tp + fn}{tp + tn + fp + fn} = \frac{|R_{category}|}{|I|}$$

With this data, the result quality of every single query can be directly compared to random picking, calculating an improvement factor τ.

Figure 14. Improvement factor

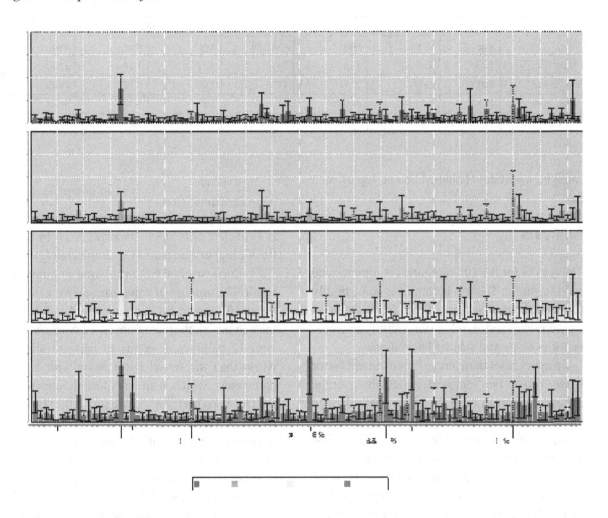

$$\tau = \frac{\rho_{normalized}}{\pi_{random}}$$

Values below 1 should never occur in realistic scenarios, as this would indicate that randomly choosing images from the repository performs better than using the benchmarked fv. The higher the improvement factor, the better. For each category, the averages and the standard deviation of the improvement factor are calculated.

Results

The findings of testing the 9144 images in 102 categories are visualized in Figure 14 and summarized in Table 2. Also, a couple of sample images from various categories are presented (Figures 28 - 32).

Figure 14 visualizes the strength of every feature to recognize a specific category. Each bar represents a single category, sorted alphabetically by the given folder name of the collection. The height of a bar represents the average improvement τ that has been achieved by using the corresponding fv. The standard deviation is indi-

Table 2. Summarized improvement

Feature	Average				Standard Deviation		
	avg	min	max	avg ≥ 10	avg	min	max
mean	7.37	1.69	37.4	20	4.51	1.14	22.3
stochastic2	6.81	1.46	27.11	17	4.01	0.72	29.73
stoch_quad	11.57	2.25	85.04	37	7.89	1.32	50.48
wavelet	14.0	1.34	71.23	50	9.07	1.09	41.04

cated by a vertical H-shaped line on top of each bar.

Analysis

The results for the 102 categories is summarized even further in Table 9. It compares some highly condensed characteristics of each fv, i.e. the *average*, *minimum* and *maximum* for both improvement factor average and standard deviation.

In many cases the average improvement factor is close to 5. For some categories, the average value ranges from 10 to 85. These peaks depend on the fv used and do not occur in every diagram equally. The amount of peaks is relatively low with the *mean* (Figure 14 a) and the *stochastic2* (Figure 14 b) fv. The number increases with the *stoch_quad* (Figure 14 c) and *wavelet* (Figure 14 d) fv. The standard deviation of each category/ feature pair varies from about 10% of the average to more than 100%. The fv used do not seem to have a large impact on this behaviour and the standard deviation seems to be closely related to the average with a factor of

$\frac{average}{standard\,deviation} \approx 1.5$. In comparison, the average improvement of the more sophisticated fv (*wavelet: 14.0, stoch_quad: 11.57*) is by a factor of 2 higher than that of the simpler ones (*mean: 7.37, stochastic2: 6.81*) in relation to a random result. The amount of categories above a threshold of 10 shows a similar tendency. According to these numbers, the histogram based fv *stochastic2* with 12 parameters seems to perform slightly worse than the trivial RBG *mean* with only 3 parameters, which is an unexpected outcome.

The worst performing category is the "BACKGROUND_Google" (Figure 15). The average improvement factor of all four fv represents the minimum in Table 2. All four values lie very close to 1. This means, there is almost no improvement compared to random picking at all. As this specific category is defined by being an unsorted collection of random images with no particular semantics, the algorithms cannot find any useful information that links any two of these images together.

One of the best recognized categories is the "car_side" (Figure 16). With some knowledge

Figure 15. Caltech 101 - category subset: BACKGROUND_Google

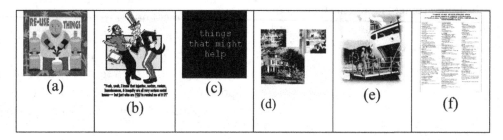

about the contained images and the fv used, the reason becomes obvious immediately. Every fv used in this investigation is analysing the image colours and this category is the only one which consists completely of gray scale images. Thus, each fv is able to cope with it very well.

The most prominent feature-dependent results are found in the category "inline_skate" (Figure 17). This is probably due to the fact that the samples this category are very homogeneous. With only 31 images, this is one of the smallest categories, but the object, background and orientation of most representations is very similar (mostly gray, white, front points to the left). While the purely colour based fv generate reasonable results, the ones which consider spatial information too are capable of retrieving most related images directly (*stoch_quad: 85.04, wavelet: 71.23*). The large standard deviation is caused by the few outliers, where background or orientation differ. Some other categories, such as "cellphone," "minaret" and "pagoda" benefit also from the spatial information and especially very similar backgrounds.

A category with a very high standard deviation is the "stop_sign" (Figure 18). This set contains 64 samples of an highly iconic motive. All over the world, stop signs look almost identical, especially according to shape and colours. Approximately half of the samples show a stop sign with only very small portions of background (e.g. Figures 18(a), 18(c), 18(e), 18(f)). These images form a very compact cluster in th feature space. On the other hand, several images show the sign embedded in scenery or from an angle. These samples form a less defined cluster, where the fv have far less distinction to samples from other categories.

In general, higher bars indicate a better performing fv for a specific category. Also, the standard deviation should be relatively low. In that case, a CBIR system would return a large set of highly similar images for every existing query image for a category. This benchmark approach could be beneficial to compare the performance of various fv and for fine tuning new ones. It compensates most of the imbalance in category sizes and also takes the repository size into account. It also indicates, which image categories can be handled easily and where the fv specific problems lie. The further summarized parameters (Table 2) can be used as a more general benchmark.

Limitations

This case study uses the well known image Caltech 101 repository (Fei-Fei et al., 2004), which has certain weaknesses. Due to limited resources, the investigation did use the complete image to extract a fv instead of applying a sophisticated regional clustering algorithm. Thus, the background of the images may have a strong influence on the results.

Also, some categories contain several sub-categories of very similar objects. The "airplanes" (Figure 19) with 800 samples contains military jets, commercial and private planes of all sizes on different backgrounds (e.g. sky, grass, concrete). These sub-categories may cause a very strong recall among each other, but other semantically related images could not be retrieved, causing a low average improvement. Very small classes with a homogeneous image set easily achieve a much better recall. Picking a more homogeneous repository would probably help to overcome these fundamental issues.

The amount of fv tested was relatively small. Each one used colour information, but not a single one is capable of extracting and matching certain objects and their shapes. In future benchmarks, additional fv implementations are going to be tested and compared.

As the benchmark performs a retrieval query with every single image in the repository and for every fv to be assessed, this benchmarking approach does not scale very well. Without further optimizations, the run time is at least linearly increasing with the repository size. If non-ideal results are also acceptable, the use of dedicated indexing structures for each fv could largely increase the scalability of this approach.

Discussion

The case study shows up a way of comparing several fv according to their classification abilities. It was attempted to minimize the influence of the inhomogeneous Caltech 101 image collection (Fei-Fei et al., 2004) in the results. The final normalized data indicated that the complex *stoch_quad* and *wavelet* features are suitable to retrieve several image categories in this repository very well. Other categories may require another fv or are simply too inhomogeneous to be retrieved. The benchmark provides feedback of how homogeneous the samples of a category are. In some cases, it might be beneficial to split a category into more detailed sub parts with additional semantic value.

Summary

The average provides evidence of how well a given category can be clustered by using the feature vector and its similarity function. The average improvement factor ranges from 1.34 up to 71.23 (both for the wavelet feature). In this case study, a suitable threshold seems to be 10. The total amount of categories above this threshold correlates with the average improvement factor and is another quality indicator.

The standard deviation visualizes, how the clusters of highly similar images are composed. A low deviation (i.e. $\lesssim 2$) indicates clusters of similar size. A high deviation (i.e. $\gtrsim 10$) in contrast indicates clusters of unequal size. This can be a problem, if for example single images of a category contain a very special representation. Then these special instances cannot be retrieved easily with the system.

SUPERVISED LEARNING

In this section, the learning algorithm described in section *Methods-Categorization-Learning Algorithm* is evaluated. This section mentions some results published in a recent conference paper (Pein & Lu, 2010).

The testing has been carried out on a Solaris 10 x86 server system with 4 CPU-cores used in parallel.

Requirements

- Image set of annotated categories

Preparation and Implementation

The image collection used is the ETH-80 collection from the ETH CogVis project (Leibe & Schiele, 2003, Leibe et al., 2004). It contains in total 3280 images of 8 different annotated object categories. Each category contains 10 different objects and have an equal size of 410 images. Each object is available from several angles and is located in front of a blue background. Additional data about the object boundaries are also available from black and white mapping files. This collection is sufficient to test the already available fv modules without

Figure 16. Caltech 101 - category subset: car_side

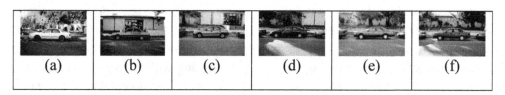

Figure 17. Caltech 101 - category subset: inline_skate

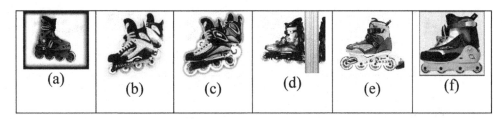

the additional need of segmentation algorithms. Further advantages of using this image set are:

1. Each image represents a single object/concept
2. The object/concept to be learned fills most of the image area, is centred and completely visible
3. The ETH-80 collection provides additional mask files which define the relevant segment

In this case study, a set of relatively simple fv is used, which are described in (Pein, Lu, & Renz, 2008a). Both the RGB and the H module are also extended and only use the relevant pixels defined by the provided map files. Both SH and W remain unchanged. They are expected to be sufficient for evaluating the learning algorithm, as they usually return better results than random guessing (see. (Schapire, 1990)). More advanced fv are currently not available for testing, but could easily be added to the system in the future, as this learning approach allows for modular extensions.

Prior to running the learning algorithm, all images were imported into the CBIR repository. At that stage, the time consuming feature extrac-

tion takes part once. The remaining computation then relies on these stored fv. To eliminate the influence of non-optimal indexing structures, a full scan over all existing fv is performed for each single retrieval step.

For each of the eight categories, the given 410 images are used as training set. To prevent over fitting, the algorithm is manually limited to a maximum of 20 SHOULD clause and at most 3 additional MUST/MUST_NOT clause for each positive one.

Testing

The testing process is split into several steps, adding more detail information each time. This is achieved by enabling more options in the learning algorithm.

1. Single Clauses
2. Multiple SHOULD Clauses
3. Additional MUST/MUST_NOT Clauses
4. Additional Boost Parameter

Every test run generates a query for each category. These queries are then analyzed in detail by

Figure 18. Caltech 101 - category subset: stop_sign

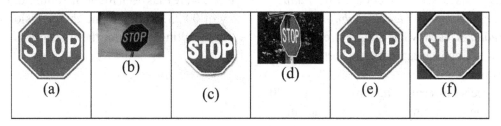

Figure 19. Caltech 101 - category subset: airplanes

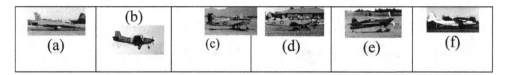

calculating the results they produce in the CBIR environment. For those results, Precision/Recall diagrams are generated. The result set size in the diagrams is normalized by the category size 410 and in some cases by twice that size (820) to the range [0.0,1.0]. Results above that size are not considered to be of high interest. The optimal retrieval would achieve a precision of $\pi = 1.0$ among the first 410 images and a precision of $\pi = 0.5$ for this result size is assumed to be reasonable in difficult cases. A searcher should browse at least these results in order to find a suitable image, simply because the repository contains that much relevant images. After this threshold, determined users should also find more relevant hits. Thus, the recall ρ should still increase, even though the precision is less crucial. If the precision is not very good for the minimum result size of 410, it is aimed to achieve an improved recall until 820.

The results of each test run are used to fine tune some learning parameters, such as the α of the F-Measure and combination rules. These parameters are also used in the subsequent runs. Further, this case study does not use the normalized similarities.

Results

Effect of Single Clauses

As already discussed in section *Case Studies-Estimating the Improvement Capabilities of Different Features*, each fv has unique strengths and weaknesses. For each category, the best available fv may vary.

The precision-recall diagrams in Figure 20 visualize the discriminative power of the single best fv found for querying each category. It is a first indication of how well a category can be learned with the available fv. The categories "apple," "pear" and "tomato" (Figure 20(a), Figure 20(g), Figure 20(h)) indicate a high achievable precision with short queries. As the category "cow" performs worst, it is used for assessing the optimization steps.

The F-Measure parameter $\alpha = 0.2$ appears to be a reasonable trade-off between precision and recall. By favouring the precision, the learning algorithm is forced to find more restrictive thresholds, filtering out more irrelevant results. This allows more complex queries to focus on multiple highly relevant clusters instead of trying to fit as much as possible into a single clause.

Effect of Additional Clauses and Tolerance

The detailed Precision/Recall and F-Measure values for four "cow" related queries are shown in Figure 21. The x-axis of the diagrams are normalized to the size of each category, i.e. 410 images. Lines ending earlier indicate result sets smaller than the expected 410 images.

Figure 21(a) represents the results for the single best clause. The precision drops relatively constantly with the increasing result set size towards a value of 0.35. The maximum quality (i.e. F-Measure) has been found at a minimum similarity of 0.823. At that point, the precision is 0.84. The resulting query for the first split is:

```
W:1750@0.823
```

Figure 34(b) shows the results for a query containing a set of several SHOULD clauses. Until a size of 76 images, the precision achieves the optimal value of 1.0. After that threshold, it quickly drops to 0.95 and after that then the precision slowly descends. The maximum result set size with this query is 360 images, containing tp = 304 true positives, fp = 56 false positives and the not retrieved false negatives fn = 106. The

resulting precision is $\pi = \dfrac{304}{304 + 56} = 0.844$ and

the recall is $\rho = \dfrac{304}{304 + 106} = 0.741$ More im-

ages cannot be retrieved, as the query contains a minimum similarity for each clause.

The highest ranked false positives are displayed in Figure 22. The first false positive is a black and white dog from different perspectives, followed by black cars with white/grey interior.

The query containing the 20 most relevant query features is:

```
W:1750@0.823   SH:2150@0.863
W:2333@0.833 W:1818@0.803
SH:1665@0.857 W:2143@0.804
W:1838@0.809 W:2083@0.773
W:2316@0.806   SH:2302@0.773
W:1921@0.814 RGB:2399@0.999
SH:1922@0.856 W:1811@0.824
W:1650@0.793 SH:1734@0.864
SH:1670@0.927 RGB:2405@0.999
W:1985@0.804 W:2151@0.799
```

Figure 21(c) is based on the full retrieved query containing additional negative clauses. In comparison to the previous query, the first false positive is already ranked at position 31, followed by a couple of other false positives. Again, the same dog and cars as from above are included in the results. As a first difference, the precision remains quite stable at a level of 0.9. Out of 323 retrieved images, tp = 286 are true positives, fp = 37 are false positives and fn = 124 related im-

ages are missing. The resulting precision is

$\pi = \dfrac{286}{286 + 37} = 0.885$ and the recall is

$\rho = \dfrac{286}{286 + 124} = 0.698$. Thus, the precision is

slightly better at the expense of the recall.

Figure 21(d) is based on an attempt to manually improve the calculated descriptor. The similarity thresholds for the first two positive clauses have been lowered by 10% in order to increase the result size and implicitly the recall rate.

```
(W:1750@0.741 -H:2908@0.988)
(SH:2150@0.776 -H:1560@0.970)
. . .
```

At a result size of 410 images, the precision is $\pi = 0.74$ and the recall is $\rho = 0.74$. While the precision is lower than for the other queries above, the recall is similar to the 20 SHOULD clauses. Yet, the total possible result set is about twice as large as for the restricted ones. Thus, the full result set contains 884 retrieved images and is separately depicted in Figure 24. The total amount of true positives is increased to tp = 356 and the still not retrieved false negatives are reduced to fn = 54. Thus, the final precision for the complete

retrieved result is $\pi = \dfrac{356}{356 + 528} = 0.403$ and

the recall is $\pi = \dfrac{356}{356 + 54} 0.868$.

The highest ranked false positives up to rank 100 are shown in Figure 25. The amount of false positives is reduced from 9 to 5. Especially the black car is ignored in this case.

Effect of Boost Parameter

The previous section indicates limitations of the retrievable results. This is mainly caused by the strict application of the similarity threshold. It is simply cutting away further relevant images with a lower similarity to the query.

Figure 20. Precision/recall of ETH-80 categories, single feature

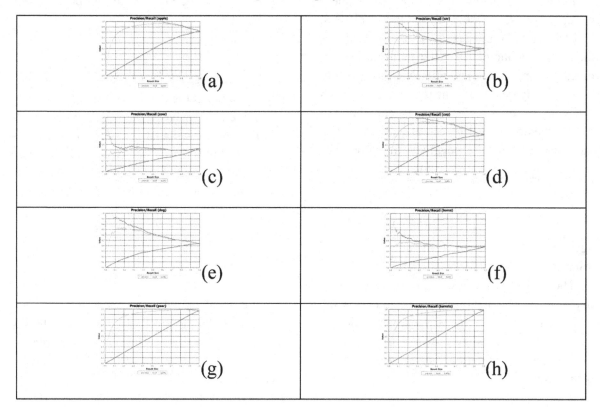

This effect can be attenuated by lowering the threshold for the most expressive query, allowing more hits to be considered. In order to enhance the query descriptor automatically, the quality of each positive top level clause is added as boost parameter. When merging multiple of those clauses, the more relevant sub results are expected to gain better ranks than the less relevant ones.

Figure 26 displays the impact of simply reducing the similarity threshold for all clauses. In this case, only the best 20 SHOULD clauses are used. The result size is $|r| = 2|R|$ to show the effects for a case, where the precision is not near 1.0.

In the upper left example, precision and recall of the result set are very good up to the point, where the query cuts off all following results. From a result size of about 0.45, no more additional data is available. The maximum recall is 0.74

The upper right result uses similarity thresholds reduced by a factor of 0.99. The precision is much lower than in the first case. The recall increases in several steps until it reaches a slightly higer value than previously ($\rho = 0.75$).

The results of the lower left diagram are generated with thresholds reduced to 0.95. This leads to a decrease of precision between the former two tests. The recall keeps increasing until it seems to reach a limit at about 0.95 of the result size. The final value is $\rho = 0.81$.

In the lower right diagram, the thresholds are reduced by a factor of 0.9. The precision drops very quickly to a value of about 0.5 where it remains until about a size of 0.5. Then it starts decreasing further at an almost constant rate. The recall increases more slowly than before, but relatively steadily. At a result size of 1.0, it is still increasing and reaches a value of $\rho = 0.73$.

Figure 21. Precision, recall and quality (F-Measure) for "cow" related queries

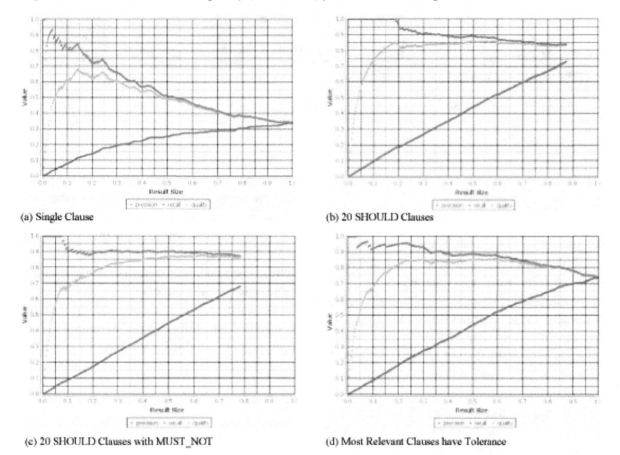

(a) Single Clause

(b) 20 SHOULD Clauses

(c) 20 SHOULD Clauses with MUST_NOT

(d) Most Relevant Clauses have Tolerance

In Figure 27 the full queries containing also negative clauses and a boost are tested. Again, the similarity threshold of each top-level Boolean clause is reduced by different amounts.

On the upper left, the diagram shows precision and recall for a threshold reduction by 0.999. The precision slowly decreases and the recall slowly increases until it is slightly higher than the precision ($\rho = 0.78$). At 425 results, the curves stop.

The upper right diagram is based on a query with reduced thresholds of 0.99. Again, the precision drops much faster than previously below 0.5. When reaching the size of the relevant set (≈ 410), there are two more points, where the precision increases again. The final recall is 0.77.

When using a factor of 0.95 (lower left), the precision does not drop as much as before and with less obvious steps. The recall reaches a maximum of $\rho = 0.84$.

In the last case, with a factor of 0.9, the precision drops very quickly towards 0.5 from where it rises up to 0.6 and then keeps dropping steadily. The best recall possible is $\rho = 0.86$.

When adding a "slack" to the thresholds of each query, the boost is used to alter its percentage. Clauses with a boost of 1.0 would be treated with the maximum additional slack and clauses with 0.0 with none at all. In between, a linear interpolated value is used.

Figure 22. Highest ranked false positives for "cow," 20 SHOULD (first 100 hits)

(a) rank 77	(b) rank 80	(c) rank 81	(d) rank 82	(e) rank 84	(f) rank 89	(g) rank 98

$$\sigma_c = 1.0 - \left(\left(1.0 - \sigma_{max}\right) * \beta_c\right)$$

where σ_c is the factor to modify a single clause c, σ_{max} is the maximum factor to be added and β_c is the boost factor assigned to clause c.

The last testing series (Figure 28) is the boost dependent variation of similarity thresholds. In this case, the new similarity threshold of each clause is reduced by the full amount of "slack" with a boost of 1.0 and with no modification for a boost of 0.0.

In the upper left case (factor 0.999), the results are comparable to the previous series, but with a slightly worse recall ($\rho = 0.77$).

The upper right diagram with a factor of 0.99, shows the same steps as in the former series with the equal decrease of the threshold. The final recall of 0.8 indicates an improvement.

The lower left test case plots the results for a factor of 0.95. Again, the steps are mostly gone. The recall curve starts relatively steep and then becomes more and more shallow with a short increase at the end. This case reaches a recall of 0.73.

In the final test with 0.9, the precision drops more quickly to 0.6 than the other curves in this series. The maximum recall is $\rho = 0.81$ with a more or less steady increase.

For each node split, the decision query term is specified. The full generated descriptor for the concept "cow," defined in the query language, is:

```
(W:1750@0.823  -H:2908@0.988)
(SH:2150@0.863 -H:1560@0.970)
 SH:1665@0.857 W:2143@0.804
(W:2084@0.743  -RGB:2738@0.912)
(W:1989@0.824 -H:4859@0.991)
SH:2302@0.773   W:1839@0.834
RGB:2399@0.999 W:1811@0.824
SH:1670@0.926   W:1985@0.799
SH:1816@0.886  W:1662@0.817
SH:1922@0.866  W:1827@0.844
W:1980@0.857   W:2151@0.799
RGB:2055@0.999  SH:1657@0.920
```

Figure 23. Highest ranked false positives for "cow," MUST NOT (first 100 hits)

(a) rank 35	(b) rank 37	(c) rank 41	(d) rank 48	(e) rank 55	(f) rank 63	(g) rank 68	(h) rank 74	(i) rank 94

Figure 24. Precision/recall of manually edited query for "cow" up to rank 900

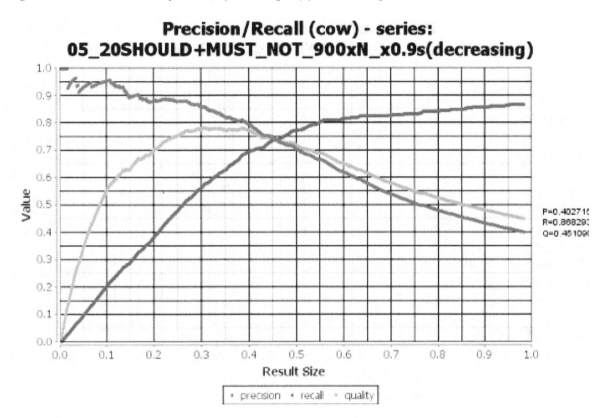

In comparison, the descriptor for the concept "tomato" only requires 3 clauses:

```
H:5793@0.988527 H:6031@0.999211
SH:6377@0.952435
```

Figure 29 shows the decision tree for the first half of the query for the learned concept "cow." The first split of the image set *I* is the query *W:1750@0.823*. It has been identified as the single query with the highest gain possible. As a result, the new left node contains a result set with an F-Measure of 0.67 and a precision of 0.84 for "cow."

As the retrieved results still contain several false positives, the query is refined by adding the negative clause *-H:2908@0.988*. This addition is filtering out a cluster of irrelevant images, i.e. a set of red cups. This second split generates a left leaf with a further improved precision and a right leaf with only irrelevant images. The node splitting is performed in the same way for the right node on the 2nd level, generating more left nodes with the highest precision possible. The right nodes contain less relevant training images for each split until the remaining training set is too small for learning or the maximum learning depth (i.e. 20 positive clauses) is reached.

Analysis

The extracted descriptors for each category show different characteristics (Table 3). The categories "tomato," "pear" and "apple" can be described with short queries. The "apple" and "tomato" queries have an emphasis on simple colour based features. The samples in the ETH-80 collection have relatively uniform colours (i.e. red and

Figure 25. Highest ranked false positives for "cow," modified MUST NOT (first 100 hits)

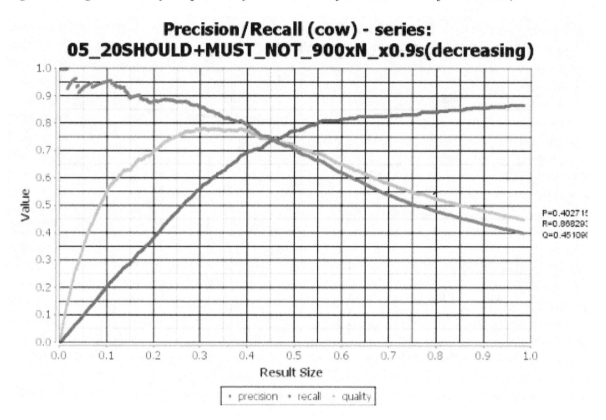

green), distinct from the other categories. The "pear" has similar colours, but it's unique shape seems to be even more distinctive, whereas the descriptor is composed of the spatially aware features. Similarly, the "cup" descriptor takes advantage of the unique handle shape, but also the distinctive plain white and brown colours can be used. The "car" seems to be much more challenging, as the colours are different for each sample, but the relatively uniform shape and size clearly favourizes the spatially aware features. The most complex shapes involved are the animals. It varies depending on the point of view, and even the colours change for each single sample object. Further, the shapes of different animals are very similar from the same angle, making it even more difficult to find a suitable feature.

An obvious property of all queries is the complete lack of MUST_HAVE clauses in the results.

Obviously, this is caused by the strict rule in the design section *Design-Learning Algorithm*. By protecting every single true positive in combination with only a small set of fv, there was no valid combination of two MUST_HAVE clauses available.

Being one of the most difficult categories in the collection (24 clauses in total Table 3), the "cow" queries are examined in more detail (Table 4). The precision for the best single clause (Figure 21(a)) is almost constantly dropping towards 0.35 for a result set of the size 410. This can be explained by the high diversity of relevant samples and a large number of similar images from other categories. Using 20 different clauses for retrieval (Figure 21(b)) results in a very high precision in the beginning. This effect is caused by the query images that usually achieve the highest possible similarity of 1.0 for at least one sub query. The

Figure 26. Precision/recall of ETH-80 "cow," max 20 SHOULD clauses, variations of "slack"

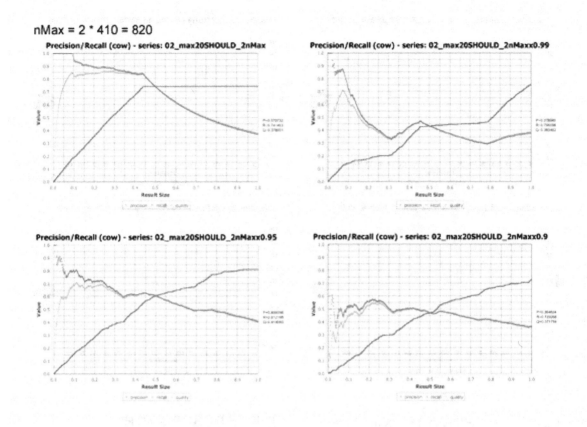

precision then drops to 0.9, but the recall keeps climbing until the threshold is cutting off the less relevant images at a recall of 0.734146. A similar effect can be seen after introducing MUST_NOT clauses (Figure 21(c)), where the final precision is higher, but the achieved recall is lower.

To overcome the limited result set size, the thresholds for the most expressive clauses are lowered by 10%. The final recall is the highest of all tests and can still increase with larger result sets. The last query appears to be the most appropriate for CBIR applications, where several results can be displayed and quickly manually scanned. In this scenario, a relatively constantly increasing recall rate is considered more important than having an extremely high precision for only the few highest ranks.

Discussion

Using the existing ranking methods of the retrieval systems indicates certain limits of this learning approach. The main issue to be solved is the cut off result set at a given threshold. In many cases, the strict similarity thresholds may be sufficient in order to generate results with a high precision. The remaining relevant images can only be found by lowering the clause thresholds which unfortunately has a negative effect on the precision of the higher ranked images. An alternative ranking approach could be derived from the category descriptor described in section *Methods-Categorization-Query Descriptors* and section *Case Studies-Query Descriptors*. This way, not a single result is cut off and at the same time, the

Figure 27. Equal application of slack

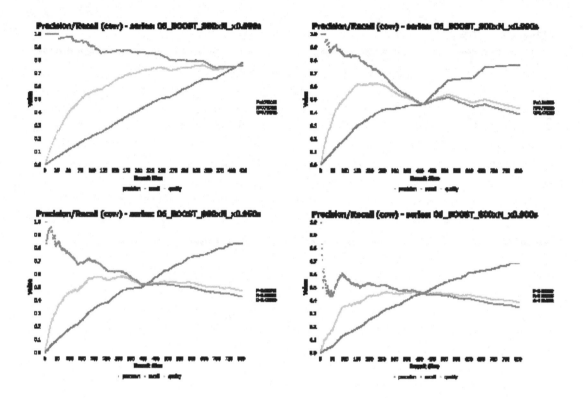

meaning of each single threshold of being the best trade-off, remains.

The learning algorithm is based on DT to find a suitable set of query terms, describing a concept as good as possible. As with most learning algorithms, the problems of over-fitting and unpredictable run times have to be addressed. Thus, suitable heuristics for this learning scenario need to be developed.

Summary

The DT based learning approach investigated above is capable of determining a set of suitable QBE clauses. It automatically chooses the best describing fv in each case and combines them into a single human-readable query. The main challenges are to achieve a better scalability and to find a reasonable trade-off between query size and over fitting.

QUERY DESCRIPTORS

The category-related queries learned in section *Case Studies-Supervised Learning* can be used for categorization tasks. Yet, the CBIR ranking algorithm is unsuitable for direct use, as it would only return similarities above 0.0 for images within the similarity tolerance specified for the clauses. Unknown images with a low similarity could not be classified at all. Thus, a category probability must be defined even for those cases section *Methods-Categorization-Query Descriptors*.

Query descriptors derived from the prototype suffer from the problem of using highly different fv. Dependent on the feature used in classification, the extracted raw probability from a single positive term may vary largely. Thus, it is required to adjust the similarity curves for each feature type to a similar behaviour (see section *Case Studies-Feature Normalization*).

Figure 28. Boost dependent application of Slack

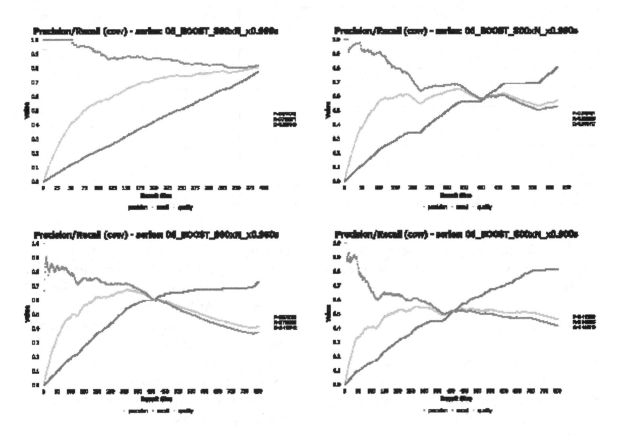

Figure 29. Decision tree for concept "cow" (most relevant clauses)

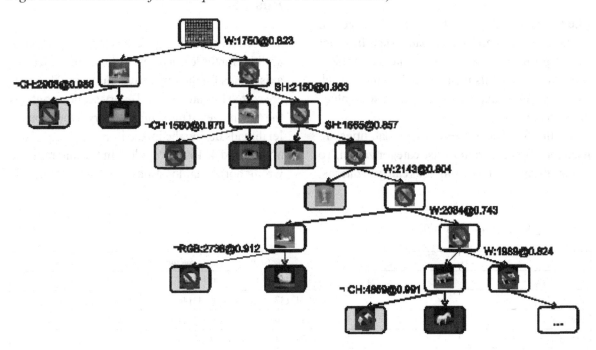

Table 3. Query composition

Category	SHOULD	MUST_NOT	RGB	H	SH	W
	clauses	clauses				
apple	10	1	8	2	1	0
car	20	0	0	0	15	5
cow	20	4	3	3	7	11
cup	15	3	1	5	4	8
dog	20	3	0	6	11	6
horse	20	4	2	9	2	11
pear	8	0	0	0	3	5
tomato	3	0	0	2	1	0

The testing has been carried out on a Solaris 10 x86 server system with 4 CPU-cores used in parallel.

Requirements

- Image set of annotated categories
- Normalized fv
- Set of descriptors, one for each category

Testing

The test is performed on the ETH-80 image set, containing 8 equally sized categories. In order to categorize a single image, the normalized probabilities for this image of belonging to each category are calculated, resulting in a list of values between 0.0 and 1.0.

At the first stage, these raw probabilities are used for a first descriptor-wise categorization. To reduce the amount of ambiguous categorizations, the range $\phi = [0.45, 0.55]$ is considered as being "unsure." Probabilities above 0.55 are interpreted as positive classification and values below 0.45 are negatives. At the second stage, all probabilities $\Phi(i)$ for a single image are merged. Out of these probabilities the highest one is selected and the "unknown" image is categorized this way. In both cases, the categorizations are compared to the real category of this image and the correctness rate for each category is calculated.

Results

The scatter plots in Figure 30 visualizes all probabilities for the learned descriptors. The horizontal axis stands for the respective image id. These ids are sorted by category and every section contains the 410 images of the same category (Due to parallel threads during the image import, image 410 is a "car" and 411 is an "apple." In the diagram, the wrong horizontal locations are barely noticeable

Table 4. Query quality parameters

	Precision	Recall	F-Measure
Figure 21(a)	0.341463	0.341463	0.341463
Figure 21(b)	0.843137	0.734146	0.838350
Figure 21(c)	0.875000	0.682927	0.865636
Figure 21(d)	0.739024	0.739024	0.739024

and the colours are correct. In the summary, the category names were used instead of the ids.). The relevant images for the respective category are highlighted by a different colour.

Generally, the plots in Figure 30 show similar characteristics. Usually, the true positives achieve probability values above the normalized threshold of 0.5. In some cases, false positives are clearly below. The negatives show similar patterns:

1. The probabilities are aggregated very close to 0.5. This is the only case, where false positives appear.
2. The probabilities are mostly lower than 0.5 but still aggregated.
3. The probabilities are spread across the whole range [0.0, 0.5]

Figure 30(a) is generated with the "apple" descriptor. The apple related images achieve a ϕ value in the upper half of the scale, in most cases clearly above the threshold of 0.5. None of the other images is located in the upper half. The images of four categories ("car," "cow," "dog" and "horse") are relatively evenly spread across the range [0.0,0.5]. The three remaining categories are mostly close to the central region around 0.5.

In Figure 30(b), the "car" related images are largely located in the upper half with a certain amount close to the threshold. Except from the "cup," which achieves several probabilities down to 0.2, most irrelevant images are located near 0.5. A few images from "apple," "cow," "dog" and "horse" achieved a ϕ clearly above 0.5.

The "cow" descriptor (Figure 30(c)) calculated about half of the relevant images close to 0.5 and quite a few irrelevant images from "car," "dog" and "horse" achieved a value above 0.5. The two results from "dog" (Figure 30(e)) and "horse" (Figure 30(f)) are similar.

For the category "cup," Figure 30(d) indicates neither clear false negatives nor false positives. The categories "apple," "pear" and "tomato" are

located close to the 0.5, while the remaining ones may drop down below $\phi = 0.1$.

The last two categories "pear" (Figure 30(g)) and "tomato" (Figure 30(h)) again share similar profiles with no false positives. Most "pear" probabilities are between 0.5 and 0.75 and "tomato," "apple" and "cup" are the categories with many values near 0.5. The "tomato" descriptor achieves more true positive probabilities up to 1.0. Again, the other fruits and "cup" are scattered around the central area.

Analysis

To provide an overview of the probability values achieved by the descriptors, Table 5 summarizes the raw probabilities for each class and descriptor. The results for every descriptor are summarized in three rows. The eight category columns represent the sets of 410 images of each category. Each box contains the amount of raw positives ($\phi > 0.55$), negatives ($\phi < 0.45$) and unclear ($\phi \in [0.45, 0.55]$) summed up to 100%. The bold numbers highlight the true positives. These values do not consider the other descriptors. The table shows the discriminative power of each single descriptor on its own.

The descriptors for "apple" (97.07%), "cup" (93.66%) and "tomato" (69.83%) and "pear" (85.61%) achieve a recognition rate of over 85% without any false positive. The remaining positive images are all in the "unsure" area, close to $\phi = 0.5$. All the images from other categories are either located in the "unsure" or the negative area.

The "car" descriptor is still in a relatively convenient area. With a rate of 77.56% of correctly categorized positives, this descriptor is quite good. A few false positives are contained ("apple," "cow," "dog" and "horse"), but the total rate is only about 1.25%. Again, all of the remaining positives are categorized as "unsure."

The animal descriptors achieve the worst results. The recognition rate for "cow" (45.61%), "dog"(60.49%) and "horse" (53.66%) are the

Figure 30. Category probabilities for ETH-80 images

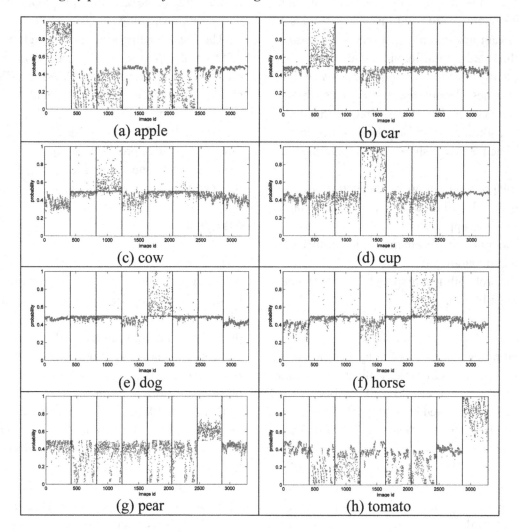

lowest ones in the test. Also the amount of false positives reaches up to ≈ 8%5. Also, the categories "cow" and "horse" are the only ones where relevant images were categorized as irrelevant.

The amount of correct categorizations is summarized in Table 6. The decision for a single category is determined by the highest probability for each image to be categorized. The recognition rate by the combined approach is higher than for the raw values, because no area of uncertainty has been defined. Because of merging the results of all eight descriptors, it is much easier to deal with probabilities close to 0.5. Even if the prob-

ability of a relevant image is below 0.5, it can still be categorized correctly, if the other descriptors return an even lower value.

Discussion

The testing results indicate that the queries generated by the learning algorithm *Methods-Categorization-Learning Algorithm* do in fact have sufficient discriminative power to be used as category descriptors. The repository specific normalization of the fv (section *Methods-Feature Normalization*), the conversion of similarities to probabilities (section *Methods-Categorization-Query Descriptors*) and choosing the maximum category seem to be sufficient to achieve reasonable recognition rates. In CBIR scenarios, these descriptors could also be applied to automatically assign a small set of labels to unknown images.

The probability calculations within the descriptor may also be an alternative to the current ranking algorithm which is cutting of all results below a certain similarity. The new approach takes this similarity threshold into account and also allows for expanding the results to any size. This behaviour would overcome the problems about the altered thresholds, discussed in section *Case Studies-Supervised Learning*.

A conspicuous amount of probabilities are very close to the threshold of 0.5. This behaviour is linked to be amount of clauses in the query and the normalization based on the clause thresholds. The more clauses are in a descriptor, the more irrelevant images are close to the determined thresholds. Equation 34 needs to be refined further in the future and also make use of the boost parameter.

Some descriptors still struggle to capture a category while others work well. This is likely to be caused by two factors. First, the query descriptors have a strictly limited size. Having a total of only 20 positive examples and a maximum of 60 (less important) negative examples restricts the system to capture at most 20 distinct clusters in the optimal case. Allowing for more clause may improve the recognition rates, but this also bears the risk of over fitting. The second factor to be considered is the small set of relatively simple fv provided. The system could only analyze the colours and histograms as well as a single wavelet approach to recognize textures. All these features are global and do not take real advantage of the additional shape information provided. The only two features using the provided pixel maps are the fv_mean (3 dimensions) and the fv_stochastic2 (12 dimensions) to ignore the blue background area. The use of additional, more sophisticated fv is expected to boost the performance of the system.

Summary

Using the retrieval queries from the supervised learning for shows a high recognition rate (92.65%). This expressiveness has been achieved by using only four global feature vectors. It is expected, that this accuracy level within a CBIR system is more than sufficient.

SEMI-SUPERVISED LEARNING

This section deals with semi-supervised learning. It compares the results of the previous section *Case Studies-Supervised Learning* to learning process with a reduced training set. A leave-one-object-out cross validation on the ETH-80 dataset has been published by Leibe and Schiele (2003). This case study compares the outcome of the semi-supervised learning within this part to the reference approach. Their categorization attempt uses seven different methods:

1. Colour – 3 colour channel histograms (Swain & Ballard, 1991)
2. Texture – first derivates in x/y direction (Schiele & Crowley, 2000)
3. Texture – gradient magnitude and Laplacian (Schiele & Crowley, 2000)
4. Global Shape – single, global eigenspace for all categories (Murase & Nayar, 1995)
5. Global Shape – class specific eigenspaces (Turk & Pentland, 1991)
6. Local Shape – "dynamic programming" contour matching (Belongie, Malik, & Puzicha, 2001)
7. Local Shape – greedy one-to-one contour matching Leibe and Schiele (2003)

The testing has been carried out on a Solaris 10 x86 server system with 4 CPU-cores used in parallel.

Table 5. Raw categorization summary

descriptor	phi	(%) by real category								
		apple	car	cow	cup	dog	horse	pear	tomato	total
apple	>0.55	**97.07**	0.00	0.00	0.00	0.00	0.00	0.00	0.00	12.13
	[0.45, 0.55]	2.93	12.20	4.88	79.76	26.34	10.24	57.80	95.12	36.16
	<0.45	0.00	87.80	95.12	20.24	73.66	89.76	42.20	4.88	51.71
car	>0.55	0.24	**77.56**	0.49	0.00	0.24	0.24	0.00	0.00	9.85
	[0.45, 0.55]	81.71	22.44	90.49	28.05	90.24	89.27	94.15	51.46	68.48
	<0.45	18.05	0.00	9.02	71.95	9.51	10.49	5.85	48.54	21.68
cow	>0.55	0.00	1.95	**45.61**	0.00	1.22	2.68	0.00	0.00	6.43
	[0.45, 0.55]	4.63	90.73	53.66	31.22	85.85	90.00	50.73	14.15	52.62
	<0.45	95.37	7.32	0.73	68.78	12.93	7.32	49.27	85.85	40.95
cup	>0.55	0.00	0.00	0.00	**93.66**	0.00	0.00	0.00	0.00	11.71
	[0.45, 0.55]	25.85	22.44	32.44	6.34	24.63	17.32	75.12	99.27	37.93
	<0.45	74.15	77.56	67.56	0.00	75.37	82.68	24.88	0.73	50.37
dog	>0.55	0.00	0.24	0.49	0.00	**60.49**	2.20	0.00	0.00	7.93
	[0.45, 0.55]	90.73	90.73	97.32	45.85	39.51	94.88	99.27	6.83	70.64
	<0.45	9.27	9.02	2.20	54.15	0.00	2.93	0.73	93.17	21.43
horse	>0.55	0.00	1.71	2.20	0.00	3.66	**53.66**	0.49	0.00	7.71
	[0.45, 0.55]	1.22	80.98	93.90	19.27	86.10	44.88	76.59	0.24	50.40
	<0.45	98.78	17.32	3.90	80.73	10.24	1.46	22.93	99.76	41.89
pear	>0.55	0.00	0.00	0.00	0.00	0.00	0.00	**85.61**	0.00	10.70
	[0.45, 0.55]	49.51	14.88	18.05	17.32	29.02	14.88	14.39	31.22	23.66
	<0.45	50.49	85.12	81.95	82.68	70.98	85.12	0.00	68.78	65.64
tomato	>0.55	0.00	0.00	0.00	0.00	0.00	0.00	0.00	**96.83**	12.10
	[0.45, 0.55]	29.76	0.98	0.00	18.29	0.00	0.00	3.41	3.17	6.95
	<0.45	70.24	99.02	100.00	81.71	100.00	100.00	96.59	0.00	80.95

Table 6. Categorization summary

category	apple	car	cow	cup	dog	horse	pear	tomato	total
size	410	410	410	410	410	410	410	410	3280
correct	408	393	351	409	346	316	406	410	3024
rate (%)	99.51	95.85	85.61	99.76	84.39	77.07	99.02	100.00	92.65

Requirements

- Image set of annotated categories
- Annotated set of objects for each category
- Normalized fv to calculate probability for an item to belong to a given descriptor

Testing

Data set sized for the leave-one-object-out cross validation for each single object:

- **Evaluation set:** 41
- **Training set:** $41 * 9 = 369$
- **Negative set:** $410 * 7 = 2870$

Evaluation steps:

1. Learn a descriptor for 9 out of 10 objects
2. calculate probability of 10th object of belonging to descriptor
3. compare probabilities for all classes/ descriptors

The learning algorithm is run for each single object from the image set. The evaluation set E is the collection of 41 images for the single object to be left out. The training set T consists of the remaining $41 * 9 = 369$ images of the same category. As negative set *N*, the $410 * 7 = 2870$ images from the other 7 categories are used. This results in a set of 80 descriptors, each one based on learning $\frac{9}{10}$ of a single category.

As in section *Case Studies-Query Descriptors*, each image is fed into 8 descriptors, one for each category. The category with the best calculated probability is selected. The difference to the descriptors from the supervised learning is the use of the new descriptors where the object to be identified is missing from the training set.

The reference results by Leibe and Schiele (2003) would require the system to learn for each single object to learn a full set of descriptors because of the negative set. Because of the large overhead, only the 80 descriptors for the modified categories to be learnt are calculated. The remaining 7 descriptors are replaced from the pool of the 8 generic descriptors. To allow for a better comparison, two separate test runs are performed. In the first one, the existing descriptors are used and in the second one, only the positive clauses from the existing descriptors are applied. This simulated loss of accuracy is expected to be larger than the benefit from having the negative sets with all 10 objects during learning.

Results

In general, the scatter plots of the 80 object specific runs are comparable to those in section *Case Studies-Query Descriptors-Results*. To provide a flavour of the differences, Figure 31 shows all 10 plots for the category "cow." The amount of false positives changes form object to object, especially in the already error-prone categories "car," "dog" and "horse." Another change is the amount of false negatives. The plots in Figure 31(c) and Figure 31(i) reveal quite a few relevant images with low probabilities. Nevertheless, most of the other plots show a smaller amount of those low values than in the fully supervised learning approach (Figure 30(c)).

Impact of removed MUST_NOT. In a second test run, all "MUST_NOT" clause were removed from the 80 descriptors and the new categorization results are compared to the previous ones. In addition to the originally wrong assigned categories, 6 additional images were mis-categorized. The total amount of traceable changes were 33 cases.

All critical changes are listed in Table 7. The table compares the original descriptor to the modified one. The first column contains the image id as well as the name of the unknown object. The second one indicates whether the following results are based on the original of the modified descriptor. The eight subsequent columns contain the probabilities for each one of the descriptors used for categorization. The last column lists the categorization result. The bold numbers highlight the changes in probability leading to the categorization error.

In four out of the six cases, the original probability for the correct class lies above 0.5. In the other two cases, it is slightly below but still above 0.49, indicating that the image is just below the threshold of the descriptor. All increased probabilities for the wrong category are above 0.5.

In 12 further cases, the result category also changed. Yet, these changes do not appear in the final result as the original results were also wrong in the first place. Finally, in 15 cases, the numerical probabilities changed, but these differences are too small to have any effect on the result.

Reference System. Table 8 summarizes the results of the reference system by Leibe and Schiele (2003) to allow for a direct comparison with the approach proposed in this part. These values are used in the analysis section below.

Analysis

Table 9 is constructed in the same way as described in section *Case Studies-Query Descriptors-Analysis*, giving an impression of how good a single descriptor is able to categorize the unknown images.

In the cross validation, the amount of false negatives is increased in comparison to the fully supervised learning (Table 5). Only the categories "car," "pear" and "tomato" are not missing any relevant images. The highest rate for false positives is the "horse" descriptor dealing with "dog" images (3.66%).

The "tomato" loses about 5% and the pear 2.5% of their previous recognition rate. A clear decrease for the "apple" and "cup" descriptors can be observed, dropping from 97.07% to 77.32% , and from 93.66% to 71.22% respectively. Most of the missing ones have been moved

to the area of uncertainty around the threshold. For the "cup," a large set of 3.9% relevant images are considered to be irrelevant.

Amongst the more difficult categories, the rate for the car dropped to 55.85% but all remaining ones are located in the area of uncertainty. The remaining animal categories share the lowest positive rates, ranging from 32.93% ("dog") down to 20.24% ("horse").

Table 10 provides an overview of the final categorization results compared to the reference by Leibe and Schiele (2003). The table shows the category-wise recognition rates as well as both the average and best results from the reference.

In two cases, the proposed learning approach slightly outperforms the best results of the reference ("apple," "tomato") and in one case, the results are close together ("pear"). For all other classes, is more or less below the average recognition rate. In total, the results are close to the average, both slightly above 80% . In case of the modified queries with the negative clause missing, the total result would be $\frac{6}{3280}100\% \approx 0.182\%$ lower than the current value.

Table 11 and Figure 32 analyze in detail, which particular objects caused most errors. These objects are collected in Figure 33.

The "apple" category was misclassified 44 times. From these errors, 30 were caused by a single object, namely "apple10" (Figure 33(a)).

The errors for each "car" are distributed between 1 and 11. "car1" (Figure 33(b)) is the one causing most errors, but there is no highly specific problem with this one. In general, the cars have much variation in colours and the features used are all related to colours, making it hard to find suitable sample images.

For the "cow," the most difficult object is "cow5" (Figure 33(c)) with 31 relevant images missing, probably caused by two reasons. First, other than the other ones, this cow is lying on the ground and thus has a different shape. Also,

Figure 31. Category probabilities for ETH-80 images (all cows)

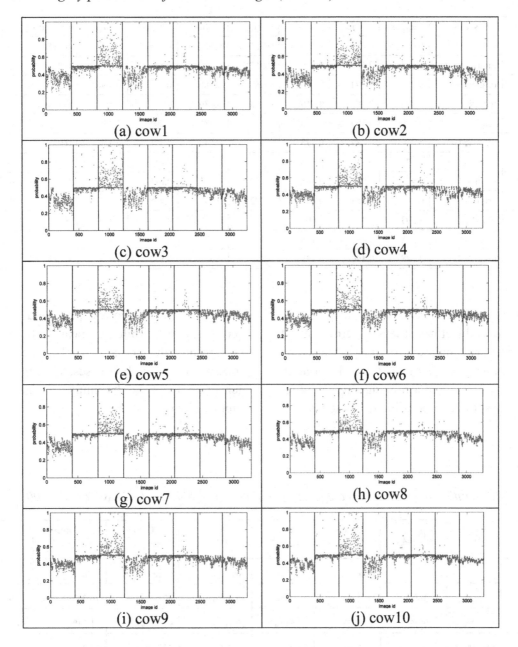

(a) cow1

(b) cow2

(c) cow3

(d) cow4

(e) cow5

(f) cow6

(g) cow7

(h) cow8

(i) cow9

(j) cow10

the black-and-white pattern is similar to a dog's pattern.

In the "cup" category, the object "cup10" (Figure 33(d)) was missed 19 times. This is probably due to the specific shape and unique gray/green color. The side views of this cup only achieved

a probability below 0.4. In 14 of these cases, the object has been mistaken as "cow."

Similar to the "cow" category, the "dog" contains multiple difficult objects. The worst one with 26 errors is "dog6" (Figure 33(e)), with a black and white pattern. Not surprisingly, it has been mistaken as a cow 15 times.

Table 7. Additional false categorizations

object	series	apple	car	cow	cup	dog	horse	pear	tomato	result
776	original	0.014	0.670	0.485	0.367	0.477	0.475	0.109	0.015	car
car7	modified	0.014	**0.670**	0.485	0.367	0.477	**0.848**	0.109	0.015	horse
813	original	0.229	0.494	0.480	0.468	0.480	0.476	0.454	0.355	car
car9	modified	0.229	**0.494**	**0.510**	0.468	0.480	0.476	0.454	0.355	cow
1104	original	0.050	0.489	0.498	0.487	0.481	0.496	0.436	0.077	cow
cow6	modified	0.050	0.489	**0.498**	0.487	**0.545**	0.496	0.436	0.077	dog
2114	original	0.473	0.443	0.468	0.429	0.590	0.611	0.417	0.385	horse
horse10	modified	0.473	0.443	0.468	0.429	**0.662**	**0.611**	0.417	0.385	dog
2248	original	0.293	0.483	0.493	0.422	0.487	0.498	0.417	0.354	horse
horse4	modified	0.293	0.483	**0.606**	0.422	0.487	**0.498**	0.417	0.354	cow
2348	original	0.248	0.490	0.498	0.396	0.495	0.577	0.437	0.319	horse
horse7	**modified**	**0.248**	**0.490**	**0.498**	**0.396**	**0.638**	**0.577**	**0.437**	**0.319**	**dog**

The most difficult category is the "horse." Every single object has at least 11 errors out of 41 samples. The highest error of 31 is caused by "horse4" Figure 33(f). Again, the high variation of colour patterns and a missing shape/contour feature seem to be responsible for these results.

The last two categories "pear" and "tomato" performed best. While the "pear" only caused 6 false results, the "tomato" has been recognized correctly always. In both cases, the highly homogeneous colours and the simple shapes could be captured by the system.

Table 8. Recognition results for the categorization of unknown objects (Leibe & Schiele, 2003)

	Color	$D_x D_y$	Mag-	PCA	PCA	Cont.	Cont.	Avg.
			Lap	Masks	Gray	Greedy	DynProg	
apple	57.56%	**85.37%**	80.24%	78.78%	**88.29%**	77.07%	76.34%	77.66%
pear	66.10%	90.00%	85.37%	**99.51%**	**99.76%**	90.73%	91.71%	89.03%
tomato	**98.54%**	94.63%	**97.07%**	67.80%	76.59%	70.73%	70.24%	82.23%
cow	86.59%	82.68%	**94.39%**	75.12%	62.44%	86.83%	86.34%	82.06%
dog	34.63%	62.44%	74.39%	72.20%	66.34%	**81.95%**	**82.93%**	67.84%
horse	32.68%	58.78%	70.98%	77.80%	77.32%	**84.63%**	**84.63%**	69.55%
cup	79.76%	66.10%	77.80%	**96.10%**	**96.10%**	**99.76%**	**99.02%**	87.81%
car	62.93%	**98.29%**	77.56%	**100.0%**	97.07%	**99.51%**	**100.0%**	90.77%
total	64.85%	79.79%	82.23%	83.41%	82.99%	86.40%	86.40%	80.87%

Table 9. Raw categorization summary

descriptor	ϕ	apple	car	cow	cup	dog	horse	pear	tomato	total
					(%) by real category					
apple	>0.55	**77.32**	0.00	0.00	0.00	0.00	0.00	0.00	0.00	9.66
	[0.45, 0.55]	20.73	12.20	4.88	79.76	26.34	10.24	57.80	95.12	38.38
	<0.45	1.95	87.80	95.12	20.24	73.66	89.76	42.20	4.88	51.95
car	>0.55	0.24	**55.85**	0.49	0.00	0.24	0.24	0.00	0.00	7.13
	[0.45, 0.55]	81.71	44.15	90.49	28.05	90.24	89.27	94.15	51.46	71.19
	<0.45	18.05	0.00	9.02	71.95	9.51	10.49	5.85	48.54	21.68
cow	>0.55	0.00	1.95	**24.88**	0.00	1.22	2.68	0.00	0.00	3.84
	[0.45, 0.55]	4.63	90.73	73.90	31.22	85.85	90.00	50.73	14.15	55.15
	<0.45	95.37	7.32	1.22	68.78	12.93	7.32	49.27	85.85	41.01
cup	>0.55	0.00	0.00	0.00	**71.22**	0.00	0.00	0.00	0.00	8.90
	[0.45, 0.55]	25.85	22.44	32.44	24.88	24.63	17.32	75.12	99.27	40.24
	<0.45	74.15	77.56	67.56	3.90	75.37	82.68	24.88	0.73	50.85
dog	>0.55	0.00	0.24	0.49	0.00	**32.93**	2.20	0.00	0.00	4.48
	[0.45, 0.55]	90.73	90.73	97.32	45.85	66.59	94.88	99.27	6.83	74.02
	<0.45	9.27	9.02	2.20	54.15	0.49	2.93	0.73	93.17	21.49
horse	>0.55	0.00	1.71	2.20	0.00	3.66	**20.24**	0.49	0.00	3.54
	[0.45, 0.55]	1.22	80.98	93.90	19.27	86.10	79.02	76.59	0.24	54.66
	<0.45	98.78	17.32	3.90	80.73	10.24	0.73	22.93	99.76	41.80
pear	>0.55	0.00	0.00	0.00	0.00	0.00	0.00	**83.17**	0.00	10.40
	[0.45, 0.55]	49.51	14.88	18.05	17.32	29.02	14.88	16.83	31.22	23.96
	<0.45	50.49	85.12	81.95	82.68	70.98	85.12	0.00	68.78	65.64
tomato	>0.55	0.00	0.00	0.00	0.00	0.00	0.00	0.00	**94.88**	11.86
	[0.45, 0.55]	29.76	0.98	0.00	18.29	0.00	0.00	3.41	5.12	7.20
	<0.45	70.24	99.02	100.00	81.71	100.00	100.00	96.59	0.00	80.95

Table 10. Categorization summary (leave-one-object-out)

category	apple	car	cow	cup	dog	horse	pear	tomato	total
size	410	410	410	410	410	410	410	410	3280
	results								
correct	366	353	279	340	270	211	404	410	2639
rate (%)	89.27	86.10	68.05	82.93	65.85	51.46	98.54	100.00	80.27
	reference (Leibe and Schiele (2003))								
avg.(%)	77.66	90.77	82.06	87.81	67.84	69.55	89.03	82.23	80.87
best (%)	88.29	100.00	94.39	99.76	82.93	84.63	99.76	98.54	93.54

Discussion

In the direct comparison with the reference system, the results are very similar. Thus, the proposed learning algorithm generating a low-level query can compete with the learning approach used in the reference. This outcome is satisfying, as the main purpose of the learning algorithm was to provide evidence for the capabilities of the query language in general.

The leave-one-object-out cross validation suffers from the same weaknesses as the supervised test (section *Case Studies-Supervised Learning*). The fv currently available are simply not capable to distinguish between the complex "animal" categories. In the reference system, these categories as well as "car" and "cup" achieved high recognition rates with the "Contour" features that were not available for this test.

Further, only having a set of existing images available for querying, restricts the possibilities of learning. Modern machine learning usually heavily relies on complex structures such as neural networks or support vector machines to learn a given concept. These approaches allow a fine grained approximation of the desired feature without the need of finding suitable query images from the existing training set. On the other hand, they usu-

Figure 32. Wrong classification by object

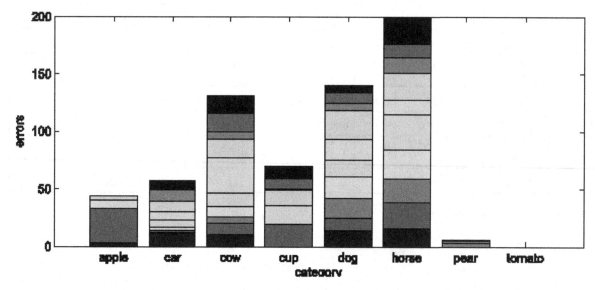

Figure 33. Most difficult objects

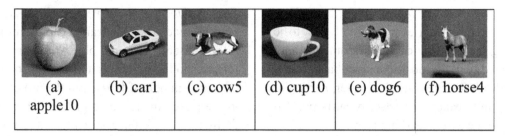

| (a) apple10 | (b) car1 | (c) cow5 | (d) cup10 | (e) dog6 | (f) horse4 |

ally require defined types of fv and a reasonable understanding of the particular meaning.

Summary

The semi-supervised learning outcome cannot compete with recent SVM approaches (e.g. (Schnitzspan, Fritz, Roth, & Schiele, 2009)). Yet, it is comparable to earlier studies that are several more complex features, such as shape information Leibe and Schiele (2003).

It is expected that adding new fv plug-ins to the proposed system makes it much more competitive without modifying the underlying theory and the need of feature specific optimizations. At the same time, the queries used within the categorization remain understandable by experienced users. This allows for subsequent and target-oriented modifications of an existing categorization query.

CONCLUSION

Before tackling the research question itself, several preconditions had to be met. Each case study described above investigates one essential aspect of CBIR. Building up on top of each other, the case studies finally allow for an analysis of how good the query language can map a set of given low-level features to a higher semantic concept. Every query descriptor learnt by the system represents a possible semantic mapping for the related category.

The extracted normalization functions in section *Case Studies-Feature Normalization* are found to be relatively accurate for the related repository, but may be unsuitable for others. The main advantage of this normalization is the better comparability of distinct fv, allowing for a more accurate fusion, which is necessary for the learning and classification tasks.

Table 11. Wrong classification by object

category	objects										total
apple	3	30	0	7	0	0	4	0	0	0	44
car	11	1	2	3	6	7	9	10	1	7	55
cow	10	10	6	9	11	31	16	7	16	15	131
cup	0	19	0	0	0	17	13	1	9	11	70
dog	14	11	17	19	14	18	26	6	9	6	140
horse	16	22	21	25	31	13	23	14	11	23	199
pear	0	0	3	0	0	0	0	2	0	1	6
tomato	0	0	0	0	0	0	0	0	0	0	0

It is shown in section *Case Studies-Estimating the Improvement Capabilities of Different Features*, that some categories are relatively easy to be learnt (e.g. the grayscale cars), while others cannot be captured (e.g. the mostly random background images) with the fv set used. Further, particular strengths and weaknesses of each fv can be pointed out before the actual learning process.

The supervised machine learning in section Case Studies-Supervised Learning works well, as long as the feature vectors have a sufficient discriminative power, as mentioned in section Case Studies-Estimating the Improvement Capabilities of Different Features. In some cases (i. e. the animals), the feature vectors used prove to be not capable of capturing highly discriminative features for a high result quality. This still seems to be sufficient for most retrieval tasks. The first 410 results can easily reach a precision of $\pi > 0.5$ and in several set-ups even $\pi > 0.8$. This can be tolerated, as users could easily filter out the false positives and only persevering users are expected to keep searching beyond this amount of images.

The section *Case Studies-Query Descriptors* shows that the categorization is more challenging than a retrieval, where the user itself is part of the final "filter." As the categorization results in a single category estimate, errors become more severe. Thus, the computation should be more accurate than during retrieval, where many true positives may well be mixed with a few false positives. An accurate calculation requires normalized fv to have the different features comparable in a comparable range. Further, the thresholds must not be used too restrictively (i.e. cutting off results with lower similarity) to acknowledge relevant images with a slightly lower similarity. To achieve this, second normalization step according to the thresholds proved to be vital.

In direct comparison of the final case study (section *Case Studies-Semi-Supervised Learn-* *ing*) to the supervised learning (section *Case Studies-Supervised Learning*), the recognition performance dropped clearly. This seems mostly to be caused by sample objects with many differences to the training set used. It is found, that the combination of fv used in the prototype can in average compete with each training on a single fv from the reference system. In the reference system, each fv performed differently well for each category.

In comparison, the relatively weak fv of the proposed system are in combination as good as the average of the reference system. The recognition rate has been achieved with a limited set of positive and negative examples (i.e. a maximum of 20 distinct clusters for a category) and without further low-level optimization of the features themselves.

REFERENCES

Al-Omari, F. A., & Al-Jarrah, M. A. (2005). Query by image and video content: A colored-based stochastic model approach. *Data Knowledge Engineering, 52*(3), 313{332.

Belongie, S., Malik, J., & Puzicha, J. (2001). *Matching shapes*. In International Conference on Computer Vision (ICCV).

Fei-Fei, L., Fergus, R., & Perona, P. (2004). *Learning generative visual models from few training examples: An incremental Bayesian approach tested on 101 object categories*. In International Conference on Computer Vision and Pattern Recognition (CVPR'04, Workshop on Generative-Model Based Vision).

Jacobs, C. E., Finkelstein, A., & Salesin, D. H. (1995). Fast multiresolution image querying. *Computer Graphics, 29*, 277–286. Retrieved from citeseer.ist.psu.edu/jacobs95fast.html

Leibe, B., Leonardis, A., & Schiele, B. (2004, May). Combined object categorization and segmentation with an implicit shape model. In *Proceedings of the Workshop on Statistical Learning in Computer Vision*, Prague, Czech Republic.

Leibe, B., & Schiele, B. (2003, June). Analyzing appearance and contour based methods for object categorization. In International Conference on Computer Vision and Pattern Recognition (CVPR'03).

Murase, H., & Nayar, S. (1995). Visual learning and recognition of 3D objects from appearance. *International Journal of Computer Vision, 14,* 5–24. doi:10.1007/BF01421486

Pein, R. P., & Lu, J. (2010). *Multi-feature query language for image classification.* In International Conference on Computational Science, ICCS 2010. Elsevier. (Accepted for publication)

Pein, R. P., Lu, J., & Renz, W. (2008, July). An extensible query language for content based image retrieval. *The Open Information Science Journal, 3*(17), 81–97.

Pein, R. P., & Lu, Z. (2006, June). Content based image retrieval by combining features and query-by-sketch. In H. R. Arabnia & R. R. Hashemi (Eds.), *International Conference on Information & Knowledge Engineering* (IKE) (p. 49-55). Las Vegas, NV: CSREA Press.

Schapire, R. E. (1990). The strength of weak learnability. *Machine Learning, 5,* 197–227. doi:10.1007/BF00116037

Schiele, B., & Crowley, J. (2000). Recognition without correspondence using multidimensional receptive field histograms. *International Journal of Computer Vision, 36*(1), 31–52. doi:10.1023/A:1008120406972

Schnitzspan, P., Fritz, M., Roth, S., & Schiele, B. (2009). Discriminative structure learning of hierarchical representations for object detection. In *Computer Vision and Pattern Recognition.* Miami, USA: CVPR. doi:10.1109/CVPR.2009.5206544

Swain, M. J., & Ballard, D. (1991). Color indexing. *International Journal of Computer Vision, 7*(1), 11–32. doi:10.1007/BF00130487

Turk, M., & Pentland, A. (1991). Eigenfaces for recognition. *Journal of Cognitive Neuroscience, 3,* 71–86. doi:10.1162/jocn.1991.3.1.71

Chapter 25
Conclusion

Raoul Pascal Pein
University of Huddersfield, UK

Joan Lu
University of Huddersfield, UK

Wolfgang Renz
Hamburg University of Applied Sciences, Germany

ABSTRACT

In this final chapter of the section, the conclusion of this book section is given. It is summarized how the initial hypothesis has been investigated and which answer has been found. A brief summary of the achievements as well as the intended future work in this area are presented.

INTRODUCTION

In order to investigate the research hypothesis several case studies have been carried out (chapter *Case Studies*). Each single case study is required to support parts of the methodology in chapter *Methods*. The final evaluation has been carried out by comparing the expressiveness of the descriptors learnt in a leave-one-object-out scenario to a traditional machine learning approach (section *Case Studies-Semi-Supervised Learning*).

It is found, that the query language used can be as powerful as a fv derived from a traditional machine learning algorithm. A Boolean query descriptor can be used to describe a single category relatively precisely. Further, it does not matter, if the category to be learnt is located in multiple disjunct clusters in the feature space, as the Boolean join can handle it easily. The weakest part of the proposed learning approach are the fv themselves. If they are not powerful enough to capture distinctive properties for a category, the whole learning process for the given category cannot be successful. Yet, as long as there is a fv available giving a slight improvement towards a random search, it is spotted by the algorithm and is used to improve the results.

In conclusion: a high-level mapping of semantics (i.e. a semantic category) can only be as good as the low-level fv are capable to distinguish positive samples from unrelated categories.

DOI: 10.4018/978-1-4666-1975-3.ch025

ACHIEVED

The proposed query language seems to be powerful enough to describe most common retrieval tasks. The search for virtually any fv is possible as long as they can be mapped to a normalized similarity of [0, 1] between two fv of the same kind. Further, merging multiple sub queries is achieved by boolean operators and parameters. Complex queries containing low-level features only, are a possible way of expressing higher-level semantics, at least to a certain extent. The query descriptors generated by the learning algorithm are mapping semantic categories to the most efficient image features available.

The tests indicated that the fv modules applied in this part are too few and not diverse enough to fully compete with recent machine learning systems. Being independent from the fv used, the results are still promising. The results indicate that by adding further plug-ins the recognition rate of the system will be improved without changing the underlying methodology. The learning algorithm has been developed as a tool to automatically generate meaningful queries. This way, it was possible to evaluate the query language in depth. Further, several techniques applied during the development and evaluation of the learning algorithm are useful in retrieval, too. One example is the fv normalization. Is important to make features of different kinds comparable. This allows for a more efficient combination of arbitrary features into a single result.

Traditional machine learning approaches often encode the derived knowledge in complex and difficult to understand data. For SVM this could be concatenating several fv into a single big data set. ANN usually create a set of weights with no obvious meaning to human perception. Unlike that, the presented DT approach generates a set of comprehensible clauses. This allows experienced users to manually modify the classification queries, e.g. to remove a set of undesired positives.

FUTURE WORK

The theoretical foundations of the part indicate several opportunities for further related research, e.g.:

- Development of an intuitive CBIR user interface
- Support for spatial information integrated into the query language handle local objects
- Integration of an efficient image segmentation algorithm
- Implementation of powerful fv, such as shape matching
- Focus on higher scalability, e.g. stronger use of index structures and heuristics
- Application of other efficient learning techniques to build query descriptors
- Use of query descriptors to replace keywords in CBIR queries or to label images with unknown content
- Improvement of the Boolean ranking mechanisms, e.g. by applying Bayesian combination rules

Section 5
Business Process in Information Retrieval

Chapter 26
An Overview of Business Process Management

Wei Zhou
Yunnan University, China

Yixuan Zhou
Yunnan University, China

Jinwu Yang
Yunnan University, China

Shaowen Yao
Yunnan University, China

ABSTRACT

BPM (Business Process Management) includes support for business process analysis, design, implementation, management methods, techniques, and tools. This chapter introduces the origin of BPM technology and development, covering four fields: Business Process Management benefits, the history of BPM, classification of Business process, the lifecycle of BPM, and Business Process Modeling Techniques. In addition, the authors also determine that the present workflow technology is not enough to exist in the root causes of some deficiencies; concluding the chapter with the future of workflow technology trends.

1 INTRODUCTION

1.1 Business Process Management Benefits

The Information community is interested in providing robust and scalable software systems to accelerate industries' performance. Due to complex business processes, an integrated solution is an important foundation for realization. Business process modeling plays an important role in today's enterprise business activities. It acts as a disciplined approach to identify, design, monitor, control, and measure business processes. Typically BPM is performed by business analysts and managers who are seeking to improve process efficiency and quality. Through Business process modeling, managers will be involved in some ac-

DOI: 10.4018/978-1-4666-1975-3.ch026

tions such as collaboration, deliberation, improvement, innovation etc, which help to create value and enable an organization to meet its business objectives with more agility. The process improvements identified by BPM may or may not require Information Technology involvement, although that is a common driver for the need to model a business process, by creating a process master.

Although early implementations of BPM have unfolded in large enterprises, managing business processes is critical for any sized organization. Today business process management is growing in popularity and widely used in most companies because it offers major business performance improvement advantages. It appears as a set of tools and services that support human and application interaction with business processes. BPM suites automate manual processes by routing tasks through departments and applications. Organizations use BPM, which will help organizations optimize business performance by discovering, documenting, and automating, to improve the effectiveness of their core operations.

The significance of BPM for enterprise lays not only a description of key business process of the enterprises, but also it can perform as a guideline for the enterprises. This will let to a series changes embodied in the optimization of resources, optimization of enterprise organization and the management system. The purpose of this optimization is to realize the companies' goal: to reduce business operating costs and increase responsiveness to market needs and strive to maximize corporate profits (Wil van der Aalst, Kees van Hee., 2002).

1.2 The History of BPM

The classic business process modeling methodologies such as the flow chart, functional flow block diagram, data flow diagram, control flow diagram, Gantt chart, PERT diagram, and IDEF have all emerged during the 20th century: The flow charts in the 1920s, Functional Flow Block Diagram and PERT in the 1950s, Data Flow Diagrams and IDEF in the 1970s. These represent just a fraction of the methodologies used over the years to document business processes. The term "business process modeling" itself was coined in the 1960s in the field of systems engineering. S. Williams in 1967 published the article "Business Process Modeling Improves Administrative Control." His idea was that techniques for obtaining a better understanding of physical control systems could be used in a similar way for business processes.

With the development of computer technology, the principle of designing software systems has also changed. Before the 1960s, information system built on a small operating system with only a special limited functionality. There is no common software and no industry-specific software; information systems at that time only have professional custom software. As time went on, in the 1970s, the software system has been continually enriched, but also faces many challenges: (1) although a variety of application layer software has been developed, the software vendors face the challenge of how to integrate these applications, how to better reuse of existing procedures? The focus of the development of software has also shifted from pure coding programming to component programming which intend to the composition of more complex systems. (2) data-driven development can't meet real business needs. As the enterprise competition increasing, business processes, management tools will update periodically. The traditional mode of development, however, cannot solve these problems. Thus system engineers have turned to process-based system development methodology research and pay attention to business process modeling (Van der Aalst, W., A. Hofstede, and M. Weske, 2003).

In the 1980s, the term workflow was first used in its modern form in the software industry. August Wilhelm-Scheer is regarded as founding the modern Business Process Modeling software industry with the development of the Y-model and the founding of IDS Scheer in the 1980s. Followed by this, many OA systems have introduced workflow conception wanting to setup a business process-based integrated software suite.

In the 1990s, Enterprise information resources appear heterogeneous, distributed, and loosely coupled characteristics. Meanwhile CS/BS architecture, distributed processing technologies became more sophisticated. These bring up challenge: how to make the inter-related tasks efficiently cooperating in a large-scale heterogeneous distributed environment? Besides its original purpose of creating a paperless office environment, Workflow technology is used to realize automatic business process in distributed environment. And then, more technology is integrated into the workflow, such as the document management system, database, MIS systems. In 1993, the international community set up the Workflow Management Coalition WfMC, marked the workflow technology has begun to enter a relatively mature stage. WfMC workflow management system in the relevant terminology, architecture, reference model and application programming interfaces has formulated a set of criteria. Since then the development of BPM has moving into the Fast Lane. New techniques and conceptions, such as Unified Modeling Language, Business Process Modeling Notation, recently appeared SOA, Cloud computing, etc, are continuously integrated into BPM.

2 RESEARCH ON BUSINESS PROCESS MANAGEMENT

2.1 Classification of Business Process

According to the various standards, business processes can be classified into different categories (Layna Fischer, 2005).

Firstly based on its location industry the business process can be divided as services process, insurance process, manufacturing process, petroleum process, and so forth.

Secondly based on its organization range the business process can be divided into departments Process, inter-process, and inter-enterprise processes. The scope of recognition will helpful to coordinate the process connection, the parallel processing work, investigate cross-departmental processes. These works will find bottlenecks in the process and be propitious to the process optimization.

- **Departments Process:** The internal processes of OA (Office automation); Inter-process: such as product release process or engineering change processes. They are usually across design, technology or manufacturing, and several other departments; Inter-enterprise processes: some business processes act as supplier or consumer processes. Such as supplier material procurement process, products sales process, etc.

Thirdly based on its contents the business process can be divided into Main Process, Support Process and Management Process. Different enterprise's activities have the multiplicity which cause enterprise's business process to present many and varied forms.

- **Main Process:** Refer to those processes that respond to customer needs in order to produce goods or provide services to customers. Such as marketing, manufacturing, service and so on, they were a direct economic benefits to the enterprise; Support Process: To support the production process, this process concentrates in the maintenance of the means of production and human resource management. Financial management is also a support process; Management Process: Generally it is located in the enterprise, used in managing and coordinating the above two kind of processes. In these processes, they determine other process manager's target and the condition, simultaneously assign the resources which other procedure execution needs.

Fourthly the Process division is based on its structural properties.

- **Production Process**: The process of producing products or services in the company, which is highly structured, rarely has model variants. However it needs to handle a large number of process instances every day, such as insurance claims process; Administrative Process: There are several pre-defined route options, well-structured, examples-driven, a large number of process instances. Ad Hoc Process: Process structure cannot be completely accurate definition, when the process instances are executed may need dynamic adjustment of the structure, need to handle the anomaly condition, such as the process of software project development management.

2.2 What Are the Components of Business Process Management?

BPM system, which offers the vision of enterprise wide process management, aims to align the employees of the organization to the customer. It produces customer value through its business processes and associated resources. A process-based organization requires an understanding of organizational components and how they relate to each other. The Components of Business Process Management can be subdivided into the following (John Jeston, Johan Nelis, 2008).

- **Customer Management**: In order to integrate and focus value delivery on the customer, the organizations need to identify what are the customer needs or wants,

develop the product & service profile, and obtain constant customer satisfaction feedback. Promoting value for customers, whether internal or external customers, is at the centre of a Business Process Model. Almost the same it starts with a customer's requirements and ends with the satisfaction of that needs.

- **Planning and Control**: Business organizations need to arrange actions to improve their current situation through planning value and establishing control measures for operational performance. The strategy of a company is specified, which describes its long-term concepts to develop a sustainable competitive advantage in the market. Its objectives include: establish goals (policies), define standards and capabilities, and develop product/service features.

- **Resource and Knowledge Management**: the resource management is in order to manage operational activities of the organization. Let the resources display own expertise, and make the similar duty continuously. However, the purpose of knowledge management is to create, share and use of a growing number of high-quality knowledge to improve organizational performance.

- **Performance Management**: The performance indicator is an important task of BPM. It is the key of evaluating and optimizing to the BPM by means of the quantitative understanding of the performance of the model. Information derived from performance metrics is critical in driving the iterative process of optimizing the business practices and policies that support organizational goals.

- **Solution**: For the purpose of achieving the level of a process-based organization, each of the business process management components needs to achieve its goals and objectives.

2.3 What is the Lifecycle of BPM?

The BPM lifecycle describes the various phases in support of operational business processes (Marta Indulska, Jan Recker, Michael Rosemann and Peter Green, 2009). It can be divided into four stages, which are organized in a cyclical structure, showing their logical dependencies. It is shown below in Figure 1.

- **Process Model and Design Phase**: The main task of this phase is to conduct process design, including problem analysis and process modeling. According to the goal, follows the enterprise unified process modeling standards and specifications, the organization responsibility department carries on the design and the modeling of business processes.

- **Process Configuration Phase**: In this phase, designs are implemented by configuring a process system, according to the organizational environment of the enterprise and the business processes. Resource carries out allocation on relevancies such as organization, personnel, instrument and so on, which needed by technological process operation, and check whether they are ready or not. This phase will help improve the effectiveness of the implementation process.

- **Process Enactment Phase**: After configuration, the enactment phase starts where the operational business processes are executed using the system configured. The first step is the deployment of process definition model. The second step is the process enactment phase instances are initiated to fulfill the business goals of a company. The third step is to monitor the process instances running. During business process enactment, valuable execution data is gathered, typically in some form of log file. Log information is basis for evaluation of processes in the next phase of the business process lifecycle.

- **Process Manage and Optimize Phase**: Based on the appropriate management software tools and techniques, managing the service and process which the operating environment, catch out the running error of system, restore the system state, get the key performance indicators, and find that the performance "bottleneck". In this phase, the data can be back to the model and design phase, which is the performance data and operating statistics, to carry out the sustained optimization.

- **Solution**: Through the cycle of the BPM lifecycle the enterprise's business processes can obtain continuous adjustment and optimization, which is quickly adapt to marketplace change rapidly.

Figure 1. The BPM lifecycle

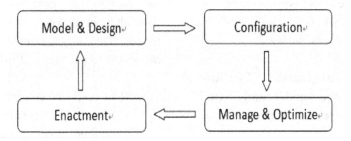

2.4 Business Process Modeling Techniques

Business Process Modeling is the formulation of business processes, which is an important basis of the process design, analysis and optimization. The business process modeling makes the relationship between the various elements and characteristics of the enterprise process become abstract, and uses graphics, formulas or text descriptions in the form to describe the characteristics of business processes. Business Process Modeling by implication focuses on processes, actions and activities, etc. (TJDLUT, 2007). Resources feature within BPM in terms of how they are processed. People (teams, departments, etc) feature in BPM in terms of what they do, to what, and usually when and for what reasons, especially when different possibilities or options exist, as in a flow diagram. Business process modeling plays an important role in the business process change throughout the life cycle, by describing the activities and the logical relationship between activities to understand the current business processes. Describe the new process to evaluate its performance. Therefore, the Accurate and complete Business Process Formal Description is very important to the Business Process Management Model.

The operation business process modeling has three essential objectives: 1. acquire explicit knowledge about the business processes of the enterprise operation; 2. exploit this knowledge in business process reengineering projects to optimize the operation; 3. support the decision making activities of the enterprise.

An appropriate business process model is the prerequisite of effective business process management, thus it is necessary to follow some business process modeling standards, such as,

- **Workflow Management Coalition (WfMC) reference model and XPDL definition language:** This is mainly devel-

oped for stream architecture and workflow definition language standard.

- **BPML & BPMN:** BPML (Business Process Modeling Language) and BPMN (Business Process Modeling Notation) is a standard developed by the Organization of BPMI, sets a graphical business process description.
- **BPEL4WS:** BPEL4WS (Business Process Executive Language for Web service) is the standard which Microsoft, BEA, IBM, SAP and so on big company formulates together, referred to as BPEL, its goal is describes and achieve inter-organizational business process interaction, it is becoming the standard which the Web service the business process is most widespread uses (Recker, Jan C. and Rosemann, Michael and Indulska, Marta and Green, Peter, 2009).
- **WSDL:** Web Services Description Language (WSDL) is the IBM developed XML-based language used to describe how to organize or co-coordinating a series of Web services invocation.
- **ebXML:** It is OASIS and the UN/CEFACT formulation about commercial coordination a series of standards.
- **UML:** Unified Modeling Language (UML) is a leading standardized specification language for object modeling in the software engineering domain by OMG.

Besides the above standards, there are also many other business process modeling techniques, such as, Flowchart. It is the most intuitive, most flexible method of process description. At present flow chart is no longer a major modeling techniques, used only for the brief description of the processes to exchange of information.

- **Role Activity Diagram (RAD) and Role Interaction Diagram (RID):** RAD is a structured process modeling techniques, emphasizing the role of the interaction between the role and activities, as well as links to external events, a comprehensive description of the process of the main features (goals, roles, decision-making, etc.) RID is the RAD method expansion

- **Petri Net:** The Petri net through place, transition, and other elements to express the process and the state, it has the solid mathematical theory support, easy to analyze and the simulation.

- **Solution**: Other technologies related to business process modeling include model-driven architecture and service-oriented architecture. People should determine to follow different standards and model at different level of granularity based on real requirements.

3 TRENDS IN BPM RESEARCH

Although BPM have achieved successful progress in current business market, it is too far to reach perfect. BPM systems are still evolving during to dynamic global market environment. Today, more companies are increasingly concerned with the business process performance and implement rather than the original operation such as processes running, doing the right process thing, easily maintaining, etc. Development of any strategic goals, if not the implementation of the enterprise's specific business processes, it has always been difficult to implement. The strategic objectives are divided into every level to correspond to the specific processes. To ensure that business processes we need to do the appropriate assurance systems and standards which include the curing process of the IT tools (Kapil Pant and Matjaz Juric, 2008).

Despite their own purpose and architecture, most BPM software in today covers the process modeling, process execution, process integration and process monitoring applications. BPM more focus on application implement. It has been integrated into some application level business such as the price management, project management to achieve greater core enterprise business.

Nowadays BPM software products present a wide range of development trends. The traditional professional BPM vendors continue to extend the function depth as well as the system architecture, such as the extension of application business event management, business rule management. More major software vendors, including IBM, Oracle, and Microsoft and so on, are set foot into the BPM field through independent research, mergers or acquisition. This trend has largely promoted the development of BPM and format a complementary situation between traditional professional BPM vendors and major software vendors. Such as the BPM field of major merger - Software AG acquisition of IDS Scheer.

Long expensive BPM development cycles along with fixed architecture quickly drains available budget resources. This seriously erodes the ability of many organizations to change and innovate as rapidly as their marketplaces demand. In order to address these challenges new methodologies for implementing and operating BPM are needed.

Recent advances in BPM technology such as SaaS, SOA, or Cloud computing will challenge the design of the future BPM systems. The goal of SOA is to achieve loose coupling among interacting software. This allows resources available as independent services on a network and can be accessed without knowledge of their underlying platform. By the services offered by SOA, BPM can use them as building blocks that can be orchestrated to model complex business processes. Through SOA, BPM can making the business process loose coupled (Leymann, F., Roller, D., Schmidt, M.-T, 2002). Therefore it is desirable to define a mechanism to integrate the SOA into BPM. Such situation also exists in SaaS and Cloud computing. In order to address these challenges new methodologies for implementing and operating business process are needed. In particular new mechanisms are required which permits to structure their architecture loosely, to define their service routing scheme, and to manage their resources independently.

REFERENCES

Fischer, L. (2005). *Workflow handbook 2005. Future Strategies Inc*. Book Division.

Indulska, M., Recker, J., Rosemann, M., & Green, P. (2009). *Business process modeling: Current issues and future challenges*. 21st International Conference on Advanced Information Systems.

Jeston, J., & Nelis, J. (2008). *Business process management: Practical guidelines to successful implementations*. Elsevier Ltd.

Leymann, F., Roller, D., & Schmidt, M.-T. (2002). Web services and business process management. *IBM Systems Journal, 41*(2), 198–211. doi:10.1147/sj.412.0198

Pant, K., & Juric, M. (2008). *Business process driven SOA using BPMN and BPEL: From business process modeling to orchestration and service oriented architecture* (pp. 208–328). Packt Publishing.

Recker, J. C., Rosemann, M., Indulska, M., & Green, P. (2009). Business process modeling: A comparative analysis. *Journal of the Association for Information Systems, 10*(4), 333–363.

TJDLUT. (2007). *Summary of business process management*. Retrieved from http://www.uml.org.cn/workclass/200710151.asp

Van der Aalst, W., Hofstede, A., & Weske, M. (2003). Business process management: A survey. *Proceedings of the 2003 International Conference on Business Process Management,* (pp. 1-12).

van der Aalst, W., & van Hee, K. (2002). *Workflow management: Models, methods and systems*. The MIT Press.

ADDITIONAL READING

Decker, G., & Puhlmann, F. (2007). *Extending BPMN for Modeling complex choreographies. On the Move to Meaningful Internet Systems 2007: CoopIS, DOA, ODBASE, GADA, and IS* (pp. 24–40). Springer. doi:10.1007/978-3-540-76848-7_4

Decker, G., & Weske, M. (2007). Behavioral consistency for B2B process integration. *Proceedings of 19th Conference on Advanced Information Systems Engineering (CAiSE 2007)* (pp. 81-95). Springer.

Dehnert, J., & Rittgen, P. (2001). Relaxed Soundness of business processes. *Proceedings of the 13th International Conference on Advanced Information Systems Engineering (CAiSE)* (pp. 157-170). Springer.

Dumas, M., & ter Hofstede, A. H. (2001). UML Activity diagrams as a workflow specification language. *Proceedings of the International Conference on the Unified Modeling Language*. Toronto, Canada.

Georgakopoulos, D., Hornick, M., & Sheth, A. (1995). An Overview of workflow management: From process modeling to workflow automation infrastructure. *Distributed and Parallel Databases, 3*(2), 119–153. doi:10.1007/BF01277643

Hoare, C. (1978). Communicating Sequential processes. *Communications of the ACM, 21*(8), 666–677. doi:10.1145/359576.359585

Krafzig, D., Karl, B., & Slama, D. (2004). *Enterprise SOA: Service-Oriented architecture best practices*. Prentice Hall PTR.

Martens, A. (2003). On Usability of web services. *Proceedings of 1st Web Services Quality Workshop (WQW 2003)*.

Martens, A. (2005). Analyzing Web Service based business processes. *Proceedings of International Conference on Fundamental Approaches to Software Engineering (FASE'05)*. Springer-Verlag.

Massuthe, P., Reisig, W., & Schmidt, K. (2005). An Operating guideline approach to the SOA. *Annals of Mathematics, Computing & Teleinformatics, 1*(3), 35–43.

Milner, R. (1991). *The polyadic Pi-calculus: A tutori*al. Technical Report ECS-LFCS-91-180. Computer Science Department, University of Edinburgh.

Milner, R. (1992). A Calculus of mobile process, part I/part II. *Journal of Information and Computation, 100*(1), 1–77. doi:10.1016/0890-5401(92)90008-4

Mulyar, N., & van der Aalst, W. (2005). *Patterns in colored petri nets*. BETA Working Paper Series, WP 139. Eindhoven, The Netherlands: Eindhoven University of Technology.

Puhlmann, F., & Weske, M. (2005). Using the Pi-Calculus for formalizing workflow patterns. *Proceedings of BPM 2005* (pp. 153-168). Springer-Verlag.

Puhlmann, F., & Weske, M. (2006). Investigations on soundness regarding lazy activities. [Springer.]. *Proceedings of Business Process Management, 2006*, 145–160. doi:10.1007/11841760_11

Sewell, P. (2000). *Applied Pi-A brief tutorial*. Technical Report Nr. 498. University of Cambridge.

van der Aalst, W. (1998). The application of Petri nets to workflow management. *The Journal of Circuits, Systems and Computers, 8*(1), 21–66.

van der Aalst, W., Hee, K., & Houben, G. (1994). Modeling and analysing workflow using a Petri-net based approach. *Proceedings of the Second Workshop on Computer-Supported Cooperative Work, Petri Nets and Related Formalisms*, (pp. 31–50).

van der Aalst, W., Navathe, S., & Wakayama, T. (1996). Three good reasons for using a Petri-net-based workflow management system. *Proceedings of the International Working Conference on Information and Process Integration in Enterprises (IPIC'96)*, (pp. 179-201).

van der Aalst, W., & ter Hofstede, A. (2002). Workflow patterns: On the expressive power of (Petri-net-based) workflow lanuages. *Proceedings of the Fourth Workshop on the Practical Use of Coloured Petri Nets and CPN Tools (CPN 2002)* (pp. 1-20). University of Aarhus.

Weske, M. (2007). *Business process management: Concepts, languages, architectures*. Springer.

Yang, D., & Zhang, S. (2003). An approach for workflow modeling using Pi-calculus. *Journal of Zhejiang University. Science, 6*.

Zaha, J., Barros, A., Dumas, M., & ter Hofstede, A. (2006). A language for service behavior modeling. *Proceedings 14th International Conference on Cooperative Information Systems (CoopIS 2006)* (pp. 145-162). Springer Verlag.

Chapter 27
Business Process Modeling:
Analysis and Evaluation

Gang He
Yunnan University, China

Gang Xue
Yunnan University, China

Kui Yu
Yunnan University, China

Shaowen Yao
Yunnan University, China

ABSTRACT

Business process modeling is that make use of graphics, formulas, tables and text to describe the characteristics of business process, and answer why to do, what to do, how to do. Business process modeling is the foundation of business process management. Implementation of business process management can improve the process and enhance competitiveness. In this chapter, the authors attempt to find current business process modeling methods' advantages and disadvantages by analyzing their feature and comparison of based on series important evaluation criteria. The goal is that it provides a reference to business process modeling methods in practice.

1 INTRODUCTION

Business process modeling is a way to express business processes, and it is the important foundation of process analysis and reengineering. The main purpose of Business process modeling is to provide an effective process model and to assist relevant staff to analyze and optimize business process. Business process management (BPM) is a management method focused on aligning all aspects of an organization with the wants and requirements of clients. It is a comprehensive management method that promotes business effectiveness and efficiency while striving for innovation, flexibility, and integration with technology. Of course, Business process modeling is the first and most important step in BPM lifecycle (van der Aalst, Hofstede., & Weske., 2003). Currently, the

DOI: 10.4018/978-1-4666-1975-3.ch027

research on business process modeling methods mostly focused on the proposal and application, and lack systemic analysis and comparison among them, thus this increase the complexity of the choice of business process modeling methods.

The remainder of this paper is organized as follows. Section 2 discusses the background of this paper, such as basic concepts of business process modeling and the primary motivation of business process modeling. Section 3 represent the main evaluation criteria of business process modeling methods which validated by some experts in related fields. Sections 4 briefly introduced these modeling methods and make the corresponding analysis; Section 5 is an overall comparison of business process modeling methods. Last make an expectation and a summary of this paper.

2 BACKGROUND

A business process is a flow of activities creating value by transforming some inputs into more valuable out puts according to a certain business goal, and a business process is a collection of related, structured activities or tasks that produce a specific service or product for a particular customer or customers. And it is the step-by-step algorithm to achieve a business objective. The steps of the process are called activities. Business process modeling is the study of the design and execution of processes (Havey, 2005).According to previous studies; we can summarize the primary motivation of business process modeling into the following points:

- Help people understand the business process and go on communication;
- Support for process improvement and management;
- Increase productivity and decrease head count;
- Support automated processes;

- Simplify regulations and compliance issues.

Although, there are many types of business modeling methods and technology, business processes and process modeling methods have their respective feature and special requirements. In other words, each business process modeling method is not a completely suitable for everywhere. Thus, selecting appropriate process modeling method become especially importance. In order to achieve this goal, the evaluation criteria of business process modeling methods which reflect their feature seem indispensable.

3 MEASUREMENT CRITERIA OF BUSINESS PROCESS MODELING METHOD

The most measurement criteria of business process modeling methods have been summarized in this paper (Lu & Sadiq., 2007).The most important criteria include the following aspects:

- **Expressibility:** the expressive power of a process modeling language that is governed by its ability to express specific process requirements reflecting the purpose of process modeling and execution. A process model is required to be complete, which should contain structure, data, execution, temporal, and transactional information of the business process (Sadiq & Orlowska., On capturing process requirements of workflow based business information systems, 1999) (Sadiq & Orlowska., On correctness issues in conceptual modeling of workflows, 1997).
- **Flexibility:** flexibility can be seen as the ability to deal with both foreseen and unforeseen changes, by varying or adapting those parts of the business process that are affected by them, whilst retaining the es-

sential format of those parts that are not impacted by the variations. Or, in other words, flexibility is as much about what should stay the same in a process as what should be allowed to change (Regev & Wegmann., 2005) (Schonenberg, 2008)

- **Adaptability:** which is the ability of the workflow processes to react to exceptional circumstances, which may or may not be foreseen, and generally would affect one or a few process instances (Sadiq, Sadiq, & Orlowska., 2005).

- **Dynamism:** the ability of the workflow process to change when the business process evolves. This evolution may be slight as for process improvements or drastic as for process innovation or process reengineering (Sadiq, Sadiq, & Orlowska., 2005).

- **Complexity:** the measures of the difficulty to model, analyze, and deploy a process model (Cardoso, 2005), as well as the support for the dynamic and changing business process.

- **Formalization:** process model require formal language to express (Renzhong, Guangmin, & T.Hongtao, 2002).

4 ANALYSIS OF BUSINESS PROCESS MODELING METHODS

There are many kinds of process modeling methods and tools at present. These process modeling methods have a wide range, from the traditional static data modeling (Eg, DFD.) to the most recent modeling of the dynamic behavior (Eg, Role Activity Diagram, Petri nets, etc.). Here, we will analyze the current relatively mature modeling methods which support for business process management, such as BPMN, Petri net, YAWL, Event-driven Process chain, Role Activity Diagrams, Data Flow Diagram.

4.1 Business Process Modeling Notation

The Business Process Modeling Notation (BPMN) is a standard for business process modeling, and provides a graphical notation for specifying business processes in a Business Process Diagram (BPD) (Simpson, 2004), which created by the Business Process Management Initiative (BPMI), the first goal of BPMN is to provide a notation that is readily understandable by all business users (Owen & Raj., 2003). The main elements of BPMN are shown in Figure 1.

A research presented in the paper (Recker, Indulska, Rosemann, & Green, 2006)uses the principles of representational analysis for an investigation into the potential and perceived shortcomings of BPMN. It uses a model of representation proposed by Wand and Weber (1995) that was originally derived from an ontology defined by Bunge (1977), the so-called BWW representation model. Another presentation about the weaknesses of BPMN as follows:

- Ambiguity and confusion in sharing BPMN models
- Support for routine work
- Support for knowledge work, and
- Converting BPMN models to executable environments

4.2 Petri Net

The Petri net, a notion devised in 1962 by the mathematician Carl Adam Petri, is a formal graphical and mathematical modeling tool, which can describe and study information processing systems that are characterized as being concurrent, asynchronous, distributed, parallel, nondeterministic, and stochastic. In Petri's original conception, the symbols are the following (Havey, 2005):

Figure 1. Main elements of BPMN

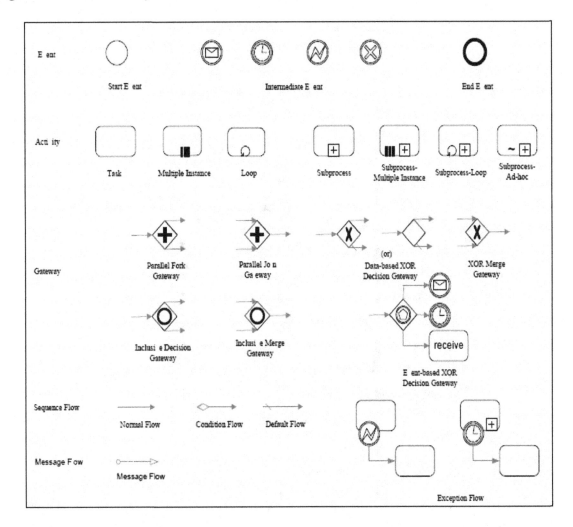

- **Place**: Drawn as a circle, a place is a stopping point in a process, representing (in many cases) the attainment of a milestone.
- **Transition**: A transition is a rectangle that represents an event or action.
- **Token**: A token is a black dot residing in a place. Collectively, the set of tokens represents the current state of the process. During the execution of the process, tokens move from place to place.
- **Arc**: An arc is a link from a transition to a place or a place to a transition.

As shown in Figure 2, it use Petri net describes the warehouse process of a company.

The strength of Petri net is their support for analysis of many properties and problems associated with concurrent systems (Kim & Kim, 1996). Petri Nets is a very general model. Finite State Machines, Process Networks and Dataflow Networks are all subclasses of Petri Nets. As a mathematical model, it is possible to set up state equations, algebraic equations and other models governing the behavior of the system. Due to its generality and permissiveness, the model can be applied to any area or system that can be described graphically. But the more general the model is,

Figure 2. Using Petri net, the figure describes the warehouse process of a company

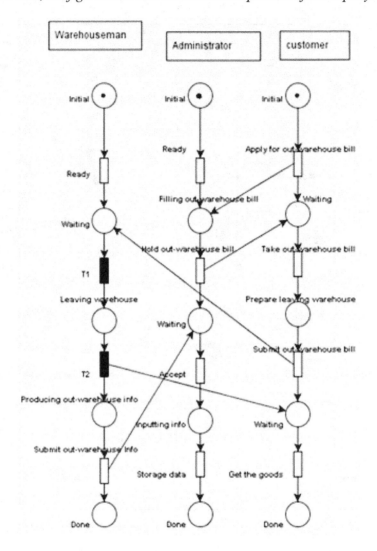

the more complex it is. A major weakness of Petri Nets is its complexity. The problem may become unsolvable even for modest sized system (Cortadella & Reisig, 2004) (Murata, 1989). Because of the link between Place and Transition is fixed, it is more suitable for expressing in a fixed structure of coupled system, but it is difficult to express loose dynamic couple system.

4.3 YAWL

YAWL (van der Aalst & Hofstede, 2005)is a workflow language especially designed to support the 20 workflow patterns proposed by Vander Aalst, etc. It is more suitable than (high-level) Petri nets in the sense that there is direct support for several patterns that are difficult to deal with using (colored) Petri nets. YAWL can be considered a very powerful workflow language, built upon experiences with languages supported by contemporary workflow management systems.

Figure 3.The main symbols of EPC

Logical connectors

YAWL to be more applicable in the area of web services and Enterprise Application Integration it is also desirable that support for communication patterns. More detail about YAWL please refers to (van der Aalst & Hofstede, 2005).YAWL has a number of advantages, but also some drawbacks. The graphical representation of process models is closely related action.In this case, the software might have already performed its work partially at the same time, the token is removed. In such situations, it is unclear, how the business process management system should behave. More detail about the weakness of YAWL in representing some advanced control flow patterns could refer to Weske, 2007.

4.4 Event-Driven Process Chain

Event-Driven Process Chains (EPC) introduced by Keller et al. (1992) is a wide-spread method for business process modeling. EPC is a business process modeling language representing temporal and logical dependencies between activities of a process (Keller, N"1ttgens., & Scheer., 1992). Event Process Chain EPC (Event Process Chains) profits from entity-relationship model (ER) model and data flow diagram (DFD) and other model approach. An EPC consists of the following elements (Van der Aalst, 1999), as shown in Figure 3:

- **Functions:** The basic building blocks are functions. A function corresponds to an activity (task, process step), which needs to be executed.
- **Events:** Events describe the situation before and/or after a function are executed. Functions are linked by events. An event

may correspond to the post-condition of one function and act as a precondition of another function.

- **Logical connectors:** Connectors can be used to connect activities and events. This way the flow of control is specified. There are three types of connectors: ^ (and), XOR (exclusive or) and (or).

We do not prepare to make excessive discussions for EPC in here,For more details about EPC, referring to (Kindler, 2006) (Mendling & N"1ttgens., 2006). Figure 4 is shown as outwarehouse process with EPC. The strength of EPC lies on its easy-to-understand notation that is capable of portraying business information sys-tem, while at the same time incorporating other important feature such as functions, data, organizational structure and information resources as already described before. This makes EPC as a widely acceptable standard to denote business processes (Zlatkin & Kaschek, 2006).However; neither the syntax nor the semantics of an EPC are well defined. The semantics of a join connector of type is not clear and subject to multiple interpretations. As a result, an EPC may be ambiguous. Moreover, it is not possible to check the model for consistency and completeness. The absence of formal semantics also hinders the exchange of models between tools of different vendors and prevents the use of powerful analytical techniques (Van der Aalst, 1999).

4.5 Role Activity Diagram

Role Activity Diagrams (RADs) are a useful way of describing processes. They are valuable

Figure 4. EPC for out-warehouse of a company

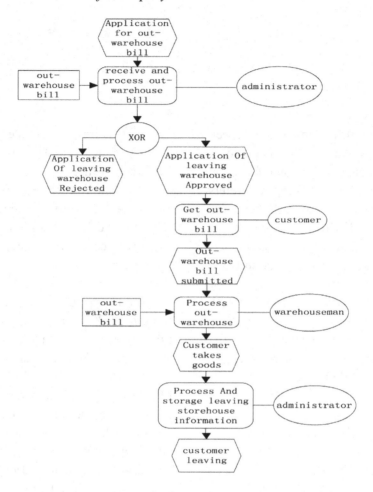

in documenting processes as they are now, and as they might be in the future. RAD is a visual notation for business process modeling. RAD is useful for modeling organized human behavior and interactions (Harrison-Broninski, 2005).

The elements of a RAD model are: roles — group together activities into units of responsibility; part refinements—describe parallel execution threads; case refinements—describe choices; activities —basic building blocks for describing work; interactions —activities requiring coordination with activities in other roles; external events—points at which state changes occurring in the environment influence on our process; states—useful to model point wise process goals; synchronization points—needed to synchronize

threads originating from the same part refinement (refer to (Badica, Badica, & Litoiu, 2003) for more details), as shown in Figure 5.

RAD describes business process by the role, purpose and rules' various aspects. The main feature that has a good description of the relationship between the activities, but RAD is just a static analysis of the relationship among the activities and less Dynamism. While, as for complex logic modeling also has certain lankness.

4.6 Data Flow Diagram

DFD is a graphical representation of logical systems that can describe the system of logic models, and data stream flowing in the system and deal

Figure 5. RAD for out-warehouse

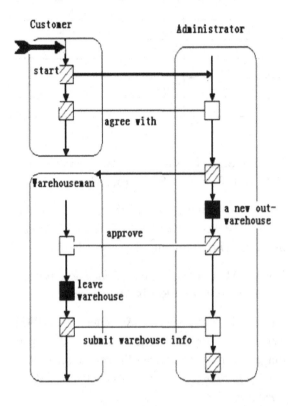

with the situation that data flow and process in the system. The main feature of DFD: visual, simple and explicit. When it comes to conveying how information data flows through systems, data flow diagram (DFD) are the method of choice over technical descriptions for three principal reasons (Donald S. Le Vie, 2000):

- DFD is easier to understand by technical and no technical audiences
- DFD can provide a high level system overview, complete with boundaries and connections to other systems
- DFD can provide a detailed representation of system components

Disadvantages: DFDs for large systems can become cumbersome, difficult to translate and read, and be time consuming in their construction. It is hard to support for Business process Re-engineering; DFD for the resource conflicts, parallel processes, and representation of effectiveness for a given period of time and behavior state is very vague. In addition, it cannot be expressed the Dynamism of processes very well.

5 COMPARISON OF BUSINESS PROCESS MODELING

In summary, we can see each modeling approach has its strength and weakness. In practice, we are unable to determine which method or technology is the best, when we actually carry out BPR, or Business Engineering (A.Curran & Ladd., 1999). In fact, people are generally based on the actual goals and circumstances to choose more than one appropriate modeling method. So it is essential to summarize and compare feature of these modeling methods. First in Here, in the form of a table shows a comparative framework, as shown in Table 1. In this table, these modeling methods which are based on some evaluation criteria of Business Process Modeling Method in Section 3. Through the comparison of the table, we can find more clearly feature and strength of various business modeling methods. It can provide some reference for people in specific business process modeling.

FUTURE RESEARCH DIRECTIONS

This paper has analyzed business process modeling methods' feature, and find their strength and weakness; In the end, make a comparison of based on series important evaluation criteria, could provides a reference for business process modeling methods in practice. Future work can focus on transforming EPC to BPEL based on a certain algorithm, and can find their weakness.

Table 1. A comparison business process modeling methods

	BPMN	Petri net	YAWL	EPC	RAD	DFD
Expressibility	Good	Good	Good	Good	Moderate	Good
Flexibility	Good	Weak	Moderate	Good	Weak	Moderate
Adaptability	Moderate	Good	Moderate	Moderate	Moderate	Moderate
Dynamism	Weak	Very good	Good	Weaker	Weak	Weak
Complexity	Easy	High	Easy	Moderate	Moderate	Easy
Formalization	Good	Good	Good	Yes	Yes	Yes

CONCLUSION

We have selected a number of classical process modeling methods, including BPMN, Petri net, YAWL, EPC, DFD, and Role Activity Diagram to specific a cited cases respectively. This paper has presented a series of important evaluation criteria of business process modeling methods, including expressibility, flexibility, adaptability, dynamism, complexity, formalization considerations, via analyzing these approaches reviews their strengths and weakness. Finally take this as the foundation, carries on an overall comparison and evaluation to the business process modeling methods.

REFERENCES

Badica, C., Badica, A., & Litoiu, V. (2003). Role activity diagrams as finite state processes. *ISP-DC'03 Proceedings of the Second international conference on Parallel and distributed computing*, (pp. 15-22).

Cardoso, J. (2005). How to measure the control-flow complexity of web processes and workflows. In *The workflow handbook* (pp. 199-212).

Cortadella, J., & Reisig, W. (2004). *Petri nets*. Bologna, Italy: Springer.

Curran, T. A., & Ladd, A. (1999). *SAP R/3 Business blueprint: Understanding enterprise supply chain management*. Pearson Education.

Donald, S., & Le Vie, J. (2000). *Understanding data flow diagrams*. STC Proceedings.

Harrison-Broninski, K. (2005). *Human interactions: The heart and soul of business process management*. Meghan-Kiffer Press Home.

Havey, M. (2005). *Essential business process modeling, part I*. O'Reilly Media, Inc.

Keller, G., Nuttgens, M., & Scheer, A. (1992). Semantische Prozessmodellierung auf der Grundlage "Ereignisgesteuerter Prozessketten (EPK). *Verffentlichungen des Instituts fur Wirtschaftsinformatik*.

Kim, Y., & Kim, T. (1996). Petri nets modeling and analysis using extended bag-theoretic relational algebra. *IEEE Transactions on Systems, Man, and Cybernetics. Part B, Cybernetics, 26*(4), 599–605. doi:10.1109/3477.517034

Kindler, E. (2006). On the semantics of EPCs: Resolving the vicious circle. *Data & Knowledge Engineering, 56*(1), 23–40. doi:10.1016/j.datak.2005.02.005

Lu, R., & Sadiq, S. (2007). A survey of comparative business process modeling approaches. *Lecture Notes in Computer Science, 4439*, 82–94. doi:10.1007/978-3-540-72035-5_7

Mendling, J., & Nuttgens, M. (2006). EPC markup language (EPML): An XML-based interchange format for event-driven process chains (EPC). *Information Systems and e-Business Management, 4*(3), 245-263.

Murata, T. (1989). Petri nets: Properties, analysis and applications. [IEEE.]. *Proceedings of the IEEE, 77*(4), 541–580. doi:10.1109/5.24143

Owen, M., & Raj, J. (2003). *Introduction to the new business process modeling standard, BPMN and business process management.*

Recker, J. C., Indulska, M., Rosemann, M., & Green, P. (2006). How good is BPMN really? Insights from theory and practice. *14th European Conference on Information Systems,* (pp. 12-14).

Regev, G., & Wegmann, A. (2005). A regulation-based view on business process and supporting system flexibility. *6th BPMDS Workshop on Business Processes and Support Systems: Design for Flexibility BPMDS'05* (pp. 13-14). CAiSE'05 Workshops.

Renzhong, T., Guangmin, Z., & Hongtao, A. T. (2002). *Analysis of process modeling methods.*

Sadiq, S., Sadiq, W., & Orlowska, M. (2005). A framework for constraint specification and validation in flexible workflows. *Information Systems, 30*(5), 349–378. doi:10.1016/j.is.2004.05.002

Sadiq, W., & Orlowska, M. (1997). On correctness issues in conceptual modeling of workflows. In *Proceedings of the 5th European Conference on Information Systems.*

Sadiq, W., & Orlowska, M. (1999). On capturing process requirements of workflow based business information systems. *3rd International Conference on Business Information Systems* (pp. 281 -294). London, UK: Springer Verlag.

Schonenberg, H. A. (2008). Process flexibility: A survey of contemporary approaches. In *Advances in Enterprise Engineering I, Part 1* (pp. 16-30).

Simpson, R. C. (2004). *An XML representation for crew procedures.* Final Report NASA Faculty Fellowship Program.

Van der Aalst, W. (1999). Formalization and verification of event-driven process chains. *Information and Software Technology, 41*(10), 639–650. doi:10.1016/S0950-5849(99)00016-6

van der Aalst, W., & Hofstede, A. (2005). YAWL: Yet another workflow language (Revised version). *Information Systems, 30*(4), 245–275. doi:10.1016/j.is.2004.02.002

van der Aalst, W., Hofstede, A., & Weske, M. (2003). Business process management: A survey. *Proceedings of the 21st International Conference on Business Process Management,* (pp. 1-12).

Weske, M. (2007). Business process management: Concepts, languages, and architectures, 1 ed. Springer.

Zlatkin, S., & Kaschek, R. (2006). *Mapping business processes models from Petri nets into event-driven process chains.*

ADDITIONAL READING

Antonio, B., & Razvan, P. (2006). From BPEL processes to YAWL workflows. In *Proceedings of the 3rd International Workshop on Web Services and Formal Methods (WS-FM 2006), Lecture Notes in Computer Science, Vol. 4184,* (pp. 107–122). Berlin, Germany: Springer.

Cassandras, C. G., & Lafortune, S. (2008). *Introduction to discrete event systems* (2nd ed.). Springer. doi:10.1007/978-0-387-68612-7

Dehnert, J., & Rittgen, P. (2001). Relaxed soundness of business processes. *Proceedings of the 13th International Conference on Advanced Information Systems Engineering (CAiSE)* (pp. 157-170). Springer.

Dufourd, C., Jancar, P., & Schnoebelen, P. (1999). Boundedness of reset P/T nets. *International Colloquium on Automata. Languages and Programming, LNCS, 1644,* 301–310.

Esparza, J. (1997). Petri nets, commutative context-free grammars and basic parallel processes. *Fundamenta Informaticae, 30,* 24–41.

Georgakopoulos, D., Hornick, M., & Sheth, A. (1995). An overview of workflow management: From process modeling to workflow automation infrastructure. *Distributed and Parallel Databases, 3*(2), 119–153. doi:10.1007/BF01277643

Hildebrandt, T., Niss, H., & Olsen, M. (2006). Formalizing business process execution with bigraphs and reactive XML. *Proceedings of the 8th International Conference on Coordination Models and Language* (pp. 113-129). Berlin, Germany: Springer.

Krafzig, D., Karl, B., & Slama, D. (2004). *Enterprise SOA: Service-oriented architecture best practices.* Prentice Hall PTR.

Langner, P., Schneider, C., & Wehler, J. (1998). Petri net based certification of event-driven process chains. *Proceedings of the 19th International Conference on Application and Theory of Petri Nets,* (pp. 286-305).

Luckham, D. (2002). *The power of events: An introduction to complex event processing in distributed enterprise systems.* Addison-Wesley Professional.

Martens, A. (2003). On usability of web services. *Proceedings of 1st Web Services Quality Workshop (WQW 2003).*

Martens, A. (2005). Analyzing Web service based business processes. *Proceedings of International Conference on Fundamental Approaches to Software Engineering (FASE'05).* Springer-Verlag.

Mendling, J., Moser, M., & Neumann, G. (2006). Transformation of yEPC business process models to YAWL. *Proceeding SAC '06 Proceedings of the 2006 ACM Symposium on Applied Computing,* (pp. 1262 – 1266).

Ouyang, C., Dumas, M., Hofstede, A., & Aalst, W. (2006). From BPMN process models to BPEL Web services. *On the 4th International Conference on Web Services (ICWS06).* Chicago, IL: IEEE.

Peterson, J. L. (1977). Petri nets. *ACM Computing Surveys, 9*(3), 223–252. doi:10.1145/356698.356702

Peterson, J. L. (1981). *Petri net theory and the modeling of systems.* Englewood Cliffs, NJ: Prentice Hall.

Recker, J., & Indulska, M. (2007). An ontology-based evaluation of process modeling with Petri nets. *Journal of Interoperability in Business Information Systems, 2*(1).

Recker, J., Rosemann, M., & Krogstie, J. (2007). Ontology- versus pattern-based evaluation of process modeling languages: A comparison. *Communications of the Association for Information Systems, 20*(48).

Reisig, W. (1985). *Petri nets: An introduction.* New York, NY: Springer-Verlag, Inc.

Remco, M., Dumas, M., & Ouyang, C. (2007). *Formal semantics and analysis of BPMN process models using Petri nets.* Queensland University of Technology, Tech. Rep.

Rosemann, M., Green, P., Indulska, M., & Recker, J. (2009). Using ontology for the representational analysis of process modeling techniques. *International Journal of Business Process Integration and Management, 4*(4). doi:10.1504/IJBPIM.2009.032282

Soffer, P., Wand, Y., & Kaner, M. (2007). Semantic analysis of flow patterns in business process modeling. In Alonso, G., Dadam, P., & Rosemann, M. (Eds.), *Business Process Management, BPM 2007* (pp. 400–407). Springer. doi:10.1007/978-3-540-75183-0_29

Stahl, C. (2004). *Transformation von BPEL4WS in Petrinetze*. Diplomarbeit, Humboldt-UniversitÄat zu Berlin.

van der Aalst. (2005). Pi calculus versus Petri nets: Let us eat "humble pie" rather than further inflate the "Pi hype". *BP Trends*, *3*(5), 1–11.

van der Aalst, W., Hee, K., & Houben, G. (1994). Modeling and analysing workflow using a Petri-net based approach. *Proceedings of the Second Workshop on Computer-Supported Cooperative Work, Petri Nets and Related Formalisms*, (pp. 31–50).

van der Aalst, W., Navathe, S., & Wakayama, T. (1996). Three good reasons for using a petri-net-based workflow management system. *Proceedings of the International Working Conference on Information and Process Integration in Enterprises (IPIC'96)*, (pp. 179-201).

Verbeek, H., & Aalst, W. (2000). Woflan 2.0: A Petri-net-based workflow diagnosis tool. In Nielsen, M., & Simpson, D. (Eds.), *Application and Theory of Petri Nets* (*Vol. 1825*, pp. 475–484). Lecture Notes in Computer Science Berlin, Germany: Springer-Verlag. doi:10.1007/3-540-44988-4_28

Weske, M. (2007). *Business process management: Concepts, languages, architectures*. Springer.

Ye, J., Sun, S., Wen, L., & Song, W. (2008). Transformation of BPMN to YAWL. *International Conference Computer Science and Software Engineering*, (pp. 354–359).

Zurawski, R., & Zhou, M. (1994). Petri nets and industrial applications: A tutorial. *IEEE Transactions on Industrial Electronics*, *41*(6), 567–583. doi:10.1109/41.334574

KEY TERMS AND DEFINITIONS

Adaptability: Adaptability is the ability of the workflow processes to react to exceptional circumstances, which may or may not be foreseen, and generally would affect one or a few process instances.

Business Process Management (BPM): BPM includes methods, techniques, and tools to support the design, enactment, management, and analysis of operational business processes. It can be considered as an extension of classical Workflow Management (WFM) systems and approaches.

Business Process Modeling: Business process modeling is that make use of graphics, formulas, tables and text to describe the characteristics of business process.

Business Process Reengineering (BPR): Business Process Reengineering is the analysis and design of workflows and processes within an organization.

Business Process: A business process consists of a set of activities, and it can are executed in organizational and technical environment. The activities jointly realize a business goal.

Complexity: The measures of the difficulty to model, analyze, and deploy a process model, as well as the sup-port for the dynamic and changing business process.

Dynamism: The ability of the workflow process to change when the business process evolves. This evolution may be slight as for process improvements or drastic as for process innovation or process reengineering.

Expressibility: The expressive power of a process modeling language that is governed by its ability to express specific process requirements reflecting the purpose of process modeling and execution.

Flexibility: Flexibility is as much about what should stay the same in a process as what should be allowed to change.

Formalization: Process model require formal language to express.

Chapter 28
Advanced Branching and Synchronization Patterns Description Using Pi-Calculus

Kui Yu
Yunnan University, China

Nan Zhang
Yunnan University, China

Gang Xue
Yunnan University, China

Shaowen Yao
Yunnan University, China

ABSTRACT

Workflow patterns contain basic features of business process. Advanced branching and synchronization patterns present a series of patterns, which characterize more complex branching and merging concepts which arise in business processes. Pi-calculus can be applied in business process modeling. In this chapter, this kind of workflow patterns is investigated using Pi-calculus.

1 INTRODUCTION

The Workflow Patterns Initiative was established with the aim of delineating the fundamental requirements that arise during business process modeling on a recurring basis and describe them in an imperative way (Russell N. A., 2006). There are eight kinds of the workflow patterns, the kind of the most patterns of which is Advanced Branching and Synchronization Patterns. Advanced Branching and Synchronization Patterns presents a series of patterns which characterize more complex branching and merging concepts which arise in business processes (Van Der Aalst, 2003).

Mobile systems are made up of components that communicate and change their structure as a result of communication (Puhlmann F. a., 2005). The Pi-calculus is a process algebra that describes mobile systems. Based on the execution semantics

DOI: 10.4018/978-1-4666-1975-3.ch028

of the Pi-calculus, the behavior of each workflow pattern has been defined precisely in (Puhlmann F. a., 2005). This paper introduces Advanced Branching and Synchronization Patterns formalizations, each with an unambiguous formal definition and execution semantics (Puhlmann F. a., 2005).

The paper is organized as follows: Section 2 discusses related work. Section 3 includes brief introduction to Advanced Branching and Synchronization Patterns and Pi-calculus. Patterns are described using Pi-calculus in section 4. In section 5, description checking sample is shown. In section 6, this paper is concluded with an outlook and directions for future work.

2 BACKGROUND

2.1 Related Work

A Ph.D. thesis by Twan Basten researches basic process algebra and Petri nets (Basten, 1998). A more practical approach of using CCS (Milner R., 1999) to formalize web service choreography can be found in (Brogi A. C., 2004). Another approach of giving a detailed representation of the workflow patterns has been made with YAWL (van der Aalst W. t., 2003). The only approach known to the authors on the use of the Pi-calculus for workflow definitions is from Yang Dong and Zhang Shen-Sheng and centers on basic control flow constructs and the definition of activities (Dong & Dadam, 2003). Pi-calculus and Petri nets provide theoretical support for most business process standard (Gang Xue, 2008). Recently, Pi-calculus is also used to formalize web service interactions. Reference (Decker G. F., 2006) describes and formalizes web services using Pi-calculus, and the model described has been verified (Decker G. F., 2006).

2.2 Advanced Branching and Synchronization Patterns

The Workflow Patterns Initiative was established with the aim of delineating the fundamental requirements that arise during business process modeling on a recurring basis and describe them in an imperative way. There are eight kinds of the workflow patterns. They are as follows (Russell N. A., 2006): Basic Control Flow Patterns, Advanced Branching and Synchronization Patterns, Multiple Instance Patterns, State-based Patterns, Cancellation and Force Completion Patterns, Iteration Patterns, Termination Patterns, Trigger Patterns. Advanced Branching and Synchronization Patterns presents a series of patterns which characterize more complex branching and merging concepts which arise in business processes. This kind of patterns contains the most pattern and changes in various forms. This paper is mainly used to describe the kind of Advanced Branching and Synchronization Patterns using Pi-calculus.

2.3 Pi- Calculus

The Pi-calculus is a modern process algebra that describes mobile systems in a broader sense (Milner R. J., 1990). We give a brief presentation of the syntax and semantics of the Pi-calculus in this section. The syntax of Pi-calculus is given below by the following equation (Milner R. J., 1990).

$$P ::= 0$$

$$\mid \overline{x}y.P$$

$$\mid x(y).P$$

$$\mid \tau.P$$

$$\mid (x)P$$

$|[x = y]P$

$|P|Q$

$|P + Q$

$|A(y_1, \ldots, y_n)$

This paper will use the concept of the counter built using the pi-calculus. Counter is defined as follows (Milner R., 1999): $Count_0 = inc.Count_1 + \overline{zero}.Count_0$ and $Count_{n+1} = inc.Count_{n+2} + \overline{dec}.Count_n$. inc is used to increase the counter and dec is used to reduce the counter until the counter is 0.

3 PATTERNS DESCRIPTION

Advanced Branching and Synchronization Patterns present a series of patterns, which characterize more complex branching and merging concepts which arise in business processes. This kind of the patterns contains fourteen patterns. As follows (Russell N. A., 2006): Multi-Choice, Structured Synchronizing Merge, Multi-Merge, Structured Discriminator, Blocking Discriminator, Cancelling Discriminator, Structured Partial Join, Blocking Partial Join, Cancelling Partial Join, Generalised AND-Join, Local Synchronizing Merge, General Synchronizing Merge, Thread Merge, Thread Split. This paper will describe the fourteen patterns in term of Pi-calculus.

3.1 Advanced Branching and Synchronization Patterns Description

- **Multi-Choice** (Russell N. A., 2006): The divergence of a branch into two or more branches such that when the incoming branch is enabled, the thread of control is immediately passed to one or more of the outgoing branches based on a mechanism that selects one or more outgoing branches.

- **Solution**: Figure 1 illustrates the behavior of this pattern. The choice between processes B or C or B and C after A is modeled by A having three possibilities of execution. Either A triggers B or C or both B and C.

$A=(v\ exec)\tau_A.(A1|A2)$

$A1=\overline{exec}.b.0+\tau.c.0+\tau.b.\overline{exec}.c.0$

$A2=!exec.0$

$B=b.\tau_B.B'$

$C=c.\tau_C.C'$

- **Structured Synchronizing Merge** (Russell N. A., 2006): the convergence of two or more branches (which diverged earlier in the process at a uniquely identifiable point) into a single subsequent branch such that the thread of control is passed to the subsequent branch when each active incoming branch has been enabled.

- **Solution**: Figure 2 illustrates the behavior of this pattern. The triggers for activating a process C can either come from A or B as well as from B and C. If A and B are executed in parallel, C has to wait on a and b, otherwise only for a or b.

Figure 1. Multi-choice

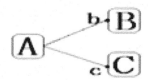

Figure 2. Structured synchronizing merge

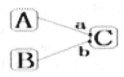

$A = \tau_A . \bar{a}.0$

$B = \tau_B . \bar{b}.0$

$C = a.\tau_C.C' + b.\tau_C.C' + a.b.\tau_C.C' + b.a.\tau_C.C'$

- **Multi-Merge** (Russell N. A., 2006): The convergence of two or more branches into a single subsequent branch such that each enablement of an incoming branch results in the thread of control being passed to the subsequent branch.

- **Solution**: Figure 3 illustrates the behavior of this pattern. Process D can be triggered arbitrary times by incoming triggers from B or C. Each time D gets triggered, a new copy of D is created by replication.

$B = \tau_B . \bar{d}.0$
$C = \tau_C . \bar{d}.0$
$D = !d . \tau_D.D'$

- **Structured Discriminator** (Russell N. A., 2006): the convergence of two or more branches into a single subsequent branch following a corresponding divergence earlier in the process model such

Figure 3. Multi-merge

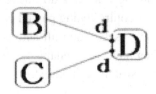

that the thread of control is passed to the subsequent branch when the first incoming branch has been enabled. Subsequent enablements of incoming branches do not result in the thread of control being passed on. The *Structured Discriminator* construct resets when all incoming branches have been enabled.

- **Solution**: Figure 4 can be used to represent Cancelling Discriminator Pattern, too. The discriminator pattern activates τ_A by triggering A2 if process A1 receives either b, c or d. After D2 has activated τ_A it waits for the triggers h from the remaining incoming branches of A1. Finally A2 resets the discriminator by using recursion.

$B = \tau_B . \bar{b}.0$

$C = \tau_C . \bar{c}.0$

$D = \tau_D . \bar{d}.0$

$A = (v\, h, exec)(A1|A2)$

$A1 = b . \bar{h}.0 | c.\bar{h}.0 | d.\bar{h}.0$

$A2 = h . \overline{exec} . h.h .A | exec . \tau_A.A'$

- **Blocking Discriminator** (Russell N. A., 2006): The convergence of two or more branches into a single subsequent branch following one or more corresponding divergences earlier in the process model. The thread of control is passed to the subsequent branch when the first active incoming branch has been enabled. The *Blocking Discriminator* construct resets when all active incoming branches have been enabled once for the same process instance. Subsequent enablements of incom-

Figure 4. Structured discriminator

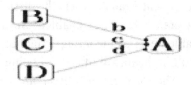

ing branches are blocked until the *Blocking Discriminator* has reset.

- **Solution**: Figure 5 can also be used to represent this pattern. This pattern is much the same as Structured Discriminator pattern, with the difference that when A2 receives a trigger h, it will trigger τ_A, and then activate process B,C and D.

$$B=\tau_B.\bar{b}.active.0$$

$$C=\tau_C.\bar{c}.active.0$$

$$D=\tau_D.\bar{d}.active.0$$

$$A=(v\,h,exec)(A1|A2)$$

$$A1=b.\bar{h}.0|c.\bar{h}.0|d.\bar{h}.0$$

$$A2=h.\overline{exec}.h.h.\overline{active}.\overline{active}.\overline{active}.A|\overline{exec}.\tau_A.A'$$

- **Cancelling Discriminator** (Russell N. A., 2006): The convergence of two or more branches into a single subsequent branch

Figure 5. Blocking discriminator

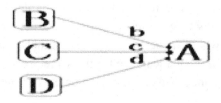

following one or more corresponding divergences earlier in the process model. The thread of control is passed to the subsequent branch when the first active incoming branch has been enabled. Triggering the *Cancelling Discriminator* also cancels the execution of all of the other incoming branches and resets the construct.

- **Solution**: Figure 6 can be used to illustrate this pattern, too. This pattern is much the same as Blocking Discriminator pattern, with the difference that when A2 receives a trigger h, it will cancel the remaining incoming branches.

$$B=\tau_B.(\bar{b}.0+cancel.0)$$

$$C=\tau_C.(\bar{c}.0+cancel.0)$$

$$D=\tau_D.(\bar{d}.0+cancel.0)$$

$$A=(v\,h,exec)(A1|A2)$$

$$A1=b.\bar{h}.0|c.\bar{h}.0|d.\bar{h}.0$$

$$A2=h.\overline{cancel}.\overline{cancel}.\overline{exec}.A|\overline{exec}.\tau_A.A'$$

- **Structured Partial Join** (Russell N. A., 2006): The convergence of two or more branches (say m) into a single subsequent branch following a corresponding divergence earlier in the process model such that the thread of control is passed to the subsequent branch when n of the incoming branches have been enabled where n is less than m. Subsequent enablements of incoming branches do not result in the thread of control being passed on. The join construct resets when all active incoming branches have been enabled. The join occurs in a structured context, i.e. there must

Figure 6. Cancelling discriminator

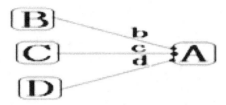

Figure 7. Structured partial join

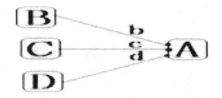

be a single *Parallel Split* construct earlier in the process model with which the join is associated and it must merge all of the branches emanating from the *Parallel Split*. These branches must either flow from the *Parallel Split* to the join without any splits or joins or be structured in form (i.e. balanced splits and joins).

- **Solution**: Figure 7 can also be used to represent this pattern. This pattern activates τ_A by triggering A2 when process A1 receives any two of b, c and d. After A2 has activated τ_A it waits for the triggers h from the remaining incoming branches of A1. Finally A2 resets the Structured Partial Join by using recursion.

$$B = \tau_B . \bar{b} . 0$$

$$C = \tau_C . \bar{c} . 0$$

$$D = \tau_D . \bar{d} . 0$$

$$A = (v\, h\, , exec\,)(A1 | A2)$$

$$A1 = b . \bar{h} . 0 | c . \bar{h}. 0 | d . \bar{h}. 0$$

$$A2 = h . h . \overline{exec} . h . A | exec . \tau_A . A'$$

- **Blocking Partial Join** (Russell N. A., 2006): The convergence of two or more branches (say m) into a single subsequent branch following one or more correspond-

ing divergences earlier in the process model. The thread of control is passed to the subsequent branch when n of the incoming branches has been enabled (where 2 = n < m). The join construct resets when all active incoming branches have been enabled once for the same process instance. Subsequent enablements of incoming branches are blocked until the join has reset.

- **Solution**: Figure 8 illustrates the behavior of this pattern, too. This pattern activates τ_A by triggering A2 when process A1 receives any two of b, c and d. After A2 has activated τ_A it waits for the triggers h from the remaining incoming branches of A1. Finally A2 activate blocked process B, C and D, and resets the blocking Partial Join by using recursion.

$$B = \tau_B . \bar{b} . active . 0$$

$$C = \tau_C . \bar{c} . active . 0$$

$$D = \tau_D . \bar{d} . active . 0$$

$$A = (v\, h\, , exec\,)(A1 | A2)$$

$$A1 = b . \bar{h} . 0 | c . \bar{h}. 0 | d . \bar{h}. 0$$

$$A2 = h . h . \overline{exec} . \overline{h} . \overline{active} . \overline{active} . \overline{active} . A | exec . \tau_A . A'$$

Figure 8. Blocking partial join

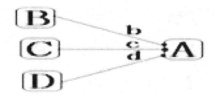

Figure 9. Cancelling partial join

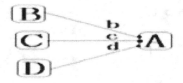

- **Cancelling Partial Join** (Russell N. A., 2006): The convergence of two or more branches (say m) into a single subsequent branch following one or more corresponding divergences earlier in the process model. The thread of control is passed to the subsequent branch when n of the incoming branches have been enabled where n is less than m. Triggering the join also cancels the execution of all of the other incoming branches and resets the construct.
- **Solution**: Figure 9 illustrates the behavior of cancelling partial join pattern. This pattern activates τ_A by triggering A2 when process A1 receives any two of b, c and d. After the remaining incoming branches are canceled, A2 will activated τ_A, and reset the Cancelling Partial Join by using recursion.

$$B = \tau_B.(\overline{b}.0 + cancel.0)$$

$$C = \tau_C.(\overline{c}.0 + cancel.0)$$

$$D = \tau_D.(\overline{d}.0 + cancel.0)$$

$$A = (\nu h, exec)(A1 | A2)$$

$$A1 = b.\overline{h}.0 | c.\overline{h}.0 | d.\overline{h}.0$$

$$A2 = h.h.\overline{cancel}.\overline{exec}.A | exec.\tau_A.A'$$

- **Generalised AND-Join** (Russell N. A., 2006): The convergence of two or more branches into a single subsequent branch such that the thread of control is passed to the subsequent branch when all input branches have been enabled. Additional triggers received on one or more branches between firings of the join persist and are retained for future firings. Over time, each of the incoming branches should deliver the same number of triggers to the AND-join construct (although obviously, the timing of these triggers may vary).
- **Solution**: Figure 10 illustrates the behavior of this pattern. First, two counters were set at the process B and C, that is, $Countb_0$ and $Countc_0$. The process B and C have storage capacity, which is represented using counter. The convergence of process B and C into a single subsequent branch, such as process D, when all input branches have been enabled. Additional triggers received on one branch, such as process B or C, between firings of the join persist and are retained for future firings through counters.

$$Countb_0 = inb.Countb_1 + \overline{bzero}.Countb_0$$

$$Countb_{n+1} = inb.Countb_{n+2} + \overline{bdec}.Countb_n$$

$$Countc_0 = inc.Countc_1 + \overline{czero}.Countc_0$$

Figure 10. Generalised AND-Join

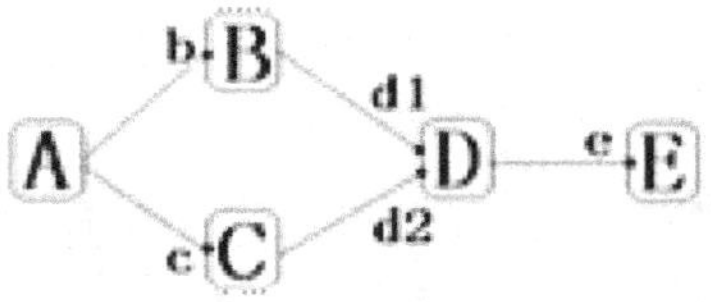

$$Countc_{n+1} = inc.Countc_{n+2} + \overline{cdec}.Countc_n$$

$$A = \tau_A.(\overline{b}.\overline{c} + \overline{c}.\overline{b}).A$$

$$B = b.\tau_B.\overline{inb}.B$$

$$C = c.\tau_C.\overline{inc}.C$$

$$DS = D1 + D2$$

$$DS1 = bdec.\overline{d1}.DS1$$

$$DS2 = cdec.\overline{d2}.DS2$$

$$D = D1 + D2 + D3$$

$$D1 = d1.d2.\tau_D.\overline{e}.D$$

$$D2 = d2.d1.\tau\,D.\,\overline{e}.D$$

$$D3 = bzero.czero.0 + czero.bzero.0$$

- **Local Synchronizing Merge** (Russell N. A., 2006): The convergence of two or more branches which diverged earlier in the process into a single subsequent branch such that the thread of control is passed to the subsequent branch when each active incoming branch has been enabled. Determination of how many branches require synchronization is made on the basis on information locally available to the merge construct. This may be communi-

cated directly to the merge by the preceding diverging construct or alternatively it can be determined on the basis of local data such as the threads of control arriving at the merge.

- **Solution**: Figure 11 can be used to illustrate the behavior of Local Synchronizing Merge pattern. This pattern is much the same as Blocking Discriminator pattern, with the difference that this pattern introduces Deferred Choice pattern. Determination of how many branches require synchronization is made on the basis on information locally available to the merge construct. The environment is modeled as an external process ε that signals either the name e_{env} or f_{env} but not both. The moment of choice is thereby as late as possible (Puhlmann F. a., 2005).

$$B = \tau_B.\overline{a1}.0$$

$$C = \tau_C.\overline{a2}.0$$

$$D = \tau_D.(\overline{d1}.0 + \overline{d2}.0)$$

$$E = d1.(e_{env}.\overline{kill}.\tau_E.\overline{a3}.0 + kill.0)$$

$$F = d2.(f_{env}.\overline{kill}.\tau_F.F' + kill.0)$$

$$A = a1.\tau_A.A' + a2.\tau_A.A' + a1.a2.\tau_A.A' + a1.a3.\tau_A.A' +$$

$$+ a2.a3.\tau_A.A' + a1.a2.a3.\tau_A.A'$$

- **General Synchronizing Merge** (Russell N. A., 2006): The convergence of two or more branches which diverged earlier in the process into a single subsequent branch such that the thread of control is passed to the subsequent branch when either (1) each

Figure 11. Local synchronizing merge

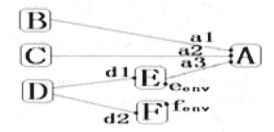

Figure 12. General synchronizing merge

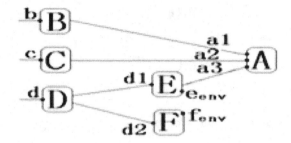

active incoming branch has been enabled or (2) it is not possible that any branch that has not yet been enabled will be enabled at any future time.

- **Solution**: Figure 12 illustrates the behavior this pattern. This pattern is much the same as Local Synchronizing Merge pattern, with the difference that process D is included in Deferred Choice pattern.

$$B = b. \, \tau_B . \overline{a1} .0$$

$$C = c. \, \tau_C . \overline{a2} .0$$

$$D = ! \, d. \, \tau_D .(\overline{d3} \, 0| \overline{d1} .0| \overline{d2} .0)$$

$$D1 = d3.(\, d \, env. \overline{kill.kill} \, . \overline{d} .0 + kill.0)$$

$$E = d1 .(e_{env}. \overline{kill} . \, \overline{kill} . \tau_E . \overline{a3} .0 + kill.0)$$

$$F = d2 .(f_{env}. \overline{kill} . \, \overline{kill} . \tau_F . F' + kill.0)$$

$$A = a1. \tau_A .A' + a2. \tau_A .A' + a1.a2. \tau_A .A' + a1.a3. \tau_A .A' +$$

$$+ a2.a3. \tau_A .A' + a1.a2.a3. \tau_A .A'$$

- **Thread Merge** (Russell N. A., 2006): At a given point in a process, a nominated number of execution threads in a single branch of the same process instance should

be merged together into a single thread of execution.

- **Solution**: Figure 13 can be used to illustrate the behavior of this pattern. At a given point in a process B, two of execution threads in a single branch of the same process instance should be merged together into a single thread of execution, such as process C.

$$A = \tau_A . \overline{bP}. \overline{bP}. \overline{bP} .0$$

$$B = b(p).p.b(p).p.b(p).p. \overline{cQ} .0$$

$$C = c(q).q.0$$

- **Thread Split** (Russell N. A., 2006): At a given point in a process, a nominated number of execution threads can be initiated in a single branch of the same process instance.

- **Solution**: Figure 14 illustrates the behavior this pattern, too. At a given point in a process B, two of execution threads can be initiated in a single branch of the same process instance.

$$A = \tau_A . \overline{b} .0$$

$$B = b. \tau_B . \overline{cQ}. \overline{cQ} .0$$

Figure 13. Thread merge

$C=!c(q).q.0$

3.2 Patterns Check

This paper uses analytical tool MWB'99(The Mobility Workbench (Victor, 1994) (Victor B., 1995) (Bundgaard M., 1994)for ensuring the correctness of patterns, which provides interactive simulation environment, to observe dynamic behaviors of process through command-line. To analyze Pattern Structured Synchronizing Merge and Structured Partial Join, for example, the whole system is simply supposed as $Ps=P_A|P_B|P_C|P_D$ and $P_T=P_A|P_B|P_C|P_D$.

Structured Synchronizing Merge Pattern is checked as follows:

- |>t.<'~v4.0|t.'~v3.0|<~v2.t.0+~v1.t.0+~v2
  .~v1.t.0+~v1.~v2.t.0>>
- |>t.<'~v4.0|'~v3.0|<~v2.t.0+~v1.t.0+~v2.
  ~v1.t.0+~v1.~v2.t.0>>
- |>'~v4.<'~v3.0|<~v2.t.0+~v1.t.0+~v2.~v1
  .t.0+~v1.~v2.t.0>>
- |>'~v3.<~v2.t.0+~v1.t.0+~v2.~v1.t.0+~v1
  .~v2.t.0>
- |>~v2.~v1.t.0
- |~v1.t.0
- |>t.0
- 0

Structured Partial Join Pattern is checked as follows:

- |>t.<'~v8.0|t.'~v7.0|t.'~v6.0|~v5.'~v2.0|~
  v4.'~v2.0|~v3.'~v2.0|~v1.~v1.'~v0.~v1.0
  |~v0.t.0>

Figure 14. Thread Split

- |[~v5=~v8]>t.<t.'~v7.0|t.'~v6.0|'~v2.0|~v
  4.'~v2.0|~v3.'~v2.0|~v1.~v1.'~v0.~v1.0
  |~v0.t.0>
- |>t.<'~v7.0|t.'~v6.0|'~v2.0|~v4.'~v2.0|~v3
  .'~v2.0|~v1.~v1.'~v0.~v1.0|~v0.t.0>
- |[~v4=~v7]>t.<t.'~v6.0|'~v2.0|'~v2.0|~v3.
  '~v2.0|~v1.~v1.'~v0.~v1.0|~v0.t.0>
- |>t.<'~v6.0|'~v2.0|'~v2.0|~v3.'~v2.0|~v1.
  ~v1.'~v0.~v1.0|~v0.t.0>
- |[~v3=~v6]>t.<'~v2.0|'~v2.0|'~v2.0|~v1.~
  v1.'~v0.~v1.0|~v0.t.0>
- |[~v1=~v2]>t.<'~v2.0|'~v2.0|~v1.'~v0.~v
  1.0|~v0.t.0>
- |[~v1=~v2]>t.<'~v2.0|~v0.~v1.0|~v0.t.0>
- |[~v0=~v2]>t.<'~v0.~v1.0|t.0>
- |>'~v0.<~v1.0|t.0>
- |>~v1.t.0
- |>t.0
- 0

Transitions of system state are showed by all tracking steps. System begins in the Ps and P_T, and the final state is Nil. In addition, all activities in process are reachable. Simultaneously, deadlocks are not found in representation of pattern Cancelling Discriminator when MWB'99 runs "deadlocks" command.

FUTURE RESEARCH DIRECTIONS

This paper discusses some advanced branching and synchronization patterns using Pi-calculus. More patterns description could be formalized based on complex Pi-calculus. My future work includes: check each pattern of Advanced Branching and Synchronization Patterns. Further study other kinds of patterns, including data patterns, resource patterns, and optimize the patterns described in this paper.

CONCLUSION

Advanced Branching and Synchronization Patterns are investigated and described using Pi-calculus in this paper. Based on the execution semantics of the Pi-calculus, the behavior of Advanced Branching and Synchronization Patterns has been defined precisely (Puhlmann F. a., 2005). The Pi-calculus has stronger ability in semantics description and the semantics of process model is more accurate. Furthermore, described Advanced Branching and Synchronization Patterns can open the door for reasoning on workflow process structures (Puhlmann F. a., 2005). This section presents a series of patterns which characterize more complex branching and merging concepts which arise in business processes. Although relatively commonplace in practice, these patterns are often not directly supported or even able to be represented in many commercial offerings (Russell N. A., 2006).

REFERENCES

Basten, A. (1998). *In terms of nets: System design with Petri nets and process algebra.*

Brogi, A. C. (2004). *Formalizing Web service choreographies.*

Bundgaard, M. (1994). *A brief introduction to mobility workbench.* MWB.

Decker, G. F. (2006). Formalizing service interactions. *Lecture Notes in Computer Science, 4102,* 414. doi:10.1007/11841760_32

Dong, Y. S.-S., & Dadam, P. (2003). Approach for workflow modeling using pi-calculus. *Journal of Zhejiang University. Science, 4*(50), 643–650.

Gang Xue, E. A. (2008). Investigating workflow resource patterns in term of Pi-calculus. In *Proceedings of the 2008 12th International Conference on Computer Supported Cooperative Word in Design, 14*(1). Xi'an,Chian.

Milner, R. (1999). *Communicating and mobile systems: The [symbol for pi]-calculus.* Cambridge University Press.

Milner, R. J. (1990). *A calculus of mobile processes-Part I/part II.*

Milner, R. (1991). *The polyadic pi-calculus: A tutorial.* Technical Report ECS-LFCS-91-180. Computer Science Department, University of Edinburgh.

Mulyar, N., & van der Aalst, W. (2005). *Patterns in colored petri nets.* BETA Working Paper Series, WP 139. Eindhoven, The Netherlands: Eindhoven University of Technology.

Puhlmann, F. a. (2005). Using the pi-calculus for formalizing workflow patterns. *Lecture Notes in Computer Science, 3649,* 153. doi:10.1007/11538394_11

Puhlmann, F., & Weske, M. (2005). Using the pi-calculus for formalizing workflow patterns. *Proceedings of BPM 2005* (pp. 153-168). Springer-Verlag.

Russell, N. A. (2006). *Workflow controlflow patterns: A revised view.*

Van Der Aalst, W. A. (2003). Workflow patterns. *Distributed and Parallel Databases, 14*(1), 5–51. doi:10.1023/A:1022883727209

van der Aalst, W. T. (2003). *YAWL: Yet another workflow language (Revised version).*

Victor, B. (1995). *The mobility workbench user's guide: Polyadic version 3.122.* Department of Information Technology, Uppsala University.

Victor, B. a. (1994). *The mobility workbench-A tool for the-calculus* (Vol. 204:11). Citeseer.

ADDITIONAL READING

Brogi, A., Canal, C., Pimentel, E., & Vallecillo, A. (2004). Formalizing Web service choreographies. *Electronic Notes in Theoretical Computer Science*, *105*, 73–94. doi:10.1016/j.entcs.2004.05.007

Dong, Y., & Shen-Sheng, Z. (2003). Approach for workflow modeling using -calculus. *Journal of Zhejiang University. Science*, *4*, 643–650. doi:10.1631/jzus.2003.0643

Dumas, M., & ter Hofstede, A. H. (2001). UML activity diagrams as a workflow specification language. *Proceedings of the International Conference on the Unified Modeling Language*. Toronto, Canada.

Georgakopoulos, D., Hornick, M., & Sheth, A. (1995). An overview of workflow management: From process modeling to workflow automation infrastructure. *Distributed and Parallel Databases*, *3*(2), 119–153. doi:10.1007/BF01277643

Milner, R. (1992). A calculus of mobile process, part I/part II. *Journal of Information and Computation*, *100*(1), 1–77. doi:10.1016/0890-5401(92)90008-4

Puhlmann, F. M., & Weske, M. (2005). Using the pi-calculus for formalizing workflow patterns. *Lecture Notes in Computer Science*, *3649*, 153. doi:10.1007/11538394_11

Puhlmann, F., & Weske, M. (2006). Investigations on soundness regarding lazy activities. [Springer.]. *Proceedings of Business Process Management*, *2006*, 145–160. doi:10.1007/11841760_11

Xue, G., et al. (2008). Investigating workflow resource patterns in term of Pi-calculus. In *Proceedings of the 2008 12th International Conference on Computer Supported Cooperative Word in Design*, Xi'an, China.

Xue, G., & Shaowen, Y. (2008). *Workflow Patterns Description in Term of Pi-calculus*. Computer Science.

KEY TERMS AND DEFINITIONS

Business Process: A business process consists of a set of activities, and it can are executed in organizational and technical environment. The activities jointly realize a business goal.

Pi-calculus: As a process calculus originally, Pi-calculus is a continuation of the body of work on the process calculus CCS(Calculus of Communicating Systems). The Pi-calculus is a modern process algebra that describes mobile systems in a broader sense.

Workflow: Workflow is the automation of a business process.

Workflow Management System (WFMS): WFMS is a software system that can define, initiate, execute, and manage workflows.

Workflow Pattern: Workflow patterns present a classification framework for workflow in the form of patterns. The framework is proposed by Nick Russell, Wil van der Aalst, and Arthur ter Hofstede.

Chapter 29
Modeling Process Exception Handling

Gang Xue
Yunnan University, China

Kun Zhang
Chuxiong Normal University, China

Yurong Hu
Yunnan University, China

Shaowen Yao
Yunnan University, China

ABSTRACT

In this chapter, process exception handling at work item level, exception handling at case level, and recovery action are discussed and represented in bigraphs for CCS. Based on the discussion, models for process exception patterns are proposed. The work intends to provide abstract models for analyzing the behavior of exception handling, and the result shows that some advanced features of bigraphs are introduced in representations.

1 INTRODUCTION

A business process consists of a set of activities, and these activities jointly realize a business goal. The activities are performed according to the execution constraints, which contain organizational and technical elements. In runtime environment, any attributes which are not conforming to process execution requirements at design time may raise errors. Exception handling aims at provid-ing facilities to handle process exceptions at runtime. Workflow exception patterns (Russell, van der Aalst, & ter Hofstede, 2006) present a classification framework for workflow exception handling in the form of patterns. The framework is independent of specific modeling approaches or technologies and as such provides an objective means of delineating the exception-handling capabilities of specific workflow systems (Russell, van der Aalst, & ter Hofstede, 2006).

DOI: 10.4018/978-1-4666-1975-3.ch029

Bigraphs and bigraphical reactive systems (BRSs) are novel theoretical tools that consider locality and connectivity (Jensen & Milner, 2004) (Milner, 2006), and they have been applied in business process management (Hildebrandt, Niss, & Olsen, 2006)(Bundgaard, Glenstrup, Hildebrandt, Højsgaard, & Niss, 2008). This chapter provides some results regarding representations of process exception handling based on bigraphs for CCS (Milner, 2009) (Milner, 1980), and the work intends to provide abstract models for analyzing the behavior of process exception handling.

The rest of chapter is organized as follows. Brief discussions on exception handling and bigraphs for CCS are included in section 2. In section 3, exception handling is represented in bigraphs for CCS. Finally, conclusion and future work are addressed in section 4 and section 5.

2 BACKGROUND

2.1 Exception Handling Patterns

In the field of Workflow Management System (WFMS), researchers analyzed the different workflow exceptions, and divided them into four classes: basic failures, application failures, expected and unexpected exceptions (Eder & Liebhart, 1995) and expected and unexpected exceptions are main topics which are addressed in WFMS. For expected exceptions, early research focuses on extensions to the classic ACID transaction model (Eder & Liebhart, 1995) (Worah & Sheth, 1997). For unexpected exceptions, adaptive workflow, workflow evolution and other technologies are proposed proposed (Rinderle, Reichert, & Dadam, 2004). In paper *Workflow Exception Patterns (Russell, van der Aalst, & ter Hofstede, 2006)*, the authors investigate the range of issues that may raise exceptions during process execution, and the paper proposed five expected types of exception: work item failure, deadline expiry, resource unavailability, external trigger

and constraint violation. There are three groups of specific handling strategy (Russell, van der Aalst, & ter Hofstede, 2006): exception handling at work item level, exception handling at case level and recovery action. For exception handling at work item level, there are 15 handling strategies. For exception handling at case level and recovery action, there are 3 handling strategies for each of them. The exception patterns take the form of tuples comprising the three elements (Russell, van der Aalst, & ter Hofstede, 2006): exception handling at work item level, exception handling at case level and recovery action. For the purpose of practice, there are 36 exception handling patterns.

Besides exception handling patterns, Researchers have summarized various kinds of Workflow-related patterns which contain Workflow Patterns (van der Aalst, ter Hofstede, Kiepuszewski, & Barros, 2003), Workflow Data Patterns (Russell, ter Hofstede, Edmond, & van der Aalst, 2004a), Workflow Resource Patterns (Russell, ter Hofstede, Edmond, & van der Aalst, Workflow Resource Patterns, 2004b), and so on.

2.2 Bigraphs for CCS

A *bigraph* consists of a set of nodes (controls) with ports. The ports can be connected to each other by links. The *place graph* represents nodes tree for spatial structure of controls. The *link graph* represents the communication between controls. Some bigraphs are shown in Figure 1, which contains three bigraphs (*G*, *F* and *H*). G^P is *place graph* for bigraph *G*, and G^L is *link graph* for bigraph *G*.

In Figure 1, the rectangles in *G* (*regions: 0, 1*) are its *roots*, and bigraph *F* has two *sites* (shaded rectangles): *0, 1*. A bigraph may have one or more *sites* where other bigraphs can be placed. Bigraphs can be built from smaller ones by composition, product, and identities. The composition of two bigraphs is formed from the combinations of place graphs and link graphs. In Figure 1, bigraph *F* and *H* can construct bigraph *G*: $G = F \circ H$.

Figure 1. Bigrah G, F, and H

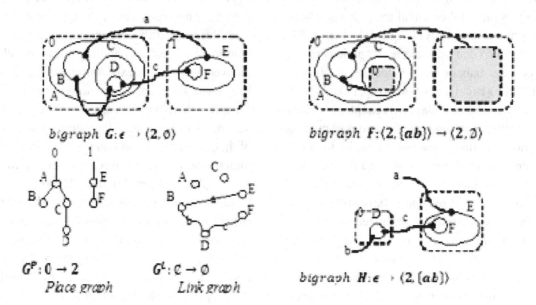

bigraph $G{:}\epsilon \rightarrow (2,\emptyset)$

$G^P{:}0 \rightarrow 2$ $G^L{:}\mathcal{C} \rightarrow \emptyset$

Place graph   Link graph

bigraph $F{:}\langle 2,\{ab\}\rangle \rightarrow \langle 2,\emptyset\rangle$

bigraph $H{:}\epsilon \rightarrow \langle 2,\{ab\}\rangle$

A node-free bigraph with no links is a *placing*, and a node-free bigraph with no places is a *linking (Milner, 2009)*. Links have two basic forms: *substitution (y/X)* and *closure (/x)* (Milner, 2009). The defined operations, which contain *parallel (∥)*, *nesting (.)* and *merge* product (|), support building bigraphs from elementary bigraphs. Bigraphs can also reconfigure themselves according to *reaction rules* which mainly consist of pre-conditions and post-conditions for transformations.

Bigraphs can use different signatures for distinct applications. A *placing sorting* Σ has a *sorts* set Θ, a *signature* $\mathcal{K}$ place-sorted over Θ, and a *formation rule* Φ (Milner, 2009). Φ is a property of augment bigraphs that is satisfied by identities and symmetries. Furthermore, it's preserved by composition and product. The augmented bigraphs satisfying Φ are called Σ_{sorted} (Milner, 2009). A sorting discipline and a set of reaction rules produce a *bigraphical reactive system* (BRS).

CCS (Calculus of Communicating Systems) (Milner, 1980), a kind of process algebra, has a strong mathematical focus on reasoning about concurrent processes. In bigraphs, the CCS place-sorting Σ_{CCS} has *sorts* $\{p, a\}$ for Θ_{CCS} and *signature* $\{alt: (p, 0), send: (a, 1), get: (a, 1)\}$ for $\mathcal{K}_{CCS}$; Σ_{CCS} is *hard* for sort p, and requires that all children of a θ type root r have sort θ, as well as all children of a θ type node v have sort opposite to θ (Milner, 2009). The sorts represents *process* and *alternation* and the *arity* in the signature means the number of ports of node. The abstract reaction rule (for CCS) R_{CCS} is a triple of form $\left(R, R', \eta\right)$, which has the *redex* (pre-condition of reaction): $R = alt.\left(send_x \mid id\right) \mid alt.(get_x \mid id)$, and the *reacutm* (post-condition of reaction): $R' = x \mid id \mid id$ (Milner, 2009). The rule is parametric, so R or R' can be filled by parameters. The two sites of R' can be filled by parameters as dictated by the instantiation map η. Concrete reaction rules `$R_{CCS}$ consist of all lean pre-images of $R_{CCS}$ by *lean-support quotient* (Milner, 2009). $\Sigma_{CCS}$ and `R_{CCS} yield concrete BRS for CCS: `BG_{CCS}. Further translations of CCS into bigraphs

Figure 2. Elemental graphical notations

and the discussion regarding relationship between original CCS theory and bigraphs for CCS can be found in (Milner, 2009).

Bigraphs and BRSs have been used for modeling context-aware system (Birkedal, Debois, Elsborg, Hildebrandt, & Niss, 2006), pervasive computing (Birkedal, et al., 2006),and so on. Furthermore, they are also applied in encompassing existing theories for concurrency and mobility, e.g. Condition-event nets (Milner, 2009), CCS (Milner, 2009), and Pi-calculus (Jensen & Milner, 2004)etc.

3 PATTERN REPRESENTATIONS

Because bigraph does not limit graphical style for representation, this chapter uses following elemental notations, as seen below, which are based on definitions of bigrah for CCS, to represent business process.

3.1 Exception Handling at Work Item Level

- **Continue-offer (OCO) (Russell, van der Aalst, & ter Hofstede, 2006):** The work item has been offered to one or more re-

sources and there is no change in its state as a consequence of the exception.

- **Solution**: This strategy requires system to take no more actions for handling exceptions. The work item can be still executed. The resources can trigger work item after exception handler detected errors. The work item is triggered by *token* link, and it can also receive *warning* message for detecting errors. This strategy can be represented in bigraphs for CCS as Figure 3.

The derived algebraic expression is (d_{oco0}, d_{oco1} and d_{oco2} are parameters or variables whose graphic notations are *sites*; $1:0 \rightarrow 1$ is a *placing* with one root, i.e.) as presented in Exhibit 1:

- **Reoffer (ORO)** (Russell, van der Aalst, & ter Hofstede, 2006): The work item has been offered to one or more resources and as a consequence of the exception, these offers are withdrawn and the work item is once again offered to one or more resources.

- **Solution**: After receiving exception message through *warning* link, resource can withdraw current work item through *halt* link. It's also supposed that work item can be triggered by other resource. Therefore, the following operations could inform system that this resource cancels the work item by using link *cancellation*. The resource uses *end* link to report that all necessary operations are completed.

Figure 3. OCO strategy

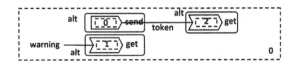

Exhibit 1.

$$Workitem_{oco} = alt.(get_{token}.d_{oco2} \mid 1)$$
$$Resource_{oco} = /token \circ \left(alt.\left(get_{warning}.d_{oco1} \mid 1 \right) \mid alt.\left(send_{token}.d_{oco0} \mid 1 \right) \mid Workitem_{oco} \right)$$

Figure 4. ORO strategy

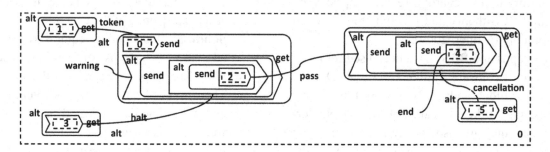

This strategy can be represented in bigraphs for CCS as Figure 4, and the derived process calculi are as follows in Exhibit 2:

- **Force-fail-o (OFF)** (Russell, van der Aalst, & ter Hofstede, 2006)**:** The work item has been offered to one or more resources, these offers are withdrawn and the state of the work item is changed to *failed*. No subsequent work items on this path are triggered.

- **Solution**: After receiving exception message through *warning* link, resource can withdraw current work item through *halt* link. Then, resource set the current execution state as "failed" for current work item by triggering *failure* link. Subsequent work items on the path are cancelled after triggered *cancellation*. Outer system continues other work after receiving *end* information.

Exhibit 2.

$$Workitem_{oro} = alt.(get_{token}.d_{oro1} \mid 1)$$
$$Handler_{oro} = alt.(get_{warning}.alt.(send_{halt}.alt.(send_{pass}.d_{oro2} \mid 1) \mid 1) \mid send_{token}.d_{oro0})$$
$$Offeror_{oro} = alt.(get_{pass}.alt.(send_{cancellation}.alt.(send_{end}.d_{oro4} \mid 1) \mid 1) \mid 1)$$
$$Resource_{other} = alt.(get_{cancellation}.d_{oro5} \mid 1)$$
$$/L \stackrel{def}{=} /\,token \parallel /pass \parallel /halt \parallel /cancellation$$
$$Resource_{oro} = /L \circ (Handler_{oro} \mid Offeror_{oro} \mid Resource_{other}$$
$$\mid Workitem_{oro} \mid alt.\left(get_{halt}.d_{oro3} \mid 1 \right))$$

Figure 5. OFF strategy

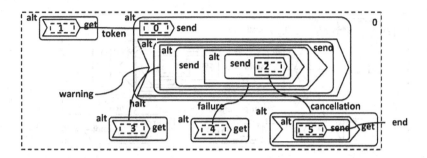

The graphical configuration is shown as Figure 5, and the corresponding representation is as presented in Exhibit 3:

- **Force-complete-o (OFC)** (Russell, van der Aalst, & ter Hofstede, 2006)**:** The work item has been offered to one or more resources, these offers are withdrawn and the state of the work item is changed to *completed*. All subsequent work items are triggered.
- **Solution**: After receiving exception message through *warning* link, resource can withdraw current work item through *halt* link. Then, resource set the current execution state as "completed" for current

work item by triggering *completeness* link. Subsequent work items on the path are triggered after sending *next* command. Outer system continues other work after receiving *end* information.

The graphical configuration is shown as Figure 6, and the derived algebraic expression is as seen in Exhibit 4:

- **Continue-allocation (ACA)** (Russell, van der Aalst, & ter Hofstede, 2006): The work item has been allocated to a specific resource that will execute it at some future time and there is no change in its state as a consequence of the exception.

Exhibit 3.

$Workitem_{off} = alt.(get_{token}.d_{off1} \mid 1)$

$Handler_{off} = alt.(get_{warning}.alt.(send_{halt}.alt.(send_{failure}.alt.(send_{cancellation}.d_{off2} \mid 1) \mid 1) \mid 1)$
$\mid send_{token}.d_{off0})$

$Canceler_{off} = alt.(get_{cancellation}.alt.(send_{end}.d_{off5} \mid 1) \mid 1)$

$Suspender_{off} = alt.(get_{halt}.d_{off3} \mid 1)$

$Setter_{off} = alt.(get_{failure}.d_{off4} \mid 1)$

$/L \overset{def}{=} / token \parallel /halt \parallel /cancellation \parallel /failure$

$Resource_{off} = /L \circ (Handler_{off} \mid Workitem_{off} \mid Canceler_{off} \mid Suspender_{off} \mid Setter_{off})$

Figure 6. OFC strategy

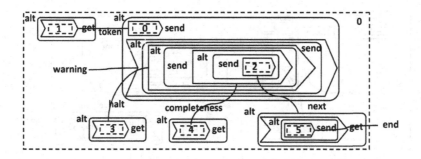

Exhibit 4.

$$Workitem_{ofc} = alt.(get_{token}.d_{ofc1} \mid 1)$$

$$Handler_{ofc} = alt.(get_{warning}.alt.(send_{halt}.alt.(send_{completeness}.alt.(send_{next}.d_{ofc2}|1)|1)|1)$$
$$\mid send_{token}.d_{ofc0})$$

$$Keeper_{ofc} = alt.(get_{next}.alt.(send_{end}.d_{ofc5} \mid 1) \mid 1)$$

$$Suspender_{ofc} = alt.(get_{halt}.d_{ofc3} \mid 1)$$

$$Setter_{ofc} = alt.(get_{completeness}.d_{ofc4} \mid 1)$$

$$/L \stackrel{def}{=} /\,token \parallel /halt \parallel /next \parallel /completeness$$

$$Resource_{ofc} = /L \circ (Handler_{ofc} \mid Workitem_{ofc} \mid Keeper_{ofc} \mid Suspender_{ofc} \mid Setter_{ofc})$$

- **Solution**: After receiving exception message through *warning* link, resource can also trigger work item through *token* link. The graphical representation is shown as Figure 7.

The derived algebraic expression is:

$$Workitem_{aca} = alt.(get_{token}.d_{aca1} \mid 1)$$

$$Resource_{aca} =$$
$$/token \circ (alt.(get_{warning}.alt.(send_{token}.d_{aca0} \mid 1) \mid 1) \mid Workitem_{aca})$$

Figure 7. ACA strategy

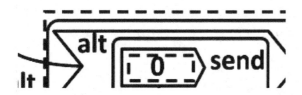

- **Reallocate (ARA)** (Russell, van der Aalst, & ter Hofstede, 2006): The work item has been allocated to a resource, this allocation is withdrawn and the work item is allocated to a different resource.
- **Solution**: the representation for this strategy is similar to the representation of ORO strategy.

Figure 8. SCE strategy

- **Reoffer-a (ARO)** (Russell, van der Aalst, & ter Hofstede, 2006): The work item has been allocated to a resource, this allocation is withdrawn and the work item is offered to one or more resources.
- **Solution**: The representation for this strategy is similar to the representation of ORO strategy.
- **Force-fail-a (AFF)** (Russell, van der Aalst, & ter Hofstede, 2006): The work item has been allocated to a resource, this allocation is withdrawn and the state of the work item is changed to *failed*. No subsequent work items are triggered.
- **Solution**: The representation for this strategy is similar to the representation of OFF strategy. This strategy can trigger no more work items after exception handling. However, OFF strategy can trigger other flow in the same workflow case.
- **Force-complete-a (AFC)** (Russell, van der Aalst, & ter Hofstede, 2006): The work item has been allocated to a resource, this allocation is withdrawn and the state of the work item is changed to *completed*. All subsequent work items are triggered.

- **Solution**: The representation for this strategy is similar to the representation of OFC strategy.
- **Continue-execution (SCE)** (Russell, van der Aalst, & ter Hofstede, 2006): The work item has been started and there is no change in its state as a consequence of the exception.
- **Solution**: The work item is started, after receiving exception message through *warning* link. Resource takes no more actions for exception handling. The graphical representation is shown as Figure 8.

Presented in Exhibit 5,t he derived algebraic expression is:

- **Restart (SRS)** (Russell, van der Aalst, & ter Hofstede, 2006): The work item has been started, progress on the current execution instance is halted and the work item is restarted from the beginning by the same resource that was executing it previously.
- **Solution**: For this strategy, a more complicated work item can be designed. The work item can be triggered through *token*. It can also be restarted for certain conditions (by using link *restart*).

The graphical configuration is shown as Figure 9, and the derived process calculi are as presented in Exhibit 6:

- **Reallocate-s (SRA)** (Russell, van der Aalst, & ter Hofstede, 2006): The work item has been started, progress on the current execution instance is halted and the

Exhibit 5.

$$Workitem_{sce} = alt.(get_{token}.d_{sce0} \mid 1)$$
$$Resource_{sce} = /token \circ (alt.(send_{token}.alt.(get_{warning}.d_{sce1} \mid 1) \mid 1) \mid Workitem_{sce})$$

Figure 9. SRS strategy

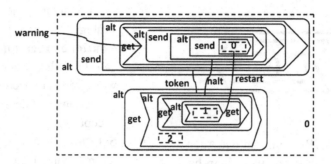

work item is reallocated to a different resource for later execution.

- **Solution**: The resource start work item through link *token*. After receiving exception message through *warning* link, resource can withdraw current work item through *halt* link. It's also supposed that work item can be triggered by other resource. Therefore, the following operations could inform system that this resource cancels the work item by using link *cancellation*. The resource uses *end* link to report that all necessary operations are completed.

The graphical configuration is shown as Figure 10, and the corresponding representation is as follows in Exhibit 7:

- **Reoffer-s (SRO)** (Russell, van der Aalst, & ter Hofstede, 2006): The work item has been started, progress on the current execution instance is halted and it is offered to one or more resources.

- **Solution**: The representation for this strategy is similar to the representation of SRA strategy.

- **Force-fail (SFF)** (Russell, van der Aalst, & ter Hofstede, 2006): The work item is being executed, any further progress on it is halted and its state is changed to *failed*. No subsequent work items are triggered.

- **Solution**: The resource start work item through link *token*. After receiving exception message through *warning* link, resource can withdraw current work item through *halt* link. Then, resource set the current execution state as "failed" for current work item by triggering *failure* link. Subsequent work items on the path are cancelled after triggering *cancellation*. Outer system continues other work after

Exhibit 6.

$$Workitem_{srs} = alt.(get_{token}.(alt.(get_{halt}.alt.(get_{restart}.d_{srs1} \mid 1) \mid 1) \mid d_{srs2}) \mid 1)$$
$$/L \overset{def}{=} / \ token \parallel /restart \parallel /halt$$
$$Resource_{rsr} = /L \circ (Workitem_{srs}$$
$$\mid alt.\big(send_{token}.alt.\big(get_{warning}.alt.\big(send_{halt}.alt.\big(send_{restart}.d_{srs0} \mid 1) \mid 1) \mid 1) \mid 1))$$

Figure 10. SRA strategy

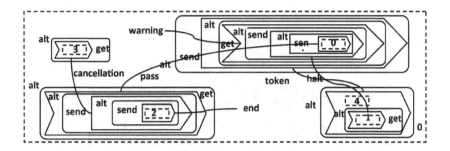

receiving *end* information. The graphical representation is shown as Figure 11.

The derived algebraic expression is presented in Exhibit 8:

- **Force-complete (SFC)** (Russell, van der Aalst, & ter Hofstede, 2006): The work item is being executed, and further progress on it is halted and its state is changed to *completed*. All subsequent work items are triggered.
- **Solution**: The resource start work item through link *token*. After receiving exception message through *warning* link, resource can withdraw current work item through *halt* link. Then, resource set the current execution state as "completed" for current work item by triggering *complete-*

ness link. Subsequent work items on the path are triggered after sending *next* command. Outer system continues other work after receiving *end* information. The corresponding representation is as follows in Exhibit 9:

3.2 Exception Handling at Case Level and Recovery Action

There are three alternatives for handling workflow cases (Russell, van der Aalst, & ter Hofstede, 2006)::Continue workflow case (CWC), Remove current case (RCC) and Remove all cases (RAC). Further, there are three operational recovery actions (Russell, van der Aalst, & ter Hofstede, 2006): no action (NIL), rollback (RBK) and compensate (COM).

Exhibit 7.

$$Workitem_{sra} = alt.(get_{token}.(alt.(get_{halt}.d_{sra1}|1) \mid d_{sra4}) \mid 1)$$

$$Resource_{other} = alt.(get_{cancellation}.d_{sra3} \mid 1)$$

$$Canceler_{sra} = alt.(get_{pass}.alt.(send_{cancellation}.alt.(send_{end}.d_{sra2} \mid 1) \mid 1)|1)$$

$$Handler_{sra} = alt.(send_{token}.alt.(get_{warning}.alt.(send_{halt}.alt.(send_{pass}.d_{sra0} \mid 1) \mid 1) \mid 1)|1)$$

$$/L \stackrel{def}{=} / token \parallel /pass \parallel /halt \parallel /cancellation$$

$$Resource_{sra} = /L \circ (Workitem_{sra} \mid Resource_{other} \mid Handler_{sra} \mid Canceler_{sra})$$

Figure 11. SFF strategy

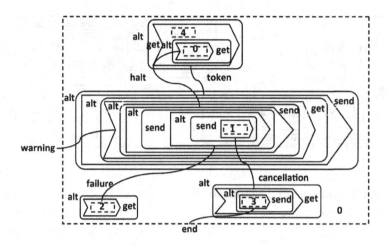

Exhibit 8.

$Workitem_{sff} = alt.(get_{token}.(alt.(get_{halt}.d_{sff0} \mid 1) \mid d_{sff4}) \mid 1)$

$Handler_{sff} = alt.(send_{token}.alt.(get_{warning}.alt.(send_{halt}.alt.(send_{failure}.alt.(send_{cancel}.d_{sff1}$
$\mid 1) \mid 1) \mid 1) \mid 1) \mid 1)$

$Canceler_{sff} = alt.(get_{cancel}.alt.(send_{end}.d_{sff3} \mid 1) \mid 1)$

$Setter_{sff} = alt.(get_{failure}.d_{sff2} \mid 1)$

$/L \overset{def}{=} / token \parallel / failure \parallel / halt \parallel / cancel$

$Resource_{sff} = /L \circ (Handler_{sff} \mid Workitem_{sff} \mid Canceler_{sff} \mid Setter_{sff})$

Exhibit 9.

$Workitem_{sfc} = alt.(get_{token}.(alt.(get_{halt}.d_{sfc0} \mid 1) \mid d_{sfc4}) \mid 1)$

$Handler_{sfc} = alt.(send_{token}.alt.(get_{warning}.alt.(send_{halt}.alt.(send_{completeness}.alt.(send_{cancel}.d_{sfc1}$
$\mid 1) \mid 1) \mid 1) \mid 1) \mid 1)$

$Keeper_{sfc} = alt.(get_{next}.alt.(send_{end}.d_{sfc3} \mid 1) \mid 1)$

$Setter_{sfc} = alt.(get_{completeness}.d_{sfc2} \mid 1)$

$/L \overset{def}{=} / token \parallel / completeness \parallel / halt \parallel / next$

$Resource_{sfc} = /L \circ (Handler_{sfc} \mid Workitem_{sfc} \mid Keeper_{sfc} \mid Setter_{sfc})$

For CWC, RCC, RAC, RBK and COM strategies, it can be simply represented as: $alt.(get_x.d \mid 1)$. Parameter d can be detailed for different strategies. The link x can also be modified for different commands. For NIL action, this chapter does not specify concrete representation.

3.3 Exception Handling Patterns

The handling patterns take three main considerations into account: exception handling at work item level, exception handling at case level, and recovery action. There are 36 patterns for exception handling. For example, the pattern ACA-CWC-NIL specifies that a resource will execute the allocated work item as a consequence of exception. No action should be taken with other work items in the same case, and no recovery actions should be executed.

Pattern ACA-CWC-NIL

For this pattern, it supposed that $Resource_{aca}$ could handle exception at work item level, and $Handler_{cwc}$ could handle exception at case level. The representation of this pattern is as follow:

$$Handler_{aca-cwc-nil} =$$
$$alt.(get_{exception}.alt.(send_{warning}.alt.(send_{cwc}.d_0 \mid 1) \mid 1) \mid 1)$$

$$Handler_{cwc} = alt.(get_{cwc}.d_1 \mid 1)$$

$$/L \overset{def}{=} / warning \parallel /cwc$$

$$Pattern_{aca-cwc-nil} =$$
$$/L \circ (Handler_{aca-cwc-nil} \mid Resource_{aca} \mid Handler_{cwc})$$

Pattern OFC-CWC-COM

For this pattern, it supposed that $Resource_{ofc}$ could handle exception at work item level, and $Handler_{cwc}$ could handle exception at case level. $Action_{com}$ executes recovery action. The representation of this pattern is as follow:

$$Handler_{cwc-com} =$$
$$alt.(get_{end}.(alt.(send_{cwc}.d_0 \mid 1) \mid alt.(send_{com}.d_1 \mid 1)) \mid 1)$$

$$Handler_{ofc-cwc-com} =$$
$$alt.(get_{exception}.(alt.(send_{warning}.d_2 \mid 1) \mid Handler_{cwc-com}) \mid 1)$$

$$Handler_{cwc} = alt.(get_{cwc}.d_3 \mid 1)$$

$$Action_{com} = alt.(get_{com}.d_4 \mid 1)$$

$$/L \overset{def}{=} / warning \parallel /cwc \parallel /com \parallel /end$$

$$Pattern_{ofc-cwc-com} =$$
$$/L \circ (Handler_{ofc-cwc-com} \mid Resource_{ofc} \mid Handler_{cwc} \mid Action_{com})$$

Pattern OFC-CWC-NIL

This pattern is similar to OFC-CWC-COM. However, recovery action is NIL.

$$Handler_{cwc-nil} = alt.(get_{end}.alt.(send_{cwc}.d_0 \mid 1) \mid 1)$$

$$Handler_{ofc-cwc-nil} =$$
$$alt.(get_{exception}.(alt.(send_{warning}.d_2 \mid 1) \mid Handler_{cwc-nil}) \mid 1)$$

$$Handler_{cwc} = alt.(get_{cwc}.d_3 \mid 1)$$

$$/L \overset{def}{=} / warning \parallel /cwc \parallel /end$$

$Pattern_{ofc-cwc-nil} =$
$/L \circ (Handler_{ofc-cwc-nil} \mid Resource_{ofc} \mid Handler_{cwc})$

Pattern OFF-CWC-COM

For this pattern, it supposed that $Resource_{off}$ could handle exception at work item level, and $Handler_{cwc}$ could handle exception at case level. $Action_{com}$ executes recovery action. The representation of this pattern is as follow:

$Handler_{cwc-com} =$
$alt.(get_{end}.(alt.(send_{cwc}.d_0 \mid 1) \mid alt.(send_{com}.d_1 \mid 1)) \mid 1)$

$Handler_{off-cwc-com} =$
$alt.(get_{exception}.(alt.(send_{warning}.d_2 \mid 1) \mid Handler_{cwc-com}) \mid 1)$

$Handler_{cwc} = alt.(get_{cwc}.d_3 \mid 1)$

$Action_{com} = alt.(get_{com}.d_4 \mid 1)$

$/L \overset{def}{=} / warning \parallel /cwc \parallel /com \parallel /end$

$Pattern_{off-cwc-com} =$
$/L \circ (Handler_{off-cwc-com} \mid Resource_{off} \mid Handler_{cwc} \mid Action_{com})$

Pattern OFF-RCC-NIL

This pattern is similar to OFF-RCC-COM. However, recovery action is NIL, and it supposed that $Handler_{rcc}$ handles exception at case level.

$Handler_{rcc-nil} =$
$alt.(get_{end}.alt.(send_{rcc}.d_0 \mid 1) \mid 1)$

$Handler_{off-rcc-nil} =$
$alt.(get_{exception}.(alt.(send_{warning}.d_2 \mid 1) \mid Handler_{rcc-nil}) \mid 1)$

$Handler_{rcc} = alt.(get_{rcc}.d_3 \mid 1)$

$/L \overset{def}{=} / warning \parallel /rcc \parallel /end$

$Pattern_{off-rcc-nil} =$
$/L \circ (Handler_{off-rcc-nil} \mid Resource_{off} \mid Handler_{rcc})$

Similarly, AFF-RCC-NIL could be represented if $Resource_{aff}$ is used to handle exception at work item level.

The representations of ARA, ARO and ORO strategies are similar. Algebraic expressions of Pattern ARA-CWC-NIL, ARO-CWC-NIL and ORO-CWC-NIL are similar too. Take ORO-CWC-NIL as an example:

$Handler_{cwc-nil} = alt.(get_{end}.alt.(send_{cwc}.d_0 \mid 1) \mid 1)$

$Handler_{oro-cwc-nil} = alt.(get_{exception}.(alt.(send_{warning}.d_2 \mid 1) \mid Handler_{cwc-nil}) \mid 1)$

$Handler_{cwc} = alt.(get_{cwc}.d_3 \mid 1)$

$/L \overset{def}{=} / warning \parallel /cwc \parallel /end$

$Pattern_{oro-cwc-nil} = /L \circ (Handler_{oro-cwc-nil} \mid Resource_{oro} \mid Handler_{cwc})$

Pattern OCO-CWC-NIL

For this pattern, it supposed that $Resource_{oco}$ could handle exception at work item level.

$Handler_{oco-cwc-nil} = alt.(get_{exception}.alt.(send_{warning}.alt.(send_{cwc}.d_0 \mid 1) \mid 1) \mid 1)$

$Handler_{cwc} = alt.(get_{cwc}.d_1 \mid 1)$

$$/L \overset{def}{=} /\,warning \parallel /cwc$$

$$Pattern_{oco-cwc-nil} = /L \circ (Handler_{oco-cwc-nil} \mid Resource_{oco} \mid Handler_{cwc})$$

Pattern SCE-CWC-COM

For this pattern, it supposed that $Resource_{sce}$ could handle exception at work item level.

$$Handler_{cwc-com} = alt.(send_{cwc}.d_0 \mid 1) \mid alt.(send_{com}.d_1 \mid 1)$$

$$Handler_{sce-cwc-com} = \\ alt.(get_{exception}.(alt.(send_{warning}.Handler_{cwc-com} \mid 1) \mid 1)$$

$$Handler_{cwc} = alt.(get_{cwc}.d_2 \mid 1)$$

$$Action_{com} = alt.(get_{com}.d_3 \mid 1)$$

$$/L \overset{def}{=} /\,warning \parallel /cwc \parallel /com$$

$$Pattern_{sce-cwc-com} = \\ /L \circ (Handler_{sce-cwc-com} \mid Resource_{sce} \mid Handler_{cwc} \mid Action_{com})$$

If recovery action is NIL, pattern SCE-CWC-NIL can be represented.

Pattern SFC-CWC-RBK

For this pattern, it supposed that $Resource_{sfc}$ could handle exception at work item level, and $Handler_{cwc}$ could handle exception at case level. $Action_{rbk}$ executes recovery action (rollback). The representation of this pattern is as follow:

$$Handler_{cwc-rbk} = \\ alt.(get_{end}.(alt.(send_{cwc}.d_0 \mid 1) \mid alt.(send_{rbk}.d_1 \mid 1)) \mid 1)$$

$$Handler_{sfc-cwc-rbk} = \\ alt.(get_{exception}.(alt.(send_{warning}.d_2 \mid 1) \mid Handler_{cwc-rbk}) \mid 1)$$

$$Handler_{cwc} = alt.(get_{cwc}.d_3 \mid 1)$$

$$Action_{rbk} = alt.(get_{rbk}.d_4 \mid 1)$$

$$/L \overset{def}{=} /\,warning \parallel /cwc \parallel /rbk \parallel /end$$

$$Pattern_{sfc-cwc-rbk} = \\ /L \circ (Handler_{sfc-cwc-rbk} \mid Resource_{sfc} \mid Handler_{cwc} \mid Action_{rbk})$$

It replaces $Action_{rbk}$ with $Action_{com}$, pattern SFC-CWC-COM could be represented. It omit recovery action, pattern SFC-CWC-NIL could be represented. The difference between SFF and SFC is that SFF set "failed" to work item, and SFC set "completed" to work item. Therefore, SFF-CWC-RBK, SFF-CWC-COM and SFF-CWC-NIL could be represented according to SFC-CWC-RBK, SFC-CWC-COM and SFC-CWC-NIL.

Pattern SFF-RAC-NIL

This pattern can be represented as:

$$Handler_{rac-nil} = alt.(get_{end}.alt.(send_{rac}.d_0 \mid 1) \mid 1)$$

$$Handler_{sff-rac-nil} = \\ alt.(get_{exception}.(alt.(send_{warning}.d_1 \mid 1) \mid Handler_{rac-nil}) \mid 1)$$

$$Handler_{rac} = alt.(get_{rac}.d_2 \mid 1)$$

$$/L \overset{def}{=} /\,warning \parallel /rac \parallel /end$$

$$Pattern_{sff-rac-nil} = \\ /L \circ (Handler_{sff-rac-nil} \mid Resource_{sff} \mid Handler_{rac})$$

Pattern SFF-RCC-RBK

This pattern can be represented as:

$$Handler_{rcc-brk} =$$
$$alt.(get_{end}.(alt.(send_{rcc}.d_0|1) \mid alt.(send_{brk}.d_1|1))$$

$$Handler_{sff-rcc-brk} =$$
$$alt.(get_{exception}.(alt.(send_{warning}.d_2 \mid 1) \mid Handler_{rcc-brk}) \mid 1)$$

$$Handler_{rcc} = alt.(get_{rcc}.d_3 \mid 1)$$

$$Action_{rbk} = alt.(get_{rbk}.d_4 \mid 1)$$

$$/L \overset{def}{=} / \, warning \parallel /rcc \parallel /end \parallel /brk$$

$$Pattern_{sff-rcc-brk} =$$
$$/L \circ (Handler_{sff-rcc-brk} \mid Resource_{sff} \mid Handler_{rcc} \mid Action_{rbk})$$

It replace $Action_{rbk}$ with $Action_{com}$, pattern SFF-RCC-COM could be represented. It omit recovery action, pattern SFF-RCC-NIL could be represented.

3.4 Discussion

In section 3.1, the work items in SRA and SRS can be designed into more complicated form. This chapter just abstracts parts of their behavior. For example: they can be cancelled after triggering. But for real application, more technical details should be considered. According to Workflow Exception Patterns(Russell, van der Aalst, & ter Hofstede, 2006). and Workflow Resource Patterns(Russell, van der Aalst, & ter Hofstede, 2004b), work item can be offered to one or more resources for execution; A resource can also send an allocating command for indicating that it wishes to execute the work item at some future time, the work item then is allocated to the resource.

Some representations treat these two behaviors similarly. For real application, resource needs to send requirement to system firstly, and then receive the allocation.

In section 3.3, some patterns are not represented. They are pattern SRA-CWC-RBK, SRA-CWC-COM, SRA-CWC-NIL, SRO-CWC-RBK, SRO-CWC-COM, SRO-CWC-NIL, SRS-CWC-COM, SRS-CWC-NIL and SRS-CWC-RBK. The first thing is that strategy SRA and SRO have similar structural characteristics. So pattern SRA-CWC-RBK and SRO-CWC-RBK, SRA-CWC-COM and SRO-CWC-COM, SRA-CWC-NIL and SRO-CWC-NIL have similar representations. The second, representations of pattern SRS-CWC-COM, SRS-CWC-NIL and SRS-CWC-RBK would also use $Resource_{srs}$, $Handler_{cwc}$ and $Action_{[com, rbk]}$ to handle exception. The last thing is that it can be abstracted two types of sequence for exception handling: simple sequence and normal sequence. Simple sequence supports that work item exception, case exception and recovery action can be handled in parallel. However, normal sequence requires system to handle exception at work item level, and then handle exception at case level, final action is recovery action. In this case, some negotiation mechanism should be chosen for managing the order of exception handling.

FUTURE RESEARCH DIRECTIONS

This chapter discusses some expected exceptions and the methods for handling them. Based on exception patterns and their models, more exception handling strategies could be found. Future work can focus on how to apply these strategies in real applications for increasing flexibility of system to deal with exceptional situations. Future research can also focus on unexpected exceptions. In this field, the range of issues that may raise exceptions during process execution can be investigated. Further, unexpected types of exception and the handling strategies should be summarized.

CONCLUSION

In this chapter, exception patterns are represented in bigraphs for CCS. The results show that using modeling method based on bigraphs for CCS is helpful for clearly presenting exception handling behavior. In addition, advanced features of bigraphs, which are compositional and extensible features, are introduced in representations.

REFERENCES

Birkedal, L., Bundgaard, M., Damgaard, T., Debois, S., Elsborg, E., Glenstrup, A., et al. (2006). Bigraphical programming languages for pervasive computing. *Proceedings of International Workshop on Combining Theory and Systems Building in Pervasive Computing*, (pp. 653-658).

Birkedal, L., Debois, S., Elsborg, E., Hildebrandt, T., & Niss, H. (2006). Bigraphical models of context-aware systems. *Proceedings of the 9th International Conference on Foundations of Software Science and Computation Structures* (pp. 187-201). Springer.

Bundgaard, M., Glenstrup, A., Hildebrandt, T., Højsgaard, E., & Niss, H. (2008). *Formalizing higher-order mobile embedded business processes with binding bigraphs. Proceedings of Coordination'08*. Berlin, Germany: Springer.

Eder, J., & Liebhart, W. (1995). The workflow activity model (WAMO). *Proceedings of the 3rd International Conference on Cooperative Information Systems (CoopIs)*. Vienna, Austria.

Hildebrandt, T., Niss, H., & Olsen, M. (2006). Formalizing business process execution with bigraphs and reactive XML. *Proceedings of the 8th International Conference on Coordination Models and Language* (pp. 113-129). Berlin, Germany: Springer.

Jensen, O. H., & Milner, R. (2004). Bigraphs and mobile processes (revised). *Technical Report UCAM-CL-TR-580.* University of Cambridge.

Milner, R. (1980). *A calculus of communicating systems.* Springer-Verlag.

Milner, R. (2006). Pure bigraphs: Structure and dynamics. *Information and Computation, 204*(11), 60–122. doi:10.1016/j.ic.2005.07.003

Milner, R. (2009). *The space and motion of communicating agents.* Cambridge University Press.

Rinderle, S., Reichert, M., & Dadam, P. (2004). Correctness criteria for dynamic changes in workflow systems: A survey. *Data & Knowledge Engineering, 50*, 9–34. doi:10.1016/j.datak.2004.01.002

Russell, N., ter Hofstede, A., Edmond, D., & van der Aalst, W. (2004a). *Workflow data patterns.* QUT Technical report FIT-TR-2004-01. Brisbane, Australia: Queensland University of Technology.

Russell, N., ter Hofstede, A., Edmond, D., & van der Aalst, W. (2004b). *Workflow resource patterns.* BETA Working Paper Series WP 127. Eindhoven, The Netherlands: Eindhoven University of Technology.

Russell, N., van der Aalst, W., & ter Hofstede, A. (2006). Workflow exception patterns. *Proceedings of the 18th International Conference on Advanced Information Systems Engineering* (pp. 288-302). Berlin, Germany: Springer-Verlag.

van der Aalst, W., ter Hofstede, A., Kiepuszewski, B., & Barros, A. (2003). Workflow patterns. *Distributed and Parallel Databases, 14*(1), 5–21. doi:10.1023/A:1022883727209

Worah, D., & Sheth, A. (1997). Transactions in transactional workflows . In Jajodia, S., & Kerschberg, L. (Eds.), *Advanced transaction models and architectures* (pp. 3–34). doi:10.1007/978-1-4615-6217-7_1

ADDITIONAL READING

Barros, A., Dumas, M., & Oaks, P. (2005). A critical overview of the web services choreography description language (WS-CDL). *BP Trends Newsletter, 3*(3).

Brogi, A., Canal, C., Pimentel, E., & Vallecillo, A. (2004). Formalizing Web service choreographies. *Electronic Notes in Theoretical Computer Science, 105*, 73–94. doi:10.1016/j.entcs.2004.05.007

Decker, G., & Puhlmann, F. (2007). *Extending BPMN for modeling complex choreographies. On the Move to Meaningful Internet Systems 2007: CoopIS, DOA, ODBASE, GADA, and IS* (pp. 24–40). Springer. doi:10.1007/978-3-540-76848-7_4

Decker, G., & Weske, M. (2007). Behavioral consistency for b2b process integration. *Proceedings of 19th Conference on Advanced Information Systems Engineering (CAiSE 2007)* (pp. 81-95). Springer.

Dehnert, J., & Rittgen, P. (2001). Relaxed soundness of business processes. *Proceedings of the 13th International Conference on Advanced Information Systems Engineering (CAiSE)* (pp. 157-170). Springer.

Dumas, M., & ter Hofstede, A. H. (2001). UML activity diagrams as a workflow specification language. *Proceedings of the International Conference on the Unified Modeling Language*. Toronto, Canada.

Georgakopoulos, D., Hornick, M., & Sheth, A. (1995). An overview of workflow management: From process modeling to workflow automation infrastructure. *Distributed and Parallel Databases, 3*(2), 119–153. doi:10.1007/BF01277643

Hoare, C. (1978). Communicating sequential processes. *Communications of the ACM, 21*(8), 666–677. doi:10.1145/359576.359585

Krafzig, D., Karl, B., & Slama, D. (2004). *Enterprise SOA: Service-oriented architecture best practices*. Prentice Hall PTR.

Martens, A. (2003). On usability of web services. *Proceedings of 1st Web Services Quality Workshop (WQW 2003)*.

Martens, A. (2005). Analyzing Web service based business processes. *Proceedings of International Conference on Fundamental Approaches to Software Engineering (FASE '05)*. Springer-Verlag.

Massuthe, P., Reisig, W., & Schmidt, K. (2005). An operating guideline approach to the SOA. *Annals of Mathematics . Computing & Teleinformatics, 1*(3), 35–43.

Milner, R. (1991). *The polyadic Pi-calculus: A tutorial*. Technical Report ECS-LFCS-91-180. Computer Science Department, University of Edinburgh.

Milner, R. (1992). A calculus of mobile process, part I/part II. *Journal of Information and Computation, 100*(1), 1–77. doi:10.1016/0890-5401(92)90008-4

Mulyar, N., & van der Aalst, W. (2005). *Patterns in colored Petri nets*. BETA Working Paper Series, WP 139. Eindhoven, The Netherlands: Eindhoven University of Technology.

Puhlmann, F., & Weske, M. (2005). Using the Pi-calculus for formalizing workflow patterns. *Proceedings of BPM 2005* (pp. 153-168). Springer-Verlag.

Puhlmann, F., & Weske, M. (2006). Investigations on soundness regarding lazy activities. [Springer.]. *Proceedings of Business Process Management, 2006*, 145–160. doi:10.1007/11841760_11

Sewell, P. (2000). *Applied Pi-A brief tutorial*. Technical Report Nr. 498. University of Cambridge.

van der Aalst, W. (1998). The application of Petri nets to workflow management. *The Journal of Circuits . Systems and Computers, 8*(1), 21–66.

van der Aalst, W., Hee, K., & Houben, G. (1994). Modeling and analysing workflow using a Petri-net based approach. *Proceedings of the Second Workshop on Computer-Supported Cooperative Work, Petri Nets and Related Formalisms*, (pp. 31–50).

van der Aalst, W., Navathe, S., & Wakayama, T. (1996). Three good reasons for using a Petri-net-based workflow management system. *Proceedings of the International Working Conference on Information and Process Integration in Enterprises (IPIC'96)*, (pp. 179-201).

van der Aalst, W., & ter Hofstede, A. (2002). Workflow patterns: On the expressive power of (Petri-net-based) workflow lanuages. *Proceedings of the Fourth Workshop on the Practical Use of Coloured Petri Nets and CPN Tools (CPN 2002)* (pp. 1-20). University of Aarhus.

Weske, M. (2007). *Business process management: Concepts, languages, architectures*. Springer.

Yang, D., & Zhang, S. (2003). An approach for workflow modeling using pi-calculus. *Journal of Zhejiang University. Science, 6*.

Zaha, J., Barros, A., Dumas, M., & ter Hofstede, A. (2006). A language for service behavior modeling. *Proceedings 14th International Conference on Cooperative Information Systems (CoopIS 2006)* (pp. 145-162). Springer Verlag.

KEY TERMS AND DEFINITIONS

Bigraphs for CCS: Bigraphs for CCS (Calculus of Communicating Systems) is a bigraphical encoding of CCS. CCS, bigraph, and bigraphs for CCS are developed by Robin Milner.

Business Process: A business process consists of a set of activities, and it can are executed in organizational and technical environment. The activities jointly realize a business goal.

Process Exception: In runtime environment, any attributes which are not conforming to process execution requirements at design time may raise errors.

Workflow Exception Handling: Exception handling aims at providing facilities to handle process exceptions at runtime.

Workflow Exception Pattern: Workflow exception patterns present a classification framework for workflow exception handling in the form of patterns. The framework is proposed by Nick Russell, Wil van der Aalst, and Arthur ter Hofstede.

Workflow Management System (WFMS): WFMS is a software system that can define, initiate, execute, and manage workflows.

Workflow: Workflow is the automation of a business process.

Chapter 30
A Rule–Based Approach to Model Business Process

Gang Xue
Yunnan University, China

Zhongwei Wu
Yunnan University, China

Kun Zhang
Chuxiong Normal University, China

Shaowen Yao
Yunnan University, China

ABSTRACT

Up to the present, the modeling of business process mainly focuses on the flow-control perspective, regardless of the logic relationships between models. Although the value of business rules in business process modeling has been recognized by many organizations, it is not fully clear how business rules can be used to model business process models. Business rules are powerful representation forms that can potentially define the semantics of business process models and business vocabulary. This chapter is committed to model the business process based on SBVR, then use the method mentioned below to transform a plain text rule statement into BPMN files.

1. INTRODUCTION

To date, business process modeling manly focuses on the flow-control perspective. There are several problems in using business process as modeling languages to define the business process, mainly that they are not understandable for business people and that they are procedural languages, which means that they specify how business processes should be executed and in what order, making the business process inflexible if implemented in a workflow management system.

Business rules define the business objects and the constraints of business objects. A business process model is called rule-based if the logic of its control flow, data flow and resource allocation is declaratively expressed by means of business rules (Goedertier, Haesen, & Vanthienen, 2008).

DOI: 10.4018/978-1-4666-1975-3.ch030

Business rules are powerful representation forms that can potentially define the semantics of business process models and business vocabulary, and it can be used directly for controlling business processes.

But business rules are usually specified in natural language. It's well-known that natural language is often ambiguous and error-prone. For this reason, there are interesting proposals of using structured natural language. Recently, OMG promoted the use of structured English in the business rules framework SBVR, short for Semantics of Business Vocabulary and Rules.

In this paper, an approach is summarized to model business process, based on SBVR statements and some metamodels (Herbst, 1995).

2. BACKGROUND

2.1 Business Rule

A business rule is a statement that aims to influence or guide behavior and information in an organization (Steinke & Nikolette, 2003). Business rules are as close to the business as we can get. For example, a life insurance company might have a business rule saying that applications for a new pension plan are decided upon within three days. A business rule in the context of immigration might be that applications for green cards are put aside if the identity of applicants cannot be established legally. The five structural categories of business rules are (Wagner, 2005):

- **Integrity** (or constraints); For example: Each project must have one and only one project manager.
- **Derivation** (conditions resulting in conclusions); For example: Platinum customers receive a 5% discount. John Doe is a platinum customer. As a conclusion, John Doe receives a 5% discount.

- **Reaction** (Event, Condition, Action, Alternative action, Post-condition); For example: An invoice is received. If the invoice amount is more than $2,000 then a supervisor must approve it.
- **Production** (condition, action); For example: If there are no defects in the last batch of cars then the batch is approved.
- **Transformation** (change of state); For example: A man's age can change from 28 to 29, but not from 29 to 28.

A variety of rule languages have been developed over the past decade, and the most common used rule modeling languages are Rule Markup Language, Simple Rule Markup Language (SRML) and Semantics of Business Vocabulary and Business Rules (SBVR). As Rule Markup Language, specification is based on xml structure, less readable than the textual representation, and SRML has less technical support, we decided to use the SBVR as the business rule modeling language.

2.2 Business Process

Business Processes are sets of activities that create value for a customer (Muehlen, 2004). While research in Business Process Management initially focused on the documentation and organizational governance of processes, organizations are increasingly automating processes using workflow systems, and are building elaborate management systems around their processes. Such management infrastructures integrate modeling, automation, and business intelligence applications. The inclusion of compliance management activities is a logical next step in governing the business process life cycle.

A variety of modeling languages exist for the specification of process models, and they can be classified according to their focal modeling construct (Muehlen, 2004):

- **Activity-centered:** Processes as a network of tasks or activities.
- **Process object centered:** Processes as the legal sequence of state changes of the process object.
- **Resource centered:** Process as a network of processing stations that interact with each other.

Process languages appear as Graph-based languages (e.g. BPMN, EPC), Net-based languages (e.g. Petri-nets, flow nets) and Workflow Programming Languages (e.g. BPEL). Such languages, in general, are considered to be of the procedural modeling type, in which they focus on specifying the step-by-step activities that are required to take place in order to perform an action. While they do not provide the same level of precision or formalism as rule modeling languages, their strengths stem from their relative user friendliness and structural properties (McBrien & Seltveit, 1995).

2.3 SBVR SE

SBVR (OMG, 2008)is a new standard from the OMG that combines aspects of ontology and of rule systems. SBVR Structured English is a structured English vocabulary developed by the Object Management Group complying with the SBVR standard. In this paper, SBVR rule examples are given in "Structured English" (explained below), using several font styles:

[Nouns] are bracketed.
Verbs are given in italics.
{Literal values} and {instance names} are shown in braces.
Keywords are shown in bold font.
Uninterrupted text is shown in normal font style.

In SBVR the distinction between an entity instance and an entity type is made by using different fonts. However, SBVR does not make a distinction between general and specific entities.

SBVR does allow one to give a definition of an entity informally, such as:

[Rental]

Definition: contract with renter specifying use of a car or a car group for a rental period and a rental movement

- **Verbs:** Verbs are used in SBVR to relate entities to each other in order to create facts, called fact types. In SBVR, several types of facts can be distinguished.
- **Keywords:** In SBVR, Keywords can be used to specify business rules. There are several types of keywords in order to specify two types of rules, namely structural rules and operative rules. Structural rules are true by definition. Operative rules can be violated, therefore, in order to fully specify an operative rule one also has to specify an enforcement level, such as strict or loose. An example of such a rule is:

It is prohibited that a [drunk person] *is* **a** [driver] *in* **a** [car]
Enforcement level: strict

2.4 Business Process Modeling Notation

The Object Management Group (OMG) has developed a standard Business Process Modeling Notation (BPMN). The primary goal of BPMN is to provide a notation that is readily understandable by all business users, from the business analysts that create the initial drafts of the processes, to the technical developers responsible for implementing the technology that will perform those processes, and finally, to the business people who will manage and monitor those processes. Thus, BPMN creates a standardized bridge for the gap between the business process design and process implementation.

BPMN defines a Business Process Diagram (BPD), which is based on a flowcharting technique tailored for creating graphical models of business process operations. A Business Process Model, then, is a network of graphical objects, which are activities (i.e., work) and the flow controls that define their order of performance. A BPD is made up of a set of graphical elements. These elements enable the easy development of simple diagrams that will look familiar to most business analysts. The four basic categories of BPD elements are (White):

1. **Flow Objects:** Flow Objects are the elements that define the behavior of a Business Process. There are three types of Flow Objects: Events, Activities and Gateways.
2. **Connection Objects:** Flow Objects can be connected to each other or other information in three ways: Sequence Flow, Message Flow and Association. A sequence flow is used to show that two flow objects are related to each other. A Message Flow is used to show the flow of messages between two flow objects. It is not allowed to use a message flow to connect a gateway to other objects. An Association is used to associate information and/or Artifacts with Flow Objects.
3. **Swimlanes:** Swimlanes are used to represent entities. Activities are assigned to entities in BPMN by drawing an activity inside a swimlane. In order to represent that a certain entity consists of several other entities BPMN has two types of swimlanes: pools and lanes.
4. **Artifacts:** BPMN was designed to allow modelers and modeling tools some flexibility in extending the basic notation and in providing the ability to additional context appropriate to a specific modeling situation, such as for a vertical market (e.g., insurance or banking). Any number of Artifacts can be added to a diagram as appropriate for the context of the business processes being modeled.

3. INTRODUCTION TO RULE-BASED PROCESS MODELING

Enterprise models are abstractions of different aspects of an enterprise, typically with a purpose to understand and share the knowledge of how the enterprise is structured and how it operates (Bajec & Krisper, 2005). In addition to the purpose of knowledge management, enterprise models can be a foundation for model driven architecture. In the context of rule-based business process modeling, three sub models of an enterprise model are particularly relevant (Goedertier & Vanthienen, Rule-based business process modeling and execution, 2005).

A Business Vocabulary Model contains the knowledge artifacts of an enterprise model. It is often argued to express Vocabulary Models using fact-oriented ontology languages rather than object-oriented ontology languages (Halpin, 2000). At this level of abstraction, little matters how attributes resort under objects. In the context of rule based modeling, fact-oriented models are particularly useful because they are closer to natural language and logic programming, than object-oriented models.

A Business Process Model consists of process descriptions that describe how the enterprise interacts with external process participants and which internal services should consequently be invoked.

Business rules models govern the dynamics of data and process resources. Consequently, Vocabulary and Process models are related to business rules models (Bajec & Krisper, A methodology and tool support for managing business rules in organisations, 2005). Vocabulary models are related to Business Rule Models, because business logic contains derivation rules and constraints that define or constrain predicates of the vocabulary model. Constraints, for instance, can define the (conditional) cardinalities of artifact relations. Derivation rules define predicates that can be logically derived from the available case data. Process models are related to Business Rule Models because business logic defines the state transitions of process instances.

4. TRANSFORMING METHODS AND APPROACHES

This chapter discusses the transforming approach to transform SBVR statements into BPMN model. These statements to be transformed must be complete and consistent. This chapter is further structured as follows: Section 4.1 describes the relationship between rules set and BPMN patterns. Section 4.2 describes the method to parse statements in plain text form into model. Section 4.3 describes the method to transform intermediate model to SBVR model. Section 4.4 discusses mapping method from SBVR instance model to BPMN model.

The whole transformation approaches are show in Figure 1.

4.1 Supported BPMN Control Flow Patterns

This part gives a selection of control flow patterns to business rules. Patterns of BPMN supported by the transformation in this paper will be introduced below, and each will be followed by its SBVR SE rules.

4.1.1 Sequence

Description: Execute two or more activities in sequence. An activity in a process is enabled after the completion of a preceding activity in the same process. The Sequence pattern serves as the fundamental building block for processes. It is used to construct a series of consecutive tasks which execute in turn one after the other. Two tasks form part of a Sequence if there is a control-flow edge from one of them to the next which has no guards or conditions associated with it (Eder, Filieri, T. Kurz, & Pezzuto). This pattern is shown in Figure 2.

The following rule leads to this pattern:

```
If A then B then C
```

Figure 1. Transforming steps

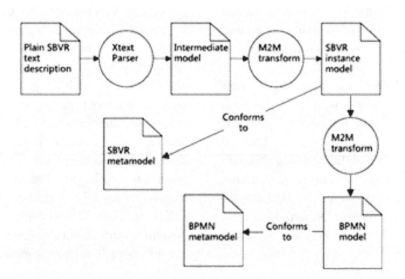

Figure 2. BPMN representation of the sequence pattern

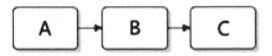

4.1.2 Parallel Split

Description: Execute two or more activities in any order or in parallel. Parallel split is the divergence of a branch into two or more parallel branches each of which execute concurrently. This pattern can be seen in Figure 3.

The following rule leads to this pattern:

```
If A then B and C
```

4.1.3 Simple Merge

Description: An activity in a process is enabled by each completion of several other preceding activities. This pattern presents a convergence of two or more branches into a single subsequent branch such that each enablement of an incoming branch results in the thread of control being passed to the subsequent branch. This pattern can be seen in Figure 4.

The following combination of rules leads to this pattern:

```
If A then C.
If B then C.
```

4.1.4 Synchronization

Description: An activity in a process is enabled only after all preceding activities are completed. It's a convergence of two or more branches into a single subsequent branch such that the thread of control is passed to the subsequent branch when

Figure 3. BPMN representation of the parallel split pattern

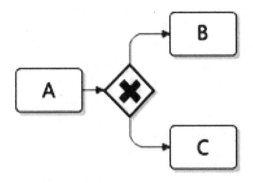

all input branches have been enabled. This pattern can be seen in Figure 5.

The following combination of rules leads to this pattern:

```
If A and B then c.
```

4.1.5 Exclusive Choice

Description: The completion of an activity enables one of several possible other activities based on some condition related to the activity. It's a divergence of a branch into two or more branches such that when the incoming branch is enabled, the thread of control is immediately passed to

Figure 4. BPMN representations of the simple merge pattern

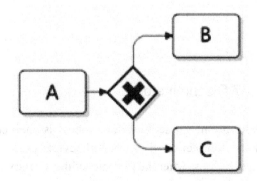

Figure 5. BPMN representation of the Synchronization pattern

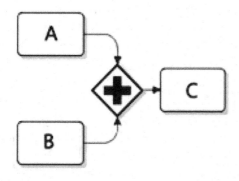

Figure 6. BPMN representation of the exclusive split pattern

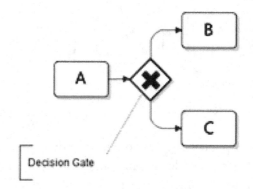

precisely one of the outgoing branches based on a mechanism that can select one of the outgoing branches. This pattern can be seen in Figure 6.

The following rule leads to this pattern:

```
If A then B else C.
```

4.1.6 Multiple Choices

Description: Multi-choice is the divergence of a branch into two or more branches such that when the incoming branch is enabled, the thread of control is immediately passed to one or more of the outgoing branches based on a mechanism that selects one or more outgoing branches. The completion of an activity enables one or more of several possible other activities based on some conditions. This pattern can be seen in Figure 7.

The following combinations of rules lead to this pattern:

```
If A then B.
If A' then C.
If A'' then B and C.
```

4.1.7 Discriminator

Description: An activity in a process is enabled by the completion of just one of several preceding activities. After the first preceding activity is completed the completion of other activities is ignored. This pattern is show in Figure 8.

BPMN don't have a standard symbol for the discriminator. We solved this by using a complex gateway combined with an annotation. The following rule leads to this pattern:

```
If A or B then C.
```

4.1.8 Structured Cycles

Description: A point in a workflow process where one or more activities can be done repeatedly. There pattern of structured cycle has one entry and exit point, which can be seen in Figure 9.

Figure 7. BPMN representation of the multiple choice pattern

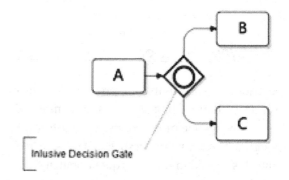

Figure 8. BPMN representation of the Discriminator pattern

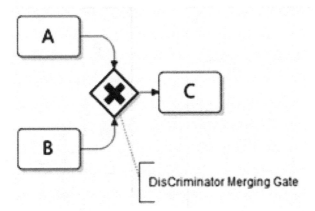

The general rule for an Activity x to be in a loop is that there is a subsequent Activity y, that can only be enabled if Activity x is completed and that triggers Activity x. An example of a set of rules that would lead to a structured cycle is:

```
If A then B
If B then C else D
If D then B
```

4.2 SBVR Statements Parsing Method

Since the input for the transformation method, SBVR is in a textual form that needs to be transformed to a model, we need text to model transformation. There are not many approaches available that support such transformation. One tool that can be found is OAW Xtext. Then we need a customized language to parse the SBVR texts. In the Xtext IDE, The language that is used in the input of the transformation must be described in an Xtext grammar language. Based on this Approach, the tool generates a metamodel, an Eclipse Text Editor and a parser. The parser is responsible for reading the text and transforming it to an instance of the generated metamodel.

Figure 10 shows some basic SBVR statements that are used as the input model for the exemplary transformation. At the beginning of the list the three concepts Bike, Rider and Wheel are introduced. After that facts about these concepts are used to add attributes and references to the concepts in order to express relationships. In order to make the xmi file generated later easy to read, I give only the vocabulary statements for example in this part.

Figure 9. BPMN representation of the structured cycle

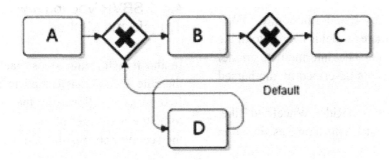

Figure 10. Sample SBVR SE statements

```
[Bike]

[Rider]

[Wheel]

[Bike] has [type]

[Bike] has [seat]

[Bike] has [Rider]

[Bike] must have 2 [Wheel]

[Wheel] has [manufacturer]

[Wheel] has [type]

[Rider] has [firstname]

[Rider] can have [middlename]

[Rider] has [lastname]

[Rider] has [age]

[Rider] has [gender]

[Rider] is identified by [lastname] and
[firstname]

[Bike] is [identified] by [type]
```

Figure 11. Sample Xtext grammar

```
... ...

   Model:

           (entities+= Entity)+

   ;

   Entity:

          name=STRING

          (attributes+= Attribute)+

        (constraints+=Constraint)*

   ;

   Attribute:

... ...
```

As mentioned below, the transforming grammar is the key point of text to model transform. The grammar defined an intermediate model which can be transformed into SBVR later. Here is a short segment of the grammar as shown in Figure 11.

Before the directly transformation to SBVR model, an intermediate model is needed to make the transform easier. The intermediate model represents the concepts described by the parsed SBVR statements.

Here are the entities of Rider, Wheel and Bike, conforming to the statements above as shown in Figure 12.

4.3 From Intermediate Model to SBVR Model

During this step, SBVR metamodel (Kleiner, Albert, & Bézivin, 2009)is needed. It can be generated by the OAW. In order to get the metamodel, you need a UML/OCL description of SBVR, and OAW can then transform it into the metamodel, shown in Figure 13.

In the transformation, three components are needed to read, transform and out put the result, as shown in Figure 14.

4.4 BPMN Transforms Method

4.4.1 SBVR Vocabulary Transforms Method

In the transforming steps, each binary fact in the rule set is transformed to an activity. The first entity mentioned by the fact is considered to be the performer of the activity, the verb and the second entity is the activity (Halpin, 2000),

Figure 12. Fragment of generated intermediate model

```
... ...

    <entities name="Rider" displayAttribute="lastname+"+firstname">

    <attributes name="firstname "required="true" defaultValue=""/>

    <attributes name="middlename"defaultValue=""/>

    <attributes name="lastname"required="true" defaultValue=""/>

    <attributes name="age"required="true" defaultValue=""/>

    <attributes name="gender" required="true" defaultValue=""/>

    </entities>

    <entities name="Wheel">

    <attributes name="manufacturer" required="true" defaultValue=""/>

    <attributes name="type" required="true" defaultValue=""/>

    </entities>

    <entities name="Bike" displayAttribute="type" hasMany="RiderRef:Rider,WheelRef:Wheel">

    <attributes name="type" required="true" defaultValue=""/>

    <attributes name="seat" required="true" defaultValue=""/>

    <references name="RiderRef" type="//@entities.0" modality="1"/>

    <references name="WheelRef" type="//@entities.1" modality="4"/>

    </entities>

    ... ...
```

and each characteristic fact is considered to be a condition that can be true or false:

Each binary fact type that has the pattern "<placeholder1> <verbPhrase> <placeholder2>"is mapped to a specific BPMN task where:

1. <placeholder1> represents the participant that performs the task;
2. <verbPhrase> <placeholder2> represents the task.

Each unary fact type that has the pattern "<placeholder> <verbPhrase>" is mapped to an Exclusive Gateway (decision point) where:

1. <placeholder> represents a concept that has a Boolean characteristic;
2. <verbPhrase> represents a Boolean characteristic of the concept that is represented by the placeholder.

Figure 13. Structure of SBVR metamodel

4.4.2 SBVR Rule Sets Transforming Method

Each rule that has the pattern "if <antecedent1> and <antecedent2> then <conscquent>", where <antecedent1> and <consequent> are both binary fact types and where <antecedent2> is a unary fact type, is mapped to a flow-path that involves a decision point (Exclusive Gateway).

Each rule that has the pattern "if <antecedent1> and <antecedent2> ... and <antecedentN> then..."

with N arbitrary and where each <antecedent> and the <consequent> are binary fact types, is mapped to a flow-path that merges N flows into one through a Join

Moreover rules that have the pattern "if <antecedent> then <consequent>"and that have the same binary fact type underpinning the <antecedent> are mapped to a Fork.

Figure 14. Transforming components

Read the xmi instance

```
<component class=" org.openarchitectureware.emf. XmiReader">

    <metaModelFile value="metamodel/metamodel.ecore"/>

    <modelFile value="${model}"/>

    <outputSlot value="model"/>

</component>
```

Transform the xmi instance

```
<component class="oaw.xtend.XtendComponent">

    <metaModel id="mm" class="org.openarchitectureware. type.emf.EmfMetaModel">

        <metaModelFile value=".../m2m/metamodels/SBVR.ecore"/>

    </metaModel>

    <invoke value="platform/resource/src/M2M::act(model)"/>

    <outputSlot value="sbvrModel"/>

</component>
```

Output the new sbvr xmi instance

```
<component id="write" class="org.eclipse.mwe.emf. Writer">

    <useSingleGlobalResourceSet value="true"/>

    <modelSlot value="sbvrModel"/>

    <uri value="platform:/resource/<NEW SBVR>.xmi"/>

</component>
```

4.4.3 Relating SBVR to BPMN

The requirement of modeling BPMN through SBVR makes it necessary to introduce the main aspects and concepts underpinning BPMN. This will be done by describing the essential elements of the BPMN metamodel, as shown in Figure 15 (a). The metamodel is the reference one for BPMN that is an xml-like language for BPMN modeling and execution. The structure of the metamodel is shown in Figure 15 (b).

Since the interest of this paper is not to provide a complete way to represent BPMN through SBVR models, only the essential elements of a BPMN will be covered. The mapping between our SBVR metamodel and the BPMN metamodel is relatively simply:

Figure 15. Simplified BPMN metamodel and structure

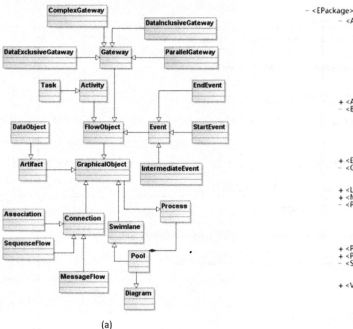

(a)   (b)

1. Sequence elements are mapped to BPMN Activity. The type of sequence element determines the BPMN activity type.
2. Activities are mapped to the BPMN activity task, and the actor of the activity is mapped to a BPMN text annotation containing the name of the actor.
3. Gateway fork and joins of the type AND are mapped to the BPMN activity type of ParallelGateway.
4. Gateway fork and joins of the type XOR are mapped to the BPMN DataExclusiveGateway.
5. Gateway fork of the type OR are mapped to the BPMN activity type of DataInclusiveGateway.
6. Gateway joins of the type Disc are mapped to the BPMN activity type of ComplexGateway with an annotation attached to it with the text 'Discriminator'.
7. SequenceFlow are mapped to a BPMN edge.
8. Connection between sequence elements is mapped to a BPMN edge. The condition, if

there is any that belongs to the connection between two sequence elements is mapped to the name of the edge.

Therefore this fact is mapped to a BPMN gateway that has two outputs, one for the true value of the condition one for the false value.

5. GENERATING PROCESS FROM RULES

In this part we are going to transform a SBVR SE statement into BPMN model, to verify that the method mentioned below is feasible.

SBVR SE statements can be edited both in the text pad and SBeaVeR. Here is the input statement about ATM, including both vocabularies and rule sets as seen in Figure 16.

Running the workflow file will result in a BPMN file, shown in Figure 17.

Figure 16. Fragment of statements for verification

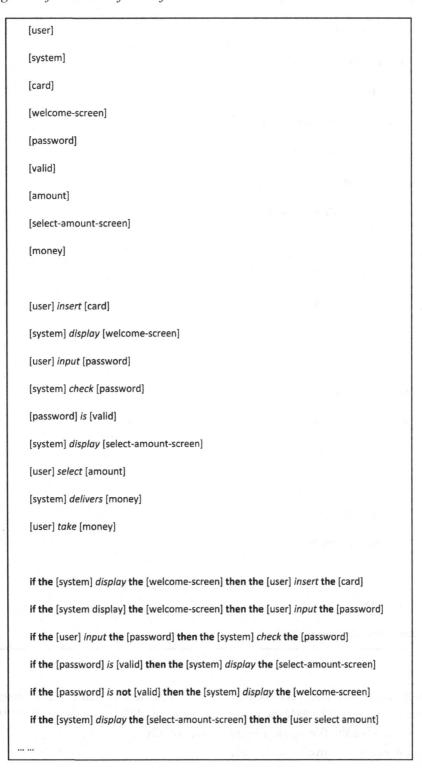

[user]

[system]

[card]

[welcome-screen]

[password]

[valid]

[amount]

[select-amount-screen]

[money]

[user] *insert* [card]

[system] *display* [welcome-screen]

[user] *input* [password]

[system] *check* [password]

[password] *is* [valid]

[system] *display* [select-amount-screen]

[user] *select* [amount]

[system] *delivers* [money]

[user] *take* [money]

if the [system] *display* **the** [welcome-screen] **then the** [user] *insert* **the** [card]

if the [system display] **the** [welcome-screen] **then the** [user] *input* **the** [password]

if the [user] *input* **the** [password] **then the** [system] *check* **the** [password]

if the [password] *is* [valid] **then the** [system] *display* **the** [select-amount-screen]

if the [password] *is* **not** [valid] **then the** [system] *display* **the** [welcome-screen]

if the [system] *display* **the** [select-amount-screen] **then the** [user select amount]

... ...

Figure 17. Fragment of generated files

```
<bpmn:BpmnDiagram ......>

<pools name="atm" ......>

<!-- vertices -->

    <vertices name="valid card" />

    <vertices name="welcomescreen" />

    <vertices name="insert card" />

<vertices name="amount screen" />

<vertices name="select amount" />

<vertices name="diliver money" />

    <vertices name="take money"/>

<vertices name="quit card" />

        ...

<vertices outgoingEdges=" "

incomingEdges=" " activityType=

"DataExclusiveGateway"/>

    ...

<!—SequenceEdges -->

    <sequenceEdges />

    ...

    </pools>

</bpmn:BpmnDiagram>
```

The only intermediate step that has to be performed is to open the generated BPMN file in the Generic editor and to save the file again. Figure 18 is the diagram generated from the sample BPMN files.

But there is still some shortages that I need some modification to make the BPMN model run correctly.

Figure 18. Generated diagram

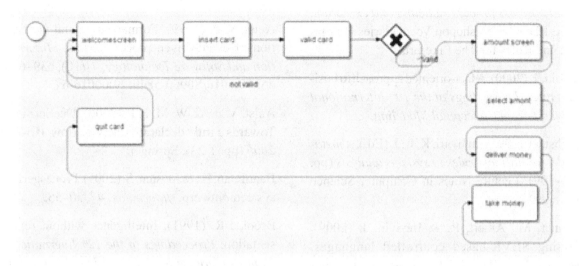

FUTURE RESEARCH DIRECTIONS

In order to figure out the limitations, some future work may aim at the semantics verification of statements, further automation, supporting of more patterns, multi-objective transformation, and so on. Some further research such as business rule engines, ontology for business rules, and more powerful parser for other kinds of input formats are also on the schedule.

CONCLUSION

In this paper, the SBVR structured English was introduced, including a plain text parsing method of it, and then the method of model to model transform was discussed. The goal of these jobs were to develop a method to automatically transform business rules into business processes, and to demonstrate an approach to model flexible and compliant business processes base on SBVR statements. To reach this goal, the parsing method and the M2M transformation were the key point of all jobs.

But I certainly do not claim to have identified and solved all the important problems. There are still many limitations in the transforming method: In some case there are some untransformed elements that don't work in the generated models, and the generated BPMN file still needs some modification to work properly. There are also some problems in solving some sequence of activities, and more complicated BPMN patterns are not supported.

REFERENCES

Bajec, M., & Krisper, M. (2005). A methodology and tool support for managing business rules in organisations. *Information Systems*, *30*(6), 423–443. doi:10.1016/j.is.2004.05.003

Eder, R., Filieri, A. T., Kurz, T. H., & Pezzuto, M. (2008). *Model-transformation-based software generation utilizing natural language notations. Digital Ecosystems and Technologies*. Thailand: IEEE DEST.

Goedertier, S., Haesen, R., & Vanthienen, J. (2008). Rule-based business process modeling and enactment. *International Journal of Business Process Integration and Management*, *3*(3), 194–207. doi:10.1504/IJBPIM.2008.023219

Goedertier, S., & Vanthienen, J. (2005). *Rule-based business process modeling and execution*. IEEE EDOC Workshopon Vocabularies Ontologies and Rules for The Enterprise.

Halpin, T. (2000). A fact-oriented approach to business rules. *Proceedings of the 19ᵗʰ International Conference on Conceptual Modeling.*

Herbst, H. (1995). In Iivari, K. L. J. (Ed.), *A metamodel for business rules in systems analysis* (pp. 186–199). Lecture Notes in Computer Science Springer.

Kleiner, M., Albert, P., & Bézivin, J. (2009). Parsing SBVR-based controlled languages. *Models'O9, ACM/IEEE 12th International Conference on Model Driven Engineering Languages and Systems* (pp. 122-136). Springer.

McBrien, P., & Seltveit, A. H. (1995). *Coupling process models and business rules*. In Information Systems Development for Decentralized Organizations. IFIP 8.1 WG Conference: Chapman.

Muehlen, M. Z. (2004). Business process and business rule modeling languages for compliance management: A representational analysis. *The 26th International Conference on Conceptual Modeling.*

OMG. (2008). *SBVR 1.0 specification*. Retrieved from http://www.omg.org/spec/SBVR/1.0/

Steinke, G., & Nikolette, C. (2003). Business rules as the basis of an organization's information systems. *Industrial Management & Data Systems, 103*(1), 3. doi:10.1108/02635570310456904

Wagner, G. (2005). Rule modeling and markup. In *Reasoning Web* (pp. 251–274). Springer. doi:10.1007/11526988_7

White, S. A. (n.d.). Introduction to BPMN. *IBM Corporation.*

ADDITIONAL READING

Aalst, V. d. (1999). Formalization and verification of event-driven process chains. *Information and Software Technology, 41*(10), 639–650. doi:10.1016/S0950-5849(99)00016-6

Aalst, V. d., & W. M. P. P. (2006). DecSerFlow: Towards a truly declarative service flow. *WS-FM 2006* (pp. 1-23). Springer.

Baardman, E., & Joosten, S. (2005). Procesgericht systeemontwerp. *Informatie, 47*, 50–55.

Brooks, R. (1991). Intelligence without representation. *Proceedings of the 12ᵗʰ International Joint Conference on Artificial Intelligence*, (pp. 139–159).

Chong, C. N., Etalle, S., Hartel, P., & Joosten, R. (2005). Service brokerage with prolog. In *7th International Conference on Enterprise Information Systems* (pp. 119-135). INSTICC Press.

Curtis, B., Kellner, M., & Over, J. (1992). Process modelling. *Communications of the ACM, 35*(9), 75–90. doi:10.1145/130994.130998

De Morgan, A. (1966). On the syllogism: Iv, and on the logic of relations. *Transactions of the Cambridge Philosophical Society, 10*, 331–358.

Dijkman, R. M., & Ferreira Pires, L. (2001). Calculating with concepts: A technique for the development of business process support. In *Proceedings of the UML 2001 Workshop on Practical UML.*

Dijkman, R. M., & Joosten, S. M. (2002). *An algorithm to derive use case diagrams from business process models*. IASTEDSEA.

F, P., & R, R. (1999). Some contributions to the metatheory of the Situation Calculus. *Journal of the ACM, 46*(3), 325-361.

Ferraiolo, D., Sandhu, R., & Gavrila, S. (2001). Proposed NIST standard for role-based access control. *ACM Transactions on Information and System Security*, *4*(3), 224–274. doi:10.1145/501978.501980

Fowler, M. (1997). *Analysis patterns - Reusable object models*. Addison-Wesley.

Goedertier, S., & Vanthienen, J. (2006). Designing compliant business processes with obligations and permissions. *Business Process Management Workshops, LNCS, 4103*, 5–14. doi:10.1007/11837862_2

Guizzardi, G., & Wagner, G. (2005). Some applications of a unified foundational ontology in business modelling. In Rosemann, M., & Green, P. (Eds.), *Ontologies and business systems analysis* (pp. 345–367). Hershey, PA: Idea Group Publisher. doi:10.4018/978-1-59140-339-5.ch013

Hale, B. V. (2001). *Business rules applied: Building better systems using the business rules approach*. John Wiley & Sons, Inc.

Jakobson, I., Booch, G., & Rumbaugh, J. (1999). *The unified software development process*. Addison-Wesley.

Joosten, S., & Purao, S. R. (2002). A rigorous approach for mapping workflows to object-oriented is models. *Journal of Database Management, 13*, 1–19. doi:10.4018/jdm.2002100101

Kilov, H., & Simmonds, I. D. (1996). Business patterns: Reusable abstract constructs for business specification. In Humphreys, P. (Eds.), *Implementing systems for supporting management decisions: Concepts, methods and experiences* (pp. 225–248).

Sadiq, S., Orlowska, M., & Sadiq, W. (2005). Specification and validation of process constraints for flexible workflows. *Information Systems, 30*(5), 349–378. doi:10.1016/j.is.2004.05.002

Vanthienen, J. (2001). Ruling the business: About business rules and decision tables. *New Directions in Software Engineering*, 103–120.

Vanthienen, J., Mues, C., & Aerts, A. (1998). An illustration of verification and validation in the modelling phase of KBS development. *Data & Knowledge Engineering, 27*(3), 337–352. doi:10.1016/S0169-023X(98)80003-7

Yolum, P., & Singh, M. (2004). Reasoning about commitments in the event calculus: An approach for specifying and executing protocols. *Annals of Mathematics and Artificial Intelligence, 42*(1-3), 227–253. doi:10.1023/B:AMAI.0000034528.55456.d9

KEY TERMS AND DEFINITIONS

BPEL: BPEL is a process language for service orchestration. It enjoys widespread industry adoption due to its status as an OASIS standard. Loosely-coupled integration through WSDL interfaces, rich process constructs, robust fault handling, and clearly defined extension points are among its salient features.

Business Process Management (BPM): BPM includes methods, techniques, and tools to support the design, enactment, management, and analysis of operational business processes. It can be considered as an extension of classical Workflow Management (WFM) systems and approaches.

Business Process: A business process consists of a set of activities, and it can are executed in organizational and technical environment. The activities jointly realize a business goal.

SBVR: The Semantics of Business Vocabulary and Business Rules (SBVR) is an adopted standard of the Object Management Group (OMG) intended to be the basis for formal and detailed natural language declarative description of a complex entity.

Workflow: Workflow is the automation of a business process.

Chapter 31

The Description and Relation of WS–CDL and BPEL

Yanjun Qian
Yunnan University, China

Wei Zhou
Yunnan University, China

Zhongwei Wu
Yunnan University, China

Shaowen Yao
Yunnan University, China

ABSTRACT

WS-CDL (Web Service Choreography Description Language) is a language to describe multiple party how to work with together to accomplish a work in the context of SOA. BEPL (Business Process Execution Language) can get the same point, but they are from different view. WS-CDL is from a global view, which describes how multiple parties communicate with each other. BPEL is from a point of view of a single role who participates to manage the process of the work. Usually these two ways work together to describe and implement the business process. But WS-CDL has more advantages to achieve the most important goal of SOA-flexibility. So, W3C gives a suggestion to create an algorithm mapping from WS-CDL to BPEL; this chapter describes such a way to accomplish this.

1 INTRODUCTION

Business process management is a very important task in industry. Especially in SOA, services are in a very loose way. If enterprises want their groups work in a highly way, they must organize these materials in scientific ways. BPEL and WS-CDL are two languages to organize these services or compose the process.

In this paper, in the second session it shows you the categories of service of SOA and two ways to compose business process; in the third session, it gives an overview of BPEL and WS-CDL; in the fourth session, this paper through an example mapping from WS-CDL to BPEL to make you understand the relation between WS-CDL and BPEL.

DOI: 10.4018/978-1-4666-1975-3.ch031

2 BACKGROUND

2.1 Categories of Service of SOA

In whole SOA, services are divided into three categories: basic services, composed services and process services (Krafzig & Dirk, 2004). Basic services provide services which are simple and can't divide into other simple services. Composed services are some basic services which compose according to certain business logic, so they are services that extend from basic service. The last kind of services is process services which are extended services from basic service too, but there are some differences between composed services and process services. The differences are as following: Composed services are working during a short period under some process logic and it can't show any state to outside. While process services are under some process logic too, but it can work during a long period and when they work, they can show some states to outside so controller can manage it with these states.

2.2 Business Process Management and Business Process Modeling

Obviously, basic services are components of SOA and process services are the final product. Usually basic services are given; if enterprises want to achieve greater efficiency in the process they must pay more attention on the designing and implementation. From this point, business process design and management play an important role in the SOA. Commonly creating a process model can simulate the state of the real world. Business process modeling is a set of practices or tasks that companies can perform to visually depict or describe all the aspects of a business process, including its flow, control and decision points, triggers and conditions for activity execution, the context in which an activity runs, and associated resources (Bloomberg, 2006). Use BPM description language, enterprise can both describe and implement business process.

3 OVERVIEW OF BPEL AND WS-CDL

We can make business process modeling by abstracting business process, through make up the various conflicts and collision analysis can obtain a higher efficiency in the implementation and better allocated resources business process model. This article assumes that this model has been established and is ready to adopt a business process modeling language to achieve the business process automation.

3.1 The Position of BPEL and WS-CDL

Throughout the SOA, all of the information transmission is based on network protocol and its concrete realization is dependent on the other side XML to prepare a simple access protocol, through the WSDL to describe the service, and through UDDI to publish and discover services, and the entire services, flow control is by the BPEL or WS-CDL to control, so BPEL and WS-CDL was higher than web service, as it show in Figure 1.

3.2 Introduction of Orchestration and Choreography

For a clearer understanding of BPEL and WS-CDL position, you must first understand the two terms in the preparation of Orchestration and choreography. Orchestration and choreography are commonly used to describe the "composite Web services in two ways" term. Although they have something in common, still there are some differences. Web services orchestration refers to business processes undertaken by Web service

Figure 1. The position of business process modeling description language

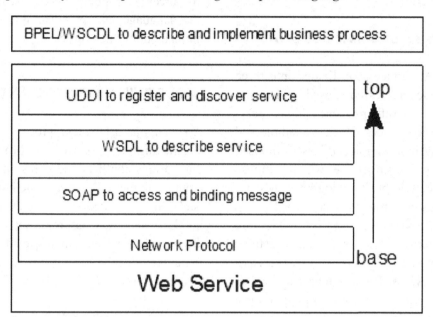

composition, while the Web Service Choreography refers to operations carried out in collaboration Web service composition (Yang D. &., 2003). Orchestration defines the services which compose to the orchestration itself, as well as the implementation of the order of these services (such as parallel events, conditional branching logic, etc.) (IBM, 2003). Therefore, orchestration can be seen as a simple process, this process itself is also a Web service. When the business process needs some services, the process will be invoked as a service for the requesting party, while other services need to call the process service, process it as a service provided by this service. Choreography focused on the definition of a larger multi-how to the business affairs collaboration. It defines how to carry out a range of services to interoperate, call services, transmission of information in order to complete a business process. In the choreography, all services are equal; each service may have multiple participants to share information to complete their adoption of a service. From the above is to know the orchestration of a centralized management approach to manage business

processes, while the choreography is based on a decentralized approach to managing business processes. The implementation orchestration of business processes rely on the advance of the implementation language, and in the choreography of business processes rely on the realization of the right for each service developed a set of rules. In some smaller systems if they rely on the orchestration of business processes, they can achieve high efficiency. But in large-scale applications, if you want to use orchestration to implement the business processes it seems too difficult. At the same it also restricting the establishment of a core purpose of SOA to achieve maximum flexibility in business services. BPEL can implement the business process by orchestration way and choreography way, but essentially BPEL is a orchestration language, because it concerns the implementation of the order of the service, while the WS-CDL is a kind of choreography language which focuses on the completion of to a business process when involved in multi-party collaboration rules. So BPEL and WS-CDL are both above Web Service and call to the services provided by the underlying Web Service in the realization of business processes, but the method was different. Therefore, they can be transformed into each other (Jensen & Milner, 2004) (Milner, 2006).

3.3 The Structure of BPEL and WS-CDL

In order to facilitate understanding of the mapping algorithm between them here, briefly describe WS-CDL and BPEL syntax structure, BPEL is a description of operational flow and order of XML language, while the business flow and the order itself can be regarded as service too (Yang D. &., 2003). Language Elements provides elements to call to service, to handle the response as well as processing variables, control structures and error. Its structure is just as in Figure 2.

Web Services Choreography Description Language version is a Web services choreography description language proposed by W3C. It defines

concurrent systems of a mutually reciprocal, cross-organization, usually with lots of interactions, from an overall perspective. It can clearly express the formal relationship between several external trading partners. Its purpose is to describe the collaboration between the services needed to comply with the rules of information and communication (Jan Mendling, 2003). Its component is just like in Figure 3.

4 THE MAPPING ALGORITHM FROM WS-CDL TO BPEL

4.1 The Generation from WS-CDL to BPEL

BPEL is a business process implementation language based on the orchestration, so its focus on the process performing on each participant, while WS-CDL is based on choreography so it is posi-

Figure 2. The structure of BPEL document

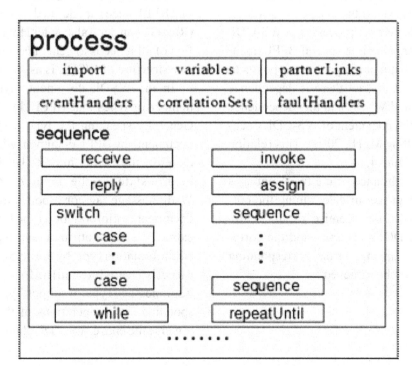

Figure 3. The structure of WS-CDL document

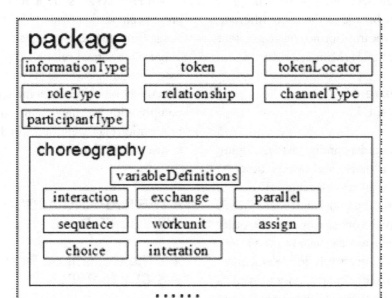

tioned in a variety of participants in co-operation rules. Because WS-CDL is from the overall view, and it involves the relationship between the various participants, it can be decomposed into multiple BPEL documents. Each participant in their own scopes of activity within the perspective of their own to deal with business processes. A WS-CDL document can mapping into several BPEL document, it means that a participant corresponds to a BPEL document. In fact there is dependence between BPEL and WSDL and this dependence also express in the document of WS-CDL document (Jan Mendling M. H., 2003). This relation can be seen in Figure 4.

Because the substance of the two languages are XML tag language, in determining the correspondence under the premise of the entire document using DOM traversal, and the corresponding node mapping, is the corresponding transformation can be achieved.

4.2 Direct Mapping

The direct mapping between WS-CDL and WSDL:

As describe above, a WS-CDL document can be mapped to several BPEL and WSDL. The services that BPEL needs are defined in WSDL document (Russell, van der Aalst, & ter Hofstede, 2006). So first of all it needs to generate WSDL document. The structure of WSDL is as shown in Figure 5.

In the WSDL document <type> defined a number of types that BPEL document can use. Generally speaking the type used in WS-CDL document, the BPEL document will use them too, therefore the use of <import> label WS-CDL can be translate to the label of <xi:include>. Wsdl:message tag corresponds to the WS-CDL document cdl:informationType label, so you can extract the name attribute and type attribute of cdl:informationType, by the help of them you can directly translate cdl:informationType to wsdl:messageType. wsdl:portType is the corresponding set of operations of the role, it must traverse the entire WS-CDL obtain the document

Figure 4. The generation relation of BPEL and WS-CDL

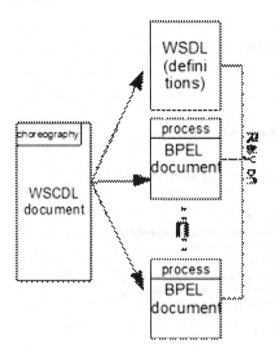

element involved in behavior. Every cdl:interaction in WS-CDL would correspond a wsdl:portType, so we should travel all cdl:interaction elements which the role works in to generate wsdl:portType elements.

The direct mapping between WS-CDL and BPEL:

By the sub element cdl:role of cdl:relationship can be directly generated to bpel:participantType.

Figure 5. The structure of WSDL documents

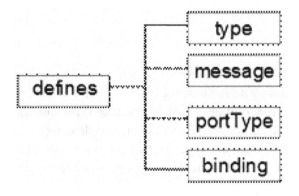

Variable elements bpel:variable can retrieve all of their role-related cdl:interaction of the cdl:channelType to obtain the corresponding mapping, According to the reason that the value of cdl:channel is rely on the elements of cdl:token and cdl:tokenLocator and just like bpel:variable cdl:tokenLocator can get its value by xQuery, so we can map cdl:channel, cdl:channelType, cdl:tokenLocator to bpel:variable. Bpel:partnerLink can be drawn from the element of cdl:relationship. If the one role was in a relationship and if this roleType is the first role attribute of cdl:relationship, then convert this role to the myRole attribute of bpel:partnerLink, if this role is the second role of a cdl:relationship then convert it to the partnerRole attribute of bpel:partnerLink.

The most important mapping relation is the mapping policy of activity between these two languages, but in fact we have abstracted behavior in WSDL document, so we just need to abstract the control logic and call for the services we defined in WSDL document. The direct mapping of control logic is as following: sequence activity cdl:sequence mapping to bpel:sequence; parallel activity cdl:parallel mapping to bpel:flow; selective structure cdl:choice could be mapped to bpel:switch, the internal branch activities which were defined in the cdl:sequence could be mapped to the activities which are defined in bpel:case; the loop structure cdl:workunit could be mapped to bpel:while or bpel:repeatUtil determined by whether the activity executes before the determination of the given Boolean expression. The activities defined in the control logic can using such a rule to mapping from CDL to BPEL: the whole cdl:interaction can map to a bpel:invoke; cdl:receive mapped to bpel:receive; cdl:send mapped to bpel:reply. If there is no action for this role, CDL will use cdl:silentAction to express this behavior, and this element can be translate to bpel:empty element. If there needed to synchronize the message to wait for an action, CDL use cdl:guard element to reach this point, while

Figure 6. The way to create WSDL and BPEL documents

```
input: WS-CDL document
output: BPEL documents & WSDL documents

Detailed steps:

The first step:
//Create the WSDL document
    Traverse the first element of WSCDL document
    while it is not the last element
        if there is a attribute of type
            Restore it into the WSDL document as a type element of WSDL
            by the given rules above;
        else
            if there is a informationType element
                Restore it into the WSDL document as a messageType
                element of WSDL by the given rules above;
                else If there is a interaction
                    Restore it into the WSDL document as a port
                    element of WSDL by the given rules above;
    Traverse the next element of WSCDL document
The second step:
    Traverse the the first relationship element
    while there is a role in relationship
            Restore it to an array;
    Travel the next relationship element;
The third step:
//create the BPEL documents
    While there is a role in the array
        Create a BPEL document
        Abstract the definition of variable, partnerLink which is involved
        with role from WSDL document as the rules given above.
        Abstract the activities in the choreography;
        if it's cdl sequence
                map it to bpel sequence;
        if it's cdl choice
                map it to bpel switch and bpel case;
        if it's cdl while
                map it to bpel guard;
        .....
    Other control logic can be mapped by the rues given above
```

BPEL use wait to achieve this objective, so we just need to translate them to each other.

Detailed mapping algorithm:

As it describes above, the first step of this transition is generating WSDL from BPEL, as it need to traverse all document looking for ele-ment cdl:type, recording them to wsdl:type; and removing redundant elements. Then navigate to the definition of cdl:informationType and use the direct mapping relation translate them to wsdl:massageType; in this point we need to note that the attribute of cdl:informationType is not

Figure 7. The business process of buying goods

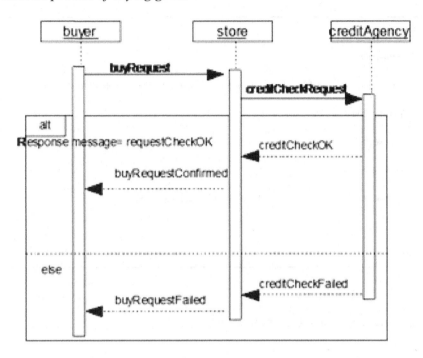

Figure 8. The WS-CDL structure of the example

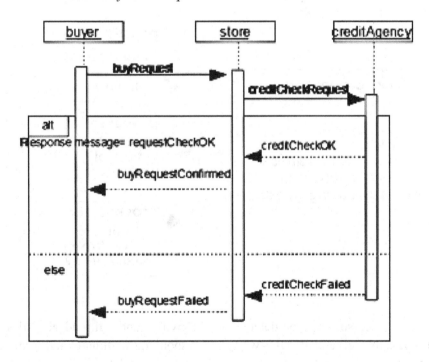

Figure 9. The structure of mapped BPEL document

```
<process>

    <partnerLinks>

        <partnerLink name="Store"partnerLinkType="tns:StoreLT"partnerRole="StoreRole"/>

    </partnerLinks>

    <variables/>

    <sequence>

        <invoke operation="buy"partnerLink="Store"portType="tns:Store"/>

    </sequence>

</process>
```

Figure 10. The generating dependency of example

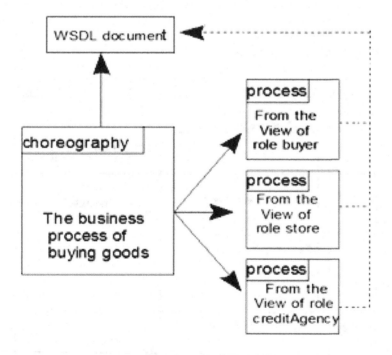

needed for wsdl:message so it can be deleted. The wsdl:portType can be generated in this way, According to the attribute of cdl:interaction to estimate whether this action is a request activity or response activity and convert their cdl:receive activities and cdl:send activities into the corresponding wsdl:input and wsdl:output tag. Because WS-CDL is focused interaction among participants so there is no corresponding mapping method to the single-channel behavior of WSDL.

The element of bind is not needed for this mapping, so there's no need to generate it. There is a 1 to n relation between WS-CDL document and BPEL document and the number of BPEL documents is depended on the number of participants defined in the WS-CDL document. So it needs to traverse the whole document to pick up kinds of roles and store them to an array. Then according to the order of role's appearance, find out the activities it participates. If the activity is a sequence according to the rules shows above translate to a BPEL sequence activities, else you can according these rules above translate all kind s of control logic to BPEL document. The flow diagram is as shown in Figure 6.

5. USING THIS ALGORITHM TO GENERATE BPEL FROM WS-CDL

Here is a WS-CDL example in Figure 7; its business process is as following sequence diagram:

If the buyer wants to buy something, the buyer can send a request which is a message express the desire to buy things, then the store will send a creditCheckRequest to check if the credit is available. If it's available then it will send a response message. After that the store can confirm this deal or refuse it.

The structure of WS-CDL document is as follows in Figure 8.

Because it relates three roles, it can be drawn to three BPEL documents and the related WSDL document. The structure of mapped BPEL documents is as shown in Figure 9.

And as it shows in Figure 10, it shows the generating dependency of this example.

FUTURE RESEARCH DIRECTIONS

Though there is a way to generate BPEL document from WSDL document in this paper, still there are lots of problem haven't been solved.

For example, we just can generate such a map, but can't prove that this mapping is correct. So next, we will be adding such a mapping algorithm as an intermediate link. (Jensen & Milner, 2004) (Milner, 2006) Firstly we'll let WS-CDL generate a BPMN diagram and then map it to BPEL documents. Using such ways we can intuitive verify if this mapping algorithm is correct (Milner, 2009) (Milner, 1980).

CONCLUSION

This chapter has presented a mapping algorithm which can generate BPEL and related WSDL documents from WS-CDL document and using this algorithm we have programmed to generate WS-CDL document automatic. This algorithm has been proved available.

REFERENCES

Barros, A., Dumas, M., & Oaks, P. (2005). A critical overview of the Web services choreography description language (WS-CDL). *BPTrends Newsletter, 3*(3).

Birkedal, L., Bundgaard, M., Damgaard, T., Debois, S., Elsborg, E., Glenstrup, A., et al. (2006). Bigraphical programming languages for pervasive computing. *Proceedings of International Workshop on Combining Theory and Systems Building in Pervasive Computing*, (pp. 653-658).

Birkedal, L., Debois, S., Elsborg, E., Hildebrandt, T., & Niss, H. (2006). Bigraphical models of context-aware systems. *Proceedings of the 9th International Conference on Foundations of Software Science and Computation Structures* (pp. 187-201). Springer.

Bloomberg. (2006). *Service orient or be doomed: How service orientation will change you business.* Vienna, Austria: John Wiley&Sons.

Brogi, A., Canal, C., Pimentel, E., & Vallecillo, A. (2004). Formalizing Web service choreographies. *Electronic Notes in Theoretical Computer Science, 105*, 73–94. doi:10.1016/j.entcs.2004.05.007

Bundgaard, M., Glenstrup, A., Hildebrandt, T., Højsgaard, E., & Niss, H. (2008). *Formalizing higher-order mobile embedded business processes with binding bigraphs. Proceedings of Coordination'08*. Berlin, Germany: Springer.

Decker, G., & Puhlmann, F. (2007). *Extending BPMN for modeling complex choreographies. On the Move to Meaningful Internet Systems 2007: CoopIS, DOA, ODBASE, GADA, and IS* (pp. 24–40). Springer. doi:10.1007/978-3-540-76848-7_4

Decker, G., & Weske, M. (2007). Behavioral consistency for B2B process integration. *Proceedings of 19th Conference on Advanced Information Systems Engineering (CAiSE 2007)* (pp. 81-95). Springer.

Dehnert, J., & Rittgen, P. (2001). Relaxed soundness of business processes. *Proceedings of the 13th International Conference on Advanced Information Systems Engineering (CAiSE)* (pp. 157-170). Springer.

Dumas, M., & ter Hofstede, A. H. (2001). UML activity diagrams as a workflow specification language. *Proceedings of the International Conference on the Unified Modeling Language.* Toronto, Canada.

Eder, J., & Liebhart, W. (1995). The workflow activity model (WAMO). *Proceedings of the 3rd International Conference on Cooperative Information Systems (CoopIs)*. Vienna, Austria.

Georgakopoulos, D., Hornick, M., & Sheth, A. (1995). An overview of workflow management: From process modeling to workflow automation infrastructure. *Distributed and Parallel Databases, 3*(2), 119–153. doi:10.1007/BF01277643

Hildebrandt, T., Niss, H., & Olsen, M. (2006). Formalizing business process execution with bigraphs and Reactive XML. *Proceedings of the 8th International Conference on Coordination Models and Language* (pp. 113-129). Berlin, Germany: Springer.

Hoare, C. (1978). Communicating sequential processes. *Communications of the ACM, 21*(8), 666–677. doi:10.1145/359576.359585

IBM. (2003). *BPWS4J*. Berlin, Germany: Springer-Verlag.

Jan Mendling, M. H. (2003). From inter-organizational workflows to process execution: Generating BPEL from WS-CDL. *Lecture Notes in Computer Science, 3762*, 506–515. doi:10.1007/11575863_70

Jensen, O. H., & Milner, R. (2004). Bigraphs and mobile processes (revised). *Technical Report UCAM-CL-TR-580*. University of Cambridge.

Josuttis, M. N. (2007). *SOA in practice*. O'Reilly.

Krafzig, D. (2004). *Enterprise SOA: Service-oriented architecture best practices*. Vienna, Austria.

Krafzig, D., Karl, B., & Slama, D. (2004). *Enterprise SOA: Service-oriented architecture best practices*. Prentice Hall PTR.

Martens, A. (2003). On usability of Web services. *Proceedings of 1st Web Services Quality Workshop (WQW 2003)*.

Martens, A. (2005). Analyzing Web service based business processes. *Proceedings of International Conference on Fundamental Approaches to Software Engineering (FASE'05)*. Springer-Verlag.

Massuthe, P., Reisig, W., & Schmidt, K. (2005). An operating guideline approach to the SOA. *Annals of Mathematics, Computing & Teleinformatics, 1*(3), 35–43.

Milner, R. (1980). *A calculus of communicating systems*. Springer-Verlag.

Milner, R. (1991). *The polyadic Pi-calculus: A tutorial*. Technical Report ECS-LFCS-91-180. Computer Science Department, University of Edinburgh.

Milner, R. (1992). A calculus of mobile process, part I/part II. *Journal of Information and Computation*, *100*(1), 1–77. doi:10.1016/0890-5401(92)90008-4

Milner, R. (2006). Pure bigraphs: Structure and dynamics. *Information and Computation*, *204*(11), 60–122. doi:10.1016/j.ic.2005.07.003

Milner, R. (2009). *The space and motion of communicating agents*. Cambridge University Press.

Mulyar, N., & van der Aalst, W. (2005). *Patterns in colored Petri nets*. BETA Working Paper Series, WP 139. Eindhoven, The Netherlands: Eindhoven University of Technology.

Puhlmann, F., & Weske, M. (2005). Using the Pi-calculus for formalizing workflow patterns. *Proceedings of BPM 2005* (pp. 153-168). Springer-Verlag.

Puhlmann, F., & Weske, M. (2006). Investigations on soundness regarding lazy activities. [Springer.]. *Proceedings of Business Process Management*, *2006*, 145–160. doi:10.1007/11841760_11

Rinderle, S., Reichert, M., & Dadam, P. (2004). Correctness criteria for dynamic changes in workflow systems: A survey. *Data & Knowledge Engineering*, *50*, 9–34. doi:10.1016/j.datak.2004.01.002

Russell, N., ter Hofstede, A., Edmond, D., & van der Aalst, W. (2004a). Workflow data patterns. *QUT* Technical report FIT-TR-2004-01. Brisbane, Australia: Queensland University of Technology.

Russell, N., ter Hofstede, A., Edmond, D., & van der Aalst, W. (2004b). Workflow resource patterns. BETA Working Paper Series WP 127. Eindhoven, The Netherlands: Eindhoven University of Technology.

Russell, N., van der Aalst, W., & ter Hofstede, A. (2006). Workflow exception patterns. *Proceedings of the 18th International Conference on Advanced Information Systems Engineering* (pp. 288-302). Berlin, Germany: Springer-Verlag.

Sewell, P. (2000). Applied Pi-A brief tutorial. Technical Report Nr. 498. University of Cambridge.

Van der Aalst, W. (1998). The application of Petri nets to workflow management. *The Journal of Circuits, Systems and Computers*, *8*(1), 21–66.

Van der Aalst, W., Hee, K., & Houben, G. (1994). Modeling and analysing workflow using a Petri-net based approach. *Proceedings of the Second Workshop on Computer-Supported Cooperative Work, Petri Nets and Related Formalisms*, (pp. 31–50).

Van der Aalst, W., Navathe, S., & Wakayama, T. (1996). Three good reasons for using a Petri-net-based workflow management system. *Proceedings of the International Working Conference on Information and Process Integration in Enterprises (IPIC'96)*, (pp. 179-201).

Van der Aalst, W., & ter Hofstede, A. (2002). Workflow patterns: On the expressive power of (Petri-net-based) workflow lanuages. *Proceedings of the Fourth Workshop on the Practical Use of Coloured Petri Nets and CPN Tools (CPN 2002)* (pp. 1-20). University of Aarhus.

Van der Aalst, W., ter Hofstede, A., Kiepuszewski, B., & Barros, A. (2003). Workflow patterns. *Distributed and Parallel Databases*, *14*(1), 5–21. doi:10.1023/A:1022883727209

Weske, M. (2007). *Business process management: Concepts, languages, architectures*. Springer.

Worah, D., & Sheth, A. (1997). *Transactions in transactional workflows* (pp. 3–34). Advanced Transaction Models and Architectures.

Yang, D. (2003). An approach for workflow modeling using Pi-calculus. *Journal of Zhejiang University. Science, 6*.

Yang, D., & Zhang, S. (2003). An approach for workflow modeling using pi-calculus. *Journal of Zhejiang University. Science, 6*.

Zaha, J., Barros, A., Dumas, M., & ter Hofstede, A. (2006). A language for service behavior modeling. *Proceedings 14th International Conference on Cooperative Information Systems (CoopIS 2006)* (pp. 145-162). Springer Verlag.

ADDITIONAL READING

Barros, A., Dumas, M., & Oaks, P. (2005). A critical overview of the web services choreography description language (WS-CDL). *BPTrends Newsletter, 3*(3).

Birkedal, L., Bundgaard, M., Damgaard, T., Debois, S., Elsborg, E., Glenstrup, A., et al. (2006). Bigraphical programming languages for pervasive computing. *Proceedings of International Workshop on Combining Theory and Systems Building in Pervasive Computing*, (pp. 653-658).

Birkedal, L., Debois, S., Elsborg, E., Hildebrandt, T., & Niss, H. (2006). Bigraphical models of context-aware systems. *Proceedings of the 9th International Conference on Foundations of Software Science and Computation Structures* (pp. 187-201). Springer.

Bloomberg. (2006). *Service orient or be doomed: How service orientation will change you business.* Vienna, Austria: John Wiley&Sons.

Brogi, A., Canal, C., Pimentel, E., & Vallecillo, A. (2004). Formalizing Web service choreographies. *Electronic Notes in Theoretical Computer Science, 105*, 73–94. doi:10.1016/j.entcs.2004.05.007

Bundgaard, M., Glenstrup, A., Hildebrandt, T., Højsgaard, E., & Niss, H. (2008). *Formalizing higher-order mobile embedded business processes with binding bigraphs. Proceedings of Coordination '08*. Berlin, Germany: Springer.

Decker, G., & Puhlmann, F. (2007). *Extending BPMN for modeling complex choreographies. On the Move to Meaningful Internet Systems 2007: CoopIS, DOA, ODBASE, GADA, and IS* (pp. 24–40). Springer. doi:10.1007/978-3-540-76848-7_4

Decker, G., & Weske, M. (2007). Behavioral consistency for B2B process integration. *Proceedings of 19th Conference on Advanced Information Systems Engineering (CAiSE 2007)* (pp. 81-95). Springer.

Dehnert, J., & Rittgen, P. (2001). Relaxed soundness of business processes. *Proceedings of the 13th International Conference on Advanced Information Systems Engineering (CAiSE)* (pp. 157-170). Springer.

Dumas, M., & ter Hofstede, A. H. (2001). UML activity diagrams as a workflow specification language. *Proceedings of the International Conference on the Unified Modeling Language.* Toronto, Canada.

Eder, J., & Liebhart, W. (1995). The workflow activity model (WAMO). *Proceedings of the 3rd International Conference on Cooperative Information Systems (CoopIs).* Vienna, Austria.

Georgakopoulos, D., Hornick, M., & Sheth, A. (1995). An overview of workflow management: From process modeling to workflow automation infrastructure. *Distributed and Parallel Databases, 3*(2), 119–153. doi:10.1007/BF01277643

Hildebrandt, T., Niss, H., & Olsen, M. (2006). Formalizing business process execution with bigraphs and reactive XML. *Proceedings of the 8th International Conference on Coordination Models and Language* (pp. 113-129). Berlin, Germany: Springer.

Hoare, C. (1978). Communicating sequential processes. *Communications of the ACM, 21*(8), 666–677. doi:10.1145/359576.359585

IBM. (2003). *BPWS4J*. Berlin, Germany: Springer-Verlag.

Jensen, O. H., & Milner, R. (2004). Bigraphs and mobile processes (revised). Technical Report UCAM-CL-TR-580. University of Cambridge.

Yang, D. (2003). An approach for workflow modeling using pi-calculus. *Journal of Zhejiang University. Science*, 6.

Zaha, J., Barros, A., Dumas, M., & ter Hofstede, A. (2006). A language for service behavior modeling. *Proceedings 14th International Conference on Cooperative Information Systems (CoopIS 2006)* (pp. 145-162). Springer Verlag.

KEY TERMS AND DEFINITIONS

BPEL: BPEL is a process language for service orchestration. It enjoys widespread industry adoption due to its status as an OASIS standard. Loosely-coupled integration through WSDL interfaces, rich process constructs, and robust fault handling and clearly defined extension points are among its salient features.

Business Process: A business process consists of a set of activities, and it can are executed in organizational and technical environment. The activities jointly realize a business goal.

Choreography: Choreography is a way to compose business process. In the business process composed in choreography way the services can communicate to each other.

Orchestration: Orchestration is a way to compose business process. In the business process composed in orchestration way most of the services can are isolated.

Workflow Management System (WFMS): WFMS is a software system that can define, initiate, execute, and manage workflows.

Workflow: Workflow is the automation of a business process.

WS-CDL: The Web Services Choreography Description Language (WS-CDL) is an XML-based language that describes peer-to-peer collaborations of participants by defining, from a global viewpoint, their common and complementary observable behavior; where ordered message exchanges result in accomplishing a common business goal.

Compilation of References

Abadi, D. J., Carney, D., Cetintemel, U., Cherniack, M., Convey, C., & Lee, S. (2003). Aurora: A new model and architecture for data stream management. *The VLDB Journal, 12*(2), 120–139. doi:10.1007/s00778-003-0095-z

Agrawal, S., Chaudhuri, S., & Das, G. (2002). DBXplorer: A system for keyword-based search over relational database. In *Proceedings of 18th International Conference on Data Engineering.*

Ahlgren, P., & Colliander, C. (2009). Document-document similarity approaches and science mapping: Experimental comparison of five approaches. *Journal of Informatrics, 3*, 49–63. doi:10.1016/j.joi.2008.11.003

Al-Hamadani, B. T., Alwan, R. F., Lu, J., & Yip, J. (2009). *Vague content and structure (VCAS) retrieval for XML electronic healthcare records (EHR).* Paper presented at the 2009 International Conference on Internet Computing, USA.

Al-Hamadani, B., Lu, J., & Alwan, R. F. (2011). (in press). A new schema-independent XML compression technique. *International Journal of Information Retrieval Research.*

Alistair, M., Radford, M. N., & Ian, H. W. (1998). Arithmetic coding revisited. *ACM Transactions on Information Systems, 16*(3), 256–294. doi:10.1145/290159.290162

Al-Khalif, A. S., Jagadish, H., Patel, J., Wu, Y., Koudas, N., & Srivastava, D. (2002). *Structural joins: A primitive for efficient XML query pattern matching.* Paper presented at the 8th International Conference on Data Engineering.

Al-Omari, F. A., & Al-Jarrah, M. A. (2005). Query by image and video content: A colored-based stochastic model approach. *Data Knowledge Engineering, 52*(3), 313{332.

Altinel, M., & Franklin, M. J. (2000). Efficient filtering of XML documents for selective dissemination of information. In *Proceedings of the 26th International Conference on Very Large Data Bases* (pp. 53-64).

Amer-Yahia, S., Du, F., & Freire, J. (2004). *A comprehensive solution to the XML-to-relational mapping problem.* In WIDM'04, Washington, DC, USA.

Amer-Yahia, S., Du, F., & Freire, J. (2004). *A comprehensive solution to the XML-to-relational mapping problem.* In WIDM'04, Washington, DC, USA.

Amer-Yahia, S., Lakshmanan, L. V. S., & Pandit, S. (2004). *FleXPath: Flexible structure and fulltext querying for XML.* Paper presented at the ACM, SIGMOD, Paris, France.

Amir-Yahya, S., Cho, S., & Srivatava, D. (2002). *Tree pattern relaxation.* Paper presented at the EDBT 8th International Conference on Extending Database Technology. Retrieved from http://citeseerx.ist.psu.edu/viewdoc/summary?doi=10.1.1.8.4952

Anders, M. (2009). *An introduction to XML and Web technologies.* Pearson Education.

Apache Software Foundation. (2006). *Apache Lucene.* Retrieved from http://lucene.apache.org/

Arion, A. (2007). *XML access modules: Towards physical data independence in XML Databases.* Paris, France: University of South Paris.

Arion, A., Bonifati, A., Manolescu, I., & Pugliese, A. (2007). XQueC: A query-conscious compressed XML database. *ACM Transactions on Internet Technology, 7*(2), 10. doi:10.1145/1239971.1239974

Arroyuelo, D., Claude, F., Maneth, S., M̈akinen, V., Navarro, G., Nguyen, K., et al. (2010). *Fast in-memory XPath search using compressed indexes.* Paper presented at the IEEE Twenty-Sixth International Conference on Data Engineering (ICDE 2010), California, USA.

Atay, M. (2006). *XML2REL: An efficient system for storing and querying XML documents using relational databases* (p. 127). Detroit, Michigan: Graduate School, Wayne State University.

Atay, M., Chebotko, A., Liu, D., Lu, S., & Fotouhi, F. (2007a). *Efficient schema-based XML-to-relational data mapping* (pp. 458–476). Elsevier Science Ltd.

Atay, M., Chebotko, A., Liu, D., Lu, S., & Fotouhi, F. (2007b). Efficient schema-based XML-to-relational data mapping. *Information Systems*, *32*, 458–476. doi:10.1016/j.is.2005.12.008

Augeri, C. J., Bulutoglu, D. A., Mullins, B. E., Baldwin, R. O., & Baird, I. (2007). *An analysis of XML compression efficiency.* Paper presented at the 2007 Workshop on Experimental Computer Science.

Augeri, C. (2008). *On some results in unmanned aerial vehicle swarms. Unpublished Ph.D.* San Diego, CA, USA: Air Force Institute of Technology.

Babcock, B., Babu, S., Datar, M., Motwani, R., & Widom, J. (2002). Models and issues in data stream systems. In *Proceedings of the 2002 ACM Symposium on Principles of Database Systems.*

Badica, C., Badica, A., & Litoiu, V. (2003). Role activity diagrams as finite state processes. *ISPDC '03 Proceedings of the Second international conference on Parallel and distributed computing,* (pp. 15-22).

Bajec, M., & Krisper, M. (2005). A methodology and tool support for managing business rules in organisations. *Information Systems*, *30*(6), 423–443. doi:10.1016/j.is.2004.05.003

Bansal, V., & Alam, A. (2001). *Study and comparison of techniques to efficiently store and retrieve XML data.*

Barros, A., Dumas, M., & Oaks, P. (2005). A critical overview of the Web services choreography description language (WS-CDL). *BPTrends Newsletter, 3*(3).

Basten, A. (1998). *In terms of nets: System design with Petri nets and process algebra.*

Beizer, B. (1990). *Software testing techniques* (2nd ed.). New York.

Belongie, S., Malik, J., & Puzicha, J. (2001). *Matching shapes*. In International Conference on Computer Vision (ICCV).

Berglund, A., Boag, S., Chamberlin, D., Fernández, M., Kay, M., Robie, J., & Siméon, J. (2007). *XML path language (XPath) 2.0.* W3 Consortium.

Berglund, A., Boag, S., Chamberlin, D., Fernandez, M. F., Kay, M., Robie, J., & Simon, J. (2002). *XML path language (XPath) 2.0 W3C working draft 16.* In World Wide Web Consortium.

Bhalotia, G., Hulgeri, A., Nakhe, C., Chakrabarti, S., & Sudarshan, S. (2002). Keyword searching and browsing in database using BANKS. In *Proceedings of 18th International Conference on Data Engineering.*

Birkedal, L., Bundgaard, M., Damgaard, T., Debois, S., Elsborg, E., Glenstrup, A., et al. (2006). Bigraphical programming languages for pervasive computing. *Proceedings of International Workshop on Combining Theory and Systems Building in Pervasive Computing,* (pp. 653-658).

Birkedal, L., Debois, S., Elsborg, E., Hildebrandt, T., & Niss, H. (2006). Bigraphical models of context-aware systems. *Proceedings of the 9th International Conference on Foundations of Software Science and Computation Structures* (pp. 187-201). Springer.

Blaser, A. D., & Egenhofer, M. J. (2000). A visual tool for querying geographic databases. In AVI '00: *Proceedings of the Working Conference on Advanced Visual Interfaces* (pp. 211-216). New York, NY: ACM.

Bloomberg. (2006). *Service orient or be doomed: How service orientation will change you business.* Vienna, Austria: John Wiley&Sons.

Boag, X., Chamberlin, D., Fernández, M., Florescu, D., Robie, J., & Siméon, J. (2007). *XQuery 1.0: An XML query language.* W3 Consortium.

Bodenhofer, U., & Küng, J. (2001). *Enriching vague queries by fuzzy orderings.* Paper presented at the European Society for Fuzzy Logic and Technology - EUSFLAT.

Bonifati, A., Lorusso, M., & Sileo, D. (2009). XML lossy text compression: A preliminary study. *Proceedings of the 6th XML Database Symposium on Database and XML Technologies* (pp. 106-113).

Bosma, M., Veltkamp, R. C., & Wiering, F. (2006). *Muugle: A modular music information retrieval framework* (pp. 330–331). The International Society for Music Information Retrieval.

Bourret, R. (2005). *XML and databases*. Retrieved September 23, 2010, from http://www.rpbourret.com/xml/XMLAndDatabases.htm

Bray, T., Paoli, J., Sperberg-McQueen, C. M., Maler, E., & Yergeau, F. (2007). *Extensible markup language (XML) 1.0* (4th ed.). W3 Consortium.

Brin, S., & Page, L. (1998). The anatomy of a large-scale hypertextual web search engine. In *Proceedings of the 7th International World Wide Web Conference.*

Brisaboa, N. R., Cerdeira-Pena, A., Navarro, G., & Pasi, G. (2010). *An efficient implementation of a flexible XPath extension.* Paper presented at the Recherche d'Information Assistee par Ordinateur - RIAO.

Brogi, A. C. (2004). *Formalizing Web service choreographies.*

Brogi, A., Canal, C., Pimentel, E., & Vallecillo, A. (2004). Formalizing Web service choreographies. *Electronic Notes in Theoretical Computer Science, 105,* 73–94. doi:10.1016/j.entcs.2004.05.007

Bruno, N., Gravano, L., Koudas, N., & Srivastava, D. (2003). Navigation- vs. index-based XML multiquery processing. In *proceedings of 19th International Conference on Data Engineering* (pp. 139-150).

Buijs, J. M., & Lew, M. S. (1999). Visual learning of simple semantics in ImageScape. In Visual '99: *Proceedings of the Third International Conference on Visual Information and Information* Systems (pp. 131-138). London, UK: Springer-Verlag.

Bundgaard, M. (1994). *A brief introduction to mobility workbench*. MWB.

Bundgaard, M., Glenstrup, A., Hildebrandt, T., Højsgaard, E., & Niss, H. (2008). *Formalizing higher-order mobile embedded business processes with binding bigraphs. Proceedings of Coordination '08.* Berlin, Germany: Springer.

Buneman, P., Grohe, M., & Koch, C. (2003). Path queries on compressed XML. In F. Johann-Christoph, L. Peter, A. Serge, C. Michael, S. Patricia & H. Andreas (Eds.), *Proceedings 2003 VLDB Conference* (pp. 141-152). San Francisco, CA: Morgan Kaufmann.

Busse, R., Carey, M., Florescu, D., & Kersten, M. (2002). *XMark- An XML benchmark project.*

Busse, R., Carey, M., Florescu, D., Kersten, M., Manolescu, I., Schmidt, A., & Waas, F. (2001). *Xmark: An XML benchmark project*. Retrieved from http://monetdb.cwi.nl/xml/index.html

BZip2. (1996). Retrieved October 10, 2009, from http://www.bzip.org/

Campi, A., Damiani, E., Guinea, S., Marrara, S., Pasi, G., & Spoletini, P. (2009). A fuzzy extension of the XPath query language. *Journal of Intelligent Information Systems, 33*(3), 285–305. doi:10.1007/s10844-008-0066-3

Cardoso, J. (2005). How to measure the control-flow complexity of web processes and workflows. In *The workflow handbook* (pp. 199-212).

Chamberlin, D. (2003). XQuery: An XML query language. *IBM Systems Journal, 41,* 597–615. doi:10.1147/sj.414.0597

Chan, C., Felber, P., Garofalakis, M., & Rastogi, R. (2002). Efficient filtering of XML documents with XPath expressions. In *Proceedings of 18th International Conference on Data Engineering* (pp. 235-244).

Chee-Yong, C., Pascal, F., Minos, G., & Rajeev, R. (2002). Efficient filtering of XML documents with XPath expressions. [Special Issue on XML Data Management]. *The VLDB Journal, 11*(4), 354–379. doi:10.1007/s00778-002-0077-6

Chen, Y., Davidson, S., Hara, C., & Zheng, Y. (2003). RRXS: Redundancy reducing XML storage in relations. In *Proceedings of the 29th International Conference on Very Large Data Bases* - Vol. 29. Berlin, Germany: VLDB Endowment.

Cheney, J. (2001). *Compressing XML with multiplexed hierarchical models*. Paper presented at the IEEE Data Compression Conference (DCC 2001).

Cheney, J. (2005). *An empirical evaluation of simple DTD conscious compression techniques*. Paper presented at the Eighth International Workshop on the Web and Databases (WebDB 2005).

Cheng, J., & Ng, W. (2004). *XQZip: Querying compressed XML using structural indexing*. Paper presented at the International Conference on Extending Data Base Technology (EDBT).

Chen, Q., Lim, A., Ong, K. W., & Tang, J. Q. (2006). Indexing graph-structured XML data for efficient structural join operation. *Data & Knowledge Engineering, 58*, 21. doi:10.1016/j.datak.2005.05.008

Chong, S., Chee-Yong, C., & Amit, K. G. (2007). Multiway SLCA-based keyword search in XML data. In *Proceedings of the 16th International Conference on World Wide Web*.

Chung, S. M., & Jesurajaiah, S. B. (2005). Schemaless XML document management in object-oriented databases. *International Conference on Information Technology: Coding and Computing, ITCC 2005*, Vol. 261, (pp. 261-266).

Clark, J. (2001). *Tree regular expressions for XML*. TREX.

Cleary, J., & Witten, I. (1984). Data compression using adaptive coding and partial string matching. *IEEE Transactions on Communications, 32*(4), 396–402. doi:10.1109/TCOM.1984.1096090

Codd, E. (1971). A database sub-language founded on the relational calculus. *ACM SIGFIDET Workshop Data Description, Access and Control* (pp. 35-61).

Codd, E. (1970). A relational model of data for large shared data banks. *Communications of the ACM, 13*, 11. doi:10.1145/362384.362685

Codd, E. (1983). *A relational model of data for large shared data banks* (pp. 64–69). ACM.

Cohen, S., Mamou, J., Kanza, Y., & Sagiv, Y. (2003). XSEarch: A semantic search engine for XML. In *Proceedings of the 29th International Conference on Very Large Data Bases* (pp. 1069–1072).

Combs, T. T. A., & Bederson, B. B. (1999). Does zooming improve image browsing? In DL '99: *Proceedings of the Fourth ACM Conference on Digital Libraries* (pp. 130-137). New York, NY: ACM.

Cortadella, J., & Reisig, W. (2004). *Petri nets*. Bologna, Italy: Springer.

Curran, T. A., & Ladd, A. (1999). *SAP R/3 Business blueprint: Understanding enterprise supply chain management*. Pearson Education.

Damiani, E., & Tanca, L. (2000). *Blind queries to XML data*. Paper presented at the 11th International Conference on Database and Expert Systems Applications.

Datta, R., Li, J., & Wang, J. Z. (2005). Content-based image retrieval: Approaches and trends of the new age. In *MIR '05: Proceedings of the 7th ACM SIGMM International Workshop on Multimedia Information Retrieval* (pp. 253-262). New York, NY: ACM.

Datta, R., Joshi, D., Li, J., & Wang, J. Z. (2008, April). Image retrieval: Ideas, influences, and trends of the new age. *ACM Transactions on Computing Surveys, 40*(2), 1–60. doi:10.1145/1348246.1348248

De Meo, P., Palopoli, L., Quattrone, G., & Ursino, D. (2007). Combining description logics with synopses for inferring complex knowledge patterns from XML sources. *Information Systems, 32*(8), 1184–1224. doi:10.1016/j.is.2007.03.003

Decker, G., & Weske, M. (2007). Behavioral consistency for B2B process integration. *Proceedings of 19th Conference on Advanced Information Systems Engineering (CAiSE 2007)* (pp. 81-95). Springer.

Decker, G. F. (2006). Formalizing service interactions. *Lecture Notes in Computer Science, 4102*, 414. doi:10.1007/11841760_32

Decker, G., & Puhlmann, F. (2007). *Extending BPMN for modeling complex choreographies. On the Move to Meaningful Internet Systems 2007: CoopIS, DOA, ODBASE, GADA, and IS* (pp. 24–40). Springer. doi:10.1007/978-3-540-76848-7_4

Dehnert, J., & Rittgen, P. (2001). Relaxed soundness of business processes. *Proceedings of the 13th International Conference on Advanced Information Systems Engineering (CAiSE)* (pp. 157-170). Springer.

Delobel, C. (1978). *Normalization and hierarchical dependencies in the relational data model* (pp. 201–222). ACM.

Diao, Y. L., & Franklin, M. J. (2003). Query processing for high-volume XML message brokering. In *Proceedings of the 29ᵗʰ International Conference on Very Large Data Bases*.

Diao, Y. L., Altinel, M., & Franklin, J., M., Zhang, H., & Fischer, P. (2003). Path sharing and predicate evaluation for high-performance XML filtering. *ACM Transactions on Database Systems*, *28*(4), 467–516. doi:10.1145/958942.958947

Diao, Y. L., Altinel, M., Franklin, M. J., Zhang, H., & Fischer, P. (2003). Path sharing and predicate evaluation for high-performance XML filtering. *ACM Transactions on Database Systems*, *28*(4), 467–516. doi:10.1145/958942.958947

Diaz, A. L., & Lovell, D. (2004). *XML generator*. Retrieved from http://www.alphaworks.ibm.com/tech/xmlgenerator

Diaz, A. L., & Lovell, D. (2004). *XML generator*. Retrieved from.

Donald, S., & Le Vie, J. (2000). *Understanding data flow diagrams*. STC Proceedings.

Dong, Y. S.-S., & Dadam, P. (2003). Approach for workflow modeling using pi-calculus. *Journal of Zhejiang University. Science*, *4*(50), 643–650.

Doulamis, N., Doulamis, A., & Kollias, S. (1999). A neural network approach to interactive content based retrieval of video databases. Proceedings 1999 International Conference on Image Processing, ICIP 99, Vol. 2, (pp. 116-120).

Dumas, M., & ter Hofstede, A. H. (2001). UML activity diagrams as a workflow specification language. *Proceedings of the International Conference on the Unified Modeling Language*. Toronto, Canada.

Dutta, A. K., Idwan, S., & Biswas, R. (2009). A study of vague search to answer imprecise query. *International Journal of Computational Cognition*, *7*(4), 70–75.

Dweib, I., Awadi, A., Alrahman, S. E. F., & Lu, J. (2008). Schemaless approach of mapping XML document into relational database. *8th IEEE International Conference on Computer and Information Technology, CIT 2008*, (pp. 167-172).

Eakins, J., & Graham, M. (1999, January). *Content-based image retrieval. A report to the JISC technology applications programme*. (Rapport technique). University of Northumbria at Newcastle. Retrieved from http://www.jisc.ac.uk/uploaded documents/jtap-039.doc

Eder, J., & Liebhart, W. (1995). The workflow activity model (WAMO). *Proceedings of the 3rd International Conference on Cooperative Information Systems (CoopIs)*. Vienna, Austria.

Eder, R., Filieri, A. T., Kurz, T. H., & Pezzuto, M. (2008). *Model-transformation-based software generation utilizing natural language notations. Digital Ecosystems and Technologies*. Thailand: IEEE DEST.

Fagin, R. (1996). Combining fuzzy information from multiple systems (extended abstract). In PODS '96: *Proceedings of the Fifteenth ACM SIGACT-SIGMOD-SIGART Symposium on Principles of Database Systems* (pp. 216-226). New York, NY: ACM.

Fallside, D., & Walmsley, P. (2004). *XML schema part 0: Primer* (2ⁿᵈ ed.). W3 Consortium.

Farrell-Vinay, P. (2008). *Manage software testing*. Auerbach. doi:10.1201/9781420013849

Fatto, V. D., Paolino, L., & Pittarello, F. (2007). A usability-driven approach to the development of a 3D web-GIS environment. *Journal of Visual Languages and Computing*, *18*, 280314.

Fazzinga, B., Flesca, S., & Pugliese, A. (2009). Retrieving XML data from heterogeneous sources through vague querying. *ACM Transactions on Internet Technology*, *9*(2), 7–35. doi:10.1145/1516539.1516542

Fei-Fei, L., Fergus, R., & Perona, P. (2004). *Learning generative visual models from few training examples: An incremental Bayesian approach tested on 101 object categories*. In International Conference on Computer Vision and Pattern Recognition (CVPR'04). (Workshop on Generative-Model Based Vision).

Feng, S., Lin, G., Chavdar, B., Anand, B., Muthiah, C., & Fan, Y. (2007). Efficient keyword search over virtual XML views. In *Proceedings of the 33ᵗʰ International Conference on Very Large Data Bases*.

Fergus, R., Perona, P., & Zisserman, A. (2003, June). Object class recognition by unsupervised scale-invariant learning. In *Proceedings of the IEEE Conference on Computer Vision and Pattern Recognition* (Vol. 2, pp. 264-271). Madison, Wisconsin.

Ferragina, P., Luccio, F., Manzini, G., & Muthukrishnan, S. (2006). *Compressing and searching XML data via two zips*. Paper presented at the 15th International Conference on World Wide Web.

Fischer, L. (2005). *Workflow handbook 2005. Future Strategies Inc*. Book Division.

Florescu, D., Hiller, C., Kossman, D., Lucas, P., Riccardi, F., & Westmann, T. … Agrawal. G. (2003). The BEA/XQRL streaming XQuery processor. In *Proceedings of the 29th International Conference on Very Large Data Bases* (pp. 997–1008).

Florescu, D., Kossmann, D., & Manolescu, I. (2000). Integrating keyword search into XML query processing. *Computer Networks, 33*(1-6), 119-135.

Franceschet, M. (2005). Lecture Notes in Computer Science: *Vol. 3671. XPathMark: Functional and performance tests for XPath* (pp. 129–143). Berlin, Germany: Springer.

Fredrick, E. J. T., & Radhamani, G. (2009). Fuzzy logic based XQuery operations for native XML database systems. *International Journal of Database Theory and Application, 2*(3).

Freund, Y., & Schapire, R. E. (1997). A decision-theoretic generalization of on-line learning and an application to boosting. *Journal of Computer and System Sciences, 55*, 119–139. doi:10.1006/jcss.1997.1504

Fuhr, N. (1999). *A probabilistic framework for vague queries and imprecise information in databases*. Paper presented at the 16TH International Conference on Very Large Databases.

Fuhr, N., Lalmas, M., & Trotman, A. (2006). *Comparative evaluation of XML information retrieval systems* (5th ed.). Springer.

Fujimoto, K., Yoshikawa, T., Kha, D. D., Yashikawa, M., & Amagasa, T. (2005). *A mapping scheme of XML documents into relational databases using schema-based path identifiers*. International Workshop on Challenges in Web Information and Integration (WIRI'05).

Gamma, E., Helm, R., Johnson, R., & Vlisides. (1994). *Design patterns - Elements of reusable object-oriented software*. Addison-Wesley.

Gang Xue, E. A. (2008). Investigating workflow resource patterns in term of Pi-calculus. In *Proceedings of the 2008 12th International Conference on Computer Supported Cooperative Word in Design, 14*(1). Xi'an, Chian.

Garber, S. R., & Grunes, M. B. (1992). The art of search: A study of art directors. *In CHI '92: Proceedings of the SIGCHI Conference on Human Factors in Computing Systems* (pp. 157-163). New York, NY: ACM.

Georgakopoulos, D., Hornick, M., & Sheth, A. (1995). An overview of workflow management: From process modeling to workflow automation infrastructure. *Distributed and Parallel Databases, 3*(2), 119–153. doi:10.1007/BF01277643

Gerlicher, A. R. S. (2007). *Developing collaborative XML editing systems*. London, UK: University of the Arts London.

Girardot, M., & Sundaresan, N. (2000). Millau: An encoding format for efficient representation and exchange of XML over the Web. *Computer Networks, 33*(1-6), 747-765.

Goedertier, S., Haesen, R., & Vanthienen, J. (2008). Rule-based business process modeling and enactment. *International Journal of Business Process Integration and Management, 3*(3), 194–207. doi:10.1504/IJBPIM.2008.023219

Goedertier, S., & Vanthienen, J. (2005). *Rule-based business process modeling and execution*. IEEE EDOC Workshopon Vocabularies Ontologies and Rules for The Enterprise.

Goldberg, K. H. (2009). *XML: Visual quickstart guide* (2nd ed.). Peachpit Press-Pearson Education.

Goldman, R., Shivakumar, N., Venkatasubramanian, S., & Garcia-Molina, H. (1998). Proximity search in database. In *Proceedings of the 24th International Conference on Very Large Data Bases*.

Goldstein, J., & Larson, P. (2001). Optimizing queries using materialized views: A practical, scalable solution. In *Proceedings of the 2001 ACM SIGMOD International Conference on Management of Data*.

Google, Inc. (2008). Picasa. Retrieved from http://picasa.google.com/

Green, T. J., Miklau, G., Onizuka, M., & Suciu, D. (2003). Processing XML streams with deterministic automata. In *Proceedings of 6th International Conference on Data Theory* (pp. 173-189).

Green, T. J., Miklau, G., Onizuka, M., & Suciu, D. (2003). Processing XML streams with deterministic automata and stream indexes. [TODS]. *ACM Transactions on Database Systems, 29*(4), 752–788. doi:10.1145/1042046.1042051

Grinev, M., Fomichev, A., & Kuznetsov, S. (2004). *Sedna: A native XML DBMS.*

Grinev, M., Fomichev, A., & Kuznetsov, S. (2004). *Sedna: A native XML DBMS.* MODIS ISPRAS.

Groppe, J. (2008). *Speeding up XML querying.* Berlin, Germany: Zugl Lübeck University.

Grust, T. (2002). *Accelerating XPath location steps.* Paper presented at the ACM SIGMOD International Conference on Management of Data.

Guo, L., Shao, F., Botev, C., & Shanmugasundaram, J. (2003). XRANK: Ranked keyword search over XML documents. In *Proceedings of the 2003 ACM SIGMOD International Conference on Management of Data* (pp. 16–27).

Guoliang, L., Beng, C. O., Jianhua, F., Jianyong, W., & Lizhu, Z. (2008). EASE: An effective 3-in-1 keyword search method for unstructured, semi-structured and structured data. In *Proceedings of the 2008 ACM SIGMOD International Conference on Management of Data.*

Guoliang, L., Jianhua, F., Jianyong, W., & Lizhu, Z. (2007). Effective keyword search for valuable LCAs over XML documents. In *Proceedings of the 16th ACM Conference on Conference on Information and Knowledge Management* (pp. 31–40).

Guoliang, L., Jianhua, F., Jianyong, W., Bei, Y., & Yukai, H. (2008). Race: Finding and ranking compact connected trees for keyword proximity search over XML documents. In *Proceedings of the 17th international conference on World Wide Web* (pp. 1045–1046).

Gupta, A., & Jain, R. (1997). Visual information retrieval. *Communications of the ACM, 40*(5), 70{79.

Gupta, A., & Suciu, D. (2003). Stream processing of XPath queries with predicates. In *Proceeding of 2003 ACM SIGMOD Conference on Management of Data.*

Gupta, A., & Jain, R. (1997). Visual information retrieval. *Communications of the ACM, 40*(5), 70–79. doi:10.1145/253769.253798

Guttman, A. (1984). R-trees: A dynamic index structure for spatial searching. In ACM SIGMOD Conference on the Management of Data (pp. 47-57).

GZip. (1992). Retrieved October 12, 2009, from http://www.gzip.org/

Halpin, T. (2000). A fact-oriented approach to business rules. *Proceedings of the 19th International Conference on Conceptual Modeling.*

Halverson, A., Burger, J., Galanis, L., Kini, A., Krishnamurthy, R., Rao, A., et al. (2003). *Mixed mode XML query processing.* Paper presented at the 29th International Conference on Very Large Data Bases.

Hao, H., Haixun, W., Jun, Y., & Philip, S. Y. (2007). BLINKS: Ranked keyword searches on graphs. In *Proceedings of the 2007 ACM SIGMOD International Conference on Management of Data* (pp. 305–316).

Harrison-Broninski, K. (2005). *Human interactions: The heart and soul of business process management.* Meghan-Kiffer Press Home.

Harrusi, S., Averbuch, A., & Yehudai, A. (2006). *XML syntax conscious compression.* Paper presented at the Data Compression Conference (DCC'06).

Havey, M. (2005). *Essential business process modeling, part I.* O'Reilly Media, Inc.

Hégaret, P. L., Whitmer, R., & Wood, L. (2005). *Document object model* (DOM). W3 Consortium.

Herbst, H. (1995). In Iivari, K. L. J. (Ed.), *A meta-model for business rules in systems analysis* (pp. 186–199). Lecture Notes in Computer Science Springer.

Hevner, A., March, S., Park, J., & Ram, S. (2004). Design science in information systems research. *Management Information Systems Quarterly, 28*(1), 75–105.

Hibino, S., & Rundensteiner, E. (1995). *A visual query language for identifying temporal trends in video data.* International Workshop on Multimedia and Database Management Systems.

Hildebrandt, T., Niss, H., & Olsen, M. (2006). Formalizing business process execution with bigraphs and reactive XML. *Proceedings of the 8th International Conference on Coordination Models and Language* (pp. 113-129). Berlin, Germany: Springer.

Hoare, C. (1978). Communicating sequential processes. *Communications of the ACM, 21*(8), 666–677. doi:10.1145/359576.359585

Holman, G. K. (2002). *XSLT and XPath.* Prentice Hall PTR.

Hristidis, V., & Papakonstantinou, Y. (2002). DISCOVER: Key-word search in relational databases. In *Proceedings of the 28ᵗʰ International Conference on Very Large Data Bases.*

Hristidis, V., Gravano, L., & Papakonstantinou, Y. (2003). Efficient IR-style keyword search over relational databases. In *Proceedings of the 29ᵗʰ International Conference on Very Large Data Bases.*

Hristidis, V., Koudas, N., Papakonstantinou, Y., & Srivastava, D. (2006). Keyword proximity search in XML trees. In *IEEE Transactions on Knowledge and Data Engineering.*

Hristidis, V., Papakonstantinou, Y., & Balmin, A. (2003). Keyword proximity search on XML graph. In *Proceedings of International Conference on Data Engineering.*

Hristidis, V., Koudas, N., Papakonstantinou, Y., & Srivastava, D. (2006). Keyword proximity search in XML trees. *IEEE Transactions on Knowledge and Data Engineering, 18*(4), 525–539. doi:10.1109/TKDE.2006.1599390

http://www.alphaworks.ibm.com/tech/xmlgenerator

Huh, S. Y., Moon, K. H., & Lee, H. (2000). A data abstraction approach for query relaxation. *Information and Software Technology, 42*(6), 407–418. doi:10.1016/S0950-5849(99)00100-7

Hung, P. C. K. (2009). *Services and business computing solution with XML.* Hershey, PA: IGI Global. doi:10.4018/978-1-60566-330-2

Hunter, D. (2000). *Beginning XML.* Wrox Press Ltd.

IBM. (2003). *BPWS4J.* Berlin, Germany: Springer-Verlag.

Indulska, M., Recker, J., Rosemann, M., & Green, P. (2009). *Business process modeling: Current issues and future challenges.* 21st International Conference on Advanced Information Systems.

Jacobs, C. E., Finkelstein, A., & Salesin, D. H. (1995). Fast multiresolution image querying. *Computer Graphics, 29*, 277–286. Retrieved from citeseer.ist.psu.edu/jacobs95fast.html

Jagadish, H., Al-Khalifa, S., Chapman, A., Lakshmanan, L., Nierman, A., & Paparizos, S. ... Yu, C. (2003). *TIMBER: A native XML database.* In SIGMOD, San Diego, CA.

Jain, A., Nandakumar, K., & Ross, A. (2005). Score normalization in multimodal biometric systems. *Pattern Recognition, 38*(12), 2270–2285. Retrieved from http://www.sciencedirect.com/science/article/B6V14-4G0DDW4-1/2/d922960ee7ed8928744113dd9494d37a-doi:10.1016/j.patcog.2005.01.012

Jan Mendling, M. H. (2003). From inter-organizational workflows to process execution: Generating BPEL from WS-CDL. *Lecture Notes in Computer Science, 3762*, 506–515. doi:10.1007/11575863_70

Jelliffe, R. (2006). *Resource directory (RDDL) for Schematron 1.5.*

Jensen, O. H., & Milner, R. (2004). Bigraphs and mobile processes (revised). *Technical Report UCAM-CL-TR-580.* University of Cambridge.

Jeston, J., & Nelis, J. (2008). *Business process management: Practical guidelines to successful implementations.* Elsevier Ltd.

Jiaheng, L. (2006). *Efficient processing of XML TWIG pattern matching.* National University of Singapore.

Jiang, H. F., Lu, H. J., & Wang, W. (2004). Efficient processing of XML twig queries with ORpredicates. In *Proceedings of the 2004 ACM SIGMOD International Conference on Management of Data.*

Jiang, H., Lu, H., Wang, W., & Yu, J. X. (2002). XParent: An efficient RDBMS-based XML database system. *International Conference of Data Engineering*, (pp. 335-336).

Jin, Y., Khan, L., Wang, L., & Awad, M. (2005). Image annotations by combining multiple evidence & wordNet. In Multimedia '05: Proceedings of the 13th Annual ACM International Conference on Multimedia (pp. 706-715). New York, NY: ACM.

Joonho, K., Praveen, R., Bongki, M., & Sukho, L. (2005). FiST: Scalable XML document filtering by sequencing twig patterns. In *Proceedings of the 31th International Conference on Very Large Data Bases* (pp. 217-228).

Joshi, D., Datta, R., Zhuang, Z., Weiss, W. P., Friedenberg, M., Li, J., et al. (2006). PARAgrab: A comprehensive architecture for web image management and multimodal querying. In VLDB '06: *Proceedings of the 32nd International Conference on Very Large Data Bases* (pp. 1163-1166). VLDB Endowment.

Josifovski, V., Fontoura, M., & Barta, A. (2005). Querying XML streams. *The VLDB Journal*, (14): 197–210. doi:10.1007/s00778-004-0123-7

Josuttis, M. N. (2007). *SOA in practice.* O'Reilly.

Kay, M. (2004). *XPath 2.0 programmers reference.* Canada: Wiley Publishing, Inc.

Keller, G., Nuttgens, M., & Scheer, A. (1992). Semantische Prozessmodellierung auf der Grundlage "Ereignisgesteuerter Prozessketten (EPK). *Ver ffentlichungen des Instituts fur Wirtschaftsinformatik.*

Kim, Y., & Kim, T. (1996). Petri nets modeling and analysis using extended bag-theoretic relational algebra. *IEEE Transactions on Systems, Man, and Cybernetics. Part B, Cybernetics*, *26*(4), 599–605. doi:10.1109/3477.517034

Kindler, E. (2006). On the semantics of EPCs: Resolving the vicious circle. *Data & Knowledge Engineering*, *56*(1), 23–40. doi:10.1016/j.datak.2005.02.005

Klarlund, N., Møller, A., & Schwartzbach, M. (2000). A schema language for XML. In *FMSP '00, ACM.* Portland, Oregon: DSD.

Kleiner, M., Albert, P., & Bézivin, J. (2009). Parsing SBVR-based controlled languages. *Models'O9, ACM/IEEE 12th International Conference on Model Driven Engineering Languages and Systems* (pp. 122-136). Springer.

Knudsen, S. U., Pedersen, T. B., Thomsen, C., & Torp, K. (2005). RelaXML: Bidirectional transfer between relational and XML data. *9th International Database Engineering* (IDEAS'05) (pp. 151-162).

Kobayashi, K., Wenxin, L., Kobayashi, D., Watanabe, A., & Yokota, H. (2005). VLEI code: An efficient labeling method for handling XML documents in an RDB. *Proceedings 21st International Conference on Data Engineering, ICDE 2005*, (pp. 386-387).

Kong, L., Gilleron, R., & Lemay, A. (2009). Retrieving meaningful relaxed tightest fragments for XML keyword search. In *Proceedings 2009 International Conference on Extended Data Base Technology* (pp.815–826).

Krafzig, D. (2004). *Enterprise SOA: Service-oriented architecture best practices.* Vienna, Austria.

Krafzig, D., Karl, B., & Slama, D. (2004). *Enterprise SOA: Service-oriented architecture best practices.* Prentice Hall PTR.

Kwon, J., Rao, P., Moon, B., & Lee, S. (2005). FiST: Scalable XML document filtering by sequencing twig patterns. In *Proceedings of the 31th International Conference on Very Large Data Bases.*

Lalmas, M., & Rolleke, T. (2004). Modelling vague content and structure querying in XML retrieval with a probabilistic object-relational framework. *Proceedings of the 6th International Conference on Flexible Query Answering Systems, LNCS 3055.* Springer.

Lee, Q., Bressan, S., & Rahayu, W. (2006). *XShreX: Maintaining integrity constraints in the mapping of XML schema to relational.* 17th International Conference on Database and Expert Systems Applications (DEXA'06).

Leibe, B., & Schiele, B. (2003, June). *Analyzing appearance and contour based methods for object categorization.* In International Conference on Computer Vision and Pattern Recognition (CVPR'03).

Leibe, B., Leonardis, A., & Schiele, B. (2004, May). Combined object categorization and segmentation with an implicit shape model. In *Proceedings of the Workshop on Statistical Learning in Computer Vision*, Prague, Czech Republic.

Leonardi, E., & Bhowmick, S. S. (2005, Nov). XANDY: A scalable change detection technique for ordered XML documents using relational databases. *Data & Knowledge Engineering, 59*, 32.

Leuski, A., & Allan, J. (2000). Improving interactive retrieval by combining ranked lists and clustering. In *Proceedings of RIAO'2000* (pp. 665{681). Retrieved from citeseer.ist.psu.edu/leuski00improving.html

Lew, M. S., Sebe, N., Djeraba, C., & Jain, R. (2006). Content-based multimedia information retrieval: State of the art and challenges. *ACM Transactions in Multimedia Computing and Communication Applications, 2*(1), 1–19. doi:10.1145/1126004.1126005

Ley, M. (2001). *DBLP DTD*. Retrieved from http://www.acm.org/sigmod/dblp/db/about/dblp.dtd

Leymann, F., Roller, D., & Schmidt, M.-T. (2002). Web services and business process management. *IBM Systems Journal, 41*(2), 198–211. doi:10.1147/sj.412.0198

Li, G., Feng, J., Wang, J., & Zhou, L. (2007). Effective keyword search for valuable LCAs over XML documents. In *Proceedings of the 16th ACM Conference on Conference on Information and Knowledge Management*.

Li, H.-G., Aghili, S. A., Agrawal, D., & Abbadi, A. E. (2006). *FLUX: Fuzzy content and structure matching of XML range queries*. Paper presented at WWW 2006, Edinburgh, Scotland.

Li, Q., & Moon, B. (2001). Indexing and querying XML data for regular path expressions. *Proceedings of the 27th International Conference on Very Large Data Bases* (pp. 361 - 370).

Liefke, H., & Suciu, D. (2000). *XMill: An efficient compressor for XML data*. Paper presented at the ACM.

Liu, F., Yu, C., Meng, W. Y., & Chowdhury, A. (2006). Effective keyword search in relational databases. In *Proceedings of the 2006 ACM SIGMOD International Conference on Management of Data*.

Liu, H., Xie, X., Tang, X., Li, Z.-W., & Ma, W.-Y. (2004). Effective browsing of web image search results. In *MIR '04: Proceedings of the 6th ACM SIGMM International Workshop on Multimedia Information Retrieval* (pp. 84-90). New York, NY: ACM.

Liu, Z. Y., Walker, J., & Chen, Y. (2007). Xseek: A semantic XML search engine using keywords. In *Proceedings of the 33th International Conference on Very Large Data Bases*.

Ludascher, B., Mukhopadhay, P., & Papakonstantinou, Y. (2002). A transducer-based XML query processor. In *Proceedings of the 28th International Conference on Very Large Data Bases*.

Lu, R., & Sadiq, S. (2007). A survey of comparative business process modeling approaches. *Lecture Notes in Computer Science, 4439*, 82–94. doi:10.1007/978-3-540-72035-5_7

Madden, S. R., Shah, M. A., & Hellerstein, J. M. (2002). Continuously adaptive continuous queries over streams. In *Proceedings of the 2002 ACM SIGMOD International Conference on Management of Data* (pp. 261–272).

Makoto, M. (2002). *RELAX (Regular Language description for XML)*.

Mandreoli, F., Martoglia, R., & Tiberio, P. (2004). *Approximate query answering for a heterogeneous XML document base*. Paper presented at the 5th International Conference on Web Information Systems Engineering, Brisbane, Australia.

Maneth, S., Mihaylov, N., & Saker, S. (2008). *XML tree structure compression*. Paper presented at the XANTEC'08, IEEE Computer Society.

Manning, C. D., Raghavan, P., & Schütze, H. (2008). *Introduction to information retrieval*. Cambridge University Press.

Markowetz, A., Yang, Y., & Papadias, D. (2007). Keyword search on relational data streams. In *Proceedings of the 2007 ACM SIGMOD International Conference on Management of Data*.

Martens, A. (2003). On usability of Web services. *Proceedings of 1st Web Services Quality Workshop (WQW 2003)*.

Martens, A. (2005). Analyzing Web service based business processes. *Proceedings of International Conference on Fundamental Approaches to Software Engineering (FASE'05).* Springer-Verlag.

Massuthe, P., Reisig, W., & Schmidt, K. (2005). An operating guideline approach to the SOA. *Annals of Mathematics. Computing & Teleinformatics, 1*(3), 35–43.

McBrien, P., & Seltveit, A. H. (1995). *Coupling process models and business rules.* In Information Systems Development for Decentralized Organizations. IFIP 8.1 WG Conference: Chapman.

McLaughlin, B., & Edelson, J. (2006). *Java and XML* (3rd ed.). O'Reilly.

Meersman, R., Tari, Z., Herrero, P., Abdelaziz, T., Elammari, M., & Branki, C. (2008). MASD: Towards a comprehensive multi-agent system development methodology. In *On the Move to Meaningful Internet Systems: OTM 2008 Workshops* (*Vol. 5333*, pp. 108–117). Berlin, Germany: Springer. doi:10.1007/978-3-540-88875-8_30

Megginson, D. (27 April 2004). *Simple API for XML.* SAX.

Mendling, J., & Nuttgens, M. (2006). EPC markup language (EPML): An XML-based interchange format for event-driven process chains (EPC). *Information Systems and e-Business Management, 4*(3), 245-263.

Microsoft Corporation. (2009). *Microsoft Office Word 2003 system requirements.* Microsoft Corporation.

Mihajlovic, V., Hiemstra, D., & Blok, H. E. (2006). Vague element selection and query rewriting for XML retrieval. *Proceedings of the 6th Dutch-Belgian Information Retrieval Workshop* (DIR 2006).

Milner, R. (1991). *The polyadic pi-calculus: A tutorial.* Technical Report ECS-LFCS-91-180. Computer Science Department, University of Edinburgh.

Milner, R. (1999). *Communicating and mobile systems: The [symbol for pi]-calculus.* Cambridge University Press.

Milner, R. J. (1990). *A calculus of mobile processes-Part I/part II.*

Milner, R. (1980). *A calculus of communicating systems.* Springer-Verlag.

Milner, R. (1992). A calculus of mobile process, part I/part II. *Journal of Information and Computation, 100*(1), 1–77. doi:10.1016/0890-5401(92)90008-4

Milner, R. (2006). Pure bigraphs: Structure and dynamics. *Information and Computation, 204*(11), 60–122. doi:10.1016/j.ic.2005.07.003

Milner, R. (2009). *The space and motion of communicating agents.* Cambridge University Press.

Min, J.-K., Park, M.-J., & Chung, C.-W. (2003). *XPRESS: A queriable compression for XML data.* Paper presented at the 2003 ACM SIGMOD International Conference on Management of data.

Min, J.-K., Lee, C.-H., & Chung, C.-W. (2008). XTRON: An XML data management system using relational database. *Information and Software Technology, 50*, 18. doi:10.1016/j.infsof.2007.05.003

Moffat, A. (1990). Implementing the PPM data compression scheme. *IEEE Transactions on Communications, 38*(11), 1917–1921. doi:10.1109/26.61469

Møller, A. (2005). *Document structure description.*

Moro, M. M., Ale, P., Vagena, Z., & Tsotras, V. J. (2008). *XML structural summaries.* Paper presented at the PVLDB '08, Auckland, New Zealand.

Morrison, J., & George, J. (1995). Exploring the software engineering component in MIS research. *Communications of the ACM, 38*(7), 80–91. doi:10.1145/213859.214802

Motwani, R., et al. (2003). Query processing, approximation, and resource management in a data stream management system. In *Proceedings of the Conference on Innovative Data Systems Research.*

Muehlen, M. Z. (2004). Business process and business rule modeling languages for compliance management: A representational analysis. *The 26th International Conference on Conceptual Modeling.*

Müldner, T., Fry, C., Miziołek, J. K., & Durno, S. (2009). *XSAQCT: XML queryable compressor.* Paper presented at the Balisage: The Markup Conference 2009.

Muller, H., Clough, P., Hersh, W., Deselaers, T., Lehmann, T., & Geissbuhler, A. (2005). Evaluation axes for medical image retrieval systems: The imageCLEF experience. In *Multimedia '05: Proceedings of the 13th Annual ACM International Conference on Multimedia* (pp. 1014-1022). New York, NY: ACM.

Muller, H., Muller, W., Marchand-Maillet, S., Pun, T., & Squire, D. (2000). Strategies for positive and negative relevance feedback in image retrieval. *Proceedings 15th International Conference on Pattern Recognition, 2000,* Vol. 1, (pp. 1043-1046). Retrieved from citeseer.ist.psu.edu/327327.html

Mulyar, N., & van der Aalst, W. (2005). *Patterns in colored petri nets.* BETA Working Paper Series, WP 139. Eindhoven, The Netherlands: Eindhoven University of Technology.

Murase, H., & Nayar, S. (1995). Visual learning and recognition of 3D objects from appearance. *International Journal of Computer Vision, 14,* 5–24. doi:10.1007/BF01421486

Murata, M., Walsh, N., & McRae, M. (2001). *TREX and RELAX unified as RELAX NG, a lightweight XML language validation specification.*

Murata, T. (1989). Petri nets: Properties, analysis and applications. [IEEE.]. *Proceedings of the IEEE, 77*(4), 541–580. doi:10.1109/5.24143

Murray, J. D., & VanRyper, W. (1996). *Encyclopedia of graphics file formats.* O'Reilly.

Natalya, F. N., & Mark, A. M. (2000). Prompt: Algorithm and tool for automated ontology merging and alignment. In *Proceedings of 17th National Conference on Artiðcial Intelligence.*

Nepal, S., & Ramakrishna, M. (1999). Query processing issues in image (multimedia) databases. *International Conference on Data Engineering,* (pp. 22-29).

Ng, W., Lam, W.-Y., & Cheng, J. (2006). Comparative analysis of XML compression technologies. *World Wide Web: Internet and Web Information Systems, 9,* 5–33.

Niblack, W., Zhu, X., Hafner, J., Breuel, T., Ponceleon, D., & Petkovic, D. (1998). Updates to the QBIC system. *Retrieval for Image and Video Databases VI, 3312,* 150–161.

Norbert, F., & Kai, G. (2004). XIRQL: An XML query language based on information retrieval concepts. *ACM Transactions on Information Systems, 22*(2), 313–356.

Nunamaker, J., & Chen, M. (1991). Systems development in information systems research. *Journal of Management Information Systems, 7*(3), 89–106.

OASIS. (2002). *SGML: General introductions and overviews.*

Olteanu, D., Kiesling, T., & Bry, F. (2003). An evaluation of regular path expressions with qualifiers against XML streams. In *Proceedings of 19th International Conference on Data Engineering.*

OMG. (2008). *SBVR 1.0 specification.* Retrieved from http://www.omg.org/spec/SBVR/1.0/

O'Neil, P., O'Neil, E., Pal, S., Cseri, I., Schaller, G., & Westbury, N. (2004) ORDPATHs: Insert-friendly XML node labels. In *Proceedings of the 2004 ACM SIGMOD International Conference on Management of Data.* Paris, France: ACM.

Oosten, J. v. (July 2002). *Basic category theory.* Department of Mathematics, Utrecht University, The Netherlands. Megginson, D. (27 April, 2004). *Simple API for XML.* SAX.

Oracle (n.d.). *Oracle XML DB developer's guide 10g.*

Oracle Technology Network. (n.d.). *Oracle XML DB.*

Owen, M., & Raj, J. (2003). *Introduction to the new business process modeling standard, BPMN and business process management.*

Pal, S., Fussell, M., & Dolobowsky, I. (December 2005). *XML support in Microsoft SQL server 2005.*

Pant, K., & Juric, M. (2008). *Business process driven SOA using BPMN and BPEL: From business process modeling to orchestration and service oriented architecture* (pp. 208–328). Packt Publishing.

Paparizos, S., Al-Khalifa, S., Chapman, A., & Jagadish, H. V., Lakshmanan, L. V. S., Nierman, A., et al. (2003). *TIMBER: A native system for querying XML.* Paper presented at the ACM SIGMOD International Conference on Management of Data.

Pein, R. P., & Lu, J. (2010). *Multi-feature query language for image classification*. In International Conference on Computational Science, ICCS 2010. Elsevier. (Accepted for publication)

Pein, R. P., & Lu, Z. (2006, June). Content based image retrieval by combining features and query-by-sketch. In H. R. Arabnia & R. R. Hashemi (Eds.), *International Conference on Information & Knowledge Engineering (IKE)* (p. 49-55). Las Vegas, NV: CSREA Press.

Pein, R. P., Amador, M., Lu, J., & Renz, W. (2008, Juillet). Using CBIR and semantics in 3D-model retrieval. In *8th IEEE International Conference on Computer and Information Technology, CIT 2008*, (pp. 173-178).

Pein, R. P., Lu, J., & Renz, W. (2008b, July). An extensible query language for content based image retrieval based on Lucene. In 8th IEEE International Conference on Computer and Information Technology, CIT 2008, (pp. 179-184).

Pein, R. P. (2005). *Multi-modal image retrieval - A feasibility study*. Diplomarbeit.

Pein, R. P. (2008). *Hot-pluggable multi-feature search engine. Memoire de Master non publie*. Hamburg University of Applied Sciences.

Pein, R. P., Lu, J., & Renz, W. (2008, July). An extensible query language for content based image retrieval. *The Open Information Science Journal*, *3*(17), 81–97.

Peng, W., & DeClaris, N. (1997, October). Heuristic similarity measure characterization for content based image retrieval. *1997 IEEE International Conference on Computational Cybernetics and Simulation, Systems, Man, and Cybernetics, 1*, (pp. 7-12).

Peng, F., & Chawathe, S. S. (2003). XSQ: A streaming XPath engine. *ACM Transactions on Database Systems*, *30*(2), 577–623. doi:10.1145/1071610.1071617

PKWare. (2003). *Website*. Retrieved March 1, 2011, from http://www.pkware.com/

Praks, P., Izquierdo, E., & Kucera, R. (2008, October). The sparse image representation for automated image retrieval. In *IEEE International Conference on Image Processing* (pp. 25-28).

Puhlmann, F., & Weske, M. (2005). Using the pi-calculus for formalizing workflow patterns. *Proceedings of BPM 2005* (pp. 153-168). Springer-Verlag.

Puhlmann, F. a. (2005). Using the pi-calculus for formalizing workflow patterns. *Lecture Notes in Computer Science*, *3649*, 153. doi:10.1007/11538394_11

Puhlmann, F., & Weske, M. (2006). Investigations on soundness regarding lazy activities. [Springer.]. *Proceedings of Business Process Management*, *2006*, 145–160. doi:10.1007/11841760_11

Quack, T., Monich, U., Thiele, L., & Manjunath, B. S. (2004). Cortina: a system for large-scale, content-based web image retrieval. In *Multimedia '04: Proceedings of the 12th Annual acm international Conference on Multimedia* (pp. 508-511). New York, NY: ACM.

Quinlan, J. R. (1986, March). Induction of decision trees. *Machine Learning*, *1*(1), 81–106. doi:10.1007/BF00116251

Ramakrishna, M. V., Nepal, S., & Srivastava, P. K. (2002). A heuristic for combining fuzzy results in multimedia databases. In *ADC '02: Proceedings of the 13th Australasian Database Conference* (pp. 141-144). Darlinghurst, Australia: Australian Computer Society, Inc.

Ramanath, M. (2006) Schema-based statistics and storage for XML, (p. 175). In Faculty of Engineering. Indian Institute of Science, Bangalore, India.

Rao, P., & Moon, B. (2004). PRIX: Indexing and querying XML using Prsfer sequences. In *Proceedings of the 20th IEEE International Conference on Data Engineering* (pp. 288–299).

Ray, E. T. (2001). *Learning XML guide to creating self-describing data*. O'Reilly Media Inc.

Ray, E. T. (2003). *Learning XML: Creating self-describing data*. O'Reilly.

Recker, J. C., Indulska, M., Rosemann, M., & Green, P. (2006). How good is BPMN really? Insights from theory and practice. *14th European Conference on Information Systems*, (pp. 12-14).

Recker, J. C., Rosemann, M., Indulska, M., & Green, P. (2009). Business process modeling: A comparative analysis. *Journal of the Association for Information Systems, 10*(4), 333–363.

Regev, G., & Wegmann, A. (2005). A regulation-based view on business process and supporting system flexibility. *6th BPMDS Workshop on Business Processes and Support Systems: Design for Flexibility BPMDS'05* (pp. 13-14). CAiSE'05 Workshops.

Renzhong, T., Guangmin, Z., & Hongtao, A. T. (2002). *Analysis of process modeling methods.*

Riecks, D. (2005). *IPTC Core schema for XMP - Version 1.0 (Rapport technique).* International Press Telecommunications Council.

Rinderle, S., Reichert, M., & Dadam, P. (2004). Correctness criteria for dynamic changes in workflow systems: A survey. *Data & Knowledge Engineering, 50*, 9–34. doi:10.1016/j.datak.2004.01.002

Rodden, K. (2002). *Evaluating similarity-based visualisations as interfaces for image browsing.* These de doctorat non publiee, University of Cambridge.

Rodden, K., Basalaj, W., Sinclair, D., & Wood, K. (2001). Does organisation by similarity assist image browsing? In *CHI '01: Proceedings of the SIGCHI Conference on Human Factors in Computing Systems* (pp. 190-197). New York, NY: ACM.

Rui, Y., & Huang, T. (2000). *Optimizing learning in image retrieval (Vol. 1,* p. 1236). IEEE Computer Society on Computer Vision and Pattern Recognition.

Runapongsa, K., Patel, J. M., Jagadish, H., Chen, Y., & Al-Khalifa, S. (2006). The Michigan benchmark: Towards XML query performance diagnostics. *Information Systems, 31*, 73–97. doi:10.1016/j.is.2004.09.004

Russell, N. A. (2006). *Workflow controlflow patterns: A revised view.*

Russell, N., ter Hofstede, A., Edmond, D., & van der Aalst, W. (2004a). *Workflow data patterns.* QUT Technical report FIT-TR-2004-01. Brisbane, Australia: Queensland University of Technology.

Russell, N., ter Hofstede, A., Edmond, D., & van der Aalst, W. (2004b). *Workflow resource patterns.* BETA Working Paper Series WP 127. Eindhoven, The Netherlands: Eindhoven University of Technology.

Russell, N., van der Aalst, W., & ter Hofstede, A. (2006). Workflow exception patterns. *Proceedings of the 18th International Conference on Advanced Information Systems Engineering* (pp. 288-302). Berlin, Germany: Springer-Verlag.

Sadiq, W., & Orlowska, M. (1997). On correctness issues in conceptual modeling of workflows. In *Proceedings of the 5th European Conference on Information Systems.*

Sadiq, W., & Orlowska, M. (1999). On capturing process requirements of workflow based business information systems. *3rd International Conference on Business Information Systems* (pp. 281 -294). London, UK: Springer Verlag.

Sadiq, S., Sadiq, W., & Orlowska, M. (2005). A framework for constraint specification and validation in flexible workflows. *Information Systems, 30*(5), 349–378. doi:10.1016/j.is.2004.05.002

Sakr, S. (2009). XML compression techniques: A survey and comparison. *Journal of Computer and System Sciences, 75*(5), 303–322. doi:10.1016/j.jcss.2009.01.004

Salomon, D. (2007). *Data compression: The complete reference* (4th ed.). Springer.

Salton, G., & McGill, M. J. (1983). *Introduction to modern information retrieval.* McGraw-Hill.

Sanz, I. (2007). *Flexible technique for heterogeneous XML data retrieval.* Universitat Jaume.

Saux, B. L., & Boujemaa, N. (2002). Unsupervised robust clustering for image database categorization. *International Conference on Pattern Recognition,* Vol. 1, (p. 10259).

Sayyadian, M., LeKhac, H., Doan, A., & Gravano, L. (2007). Efficient keyword search across heterogeneous relational database. In *Proceedings of 23th International Conference on Data Engineering.*

Schapire, R. E. (1990). The strength of weak learnability. *Machine Learning, 5*, 197–227. doi:10.1007/BF00116037

Schiele, B., & Crowley, J. (2000). Recognition without correspondence using multidimensional receptive field histograms. *International Journal of Computer Vision, 36*(1), 31–52. doi:10.1023/A:1008120406972

Schietse, J., Eakins, J. P., & Veltkamp, R. C. (2007). Practice and challenges in trademark image retrieval. In CIVR '07: Proceedings of the 6th ACM International Conference on Image and Video Retrieval (pp. 518-524). New York, NY: ACM.

Schlieder, T. (2001). *Similarity search in XML data using cost-based query transformations.* Paper presented at ACM SIGMOD WebDB.

Schnitzspan, P., Fritz, M., Roth, S., & Schiele, B. (2009). Discriminative structure learning of hierarchical representations for object detection. In *Computer Vision and Pattern Recognition.* Miami, USA: CVPR. doi:10.1109/CVPR.2009.5206544

Schonenberg, H. A. (2008). Process flexibility: A survey of contemporary approaches. In *Advances in Enterprise Engineering I, Part 1* (pp. 16-30).

Sewell, P. (2000). Applied Pi-A brief tutorial. Technical Report Nr. 498. University of Cambridge.

Shanmugasundaram, J., Tufte, K., Zhang, C., He, G., DeWitt, D. J., & Naughton, J. F. (1999). Relational databases for querying XML documents: Limitations and opportunities. *Conference on Very Large Data Bases,* (pp. 302–314).

Shannon, C. E. (1948). A mathematical theory of communication. *The Bell System Technical Journal, 27,* 379–423.

Sheikholeslami, G., Chatterjee, S., & Zhang, A. (1998, August). NeuroMerge: An approach for merging heterogeneous features in content-based image retrieval systems. *Proceedings International Workshop on Multi-Media Database Management Systems, 1998,* (pp. 106-113).

Sigurbjornsson, B., & Trotman, A. (2003). *Queries: INEX 2003 working group report.* Paper presented at the 2nd Workshop of the Initiative for the Evaluation of XML Retrieval (INEX).

Simpson, R. C. (2004). *An XML representation for crew procedures.* Final Report NASA Faculty Fellowship Program.

Smeulders, A. W., Worring, M., Santini, S., Gupta, A., & Jain, R. (2000). Content-based image retrieval at the end of the early years. *IEEE Transactions on Pattern Analysis and Machine Intelligence, 22*(12), 1349–1380. doi:10.1109/34.895972

Smith, J. R. (2004). *MARVEL: Multimedia analysis and retrieval system (Whitepaper).* Hawthorne, NY: IBM T. J. Watson Research Center Intelligent Information Management Dept.

Soltan, S., & Rahgozar, M. (2006). A clustering-based scheme for labeling XML trees. *International Journal of Computer Science and Network Security, 6,* 84–89.

Spy, X. M. L. (2008). *SAX & DOM.* Retrieved from www.Altova.com/XMLSpy

Stamatina, B., Mounia, L., Anastasios, T., & Theodora, T. (2006). *User expectations from XML element retrieval.* Paper presented at the 29th Annual International ACM SIGIR Conference on Research and Development in Information Retrieval.

Steinke, G., & Nikolette, C. (2003). Business rules as the basis of an organization's information systems. *Industrial Management & Data Systems, 103*(1), 3. doi:10.1108/02635570310456904

Su, H., Jinhui, J., & Rundensteiner, A. E. (2003). RAINDROP: A uniform and layered algebraic framework for XQueries on XML streams. In *Proceedings of the 12th International Conference on Information and Knowledge Management* (pp. 279 - 286).

Swain, M. J., & Ballard, D. (1991). Color indexing. *International Journal of Computer Vision, 7*(1), 11–32. doi:10.1007/BF00130487

Tan, Z., Xu, J., Wang, W., & Shi, B. (2005). Storing normalized XML documents in normalized relations. *The Fifth International Conference on Computer and Information Technology* (CIT'05) (pp. 123-129).

Tatarinov, I., Viglas, S. D., Beyer, K., Shanmugasundaram, J., Shekita, E., & Zhang, C. (2002). *Storing and querying ordered XML using a relational database system* (pp. 204–215). SIGMOD.

Thompson, H. S., Beech, D., Maloney, M., & Mendelsohn, N. (2004). *XML schema part 1: Structures,* 2nd ed. W3 Consortium.

Tian, F., Reinwald, B., Pirahesh, H., Mayr, T., & Myllymaki, J. (2004). Implementing a scalable XML publish/subscribe system using a relational database system. In *Proceedings of the 2004 ACM SIGMOD International Conference on Management of Data* (pp. 479-490).

TJDLUT. (2007). *Summary of business process management.* Retrieved from http://www.uml.org.cn/work-class/200710151.asp

Tolani, P. M., & Haritsa, J. R. (2000). *XGRIND: A query-friendly XML compressor.* Paper presented at the IEEE 18th International Conference on Data Engineering.

Torres, R. S., Silva, C. G., Medeiros, C. B., & Rocha, H. V. (2003). Visual structures for image browsing. In *CIKM '03: Proceedings of the Twelfth International Conference on Information and Knowledge Management* (pp. 49-55). New York, NY: ACM.

Torsten, G. (2002) Accelerating XPath location steps. In *Proceedings of the 2002 ACM SIGMOD International Conference on Management of Data.* Madison, WI: ACM.

Torsten, G., Keulen, M. V., & Jens, T. (2004). Accelerating XPath evaluation in any RDBMS. *ACM Transactions on Database Technology, 29,* 40.

Town, C., & Sinclair, D. (2001, 14 December). Ontological query language for content based image retrieval. In IEEE Workshop on Content-Based Access of Image and Video Libraries, CBAIVL 2001, (pp. 75-80).

Trotman, A., & Sigurbjornsson, B. (2005). *Narrowed extended XPath I (NEXI).* Paper presented at the Advances in XML Information Retrieval, Berlin.

Turk, M., & Pentland, A. (1991). Eigenfaces for recognition. *Journal of Cognitive Neuroscience, 3,* 71–86. doi:10.1162/jocn.1991.3.1.71

Vakali, A., Catania, B., & Maddalena, A. (2005). XML data stores: Emerging practices. *IEEE Internet Computing, 9*(2). doi:10.1109/MIC.2005.48

van der Aalst, W. T. (2003). *YAWL: Yet another workflow language (Revised version)..*

Van der Aalst, W., & ter Hofstede, A. (2002). Workflow patterns: On the expressive power of (Petri-net-based) workflow lanuages. *Proceedings of the Fourth Workshop on the Practical Use of Coloured Petri Nets and CPN Tools (CPN 2002)* (pp. 1-20). University of Aarhus.

Van der Aalst, W., Hee, K., & Houben, G. (1994). Modeling and analysing workflow using a Petri-net based approach. *Proceedings of the Second Workshop on Computer-Supported Cooperative Work, Petri Nets and Related Formalisms,* (pp. 31–50).

Van der Aalst, W., Hofstede, A., & Weske, M. (2003). Business process management: A survey. *Proceedings of the 2003 International Conference on Business Process Management,* (pp. 1-12).

Van der Aalst, W., Navathe, S., & Wakayama, T. (1996). Three good reasons for using a Petri-net-based workflow management system. *Proceedings of the International Working Conference on Information and Process Integration in Enterprises (IPIC'96),* (pp. 179-201).

Van der Aalst, W. (1998). The application of Petri nets to workflow management. *The Journal of Circuits. Systems and Computers, 8*(1), 21–66.

Van der Aalst, W. (1999). Formalization and verification of event-driven process chains. *Information and Software Technology, 41*(10), 639–650. doi:10.1016/S0950-5849(99)00016-6

Van Der Aalst, W. A. (2003). Workflow patterns. *Distributed and Parallel Databases, 14*(1), 5–51. doi:10.1023/A:1022883727209

van der Aalst, W., & Hofstede, A. (2005). YAWL: Yet another workflow language (Revised version). *Information Systems, 30*(4), 245–275. doi:10.1016/j.is.2004.02.002

van der Aalst, W., ter Hofstede, A., Kiepuszewski, B., & Barros, A. (2003). Workflow patterns. *Distributed and Parallel Databases, 14*(1), 5–21. doi:10.1023/A:1022883727209

van der Aalst, W., & van Hee, K. (2002). *Workflow management: Models, methods and systems.* The MIT Press.

van Rijsbergen, C. (1979). *Information retrieval.* London, UK: Butterworths.

Victor, B. a. (1994). *The mobility workbench-A tool for the-calculus* (Vol. 204:11). Citeseer.

Victor, B. (1995). *The mobility workbench user's guide: Polyadic version 3.122*. Department of Information Technology, Uppsala University.

Violleau, T. (2001). *Java technology and XML*. Retrieved October 1, 2010, from http://java.sun.com/developer/technicalArticles/xml/JavaTechandXML/

W3C. (1999). *XML path language (XPath) - Version 1.0*. Retrieved from http://www.w3.org/TR/xpath/

W3C. (2002). *XML pointer language (XPointer)*. Retrieved from http://www.w3.org/TR/xptr/

W3C. (2005). *Document object model* (DOM).

W3C. (2008). *Extensible markup language (XML) 1.0* (5th ed.). Retrieved September 22, 2010, from http://www.w3.org/TR/REC-xml/

W3C. (2010a). *XML path language (XPath) 2.0*. Retrieved October 19, 2010, from http://www.w3.org/TR/xpath20/

W3C. (2010b). *XQuery 1.0 and XPath 2.0 functions and operators*. Retrieved September 26, 2010, from http://www.w3.org/TR/xpath-functions/

W3C Working Draft. (2001). *XQuery 1.0: An XML query language*. Retrieved from www.w3.org/TR/xquery/

W3Schools.com. (2006). *XLink and XPointer*. Retrieved September 27, 2010, from http://www.w3schools.com/xlink/default.asp

W3Schools.com. (2006). *XML examples*. Retrieved October 7, 2010, from http://www.w3schools.com/XML/cd_catalog.xml

Wagner, G. (2005). Rule modeling and markup. In *Reasoning Web* (pp. 251–274). Springer. doi:10.1007/11526988_7

Wang, H., & Meng, X. (2005). *On the sequencing of tree structures for XML indexing*. 21st International Conference on Data Engineering (ICDE 2005).

Wang, J. Z., Boujemaa, N., Bimbo, A. D., Geman, D., Hauptmann, A. G., & Tesic, J. (2006). Diversity in multimedia information retrieval research. In *MIR '06: Proceedings of the 8th ACM International Workshop on Multimedia Information Retrieval* (pp. 5-12). New York, NY: ACM.

Wang, J. Z., Boujemaa, N., & Chen, Y. (2007). High diversity transforms multimedia information retrieval into a cross-cutting field: Report on the 8th Workshop on Multimedia Information Retrieval. *SIGMOD Record*, *36*(1), 57–59. doi:10.1145/1276301.1276315

Washington University. (2002). *XML data repository*.

Web Ontology Language (OWL). (2007). Retrieved from http://www.w3.org/2004/OWL/.

Weidong, Y., Hao, Z., Nan, L., & Guansheng, Z. (2011). Adaptive and effective keyword search for XML. In *Proceedings of 15th Pacific-Asia Conference on Knowledge Discovery and Data Mining*.

Weske, M. (2007). Business process management: Concepts, languages, and architectures, 1 ed. Springer.

White, S. A. (n.d.). Introduction to BPMN. *IBM Corporation.*

Williams, I. (2009). *Beginning XSLT and XPath: Transforming XML documents and data*. Wrox Press.

WinZip. (1990). Retrieved November 15, 2009, http://www.winzip.com/

Woods, K., Bowyer, K., & Jr, W. P. K. (1996). Combination of multiple classifiers using local accuracy estimates. In *CVPR '96: Proceedings of the 1996 Conference on Computer Vision and Pattern Recognition* (p. 391). Washington, DC: IEEE Computer Society.

Worah, D., & Sheth, A. (1997). *Transactions in transactional workflows* (pp. 3–34). Advanced Transaction Models and Architectures.

Wu, B., & Nevatia, R. (2007, Oct.). Cluster boosted tree classifier for multi-view, multi-pose object detection. In *IEEE 11th international Conference on Computer vision, ICCV 2007* (pp. 1-8).

Wu, X., Lee, M. L., & Hsu, W. (2004). A prime number labelling scheme for dynamic ordered XML trees. *Proceedings 20th International Conference on Data Engineering*, 2004, (pp. 66-78).

Xing, G., Xia, Z., & Ayers, D. (2007a). X2R: A system for managing XML documents and key constraints using RDBMS. In *Proceedings of the 45th Annual Southeast Regional Conference*. ACM, Winston-Salem, North Carolina.

Xing, G., Xia, Z., & Ayers, D. (2007b). *X2R: A system for managing XML documents and key constraints using RDBMS. Winston.* Salem, NC: ACMSE.

XML Data Repository. Retrieved from http://www.cs.washington.edu/research/xmldatasets/www/repository.html

XQuery 1.0: An XML query language (2nd ed.). (2011). Retrieved from http://www.w3.org/TR/xquery/

Xu, Y., & Papakonstantinou, Y. (2005). Efficient keyword search for smallest LCAs in XML database. In *Proceedings of the 2005 ACM SIGMOD International Conference on Management of Data*.

Xu, Y., & Papakonstantinou, Y. (2008). Efficient LCA based keyword search in XML data. In *Proc. 2008 International Conference on Extended Data Base Technology* (pp. 535–546).

Xu, J. J., Lu, J. H., Wang, W., & Shi, B. L. (2006). Effective keyword search in XML documents based on MIU. In Lee, M. L., Tan, K. L., & Wuwongse, V. (Eds.), *Database system for advanced applications* (pp. 702–716). doi:10.1007/11733836_49

Yahoo. Inc. (2006). *Flickr - Photo sharing*. Retrieved from http://www.flickr.com/

Yang, Y., Ng, W., Lau, H. L., & Cheng, J. (2006). *An efficient approach to support querying secure outsourced XML information*. Paper presented at the 18th Conference on Advanced Information Systems Engineering (CAiSE).

Yang, D. (2003). An approach for workflow modeling using Pi-calculus. *Journal of Zhejiang University. Science*, 6.

Yang, D., & Zhang, S. (2003). An approach for workflow modeling using pi-calculus. *Journal of Zhejiang University. Science*, 6.

Yoshikawa, M., Amagasa, T., Shimura, T., & Uemura, S. (2001). XRel: A path-based approach to storage and retrieval of XML documents using relational databases. *ACM Transactions on Internet Technology*, *1*, 32. doi:10.1145/383034.383038

Yousof, M. M., Shukur, Z., & Abdullah, A. L. (2011). CuQuP: A hybrid approach for selecting suitable information systems development methodology. *Information Technology Journal, 10*(5).

Yuan, Y., & Shaw, M. J. (1995). Induction of fuzzy decision trees. *Fuzzy Sets and Systems*, *69*(2), 125–139. Retrieved from http://www.sciencedirect.com/science/article/B6V05-4007D5X-C/2/62fa7de5b67d27ad22a38a1f4e6ba0e6doi:10.1016/0165-0114(94)00229-Z

Yun, J.-H., & Chung, C.-W. (2008). Dynamic interval-based labelling scheme for efficient XML query and update processing. *Journal of Systems and Software, 81*, 56–70. doi:10.1016/j.jss.2007.05.034

Yunyal, L., Cong, Y., & Jagadish, H. V. (2004). Schema-free XQuery. In *Proceedings of the 30th International Conference on Very Large Data Bases*.

Yunyal, L., Cong, Y., & Jagadish, H. V. (2008). Enabling schema-free XQuery with meaningful query focus. *The VLDB Journal, 17*(3), 355–377. doi:10.1007/s00778-006-0003-4

Yunyao, L., Cong, Y., & Jagadish, H. V. (2004). Schema-free XQuery. In *Proceedings of the 30th International Conference on Very Large Data Bases* (pp. 72–83).

Zadeh, L. A. (1965). Fuzzy sets. *Information and Control*, *8*, 338–353. doi:10.1016/S0019-9958(65)90241-X

Zadeh, L. A. (1996). *Fuzzy sets*. River Edge, NJ: World Scientific Publishing Co., Inc.

Zaha, J., Barros, A., Dumas, M., & ter Hofstede, A. (2006). A language for service behavior modeling. *Proceedings 14th International Conference on Cooperative Information Systems (CoopIS 2006)* (pp. 145-162). Springer Verlag.

Zhang, H., & Tompa, F. W. (2004a). Querying XML documents by dynamic shredding. In *Proceedings of the 2004 ACM Symposium on Document Engineering*. Milwaukee, WI: ACM.

Zhang, H., & Tompa, F. W. (2004b). *Querying XML documents by dynamic shredding.* In DocEng'04, Milwaukee, Wisconsin, USA.

Zhang, Q., & Izquierdo, E. (2006, April). *A new approach to image retrieval in a multi-feature space.* In International Workshop on Image Analysis for Multimedia Interactive Services.

Zhang, Q., & Kankanhalli, M. S. (2003). *Semantic video annotation and vague query.* Paper presented at the 9th International Conference on Multimedia Modeling (MMM 2003)

Zhao, F., & Ma, Z. M. (2009). *Vague query based on vague relational model.* Paper presented at the AISC.

Zhao, R., & Grosky, W. I. (2002). Bridging the semantic gap in image retrieval. In Shih, T. K. (Ed.), *Distributed multimedia databases: Techniques & applications* (pp. 14–36). doi:10.4018/978-1-930708-29-7.ch002

Zhou, J., Zhang, S., Wang, M., & Sun, H. (2006). XML-RDB driven semi-structure data management. *Journal of Information and Computing Science, 1*, 9.

Ziyang, L., & Cheng, Y. (2001). Exploiting and maintaining views for XML keyword search. In *Proceedings of the 2001 ACM SIGMOD International Conference on Management of Data.*

Ziyang, L., & Yi, C. (2007). Identifying meaningful return information for XML keyword search. In *Proceedings of the 2007 ACM SIGMOD International Conference on Management of Data* (pp. 329–340).

Ziyang, L., Jeffrey, W., & Yi, C. (2007). XSeek: A semantic XML search engine using keywords. In *Proceedings of the 33rd International Conference on Very Large Data Bases* (pp. 1330–1333).

Zlatkin, S., & Kaschek, R. (2006). *Mapping business processes models from Petri nets into event-driven process chains.*

About the Contributors

Joan Lu is Professor in the Department of Informatics at the University of Huddersfield (UK). Her extensive research covers information access, retrieval and visualization, XML technology, object oriented technologies, agent technology, data management system, security issues, response technologies in wire and wireless computing, and Internet computing. Specifically for these areas, she has been an invited speaker for industrial-oriented events and published three books in XML technology, Spatial Data mining, Learning with Mobile Technologies, Handheld Devices, and Smart Phones and more than 150 academic papers. Professor Lu is Leader of research group in XML, Database and Information Retrieval, University of Huddersfield, UK. Professor Lu has acted as the founder and a program chair for the International XML Technology workshop and XMLTech (USA) for 11 years (2003-2011). She also serves as 7 international conference chairs, is a regular paper reviewer for international journals and a committee member for sixteen international conferences in her subject area. Professor Lu is involved in both internal and external research projects. The EU projects she involved are Edumecca for leading to develop an open mobile based Student Response System – SRS, DO-IT for leading to internationalise Student Response System with EU languages and DONE-IT for leading to develop a mobile examination system – MES, collaborating with partners from 5 EU countries. She is specializing in XML technology, database, response technologies in wire and wireless computing with the latest mobile devices, such as Smartphone. Professor Lu serves as a member of the British Computer Society (BCS), BCS examiner of Advanced Database Management Systems; the Fellow of the Higher Education Academy (UK), funding reviewer for professional bodies, PhD examiners nationally and internationally.

***

Baydaa Al-Hamadani is a PhD holder in Computer Science. She has got her last degree from the University of Huddersfield, UK at 2011 in Retrieving Information from Compressed XML Documents. Before that she was a Lecturer in Philadelphia University, Jordan for 5 years upon finishing her second degree (MSc) in Computer Science from the University of Technology, Iraq. She has got her first (Bachelor) degree from the same University and in the same field. Now she is an honorary Researcher in XDIR research group, University of Huddersfield, UK.

Ibrahim Mohammad Dweib is working as a Lecturer in the Department of Computer Science of Sultan Qaboos University (SQU). Prior to joining SQU, he worked as an Instructor in King Khaled University and Ibri Teachers College –Ministry of Higher Education. Ibrahim holds BSc in Computer Science from Yarmouk University (1989), MSc in Computer Information Systems from Arab Academy for Financial & Banking Science (2003) and PhD in Computer Science -XML Database and Relational Database from the University of HuddersField (2011). His research interests include XML database, relational database, XML security, performance evaluation, and information systems.

Gang He is a postgraduate student in School of Software Engineering, Yunnan University, Kunming, China. He received his Bachelor's Degree in 2008. During his Postgraduate study, business process modeling and methodology are his research fields.

Raoul Pascal Pein works as Associate Prof. at Sør-Trøndelag University College, Faculty of Technology. He received a PhD in Computing Sciences (2010) from the University of Huddersfield in the UK. He has been working in the field of content-based image retrieval for several years. The aim was to simplify the user interface for retrieving pixel-based images from large repositories. The key methods employed were feature vector extraction, analysis of distinct feature vector characteristics, query languages, and decision tree based machine learning. He currently works as Software Engineer in the development of innovative software solutions for various European R&D projects within the lifelong learning sector. The main area is to coordinate the design and implementation of cooperating software modules required in the projects. His research interests include efficient information retrieval, the use of platform independent communication standards, as well as mobile computing.

Yanjun Qian studied in Hennan Normal University majoring in Computer Science, and was granted Bachelor's Degree in 2008. From 2008-2011, he studied in Yunnan University majoring in computer organization and architecture, and was granted Master's Degree in 2011. His research interests include business process organization and optimization.

Wolfgang Renz is Professor of Practical Computer Science and Applied Mathematics in the Department of Information and Electrical Engineering at the Hamburg University of Applied Sciences, Germany. He is Head of the section of Distributed Systems in multi-agent systems in logistics in smart grid, virtual and augmented reality, and stochastic process, simulation, and self-organization. He is Founder and Director of the Laboratory for Multi Media Systems.

Zhongwei Wu works at the School of Information Science and Engineering, Yunnan University, in Kunming, China. He has published several conference proceedings papers with the IEEE, including "Pollution Purifying Agriculture in China," published in the *Proceedings of the 2011 International Conference on Remote Sensing, Environment, and Transportation Engineering* (RSETE), and "Comparison Investigation of Thermal Fatigue and Mechanical Fatigue Behavior of Board Level Solder Joint" in *Proceedings of the 2010 International Conference on Electronic Packaging Technology and High Density Packaging* (ICEPT-HDP) to name a few.

Gang Xue is a Lecturer at Yunnan University, Kunming, China. He received his Bachelor of Engineering in 2000. From 2000-2003, he was a Software Engineer in Fundamental Geographic Information Center of Jiangsu Province, China. He received his M.D. and Ph.D. of Engineering in 2006 and 2009. Since 2009 he has been with the Software School of Yunnan University. His research interests include service computing and business process (or workflow) management technology.

Jinwu Yang studied in Beijing University of Chemical Technology majoring in Automation, and granted Bachelor's Degree in 2009. From 2010-2013, he studied in Yunnan University majoring in Computer Application Technology. His research interests include business process re-engineering and business process modeling.

Weidong Yang is an Associate Professor at the school of Computer Science at University of Fudan. His current research is focused on XML data management and database system. He is also interested in data stream management system, Web engineering, and data integration. He received a PhD degree in Computer Science from Xiandian University. He won the Award of Science and Technology Advancement of Shanghai, 1st Class, 2003.

Shaowen Yao, born in 1966, received the Bachelor's and Master's degree from Yunnan University in 1988 and 1991, respectively. He graduated from University of Electronic Science and Technology of China and received his Doctor's degree in 2002. In June, 1998, as a visiting scholar, he started one years' learning in ITR (Institute of Telecom Research) in University of South Australia. He is the Vice Dean of the National Pilot School of Software, Yunnan University. He is also the Director of the Laboratory of Network Intelligence Computing. He is the Vice Director of the China Computer Federation Southwestern Network and MIS Committee and Network Committee of Yunnan Federation of Computers. He is the Technical Advisor of the Yunnan High People's Court, Yunnan Provincial Bureau of Statistics, and so on. His research interests include Semantic Web technology, network distributed processing, CPN modeling and network protocol engineering, e-government processing, and so on.

Kui Yu studied in Chuxiong Normal University majoring in Computer Science, and granted Bachelor's Degree in 2008. From 2008-2011, he studied in Yunnan University majoring in computer theory and software, and was granted Master's Degree in 2011. His research interests include business process organization and optimization.

Kun Zhang is a Lecturer at Chuxiong normal university, Chuxiong, China. He received his M.D. of Engineering in 2006. His research interests include artificial neural networks and particle swarm optimization algorithms.

Nan Zhang studied in Yunnan University majoring in Software Engineering, and granted Bachelor's Degree in 2010. From 2010-2013, she studied in Yunnan University majoring in System Integration and Analysis. Her research interests include process mining and process optimization.

Wei Zhou received the B.Engr. degree from the Department of Optoelectronic Techniques, Nanjing University of Science and Technology, China, in 1996 and Ph.D. degrees from the Network Information Center of Chinese Academy of Science, China, in 2008. Since 2008, he has been with the Software school of the Yunnan University, where he is currently an Associate Professor. His research interests include large-scale distributed systems, cloud computing, peer-to-peer networks, and applications of network coding.

Yixuan Zhou studied in The PLA Information Engineering University majoring in Network Engineering, and was granted Bachelor's Degree in 2009. From 2009-2012, she studied in Yunnan University majoring in Computer Application Technology. Her research interests include process mining and process optimization.

Index